THE SERVICE-DOMINANT LOGIC OF MARKETING

DIALOG, DEBATE, AND DIRECTIONS

ROBERT F. LUSCH AND STEPHEN L. VARGO, EDITORS

FOREWORDS BY RUTH N. BOLTON AND FREDERICK E. WEBSTER JR.

M.E.Sharpe
Armonk, New York
London, England

To Virginia, my closest and dearest friend.
—Robert F. Lusch

To Jean and Marty, thank you.
—Stephen L. Vargo

Library of Congress Cataloging-in-Publication Data

The service-dominant logic of marketing : dialog, debate, and directions / edited by Robert F. Lusch and
Stephen L. Vargo.
    p. cm.
Includes bibliographical references and index.
ISBN 0-7656-1490-1 (cloth : alk. paper) — ISBN 0-7656-1491-X (pbk. : alk. paper)
  1. Marketing—Philosophy. 2. Customer services. 3. Relationship marketing. I. Lusch, Robert F.
II. Vargo, Stephen L., 1945–

HF5415.S377 2006
658.8'12—dc22   2005024992

Printed in the United States of America

The paper used in this publication meets the minimum requirements of
American National Standard for Information Sciences
Permanence of Paper for Printed Library Materials,
ANSI Z 39.48-1984.

∞

BM (c) 10   9   8   7   6   5   4   3   2   1
BM (p) 10   9   8   7   6   5   4   3   2   1

THE SERVICE-DOMINANT
LOGIC OF MARKETING

CONTENTS

FOREWORD

Ruth N. Bolton

This collection of essays was preceded by an article titled "Evolving to a New Dominant Logic for Marketing," by Stephen L. Vargo and Robert F. Lusch, published in the *Journal of Marketing*, Volume 68, Number 1, in January 2004. The article is packed with "big ideas" so—not surprisingly—its publication was the culmination of an unusually lengthy review and revision process that spanned five years and the tenure of two *Journal* editors (David W. Stewart and myself). The iterations of the review process sustained an intellectual debate through which the expert reviewers challenged the authors to deepen and refine their perspective on a new dominant logic (NDL) for marketing. Subsequently, with the goal of stimulating public discussion and debate, I invited some distinguished scholars—George Day, John Deighton, Evert Gummesson, Shelby D. Hunt, C. K. Prahalad, Roland T. Rust, and Steven M. Shugan—to write brief commentaries for publication in the same issue of the *Journal*.

The *Journal* article and accompanying commentaries galvanized debate about the NDL among marketing academics, both in formal forums (e.g., conferences) and informal settings. Now, with the publication of *The Service-Dominant Logic of Marketing: Dialog, Debate, and Directions*, the intellectual debate has broadened and deepened, as represented by this collection of essays by eminent scholars from throughout the global marketing community. In this foreword, I offer a few observations—based on my knowledge of the history of the article's development—on the diversity of viewpoints expressed in this volume.

DEFINITION OF THE TERM *SERVICE*

This volume is titled *The Service-Dominant Logic of Marketing: Dialog, Debate and Directions*. The term *service-dominant logic* is controversial—even among scholars who believe that a new dominant logic is emerging for marketing. It is noteworthy that the authors offer a very specific definition of *service* that extends the conventional definition, specifically: "We define *service* as the application of specialized competences (knowledge and skills), through deeds, processes, and performances for the benefit of another entity or the entity itself." This definition is the keystone to the authors' argument that marketing is in the midst of an evolution to a new dominant logic. Consequently, the essays collected in this volume reveal the diverse ways that distinguished marketing scholars think about service—and, more importantly, how they think about the content and boundaries of marketing.

NEW INTELLECTUAL INSIGHTS

The article published in the *Journal* evolved from a monograph-length manuscript that traced the history of marketing thought from its earliest beginnings and synthesized the threads of many research streams, including resource-advantage theory and relationship marketing. Given that many of these ideas have long histories in the marketing literature, the thoughtful reader might be tempted to inquire, "What new intellectual insights are offered by the NDL perspective?" The short answer is that, by integrating diverse topics in business and marketing, the article identifies eight foundational premises that outline a "patchwork" (as its authors say) of the emerging dominant logic.

Given the specialization (and, some might say, fragmentation) of the marketing discipline in the past few decades, the article makes a remarkable contribution by synthesizing key aspects of marketing thought to develop a succinct framework that offers new and compelling insights for marketing. The essays in this volume contribute to an energizing and instructive debate (that still continues) about the conceptual underpinnings of the NDL. Three topics provoke considerable discussion in this volume: the distinction between operand and operant resources, co-production, and the relationship of the NDL to other perspectives.

IMPLICATIONS FOR MARKETING THEORY

The wide range of opinions expressed in this volume gives some indication of the fruitfulness of elaborating the NDL. Some authors explore its implications for marketing practice within organizations or networks, focusing on organizational activities such as customer equity management, integrated marketing communications, value chain management, cross-functional business processes, customer–firm co-production, and so forth. Other authors locate the NDL within the current business landscape and consider its alignment with organizational objectives regarding marketing productivity and long-run (financial) business performance. These essays are leavened by a pragmatic concern with NDL as a normative theory that can help identify "best practices" for business practice and pedagogy.

These "multiple logics" can be challenging as academics attempt to flesh out the NDL. For example, some authors question how the NDL helps researchers think about issues related to marketing and society, including the social and ethical dimensions of marketing, the evolution of aggregate marketing systems in different societies, the value created by markets, and so forth. There is yet another layer of complexity when one considers how the essays represent different traditions of marketing thought from around the world.

IMPLICATIONS FOR MANAGERIAL PRACTICE

Many business leaders believe that "enterprise integration"—that is, connecting and leveraging business processes that cut across traditional organizational silos—is (now) the key to business success. They are exploring the opportunities for competitive advantage that can be obtained by integrating supply chain management, customer relationship management, brand management, and so forth. The eight foundational premises of the NDL provide a useful starting point for considering how enterprise integration creates new capabilities for excellence in strategy and execution—thereby leading to superior business performance. Hence, the ideas expressed in this volume are likely to resonate strongly with executive-level managers.

CONTENT AND BOUNDARIES OF MARKETING

As editor of the *Journal of Marketing,* I have had many opportunities to read and discuss marketing science and practice with a wide range of academic researchers and business leaders, and it is my sense that we are in the midst of a change in the content and boundaries of the marketing discipline.[1] This volume of essays brings us closer to developing a comprehensive account of marketing phenomena. However, explanations of marketing phenomena, like explanations in the physical sciences, inevitably raise new questions for science and practice. Clearly, there is more work to be done. An NDL has important implications for marketing science, practice, and pedagogy —as well as for organizations and society. I invite you, in your own work, to consider the challenges and opportunities that an NDL offers for enhancing marketing thought and practice.

NOTE

1. See *Journal of Marketing* (Volume 69, Issue Number 4) for a collection of essays addressing this issue.

FOREWORD

FREDERICK E. WEBSTER, JR.

The service-dominant logic (SDL) model is exciting, important, and controversial. Going back to the roots of economic reasoning in moral philosophy and Adam Smith's *Wealth of Nations,* Vargo and Lusch propose a way of viewing marketing that is fundamentally different from, and often at odds with, the conventional wisdom of marketing that is based on the classical economic model. This new view of the marketing world is both promising and threatening, depending on how strongly one is committed to the microeconomics-based theoretical view of marketing as behavioral and quantitative science and the firm-based view of marketing management as an attempt to influence customers. As the range of excellent essays in this collection attests, the dialog about the strengths and weaknesses, promise and problems inherent in the SDL model is already in full swing and will undoubtedly continue for some time. The final outcome of that debate, and the shape of a new paradigm, is anything but certain.

For the past decade or so, marketing thought leaders, both in academe and business, have expressed increasing concerns about the state of marketing, both as a science and as a practice, and the strained relationship between the two. There is more agreement about the nature of the problems facing the field than there is about required changes and future direction. Certainly, no one is clear about the general theory that will emerge to replace current understanding of marketing as an academic discipline, field of practice, and intellectual domain.

It seems increasingly likely, however, that marketing is moving toward a new, or at least radically modified, dominant paradigm. Some would argue that the SDL model is a strong candidate to provide that conceptual framework because it is highly abstract and broad. Lusch and Vargo are, however, not among them; they specifically disclaim SDL as being a new theory or a paradigm shift in marketing. However, they do suggest in their concluding essay that SDL can potentially serve as the foundation for more integrative marketing theory to include perhaps a general theory. The reader will find it productive to read these essays in the context of this general question: Is the SDL model a robust alternative to the traditional view? As evidenced by the chapters that follow, there is a wide range of opinion on this question; this demonstrates that, at the minimum, the SDL approach provides a valuable contribution to the dialogue about necessary and evolving change in marketing.

The editors have assembled some of the world's preeminent scholars, whose thoughts have great value not just as commentaries on the SDL model but also for their fundamental understanding of marketing thought and practice. Uniquely valuable insights bubble up in every essay. The authors' comments reflect their own experience and point of view, each bringing a different perspective to the SDL paradigm. Several of the authors present their own (some old, some new) viewpoints as complementary frameworks to SDL. Among those junctions are customer value, resource-advantage theory, interaction, communication, relationships and networks, customer equity, and neoclassical economics itself, all of which have analogues in the Vargo and Lusch SDL paradigm. Other authors forcefully argue for their own ideas as competitors and contradictions to the SDL model.

It is useful to approach these essays with an eye out for points in the discussion of marketing theory that perhaps go beyond the appropriate boundaries on marketing as an intellectual domain whose roots, as argued by Lehmann and others, must be in business (or, more generally, economic organization) practice and related ultimately to financial performance. Ambler warns us to be wary when the discussion veers into a consideration of theory for its own sake, not of marketing itself.

The most basic question might be whether marketing theory should always reflect, and be able to inform and guide, marketing practice. Venkatesh, Peñaloza, and Firat believe that a managerial perspective actually has hindered the development of marketing, which they say should focus on the value created by markets, not by producers, and they evaluate SDL in that light. Wilkie and Moore would prefer that SDL focus not on firms but on the "aggregate marketing system" of marketers, consumers, and government entities. Most of the other commentators assess the validity of SDL against marketing practice and the actual problems facing marketing managers in an increasingly competitive marketplace, where the information available to more and more powerful customers is growing exponentially. Many commentators extend the SDL model in ways that show its potential for reshaping scholars' understanding of marketing. Defenders of the economics-based paradigm argue that it too is evolving, incorporating developments from strategic management and other disciplines, in directions consistent with SDL. Whereas some essays offer strong advocacy for the SDL formulation, others criticize it and defend important aspects of currently accepted marketing paradigms.

Readers who are familiar with the traditions of the marketing literature will recognize that many of the ideas contained in these chapters have long histories, a fact not always clearly acknowledged. Levy, however, notes that "even the innovators stand on the shoulders of those who came before." Furthermore, as some correctly point out, there are many innovative ideas about marketing that have their origins in business practice, not in academe. If current marketing thought development initiatives are focused on customer value and involve seeing products as bundles of user benefits, which is to say service (ideas that first appeared in the literature more than half a century ago), business practice has arguably raced ahead of marketing theory, as firms have sought more sustainable sources of differentiation and competitive advantage. For decades, as Brown and Bitner note, the most successful marketers have recognized that their superior knowledge of customers' perceptions, use systems, and buying behavior can be the most valuable, and hardest to duplicate, source of competitive advantage and superior business performance. Scholars focused on problems amenable to rigorous methodologies have lagged behind in the development of conceptual knowledge required to keep marketing science in step with and potentially leading management practice. The SDL paradigm is built around such important and fundamental concepts and derives much of its strength from its ability to integrate so many diverse but related ideas.

Do Vargo and Lusch go too far in dichotomizing the product-centric and customer-centric viewpoints? Is the SDL concept of co-production really different from the central idea in the industrial marketing strategy literature that no two customers ever buy the exact same product because product offerings are always tailored to each customer's specific needs and use system?

Do Vargo and Lusch discount too strongly the value of technology-driven innovation and manufacturing capabilities as bases for delivering customer value and building the value of firms for owners? Isn't selling (i.e., communication directed at potential customers as targets) ultimately a necessary step in delivering value to customers? Each reader will come to his or her own conclusion. Some of these authors think SDL does go too far, whereas others agree with Vargo and Lusch that this fundamental shift in perspective is the key to restoring the health of marketing as business function and academic discipline.

A good number of these essays accept the fundamental propositions of SDL and suggest theoretical extensions and business applications in such areas as market research, product development and pricing, and marketing communications. These extensions show that a successful evolution of the fundamental concepts of marketing has not only begun but is well underway. These essays provide a broad perspective on the many dimensions of change and the diversity of viewpoints pushing the boundaries of the marketing discipline. We can optimistically expect a burst of creativity in reconceptualizing the field of marketing to be stimulated by the recent work of the authors represented here. Teaching, practice, research, and theory development will all be changed for the better as a result.

PREFACE

Trying too hard to get things right sometimes results in restraining creativity. Even as we put the finishing touches on "Evolving to a New Dominant Logic for Marketing," which appeared in the January 2004 issue of the *Journal of Marketing,* we simultaneously felt that (1) we had successfully challenged the central tenets of marketing practice and theory, and (2) our writing and thought development had not been as creative as possible. In part, this dual evaluation was the outcome of the normal, somewhat regressive, scholarly journal review process in which multiple authors, multiple reviewers, and, in our case, multiple editors work together to "get it right"—in this instance a process that extended over five years and five manuscript revisions. At the same time, part of this was a function of the unfolding nature and the discovery process associated with our task. Our primary purpose in initiating this book of essays is to extend and expand the creative exploration and development of this "new dominant logic" for marketing, and thus to take one additional step in a continuing process of "getting it right."

Within weeks of the publication of "Evolving to a New Dominant Logic for Marketing" the number of inquiries and comments, positive and skeptical, signaled to us both the potential impact of our work and the scope of the additional effort required. One matter that became immediately apparent was the need to brand this new logic, because "new" had only short-term applicability and because it was being referred to by a variety of names with variously nuanced connotations. The essential notion behind what we originally identified as the "new dominant logic" is that it is service centered rather than goods centered. Thus, simply but appropriately, we branded it "Service-Dominant Logic."

The use of the singular *service* as opposed to the more common reference *services* is subtle but intentional. *Service* implies a process—applying operant resources for the benefit of another entity—whereas *services* implies units of output and therefore reflects the goods-dominant logic that we believe is flawed.

The essence of service-dominant (S-D) logic, then, is that service provision is the fundamental purpose of economic exchange and marketing—that is, service is exchanged for service. We believe this logic is applicable not only to markets and marketing, but also to society. Goods, money, organizations, and networks are intermediaries in the process of exchanging service for service. They are an important part of marketing and a market-based economy; however, they are collateral institutions.

Embracing S-D logic motivates one to view marketing differently. In fact, with an S-D logic lens, we define marketing as "the process in society and organizations that facilitates voluntary exchange through collaborative relationships that create reciprocal value through the application of complementary resources." Importantly, this view of marketing has three essential elements: (1) marketing is not only an organizational process but also a societal process; (2) marketing emphasizes voluntary exchange and collaborative relationships; and (3) parties obtain value by the application of complementary resources.

Over the past decade, and especially over the past eighteen-month development of this book, we have been very strong advocates of what we now call S-D logic. As we read the completed essays in this book, our belief in S-D logic has grown stronger. We believe the latitude we granted the contributors for exercising their creativity and providing their voice stimulated us to be more creative in our effort to deepen and expand the logic of S-D logic. Regardless of whether a particular author or authors offered agreement and extension or thoughtful critique and an alternative direction, all of the essays afforded us an opportunity to improve and extend our original thinking and commitment.

We believe that S-D logic has important implications that extend beyond the discipline of marketing, to customers, the firm, and society. We submit that with S-D logic, *finally,* customers are explicitly given equal importance to the firm, as they are recognized as co-creators of value and potentially of the firm's entire marketing strategy and program. *Finally,* the firm has a theoretical foundation that is applicable regardless of its offering and a theory of marketing that positions marketing as the dominant, harmonizing force behind both marketing strategy and overall business strategy. *Finally,* the role of marketing in society is clarified because S-D logic aligns society, markets, networks, organizations, and marketing, all as institutions for the exchange of applied operant resources (mental and physical skills)—service. *Finally,* marketing has a theoretical basis that informs marketing action (both micro and macro) that is liberated from the unrealistic assumptions of the standard microeconomic paradigm, one that has the potential of providing a foundation for a general theory of marketing. We think that perhaps the ultimate hallmark of S-D logic is this unification potential, through the simultaneous understanding of buyer behavior, seller behavior, institutional mechanisms that bring buyers and sellers together, and the role of marketing in society.

We would like to express our gratitude to the many people who read early drafts—going back nearly ten years—of our original work on S-D logic. We particularly recognize our prior colleagues at the University of Oklahoma: Mike Bolen, Pat Daugherty, Fred Morgan, Matthew O'Brien, and Dan Wren. Early readers of our work at other institutions included Shelby Hunt, Alan Malter, Lisa Scheer, and Gunter Wessels. More recently, we have also benefited from the advice of Ruth Bolton, George Day, Roland Rust, and Tor Andreassen who provided valuable guidance and advice in crafting and positioning either the final manuscript for our 2004 *Journal of Marketing* article on S-D logic or the essays for this book. We are also indebted to our editor, Harry Briggs, who recognized early the potential contribution of our work with S-D logic and the need for a collection of original essays to further expand thinking on the topic. At M.E. Sharpe we would also like to thank Elizabeth Granda and Angela Piliouras (managing editor) for their careful attention and dedication to this project.

Finally, we have gathered together in this book one of the largest collections of original essays by prominent marketing thought leaders ever assembled. Without their participation this book would not have been possible, and therefore our thanks go out to each contributor.

Consistent with S-D logic's advocacy of co-production and the co-creation of value, we invite the entire marketing community—including educators, students, researchers, managers, practitioners, and public policy makers—to participate in the continuing development of S-D logic. Only an open-source, collaborative effort can "get right" a fully developed theoretical framework that can serve the long-term needs of the discipline.

Robert F. Lusch   Stephen L. Vargo
Tucson, Arizona   Honolulu, Hawaii

PART I

FOUNDATIONAL ASPECTS OF THE SERVICE-DOMINANT LOGIC OF MARKETING

As we begin to explore the dialog, debate, and suggested directions the service-dominant (S-D) logic of marketing has stimulated, it is useful to examine the foundational aspects of S-D logic. We start with the reprinting, as Chapter 1, of "Evolving to a New Dominant Logic for Marketing," which appeared in the January 2004 issue of the *Journal of Marketing*. Ruth Bolton was editor of the *Journal* at the time and had the courage to publish this controversial article and the foresight to include a series of commentaries by marketing thought leaders. From the outset, we knew the article would be contentious; however, it stimulated even more dialog and debate than we had imagined. As we presented the central ideas and philosophy of S-D logic at dozens of forums and conferences around North America and beyond, we found, similar to what we had found in the review process associated with the original article, that people variously thought the article (1) was seminal and offered ideas that, if not revolutionary, certainly represented an positive inflection point in normal discourse in marketing thought; (2) communicated ideas that had already been presented, if not accepted; or (3) was outright wrong.

Because we were so constrained by space in our initial article, we felt it necessary to provide an expanded treatment of the historical perspectives of the S-D logic; joining us in this effort is Fred W. Morgan. "Historical Perspectives on Service-Dominant Logic" appears as Chapter 2. Some of the material in this chapter was in the original submission to the *Journal of Marketing* and was removed due to space constraints. Other parts are expanded on in an article by Steve Vargo and Fred Morgan in the June 2005 issue of the *Journal of Macromarketing*. And yet other parts attempt to show how many of the early approaches to the study of marketing, such as the functional and institutional approaches, were essentially service based. That is, the traditional functions of marketing—buying, selling, transportation, storage, information gathering, sorting, financing, and risk taking—all represented the performance of service by the seller, although often associated with a tangible product. Overall, it suggests that S-D logic represents the confluence of a number of streams of thought and research that were previously viewed as diverse.

From the start of the dialog and debate around the rather simple idea of the need for a service-dominant logic of marketing, we also noted considerable misunderstanding in just what S-D logic represents. We attempt to clarify and correct these misunderstandings and occasional misattributions in Chapter 3, "Service-Dominant Logic: What It Is, What It Is Not, What It Might Be."

Most of the confusion has involved issues of what S-D logic is versus what it is not. We have repeatedly seen—including in some of the essays in this collection—that the following impre-cise, if not inaccurate, statements have been attributed to S-D logic: (1) It is a reflection of the transition from an industrial era to a services era; (2) it portrays service(s) as more important than goods; (3) it is merely a restatement of customer orientation; (4) it is justified by the superior customer responsiveness of services firms; (5) it is an alternative to the exchange paradigm; (6) it employs *service* as another word for *utility* or *value-added*; (7) it argues against and does not acknowledge the role of value-in-exchange; (8) it is only applicable to profit-oriented firms be-cause financial feedback implies profit; and (9) it is primarily managerial in orientation. We try to explain why none of these characterizations of S-D logic is accurate or valid. Looking to the future, we offer our vantage point on what S-D logic might be. We argue that S-D logic is perhaps the foundation of a paradigm shift in marketing, the basis of a new theory of the firm, a prescrip-tion for a reorientation of economic theory, and a rationale for a theory of society.

Part I concludes with Chapter 4, "How New, How Dominant?" a provocative essay by Sidney Levy. Few scholars in their eighth decade of life continue to come to the office almost daily, lecture around the world, read daily, and write often. As winner of virtually every major award for scholarship in marketing and consumer behavior and simply as a wise older one, we should listen carefully. Professor Levy observes, "Even the innovators stand on the shoulder of those who came before"; we wholeheartedly agree. As with the reactions to "Evolving to a New Domi-nant Logic for Marketing" during the review process and since, we found in reading the essays for this volume that people often have strong, varied views about S-D logic. As Professor Levy states it: S-D logic will be met with "interest and mixed support." We would rather have it this way than to just have total agreement, which would suggest we were not upsetting the status quo, or total rejection, which would suggest our ideas are not worthy of further dialog and debate. In fact, it is our goal with this collection of essays by marketing thought leaders to provide a plat-form for the identification and exploration of the areas of agreement and disagreement. In the spirit of S-D logic, our value proposition is to co-create a new paradigm for marketing—one that is generalizable to marketing practices, offerings, industries, and societies of varied types. For this to occur a dialog and continuing conversation is of paramount importance.

EVOLVING TO A NEW DOMINANT LOGIC FOR MARKETING

STEPHEN L. VARGO AND ROBERT F. LUSCH

The formal study of marketing focused at first on the distribution and exchange of commodities and manufactured products and featured a foundation in economics (Marshall 1927; Shaw 1912; Smith 1904). The first marketing scholars directed their attention toward commodities exchange (Copeland 1923), the marketing institutions that made goods available and arranged for possession (Nystrom 1915; Weld 1916), and the functions that needed to be performed to facilitate the exchange of goods through marketing institutions (Cherington 1920; Weld 1917).

By the early 1950s, the functional school began to morph into the marketing management school, which was characterized by a decision-making approach to managing the marketing functions and an overarching focus on the customer (Drucker 1954; Levitt 1960; McKitterick 1957). McCarthy (1960) and Kotler (1967) characterized marketing as a decision-making activity directed at satisfying the customer at a profit by targeting a market and then making optimal decisions on the marketing mix, or the "4 P's." The fundamental foundation and the tie to the standard economic model continued to be strong. The leading marketing management textbook in the 1970s (Kotler 1972, p. 42, emphasis in original) stated that "marketing management seeks to determine the settings of the company's *marketing decision variables* that will maximize the company's objective(s) in the light of the expected behavior of noncontrollable *demand variables.*"

Beginning in the 1980s, many new frames of reference that were not based on the 4 P's and were largely independent of the standard microeconomic paradigm began to emerge. What appeared to be separate lines of thought surfaced in relationship marketing, quality management, market orientation, supply and value chain management, resource management, and networks. Perhaps most notable was the emergence of services marketing as a subdiscipline, following scholars' challenges to "break free" (Shostack 1977) from product marketing and recognize the inadequacies of the dominant logic for dealing with services marketing's subject matter (Dixon 1990). Many scholars believed that marketing thought was becoming more fragmented. On the surface, this appeared to be a reasonable characterization.

In the early 1990s, Webster (1992, p. 1) argued, "The historical marketing management function, based on the microeconomic maximization paradigm, must be critically examined for its relevance to marketing theory and practice." At the end of the twentieth century, Day and Montgom-

From *The Journal of Marketing,* vol. 68, no. 1 (January 2004): 1–17. Copyright © 2004 American Marketing Association. Reprinted with permission.

ery (1999, p. 3) suggested that "with growing reservation about the validity or usefulness of the Four P's concept and its lack of recognition of marketing as an innovating or adaptive force, the Four P's now are regarded as merely a handy framework." At the same time, advocating a network perspective, Achrol and Kotler (1999, p. 162) stated, "The very nature of network organization, the kinds of theories useful to its understanding, and the potential impact on the organization of consumption all suggest that a paradigm shift for marketing may not be far over the horizon." Sheth and Parvatiyar (2000, p. 140) suggested that "an alternative paradigm of marketing is needed, a paradigm that can account for the continuous nature of relationships among marketing actors." They went as far as stating (p. 140) that the marketing discipline "give up the sacred cow of exchange theory." Other scholars, such as Rust (1998), called for convergence among seemingly divergent views.

Fragmented thought, questions about the future of marketing, calls for a paradigm shift, and controversy over services marketing being a distinct area of study—are these calls for alarm? Perhaps marketing thought is not so much fragmented as it is evolving toward a new dominant logic. Increasingly, marketing has shifted much of its dominant logic away from the exchange of tangible goods (manufactured things) and toward the exchange of intangibles, specialized skills and knowledge, and processes (doing things for and with), which we believe points marketing toward a more comprehensive and inclusive dominant logic, one that integrates goods with services and provides a richer foundation for the development of marketing thought and practice.

Rust (1998, p. 107) underscores the importance of such an integrative view of goods and services: "[T]he typical service research article documented ways in which services were different from goods. . . . It is time for a change. Service research is not a niche field characterized by arcane points of difference with the dominant goods management field." The dominant, goods-centered view of marketing not only may hinder a full appreciation for the role of services but also may partially block a complete understanding of marketing in general (see, e.g., Grönroos 1994; Kotler 1997; Normann and Ramirez 1993; Schlesinger and Heskett 1991). For example, Gummesson (1995, pp. 250–51, emphasis added) states the following:

> Customers do not buy goods or services: [T]hey buy offerings which render services which create value. . . . The traditional division between goods and services is long outdated. It is not a matter of redefining services and seeing them from a customer perspective; *activities render services, things render services*. The shift in focus to services is a shift from the means and the producer perspective to the utilization and the customer perspective.

The purpose of this article is to illuminate the evolution of marketing thought toward a new dominant logic. A summary of this evolution over the past 100 years is provided in Figure 1.1 and Table 1.1. Briefly, marketing has moved from a goods-dominant view, in which tangible output and discrete transactions were central, to a service-dominant view, in which intangibility, exchange processes, and relationships are central. It is worthwhile to note that the service-centered view should not be equated with (1) the restricted, traditional conceptualizations that often treat services as a residual (that which is not a tangible good; e.g., Rathmell 1966); (2) something offered to enhance a good (value-added services); or (3) what have become classified as services industries, such as health care, government, and education. Rather, we define services as the application of specialized competences (knowledge and skills) through deeds, processes, and performances for the benefit of another entity or the entity itself. Although our definition is compatible with narrower, more traditional definitions, we argue that it is more inclusive and that it captures the fundamental function of all business enterprises.[1] Thus, the service-centered dominant logic represents a reoriented philosophy that is applicable to all marketing offerings, including those that involve tangible output (goods) in the process of service provision.

Figure 1.1 **Evolving to a New Dominant Logic for Marketing**

Pre-1900

Goods Centered Model of Exchange (concepts: tangibles, statics, discrete transactions, operand resources).

Thought leaders in marketing continually move away from tangible output with embedded value where the focus was on activities directed at discrete or static transactions. In turn they move toward dynamic exchange relationships that involve performing processes and exchanging skills and/or services where value is co-created with the consumer. The worldview changes from a focus on resources upon which an operation or act is performed (operand resources) to resources that produce effects (operant resources).

Twenty-first Century

Services Centered Model of Exchange (concepts: intangibles, competences, dynamics, exchange processes and relationships, operant resources)

Classical and Neoclassical Economics (1800–1920)

Formative Marketing Thought (Descriptive: 1900–1950)

- Commodities
- Marketing institutions
- Marketing functions

Marketing Management School of Thought (1950–2000)

- Customer orientation and marketing concept
- Value determined in marketplace
- Manage marketing functions to achieve optimal output
- Marketing science emerges and emphasizes use of optimization techniques

Marketing as a Social & Economic Process (Emerging Paradigm: 1980–2000+)

- Market orientation processes
- Services marketing processes
- Relationship marketing processes
- Quality management processes
- Value and Supply management processes
- Resource management and competitive processes

Table 1.1

Schools of Thought and Their Influence on Marketing Theory and Practice

Timeline and stream of literature	Fundamental ideas or propositions
1800–1920: Classical and Neoclassical Economics • Marshall (1890); Say (1821); • Shaw (1912); Smith (1776)	Economics became the first social science to reach the quantitative sophistication of the natural sciences. Value is embedded in matter through manufacturing (value-added, utility, value-in-exchange); goods come to be viewed as standardized output (commodities). Wealth in society is created by the acquisition of tangible "stuff." Marketing as matter in motion.
1900–1950: Early/Formative Marketing • Commodities (Copeland 1923) • Institutions (Nystrom 1915; Weld 1916) • Functional (Cherington 1920; Weld 1917)	Early marketing thought was highly descriptive of commodities, institutions, and marketing functions: commodity school (characteristics of goods), institutional school (role of marketing institutions in value-embedding process), and functional school (functions that marketers perform). A major focus was on the transaction or output and how institutions performing marketing functions added value to commodities. Marketing primarily provided time and place utility, and a major goal was possession utility (creating a transfer of title and/or sale). However, a focus on functions is the beginning of the recognition of operant resources.
1950–1980: Marketing Management • Business should be customer focused (Drucker 1954; McKitterick 1957) • Value "determined" in marketplace (Levitt 1960) • Marketing is a decision-making and problem-solving function (Kotler 1967; McCarthy 1960)	Firms can use analytical techniques (largely from microeconomics) to try to define the marketing mix for optimal firm performance. Value "determined" in marketplace; "embedded" value must have usefulness. Customers do not buy things but need or want fulfillment. Everyone in the firm must be focused on the customer because the firm's only purpose is to create a satisfied customer. Identification of the functional responses to the changing environment that provide competitive advantage through differentiation begins to shift toward value in use.
1980–2000 and Forward: Marketing as a Social and Economic Process • Market orientation (Kohli and Jaworski 1990; Narver and Slater 1990) • Services marketing (Grönroos 1984; Zeithaml, Parasuraman, and Berry 1985) • Relationship marketing (Berry 1983; Duncan and Moriarty 1998; Gummesson 1994, 2002; Sheth and Parvatiyar 2000)	A dominant logic begins to emerge that largely views marketing as a continuous social and economic processin which operant resources are paramount. This logic views financial results not as an end result but as a test of a market hypothesis about a value proposition. The marketplace can falsify market hypotheses, which enables entities to learn about their actions, find ways to better serve their customers and to improve financial performance.

(continued)

Table 1.1 *(continued)*

Timeline and stream of literature	Fundamental ideas or propositions
• Quality management (Hauser and Clausing 1988; Parasuraman, Zeithaml, and Berry 1988) • Value and supply chain management (Normann and Ramirez 1993; Srivastava, Shervani, and Fahey 1999) • Resource management (Constantin and Lusch 1994; Day 1994; Dickson 1992; Hunt 2000; Hunt and Morgan 1995) • Network analysis (Achrol 1991; Achrol and Kotler 1999; Webster 1992)	This paradigm begins to unify disparate literature streams in major areas such as customer and market orientation, services marketing, relationship marketing, quality management, value and supply chain management, resource management, and network analysis. The foundational premises of the emerging paradigm are (1) skills and knowledge are the fundamental unit of exchange, (2) indirect exchange masks the fundamental unit of exchange, (3) goods are distribution mechanismsfor service provision, (4) knowledge is the fundamental source of competitive advantage, (5) all economies are services economies, (6) the customer is always a co-producer, (7) the enterprise can only make valuepropositions, and (8) a service-centered view is inherently customer oriented and relational.

A FUNDAMENTAL SHIFT IN WORLDVIEW

To unravel the changing worldview of marketing or its dominant logic, we must see into, through, and beyond the extant marketing literature. A worldview or dominant logic is never clearly stated but more or less seeps into the individual and collective mind-set of scientists in a discipline. Predictably, this requires viewing the world at a highly abstract level. We begin our discussion with the work of Thomas Malthus.

In his analysis of world resources, Thomas Malthus (1798) concluded that with continued geometric population growth, society would soon run out of resources. In a Malthusian world, "resources" means natural resources that humans draw on for support. Resources are essentially "stuff" that is static and to be captured for advantage. In Malthus's time, much of the political and economic activity involved individual people, organizations, and nations working toward and struggling and fighting over acquiring this stuff. Over the past fifty years, resources have come to be viewed not only as stuff but also as intangible and dynamic functions of human ingenuity and appraisal, and thus they are not static or fixed. Everything is neutral (or perhaps even a resistance) until humankind learns what to do with it (Zimmerman 1951). Essentially, resources are not; they become. As we discuss, this change in perspective on resources helps provide a framework for viewing the new dominant logic of marketing.

Constantin and Lusch (1994) define operand resources as resources on which an operation or act is performed to produce an effect, and they compare operand resources with operant resources, which are employed to act on operand resources (and other operant recourses). During most of civilization, human activity has been concerned largely with acting on the land, animal life, plant life, minerals, and other natural resources. Because these resources are finite, nations, clans, tribes, or other groups that possessed natural resources were considered wealthy. A goods-centered dominant logic developed in which the operand resources were considered primary. A firm (or nation) had factors of production (largely operand resources) and a technology (an operant resource), which had value to the extent that the firm could convert its operand resources into outputs at a low cost. Customers, like resources, became something to be captured or acted on, as English vocabulary would eventually suggest; we "segment" the market, "penetrate" the market, and "promote to" the market all in hope of attracting customers. Share of operand resources and share of (an operand) market was the key to success.

Operant resources are resources that produce effects (Constantin and Lusch 1994). The relative role of operant resources began to shift in the late twentieth century as humans began to realize that skills and knowledge were the most important types of resources. Zimmermann (1951) and Penrose (1959) were two of the first economists to recognize the shifting role and view of resources. As Hunt (2000, p. 75) observes, Penrose did not use the popular term *factor of production* but rather used the term *collection of productive resources*. Penrose suggested (pp. 24–25; emphasis in original) that "it is never *resources* themselves that are the 'inputs' to the production process, but only the *services* that the resources can render."

Operant resources are often invisible and intangible; often they are core competences or organizational processes. They are likely to be dynamic and infinite and not static and finite, as is usually the case with operand resources. Because operant resources produce effects, they enable humans both to multiply the value of natural resources and to create additional operant resources. A well-known illustration of operant resources is the microprocessor: Human ingenuity and skills took one of the most plentiful natural resources on Earth (silica) and embedded it with knowledge. As Copeland (qtd. in Gilder 1984) has observed, in the end the microprocessor is pure idea. As we noted previously, resources are not; they become (Zimmermann 1951). The service-centered dominant logic perceives operant resources as primary, because they are the producers of effects. This shift in the primacy of resources has implications for how exchange processes, markets, and customers are perceived and approached.

GOODS VERSUS SERVICES: RETHINKING THE ORIENTATION

Viewed in its traditional sense, marketing focuses largely on operand resources, primarily goods, as the unit of exchange. In its most rudimentary form, the goods-centered view postulates the following:

1. The purpose of economic activity is to make and distribute things that can be sold.
2. To be sold, these things must be embedded with utility and value during the production and distribution processes and must offer to the consumer superior value in relation to competitors' offerings.
3. The firm should set all decision variables at a level that enables it to maximize the profit from the sale of output.
4. For both maximum production control and efficiency, the good should be standardized and produced away from the market.
5. The good can then be inventoried until it is demanded and then delivered to the consumer at a profit.

Because early marketing thought was concerned with agricultural products and then with other physical goods, it was compatible with this rudimentary view. Before 1960, marketing was viewed as a transfer of ownership of goods and their physical distribution (Savitt 1990); it was viewed as the "application of motion to matter" (Shaw 1912, p. 764). The marketing literature rarely mentioned "immaterial products" or "services," and when it did, it mentioned them only as "aids to the production and marketing of goods" (Converse 1921, p. vi; see Fisk, Brown, and Bitner 1993). An early fragmentation in the marketing literature occurred when Shostack (1977, p. 73) noted, "The classical 'marketing mix,' the seminal literature, and the language of marketing all derive from the manufacture of physical-goods."

Marketing inherited the view that value (utility) was embedded in a product from economics. One of the first debates in the fledgling discipline of marketing centered on the question, If value was something added to goods, did marketing contribute to value? Shaw (1912, p. 12; see also Shaw 1994) argued that "Industry is concerned with the application of motion to matter to change its form and place. The change in form we term production; the change in place, distribution." Weld (1916) more formally defined marketing's role in production as the creation of the time, place, and possession utilities, which is the classification found in current marketing literature.

The general concept of utility has been broadly accepted in marketing, but its meaning has been interpreted differently. For example, discussing Beckman's (1957) and Alderson's (1957) treatments of utility, Dixon (1990, pp. 337–38, emphasis in original) argues that "each writer uses a different concept of value. Beckman is arguing in terms of *value-in-exchange*, basing his calculation on value-added, upon 'the selling value' of products. . . . Alderson is reasoning in terms of *value-in-use*." Drawing on Cox (1965), Dixon (1990, p. 342) believes the following:

> The "conventional view" of marketing as adding properties to matter caused a problem for Alderson and "makes more difficult a disinterested evaluation of what marketing is and does" (Cox 1965). This view also underlies the dissatisfaction with marketing theory that led to the services marketing literature. If marketing is the process that adds properties to matter, then it can not contribute to the production of "immaterial goods."

Alderson (1957, p. 69) advised, "What is needed is not an interpretation of the utility created by marketing, but a marketing interpretation of the whole process of creating utility." Dixon (1990, p. 342) suggests that "the task of responding to Alderson's challenge remains."

The service-centered view of marketing implies that marketing is a continuous series of social and economic processes that is largely focused on operant resources with which the firm is constantly striving to make better value propositions than its competitors. In a free enterprise system, the firm primarily knows whether it is making better value propositions from the feedback it receives from the marketplace in terms of firm financial performance. Because firms can always do better at serving customers and improving financial performance, the service-centered view of marketing perceives marketing as a continuous learning process (directed at improving operant resources). The service-centered view can be stated as follows:

1. Identify or develop core competences, the fundamental knowledge and skills of an economic entity that represent potential competitive advantage.
2. Identify other entities (potential customers) that could benefit from these competences.
3. Cultivate relationships that involve the customers in developing customized, competitively compelling value propositions to meet specific needs.
4. Gauge marketplace feedback by analyzing financial performance from exchange to learn how to improve the firm's offering to customers and improve firm performance.

This view is grounded in and largely consistent with resource-advantage theory (Conner and Prahalad 1996; Hunt 2000; Srivastava, Fahey, and Christensen 2001) and core competency theory

(Day 1994; Prahalad and Hamel 1990). Core competences are not physical assets but intangible processes; they are "bundles of skills and technologies" (Hamel and Prahalad 1994, p. 202) and are often routines, actions, or operations that are tacit, causally ambiguous, and idiosyncratic (Nelson and Winter 1982; Polanyi 1966). Hunt (2000, p. 24) refers to core competences as higher-order resources because they are bundles of basic resources. Teece and Pisano (1994, p. 537) suggest that "the competitive advantage of firms stems from dynamic capabilities rooted in high performance routines operating inside the firm, embedded in the firm's processes, and conditioned by its history." Hamel and Prahalad (pp. 202, 204) discuss "competition for competence," or competitive advantage resulting from competence making a "disproportionate contribution to customer-perceived value."

The focus of marketing on core competences inherently places marketing at the center of the integration of business functions and disciplines. As Prahalad and Hamel (1990, p. 82) suggest, "core competence is communication, involvement, and a deep commitment to working across organizational boundaries." In addition, they state (p. 82) that core competences are "collective learning in the organization, especially [about] how to coordinate diverse production skills." This cross-functional, intraorganizational boundary-spanning also applies to the interorganizational boundaries of vertical marketing systems or networks. Channel intermediaries and network partners represent core competences that are organized to gain competitive advantage by performing specialized marketing functions. The firms can have long-term viability only if they learn in conjunction with and are coordinated with other channel and network partners.

The service-centered view of marketing is customer-centric (Sheth, Sisodia, and Sharma 2000) and market driven (Day 1999). This means more than simply being consumer oriented; it means collaborating with and learning from customers and being adaptive to their individual and dynamic needs. A service-centered dominant logic implies that value is defined by and co-created with the consumer rather than embedded in output. Haeckel (1999) observes successful firms moving from practicing a "make-and-sell" strategy to a "sense-and-respond" strategy. Day (1999, p. 70) argues for thinking in terms of self-reinforcing "value cycles" rather than linear value chains. In the service-centered view of marketing, firms are in a process of continual hypothesis generation and testing. Outcomes (e.g., financial) are not something to be maximized but something to learn from as firms try to serve customers better and improve their performance. Thus, a market-oriented and learning organization (Slater and Narver 1995) is compatible with, if not implied by, the service-centered model. Because of its central focus on dynamic and learned core competences, the emerging service-centered dominant logic is also compatible with emerging theories of the firm. For example, Teece and Pisano (1994, p. 540) emphasize that competences and capabilities are "ways of organizing and getting things done, which cannot be accomplished by using the price system to coordinate activity."

Having described the goods- and service-centered views of marketing, we turn to ways that the views are different. Six differences between the goods- and service-centered dominant logic, all centered on the distinction between operand and operant resources, are presented in Table 1.2. The six attributes and our eight foundational premises (FPs) help present the patchwork of the emerging dominant logic.

FP$_1$: THE APPLICATION OF SPECIALIZED SKILLS AND KNOWLEDGE IS THE FUNDAMENTAL UNIT OF EXCHANGE

People have two basic operant resources: physical and mental skills. Both types of skills are distributed unequally in a population. Each person's skills are not necessarily optimal for his or

Table 1.2

Operand and Operant Resources Help Distinguish the Logic of the Goods- and Service-Centered Views

	Traditional goods-centered dominant logic	Emerging service-centered dominant logic
Primary unit of exchange	People exchange for goods. These goods serve primarily as operand resources.	People exchange to acquire the benefits of specialized competences (knowledge and skills), or services. Knowledge and skills are operant resources.
Role of goods	Goods are operand resources and end products. Marketers take matter and change its form, place, time, and possession.	Goods are transmitters of operant resources (embedded knowledge); they are intermediate "products" that are used by other operant resources (customers) as appliances in value-creation processes.
Role of customer	The customer is the recipient of goods. Marketers do things to customers; they segment them, penetrate them, distribute to them, and promote to them. The customer is an operand resource.	The customer is a co-producer of service. Marketing is a process of doing things in interaction with the customer. The customer is primarily an operant resource, functioning only occasionally as an operand resource.
Determination and meaning of value	Value is determined by the producer. It is embedded in the operand resource (goods) and is defined in terms of "exchange value."	Value is perceived and determined by the consumer on the basis of "value in use." Value results from the beneficial application of operant resources sometimes transmitted through operand resources. Firms can only make value propositions.
Firm–customer interaction	The customer is an operand resource. Customers are acted on to create transactions with resources.	The customer is primarily an operant resource. Customers are active participants in relational exchanges and co-production.
Source of economic growth	Wealth is obtained from surplus tangible resources and goods. Wealth consists of owning, controlling, and producing operand resources.	Wealth is obtained through the application and exchange of specialized knowledge and skills. It represents the right to the future use of operant resources.

her survival and well-being; therefore, specialization is more efficient for society and for individual members of society. Largely because they specialize in particular skills, people (or other entities) achieve scale effects. This specialization requires exchange (Macneil 1980; Smith 1904). Studying exchange in ancient societies, Mauss (1990) shows how division of labor within and between clans and tribes results in the tendering of "total services" by gift giving among clans and tribes. Not only do people contract for services from one another by giving and receiving gifts, but, as Mauss (p. 6) observes, "there is total service in the sense that it is indeed the whole clan that contracts on behalf of all, for all that it possesses and for all that it does."

This exchange of specializations leads to two views about what is exchanged. The first view involves the output from the performance of the specialized activities; the second involves the performance of the specialized activities. That is, if two parties jointly provide for each other's carbohydrate and protein needs by having one party specialize in fishing knowledge and skills and the other specialize in farming knowledge and skills, the exchange is one of fish for wheat or of the application of fishing knowledge or competence (fishing services) for the application of farming knowledge or competence (farming services).

The relationships between specialized skills and exchange have been recognized as far back as Plato's time, and the concept of the division of labor served as the foundation for Smith's (1904) seminal work in economics. However, Smith focused on only a subclass of human skills: the skills that resulted in surplus tangible output (in general, tangible goods and especially manufactured goods) that could be exported and thus contributed to national wealth. Smith recognized that the foundation of exchange was human skills as well as the necessity and usefulness of skills that did not result in tangible goods (i.e., services); they were simply not "productive" in terms of his national wealth standard. More than anything else, Smith was a moral philosopher who had the normative purpose of explaining how the division of labor and exchange should contribute to social well-being. In the sociopolitical milieu of his time, social well-being was defined as national wealth, and national wealth was defined in terms of exportable things (operand resources). Thus, for Smith, "productive" activity was limited to the creation of tangible goods, or output that has exchange value.

At that time, Smith's focus on exchange value represented a departure from the more accepted focus on value in use, and it had critical implications for how economists, and later marketers, would view exchange. Smith was aware of the schoolmen's and early economic scholars' view that "The Value of all Wares arises from their use" (Barbon 1903, p. 21) and that "nothing has a price among men except pleasure, and only satisfactions are purchased" (Galiani qtd. in Dixon 1990, p. 304). But this use-value interpretation was not consistent with Smith's national wealth standard. For Smith, "wealth consisted of tangible goods, not the use made of them" (Dixon 1990, p. 340). Although most early economists (e.g., Mill 1929; Say 1821) took exception to this singular focus on tangible output, they nonetheless acquiesced to Smith's view that the proper subject matter for economic philosophy was the output of "productive" skills or services, that is, tangible goods that have embedded value.

Frederic Bastiat was an early economic scholar who did not acquiesce to the dominant view. Bastiat criticized the political economists' view that value was tied only to tangible objects. For Bastiat (1860, p. 40), the foundations of economics were people who have "wants" and who seek "satisfactions." Although a want and its satisfaction are specific to each person, the effort required is often provided by others. For Bastiat (1964, pp. 161–62), "the great economic law is this: *Services are exchanged for services*. . . . It is trivial, very commonplace; it is, nonetheless, the beginning, the middle, and the end of economic science." He argued (1860, p. 43) the following: "[I]t is in fact to this faculty . . . *to work the one for the other*; it is this *transmission of efforts, this exchange of services* [this emphasis added], with all the infinite and involved combinations to which it gives rise . . . which constitutes Economic Science, points out its origin, and determines its limits."

Therefore, value was considered the comparative appreciation of reciprocal skills or services that are exchanged to obtain utility; value meant "value in use." As Mill (1929) did, Bastiat recognized that by using their skills (operant resources), humans could only transform matter (operand resources) into a state from which they could satisfy their desires.

However, the narrower focus on the tangible output with exchange value had several advantages for the early economists' quest of turning economic philosophy into an economic science, not the least of which was economics' similarity to the subject matter of the archetypical science of the day: Newtonian mechanics. The treatment of value as embedded utility, or value added (exchange value), enabled economists (e.g., Marshall 1927; Walras 1954) to ignore both the application of mental and physical skills (services) that transformed matter into a potentially useful state and the actual usefulness as perceived by the consumer (value in use). Thus, economics evolved into the science of matter (tangible goods) that is embedded with utility, as a result of manufacturing, and has value in exchange.

It was from this manufacturing-based view of economics that marketing emerged 100 years later. Throughout the period that marketing was primarily concerned with the distribution of physical goods, the goods-centered model was probably adequate. However, as the focus of marketing moved away from distribution and toward the process of exchange, economists began to perceive the accepted idea of marketing adding time, place, and possession utility (Weld 1916) as inadequate. As we noted previously, Alderson (1957, p. 69) advised, "What is needed is not an interpretation of the utility created by marketing, but a marketing interpretation of the whole process of creating utility." Shostack (1977, p. 74) issued a much more encompassing challenge than to "break [services marketing] free from product marketing"; she argued for a "new conceptual framework" and suggested the following:

> One unorthodox possibility can be drawn from direct observation of the nature of market "satisfiers" available to it. . . . How should the automobile be defined? Is General Motors marketing a service, a service that happens to include a by-product called a car? Levitt's classic "Marketing Myopia" exhorts businessmen to think exactly this generic way about what they market. Are automobiles "tangible services"?

Shostack concluded (p. 74) that "if 'either–or' terms (product [versus] service) do not adequately describe the true nature of marketed entities, it makes sense to explore the usefulness of a new structural definition." We believe that the emerging service-centered model meets Shostack's challenge, addresses Alderson's argument, and elaborates on Levitt's (1960) exhortation.

FP$_2$: INDIRECT EXCHANGE MASKS THE FUNDAMENTAL UNIT OF EXCHANGE

Over time, exchange moved from the one-to-one trading of specialized skills to the indirect exchange of skills in vertical marketing systems and increasingly large, bureaucratic, hierarchical organizations. During the same time, the exchange process became increasingly monetized. Consequently, the inherent focus on the customer as a direct trading partner largely disappeared. Because of industrial society's increasing division of labor, its growth of vertical marketing systems, and its large bureaucratic and hierarchical organizations, most marketing personnel (and employees in general) stopped interacting with customers (Webster 1992). In addition, because of the confluence of these forces, the skills-for-skills (services-for-services) nature of exchange became masked.

The Industrial Revolution had a tremendous impact on efficiency, but this came at a price, at least in terms of the visibility of the true nature of exchange. Skills (at least "manufacturing" skills, such as making sharp sticks) that had been tailored to specific needs were taken out of cottage industry and mechanized, standardized, and broken down into skills that had increasingly narrow purposes (e.g., sharpening one side of sticks). Workers' specialization increasingly became microspecialization (i.e., the performance of increasingly narrow-skilled proficiencies). Organizations acquired and organized microspecializations to produce what people wanted, and thus it became easier for people to engage in exchange by providing their microspecializations to organizations. However, the microspecialists seldom completed a product or interacted with a customer. They were compensated indirectly with money paid by the organization and exchangeable in the market for the skills the microspecialists needed rather than with direct, reciprocal skill-provision by the customer. Thus, organizations further masked the skills-for-skills (services-for-services) nature of exchange. Organizations themselves specialized (e.g., by making sticks but relying on other organizations such as wholesalers and retailers to distribute them), thus further masking the nature of exchange.

As organizations continued to increase in size, they began to realize that virtually all their workers had lost sense of both the customer (Hauser and Clausing 1988) and the purpose of their own service provision. The workers, who performed microspecialized functions deep within the organization, had internal customers, or other workers. One worker would perform a microspecialized task and then pass the work product on to another worker, who would perform an activity; this process continued throughout a service chain. Because the workers along the chain did not pay one another (reciprocally exchange with one another) and did not typically deal directly with external customers, they could ignore quality and both internal and external customers. To correct for this problem, various management techniques were developed under the rubric of total quality management (Cole and Mogab 1995). The techniques were intended to reestablish the focus of workers and the organization on both internal and external customers and quality.

The problem of organizations and their workers not paying attention to the customer is not unique to manufacturing organizations. If an organization simply provides intangibles, has some microspecialists who interact with customers, and is in an industry categorized as a "service" industry, it is not necessarily more customer focused. Many non-goods-producing organizations, especially large bureaucracies, are just as subject as goods-producing institutions to the masking effect of indirect exchange; they also provide services through organized microspecializations that are focused on minute and isolated aspects of service provision.

Regardless of the type of organization, the fundamental process does not change; people still exchange their often collective and distributed specialized skills for the individual and collective skills of others in monetization and marketing systems. People still exchange their services for other services. Money, goods, organizations, and vertical marketing systems are only the exchange vehicles.

FP₃: GOODS ARE DISTRIBUTION MECHANISMS FOR SERVICE PROVISION

The view of tangible products as the fundamental components of economic exchange served reasonably well as Western societies entered the Industrial Revolution, and the primary interest of the developing science of economics was manufacturing. Given its early concerns with the distribution of manufactured and agricultural goods, the view also worked relatively well when it was adopted by marketing. However, marketing has moved well beyond distribution and is now concerned with more than the exchange of goods. Goods are not the common denominator of exchange; the common denominator is the application of specialized knowledge, mental skills, and, to a lesser extent, physical labor (physical skills).

Knowledge and skills can be transferred (1) directly, (2) through education or training, or (3) indirectly by embedding them in objects. Thus, tangible products can be viewed as embodied knowledge or activities (Normann and Ramirez 1993). Wheels, pulleys, internal combustion engines, and integrated chips are all examples of encapsulated knowledge, which informs matter and in turn becomes the distribution channel for skill application (i.e., services).

The matter, embodied with knowledge, is an "appliance" for the performance of services; it replaces direct service. Norris (1941, p. 136) was one of the first scholars to recognize that people want goods because they provide services. Prahalad and Hamel (1990, p. 85) refer to products (goods) as "the physical embodiments of one or more competencies." The wheel and pulley reduce the need for physical strength. A pharmaceutical provides medical services. A well-designed and easy-to-use razor replaces barbering services, and vacuum cleaners and other household appliances make household chores less labor intensive. Computers and applications software can substitute for the direct services of accountants, attorneys, physicians, and teachers. Kotler (1977, p. 8) notes that the "importance of physical products lies not so much in owning them as in obtaining the services they render." Gummesson (1995, p. 251) argues that "activities render services, things render services." Hollander (1979, p. 43) suggests that "services may be replaced by products" and compares barber shaves to safety razors and laundry services to washing machines.

In addition to their direct service provision, the appliances serve as platforms for meeting higher-order needs (Rifkin 2000). Prahalad and Ramaswamy (2000, p. 84) refer to the appliances as "artifacts, around which customers have experiences" (see also Pine and Gilmore 1999). Gutman (1982, p. 60) has pointed out that products are "means" for reaching "end-states," or "valued states of being, such as happiness, security, and accomplishment." That is, people often purchase goods because owning them, displaying them, and experiencing them (e.g., enjoying knowing that they have a sports car parked in the garage, showing it off to others, and experiencing its handling ability) provide satisfactions beyond those associated with the basic functions of the product (e.g., transportation). As humans have become more specialized as a species, use of the market and goods to achieve higher-order benefits, such as satisfaction, self-fulfillment, and esteem, has increased. Goods are platforms or appliances that assist in providing benefits; therefore, consistent with Gutman, goods are best viewed as distribution mechanisms for services, or the provision of satisfaction for higher-order needs.

FP$_4$: KNOWLEDGE IS THE FUNDAMENTAL SOURCE OF COMPETITIVE ADVANTAGE

Knowledge is an operant resource. It is the foundation of competitive advantage and economic growth and the key source of wealth. Knowledge is composed of propositional knowledge, which is often referred to as abstract and generalized, and prescriptive knowledge, which is often referred to as techniques (Mokyr 2002). The techniques are the skills and competences that entities use to gain competitive advantage. This view is consistent with current economic thought that the change in a firm's productivity is primarily dependent on knowledge or technology (Capon and Glazer 1987; Nelson, Peck, and Kalachek 1967). Capon and Glazer (1987) broadly define technology as know-how, and they identify three components of technology: (1) product technology (i.e., ideas embodied in the product), (2) process technology (i.e., ideas involved in the manufacturing process), and (3) management technology (i.e., management procedures associated with business administration and sales). Mokyr (2002) reviews historical developments in science and technology to demonstrate that the Industrial Revolution was essentially about the creation and dissemination of propositional and prescriptive knowledge.

In the neoclassical model of economic growth, the development of knowledge in society is exogenous to the competitive system. However, in Hunt's (2000) general theory of competition, knowledge is endogenous. The process of competition and the information provided by profits result in competition being a knowledge-discovery process (Hayek 1945; Hunt 2000). Therefore, not only are mental skills the fundamental source of competitive advantage, but competition also enhances mental skills and learning in society. Dickson (1992) suggests that the firms that do the best are the firms that learn most quickly in a dynamic and evolving competitive market.

Quinn, Doorley, and Paquette (1990, p. 60) state that "physical facilities—including a seemingly superior product—seldom provide a sustainable competitive edge." Quinn, Doorley, and Paquette's suggestion that "a maintainable advantage usually derives from outstanding depth in selected human skills, logistics capabilities, knowledge bases, or other service strengths that competitors cannot reproduce and that lead to greater demonstrable value for the customer" is consistent with our own views. Normann and Ramirez (1993, p. 69) state, "the only true source of competitive advantage is the ability to conceive the entire value-creating system and make it work." Day (1994) discusses competitive advantage in terms of capabilities or skills, especially those related to market sensing, customer linking, and channel bonding. Barabba (1996, p. 48) argues that marketing-based knowledge and decision making provide the core competence that "gives the enterprise its competitive edge." These views imply that operant resources, specifically the use of knowledge and mental competences, are at the heart of competitive advantage and performance.

The use of knowledge as the basis for competitive advantage can be extended to the entire "supply" chain, or service-provision chain. The goods-centered model necessarily assumes that the primary flow in the chain is a physical flow, but it acknowledges the existence of information flows. We argue that the primary flow is information; service is the provision of the information to (or use of the information for) a consumer who desires it, with or without an accompanying appliance. Evans and Wurster (1997, p. 72) state this idea as follows: "[T]he value chain also includes all the information that flows within a company and between a company and its suppliers, its distributors, and its existing or potential customers. Supplier relationships, brand identity, process coordination, customer loyalty, employee loyalty, and switching costs all depend on various kinds of information." Evans and Wurster suggest that every business is an information business. It is through the differential use of information, or knowledge, applied in concert with the knowledge of other members of the service chain that the firm is able to make value propositions to the consumer and gain competitive advantage. Normann and Ramirez (1993, pp. 65–66) argue that value creation should not be considered in terms of the "outdated" value-added notion, "grounded in the assumptions and models of an industrial economy," but in terms of the value created through "co-production with suppliers, business partners, allies, and customers."

The move toward a service-dominant logic is grounded in an increased focus on operant resources and specifically on process management. Webster (1992) and Day (1994) emphasize the importance of marketing being central to cross-functional business processes. To better manage the processes, Moorman and Rust (1999) suggest that firms are shifting away from a functional marketing organization and toward a marketing process organization. Taking this even further, Srivastava, Shervani, and Fahey (1999, p. 168) contend that the enterprise consists of three core business processes: (1) product development management, (2) supply chain management, and (3) customer relationship management. They also contend that marketing must be a critical part of all these core business processes "that create and sustain customer and shareholder value." Similarly, Barabba (1996) argues that marketing is an organizational "state of mind."

FP$_5$: ALL ECONOMIES ARE SERVICES ECONOMIES

As we have argued, the fundamental economic exchange process pertains to the application of mental and physical skills (service provision), and manufactured goods are mechanisms for service provision. However, economic science, as well as most classifications of economic exchange that are based on it, is grounded on Smith's narrowed concern with manufactured output. Consequently, services have traditionally been defined as anything that does not result in manufactured (or agricultural) output (e.g., Rathmell 1966).

In addition, as we have suggested, specialization breeds microspecialization; people are constantly moving toward more specific specialties. Over time, activities and processes that were once routinely performed internally by a single economic entity (e.g., a manufacturing firm) become separate specializations, which are then often outsourced (Shugan 1994). Giarini (1985, p. 134) refers to this increasing specialization as "complification." The complification process causes distortions in national economic accounting systems, such as the one used in the United States, that are based on types of output (e.g., agricultural, manufacturing, intangible). The U.S. government is aware of these distortions, as is evidenced in the Economic Classification Policy Committee of the Bureau of Economic Analysis's (1994, pp. 3–4) citation of Hill (1977, p. 320) on the issue:

> [O]ne in the same activity, such as painting, may be classified as goods or service production depending purely on the organization of the overall process of production . . . If the painting is done by employees within the producer unit [that] makes the good, it will be treated as [part of] the goods production, whereas if it is done by an outside painting company, it will be classified as an intermediate input of services. Thus, when a service previously performed in a manufacturing establishment is contracted out, to a specialized services firm, data will show an increase in services production in the economy even though the total activity of "painting," may be unchanged.

It is because of the differentiation of specialized skills (services) in an output-based classification model rather than a fundamental economic shift that scholars definitionally, rather than functionally, have only recently considered that a shift is occurring toward a "services economy" (see Shugan 1994).

Similarly, economists have taught marketing scholars to think about economic development in terms of "eras" or "economies," such as hunter-gatherer, agricultural, and industrial. Formal economic thought developed during one of these eras, the industrial economy, and it has tended to describe economies in terms of the types of output, or operand resources (game, agricultural products, and manufactured products), associated with markets that were expanding rapidly at the time. However, the "economies" might be better viewed as macrospecializations, each characterized by the expansion and refinement of some particular type of competence (operant resource) that could be exchanged. The hunter-gatherer macrospecialization was characterized by the refinement and application of foraging and hunting knowledge and skills; the agricultural macrospecialization by the cultivation of knowledge and skills; the industrial economy by the refinement of knowledge and skills for large-scale mass production and organizational management; and the services and information economies by the refinement and use of knowledge and skills about information and the exchange of pure, unembedded knowledge.

In both the classification of economic activity and the economic eras, the common denominator is the increased refinement and exchange of knowledge and skills, or operant resources. Virtually all the activities performed today have always been performed in some manner; however, they have become increasingly separated into specialties and exchanged in the market.

All this may seem to be an argument that traditional classificatory systems underestimate the historical role and rise of services. In a sense, it is. Services are not just now becoming important, but just now they are becoming more apparent in the economy as specialization increases and as less of what is exchanged fits the dominant manufactured-output classification system of economic activity. Services and the operant resources they represent have always characterized the essence of economic activity.

FP$_6$: THE CUSTOMER IS ALWAYS A CO-PRODUCER

From the traditional, goods-based, manufacturing perspective, the producer and consumer are usually viewed as ideally separated in order to enable maximum manufacturing efficiency. However, if the normative goal of marketing is customer responsiveness, this manufacturing efficiency comes at the expense of marketing efficiency and effectiveness. From a service-centered view of marketing with a heavy focus on continuous processes, the consumer is always involved in the production of value. Even with tangible goods, production does not end with the manufacturing process; production is an intermediary process. As we have noted, goods are appliances that provide services for and in conjunction with the consumer. However, for these services to be delivered, the customer still must learn to use, maintain, repair, and adapt the appliance to his or her unique needs, usage situation, and behaviors. In summary, in using a product, the customer is continuing the marketing, consumption, and value-creation and delivery processes.

Increasingly, both marketing practitioners and academics are shifting toward a continuous-process perspective, in which separation of production and consumption is not a normative goal, and toward a recognition of the advantages, if not the necessity, of viewing the consumer as a co-producer. Among academics, Normann and Ramirez (1993, p. 69) state that "the key to creating value is to co-produce offerings that mobilize customers." Lusch, Brown, and Brunswick (1992) provide a general model to explain how much of the co-production or service provision the customer will perform. Oliver, Rust, and Varki (1998) echo and extend the idea of co-production in their suggestion that marketing is headed toward a paradigm of "real-time" marketing, which integrates mass customization and relationship marketing by interactively designing evolving offerings that meet customers' unique, changing needs. Prahalad and Ramaswamy (2000) note that the market has become a venue for proactive customer involvement, and they argue for co-opting customer involvement in the value-creation process. In summary, the customer becomes primarily an operant resource (co-producer) rather than an operand resource ("target") and can be involved in the entire value and service chain in acting on operand resources.

FP$_7$: THE ENTERPRISE CAN ONLY MAKE VALUE PROPOSITIONS

As we noted previously, marketing inherited a view that value was something embedded in goods during the manufacturing process, and early marketing scholars debated the issue of the types and extent of the utilities, or value added, that were created by marketing processes. This value-added view functioned reasonably well as long as the focus of marketing remained the tangible good. However, arguably, it was the inadequacy of the value-added concept that necessitated the delineation of the consumer orientation—essentially, the admonition that the consumer ultimately needed to find embedded value (value-in-exchange) useful (value-in-use). As Dixon (1990, p. 342) notes, the "conventional view of marketing adding properties to marketing . . . underlies the dissatisfaction with marketing theory that led to the services marketing literature" (see also Shaw 1994).

Services marketing scholars have been forced both to reevaluate the idea of value being embedded in tangible goods and to redefine the value-creation process. As with much of the reexamination and redefinition that has originated in the services marketing literature, the implications can be extended to all of marketing. For example, Gummesson (1998, p. 247) has argued that "if the consumer is the focal point of marketing, value creation is only possible when a good or service is consumed. An unsold good has no value, and a service provider without customers cannot produce anything." Likewise, Grönroos (2000, pp. 24–25; emphasis in original) states,

Value for customers is created throughout the relationship by the customer, partly in inter-
actions between the customer and the supplier or service provider. The focus is not on
products but on the customers' *value-creating processes* where value emerges for customers and is perceived by them, . . . the focus of marketing is value creation rather than value
distribution, and facilitation and support of a value-creating process rather than simply
distributing ready-made value to customers.

We agree with both Gummesson and Grönroos, and we extend their logic by noting that the
enterprise can only offer value propositions; the consumer must determine value and participate
in creating it through the process of co-production.

If a tangible good is part of the offering, it is embedded with knowledge that has value potential for
the intended consumer, but it is not embedded with value (utility). The consumer must understand
that the value potential is translatable to specific needs through co-production. The enterprise can
only make value propositions that strive to be better or more compelling than those of competitors.

FP$_8$: A SERVICE-CENTERED VIEW IS CUSTOMER ORIENTED AND RELATIONAL

Interactivity, integration, customization, and co-production are the hallmarks of a service-centered
view and its inherent focus on the customer and the relationship. Davis and Manrodt (1996, p. 6)
approach a service-centered view in their discussion of the customer-interaction process:

[It] begins with the interactive definition of the individual customers' problem, the development of a customized solution, and delivery of that customized solution to the customer.
The solution may consist of a tangible product, an intangible service, or some combination
of both. It is not the mix of the solution (be it product or service) that is important, but that
the organization interacts with each customer to define the specific need and then develops
a solution to meet the need.

It is in this sense of doing things, not just for the customer but also in concert with the customer, that the service-centered view emerges. It is a model of inseparability of the one who
offers (and the offer) and the consumer. Barabba (1995, p. 14) extends the customer-centric idea
to the "integration of the voice of the market with the voice of the enterprise," and Gummesson
(2002) suggests the term *balanced centricity*, concepts that may be particularly compatible with a
services-for-services exchange perspective. We also suggest that the interactive and integrative
view of exchange is more compatible with the other normative elements of the marketing concept, the idea that all activities of the firm be integrated in their market responsiveness and the
idea that profits come from customer satisfaction (rather than units of goods sold) (Kohli and
Jaworski 1990; Narver and Slater 1990). Notably, this view harks back to pre–Industrial Revolution days, when providers were close to their customers and involved in relationships that offered
customized services. Hauser and Clausing (1988, p. 64) observe the following:

Marketing, engineering, and manufacturing were integrated—in the same individual. If a
knight wanted armor, he talked directly to the armorer, who translated the knight's desires
into a product, the two might discuss the material—plate rather than chain armor—and
details like fluted surface for greater bending strength. Then the armorer would design the
production process.

Consistent with this view, Gummesson (1998, p. 243) suggests that services marketing research, and its emphasis on relationships and interaction, is one of the two "most crucial contributions" to relationship marketing; the other is the network approach to industrial marketing. Similarly,

Glynn and Lehtinen (1995) note that services scholars' recognition of characteristics of intangibility, inseparability, and heterogeneity has forced a focus on interaction and relationships. At least in the U.S. marketing literature (Berry 1983), the term *relationship marketing* originated in the services literature (Grönroos 1994).

Although the output-based, goods-centered paradigm is compatible with deterministic models of moving things through spatial dimensions (e.g., distribution of goods), it is considerably less compatible with models of relationship. In their role as distribution mechanisms for service provision (FP3), goods may be instrumental in relationships, but they are not parties to the relationship; inanimate items of exchange cannot have relationships. Over the past fifty years, marketing has been transitioning from a product and production focus to a consumer focus and, more recently, from a transaction focus to a relationship focus. The common denominator of this customer-centric, relational focus is a view of exchange that is driven by the individual consumer's perceived benefits from potential exchange partners' offerings. In general, consumers do not need goods. They need to perform mental and physical activities for their own benefit, to have others perform mental and physical activities for them (Gummesson 1995; Kotler 1977), or to have goods that assist them with these activities. In summary, they need services that satisfy their needs.

It might be argued that at least some firms and customers seek single transactions rather than relationships. If "relationship" is understood in the limited sense of multiple transactions over an extended period, the argument might be persuasive. However, even in the cases when the firm does not want extended interaction or repeat patronage, it is not freed from the normative goal of viewing the customer relationally. Even relatively discrete transactions come with social, if not legal, contracts (often relatively extended) and implied, if not expressed, warranties. They are promises and assurances that the exchange relationship will yield valuable service provision, often for extended periods. The contracts are at least partially represented by the offering firm's brand. Part of the compensation for the service provision is the creation and accumulation of brand equity (an off-balance-sheet resource).

Customers also might not desire multiple discrete transactions; however, a customer is similarly not freed of relational participation. Regardless of whether the service is provided interactively or indirectly by a tangible good, we argue that value is co-produced (FP6), and in the case of all tangible goods, the customer must interact with them over some period that extends beyond the transaction. Service provision and the co-creation of value imply that exchange is relational.

In a service-centered model, humans both are at the center and are active participants in the exchange process. What precedes and what follows the transaction as the firm engages in a relationship (short- or long-term) with customers is more important than the transaction itself. Because a service-centered view is participatory and dynamic, service provision is maximized through an iterative learning process on the part of both the enterprise and the consumer. The view necessarily assumes the existence of emergent relationships and evolving structure (e.g., relational norms of exchange learned through reinforcement over time; see Heide and John 1992). The service-centered view is inherently both consumer-centric and relational.

DISCUSSION

Perhaps the central implication of a service-centered dominant logic is the general change in perspective. The goods-centered view implies that the qualities of manufactured goods (e.g., tangibility), the separation of production and consumption, standardization, and nonperishability are normative qualities (Zeithaml, Parasuraman, and Berry 1985). Thus, even many services marketers have taken up the implied challenge of trying to make services more like goods. These qualities are primarily true of goods only when they are viewed from the manufacturer's perspective (e.g., Beaven and Scotti 1990). From what we argue the marketing perspective should be, the qualities are often neither valid nor desirable. That is, standardized goods, produced without consumer involvement and requiring physical distribution and inventory, not only add to marketing costs but also are often extremely perishable and nonresponsive to changing consumer needs.

A service-centered view of exchange points in an opposing normative direction. It implies that the goal is to customize offerings, to recognize that the consumer is always a co-producer, and to strive to maximize consumer involvement in the customization to better fit his or her needs. It suggests that for many offerings, tangibility may be a limiting factor, one that increases costs and that may hinder marketability. A service-centered perspective disposes of the limitations of thinking of marketing in terms of goods taken to the market, and it points to opportunities for expanding the market by assisting the consumer in the process of specialization and value creation.

A service-centered view identifies operant resources, especially higher-order, core competences, as the key to obtaining competitive advantage. It also implies that the resources must be developed and coordinated to provide (to serve) desired benefits for customers, either directly or indirectly. It challenges marketing to become more than a functional area and to represent one of the firm's core competences; it challenges marketing to become the predominant organizational philosophy and to take the lead in initiating and coordinating a market-driven perspective for all core competences. As Srivastava, Shervani, and Fahey (1999) suggest, marketing must play a critical role in ensuring that product development management, supply chain management, and customer relationship management processes are all customer-centric and market driven. If firms focus on their core competences, they must establish resource networks and outsource necessary knowledge and skills to the network. This means that firms must learn to be simultaneously competitive and collaborative (Day 1994), and they must learn to manage their network relationships.

Ultimately, the most successful organizations might be those whose core competence is marketing and all its related market-sensing processes (Day 1999; Haeckel 1999). In a service-centered view of marketing, in which the purpose of the firm is not to make and sell (Haeckel 1999) units of output but to provide customized services to customers and other organizations, the role of manufacturing changes. Investment in manufacturing technologies constrains market responsiveness. Together with many goods becoming commodities, as evidenced by the rise in globalized, contract manufacturing services, firms will increasingly become more competitive by outsourcing the manufacturing function. Achrol (1991, pp. 88, 91) identifies "transorganizational firms," which he refers to as "marketing exchange" and "marketing coalition" companies, both of which have "one primary function—all aspects of marketing." Achrol suggests that "the true marketing era may be just over the horizon." Achrol and Kotler (1999) envision marketing as largely performing the role of a network integrator that develops skills in research, forecasting, pricing, distribution, advertising, and promotion, and they envision other network members as bringing other necessary skills to the network.

In a service-centered view, tangible goods serve as appliances for service provision rather than ends in themselves. In this perspective, firms may find opportunities to retain ownership of goods and simply charge a user fee (Hawken, Lovins, and Lovins 1999; Rifkin 2000), thus finding a competitive advantage by focusing on the total process of consumption and use. For example, *chauffagistes* in France have realized that buyers do not want to buy furnaces and air conditioners and units of energy, but comfort, so they now contract to keep floor space at an agreed temperature range and an agreed cost. They are paid for "warmth service," and they profit by finding innovative and efficient ways to provide these services rather than sell more products. Similar examples are found in the United States, where Carrier is testing "comfort leasing" and Dow Chemical is providing "dissolving services" while maintaining the responsibility for disposing and recycling toxic chemicals. Hawken, Lovins, and Lovins (1999, pp. 125–27) cite these and other examples as indicative of the way firms benefit themselves, their customers, and society by increasing this "service flow," or the "continuous flow of value" as "defined by the customer." The observation of the market in terms of processes and service flows rather than units of output opens many strategic marketing opportunities.

From a service-provision perspective, economic exchange in the marketplace has a competitor: the potential customer (individual or organization) (Lusch, Brown, and Brunswick 1992; Prahalad and Ramaswamy 2000). The potential customer has a choice: engage in self-service (e.g., do-it-yourself activity) or go to the marketplace. However, to be successful at self-service, the entity must have sufficient physical and mental skills and/or the appliances (embedded with knowledge) to make self-service possible. Organizations that recognize this can find opportunities in developing offerings that enable the entity's increasing self-service.

As individual people continue to progress toward finer degrees of specialization, they will find themselves increasingly dependent on the market, both for service provision and for the ability to self-serve. Consequently, consumers will seek to domesticate or tame the market by adopting and developing a relationship with a limited number of organizations. This domestication process increases the consumer's efficiency in dealing with the marketplace and decreases the impact of opportunistic behavior by potential service providers. Consumers will develop relationships with organizations that can provide them with an entire host of related services over an extended period (Rifkin 2000). For example, in providing for individual transportation, the automobile has associated needs for car insurance, maintenance, repair, and fuel. There will be opportunities for organizations that can offer all these services bundled into periodic user fees. The success of organizations in capitalizing on this need for domesticated market relationships does not come from finding ways to provide efficient, standardized solutions but from making it easier for consumers to acquire customized service solutions efficiently through involvement in the value-creation process.

Achrol and Kotler (1999) extend this service perspective by suggesting that the marketing function may become a customer-consulting function. The marketer would become the buying agent on a long-term, relational basis to source, evaluate, and purchase the skills (either as intangibles or embedded in tangible matter) that the customer needs, wants, or desires. This could be extended to marketers who also serve as selling agents, enabling a customer to exchange his or her skills in the marketplace. This position would enable the marketer not only to evaluate the skills (services) the customer needs but also to advise the customer about which skills (services) he or she can best specialize and exchange in the marketplace and the services (intangible or provided through goods) that might be acquired to leverage his or her own service provision and exchange processes.

Historically, most communication with the market can be characterized as one-way mass communication that flows from the offering firm to the market or to segments of markets. A service-centered view of exchange suggests that individual customers increasingly specialize and turn to their domesticated market relationships for services outside of their own competences. Therefore, promotion will need to become a communication process characterized by dialogue, asking and answering questions. Prahalad and Ramaswamy (2000) argue that consumers rather than corporations are increasingly initiating and controlling this dialogue. Duncan and Moriarty (1998, p. 3) believe that marketing theory and communications theory are at an intersection; "[They are] in the midst of fundamental changes that are similar in origin, impact, and direction.

Parallel paradigm shifts move both fields from a functional, mechanistic, production-oriented model to a more humanistic, relationship-based model." They point out (p. 2) that "many marketing roles, particularly in services, are fundamentally communications positions that take communication deeper into the core of marketing activities, . . . which involves the process of listening, aligning, and matching." The normative goal should not be communication to the market but developing ongoing communication processes, or dialogues, with micromarkets and ideally markets of one.

Shostack (1977) and others (e.g., Beaven and Scotti 1990; Schlesinger and Heskett 1991) have indicated that the basic lexicon of marketing is derived from a goods-based, manufacturing exchange perspective. As we believe, if contemporary marketing thought is evolving from an operand-resource-based, good-centered dominant logic to an operant-resource-based, service-centered dominant logic, academic marketing may need to rethink and revise some of the lexicon. The seemingly diverse literature that we cite as converging on this new dominant logic provides the foundation for the revised lexicon. Notably, the need and its existence do not necessarily require discarding the goods-centered counterpart. Its function should be to refocus perspective through reorientation rather than reinvention. For example, the treatment of quality in the services literature has resulted in the distinction between manufactured quality and perceived quality; the former arguably has become a necessary but not sufficient component of the latter. The concept of transaction becoming subordinated to the concept of relationship is another example. Similarly, Rust, Zeithaml, and Lemon (2000) have suggested that the customer-focused term *customer equity* be superordinated to the more traditional, product-focused term *brand equity*, which is a component of the former (along with "value equity" and "retention equity").

Marketing educators and scholars should be proactive in leading industry toward a service-centered exchange model. As with the lexicon, this implies reorientation rather than reinvention. This reorientation would not necessitate abandonment of most of the traditional core concepts, such as the marketing mix, target marketing, and market segmentation, but rather it would complement these with a framework based on the eight FPs we have discussed.

A service-centered college curriculum would be grounded by a course in principles of marketing, which would subordinate goods to service provision, emphasizing the former as distribution mechanisms for the latter. The marketing strategy course might be centered on resource advantage theory, building on the role of competences and capabilities in the co-production of value and competitive advantage. The course could be followed by a new course, one focused on the management of cross-functional businesses processes that support the development of the capabilities and competences needed in a market-driven organization. Integrated marketing communication would continue to replace limited-focus, promotional courses such as advertising. In addition, the course would emphasize both the means and the mechanisms for initiating and maintaining a continuing dialogue with the customer and for enhancing the relationship by using tools such as branding. Likewise, the consumer behavior course might evolve to increased emphasis on relational phenomena such as brand identification, value perception, and the role of social and relational norms in co-production and repeat patronage. Similarly, courses in pricing would evolve to focus on strategies for building and maintaining value propositions, including the management of long-term customer equity. The marketing channels course would become a course that addressed coordinating marketing networks and systems. Supply chain management concepts would become subordinated to the management of value constellations and service flows.

Complementing this college curriculum could be the emergence of executive education offerings with similar perspectives and frames of references. It is perhaps in the executive education classroom where the rapid dissemination of the service-centered model of exchange is most likely.

If adopted and diffused throughout industry, what does the service-centered model mean for the role of marketing in the firm? It positions service, the application of competences for the benefit of the consumer, as the core of the firm's mission. Marketing's role as the facilitator of exchange becomes one of identifying and developing the core competences and positioning them as value propositions that offer potential competitive advantage. To do this, marketing should lead the effort of designing and building cross-functional business processes. Therefore, marketing should be positioned at the core of the firm's strategic planning. Relationship building with customers becomes intrinsic not only to marketing but also to the enterprise as a whole. All employees are identified as service providers, with the ultimate goal of satisfying the customer. Everyone in the organization is encouraged to reflect on the firm's value proposition. Indeed, from a service-centered dominant logic, a firm's mission statement should communicate the firm's overall value proposition.

Finally, in the service-centered model, marketplace feedback not only is obtained directly from the customer but also is gauged by analyzing financial performance from exchange relationships to learn how to improve both firms' offering to customers and firm performance. Marketing practice accepts responsibility for firm financial performance by taking responsibility for increasing the market value rather than the book value of the organization as it builds off-balance-sheet assets such as customer, brand, and network equity.

CONCLUSION

The models on which much of the understanding of economics and marketing are based were largely developed during the nineteenth century, a time when the focus was on efficiencies in the production of tangible output, which was fundamental to the Industrial Revolution. Given that focus, perhaps appropriately, the unit of analysis was the unit of output, or the product (good). The central role of the good also fits well with the political goals of exporting manufactured products to the developing and often colonized regions of the world in exchange for raw materials for the purpose of increasing national wealth. In addition, making the good, characterized as "stuff" with embedded properties, the unit of analysis fits well with the academic goals of turning economics into a deterministic science such as Newtonian mechanics. The goods-oriented, output-based model has enabled advances in the common understanding, and it has reached paradigm status.

However, times have changed. The focus is shifting away from tangibles and toward intangibles, such as skills, information, and knowledge, and toward interactivity and connectivity and ongoing relationships. The orientation has shifted from the producer to the consumer. The academic focus is shifting from the thing exchanged to one on the process of exchange. Science has moved from a focus on mechanics to one on dynamics, evolutionary development, and the emergence of complex adaptive systems. The appropriate unit of exchange is no longer the static and discrete tangible good.

As more marketing scholars seem to be implying, the appropriate model for understanding marketing may not be one developed to understand the role of manufacturing in an economy, the microeconomic model, with its focus on the good that is only occasionally involved in exchange. A more appropriate unit of exchange is perhaps the application of competences, or specialized human knowledge and skills, for and to the benefit of the receiver. These operant resources are intangible, continuous, and dynamic. We anticipate that the emerging service-centered dominant logic of marketing will have a substantial role in marketing thought. It has the potential to replace the traditional goods-centered paradigm.

NOTES

The authors contributed equally to this manuscript. The authors thank the anonymous JM reviewers and Shelby Hunt, Gene Laczniak, Alan Malter, Fred Morgan, and Matthew O'Brien for comments on various drafts of this manuscript.

1. Typical traditional definitions include those of Lovelock (1991, p. 13), "services are deeds, processes, and performances"; Solomon and colleagues (1985, p. 106), "services marketing refers to the marketing of activities and processes rather than objects"; and Zeithaml and Bitner (2000), "services are deeds, processes, and performances." For a definition consistent with the one we adopt here, see Grönroos (2000).

REFERENCES

Achrol, Ravi S. (1991), "Evolution of the Marketing Organization: New Frontiers for Turbulent Environments," *Journal of Marketing,* 55 (October), 77–93.

———— and Philip Kotler (1999), "Marketing in the Network Economy," *Journal of Marketing,* 63 (Special Issue), 146–63.

Alderson, Wroe (1957), *Marketing Behavior and Executive Action: A Functionalist Approach to Marketing Theory.* Homewood, IL: Richard D. Irwin.

Barabba, Vincent P. (1995), *Meeting of the Minds: Creating a Market-Based Enterprise.* Boston: Harvard Business School Press.

———— (1996), "Meeting of the Minds," *American Demographics,* 18 (March–April), 48–55.

Barbon, Nicholas (1903), *A Discourse on Trade,* (1690). Reprint, Baltimore: The John Hopkins Press.

Bastiat, Fredric (1860), *Harmonies of Political Economy,* Patrick S. Sterling, trans. London: J. Murray.

———— (1964), *Selected Essays on Political Economy,* (1848), Seymour Cain, trans., George. B. de Huszar, ed. Reprint, Princeton, NJ: D. Van Nordstrand.

Beaven, M.H. and D.J. Scotti (1990), "Service-Oriented Thinking and Its Implications for the Marketing Mix," *Journal of Services Marketing,* 4 (Fall), 5–19.

Beckman, Theodore N. (1957), "The Value Added Concept as a Measurement of Output," *Advanced Management,* 22 (April), 6–9.

Berry, Leonard L. (1983), "Relationship Marketing," in *Emerging Perspectives of Services Marketing,* Leonard L. Berry, Lynn Shostack, and G.D. Upah, eds. Chicago: American Marketing Association, 25–28.

Bureau of Economic Analysis, Economic Classification Policy Committee (1994), *Issues Paper No. 6: Services Classifications.* Washington, DC: U.S. Department of Commerce.

Capon, Noel and Rashi Glazer (1987), "Marketing and Technology: A Strategic Coalignment," *Journal of Marketing,* 51 (July), 1–14.

Cherington, Paul T. (1920), *The Elements of Marketing.* New York: Macmillan.

Cole, William E. and John W. Mogab (1995), *The Economics of Total Quality Management: Clashing Paradigms in the Global Market.* Cambridge, MA: Blackwell.

Conner, Kathleen and C.K. Prahalad (1996), "A Resource-Based Theory of the Firm: Knowledge Versus Opportunism," *Organizational Science,* 7 (September–October), 477–501.

Constantin, James A. and Robert F. Lusch (1994), *Understanding Resource Management.* Oxford, OH: The Planning Forum.

Converse, Paul D. (1921), *Marketing Methods and Politics.* New York: Prentice Hall.

Copeland, Melvin T. (1923), *Marketing Problems.* New York: A.W. Shaw.

Cox, Reavis (1965), *Distribution in a High-Level Economy.* Englewood Cliffs, NJ: Prentice Hall.

Davis, Frank W. and Karl B. Manrodt (1996), *Customer-Responsive Management: The Flexible Advantage.* Cambridge, MA: Blackwell.

Day, George (1994), "The Capabilities of Market-Driven Organization," *Journal of Marketing,* 58 (October), 37–52.

———— (1999), *The Market-Driven Organization: Understanding, Attracting, and Keeping Valuable Customers.* New York: The Free Press.

———— and David Montgomery (1999), "Charting New Directions for Marketing," *Journal of Marketing,* 63 (Special Issue), 3–13.

Dickson, Peter R. (1992), "Toward a General Theory of Competitive Rationality," *Journal of Marketing,* 56 (January), 69–83.

Dixon, Donald F. (1990), "Marketing as Production: The Development of a Concept," *Journal of the Academy of Marketing Science,* 18 (Fall), 337–43.

Drucker, Peter F. (1954), *The Practice of Management.* New York: Harper and Row.

Duncan, Tom and Sandra E. Moriarty (1998), "A Communication-Based Marketing Model for Managing Relationships," *Journal of Marketing,* 62 (April), 1–12.

Evans, Philip B. and Thomas S. Wurster (1997), "Strategy and the New Economics of Information," *Harvard Business Review,* 75 (September–October), 71–82.

Fisk, Raymond P., Stephen W. Brown, and Mary Jo Bitner (1993), "Tracking the Evolution of the Services Marketing Literature," *Journal of Retailing,* 69 (Spring), 61–103.

Giarini, Orio (1985), "The Consequences of Complexity in Economics: Vulnerability, Risk, and Rigidity Factors in Supply," in *The Science and Praxis of Complexity: Contributions to the Symposium held at Montpellier, France,* S. Aida, et al., eds. Tokyo: The UN University, 133–45.

Gilder, George (1984), *The Spirit of Enterprise.* New York: Simon and Schuster.

Glynn, William J. and Uolevi Lehtinen (1995), "The Concept of Exchange: Interactive Approaches in Services Marketing," in *Understanding Services Management,* William J. Glynn and James G. Barnes, eds. New York: John Wiley & Sons, 89–118.

Grönroos, Christian (1994), "From Marketing Mix to Relationship Marketing: Towards a Paradigm Shift in Marketing," *Asia-Australia Marketing Journal,* 2 (August), 9–29.

——— (2000), *Service Management and Marketing: A Customer Relationship Management Approach.* West Sussex, UK: John Wiley & Sons.

Gummesson, Evert (1994), "Broadening and Specifying Relationship Marketing," *Asia-Australia Marketing Journal,* 2 (August), 31–43.

——— (1995), "Relationship Marketing: Its Role in the Service Economy," in *Understanding Services Management,* William J. Glynn and James G. Barnes, eds. New York: John Wiley & Sons, 244–68.

——— (1998), "Implementation Requires a Relationship Marketing Paradigm," *Journal of the Academy of Marketing Science,* 26 (Summer), 242–49.

——— (2002), "Relationship Marketing and a New Economy: It's Time for Deprogramming," *Journal of Services Marketing,* 16 (7), 585–89.

Gutman, Jonathan (1982), "A Means–End Chain Model Based on Consumer Categorization Processes," *Journal of Marketing,* 46 (Spring), 60–72.

Haeckel, Stephen H. (1999), *Adaptive Enterprise: Creating and Leading Sense-and-Respond Organizations.* Boston: Harvard School of Business.

Hamel, Gary and C.K. Prahalad (1994), *Competing for the Future.* Boston: Harvard Business School Press.

Hauser, John R. and Don Clausing (1988), "The House of Quality," *Harvard Business Review,* 66 (May–June), 63–73.

Hawken, Paul, Amory Lovins, and L. Hunter Lovins (1999), *Natural Capitalism: Creating the Next Industrial Revolution.* Boston: Little, Brown.

Hayek, Friedrich A. (1945), "The Use of Knowledge in Society," *American Economic Review,* 35 (September), 519–30.

Heide, Jan B. and George John (1992), "Do Norms Matter in Marketing Relationships?" *Journal of Marketing,* 56 (April), 32–44.

Hill, T.P. (1977), "On Goods and Services," *Review of Income and Wealth,* 23 (December), 315–38.

Hollander, Stanley C. (1979), "Is There a Generic Demand for Services?" *MSU Business Topics,* 79 (Spring), 41–46.

Hunt, Shelby D. (2000), *A General Theory of Competition: Resources, Competences, Productivity, Economic Growth.* Thousand Oaks, CA: Sage Publications.

——— and Robert M. Morgan (1995), "The Comparative Advantage Theory of Competition," *Journal of Marketing,* 59 (April), 1–15.

Kohli, Ajay K. and Bernard J. Jaworski (1990), "Market Orientation: The Construct, Research Propositions, and Managerial Implications," *Journal of Marketing,* 54 (April), 1–18.

Kotler, Philip (1967), *Marketing Management Analysis, Planning, and Control.* Englewood Cliffs, NJ: Prentice Hall.

——— (1972), *Marketing Management,* 2d ed. Englewood Cliffs, NJ: Prentice Hall.

——— (1977), *Marketing Management: Analysis, Planning, Implementation, and Control,* 3d ed. Upper Saddle River, NJ: Prentice Hall.

———— (1997), *Marketing Management: Analysis, Planning, Implementation, and Control,* 9th ed. Upper Saddle River, NJ: Prentice Hall.

Levitt, Theodore (1960), "Marketing Myopia," *Harvard Business Review,* 38 (July–August), 26–44, 173–81.

Lovelock, Christopher H. (1991), *Services Marketing,* 2d ed. Englewood Cliffs, NJ: Prentice Hall.

Lusch, Robert F., Stephen W. Brown, and Gary J. Brunswick (1992), "A General Framework for Explaining Internal vs. External Exchange," *Journal of the Academy of Marketing Science,* 20 (Spring), 119–34.

Macneil, Ian R. (1980), *The New Social Contract: An Inquiry into Modern Contractual Relations.* New Haven, CT: Yale University Press.

Malthus, Thomas (1798), *An Essay on the Principle of Population.* London: Printed for J. Johnson, in St. Paul's Church-Yard.

Marshall, Alfred (1927), *Principles of Economics,* (1890). Reprint, London: Macmillan.

Mauss, Marcel (1990), *The Gift,* (1950). Reprint, London: Routledge.

McCarthy, E. Jerome (1960), *Basic Marketing, A Managerial Approach.* Homewood, IL: Richard D. Irwin.

McKitterick, J.B. (1957), "What Is the Marketing Management Concept?" in *Frontiers of Marketing Thought and Science,* Frank M. Bass, ed. Chicago: American Marketing Association, 71–81.

Mill, John Stuart (1929), *Principles of the Political Economy,* (1885). Reprint, London: Longmans, Green.

Mokyr, Joel (2002), *The Gifts of Athena: Historical Origins of the Knowledge Economy.* Princeton, NJ: Princeton University Press.

Moorman, Christine and Roland T. Rust (1999), "The Role of Marketing," *Journal of Marketing,* 63 (Special Issue), 180–97.

Narver, John C. and Stanley F. Slater (1990), "The Effect of a Market Orientation on Business Profitability," *Journal of Marketing,* 54 (October), 20–35.

Nelson, Richard, Merton J. Peck, and Edward D. Kalachek (1967), *Technology, Economic Growth, and Public Policy.* Washington, DC: The Brookings Institution.

———— and Sidney G. Winter (1982), *An Evolutionary Theory of Economic Change.* Cambridge, MA: Belknap Press.

Norris, Ruby Turner (1941), *The Theory of Consumer's Demand.* New Haven, CT: Yale University Press.

Normann, Richard and Rafael Ramirez (1993), "From Value Chain to Value Constellation: Designing Interactive Strategy," *Harvard Business Review,* 71 (July–August), 65–77.

Nystrom, Paul (1915), *The Economics of Retailing,* Vols. 1 and 2. New York: Ronald Press.

Oliver, Richard W., Roland T. Rust, and Sanjeev Varki (1998), "Real-Time Marketing," *Marketing Management,* 7 (Fall), 28–37.

Parasuraman, A., Valarie A. Zeithaml, and Leonard L. Berry (1988), "SERVQUAL: A Multiple-Item Scale for Measuring Customer Perceptions of Service Quality," *Journal of Retailing,* 64 (Spring), 12–40.

Penrose, Edith T. (1959), *The Theory of the Growth of the Firm.* London: Basil Blackwell and Mott.

Pine, B. Joseph and James H. Gilmore (1999), *The Experience Economy: Work Is Theater and Every Business a Stage.* Boston: Harvard Business School Press.

Polanyi, Michael (1966), *The Tacit Dimension.* Garden City, NY: Doubleday.

Prahalad, C.K. and Gary Hamel (1990), "The Core Competence of the Corporation," *Harvard Business Review,* 68 (May–June), 79–91.

———— and Venkatram Ramaswamy (2000), "Co-opting Customer Competence," *Harvard Business Review,* 78 (January–February), 79–87.

Quinn, James Brian, Thomas L. Doorley, and Penney C. Paquette (1990), "Beyond Products: Services-Based Strategy," *Harvard Business Review,* 68 (March–April), 58–66.

Rathmell, John M. (1966), "What Is Meant by Services?" *Journal of Marketing,* 30 (October), 32–36.

Rifkin, Jeremy (2000), *The Age of Access: The New Culture of Hypercapitalism, Where All of Life is a Paid-For Experience.* New York: Putnam.

Rust, Roland (1998), "What Is the Domain of Service Research?" *Journal of Service Research,* 1 (November), 107.

————, Valarie A. Zeithaml, and Katherine N. Lemon (2000), *Driving Customer Equity: How Customer Lifetime Value Is Reshaping Corporate Strategy.* New York: The Free Press.

Savitt, Ronald (1990), "Pre-Aldersonian Antecedents to Macromarketing: Insights from the Textual Literature" *Journal of the Academy of Marketing Science,* 18 (Fall), 293–301.

Say, J. (1821), *A Treatise on the Political Economy.* Boston: Wells and Lilly.

Schlesinger, Leonard A. and James L. Heskett (1991), "The Service-Driven Company," *Harvard Business Review,* 69 (September–October), 71–81.

Shaw, A. (1912), "Some Problems in Market Distribution," *Quarterly Journal of Economics,* 12 (August), 703–765.

Shaw, Eric (1994), "The Utility of the Four Utilities Concept," in *Research in Marketing, Supplement 6,* J. Sheth and R. Fullerton, eds. Greenwich, CT: JAI Press.

Sheth, Jagdish and A. Parvatiyar (2000), "Relationship Marketing in Consumer Markets: Antecedents and Consequences," in *Handbook of Relationship Marketing,* Jagdish Sheth and A. Parvatiyar, eds. Thousand Oaks, CA: Sage Publications.

———, Rajendra S. Sisodia, and Arun Sharma (2000), "The Antecedents and Consequences of Customer-Centric Marketing," *Journal of the Academy of Marketing Science,* 28 (Winter), 55–66.

Shostack, G. Lynn (1977), "Breaking Free from Product Marketing," *Journal of Marketing,* 41 (April), 73–80.

Shugan, Steven M. (1994), "Explanations for the Growth of Service," in *Service Quality: New Directions in Theory and Practice,* Roland T. Rust and Richard L. Oliver, eds. Thousand Oaks, CA: Sage Publications, 223–40.

Slater, Stanley F. and John C. Narver (1995), "Market Orientation and the Learning Organization," *Journal of Marketing,* 59 (July), 63–74.

Smith, A. (1904), *An Inquiry into the Nature and Causes of the Wealth of Nations,* (1776). Reprint, London: Printed for W. Strahan and T. Cadell.

Solomon, Michael R., Carol Surprenant, John A. Czepiel, and Evelyn G. Gutman (1985), "A Role Theory Perspective on Dynamic Interactions: The Service Encounter," *Journal of Marketing,* 49 (Winter), 99–111.

Srivastava, Rajendra K., Liam Fahey, and H. Kurt Christensen (2001), "The Resource-Based View and Marketing: The Role of Market-Based Assets in Gaining Competitive Advantage," *Journal of Management,* 27 (6), 777–802.

———, Tasadduq A. Shervani, and Liam Fahey (1999), "Marketing, Business Processes, and Shareholder Value: An Organizationally Embedded View of Marketing Activities and the Discipline of Marketing," *Journal of Marketing,* 63 (Special Issue), 168–79.

Teece, David and Gary Pisano (1994), "The Dynamic Capabilities of Firms: An Introduction," *Industrial and Corporate Change,* 3 (3), 537–56.

Walras, Leon (1954), *Elements of the Political Economy,* (1894). Reprint, Homestead, NJ: Richard D. Irwin.

Webster, Frederick E., Jr. (1992), "The Changing Role of Marketing in the Corporation," *Journal of Marketing,* 56 (October), 1–17.

Weld, Louis D.H. (1916), *The Marketing of Farm Products.* New York: Macmillan.

——— (1917), "Marketing Functions and Mercantile Organizations," *American Economic Review,* 7 (June), 306–318.

Zeithaml, Valarie A. and Mary Jo Bitner (2000), *Services Marketing: Integrating Customer Focus Across the Firm,* 2d ed. Boston: Irwin/McGraw-Hill.

———, A. Parasuraman, and Leonard L. Berry (1985), "Problems and Strategies in Services Marketing," *Journal of Marketing,* 49 (Spring), 33–46.

Zimmermann, Erich W. (1951), *World Resources and Industries.* New York: Harper and Row.

2

HISTORICAL PERSPECTIVES ON SERVICE-DOMINANT LOGIC

STEPHEN L. VARGO, ROBERT F. LUSCH, AND FRED W. MORGAN

INTRODUCTION

Histories have no beginnings. Every history has its own history, usually a series of divergences and convergences that are in turn driven by other events. This pattern aptly describes the history of the treatment of exchange phenomena in academic and applied thought. It can, however, be characterized by a major bifurcation that resulted in the development of a paradigm of economic exchange built upon the idea of tangible goods being embedded with value and exchanged for other goods that are also so embedded, thus increasing each trading party's wealth by improving its assortment of goods.

In the development of this paradigm, some types of exchange phenomena, usually categorized as services, were mostly ignored and later partially dealt with as special cases of goods by forcing their conceptualization to comply with the then-established logic. This perverted view of services as "immaterial goods" has caused problems for economic scholars for more than 150 years, and marketing scholars for much of that time. We contend that dealing with this distorted view of services has required, or at least resulted in, more bifurcations in thought. These rifts reveal themselves in apparently divergent orientations, models, and theories of exchange, and the creation of subdisciplines that led to more and more fragmentation in marketing thought. Particularly for marketing, we argue that these distractions have inhibited the full understanding of the fundamental subject matter—exchange.

Recently, these seemingly divergent views appear to be converging on a more inclusive and integrative logic of exchange, one that is centered on the same phenomena that had been previously orphaned, if not ignored. We (Vargo and Lusch 2004a) label this emergent logic and potential paradigm "service-dominant" (S-D) logic in contrast to "goods-dominant" (G-D) logic. The purpose of this chapter is to explore the primary divergences, convergences, and forces behind S-D logic's emergence. The story includes bifurcations of goods and services, productive and unproductive activities, value-in-use and value-in-exchange, product orientation and consumer orientation, and transactions and relationships.

GOODS, PRODUCTIVITY, AND VALUE-IN-EXCHANGE: THE DEVELOPMENT OF AN ECONOMIC PARADIGM

Viewing exchange in terms of innate properties of tangible things that are only sometimes used as vehicles for exchange is a relatively recent paradigmatic development. The perspective is attributable to the convergence of the philosophical, sociopolitical, and scientific thought that dominated the Industrial Revolution and is a direct result of intellectual choice associated with the development of formal "economic science" that emerged during this period.

Adam Smith's (1776/1904) *The Wealth of Nations* marked the beginning of modern economic thought. Smith explicated and elaborated the dominant views of his era (see Bell 1953; Delaunay and Gadrey 1992; Schumpeter 1954; Vargo and Morgan 2005):

1. The Aristotelian view of *social virtue,* described in terms of how an individual's service contributed to the common benefit of society.
2. The mercantilist notion that society benefited from the production of surplus tangible commodities that could be exported in exchange for precious metals.
3. The physiocratic notion that activities other than agriculture were sterile because they did not create anything of value.
4. The philosophy that *natural law* governed social exchange and civilization and that the normative laws of society should be derived from the laws of nature.
5. The related view that humans could master the *laws of nature* through scientific discovery and rationality. *Newtonian mechanics* served as the model for this mastery of nature by providing that things (matter) have innate properties and relationships to other things that could be manipulated by human effort.

Smith (1776/1904) is commonly considered the "father of economic thought," though this was not his intention. His purpose was to integrate and expand the preceding views into a model of the *normative economics* of national wealth creation. In so accomplishing this objective, he created bifurcations in the treatment of the concepts of "productive" services and "value" that would influence economics and its descendent disciplines for the next several hundred years.

Smith derived his political economic views from the essential proposition of the efficiency of the "division of labor" resulting in the necessity of "exchange." For Smith (1776/1904, p. 1), labor is the "fund which originally supplies (the nation) with all the necessities and conveniences of life which it annually consumes." Thus labor, the application of mental and physical skills (parties doing things for other parties—what both Smith and we call *service*), served as the foundation for exchange.

Though he initially laid a foundation for a broad explanation of exchange and value, Smith then shifted attention to a normative explanation for how some services (types of labor) *could contribute to national well-being* through the production of surplus commodities that could be exported for trade. In effect, Smith, a moral philosopher, drew upon Aristotle's theme of virtuous services and the physiocrats' focus on agriculture and added the tangible products of the increasingly developing industry to derive a formula for *productivity* in terms of its contribution to national wealth.

Smith's (1776/1904) reasoning is evident in his discussion, often misquoted, of "productive" and "unproductive" services. Frequently credited with the view that services are not valuable, Smith (1776/1904, p. 314) asserted that

> The labor of some of the most respectable orders in society is . . . unproductive of any value, and does not fix or realize itself in any permanent subject, or venerable commodity which endures after that labor is past, and for which an equal quantity of labor could afterwards be produced. The sovereign, for example . . . produces nothing for which an equal quantity of service can be afterwards procured.

Smith (1776/1904) argued only that some services were *unproductive* in terms of his national wealth standard, not that services were unnecessary or not useful for individual well-being. He asserted that physicians and lawyers were "useful," "respectful," and "deserving of higher wages"; they just were not productive in terms of contributing to the national surplus. Smith did specifically identify some useful and productive services: those that were essential for the production and trade of commodities. These included retailers, wholesale merchants, manufacturers, and "those who undertake the improvement or cultivation of lands, mines, and fisheries" (pp. 340–341).

Smith (1776/1904, pp. 30–31) defined "real value" as the labor required to afford the "necessities, conveniences, and amusements of human life" through the labor of others. However, having established that labor, or service, was the fundamental value source, he moved his attention to "nominal value"—the price paid in the marketplace. Smith believed that people could more easily think about quantities of things rather than quantities of labor, and he was concerned with the former. Smith now faced the paradox of dual standards of *value-in-use,* based on consumption, and *value-in-exchange,* based on trade, which had been discussed since the time of Aristotle. This limited the generalizability of the economic philosophy, economic science, and other academic descendents of his work.

Not all who followed Smith agreed with his productive/unproductive standards. For example, Say (1821) saw production as the creation of "utility," not matter. Thus, he defined services as those activities that are "consumed at the time of production itself" and described them as "immaterial products," laying the groundwork for more contemporary conceptualizations (Lovelock and Gummesson 2004). Likewise, Mill (1848, p. 44) disagreed with political economists who classified labor as unproductive unless it resulted in some material object capable of being transferred. Mill (1848, p. 45) contended that production of objects represented the *rearrangement of matter* because "no human being can produce one particle of matter." Like Say, Mill (1848, p. 45–46) believed that the value of production was not in the objects themselves but in their *usefulness*; therefore, labor was "not creative of objects, but of utilities." He asked, "Why should not all labor which produces utility be accounted productive," including labor "consisting of a mere service rendered?" Nonetheless, he acquiesced to the dominant logic of productive labor, referring only to those kinds of exertion that produce utilities embodied in material objects. Like other political economists, he tried to *break free* from the developing paradigmatic constraint of production and value being centered on tangible resources, but could not. As Kuhn (1962) pointed out, paradigms are perceptually potent and normatively prescriptive.

Frédéric Bastiat did not accept the conventional wisdom. He criticized political economists' position tying value to tangible objects. For Bastiat (1860, p. 40) people had "wants" and sought "satisfactions" that could be appeased by (1) "gratuitous utilities," which were provided by Providence, and (2) "onerous utilities," which must be purchased with effort. A single person generated a want and its satisfaction, whereas the effort required for the associated onerous utility was seen to often reside in other individuals. Bastiat (1860, p. 43) believed "it is in fact to this faculty . . . to work the one for the other; it is this transmission of efforts, this exchange of services, with all the infinite and involved combinations to which it gives rise, through time and through space, it is *this* precisely which constitutes Economic Science, points out its origin, and determines its limits"(italics in the original). Value was thus seen as the "comparative appreciation of reciprocal services" exchanged to obtain utility. Bastiat, like Mill (1848), recognized that humans, rather than creating matter, transformed it through service into a state that could provide satisfaction.

Because the value of matter resided in the service rendered upon it by labor, and since material things that required no effort to provide utility (gratuitous) could not have value, material things could not possess value. Bastiat (1848/1964, p. 162) summarized his view:

The great economic law is this: Services are exchanged for services. . . . It is trivial, very commonplace; it is, nonetheless, the beginning, the middle, and the end of economic science. . . . Once this axiom is clearly understood, what becomes of such subtle distinctions as use-value and exchange-value, material products and immaterial products, productive classes and unproductive classes? . . . Now since these reciprocal services alone are commensurate with one another, it is in them alone that value resides, and not the gratuitous raw materials and in the gratuitous natural resources that they put to work.

Fellow economists criticized Bastiat's views as not being economic theory (Schumpeter 1954). He had rejected the dominant paradigm and offered an alternative paradigm that challenged the fundamental logic of exchange. Thus, he was largely ignored.

ECONOMIC SCIENCE

By the middle of the nineteenth century, Say's concept of utility stood as the primary unit of analysis in economics and could be viewed as an embedded property of matter. Thus, the issue of use value versus exchange value could largely be ignored, since value-in-use had been transformed into an embodied property that was represented by, if not essentially equivalent to, value-in-exchange. This revised concept of utility set the stage for turning economic philosophy into economic "science" in the Newtonian tradition.

Leon Walras (1894/1954) described the function of pure economics as the theoretical determination of price and saw services as the source of all production. He separated "services of capital goods" into "consumers' services" that possess direct utility and "producer services" that have indirect utility. Walras's primary goal was the development of a pure theory of economics with pure economics as "a physio-mathematical science like mechanics and hydraulics and its practitioners should not fear to employ the methods and language of mathematics" (Walras 1894/1954, pp. 29–30).

Walras (1894/1954) derived a mathematical relationship among supply, demand, and price based on the then well-established "ideal-type" concept of utility, after employing a number of assumptions. Walras believed that economic thought had finally caught up with the Newtonian model of a mechanistic, deterministic, rational, and certain world; hence, economics could be deemed a legitimate "science." A hypothetical "economic man" had been fashioned and substituted for the "inanimate Newtonian body in motion." The former was motivated by utility and profit maximization, whereas the latter's behavior was determined by Newton's laws of motion.

Alfred Marshal, more than Walras, has been credited with the advancement of equilibrium theory (Schumpeter 1954). Marshall (1890/1927) saw "tendencies" toward equilibrium that were discernible through the science of economics. These tendencies could be written as normative "laws" if the caveat ceteris paribus, were applied. He did not dwell on the distinctions between unproductive and productive labor. Marshall used the word *productive*, but he cautioned "it is a slippery term, and should not be used where precision is needed."

Thus, by the beginning of the twentieth century, economics scholars often proffered parallel models describing economic activity (see Delaunay and Gadrey 1992). One perspective essentially touted a service-dominant model that viewed economics in terms of the discrete and collective relationships among specialized service providers exchanging services with other specialized services providers. Smith outlined and then abandoned the model in favor of his more immediate purpose. Political economists and economic scientists following Smith first acknowledged and then deserted the model, except for Bastiat, who actively elaborated upon and promoted it.

The second perspective featured a G-D model describing economics in terms of the demand and supply of "goods" to which consumers attribute an abstract property of utility or value. A demand function for a good represented the aggregation of consumers' utility curves for the good. A supply function for the good represented the aggregation of firms' cost curves for that good. The "good" was the unifying construct.

The G-D model of economic activity was more congruent with the political underpinnings of the political economists' view of materialistic virtue and with the economic scientists' desire to be compatible with the "scientific" and mathematical prerequisite of the natural sciences. Because of the desire for scientific respectability in the Newtonian tradition, the G-D paradigm survived and the S-D model was relegated to footnote status, at least temporarily. Economics and the derivative disciplines of marketing and management inherited this G-D paradigm.

THE IMPACT OF ECONOMICS ON MARKETING THOUGHT

Economic science provided the foundation for marketing thought and the impetus for its development. As production moved out of the household and into the factory, consumer and producer were separated. Marketing's role was to generate and fulfill demand. Marketing thought focused on all of the institutions, both title carrying and facilitating, that performed the marketing functions that brought buyers and sellers together. These functions included buying, selling, sorting, financing, transporting, storing, information gathering, and risk taking. Economic science largely ignored these and focused on a simplified model of production (manufacturing) and consumption. "Scientific management" had resolved issues of production efficiency and worsened problems regarding distribution and oversupply. Bartels (1986, p. 32) opined:

> There remained, therefore, a gap in the theoretical explanation as social and economic conditions departed increasingly from the assumptions concerning the market on which trade theory was built. Competition no longer characterized some markets; demanders and suppliers were further removed from each other; customary relations of demand and supply were becoming reversed; and new patterns of living were evolving. New interpretations of economic activity were needed, as were new applications of management science to distributive business. These needs nurtured the discovery of "marketing."

Typical of emerging disciplines, early efforts in marketing focused on justification, differentiation, and classification. The influence of G-D logic, emphasizing "productive" goods as opposed to "unproductive" services and the associated notion of value being embedded during the manufacturing (or agricultural or extraction) process, was apparent if not problematic.

Shaw (1912) is usually acknowledged to have written the first scholarly marketing article (Sheth and Gross 1988). This issue of the value-creation role of marketing occupied much of Shaw's early scholarly effort. The sway of the manufacturing perspective from economics was evident in Shaw's (1912, p. 12) contention that "industry is concerned with the application of motion to matter to change its form and place. The change in form we term production; the change in place, distribution" (see also Shaw 1994).

Similarly, Weld (1916, p. 317) viewed marketing as a production function. He contended that production was "the creation of utilities," specifically form, time, place, and possession utility, with marketing involved with the last three. For Weld, an economist, marketing was a further division of labor utilized for greater efficiency. He wondered why the division of labor was mistrusted when used in distribution but praised in manufacturing. Weld insisted that the problem was the absence of a body of knowledge about the role of marketing in creating utility in economic systems. He delineated the roles of wholesale and retail agents who specialized in different parts of the efficient marketing of commodities.

The positions established by these early marketing scholars were later designated the functional and institutional schools, respectively (Bartels 1986; Sheth and Gross 1988). A third school of analysis involved viewing marketing as the distribution of commodities. These perspectives centered on how marketing can have or add value given that marketing is a service.

For early marketing scholars the answer clearly had to do with how marketing added value to goods. That is, what were the functions (services) provided by marketers; what were the value-adding roles of the services of marketing? This goods-dominant, supporting role of services in the economy can be seen in the typical reference describing them in terms of "aids to the production and marketing of goods" (Converse 1930, p. vi; see Fisk, Brown, and Bitner 1993). Given that G-D logic of economic science was the dominant paradigm for understanding exchange and that marketing was initially focused on the distribution of goods, this supporting role is not surprising. Regardless, given the dominant logic of the time, much of the exchange taking place in the market was mainly being overlooked by the fledgling discipline.

Notable exceptions, at least on the surface, include Converse (1930, 1936), who included a chapter on the selling and marketing of intangible services in his texts. Converse (1936, p. 492) conceived service to include "all of those nonphysical things for which we spend money." He examined specific marketing methods applicable to these "radically different" types of services, including telephone and electric services, defined as intangible goods (e.g., Breyer 1931, 1934).

Additional references to other "service" businesses can also be found. Macklin (1922, pp. 26–28) provided a more integrative view, as well as presaging contemporary calls for co-production and co-creation of value, by identifying both production and marketing as "rendering of essential services." Macklin maintained that production is incomplete until all of these services have been provided. Even in these exceptions, however, services were viewed as a special type of good, that is, intangible goods.

Nonetheless, the attitude prevailed that value was in goods and that distribution (marketing) was something that added costs and waste. This view later motivated the Twentieth Century Fund investigation, "Does Distribution Cost Too Much?" (Stewart and Dewhurst, 1939/1976). This nationally debated study was published toward the end of the 1930s, which had witnessed one of the most prolonged economic depressions the United States and the world had ever experienced. Thus, prices consumers paid for goods were a major concern, and the free enterprise system of capitalism was beginning to be questioned by many. Stewart and Dewhurst (1939/1976, p. 3) open with the following:

> The idea that it costs too much to distribute goods and that modern methods of distribution are wasteful and inefficient has taken root in the public mind. Every day the consumer is exposed to sights and sounds which seem to confirm this impression—the spectacle of four gasoline stations, one on each corner of a crossroads, the constant bombardment of costly radio programs selling everything from cigarettes to pianos, and the frequent complaint of the farmer who gets only four or five cents of the fifteen cents we pay for a quart of milk.

This report manifests vivid indicators of how strongly G-D logic and the Newtonian elegance of equilibrium economics had pervaded thinking. Recognizing the difficulty in determining the excess cost or waste due to marketing and distribution, Stewart and Dewhurst (1939/1976, p. 346) propose a workable criterion: "to prepare a blueprint of the potential efficiency of an imaginary, perfectly functioning planned economy, and draw a contrast." They believed that the analysis would show tremendous waste in the economic system of that era.

That services were generally wasteful was deeply ingrained in the thinking of the day. The ideal—to help identify waste of distribution (marketing)—would be a perfectly planned equilibrium economy that featured mass-produced high-efficiency production that limits consumer choice—which shortly thereafter the Soviet Union attempted to implement.

Mid-Century Perturbations

Beginning approximately with the second quarter of the twentieth century, the world of exchange progressed through a series of important changes. The late 1920s saw rapid economic expansion; the 1930s a worldwide depression; the 1940s a major world war; and the late 1940s and 1950s a rapid recovery and the beginning of a new prosperity. The changes affected markets and the way marketing was approached, both practically and academically. With economic expansion came increased specialization. Activities that had traditionally been classified as manufacturing were increasingly outsourced and classified as services. During the depression, governments' role in what had previously largely been communal and market activities was amplified, accelerating what was normally classified as the service sector.

Partly in response, Fisher (1935) differentiated among the roles of primary (agriculture), secondary (manufacturing), and tertiary stages or sectors in evolutionary economics. He did not argue that services correspond to the tertiary sector. Fisher declared that some of Smith's unproductive activities could be considered productive—for example, useful labor in societies that have advanced beyond basic agriculture and manufacturing. Still, the views that services are tertiary and of growing importance are often attributed to Fisher.

The postwar years brought an additional rapid economic expansion. Consumer demand increased, as did production and competition. Marketing thought shifted toward issues focused on the exchange process and away from aggregate analyses (e.g., Alderson 1957; McInnis 1964). Two influential initiatives emerged: the "consumer behavior" and "marketing management" schools of thought (Sheth and Gross 1988). The "marketing concept"—the belief that markets are energized by consumers' desires (consumer orientation), that firms seek profitable sales, and that all activities of the firm should be directed toward satisfying these desires—underlies both schools.

A similar shift in thought was later attempted from deep within the walls of the factory where G-D logic had thrived and motivated mass production, emphasizing efficiency in manufacturing techniques. Effectiveness was a second or third priority. A low enough price would move consumers to compromise and accept a good not composed of their ideal set of attributes. The emphasis on efficiency overwhelmed other goals, including quality. Customers had to check for quality and return defective goods for replacement.

The emergence of the total quality management (TQM) framework placed customers' perception of quality as a prime driver of production techniques (Garvin 1987; Juran 1988). TQM, had it worked, was supposed to improve quality and lower costs by orienting the firm toward customer satisfaction and customer perceptions of quality. Costs would be decreased because repairing goods in the factory is cheaper than waiting until customers found defects and either returned goods for replacement or switched to competitive offerings. TQM was generally applied within functional areas of the firm and not across functions, processes that S-D logic emphasizes. Workers continued to be specialized and were not cross-trained and developed to perform more broadly defined skills (Schonberger 1992).

Presumably, these shifts to the consumer orientation and TQM represented a major reorientation not only from manufactured quality to customer perception of quality (satisfaction) as the major determinant of exchange but also conceivably toward a correction in the underlying economic model. These shifts appeared to represent significant departures from economic thought and the foundation upon which economic science was built. For marketing, the orientation was becoming not so much national well-being as the individual's perception of well-being.

But did these shifts represent corrections in the foundation of the model or just a superficial change to the facade? In part, the answer can be seen in another schism regarding the meaning of *value*, even as a more marketing-relevant, unified meaning was being sought. The evolution in orientation that marketing was experiencing implied the need for a parallel shift in the concepts of value and utility toward *usefulness* or *value-in-use* and away from *value-in-exchange*. However, as Dixon (1990, pp. 337–38) noted, although scholars like Beckman and Alderson both called for a unifying concept of utility, "each writer uses a different concept of value. Beckman is arguing in terms of *value-in-exchange,* basing his calculation on value added, upon 'the selling value' of products. On the other hand, Alderson is reasoning in terms of *value-in-use.*" Dixon (1990, p. 342) remarked that

> The "conventional view" of marketing as adding properties to matter, caused a problem for Alderson and "makes more difficult a disinterested evaluation of what marketing is and does" (Cox 1965). This view also underlies the dissatisfaction with marketing theory that led to the services marketing literature. If marketing is the process that adds properties to matter, then it can not contribute to the production of "immaterial goods."

Alderson (1957, p. 69) claimed, "What is needed is not an interpretation of the utility created by marketing, but a marketing interpretation of the whole process of creating utility." During this time Drucker (1958, pp. 253, 255) identified marketing, itself a service, as the catalyst in economic development and rejected standard theories focused on production, labor, and government policy.

> Marketing is thus the process through which economy is integrated into society to serve human needs . . . the essential aspect of an "underdeveloped" economy and the factor the absence of which keeps it "under-developed," is the inability to organize economic efforts and energies, to bring together resources, wants, and capacities, and so to convert a self-limiting static system into creative, self-generating organic growth.

Drucker identified a major issue in these underdeveloped countries as a "strong, pervasive prejudice against the 'middleman'" (p. 255). In brief, marketing and distribution were viewed as relatively useless and wasteful services, with wealth coming from embedding goods with value during the production process.

Alderson and Drucker had it "right," but economic theory, based on the concept of embedded value, was itself deeply embedded in marketing thought. Thus, two logics of exchange coexisted, one built upon economic theory inherited by marketing and the other emerging as marketing scholars began rethinking their orientations. Within this context, as noted by Dixon (1990), service marketing as an academic marketing concern began to take on an increasingly separate identity from goods marketing, and thus we see a further bifurcation.

SERVICE MARKETING AS A SUBDISCIPLINE

Services marketing began to take shape as a subdiscipline in the context of the following:

1. The consumer behavior movement and the recognition that consumer choice was more than just a function of the utilitarian benefits of goods and the motivation to maximize utility;
2. The apparent increased salience of services in society and exchange and the related view that economies evolve into services economies;
3. The realization that marketing was concerned with the process of exchange, which could not be adequately understood from the economic science perspective of goods embedded with utility; and
4. The idea that the customer and producer could not be necessarily separated and viewed as distinct entities but were involved in co-producing.

Services marketing emerged slowly as a subdiscipline. Fisk, Brown, and Bitner (1993) labeled the pre-1980s as the "crawling out" period for services marketing. Early scholars sought to delineate services from goods and to understand management of the marketing of intangibles. The influence of G-D logic, with its manufacturing perspective, is apparent in the way service was initially defined. Definitions first involved an explicit description of a "good" and then depicted services as anything else (e.g., a process rather than a thing). Judd (1964, p. 58) called it "definition by exclusion" (see also Rathmell 1966). Still relying on residual approaches, Lovelock (1983, p. 13; see also Solomon et al. 1985) added more positive terms such as "performance," and Bateson (1991, p. 7) added "interactive experience" on the part of the consumer. However, generally, services were considered to be what goods were not.

The G-D logic and manufacturing-based frame of reference are also evident in the four commonly cited differences between goods and services condensed from the service marketing literature by Zeithaml, Parasuraman, and Berry (1985):

1. Intangibility—lacking the physical or concrete quality of goods;
2. Heterogeneity—the relative difficulty of standardizing services in comparison to goods;
3. Inseparability of production and consumption—the simultaneous nature of service production and consumption as compared to the sequential nature of production, purchase, and consumption that characterizes physical products; and
4. Perishability—the relative inability to stockpile services as compared to goods.

These characteristics are usually thought to be disadvantages of services relative to goods and thus suggest normative steps for service marketing managers to take (Zeithaml, Parasuraman, and Berry 1985, p. 44).

Others have questioned defining services as the antitheses of goods and utilizing these four characteristics. Gummesson (1993, p. 32) notes that using physical products as a definitional foundation "presupposes that there is a fairly unambiguous definition of goods" and "forces services to exist on goods' conditions instead of allowing them to exist on their own conditions." Beaven and Scotti (1990, pp. 7–8) believe that common descriptors fail "to differentiate between these two production processes and confuse(s) outputs with outcomes" and "inhibits the development of services as a truly distinct subdiscipline."

Ironically, Berry and Parasuraman (1993) compared the evolution of services marketing to the "growth of a new product," though an intangible one. As Shostack (1977) concluded, "The classical 'marketing mix,' the seminal literature, and the language of marketing all derive from the manufacture of physical-goods" and urged services to "break free from product marketing."

Following this period of unresolved goods versus services debate, the focus turned toward more substantive issues. In the United States, Zeithaml, Parasuraman, and Berry (1985) proffered a conceptual model and standardized instrument for assessing perceptions of service quality. Solomon et al. (1985) sketched the elements necessary for understanding the service encounter; and Berry (1983) coined the term *relationship marketing*.

At the same time, European scholars, particularly in the Nordic countries, were rethinking the concepts of service quality (Grönroos 1984) and relationships independent of similar work in the United States. European service marketing scholars extended the notion of relationship to the development of an interactive logic of "service management" (Grönroos 2000b; Normann 1988).

To appreciate fully the significance of these developments, both their antithetical intentions and subsequent impact should be studied. Concepts like service quality, relationship marketing, and service management were intended as perspectives for understanding service and service marketing, which were necessitated by the inadequacies of their G-D logic counterparts. Service quality, as well as TQM, shifted the focus from engineering specifications of goods to the perceived evaluations of the consumer. Relationship marketing shifted the focus of successful exchange from the discrete transaction to ongoing interactivity. Service management shifted the focus from the highly structured, mass production, and standardization economies of scale of Taylor's (1947) "scientific management" to the "teamwork, interfunctional collaboration, and interorganizational partnership" (Grönroos 1994) perspective necessary for "service firms."

In each case, these "services" conceptualizations gradually began to displace, or at least subordinate, their G-D logic counterparts. Instead of serving as differentiators of service from goods phenomena, as originally intended, they took on the role of unifiers as they were adopted and applied by marketers who did not identify themselves as having a service focus. Now these same concepts are reshaping the logic of mainstream marketing.

Fisk, Brown, and Bitner (1993) and Berry and Parasuraman (1993) specify that services marketing succeeded in "breaking free from products marketing" (Shostack 1977). The major contributions of service scholars ensured that service marketing had evolved into a full-fledged subdiscipline. Perhaps a more general breaking free was also taking place (see Vargo and Lusch 2004b) or at least being signaled. Perhaps marketing in general was beginning to show signs of breaking free from G-D logic.

SIGNS OF DIVERGENCE FROM G-D LOGIC

As marketing was adopting service marketing perspectives, other signs of change in marketing could be observed. For example, Pine (1993) argued that mass customization as opposed to mass production was becoming the new frontier of competition. Prahalad and others (e.g., Prahalad and Ramaswamy 2000) shifted attention away from the notion of separately produced value to the idea of value being co-produced. Pine and Gilmore (1999) urged a focus on experiences and away from goods, even when tangible products were involved. Prahalad and Hamel (1990; see also Day 1994) espoused core competency (collective learning in the organization) theory, in which competitive advantage resulting from competence makes a "disproportionate contribution to customer-perceived value" (Hamel and Prahalad 1994, pp. 202, 204).

Hunt (e.g., 2002) offered a resource-advantage view of competition as a framework for a more market-relevant general theory of competition while identifying specific problems with the microeconomic model that had served as the foundation for marketing. Zuboff and Maxmin (2002) took exception with the "old enterprise logic" and its "managerial capitalism" (p. 280) that had provided the value-distributing, transactional logic for approaching markets for the past century and suggested a new relational logic of "distributed capitalism" (p. 323) in which value originated with the individual and marketing's role is to provide "deep support." Sheth and Parvatiyar (2000, p. 126) noted a "change in focus from value exchanges to value-creation relationships," pointing to "partnering relationships."

As the Nordic service scholars were moving toward relationship rather than transaction as the core marketing process, almost independently, an alternative relational approach, developed under the rubric of the "network approach," was being developed by the Industrial Marketing and Purchasing (IMP) Group in Sweden. This IMP-inspired model also was gaining wider acceptance and application. For example, Achrol and Kotler (1999, p.162), advocating a network perspective, suggested, "The very nature of network organization, the kinds of theories useful to its understanding, and the potential impact on the organization of consumption all suggest that a paradigm shift for marketing may not be far over the horizon." Much of this appeared under the heading of supply and value chain management or value constellations (Normann and Ramirez 1993), a significant move away from the standard integrated logistics management model of moving "matter" to market.

Parallel shifts in related disciplines can also be seen, some of which served pedigree roles for emerging marketing thought. Resource-based views of the firm (e.g., Penrose 1959) had been developing for some time. Some economists challenged "orthodox" economic theory and suggested a model of evolutionary economics based on capability-driven organizational "routines" (see, e.g., Nelson and Winter 1982). Teece and Pisano (1994, p. 537) suggested that "the competitive advantage of firms stems from dynamic capabilities rooted in high performance routines operating inside the firm, embedded in the firm's processes, and conditioned by its history." By the end of the twentieth century, Webster (1992, p. 1) contended, "The historical marketing management function, based on the microeconomic maximization paradigm, must be critically examined for its relevance to marketing theory and practice." Similarly, Day and Montgomery (1999, p. 3) thought the logic of the Four P's should now be "regarded as merely a handy framework." Sheth and Parvatiyar (2000, p. 140) believed that "an alternative paradigm of marketing is needed, a paradigm that can account for the continuous nature of relationships among marketing actors."

These and other divergences from conventional thinking and calls for new paradigms can alternatively be interpreted as signaling the fragmentation of logics or a convergence on a newer, more integrative logic of exchange and related phenomena. We believe the latter is indicated.

Alderson's (1957, p. 69) request for "a marketing interpretation of the whole process of creating utility" and Shostack's (1977) call to "break free from product marketing" argued for more than the recognition of a subdiscipline. Likewise, Gummesson (1993, p. 250) argues that:

> Customers do not buy goods or services: they buy *offerings* which render services which create value. . . . The traditional division between goods and services is long outdated. It is not a matter of redefining services and seeing them from a customer perspective; *activities render services, things render services.* The shift in focus to services is a shift from the means and the producer perspective to the utilization and the customer perspective. [emphasis ours]

In agreement with Alderson, Shostack, and Gummesson, we see a movement toward a value-in-use perspective and away from the good-centered, value-in-exchange model of economics. We also agree with Rust's (1998) and Grönroos's (2000a) call for convergence of goods and services thinking. We believe that all of this apparently disparate thought is converging on a unifying logic of exchange, one in which service plays a more central role.

TOWARD CONVERGENCE ON A NEW DOMINANT LOGIC

These shifts share common features:

1. What parties exchange is less well characterized as "goods" than as applied specialized resources;
2. Most critical resources are often not tangible but rather intangible resources like human knowledge and skills (competences);
3. Value creation cannot occur in factories or through distribution but rather only through the interactions of the parties sharing these resources—that is, through service provision;
4. Marketing is less about units of output than the process of sharing of the application of resources among parties;
5. Customers are not static resources to be targeted or marketed to but active and creative resources to be collaborated and marketed with;
6. Competitive advantage is a function of resources that are better able to provide service for some portion of the market;
7. Value is co-created and ultimately can only be determined by the customer;
8. Markets represent opportunities for value creation and value sustainability rather than value delivery; and
9. When goods are involved, they are tools for the delivery and application of resources— that is, service provision.

We believe that these commonalities can be integrated via a new dominant logic, one in which service—*the application of specialized competences (knowledge and skills), through deeds, processes, and performances for the benefit of another entity or the entity itself* (Vargo and Lusch 2004a)—replaces goods as the common denominator. We intentionally use the singular word *service*, rather than the plural *services*. The former represents S-D logic and implies doing something for and with another party, whereas the latter, as normally employed, implies an intangible unit of output and has meaning only in the context of G-D logic.

We believe that S-D logic represents the convergence of contemporary marketing thought. Importantly, it therefore represents a view of exchange and marketing that has been generated by marketing scholars, rather than inherited from economics and industrialization. Perhaps it is what Alderson (1957, p. 69) had in mind: "a marketing interpretation of the whole process of creating utility." But it also represents a logic that is consistent with the logic of exchange from which economic models were derived, though for more limited purposes. Thus, we suggest it is also a broad, confirmatory convergence that provides a better foundation for marketing and for understanding exchange in general and its role in society.

REFERENCES

Achrol, Ravi S. and Philip Kotler (1999), "Marketing in the Network Economy," *Journal of Marketing,* 63 (Special Issue), 146–163.

Alderson, Wroe (1957), *Marketing Behavior and Executive Action: A Functionalist Approach to Marketing Theory.* Homewood, IL: Richard D. Irwin.

Bartels, Robert (1986), "Development of Marketing Thought: A Brief History," in *Marketing Thought,* J.N. Sheth and D.E. Garrett, eds. Cincinnati, OH: Southwestern.

Bastiat, Frédéric (1848/1964), *Selected Essays on Political Economy,* S. Cain, trans., G.B. de Huszar, ed. Princeton, NJ: D. Van Nordstrand.

—— (1860), *Harmonies of Political Economy*. Patrick S. Sterling, trans. London: J. Murray.

Bateson, John E.G. (1991), *Managing Services Marketing*. Fort Worth, TX: Dryden.

Beaven, Mary H. and Dennis J. Scotti (1990), "Service-Oriented Thinking and Its Implications for the Marketing Mix," *Journal of Services Marketing*, 4 (Fall): 5–19.

Bell, J.B. (1953), *A History of Economic Thought*. New York: Ronald Press.

Berry, Leonard L. (1983), "Relationship Marketing," in *Emerging Perspectives in Services Marketing*, L. L. Berry, G. L. Shostack, and G. D. Upah, eds. Chicago: American Marketing Association, 25–38.

—— and A. Parasuraman (1993), "Building a New Academic Field—The Case of Services Marketing," *Journal of Retailing*, 69 (1), 13–60.

Breyer, Ralph F. (1931), *Commodity Marketing*. New York: McGraw-Hill.

—— (1934), *The Marketing Institution*. New York: McGraw-Hill.

Converse, Paul D. (1930), *The Elements of Marketing*. New York: Prentice Hall.

—— (1936), *Essentials of Distribution*. New York: Prentice Hall.

Cox, Reavis (1965), *Distribution in a High-Level Economy*. Englewood Cliffs, NJ: Prentice Hall.

Day, George (1994), "The Capabilities of Market-Driven Organization," *Journal of Marketing*, 58 (October), 37–52.

—— and David Montgomery (1999), "Charting New Directions for Marketing," *Journal of Marketing*, 63 (Special Issue), 3–13.

Delaunay, Jean-Claude and Jean Gadrey (1992), *Services in Economic Thought*. Boston: Kluwer Academic Press.

Dixon, Donald F. (1990), "Marketing as Production: The Development of a Concept," *Journal of the Academy of Marketing Science*, 18 (4), 337–43.

Drucker, Peter (1958), "Marketing and Economic Development," *Journal of Marketing*, 22 (1958), 252–59.

Fisher, Allan G.B. (1935), *The Class of Progress and Society*. New York: Augustus M. Kelley Publishers.

Fisk, Raymond P., Steven W. Brown, and Mary Jo Bitner (1993), "Tracking the Evolution of the Services Marketing Literature," *Journal of Retailing*, 69 (1), 61–103.

Garvin, David A. (1987), "Competing on the Eight Dimensions of Quality," *Harvard Business Review*, (November-December), 101–9.

Grönroos, Christian (1984), "A Service Quality Model and Its Marketing Implications," *European Journal of Marketing*, 18 (4), 36–44.

——. (1994), "From Scientific Management to Service Management," *International Journal of Service Industry Management*, 5 (1), 5–20.

—— (2000a), *Service Management and Marketing: A Customer Relationship Management Approach*. West Sussex, UK: John Wiley & Sons.

—— (2000b), "Relationship Marketing: The Nordic School Perspective," in Jagdish N. Sheth and Atul Parvatiyar, eds. *Handbook of Relationship Marketing*, Thousand Oaks, CA: Sage Publications, 95–117.

Gummesson, Evert (1993), *Quality Management in Service Organization*. New York: International Service Quality Association.

Hamel, Gary and C. K. Prahalad (1994), *Competing for the Future*. Boston: Harvard Business School Press.

Hunt, Shelby D. (2002), *Foundations of Marketing Theory: Toward a General Theory of Marketing*. Thousand Oaks, CA: Sage Publications.

Judd, Robert C. (1964), "The Case for Redefining Services," *Journal of Marketing*, 18 (January), 58–59.

Juran, J.M. (1988), *Juran on Planning for Quality*. New York: The Free Press.

Kuhn, Thomas S. (1962), *The Structure of Scientific Revolutions*. Chicago: University of Chicago Press.

Lovelock, Christopher H. (1983), "Classifying Services to Gain Strategic Marketing Insights," *Journal of Marketing*, 47 (Summer), 9–20.

—— and Evert Gummesson (2004), "Whither Services Marketing? In Search of a New Paradigm and Fresh Perspectives," *Journal of Service Research*, 7 (1), 20–41.

Macklin, T. (1922), *Efficient Marketing for Agriculture*. New York: Macmillan.

Marshall, Alfred (1890/1927), *Principles of Economics*. London: Macmillan.

McInnis, W.J. (1964), "A Conceptual Approach to Marketing," in *Theory in Marketing*, Reavis Cox, Wroe Alderson, and Stanley Shapiro, eds. Homewood, IL: Richard D. Irwin.

Mill, John Stuart (1848), *Principles of Political Economy*. London: J. P. Parker.

Nelson, Richard and Sidney G. Winter (1982), *An Evolutionary Theory of Economic Change*. Cambridge, MA: Belknap Press.

Normann, Richard (1988), *Service Management: Strategy and Leadership in Service Business.* New York: John Wiley & Sons.

———— and Rafael Ramirez (1993), "From Value Chain to Value Constellation: Designing Interactive Strategy," *Harvard Business Review,* 71 (July-August), 65–77.

Penrose, Edith T. (1959), *The Theory of the Growth of the Firm.* London: Basil Blackwell and Mott.

Pine, Joseph B. (1993), *Mass Customization: New Frontiers in Business Competition.* Cambridge, MA: Harvard Business School Press

———— and James H. Gilmore (1999), *The Experience Economy: Work as Theater and Every Business a Stage.* Cambridge, MA: Harvard University Press.

Prahalad, C. K. and Gary Hamel (1990), "The Core Competence of the Corporation," *Harvard Business Review,* 68 (May/June), 79–91.

———— and Venkatram Ramaswamy (2000), "Co-opting Customer Competence," *Harvard Business Review,* 78 (January/February), 79–87.

Rathmell, John M. (1966), "What Is Meant by Services?" *Journal of Marketing,* 30 (October), 32–36.

Rust, Roland (1998), "What Is the Domain of Service Research?" *Journal of Service Research,* 1 (November), 107.

Say, Jean-Baptiste (1821), *A Treatise on the Political Economy.* Boston: Wells and Lilly.

Schonberger, Richard J. (1992), "Total Quality Management Cuts a Broad Swath—Through Manufacturing and Beyond," *Organizational Dynamics,* 20 (Spring), 16–28.

Schumpeter, Joseph (1954), *History of Economic Analysis.* New York: Oxford University Press.

Shaw, Arch W. (1912), "Some Problems in Market Distribution," *Quarterly Journal of Economics,* (August), 706–65.

Shaw, Eric (1994), "The Utility of the Four Utilities Concept," in *Research in Marketing,* Jagdish Sheth and Ronald Ferguson, eds. Greenwich, CT: JAI Press.

Sheth, Jagdish N. and Barbara L. Gross (1988), "Parallel Development of Marketing and Consumer Behavior: A Historical Perspective," in *Historical Perspectives in Marketing,* T. Nevett and R.A. Fullerton, eds. Lexington, MA: Lexington Books, 9–33.

———— and A. Parvatiyar (2000), "Relationship Marketing in Consumer Markets: Antecedents and Consequences," in Jagdish Sheth and A. Parvatiyar, eds. *Handbook of Relationship Marketing,* Thousand Oaks, CA: Sage Publications.

Shostack, G. Lynn (1977), "Breaking Free from Product Marketing," *Journal of Marketing,* 41 (April), 73–80.

Smith, Adam (1776/1904), *An Inquiry into the Nature and Causes of the Wealth of Nations.* London: Printed for W. Strahan and T. Cadell.

Solomon, Michael R., Carol F. Surprenant, John A. Czepiel, and Evelyn G. Gutman (1985), "A Role Theory Perspective on Dyadic Interactions," *Journal of Marketing,* 49 (Winter), 99–111.

Stewart, Paul W. and J. Fredric Dewhurst (1939/1976), *Does Distribution Cost too Much?* New York: Arno Press.

Taylor, Fredrick W. (1947), *Scientific Management.* London: Harper and Row.

Teece, David and Gary Pisano (1994), "The Dynamic Capabilities of Firms: An Introduction," *Industrial and Corporate Change,* 3 (3), 537–56.

Vargo, Stephen L. and Robert F. Lusch (2004a), "Evolving to a New Dominant Logic for Marketing," *Journal of Marketing,* 68 (January), 1–17.

———— and ———— (2004b), "The Four Service Marketing Myths: Remnants of a Goods-Based, Manufacturing Model," *Journal of Service Research,* 6 (May), 324–335.

———— and Fred W. Morgan (2005), "Services in Society and Academic Thought: An Historical Analysis," *Journal of Macromarketing,* 25 (June), 42–53.

Walras, Leon (1894/1954), *Elements of the Political Economy.* Homestead, NJ: Richard D. Irwin.

Webster, Frederick E., Jr. (1992), "The Changing Role of Marketing in the Corporation," *Journal of Marketing,* 56 (October), 1–17.

Weld, Louis D.H. (1916), *The Marketing of Farm Products.* New York: Macmillan.

Zeithaml, Valerie A., A. Parasuraman, and Leonard L. Berry (1985), "Problems and Strategies in Services Marketing," *Journal of Marketing,* 49 (Spring), 33–46.

Zuboff, Shoshana and James Maxmin (2002), *The Support Economy: Why Corporations Are Failing Individuals and the Next Episode of Capitalism.* New York: Viking Press.

3

SERVICE-DOMINANT LOGIC

What It Is, What It Is Not, What It Might Be

S<small>TEPHEN</small> L. V<small>ARGO AND</small> R<small>OBERT</small> F. L<small>USCH</small>

WHAT IT IS

Service-dominant (S-D) logic represents a departure from the traditional, foundational, goods-dominant (G-D) logic of exchange, in which goods were the focus of exchange and services represented a special case of goods—a logic that marketing inherited from economics a little more than 100 years ago. It represents a shift from an emphasis on the exchange of *operand resources,* usually tangible, inert resources, to an emphasis on *operant resources,* dynamic resources that act upon other resources.

Service-dominant logic views applied, specialized skills and knowledge as the focus of economic exchange and one of the fundamental foundations upon which society is built. Thus, it rests on the premise that, in order to improve their individual and collective well-being, humans exchange the service—the application of specialized skills and knowledge—that they can provide to others for the service that they need from others. If goods are involved in the exchange, they are seen as mechanisms for service provision.

Consistent with this shift, S-D logic challenges the joint, central logic of the G-D paradigm of (1) units of output being embedded with value and (2) units of output (e.g., "products," "goods," "services") representing the fundamental unit(s) of exchange. Instead, S-D logic specifies that it is *service*—defined as *the application of specialized competences (operant resources—knowledge and skills), through deeds, processes, and performances for the benefit of another entity or the entity itself*—that is exchanged for service. It is important to note that we use the singular term, *service,* which we feel better reflects the notion of *doing* something beneficial, for rather than units of, output—immaterial goods—as the more commonly used plural, *services,* implies.

As a corollary, we see S-D logic rejecting the traditional classification of goods and services (i.e., alternative forms of products). Service (or services) is not an alternative (to goods) form of product (cf. e.g., Ambler, chapter 22; Brodie, Pels, and Saren, chapter 25, Achrol and Kotler, chapter 26). Goods are *appliances* (tools, distribution mechanisms) that serve as alternatives to direct service provision. In this sense, S-D logic represents an inversion of G-D logic. Goods are a special case, or at least a special method, of service provision. Service, then, represents the general case, the common denominator, of the exchange process; *service* is what is *always* exchanged. The following eight foundational premises (Vargo and Lusch 2004a, reprinted as chapter 1 of this book) summarize S-D logic:

FP1. The application of specialized skill(s) and knowledge is the fundamental unit of exchange:
- Service is exchanged for service.

FP2. Indirect exchange masks the fundamental unit of exchange:
- Microspecialization, organizations, goods, and money obscure the service-for-service nature of exchange.

FP3. Goods are distribution mechanisms for service provision:
- "Activities render service; things render service" (Gummesson 1995, p. 251)—goods are appliances.

FP4. Knowledge is the fundamental source of competitive advantage:
- Operant resources, especially know-how, are the essential component of differentiation.

FP5. All economies are services economies:
- Service is only now becoming more *apparent* with increased specialization and outsourcing; it has always been what is exchanged.

FP6. The customer is always a co-creator of value:
- There is no value until an offering is used—experience and perception are essential to value determination.

FP7. The enterprise can only make value propositions:
- Since value is always determined by the customer (value-in-use), it cannot be embedded through manufacturing (value-in-exchange).

FP8. A service-centered view is customer oriented and relational:
- Operant resources being used for the benefit of the customer places the customer inherently in the center of value creation and implies relationship.

It should be noted that FP6 now uses the term *co-creator of value* instead of the original term *co-producer*. We now believe that the term co-producer brings forth too much of a goods-dominant and production-oriented logic. Rather, we prefer co-creator which is much more in line with service-dominant logic. Collectively, these foundational premises provide a framework for reexamining and potentially extending knowledge about the exchange process and its role, not only in commerce, but also in society.

Importantly, S-D logic makes the consumer endogenous to the value-creation process (see also Arnould, Price, and Malshe, chapter 7; Grönroos, chapter 28; Woodruff and Flint, chapter 14). Value, then, becomes a joint function of the actions of the provider(s) and the consumer(s) but is always determined by the consumer (see Venkatesh, Peñaloza, and Firat, chapter 19; Woodruff and Flint, chapter 14). This orientation has strikingly different normative implications for the way that the enterprise approaches the market than does G-D logic.

WHAT IT IS NOT

From the time of the receipt of the initial reviews of our first submission of "Evolving to a New Dominant Logic for Marketing" to the *Journal of Marketing* (Vargo and Lusch 2004a), through the drafts of the commentaries invited by the editor following its acceptance, to the proposals and final essays for this volume, we have witnessed misstatements about the underlying thesis of S-D logic. This is not entirely surprising. No doubt some of this is partially a reflection of our own imprecision in composition. But, perhaps as important, it is also likely a reflection of the paradigmatic strength of G-D logic, or for that matter, any paradigm. As noted, at the heart of the G-D paradigm is the notion of tangible goods, output from "productive activity," as the unit of exchange and the co-notion of services as "immaterial goods." Although that notion has been modified fairly recently to portray goods and services as alternative forms of products, the contemporary term *product* is essentially equivalent in meaning to the term *goods*—output embedded with value— with *services* referring to productive output that is lacking in certain desirable characteristics (see Vargo and Lusch 2004b).

Given that S-D logic inverts a paradigm that has served as the foundation for not only the scientific study of economics, and subsequently marketing, but also as a foundation for more mundane musings, it is probably not surprising that the nuances of S-D logic are often overlooked, if not misunderstood. Necessarily, S-D logic is essentially always first encountered by peering through a lens honed by G-D logic (see, e.g., Achrol and Kotler, chapter 26). In the following sections, we highlight some of the most consistent misconceptions and misunderstandings that we have encountered.

S-D Logic Is a Reflection of the Transition from an Industrial Era to a Services Era

One of the most consistent restatements, and misstatements, of the S-D thesis is that because services, rather than goods, now dominate many economies, it is appropriate for marketing to adopt models that reflect this transition (see, e.g., Achrol and Kotler, chapter 26; Ambler, chapter 22; Brodie, Pels, and Saren, chapter 25). We, of course, have no argument with the idea that service dominates exchange today, but the statement does not go far enough. S-D logic implies that service is the foundation for *all* of exchange; the function of goods is to enable service—that is, goods represent a special case of service provision, one that has always been a fairly small subset. It is only from the perspective of a model that includes the fundamental assumption that exchange is driven by goods (G-D logic) that the importance of service is just now becoming apparent and that the economy is perceived to be transitioning from goods focused to service focused.

The fundamental subject matter of marketing is exchange (Hunt 1991). Exchange, in turn, is a corollary of the division of labor, or more precisely, specialization—Macneil (1980) calls it the "shadow of specialization." Specialization implies the refinement of operant resources, the ability to cause something to happen; it is about doing things, the application of specialized skills and knowledge; it is about service provision. This is not to say that operand resources—normally tangible matter—are not important. Many of them are extremely beneficial, if not essential, to human welfare. But we argue that the key to deriving their benefit resides with the knowledge and skills necessary to learn about, find, extract, cultivate, invent, manufacture, and use the operand resources. That is, the benefits are derived from the *application of operant resources* to operand and other operant resources—service as we define it.

From this perspective, industrialization or manufacturing is a form of service provision, the services concerned with the synchronized application of advanced specialized extraction, design, management, financial, accounting, and distribution of knowledge and skills, among others. Much of the *apparent* move to a service economy is nothing more than the further refinement and subsequent outsourcing of these operant resources.

This operant-resource-driven perspective of economic activity is not entirely new. Largely, G-D logic is the result of the confluence of several normative rationales that developed over the past several centuries and formed the foundation for economic science, rather than the result of more positive attempts at modeling exchange. This logic, which was later adopted by marketing, was grounded in the idea that goods were embedded with value and then exchanged in the marketplace.

As discussed more fully elsewhere (e.g., Vargo, Lusch, and Morgan, chapter 2), this goods-centered logic became dominant for two fundamental reasons. First, Adam Smith, on whose work economics was grounded, was primarily concerned with tangible things because they could be exported to increase the wealth of nations. Smith captured the fundamental role of the application of operant resources in his acknowledgment of the central role of the concomitant notions of the division of labor and exchange in value creation. But Smith did not know that he was eventually to become the "father of economics"; he was a moral philosopher concerned with a normative theory of national wealth accumulation rather than a positive theory of exchange.

Second, the model of tangible stuff, once the notion of its being embedded with utility, or value, was introduced, fit the proscriptive requirements of the economic scientists who followed Smith. It was compatible with the normative model for doing "real" science in the tradition of Newtonian mechanics. Even they wrestled with the difficulty of viewing productivity and exchange only in terms of these tangible goods, but having noted their objections, they acquiesced to what was becoming the accepted view. Thus, the G-D logic of exchange became the dominant logic of economics and its academic offspring, including marketing.

But as the division of labor increases, the fact that it is primarily concerned with operant resources, rather than the operand resources, on which they are acting only occasionally, becomes increasingly compelling. Specialization begets specialization—that is, operant resources create additional operant resources, which are increasingly refined, then outsourced, and finally exchanged in the market. As noted, we believe that the essential transition is not from a goods economy to a service economy; it is from internally supplied, applied operant resources to the outsourcing and exchange of applied operant resources.

Service(s) Is (Are) More Important Than Goods

S-D logic places service *superordinate* to goods in terms of classification and function, but not superior in terms of importance. Given the nested relationship between service and goods that is part of the fabric of S-D logic, it would be almost incoherent for us to suggest that service is superior to goods. Thus, we also are not saying that S-D logic is about substituting the concept of "service" for the concept of "good" (or product) (cf. Achrol and Kotler, chapter 26; Brodie, Pels, and Saren, chapter 25).

According to S-D logic, the function of goods is to deliver service. There is nothing in S-D logic that suggests inherently whether a particular service is best provided directly or through an appliance. The question is how to simultaneously optimize the benefits—the joint value co-created—for the exchange partners, and the solution is context and exchange-partner specific.

Service-Dominant Logic Is a Restatement of the Consumer Orientation

Some have suggested that S-D logic is not necessary because the "product orientation" of G-D logic now represents a "straw man." That is, although it may have been true that early marketing was "myopic" (Levitt 1960) in focusing on the product, this situation has long ago been corrected by adopting consumer orientation. We disagree. In fact, perhaps ironically, we suggest that the consumer orientation is evidence of the continued existence of the inherently myopic orientation of G-D logic.

G-D logic, by definition, puts goods, units of output, at the center of exchange. The consumer orientation represents an attempt, appropriately, at shifting the focus from the good to the needs and desires of the consumer, but it is a modification—arguably a contradictory one—of G-D logic, not a reconstruction of the foundation. Together, G-D logic and the consumer orientation say that goods are *embedded with value* during manufacturing (or extraction) and that value is *determined by the consumer*. At best, this co-foundational source of value is paradoxical; at worst, it is incoherent. Value cannot be created independently in manufacturing and consumption.

S-D logic, on the other hand, *implies* a consumer orientation. Because service is defined in terms of benefit being co-created with the consumer, rather than embedded in output, no separate explication or modification is necessary. The consumer, or more precisely, consumers—multiple parties in an exchange—are the foundation of S-D logic. With S-D logic, the consumer orientation becomes redundant.

Service-Dominant Logic Is Justified by the Superior Customer Responsiveness of "Service" Companies

Service-dominant logic is not necessarily the dominant logic of "service" enterprises and thus does not necessarily lead them to an implicit customer orientation or superior service provision. Goods-dominant logic is much more than an alternative philosophy or model of exchange. As noted, long ago it reached paradigmatic status. In fact, together with the Newtonian mechanics paradigm for doing science, with which G-D logic is closely tied, it might be one of the most deeply ingrained paradigms in both academic and managerial thought. Accordingly, enterprises that would be classified as service firms by most contemporary categorization schema, such as banks, hospitals, and universities, are just as likely to be guided by G-D logic as are "goods" firms. Consequently, they are just as likely to miss the customer's roles in value creation and value determination that are implied by a service-driven model, as are their goods-producing counterparts.

S-D logic, of course, implies that all firms are service firms. Thus, it has normative implications for all types of firms, including those that are traditionally classified as goods firms, such as manufacturers. Interestingly, many of these goods firms (e.g., Dell, GE, and IBM) are more service and customer oriented than firms that are more normally classified as service firms.

Likewise, academics with a specialization in service marketing and management are not necessarily guided by S-D logic. Nowhere is the paradigmatic power of G-D logic more evident than in the traditional academic treatment of the distinction between goods and services. Typically, service is treated as a kind of good (subset of product) that differs from other goods by lacking in certain qualities—tangibility, separability of production and consumption, standardizability, and inventoriability. Either implicitly or explicitly, these qualities are typically seen as advantageous, and thus, by implication, services (service provided directly) are somewhat deficient.

We have argued elsewhere (Vargo and Lusch 2004b) that these goods-versus-services distinctions are meaningful only from the perspective of G-D logic. From an S-D logic perspective, the distinctions are not only often mythical, but to the extent that they exist, *may* represent advantages rather than deficiencies. There is growing evidence and emphasis in the literature that tangibility is not what is typically being purchased, co-creation is preferable to separate production, heterogeneity in offerings is more likely to meet the idiosyncratic desires of consumers than homogeneity, and inventoriability is often expensive and a limiting factor in marketing efficiency. We suggest that, as with the consumer orientation, this literature reflects deficiencies in G-D logic, deficiencies that are corrected through the adoption of the fundamental model of S-D logic, rather than through patchwork modification to G-D logic.

Service-Dominant Logic Is an Alternative to the Exchange Paradigm

The exchange paradigm, grounded in the idea of exchange as the fundamental subject matter of marketing (e.g., Hunt 1991), has been increasingly questioned, if not maligned. Gummesson (1994, 1995), Grönroos (1994, 2000), and Sheth and Parvatiyar (2000) have called for a paradigm shift in marketing. Often, the suggestion is that the *exchange paradigm* should be replaced by a *relationship paradigm*.

Perhaps, given S-D logic's close alignment with relational models of exchange, it is natural to see it as an alternative to the exchange paradigm. However, we suggest that it should not be. Rather, we believe that the underlying discontent with exchange as the fundamental subject matter of marketing is actually a reflection of the inadequacies of G-D logic and its implication that exchange must be about output embedded with value (i.e., goods). Therefore, though we agree with relationship marketing scholars' (e.g., Grönroos 2000; Sheth and Parvatiyar 2000) call for a paradigm shift, we do not agree that the shift needs to abandon exchange—just the notion of the centrality of the good. We suggest that service is more fundamental than relationship. Given specialization, mutual service provision is required (desired); relationship, particularly in the normative sense in which it is most often used, is the means. That is, service is exchanged for service, *through* relationship.

Similar to our position, Gummesson (1995, p. 251) sees the need for a shift to a "service-centered" model as a necessary part of a relationship focus. We agree and argue that the shift in focus from the exchange of output to the exchange of applied, specialized competences (service) not only allows but also implies a relational perspective. We believe that S-D logic bridges the exchange and relationship perspectives and therefore obviates the apparent need for abandoning the exchange paradigm. As noted, we think the S-D logic of exchange is more fundamental than relationship. S-D logic is inherently relational; however, a relationship paradigm is not inherently service centered.

One additional clarification about relationship should be offered. Some see relationship as an optional strategy both on the part of the enterprise and the consumer. That is, in some cases only a transaction, rather than a relationship, is desired. If *relationship* has the limited meaning of multiple transactions, this argument might have some validity, but we use the term *relationship* more broadly in several ways. First, since S-D logic specifies that value is co-created by both parties and for both parties, it implies relationship, even when repeat patronage is not a goal. Furthermore, we (Vargo and Lusch 2004a, p. 12) have argued "even relatively discrete transactions come with social, if not legal, contracts and implied, if not expressed, warranties. These are promises and assurances that the exchange relationships will yield valuable service provision, often for extended periods of time."

Service Is Another Word for Utility or Value-Added

The term *utility* has two meanings. The first relates to usefulness, the ability to derive benefit from something. If its meaning was always so denoted, we would have no argument with the term being used as essentially equivalent with service. But that is not the case. Utility, as it is more frequently used in marketing, derives from economic science and, though its original meaning was tied to usefulness, the term has morphed to a connotation, if not denotation, of an embedded property of matter. That is, it suggests that things, usually extracted, cultivated, and manufactured goods, have various amounts of "utiles." This newer, morphed meaning of utility allowed the development of marginal utility theory by providing economic goods with a quasi-quantifiable, differentiable property. It also enabled economists to largely ignore the millenniums-old debate concerning value-in-exchange versus value-in-use.

Marketing, in an effort to legitimize itself, quickly adopted this newer meaning of utility, distinguishing the time and place utility provided by distribution from the form utility provided by manufacturing. Beckman (1954) more fully developed the idea of embedded utility into "value added," especially by marketing. *Service* subsequently became partially understood in terms of a form of value added, usually to manufactured goods.

We are uncomfortable with the notion of utility, at least as it is presently used to mean "embedded value," as well as the associated notion of value added. S-D logic implies that value cannot be embedded in either the factory or the distribution process. Value determination resides with the consumer. S-D logic directs the firm to make value propositions to potential customers who need the benefit of the firm's competences and then to heterogeneously co-create value with consumers.

S-D Logic Argues Against Value-in-Exchange

S-D logic embraces value-in-use and posits that only the customer can determine value; this occurs as the customer uses the offerings of the service provider (firm). It does not propose that value-in-exchange is irrelevant. First, S-D logic argues that value-in-exchange could not continue to exist if value-in-use did not occur. However, things can have value-in-use but not value-in-exchange; for instance, the biosphere has value-in-use but has generally not been subject to economic exchange.

Second, S-D logic recognizes the importance of financial feedback from the marketplace (exchange value) as a learning mechanism. In brief, S-D logic is compatible with the idea that financial feedback is tied to accounting systems that capture value-in-exchange. When a firm sells its service (with or without a tangible good), it receives a monetary instrument (cash or the promise to pay). These monetary instruments are used to acquire other service (with or without tangible good) from suppliers, including employees. Nonetheless, designing marketing strategy around this limited view of exchange (value-in-exchange) is myopic for reasons elaborated in Vargo and Lusch (2004a, 2004b, and this book).

Service Provision Relates Only to "Functional Benefits"

We have been presented with several objections to S-D logic that are based on an understanding that we are saying that our link between service and benefits is limited to functional benefits. These objections appear to become amplified when dealing with our contention that goods are service-delivery mechanisms, or appliances. Arguments range from something like "my car is much more than transportation; I like knowing it is in the garage and having other people know that I own it," to "I may not have a use for an object, but just knowledge that I own it and perhaps could get a loan for it at the bank, has value to me" (cf. Venkatesh, Peñaloza, and Firat, chapter 19).

Not only do we not make any claim that service benefits are limited to functional benefits, we embrace strongly the claim that hedonic, or expressive, benefits are often more important than more utilitarian ones. Actually, we find it odd, given our inversion of the goods-service relationship, that this emphasis on intangible benefits would be overlooked. We (Vargo and Lusch 2004a) have cited Prahalad and Ramaswamy's (2000, p. 84) reference to goods as "artifacts, around which customers have experiences" and Pine and Gilmore's (1999) *The Experience Economy* as support for our view of the service role of goods. We also tied the discussion to Gutman's (1982), contention that products are "means" for reaching "end-states, " or "valued states of being, such as happiness, security, and accomplishment" and pointed out that individuals often purchase goods because owning them and displaying them provide satisfactions *beyond* those associated with the basic functions of the product. We thus agree with Venkatesh, Peñaloza, and Firat (chapter 19) that "signs" play a critical role in value determination. We just believe that the co-creation of sign value is captured in S-D logic and that service is more primary than signs.

We suspect that our emphasis on service satisfying higher-order needs is missed because, as with many misperceptions about S-D logic, the dominant paradigmatic perspective is G-D logic. Arguably, G-D logic implies functional benefits, and its dominance is why the literature is just now evolving toward grasping the role of more experiential, expressive, phenomenological, and emotional benefits.

Financial Feedback Equals Profits

Given S-D logic's foundational model of service being exchanged for service, typically through indirect (usually monetary) exchange and its emphasis on the application of improvable operant resources (knowledge and skills) as the basis for the co-creation of value, financial feedback plays several important roles. Among these are providing information for resource improvement through learning and functioning as "rights" to additional applied resources—that is, service. Although this financial feedback might be reflected in profit to a firm, it does not necessarily do so. Financial feedback is a considerably more general concept than profit.

S-D logic is relevant for both profit-oriented and non-profit-oriented organizations. However, some who have critiqued S-D logic have equated its focus on financial feedback as either (1) a paradigm restricted to only profit-driven firms or (2) not encompassing the generally accepted broadened domain of marketing, comprising ideas, people, and places.

First, we intentionally stress, "[m]arketplace feedback not only is obtained directly from the customer but also is gauged by analyzing financial performance from exchange relationships to learn how to improve both firms' offering to customers and firm performance" (Vargo and Lusch 2004a, p. 14). For some firms, financial feedback is indeed "profit." However, for other firms it can be market share, sales growth, or cash flow. However, over the longer term "cash in" must exceed "cash out." And for this reason many scholars are emphasizing the importance of cash flow (Ambler, chapter 22; Srivastava, Shervani, and Fahey 1999). Although we do indeed argue that value is only created through co-creation and in interaction with the customer, we recognize that monetary flows are critical. Cash (or its equivalent) provides the firm options on future service flows and relationships. Importantly, S-D logic also places the responsibility for firm financial performance on the marketing function and for "increasing the market value rather than the book value of the organization as it builds off-balance-sheet assets such as customer, brand, and network equity" (Vargo and Lusch 2004a, p. 14).

Second, S-D logic and the role that financial feedback and off-balance-sheet assets (e.g., customer, brand, and network equity) play are very relevant for the marketing of ideas, people, and places. In contemporary society the marketing of ideas, people, and places occurs through organizations that have inflows and outflows of cash and other financial resources (i.e., debt capacity). For instance, political candidates do frequent political polling and use this to better position and establish their political platform. However, these candidates usually do not drop out of political races due to polling statistics; they drop out because they run out of financial resources. S-D logic is interactive; it requires and depends upon constant feedback from customers, and customers vote with their dollars regardless of if one operates a non-profit- or profit-directed organization.

However, one must recognize financial accounting systems, by their very nature, are transactional, and financial accounting standards do not enable a firm to capitalize most marketing investments. Thus, the financial feedback a firm receives from the marketplace is a fuzzy signal and should be treated as lacking in substantive validity. This opens up a huge research opportunity for integrating financial, accounting, and marketing theory.

Service-Dominant Logic Is Primarily Managerially Oriented

Some (e.g., Venkatesh, Peñaloza, and Firat, chapter 19; Wilkie and Moore, chapter 20) have either implicitly or explicitly indicated that S-D logic does not go far enough because it does not move marketing beyond its present managerial, or firm-centric, orientation. We agree that marketing is largely managerial. This is understandable given its origin and its original focus on application. Even the word *marketing* implies doing something—going to market, acting on the market, and so on—as opposed to a more positive term like *market science*. Also, we originally wrote "Evolving to a New Dominant Logic for Marketing" for the *Journal of Marketing,* which has an editorial policy of managerial relevance. Even then, we had focused much of the effort toward macro-positive implications but had to cut most of that material because of space limitations.

We believe, however, that S-D logic has much broader relevance than managerial. The basic premise that it is the mutual application of specialized skills and knowledge that is exchanged has implications not only for a better grounded theory of the firm, but also for a general theory of marketing or, as Venkatesh, Peñaloza, and Firat (chapter 19) probably appropriately suggest, of "markets," and possibly for a process-centered theory of economics and society (see the following section). Thus, though we freely acknowledge that some of our initial presentation of S-D logic was couched in managerial terms, we do not agree that it is *inherently* managerial and completely agree that its nonmanagerial implications need to be more fully explored (see e.g., Gummesson, chapter 27; Laczniak, chapter 21; Venkatesh, Peñaloza, and Firat, chapter 19; Wilkie and Moore, chapter 20; and Lusch and Vargo, chapter 32).

WHAT IT MIGHT BE

S-D logic represents a somewhat subtle but, we believe, potentially significant departure from the way that we have been taught, both explicitly and implicitly, about exchange. As we have noted, it shifts the focus away from goods to service, from operand resources to operant resources, from being to doing, and, somewhat less precisely, from what is exchanged to the process of exchange and from the tangible to the intangible. Arguably, it also refocuses us on the role of exchange in general, not only as it relates to marketing, but also in terms of its role in commerce and society. As such, S-D logic might provide insights useful for reconsidering and reformulating the models, theories, and paradigms that guide thought about these activities and institutions.

We stress the use of the terms *potentially* and *arguably* here. S-D logic is a work in progress. We do not claim to have invented it and do not claim ownership. We only claim to have identified what we consider to represent the convergence of previously apparently divergent streams of research in academic marketing—the migration from operand resources to applied operant resources as the primary focus of exchange. S-D logic is still evolving and in "open source" development—thus the purpose of and approach to this book. It is too early to make claims about S-D logic being a new theory, let alone a "general theory" or a paradigm shift for marketing. However, arguably, it might be worthwhile to muse about the *potential* of S-D logic in these regards.

The Foundation of a Paradigm Shift in Marketing

We have characterized G-D logic as paradigmatic. Kuhn (1970, p. 10) defines *paradigms* as "accepted examples of actual scientific practice that provide models from which spring particular coherent traditions of scientific research." Drawing on Kuhn, Arndt (1985, p. 11) views paradigms as "social constructions reflecting the values and interests of the dominant researchers in a science and their reference groups." Hunt (1991), in keeping with popular use, uses the term in the broad sense to connote *weltanschauung,* or worldview.

By either of these definitions, we believe that G-D logic represents a paradigm for marketing. As Shostack (1977, p. 73) notes, "The classical 'marketing mix,' the seminal literature, and the language of marketing all derive from the manufacture of physical goods." The impact of this G-D paradigm can be seen in the basic language of marketing. For example, the terms *product*; *form, time, place,* and *possession* utilities; *distribution*; *channels of distribution*; *targeting*; the *marketing mix*; *producer*; and *consumer,* in the dominant ways they have been used, all imply to varying extents that the tangible good is the central focus of marketing. Elsewhere (Vargo and Lusch 2004b), we argue that the view that services are characterized by nongoods characteristics such as intangibility, perishability, heterogeneity, and inseparability of production and consumption (Zeithaml, Parasuraman, and Berry 1985) is further evidence.

Does S-D logic represent a paradigm shift? We do not think it does, at least not presently. Although we argue that S-D logic provides a broader, more generalizable framework than G-D logic of exchange and even note that some marketing scholars seem to have adopted an S-D logic view, at least at the present time S-D logic does not meet the criterion of reflecting the values and interests of the dominant researchers in the science of marketing as a whole and does not represent a worldview (see Levy, chapter 4). However, as we have discussed, except for the convergence of a particular set of events and preexisting paradigms, S-D logic *could* have emerged as the basis for the guiding paradigm of economics and thus for marketing and, as S-D logic evolves, it might serve as a more solid foundation than G-D logic for the better understanding of marketing, both academically and strategically. Thus, S-D logic *might* be a candidate for the foundation for the paradigmatic shift that has been called for by a number of marketing scholars (e.g., Grönroos 1994; Gummesson 1995; Hunt and Morgan 1995; Schlesinger and Heskett 1991; Shostack 1977).

Theory of the Firm

Coase (1937) theorized that organizations exist and get larger because the costs of market transactions often exceed the costs of internal organization. We believe S-D logic offers a different perspective on this. S-D logic recognizes that there is an acceleration in the division of labor in society as individuals become increasingly microspecialized. As entities become more and more specialized, their marketplace options become restricted. That is, if one becomes highly specialized (as opposed to a generalist), there often is no efficient market for the direct exchange of his or her specialized competences for the competences desired from another entity. For instance, consider a person who is an expert on multivariate statistics, theoretical physics, or counseling students about their curriculum. This person will infrequently run across people who want the direct application of his or her services and, if so, the other party will seldom have the bundle of competences that the microspecialist needs. In contrast, S-D logic views the microspecializations of individuals as inputs the entrepreneur combines to create service that people want (e.g., a market research study, a computer system, transportation, or a college education). Organizations are thus integrators of individual competences that they transform into service people want and/or need. For this reason, S-D logic is heavily grounded in and aligned with resource advantage theory (Hunt 2000) and Penrose's (1959) resource-based theory of the firm.

S-D logic suggests that organizations exist because the entrepreneur, with his or her bundle of skills, is able to (1) envision service that people want and will pay to obtain and (2) integrate together microspecialists to offer and provide this service. In this sense one of the most important operant resources in society and the economy is the entrepreneurial spirit, and mental skills of individual entrepreneurs and their collectivity. These entrepreneurs can multiply resources by combining them in an organization and exchanging applied organizational competences with customers.

All of this boils down to what might be considered to be a ninth foundational premise of S-D logic that we did not report in our initial publication.

FP9. Organizations exist to integrate and transform microspecialized competences into complex services that are demanded in the marketplace.

This foundational premise implies that S-D logic could provide a framework for a theory of the firm.

A Reorientation for Economic Theory

If marketing inherited its G-D logic from economics and if G-D logic is flawed, as others and we have suggested, it is natural to consider the following question: Would S-D logic provide a better foundation, not only for marketing, but also for economic science? We believe that there are compelling reasons to think that the answer is yes. Perhaps one need look no further than Smith's (1776/1965) work, on which economic science is based. As we have argued here and elsewhere, Smith actually comes very close to S-D logic in the beginning of *The Wealth of Nations*. Consider the first paragraph in chapter 5 (Smith 1776/1965, p. 30):

> Every man is rich or poor according to the degree in which he can afford to enjoy the necessities, conveniences, and amusements of human life. But after the division of labour has once thoroughly taken place, it is but a very small part of these with which a man's own labour can supply him. The far greater part of them he must derive from the labour of other people, and he must be rich or poor according to the *quantity of that labor which he can command* or which he can afford to purchase. *The value of any commodity,* therefore, to the person who possesses it, and who means not to use or consume it himself, but to exchange it for other commodities, *is equal to the quantity of labour which it enables him to purchase or command. Labour, therefore, is the real measure of the exchange value of all commodities* [emphasis added].

Compare this with our first two foundational premises, which say essentially that service (the application of competences) is exchanged for service, and indirect exchange, including monetary exchange, obscures the service-for-service nature of exchange. All one has to do is substitute "the application of competences" for "labor" and Smith's initial arguments translates into S-D logic.

Or compare it to Bastiat's (1860, p. 43) attempt to restate the nature of exchange:

> It is in fact to this faculty . . . *to work the one for the other* [italics in the original]; it is this *transmission of efforts, this exchange of services* [emphasis added], with all the infinite and

involved combinations to which it gives rise . . . which constitutes Economic Science, points out its origin, and determines its limits.

Value therefore is seen as the "comparative appreciation of *reciprocal services*" (p. 44)

And consider the similarity of the views of Walras (1954, p. 225)—generally considered the father of equilibrium theory, if not economic science: "We may . . . simply consider the *productive services* as being *exchanged directly for one another,* instead of being exchanged first against products, and then productive services" [emphasis added]. He acknowledged that this had been Bastiat's original concept but felt that Bastiat "meant only personal services."

The point of this is to suggest that a call for S-D logic is not so much a call for the abandonment of all economic thought as it is a call for the return to a logic of economics that had been previously abandoned for G-D logic's simplicity, normative purposes, and fit with the Newtonian model of science. The early economic philosophers and scientists understood S-D logic; in the social and scientific milieu of the time, they just did not fully embrace and elaborate it. As many of them implied, if not acknowledged, S-D is more fundamental than G-D logic. Thus, it might provide a basis for a richer and more robust science of economics.

A Reorientation for a Theory of Society

The central notions of S-D logic are that fundamental to human well-being, if not survival, is specialization by individuals in a subset of knowledge and skills (operant resources) and exchanging the application of these resources for the application of knowledge and skills in which they do not specialize. In short, the fisherman fishes for the farmer in exchange for the farmer farming for the fisherman. These joint ideas of specialization and exchange are not new. But the contention that it is the application of operant resources that is exchanged for the application of other operant resources—rather than the operand resources on which operant resources have acted being exchanged for other operand resources—is relatively new, if not unique. S-D logic further suggests that organizations and money emerged in societal evolution as vehicles to help accomplish the exchange of service for service. This shift in focus from operand to operant resources has implications for understanding social interaction and structure that are markedly different from the ones suggested by a focus on the exchange of operand resources and potentially has ramifications for understanding exchange processes, dynamics, structures, and institutions beyond commerce.

As we explore in chapter 32, "Service-Dominant Logic as a Foundation for a General Theory," S-D logic is very rich as a foundation for the development of macromarketing theory and ultimately a theory of society. There are many things that hold a society together, but four are language, norms, paradigms, and institutions. For each of these, co-creation is determinant. A language cannot be developed without co-creation of the parties that will use the language to communicate. Norms require a co-creation by definition. A paradigm involves a worldview and social construction that is co-created and provides the lens upon which a domain is viewed by a society or a dominant group in society. And institutions involve a complex web of interactive behavior directed at co-creation of regulatory mechanisms in society. Language, norms, and institutions are emergent phenomena that result in macrostructures. Furthermore, these emergent phenomena converge with other phenomena, proliferate, and finally decouple and diverge to create new emergent forms. This cycle repeats over and over again to evolve new macrostructures. Thus, S-D logic, with its focus on the micro-activity of the exchange of service for service, is the building block via co-creation for the creation and development of society.

SUMMARY

Necessarily, for most people, the first glance at S-D logic occurs by focusing on the concepts that are familiar from G-D logic, as seen through a lens honed by G-D logic. The most common error is to think that S-D logic represents the replacement of one form of output or product, goods, with another form of output, services. S-D logic is a shift in logic in a real sense. It represents an inversion that places activities driven by specialized knowledge and skills, rather than units of output, at the center of exchange processes. Hunt (2004, p. 22) argues that S-D logic "deserves a careful read and thoughtful evaluation, not a quick skim and hasty judgment." Given its work-in-progress status, this may be especially true. A full understanding of its substance and complete grasp of its nuances require re-honing and refocusing. We hope this chapter adds illumination for that process.

REFERENCES

Arndt, Johan (1985), "On Making Marketing Science More Scientific: Role Orientations, Paradigms, Metaphors, and Puzzle Solving," *Journal of Marketing.* 49 (Summer), 11–23.

Bastiat, F. (1860), *Harmonies of Political Economy.* London: J. Murray.

Beckman, Theodore N. (1954), "The Value Added Concept as Applied to Marketing and Its Implications," in *Frontiers in Marketing Thought,* Stewart H. Rewoldt, ed. Bloomington, IN: Bureau of Business Research, Indiana University, 83–145.

Coase, R.H. (1937), "The Nature of the Firm," *Econometrica,* 4, 386–405.

Grönroos, Christian (1994), "From Marketing Mix to Relationship Marketing: Towards a Paradigm Shift in Marketing," *Asia-Australia Marketing Journal,* 2 (August), 9–29.

——— (2000), *Service Management and Marketing: A Customer Relationship Management Approach.* West Sussex, UK: John Wiley & Sons.

Gummesson, E. (1994), "Broadening and Specifying Relationship Marketing," *Asia-Australia Marketing Journal,* 2 (August), 31–43.

——— (1995), "Relationship Marketing; Its Role in the Service Economy," in *Understanding Services Management,* W. J. Glynn and J. G. Barns, eds. New York: John Wiley & Sons, 224–68.

Gutman, Jonathan (1982), "A Means-End Chain Model Based on Consumer Categorization Processes," *Journal of Marketing,* 46 (Spring), 60–72.

Hunt, Shelby D. (1991), *Modern Marketing Theory: Critical Issues in the Philosophy of Marketing Science.* Cincinnati: Southwest Publishing.

——— (2000), *A General Theory of Competition: Resources, Competences, Productivity, Economic Growth.* Thousand Oaks, CA: Sage Publications

——— (2004), "On the Service-Centered Dominant Logic of Marketing," *Journal of Marketing,* 68, 18–27.

——— and R. M. Morgan (1995), "The Comparative Advantage Theory of Competition," *Journal of Marketing* 59 (2): 1–15.

Kuhn, Thomas (1970), *The Structure of Scientific Revolutions.* Chicago: University of Chicago Press.

Levitt, Theodore (1960), "Marketing Myopia," *Harvard Business Review,* 38 (July–August), 26–44, 173–81.

Macneil, Ian R. (1980), *The New Social Contract: An Inquiry into Modern Contractual Relations.* New Haven, CT: Yale University Press.

Penrose, Edith T. (1959), *The Theory of the Growth of the Firm.* London: Basil, Blackwell, and Mott.

Pine, B. Joseph and James H. Gilmore (1999), *The Experience Economy: Work Is Theater and Every Business a Stage.* Boston: Harvard Business School Press.

Prahalad, C.K. and Venkatram Ramaswamy (2000), "Co-opting Customer Competence," *Harvard Business Review,* 78 (January/February), 79–87.

Schlesinger, Leonard A. and James L. Heskett (1991), "The Service-Driven Company," *Harvard Business Review,* (September–October), 71–81.

Sheth, Jagdish and A. Parvatiyar (2000), "Relationship Marketing in Consumer Markets: Antecedents and Consequences," in *Handbook of Relationship Marketing,* Jagdish Sheth and A. Parvatiyar, eds. Thousand Oaks, CA: Sage Publications, 171–208.

Shostack, G.L. (1977). "Breaking Free from Product Marketing." *Journal of Marketing,* 41: 73–80.

Smith, A. (1776/1965), *An Inquiry into the Nature and Causes of the Wealth of Nations.* New York: Random House.

Srivastava, Rajendra K., Tasadduq A. Shervani, and Liam Fahey (1999), "Marketing, Business Processes, and Shareholder Value: An Organizationally Embedded View of Marketing Activities and the Discipline of Marketing," *Journal of Marketing* 63 (Special Issue), 168–79.

Vargo, Stephen L. and Robert F. Lusch (2004a), "Evolving to a New Dominant Logic for Marketing," *Journal of Marketing,* 68 (January), 1–17.

———— and ———— (2004b), "The Four Services Marketing Myths: Remnants from a Manufacturing Model," *Journal of Service Research* (May), 324–35.

Walras, Leon (1954), *Elements of the Political Economy.* Homestead, NJ: Richard D. Irwin.

Zeithaml, V.A., A. Parasuraman, and L.L. Berry (1985), "Problems and Strategies in Services Marketing," *Journal of Marketing,* 49 (Spring), 33–46.

4

HOW NEW, HOW DOMINANT?

SIDNEY J. LEVY

EVOLUTION IN MARKETING THOUGHT

Intellectual stimulation and change, with their behavioral consequences, occur in various ways. Sometimes they seem sudden and dramatic, and make the world seem different, due to notable events such as the attacks of September 11, 2001, or the launch of *Sputnik I* on October 4, 1957. Even then, as George Day (2004) points out, preceding such events is a gradual accretion and convergence of responses to shifts in technology and communication. Few people create; most emulate. But even the innovators stand on the shoulders of those who came before. In the flow of history, this gradual process, with its accumulation of instances of the new behaviors, culminates at intervals with a summing up by an event, a person, or persons. Statements that tell what has been happening and what it means crystallize into an article, a book, a speech. Most famously and profoundly in their effects, oral transmissions that, written, became the Hebrew Bible, the New Testament, and the Koran, came into being as the ripened expression and furthering of Judaism, Christianity, and Islam, respectively. Notable legislations and Supreme Court decisions also provide such special moments. The word is then spread in accelerated fashion by making audiences self-conscious about the new ideas and their implications through more writing, citation, and discussion.

Within the marketing field, as Vargo and Lusch (2004; hereafter V&L) indicate, there are outstanding instances of writings that reflected and influenced the evolving dominant logic of the day; I played a role and know some of the history. Some dominant logics defining marketing arose over time in a sequential way; other governing ideas were and are concurrent or are perhaps sublogics that prevail in a particular sphere such as pricing or consumer research. The importance of satisfying customers came to the fore in the post–World War II period with the growth of resources, productivity, consumer demand, and competition. Companies and their executives led the way in the late 1940s and 1950s by studying consumers, sponsoring the consumer research that was called Motivation Research, and writing articles about their experience. Influential examples delineating in action what came to be called The Marketing Concept were "What Is the Marketing Management Concept?" by J. B. McKitterick (1957) of General Electric and "The Marketing Revolution" by Robert J. Keith (1960) of Pillsbury. Academia tended to lag, showing the difference between logics operative among marketing practitioners and those that scholars think about.

Working at Social Research, Inc., starting in 1948, I found that managers tended to ask, in a one-to-one fashion, if a particular marketing action—an advertisement, a change in price, or a new package design—would increase sales. However, I noticed also that consumers, when asked, used a more contextual and integrated perception of the product, the brand, and their existing relationship with it to determine their response. These observations led to my writing the article "The Product and the Brand." Published in the *Harvard Business Review* (Gardner and Levy 1955), it introduced the concept of the brand image. This idea spread through the marketing community and was given a major boost by David Ogilvy in a keynote speech to the American Association of Advertising Agencies. It was elaborated in "Symbols for Sale" (Levy 1959), an article still frequently cited and recognized for its impact by the Converse Award in 2000 (Griffin and Hess 2001). (It also led to my being hired by Northwestern University to join its marketing department.) Consideration of branding and its symbolic character became a common part of management thought and continues to be a dominant logic fostered lately in books by David Aaker (1996) and Kevin Keller (2003).

In 1957, the sophisticated writing of Wroe Alderson, well represented in his *Marketing Behavior and Executive Action: A Functionalist Approach to Marketing Theory,* was part of the familiar sequence of marketing foci: commodities, institutions, and functions. When I first taught an introductory marketing course in 1961, I used the easier popular text, *Basic Marketing* by Jerome McCarthy. Although just published in April 1960, it was already in its fourth edition. In that volume, as V&L note, the dominant logic of marketing was about management of the Four P's—Product, Place, Price, and Promotion (McCarthy 1960)—and emphasized "satisfying target customers" (p. vi). That year, also, the often-cited and anthologized "Marketing Myopia" by Theodore Levitt (1960) in the *Harvard Business Review,* noted managers' traditionally narrow views and provided a rationale for enlarging their understanding of their role.

Scholars recognized that the late 1940s and the 1950s had spawned a Consumption Revolution, and they studied and taught the thinking that burgeoned in the 1960s. This followed the Drucker (1954) dictum, "to create a customer," (p. 37) and "satisfying the consumer, no matter what," as Levitt recalls (1983, p. 8). This focus on customers intensified, and was crystallized at the end of the decade in such major volumes as *Consumer Behavior* by Engel, Kollat, and Blackwell (1968) and *The Theory of Buyer Behavior* by Howard and Sheth (1969). Hard on their heels, and consolidating the importance of the consumer, there emerged the Association for Consumer Research in 1970 and the *Journal of Consumer Research* in 1974. Richard Bagozzi's "Marketing as Exchange" (1974) explicated the central importance of exchange theory in exploring interaction in the marketplace.

The end of the sixties also saw the emergence of another major idea that affected the general perception and practice of marketing. Based on my twenty years of experience doing marketing research for many kinds of organizations, "Broadening the Concept of Marketing" appeared in the *Journal of Marketing* (Kotler and Levy 1969) and created a big stir. The ideas put forth in the article—that all organizations and individuals inevitably engage in marketing and should therefore give thought to doing it well—were widely embraced. In 1970, the American Marketing Association Fall Conference (Sparks 1970) was titled "Broadening the Concept of Marketing." The broadening idea had seemed self-evident to me, and some people at the conference thought so, too. A colleague told me he had "always thought that"; I said he should have written an article. Its impact became visible, perhaps surprisingly so soon: The 1970 AMA program included such topics as marketing strategies for higher education (Naidu 1970), health practices (Zaltman and Vertinsky 1970), family planning (O'Connor 1970), and political candidates (Ward 1970). Then again, perhaps not so surprising, this quick response showed the readiness that already existed for the broadening idea. The application of the broadening concept to the marketing of education, politics, health, public policy, government, the arts, and so on, has become a largely taken-for-granted part of modern life. For example, the University of Arizona currently has a Director of Advancement and has just hired a Director of Marketing. The nature of this dominant logic was debated: Bartels (1974) considered "The Identity Crisis in Marketing"; Tucker (1974) was concerned about the effects of the broadening concept on "Future Directions in Marketing Theory"; and Laczniak and Michie (1979) attested to the impact of broadening the concept of marketing by accusing it of contributing to social disorder.

As new concepts evolve into marketing thought, they show a common pattern. For example, the changing circumstances of the post–World War II period led to the great interest in consumers. The need to study consumers led marketing scholars to adopt behavioral science concepts and methods, with a flare-up of ideas and their associated pioneers, such as diffusion of innovation (Rogers 1962), cognitive dissonance (Festinger 1957), and information processing (Bettman 1974). Each main idea had a vogue, then settled down as part of the common wisdom, as a subdominant logic that some people call upon when it seems relevant, and in which others specialize. Similarly, as marketing study—and the academic curriculum—grew, other various ideas were added.

When Northwestern University's marketing department first introduced an elective course in international marketing in the MBA program, only five students signed up for it. Also, although there were occasional articles in the *Journal of Marketing* describing marketing in Poland or in Spain, the common view was that marketing principles were basically the same everywhere and all that was necessary were a few cases about international issues, not a whole course. Although no single article stands out as the defining moment in launching more general interest in international marketing, some pioneers such as Cateora and Hess (1971) and Terpstra (1972) were steadfast in nurturing this topic, with a strong impetus from Michael Porter (1980). Now many schools offer full courses in international or global marketing, MBA students travel abroad to observe other cultures, and research about diversity among societies is frequent fare in journals and at conferences. Some authors try to make globalization and its discontents a dominant logic. In a recent book review of the writings of Hardt and Negri (2001, 2004), Gary Rosen (2004) in the *Wall Street Journal* noted that "their theme was being talked about as the Next Big Idea, sending 'frissons of excitement through campuses from Sao Paulo to Tokyo.'" But he calls their work "a ramshackle, theory-stuffed disquisition . . . [that] lacked what many of its readers most wanted" (p. 8).

Analogously, when the marketing of services first began to gain attention, it was said to be just a part of basic marketing, that the same principles applied to the marketing of anything—goods, services, people, ideas, people, places, causes. But the economy was said to be moving from a manufacturing economy to a services economy. Some writers persisted in making the distinction and addressed themselves to the service sector. Notably leading the way were Berry and Parasuraman (1991), Zeithaml (1990), and Shostack (1977). Now there are courses dedicated to services marketing and enough studies to warrant a handbook anthology by Swartz and Iacobucci (1999).

THE NEW LOGIC

When new insights come along, some scholars say that the established ideas have been superseded by the new logics, although usually they do not actually go away. People still manage, work with, and study commodities, institutions, functions, and the marketing mix. The alleged demise of Motivation Research of the fifties saw a vigorous rebirth—or merely renaming—and continuing practice as qualitative research. Brand images and marketing exchanges all remain undeniably present, despite the criticism or challenge to them in the comments by Gummesson (2004) and Prahalad (2004).

New dominant logics usually assimilate what came before, claiming an insight that is more encompassing. A comprehensive view of brand imagery says that all offerings are brands, as even the word for a commodity may be considered a branding of it. The Four P's, fully understood as encompassing all marketing activities, give managers all the marketing mix issues they need to think about. Broadening says that all people, whether groups or individuals, must inevitably engage in marketing, implying that Everything Is Marketing. Exchange theory says that all marketing involves exchanges or, more debatably, that all exchanges, whether physical, financial, emotional, or social, and so forth, are forms of marketing.

Now come V&L asserting the crystallized service-centered dominant logic that Rust (2004) characterizes as "Everything Is Service" (p. 23). Their article is thoughtful and detailed in explaining the nature of this concept and how it has converged to be necessary and suitable to this stage in the development of marketing thought. Of central importance is the distinction between the traditional definition of service and their extension of it. Formerly limited to the intangible activities that only some marketers offer, involving the marketing of performances and processes rather than or only incidentally the sale of objects, the reoriented philosophy applies to all marketing offerings. It shifts attention from the goods (operand resources) to the skills and knowledge (operant resources) necessary to the creation of and utilization of wealth. They join this idea to the recent vogues emphasizing customer satisfaction and customer relationships, seeking to arrive at a more comprehensive and penetrating understanding of the marketplace and the changes within practice and research that such a fuller awareness would entail.

NOVELTY, DOMINANCE, IMPACT?

How new is the V&L logic? How dominant is the logic? And what is its likely acceptance and impact? To answer these questions, I will take advantage of the information provided by the authors of the invited commentaries included with the V&L article. These authors, Day, Deighton and Narayandas, Gummesson, Hunt, Prahalad, Rust, and Shugan are naturally scholars likely to be concerned with the definition of marketing and the meaning of service-centeredness. Their reactions may be characterized as follows. They show general receptivity to the article and its main theses. They say they support the intention and the effort, and agree with this part or that. Some praise is extravagant: "V&L's brilliantly insightful article," "[they] eloquently and provocatively detail," "I want to congratulate the authors," "V&L's argument is historically informed, finely crafted, properly interdisciplinary, and logically sound."

Then the scholars become more equivocal and take issue with V&L. A main way is to question whether V&L's dominant logic is new. Day (2004, p. 18) puts the "new" in quotation marks and says, "The crux of V&L's argument (p. 12) . . . is not a new insight." Deighton and Narayandas (2004) express uncertainty, and tell a story hinting that V&L's argument fits just a familiar set of contingencies rather than a new dominant logic. Hunt (2002) sympathizes with the difficulty of the task V&L have undertaken, saying he and Robert M. Morgan tried to do it ten years ago; and he indicates that what V&L lack can be found in his *Foundations of Marketing Theory* (2002). Prahalad (2004) says V&L do not go far enough. Shugan (2004) appreciates V&L's intentions and spirit, but fears that research faces many "nontrivial impediments and perilous obstacles" (p. 25).

I could begrudgingly say V&L is a reworking or updating of what Boyd and Levy (1963) wrote about in a simpler way in "New Dimensions in Consumer Analysis," the point being that people consume for purposes in a consumption system beyond handling the goods themselves. We prepare meals, bake cakes, buy cars, and so on to further our goals. We eat to feel good, to celebrate birthdays, and when we get obese and want to lose weight, the manufacturers change the food offerings to serve that goal. Once we said that, no one doubted it, and despite the title *HBR* gave it to hype it, that was about the end of it.

With V&L, the commentators' tone of qualified acceptance is buttressed by the distinction between what marketing scholars themselves think and what they believe goes on among managers. Generally, they think that marketing scholars can of course understand and appreciate what V&L are saying. They can go along with the idea that there is convergence toward a service-centered logic and enjoy dialogue about it. But they doubt that it can be truly characterized as dominant, even if one grants that all marketing offerings, including tangible products, are in the service of providing service. Too many people just lag behind in their product-oriented thinking. For example, Prystay (2004, p. B1) reports, "That attitude, though, is precisely the problem many Asian companies face. . . . They often stumble at branding and marketing . . . feel it's about the product and about pricing. . . . It's hard for them to see what's changed." They are necessarily wedded to that view, given their place in the system, or do not have the capacity or skill to comprehend or implement such a thoroughgoing service-centered logic. Or they do not see what difference it would make to what they do.

Day and Montgomery (1999) know the difficulties of truly implementing the market-driven organization. Gummesson (2004) says the literature clings to the Four P's of marketing management. Hunt (2004) appears to prefer his own better understanding of resource advantage theory. Shugan (2004) pragmatically thinks V&L's theorizing is too abstract and general, and takes insufficient account of the realities in organizations and the resistance from other business functions. That is probably especially true for rule-oriented accountants; for operations, which is so product focused; and for finance, which dislikes facing that it is just a specialization of the marketing of money and its instruments. In addition, those in finance tend to firmly believe the logic that should dominate the organization is to "enhance shareholder wealth." This maxim ignores the reality that this goal may conflict with satisfying consumers, as marketers urge, or with the greed of the managers. Similarly, economists' devotion to the logic of the free market and perfect competition ignores the actualities that often distort those ideals.

It is likely that the V&L thesis will continue to be met with interest (their article won the Maynard Award) and mixed support. Scholars and managers who are already imbued with a service-centered frame of mind will feel reinforced, maybe enthusiastic, as is Rust (2004), or annoyed because they "always thought that" anyway. Many marketing scholars and managers will give some lip service to the pervasiveness of service, but still prefer mainly to keep defining services as a sector or activities distinct from concern with products. Buyer behaviorists may think that "relationships" and "customer satisfaction" can handle most of the problems they face, or find the distinction between their view of The Marketing Concept and the new logic too abstract. Consumer-oriented scholars, absorbed in their social surveys and psychological experiments, may not see what is added to their own focus.

The most successful dominant logics over time are those that are embraced by both managers and scholars. When they come together in conferences, executive education programs, and consulting relationships, the managers want to know what academics can teach them from their cutting-edge research, broader point of view, and general smarts. The scholars want to know what the managers are doing so they can teach their students about current practice and generate theories about management thought. Thus, they reinforce each other. For a time, all marketing professors taught the Four P's and made them coin of the realm. David Ogilvy, the great advertising man, promoted Gardner and Levy's brand image idea. It became common parlance and was reinforced by popular writing like *Positioning: The Battle for Your Mind* by Ries and Trout (1981) and "Branding" online at the *CEO Refresher* (2004).

Shugan emphasizes the practicalities that dominate managers' thinking. Managers latched onto qualitative research, especially manifested in the use of focus groups, because they thought it cheap, convenient, and useful; some scholars went along, but most were reluctant, critical, or indifferent. Managers find it easy to stick with Peters (1982) when he elaborates the idea of excellence (1982). Collins (2001) stays on top of the best-sellers' list with his understandable advice: be disciplined and consistent. The service-centered distinction between *operand* and *operant* is language that probably will not help managers: I fear that it is easy to say, or to agree with Penrose (1959, pp. 24–25), that "it is never *resources* themselves that are the 'inputs' to the production process, but only the *services* that the resources can render"(emphasis in the original) and then just go on about one's business. V&L may cope with these various obstacles by doing a superior job of promoting their thesis among scholars, as they have been doing, and especially by delineating its practical implications so as to engage the managers.

Still, it will not be easy. At intervals, the American Marketing Association publishes in the *Marketing News* (2004) a contemporary redefinition of marketing, arrived at by a group of outstanding marketing thinkers. The most recent version (led, curiously enough, by Robert Lusch) reads:

> "Mar-ket-ing \ *noun*. An organizational function and a set of processes for creating, communicating, and delivering value to customers and for managing customer relationships in ways that benefit the organization and its stakeholders" (*Marketing News* 2004, p. 1).

This definition shows the tenacity of a traditional viewpoint of marketing. It is not superior to Brown's (1925) definition of marketing "as the process of transferring goods through commercial channels from producer to consumer" (p. 3). The AMA's is an old-fashioned prescription for an organization to make offerings in a virtuous way: "value," "benefit." It ignores the fact that bad marketing is also marketing, that individuals as well as organizations market, and that buying is marketing, too. Although it mentions customers twice, it certainly does not recognize the new dominant logic put forth by Vargo and Lusch.

REFERENCES

Aaker, David (1996), *Building Strong Brands.* New York: The Free Press.
Alderson, Wroe (1957), *Marketing Behavior and Executive Action: A Functionalist Approach to Marketing Theory.* Homewood, IL: Richard D. Irwin, Inc.
Bagozzi, Richard P. (1974), "Marketing as Exchange," *Journal of Marketing,* 38 (October), 77–81.
Bartels, Robert (1974), "The Identity Crisis in Marketing," *Journal of Marketing,* 38 (October) 73–76.
Berry, Leonard L. and A. Parasuraman (1991), *Marketing Services: Competing through Quality.* New York: The Free Press.
Bettman, James R. (1974), "Relationship of Information Processing Attitude Structures to Private Brand Purchasing Behavior," *Journal of Applied Psychology,* 59, 79–83.
Boyd, Harper Jr., and Sidney J. Levy (1963), "New Dimensions in Consumer Analysis," *Harvard Business Review,* 41 (November–December), 129–140.
Brown, Edmund, Jr. (1925), *Marketing.* New York: Harper and Brothers.
Cateora, Philip R. and John M. Hess (1971), *International Marketing.* Homewood, IL: Richard D. Irwin.
CEO Refresher (2004), "Branding," www.refresher.com/archives43.html. Accessed on March 15, 2005.
Collins, Jim (2001), *Good to Great: Why Some Companies Make the Leap . . . and Others Don't.* New York: Harper Business.

Day, George S. and David Montgomery (1999), "Fundamental Issues and Marketing," *Journal of Marketing,* 63 (October), 3–13.

Day, George S. (2004), "Achieving Advantage with a New Dominant Logic," *Journal of Marketing,* 68 (January), 18–19.

Deighton, John and Das Narayandas (2004), "Stories and Theories," *Journal of Marketing,* 68 (January), 19–20.

Drucker, Peter F. (1954), *The Practice of Management.* New York: Harper & Row.

Engel, James F., David T. Kollat, and Robert D. Blackwell (1968), *Consumer Behavior.* Chicago: The Dryden Press.

Festinger, Leon (1957), *A Theory of Cognitive Dissonance.* Stanford, CA: Stanford University Press.

Gardner, Burleigh B. and Sidney J. Levy (1955), "The Product and the Brand," *Harvard Business Review,* 33 (March–April), 33–39.

Griffin, Abbie and James D. Hess, eds. (2001), *15th Paul D. Converse Symposium.* Chicago: American Marketing Association.

Gummesson, Evert (2004), "Service Provision Calls for Partners Instead of Parties," *Journal of Marketing,* 68 (January), 18–27.

Hardt, Michael and Antonio Negri (2001), *Empire.* Cambridge, MA: Harvard University Press.

——— and ——— (2004), *Multitude.* New York: Penguin Press.

Howard, John A. and Jagdish N. Sheth (1969), *The Theory of Buyer Behavior.* New York: John Wiley & Sons.

Hunt, Shelby D. (2002), *Foundations of Marketing Theory: Toward a General Theory of Marketing.* Armonk, NY: M.E. Sharpe.

——— (2004), "On the Service-Centered Dominant Logic for Marketing," *Journal of Marketing,* 68 (January), 21–22.

Keith, Robert J. (1960), "The Marketing Revolution," *Journal of Marketing* (January), 35–38.

Keller, Kevin Lane (2003), *Strategic Brand Management: Building, Measuring, and Managing Brand Equity,* 2d ed. Upper Saddle River, NJ: Prentice Hall.

Kotler, Philip and Sidney J. Levy (1969), "Broadening the Concept of Marketing," *Journal of Marketing.* 33 (July), 10–15.

Laczniak, G.R. and D.A. Michie (1979), "The Social Disorder of the Broadened Concept of Marketing," *Journal of the Academy of Marketing Science,* 7, 214–232.

Levitt, Theodore (1960), "Marketing Myopia," *Harvard Business Review,* 38 (July–August), 45–56.

——— (1983), *The Marketing Imagination.* New York: The Free Press.

Levy, Sidney J. (1959), "Symbols for Sale," *Harvard Business Review,* 37 (July–August), 117–124.

Marketing News (2004), "Marketing Redefined," (September 15), 1.

McCarthy, Jerome (1960), *Basic Marketing: A Managerial Approach.* Homewood, IL: Richard D. Irwin.

McKitterick, J.B. (1957), "What Is the Marketing Management Concept?" in *The Frontiers of Marketing Thought and Science,* Frank M. Bass, ed. Chicago: American Marketing Association, 71–81.

Naidu, G.M. (1970), "Marketing Strategies for Higher Education," in *Broadening the Concept of Marketing, Fall Conference,* David L. Sparks, ed. Chicago: American Marketing Association, Series 32, 28.

O'Connor, Ronald W. (1970), "An Approach to Information Flow in a Public Family Planning Program," in *Broadening the Concept of Marketing, Fall Conference,* David L. Sparks, ed. Chicago: American Marketing Association, Series 32, 17.

Penrose, Edith T. (1959), *The Theory of the Growth of the Firm.* London: Basil Blackwell and Mott.

Peters, Tom (1982), *In Search of Excellence.* New York: Harper Collins.

Porter, Michael E. (1980), *Competitive Advantage: Techniques for Analyzing Industries and Competitors.* New York: The Free Press.

Prahalad, C.K. (2004), "The Co-creation of Value," *Journal of Marketing,* 68 (January), 23.

Prystay, Cris (2004), "When Being First Doesn't Make You No. 1," *Wall Street Journal,* August 12, B1.

Ries, Al and Jack Trout (1981), *Positioning: The Battle for Your Mind.* New York: Warner Books.

Rogers, Everett M. (1962), *Diffusion of Innovations.* New York: The Free Press.

Rosen, Gary (2004), "They Say They Want a Revolution," *Wall Street Journal* (August 2), 8.

Rust, Roland T. (2004), "If Everything Is Service, Why Is this Happening Now, and What Difference Does It Make?" *Journal of Marketing,* 68 (January), 23–24.

Shostack, G. Lynn (1977), "Breaking Free from Product Marketing," *Journal of Marketing,* 41 (April), 73–80.

Shugan, Steven M. (2004), "Finance, Operations, and Marketing Conflicts in Service Firms," *Journal of Marketing,* 68 (January), 24–26.

Sparks, David L., ed. (1970), *Broadening the Concept of Marketing, Fall Conference.* Chicago: American Marketing Association, Series 32.

Swartz, Teresa and Dawn Iacobucci (1999), *Handbook of Services Marketing and Management.* Thousand Oaks, CA: Sage Publications, Inc.

Terpstra, Vern (1972), *International Marketing.* New York: Holt, Rinehart.

Tucker, W. T. (1974), "Future Directions in Marketing Theory," *Journal of Marketing,* 39 (April), 58–66.

Vargo, Stephen L. and Robert F. Lusch (2004), "Evolving to a New Dominant Logic for Marketing," *Journal of Marketing,* 68 (January), 1–17.

Ward, Scott (1970), "Marketing of Political Candidates: The Ethical Issues," in *Broadening the Concept of Marketing, Fall Conference,* David L. Sparks, ed. Chicago: American Marketing Association, Series 32, 88.

Zaltman, Gerald and Hans Vertinsky (1970), "The Marketing of Health Practices: A Case in Nutrition," in *Broadening the Concept of Marketing, Fall Conference,* David L. Sparks, ed. Chicago: American Marketing Association, Series 32, 16.

Zeithaml, Valerie (1990), *Delivering Quality Service.* New York: The Free Press.

PART II

DIALOG: THE CENTRALITY
OF RESOURCES

The concept of resources is central to service-dominant (S-D) logic. Resources are anything one can draw upon for support, either tangible or intangible. As humans began to specialize and the division of labor increased in society, they became more and more dependent upon each other as sources of support, for the application of their resources, and for service. Thus, humans exchange some combination of mental and physical skills that they use to benefit others for the service they require from others. Of course, as explicated in chapter 1 (Vargo and Lusch), as this exchange process becomes more complex, goods, money, and organizations become intermediaries in this service-exchange process, often masking the true service nature of exchange.

In chapter 5, "The Service-Dominant Logic of Marketing: Theoretical Foundations, Pedagogy, and Resource-Advantage Theory," Hunt and Madhavaram clearly demonstrate how resource-advantage theory can be a guiding framework for the S-D logic of marketing. Perhaps more important, they elaborate on how it can be used as an integrative framework to teach business and marketing strategy. In our opinion, it can also be a platform for a substantial research program embracing S-D logic. Hunt's resource-advantage theory can take us in the direction of a general theory of marketing by providing a general theory of competition. However, for a general theory to be complete, it is essential that it be capable of explaining and addressing not only seller behavior but also customer and consumer behavior, the institutional framework that is a part of marketing, and the influence of marketing on society. In the last part of this book, we suggest that S-D logic can potentially provide a foundational framework for not only a general theory of marketing, but also a theory of society.

Day's arguments in chapter 6 on achieving advantage with S-D logic are persuasive. He argues that there is path dependency in any system. Consequently, for S-D logic to be fully embraced, these path dependencies, which can be sources of resistance, must be overcome. His views echo our belief that "resources are not; they become," and for resources to "become" it is essential that "resistances" be overcome. It is probably for this reason that Levy, in chapter 4, suggested change may come slowly. In the case of a potential cultural resource, such as S-D logic, the resistance that must be overcome is the old way of thinking, as Day suggests. He concludes that marketing must become a general, senior-management responsibility if S-D logic is to be successful. We agree!

Contemporary authors in the business and marketing literature view resources from the firm's perspective. However, S-D logic argues that the customer is a resource and can be drawn upon for support. Arnould, Price, and Malshe in chapter 7, "Toward a Cultural Resource-Based Theory of the Customer," argue that the customer can, in turn, view the firm, marketplace, and culture as resources to draw upon for support. Importantly, they make the insightful contribution to S-D logic that operant resources (i.e., dynamic resources that act upon other resources) of customers and firms converge to "co-create value through patterns of experiences and meanings embedded in the cultural life-worlds of consumers." They convincingly argue that "through the deployment of consumer operant resources, consumers engage brands and organizations to co-create value in interactive and sometimes unanticipated ways." We are indebted to them for bringing attention to the lack of solid conceptualization on consumers' rich value-creative competences and suggesting a unifying conceptual framework. We believe that firms and managers can benefit from a conceptualization of consumer's value-creative competences. With such a framework, the firm can more effectively adopt S-D logic. We agree with Arnould, Price, and Malshe that the conceptual framework of firm and consumer resource interaction provides direction for much needed research.

5

THE SERVICE-DOMINANT LOGIC
OF MARKETING

Theoretical Foundations, Pedagogy,
and Resource-Advantage Theory

SHELBY D. HUNT AND SREEDHAR MADHAVARAM

The insightful and provocative article by Vargo and Lusch (2004; hereafter V&L) argues that, because marketing has historically been informed by static-equilibrium economics, it has had a goods-centered, "value is embedded in output," dominant logic. This logic has been based on an "understanding of economics and marketing . . . [that was] largely developed during the nineteenth century, a time when the focus was on the efficiencies in the production of tangible output, which was fundamental to the Industrial Revolution" (V&L, p. 14). Now, they argue, "times have changed" (p. 15), and marketing is evolving toward a dynamic, evolutionary process, service-centered view that is informed by resource-advantage theory, competences, knowledge, and relationship marketing. In this view, "value is defined by and co-created in concert with the consumer" (p. 6).

For V&L, marketing not only *is* shifting, but it *should* shift toward this customer-centric, market-driven, services-centered view. Therefore, marketing should (1) focus on specialized skills and knowledge as operant resources that provide competitive advantage, (2) strive to maximize consumers' involvement in developing customized offerings, and (3) aim to be "the predominant organizational philosophy . . . [that] leads in initiating and coordinating a market-driven perspective for all core competences" (p. 13). Furthermore, marketing scholars should "lead industry toward a service-centered model of exchange" (p. 14).

It is true, as Shugan (2004, p. 24) points out, that the "insightful observations of V&L should dramatically influence academic research in marketing and other disciplines." However, what many readers may underestimate is the significance of the service-dominant logic's implications for marketing pedagogy (Hunt 2004). Among V&L's recommendations is that the principle course should "subordinate goods to service provision, emphasizing the former as a distribution mechanism for the latter" (p. 14). Furthermore, the marketing strategy course should be "centered on resource-advantage theory, building on the role of competences and capabilities in the co-production of value and competitive advantage" (p. 14).

The purpose of this chapter is to use resource-advantage (R-A) theory to explicate further the service-dominant (S-D) logic of marketing. First, we overview R-A theory and show how it provides a theoretical foundation for the S-D logic of marketing. Then, we show how, as V&L prescribe, strategy courses within the S-D logic can be taught by means of R-A theory.

Figure 5.1 **A Schematic of the Resource-Advantage Theory of Competition**

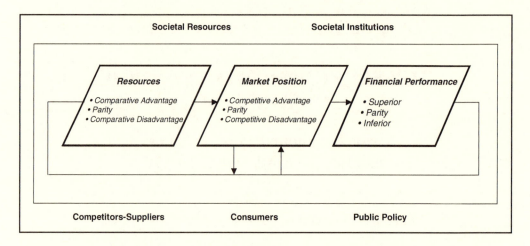

Source: Hunt and Morgan (1997). Reprinted by permission of the American Marketing Association.

Note: Competition is the disequilibrating, ongoing process that consists of the constant struggle among firms for a comparative advantage in resources that will yield a marketplace position of competitive advantage and, thereby, superior financial performance. Firms learn through competition as a result of feedback from relative financial performance "signaling" relative market position, which, in turn, signals relative resources.

R-A THEORY AND THE S-D LOGIC OF MARKETING

Resource-advantage theory is an evolutionary, process theory of competition that is interdisciplinary in the sense that it has been developed in the literatures of several different disciplines. These disciplines include marketing (Falkenberg 2000; Foss 2000; Hodgson 2000; Hunt 1997a, 1999, 2000b, 2000c, 2001, 2002a, 2002b; Hunt and Arnett 2001, 2003, 2004; Hunt and Derozier 2004; Hunt, Lambe, and Wittmann 2002; Hunt and Morgan 1995, 1996, 1997; Morgan and Hunt 2002), management (Hunt 1995, 2000a; Hunt and Lambe 2000), economics (Hunt 1997b, 1997c, 1997d, 2000d, 2002c), ethics (Arnett and Hunt 2002), and general business (Hunt 1998; Hunt and Duhan 2002).

Resource-advantage theory is also interdisciplinary in that it draws on, and has affinities with, numerous other theories and research traditions, including evolutionary economics, "Austrian" economics, the historical tradition, industrial-organization economics, the resource-based tradition, the competence-based tradition, institutional economics, transaction cost economics, and economic sociology. Resource-advantage theory is a general theory of competition that describes the process of competition. Figures 5.1 and 5.2 provide schematic depictions of R-A theory's key constructs. The purpose of this section is to show how R-A theory provides a theoretical foundation for the S-D logic.

R-A Theory as a Foundation for the S-D Logic

Using Hodgson's (1993) taxonomy, R-A theory is an evolutionary, disequilibrium-provoking, process theory of competition, in which innovation and organizational learning are endogenous, firms and consumers have imperfect information, and entrepreneurship, institutions, and public

Figure 5.2 **Competitive Position Matrix**

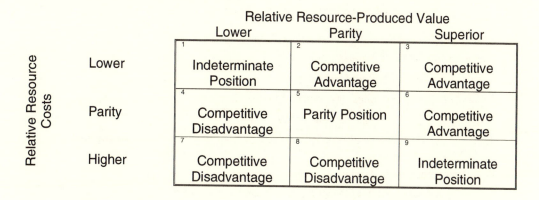

| | | Relative Resource-Produced Value | | |
		Lower	Parity	Superior
Relative Resource Costs	Lower	1 Indeterminate Position	2 Competitive Advantage	3 Competitive Advantage
	Parity	4 Competitive Disadvantage	5 Parity Position	6 Competitive Advantage
	Higher	7 Competitive Disadvantage	8 Competitive Disadvantage	9 Indeterminate Position

Source: Adapted from Hunt and Morgan (1995). Reprinted by permission of the American Marketing Association.

Note: The marketplace position of competitive advantage identified as Cell 3 results from the firm, relative to its competitors, having a resource assortment that enables it to produce an offering for some market segment(s) that (a) is perceived to be of superior value and (b) is produced at lower costs.

policy affect economic performance. Evolutionary theories of competition require units of selection that are (1) relatively durable—that is, they can exist, at least potentially, through long periods of time and (2) heritable—that is, they can be transmitted to successors. For R-A theory, both firms and resources are proposed as the heritable, durable units of selection, with competition for comparative advantages in resources constituting the selection process.

At its core, R-A theory combines heterogeneous demand theory with a resource-based theory of the firm (see premises P1, P6, and P7 in Table 5.1). Contrasted with perfect competition, heterogeneous demand theory views intra-industry demand as significantly heterogeneous with respect to consumers' tastes and preferences. Therefore, viewing products as bundles of attributes, different market offerings, or "bundles," are required for different market segments within the same industry. Contrasted with the view that the firm is a production function that combines homogeneous, perfectly mobile "factors" of production, the resource-based view holds that the firm is a combiner of heterogeneous, imperfectly mobile entities that are labeled "resources." These heterogeneous, imperfectly mobile resources, when combined with heterogeneous demand, imply significant diversity as to the sizes, scopes, and levels of profitability of firms within the same industry.

As diagrammed in Figures 5.1 and 5.2, R-A theory stresses the importance of (1) market segments, (2) heterogeneous firm resources, (3) comparative advantages/disadvantages in resources, and (4) marketplace positions of competitive advantage/disadvantage. In brief, market segments are defined as intra-industry groups of consumers whose tastes and preferences with regard to an industry's output are *relatively* homogeneous. Readers should note at this point in our discussion that central to the S-D logic of marketing is the distinction between *operand* resources (those upon which an operation or act is performed) and *operant* resources (those that act upon other resources). However, for the S-D logic of marketing, how is *resource* to be defined? For R-A theory, resources are defined as the tangible and intangible entities available to the firm that enable it to produce efficiently and/or effectively a market offering that has value for some marketing segment(s). This conceptualization of *resource* develops further the S-D logic of marketing.

Table 5.1

Foundational Premises of Resource-Advantage Theory

P_1: Demand is heterogeneous across industries, heterogeneous within industries, and dynamic.

P_2: Consumer information is imperfect and costly.

P_3: Human motivation is constrained self-interest seeking.

P_4: The firm's objective is superior financial performance.

P_5: The firm's information is imperfect and costly.

P_6: The firm's resources are financial, physical, legal, human, organizational, informational, and relational.

P_7: Resource characteristics are heterogeneous and imperfectly mobile.

P_8: The role of management is to recognize, understand, create, select, implement, and modify strategies.

P_9: Competitive dynamics are disequilibrium-provoking, with innovation endogenous.

Source: Adapted from Hunt and Morgan (1997). Reprinted by permission of the American Marketing Association.

For R-A theory, resources are not just land, labor, and capital, as in neoclassical theory. Rather, resources can be categorized as financial (e.g., cash resources, access to financial markets), physical (e.g., plant, equipment), legal (e.g., trademarks, licenses), human (e.g., the skills and knowledge of individual employees), organizational (e.g., competences, controls, policies, culture), informational (e.g., knowledge from consumer and competitive intelligence), and relational (e.g., relationships with suppliers and customers). Therefore, returning again to the S-D logic, R-A theory both conceptualizes "resource" and explicates the kinds of resources that may be "operand" or "operant." That is, operand resources are typically physical, whereas operant resources are typically human, organizational, informational, and relational.

For the S-D logic, operant resources such as competences are valuable to the firm. How, though, is their value determined? R-A theory provides an answer to the value question. For R-A theory, not all resources that have value to the firm have an exchange value or price. That is, relatively immobile resources such as competences are not commonly or easily bought and sold in the marketplace (save when firms themselves are bought and sold). Therefore, the value of such operant resources is determined not by exchange, but by the extent to which each contributes to the firm's ability to produce efficiently/effectively market offerings that are perceived by some market segment(s) to have value. Also, because "relative resource costs" in the competitive position matrix are *accounting* costs, readers should note that such costs may be related only indirectly to key, operant, value-producing resources.

For R-A theory, each firm in the marketplace will have at least some resources that are unique to it (e.g., very knowledgeable employees, efficient production processes) that could constitute a comparative advantage in resources that could lead to positions of advantage (i.e., cells 2, 3, and 6 in Figure 5.2) in the marketplace. Some of these resources are not easily copied or acquired (i.e., they are relatively immobile). Therefore, such resources (e.g., culture, processes) may be a source of long-term competitive advantage in the marketplace.

Just as international trade theory recognizes that nations have heterogeneous, immobile resources and focuses on the importance of comparative advantages in resources to explain the benefits of trade, R-A theory recognizes that many of the resources of firms within the same industry are significantly heterogeneous and relatively immobile. Therefore, analogous to nations, some firms will have a comparative advantage and others a comparative disadvantage in efficiently and/or effectively producing particular market offerings that have value for particular market segments.

Specifically, as shown in Figure 5.1 and further explicated in Figure 5.2, when firms have, on balance, a comparative advantage in resources, they will occupy marketplace positions of competitive advantage for some market segment(s). Marketplace positions of competitive advantage then result in *superior* financial performance. Similarly, when firms have, on balance, a comparative disadvantage in resources, they will occupy positions of competitive disadvantage, which will then produce *inferior* financial performance. Therefore, firms compete for comparative advantages in resources that will yield marketplace positions of competitive advantage for some market segment(s) and, thereby, superior financial performance. As Figure 5.1 shows, how well competitive processes work is significantly influenced by five environmental factors: the societal resources on which firms draw, the societal institutions that form the "rules of the game" (North 1990), the actions of competitors, the behaviors of consumers and suppliers, and public policy decisions.

Returning to the S-D logic, because the "consumer must perceive that the value-potential [of an offering] is translatable to specific needs through co-production, the firm can only make value propositions that strive to be better or more compelling than competitors" (V&L, p. 11). As to what this means, note that the axes of the nine-celled, competitive position matrix (Figure 5.2) are "relative, resource-produced value" and "relative resource costs." Because "value refers to the sum total of all benefits that consumers perceive they will receive if they accept a particular firm's market offering" (Hunt 2000b, p. 138), the positions of competitive advantage/disadvantage in the matrix further explicate V&L's stress on "value propositions" that are "more compelling."

Consistent with its Schumpeterian heritage, R-A theory places great emphasis on innovation, both proactive and reactive. The former is innovation by firms that, though motivated by the expectation of superior financial performance, is not prompted by specific competitive pressures— it is genuinely entrepreneurial in the classic sense of *entrepreneur*. In contrast, the latter is innovation that is directly prompted by the learning process of firms competing for the patronage of market segments. Both proactive and reactive innovation contribute to the dynamism of R-A competition.

For the S-D logic, competition is a knowledge-discovery process because "in the services-centered model, marketplace feedback is obtained not only directly from the customer but is also gauged by analyzing financial performance from exchange relationships in order to learn" (V&L 2004, p. 31). Similarly, for R-A theory, firms (attempt to) learn in many ways—by formal market research, seeking out competitive intelligence, dissecting competitor's products, benchmarking, and test marketing. However, as does the S-D logic, R-A theory stresses that the process of competition itself contributes to organizational learning. As the feedback loops in Figure 5.1 show, firms learn through competition as a result of the feedback from relative financial performance signaling relative market position, which in turn signals relative resources. When firms competing for a market segment learn from their inferior financial performance that they occupy positions of competitive disadvantage (see Figure 5.2), they attempt to neutralize and/or leapfrog the advantaged firm(s) by acquisition and/or innovation. That is, they attempt to acquire the same resource as the advantaged firm(s) and/or they attempt to innovate by imitating the resource, finding an equivalent resource, or finding (creating) a superior resource. Here, *superior* implies that the innovating firm's new resource enables it to surpass the previously advantaged competitor in terms of either relative costs (i.e., an *efficiency* advantage) or relative value (i.e., an *effectiveness* advantage), or both.

The importance at the macro level of the process of R-A competition promoting organizational learning cannot be stressed enough. For example, it is "because command economies lack the process of competition, their firms lack a powerful means (i.e., financial performance stemming from marketplace positions) for determining how efficient and effective they are. Indeed, it . . . was the premium prices of Western imports that communicated to socialist planners just how ineffective socialist firms were" (Hunt 2000b, p. 174).

For R-A theory, firms occupying positions of competitive advantage (see Figure 5.2) can continue to do so if (1) they continue to reinvest in the resources that produced the competitive advantage, and (2) rivals' acquisition and innovation efforts fail. Rivals will fail (or take a long time to succeed) when an advantaged firm's resources are either protected by such societal institutions as patents or the advantage-producing resources are causally ambiguous, socially or technologically complex, tacit, or have time-compression diseconomies.

Competition, then, for R-A theory, is viewed as an evolutionary, disequilibrium-provoking process. It consists of the constant struggle among firms for comparative advantages in resources that will yield marketplace positions of competitive advantage and, thereby, superior financial performance. Once a firm's comparative advantage in resources enables it to achieve superior performance through a position of competitive advantage in some market segment(s), competitors attempt to neutralize and/or leapfrog the advantaged firm through acquisition, imitation, substitution, or major innovation. R-A theory is, therefore, inherently dynamic. Disequilibrium, not equilibrium, is the norm. In the terminology of Hodgson's (1993) taxonomy of evolutionary economic theories, R-A theory is non-consummatory: It has no end stage, only a never-ending process of change. The implication is that, though market-based economies are *moving*, they are not moving toward some final state, such as a Pareto-optimal, general equilibrium.

PEDAGOGY, STRATEGY, AND THE S-D LOGIC OF MARKETING

The preceding section shows how R-A theory provides a theoretical foundation for the S-D logic. Indeed, they reinforce each other so well that teaching them together comes naturally. V&L (2004, p.14) claim that the S-D logic of marketing implies that marketing strategy courses should be "centered on resource-advantage theory." Therefore, the purpose of this section is to show how R-A theory can be used as an integrative theory to teach business and marketing strategy. Before beginning, however, is there a *need* for such an integrative theory? Hunt (1992, 2002a) argues that the marketing discipline has a responsibility to marketing practice to provide a continuous supply of competent, responsible entrants to the marketing profession. Similarly, commenting on an American Marketing Association task force report, Garda (1988) maintains that, in order for firms to be market focused, practitioners need concepts, models, and integrative theoretical frameworks. Therefore, if marketing is, indeed, evolving toward an S-D logic, academicians need an integrative theory as a pedagogical tool for preparing knowledgeable entrants for the marketing profession.

Most normative theories of business strategy can be grouped into one of four categories: industry-based, resource-based, competence-based, and knowledge-based. Figure 5.3 shows each of these four, as well as four specific theories of marketing strategy: market orientation, market segmentation, relationship marketing, and brand equity. As depicted in Figure 5.3, R-A theory provides a positive theoretical foundation for an *integrative* understanding of all eight normative theories of strategy. That is, because the implementation of normative strategies occurs in the context of competition, and R-A theory best describes the nature of competition

Figure 5.3 **Integrating Business and Marketing Strategy**

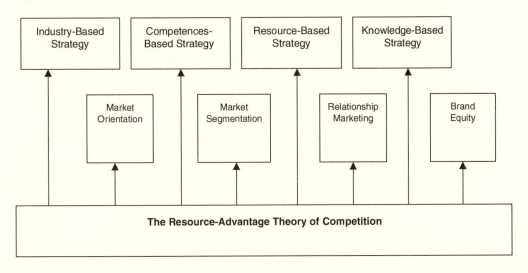

Source: Hunt (2004b). Reprinted by permission of the author.

in market-based economies, R-A theory can *ground* business and marketing strategy (Hunt 2002a; Hunt and Derozier 2004). Because it fosters an integrative understanding of business and marketing strategy, R-A theory can be used to teach these subjects, for to understand how competition *works* is to understand which normative theory of strategy might *work well* in particular competitive contexts.

BUSINESS AND MARKETING STRATEGY

Page limitations dictate that we cannot discuss all eight of the approaches to business and marketing strategy shown in Figure 5.3. Instead we focus on just two approaches to business strategy, resource-based and competence-based, and two approaches to marketing strategy, market orientation and relationship marketing. (For discussions of industry-based strategy and market segmentation strategy, see Hunt [2002a, b], Hunt and Derozier [2004], and Hunt and Arnett [2004].)

Resource-Based Strategy

Resource-based business strategy traces to the long-neglected work of Edith Penrose (1959). Avoiding the term *factor of production* because of its ambiguity, she viewed the firm as a "collection of productive resources" and pointed out: "It is never *resources* themselves that are the 'inputs' to the production process, but only the *services* that the resources can render" (pp. 24–25; emphasis in original). Viewing resources as bundles of possible services that an entity can provide, "[i]t is the heterogeneity . . . of the productive services available or potentially available from its resources that gives each firm its unique character" (pp. 75, 77). Therefore, contrasted with the neoclassical notion of an *optimum* size of firm, "the expansion of firms is largely based on opportunities to use their existing productive resources more efficiently than they are being used" (p. 88).

Works drawing on Penrose (1959) to explicate resource-based theory in business strategy include the seminal articles of Lippman and Rumelt (1982), Rumelt (1984), and Wernerfelt (1984) in the early 1980s, followed by the efforts of Dierickx and Cool (1989), Barney (1991, 1992), and Conner (1991). Resource-based strategy maintains that resources (to varying degrees) are both significantly heterogeneous across firms and imperfectly mobile. "Resource heterogeneity" means that each and every firm has an assortment of resources that is at least in some ways unique. "Imperfectly mobile" implies that firm resources, to varying degrees, are not commonly, easily, or readily bought and sold in the marketplace (the neoclassical factor markets). Because of resource heterogeneity, some firms are more profitable than others. Because of resource immobility, resource heterogeneity can persist through time despite firms' attempts to acquire the same resources of particularly successful competitors. *Therefore, the fundamental strategic imperative of resource-based strategy is that, to achieve competitive advantage and, thereby, superior financial performance, firms should seek resources that are valuable, rare, imperfectly mobile, inimitable, and nonsubstitutable.*

Resource-Based Strategy and R-A Theory

A positive theory of competition that could ground normative, resource-based strategy (1) must have competitive circumstances that permit such a strategy to be successful and (2) contribute to explaining why and when (i.e., under what circumstances) such a strategy may be successful. First, R-A theory permits resource-based strategy to be successful because it specifically adopts a resource-based view of the firm. As premise P7 in Table 5.1 notes, firms are viewed as combiners of heterogeneous and imperfectly mobile resources—which is the fundamental tenet of the "resource-based view" (Conner 1991). Indeed, competition for R-A theory consists of the constant struggle among firms for comparative advantages in such resources.

Note, however, that R-A theory adopts *a* resource-based view of the firm, not *the* view. As discussed by Schulze (1994), many resource-based theorists view competition as an equilibrium-seeking process. Indeed, firms are often described as seeking "abnormal profits" or "economic rents," which in the neoclassical tradition imply profits different from that of a firm in an industry characterized by perfect competition and/or profits in excess of the minimum necessary to keep a firm in business in long-run competitive equilibrium. Thus, because *perfect* is posited as *ideal* (i.e., it views competition as equilibrium-seeking and the goal of the firm as *abnormal* profits or *rents*), this implies that the achievement of sustained, superior financial performance by firms is detrimental to social welfare.

In contrast, R-A theory maintains that competition is dynamic and disequilibrium-provoking (see premise P9 in Table 5.1). In a critique of resource-based strategy, Priem and Butler (2001, p. 35) argue for dynamic theory and suggest that in order for a resource-based view "to fulfill its potential in strategic management, its idea must be integrated with an environmental demand model." They point out that R-A theory's incorporation of heterogeneous demand in a dynamic theory is in the right direction. Barney (2001) agrees that a dynamic analysis using the resource-based view of the firm is important for the further development of strategic research, and he cites R-A theory as an example of an evolutionary approach that incorporates the necessary dynamics.

Also in contrast, R-A theory denies that perfect competition is the ideal competitive form. The achievement of superior financial performance—both temporary and sustained—is pro-competitive when it is consistent with and furthers the disequilibrating, ongoing process that consists of the constant struggle among firms for comparative advantages in resources that will yield marketplace positions of competitive advantage and, thereby, superior financial performance. It is anticompetitive when it is inconsistent with and thwarts this process. Therefore, R-A theory maintains that when superior financial performance results from pro-competitive (*pro* in the sense of R-A theory) factors, it contributes to social welfare because the dynamic process of R-A competition furthers productivity and economic growth through both the efficient allocation of scarce tangible resources and, more importantly, the creation of new tangible and intangible resources.

Specifically, the ongoing quest for superior financial performance, coupled with the fact that all firms cannot be simultaneously superior, implies not only that the process of R-A competition will allocate resources in an efficient manner but also that there will be both proactive and reactive innovations developed that will contribute to further increases in efficiency and effectiveness.[1] Indeed, it is the process of R-A competition that provides an important mechanism for firms to learn how efficient/effective, inefficient/ineffective, they are. (See the learning, feedback loops in Figure 5.1.) Similarly, it is the quest for superior performance by firms that results in the proactive and reactive innovations that, in turn, promote the very increases in firm productivity that constitute the technological progress that results in economic growth.

As to why and when a strategy of seeking resources that are "valuable, rare, imperfectly mobile, inimitable, and nonsubstitutable" will be successful, consider the "valuable" criterion. An entity can be valuable in many ways. For example, a firm's assets could include a section of land, a building, or a painting that has value in the marketplace (and appears on the firm's balance sheet). But what R-A theory highlights is that *marketplace value* is not the key for understanding the nature of competition. Rather, a resource is "valuable" when it contributes to a firm's ability to efficiently and/or effectively produce a marketplace offering that *has value* for some market segment or segments. And, R-A theory maintains, consumer perceptions of value are dispositive. That is, consumer perceptions are the ultimate authority as to the value of a firm's market offering.

Now consider the recommendation that valuable resources should be *rare*. Entities can be rare in many ways. What R-A theory highlights and emphasizes is that a valuable, rare resource is one that enables a firm, when competing for a market segment's patronage, to move upward and/or to the right in the marketplace position matrix (Figure 5.2). That is, valuable, *rare* resources enable firms to compete by being, relative to competitors, more efficient and/or more effective.

Now, in light of R-A theory's emphasis on proactive and reactive innovation, consider the recommendation that resources should be "inimitable and nonsubstitutable." To the list, R-A theory adds "nonsurpassable" (Hunt 1999). Firms occupying positions of competitive disadvantage (cells 4, 7, and 8 in Figure 5.2) will be motivated to engage in three forms of reactive innovation: (1) imitating the resource of an advantaged competitor, (2) finding (creating) an equivalent resource, or (3) finding (creating) a superior resource. Many authors have tended to focus on the equilibrating behavior of resource imitation and substitution. Although imitation and substitution are important forms of competitive actions, R-A theory highlights the fact that reactive innovation can also prompt disequilibrium-provoking behaviors. That is, reactive innovation in the form of finding (creating) a *superior* resource results in the innovating firm's new resource assortment enabling it to *surpass* the previously advantaged competitor in terms of either relative efficiency or relative value, or both. By leapfrogging competitors, firms realize their objective of *superior* returns, make competition dynamic, shape their environments, and renew society. In doing so, the process of reactive innovation contributes to the kinds of major innovations described as creative destruction by Schumpeter (1950). Imitation brings parity returns; parity returns are never enough.

Competence-Based Strategy

The term *distinctive competence* traces to Selznick (1957) and was used by Andrews (1971/1980/1987) and his colleagues in the strengths, weaknesses, opportunities, and threats model to refer to what an organization could do particularly well, relative to its competitors. Stimulating the development of competence-based theory in the early 1990s were the works of Chandler (1990), Hamel and Prahalad (1989, 1994a, b), Prahalad and Hamel (1990, 1993), Reed and De Fillippi (1990), Lado, Boyd, and Wright (1992), and Teece and Pisano (1994). Numerous other theoretical and empirical articles have been developing competence-based theory (Aaker 1995; Bharadwaj, Varadarajan, and Fahy 1993; Day and Nedungadi 1994; Hamel and Heene 1994; Heene and Sanchez 1997; Sanchez and Heene 1997, 2000; Sanchez, Heene, and Thomas 1996).

Prahalad and Hamel (1990, p. 81) argue that "the firm" should be viewed as both a collection of products or strategic business units and a collection of competences because "in the long run, competitiveness derives from an ability to build, at lower cost and more speedily than competitors, the core competencies that spawn unanticipated products." For Hamel and Prahalad (1994a), business strategy should focus on industry foresight and competence leveraging. *Industry foresight* involves anticipating the future by asking what new types of benefits firms should provide their customers in the next five to fifteen years and what new competences should be acquired or built to offer such benefits. *Resource leveraging* focuses on the numerator in the productivity equation (i.e., value of output / cost of input). Specifically, they argue that too much attention in analyses of firm productivity has been devoted to resource efficiency—the denominator—and too little on resource effectiveness—the numerator.

For competence-based theorists, productivity gains and competitive advantage come through the resource-leveraging that results from "more effectively concentrating resources on key strategic goals, . . . more efficiently accumulating resources, . . . complementing resources of one type with those of another to create higher-order value, . . . conserving resources whenever possible, and . . . rapidly recovering resources by minimizing the time between expenditure and payback" (Hamel and Prahalad 1994a, p. 160*). Therefore, the fundamental strategic imperative of the competence-based view of strategy is that, to achieve competitive advantage and, thereby, superior financial performance, firms should identify, seek, develop, reinforce, maintain, and leverage distinctive competences.*

Competence-Based Strategy and R-A Theory

Organizational competences, all strategy theorists agree, have components that are significantly intangible (e.g., knowledge and skills) and are not *owned* by the firm (i.e., not capable of being *sold* by the firm, except, of course, by selling the division of the firm that houses the competence). Recall that R-A theory acknowledges that both tangible and intangible entities can be resources. Recall also that entities need not be owned by firms to be resources. Rather they need only be *available* to firms.

Premise P6 in Table 5.1 classifies firm resources as financial, physical, legal, human, organizational, informational, and relational. For R-A theory, therefore, a firm competence is a kind of *organizational* resource. Specifically, competences are "higher order" resources that are defined as socially and/or technologically complex, interconnected combinations of tangible basic resources (e.g., basic machinery) and intangible basic resources (e.g., specific organizational policies and procedures and the skills and knowledge of specific employees) that fit together coherently in a synergistic manner. Competences are distinct resources because they exist as distinct packages of basic resources. Because competences are causally ambiguous, tacit, complex, and highly interconnected, they are likely to be significantly heterogeneous and asymmetrically distributed across firms in the same industry. Therefore, R-A theory permits competence-based strategy to be successful.

Differences in specific competences explain why some firms are simply better than others at *doing* things (Hamel and Heene 1994; Heene and Sanchez 1997; Langlois and Robertson 1995; Sanchez and Heene 1997; Sanchez, Heene, and Thomas 1996). For example, firms can have superior entrepreneurial competences (Foss 1993), research and development competences (Roehl 1996), production competences (Prahalad and Hamel 1990), marketing competences (Conant, Mokwa, and Varadarajan 1990; Day 1992), and competitive agility competences (Nayyan and Bantel 1994).

Highlighted by R-A theory is the role of *renewal* competences, such as those described by Teece and Pisano (1994) and Teece, Pisano, and Shuen (1997) as "dynamic capabilities"; by Dickson (1996) as "learning how to learn"; and by Hamel and Prahalad (1994a, b) as "industry foresight." Specifically, renewal competences prompt proactive innovation by enabling firms to (1) anticipate potential market segments (unmet, changing, and/or new needs, wants, and desires), (2) envision market offerings that might be attractive to such segments, and (3) foresee the need to acquire, develop, or create the required resources, including competences, to produce the envisioned market offerings. Therefore, because firms are not viewed by R-A theory as just passively responding to changing environment or looking for the best "fit" between existing resources and market "niches," it contributes to explaining why and when a firm developing a renewal competence will be successful. A strategy of developing a renewal competence will be successful (or more successful) when (1) the marketplace is turbulent, (2) competitors are "sleepy," and/or (3) the proactive innovations spawned by a renewal competence promote turbulence.

Market Orientation Strategy

The idea of market orientation traces to the marketing concept, which has been considered a marketing cornerstone since its articulation and development in the 1950s and 1960s. The marketing concept maintains that (1) all areas of the firm should be customer oriented, (2) all marketing activities should be integrated, and (3) profits, not just sales, should be the objective. As conventionally interpreted, the concept's customer-orientation component—that is, knowing one's customers and developing products to satisfy their needs, wants, and desires—has been considered paramount. Historically contrasted with the production and sales orientations, the marketing concept is considered to be a philosophy of doing business that should be a major part of a successful firm's culture (Baker, Black, and Hart 1994; Wong and Saunders 1993). For Houston (1986, p. 82), it is the "optimal marketing management philosophy." For Deshpandé and Webster (1989, p. 3), "the marketing concept defines a distinct organizational culture . . . that put[s] the customer in the center of the firm's thinking about strategy and operations."

In the 1990s, the marketing concept morphed into market orientation. In this view, for Webster (1994, pp. 9, 10), "the customer must be put on a pedestal, standing above all others in the organization, including the owners and the managers." Nonetheless, he maintains, "having a customer orientation, although still a primary goal, is not enough. Market-driven companies also are fully aware of competitors' product offerings and capabilities and how those are viewed by customers." At the same time, Narver and Slater (1990) and Slater and Narver (1994) were characterizing a market orientation as having the three components of customer orientation, competitor orientation, and interfunctional coordination. And Kohli and Jaworski (1990, p. 6) defined a market orientation as "the organizationwide *generation* of market intelligence pertaining to current and future customer needs, *dissemination* of the intelligence across departments, and organizationwide *responsiveness* to it" [emphasis in original]. *Therefore, the fundamental imperative of market orientation strategy is that, to achieve competitive advantage and, thereby, superior financial performance, firms should systematically (1) gather information on present and potential customers and competitors and (2) use such information in a coordinated way across departments to guide strategy recognition, understanding, creation, selection, implementation, and modification.*

Market Orientation Strategy and R-A Theory

R-A theory permits market orientation (MO) strategy to succeed because premise P5 in Table 5.1 assumes that the firm's information is imperfect and premise P6 indicates that information can be a resource. That is, the (1) systematic acquisition of information about present and potential customers and competitors and (2) coordinated use of such information to guide strategy may contribute to the firm's ability to efficiently and/or effectively produce market offerings that have value for some market segments.

If a firm is market oriented and its competitors are not, then an MO strategy may be a resource that moves the firm's marketplace position upward and to the right in Figure 5.2. Note, however, premise P5 in Table 5.1 also points out that information acquisition is costly. The implication is that if implementing an MO strategy is *too* costly, then the firm's position in Figure 5.2 will shift downward toward positions of competitive disadvantage. Therefore, whether an MO strategy provides a resource that leads to a position of competitive advantage in Figure 5.2 depends on the relative value to relative cost ratio of MO implementation.

Because it consists of a synergistic combination of more basic resources (Hunt and Lambe 2000), the effective implementation of an MO can be viewed as an organizational competence. To implement an MO strategy, firms deploy tangible resources, such as information systems to store, analyze, and disseminate information about competitors and customers. In addition, firms use intangible resources to implement MO. That is, organizational policies must be in place to encourage MO action, and managers must have the knowledge and experience required to utilize customer and competitor information effectively.

Specifically, a market orientation can be viewed as a kind of *renewal* competence. That is, a competence in MO will prompt proactive innovation by enabling firms to anticipate potential market segments, envision market offerings that might be attractive to such segments, and prompt the need to acquire, develop, or create the required resources to produce the offerings. Furthermore, a competence in MO will assist efforts at reactive innovation because it provides valuable information about existing competitors and customers.

Relationship Marketing Strategy

The strategic area of relationship marketing was first defined by Berry (1983, p. 25) as "attracting, maintaining, and—in multi-service organizations—enhancing customer relationships." Since then, numerous other definitions have been offered. For example, Berry and Parasuraman (1991) propose that "relationship marketing concerns attracting, developing, and retaining customer relationships." Gummesson (1999, p. 1) proposes that "relationship marketing (RM) is marketing seen as relationships, networks, and interaction." Grönroos (1996, p. 11) states that "relationship marketing is to identify and establish, maintain, and enhance relationships with customers and other stakeholders, at a profit, so that the objectives of all parties involved are met; and that this is done by a mutual exchange and fulfillment of promises." Also for him, relationship marketing is "marketing . . . seen as the management of customer relationships (and of relationships with suppliers, distributors, and other network partners as well as financial institutions and other parties)" (Grönroos 2000, pp. 40–41). Sheth (1994, p.2) defines relationship marketing as "the understanding, explanation, and management of the ongoing collaborative business relationship between suppliers and customers." Sheth and Parvatiyar (1995, p. 399) view relationship marketing as "attempts to involve and integrate customers, suppliers, and other infrastructural partners into a firm's developmental and marketing activities," and Morgan and Hunt (1994, p. 22) propose that "relationship marketing refers to all marketing activities directed towards establishing, developing, and maintaining successful relational exchanges."

Although the various perspectives on relationship marketing differ, one common element is that all view relationship marketing as implying that, increasingly, firms are competing through developing relatively long-term relationships with stakeholders such as customers, suppliers, employees, and competitors. Consistent with the Nordic School (Grönroos 2000; Grönroos and Gummesson 1985) and the IMP Group (Axelsson and Easton 1992; Ford 1990; Hakansson 1982), the emerging thesis seems to be as follows: To be an effective *competitor* (in the global economy) requires one to be an effective *cooperator* (in some network) (Hunt and Morgan 1994). Indeed, for Sheth and Parvatiyar (1995, p. 400), the "purpose of relationship marketing is, therefore, to enhance marketing productivity by achieving efficiency and effectiveness."

It is important to point out that none of the previously cited authors naïvely maintains that a firm's efficiency and effectiveness are always enhanced by establishing relationships with all potential stakeholders. Clearly, advocates of relationship marketing recognize that firms should at times avoid developing certain relationships. As Gummesson (1994, p. 17) observes, "Not all relationships are important to all companies all the time. . . . Some marketing is best handled as transaction marketing." Indeed, he counsels: "Establish which relationship portfolio is essential to your specific business and make sure it is handled skillfully" (p. 17). *Therefore, the fundamental strategic imperative of relationship marketing strategy is that, to achieve competitive advantage and, thereby, superior financial performance, firms should identify, develop, and nurture a relationship portfolio.*

Relationship Marketing Strategy and R-A Theory

Consider what is required for a theory of competition to permit a relationship marketing strategy to succeed. First, because relationships are intangible, the theory must permit intangibles to be resources. Second, because relationships are not owned (and, therefore, firms cannot buy and sell relationships in the "factor" markets), firm ownership must not be a criterion for an entity to be a firm resource. Third, because each relationship has unique characteristics (and, therefore, one cannot take the first derivative of any equation in which a relationship appears), unique entities must be allowed. Fourth, because (at least some) relationships involve cooperation among firms in order for them to compete, the theory must permit some relationships to be pro-competitive (and not presumptively assume all instances of cooperation to be anti-competitive collusion).

Now consider R-A theory with regard to its view of resources. A firm resource is any tangible or intangible entity available to the firm that enables it to produce efficiently and/or effectively a market offering that has value for some market segment(s). Therefore, R-A theory satisfies criteria 1 and 2. Now recall that R-A theory views firm resources as significantly heterogeneous (premise P7 in Table 5.1). Therefore, it satisfies criterion 3. Finally, because R-A theory assumes that (at least some) firm resources are imperfectly mobile (premise P7), yet such resources can nonetheless enable firms to produce offerings efficiently and/or effectively, the theory satisfies criterion 4. That is, at least some cooperative relationships are *relational* resources (premise P6), making them pro-competitive.

As discussed in Hunt (1997a), R-A theory implies that firms should periodically conduct a strategic resource audit as a standard part of their corporate planning. The strategic resource audit should pay close attention to the competences of the organization and the role that relationships with suppliers, customers, employees, and competitors can play in enhancing the total "mix" of strategic competences. From the perspective of relationship marketing, therefore, firms should develop a relationship portfolio or "mix" that complements existing competences and enables them to occupy positions of competitive advantage, as identified in Figure 5.2. However, it is important to recognize that relationship portfolios are developed, not selected.

Because it conjures the image of being like a portfolio of stocks, Gummesson's (1999) concept of a relationship portfolio has the same systemic ambiguity as the marketing mix. The standard, textbook versions of the marketing mix concept often imply that some marketing manager sits down at a specific point in time and *selects* both a target market and a particular combination of price, product, place, and promotion that is believed to be optimal. Although this may occur on rare occasions, much more commonly these decisions are made sequentially, that is, through time. For example, it could well be the case that the first decision actually made was the nature of the product. Then a market segment is targeted for the product. Following that, the price, channels of distribution, and promotional programs are developed. The point is that, in contrast with standard textbook treatments, marketing mixes are most often developed through time, not selected at a point in time.

A similar ambiguity emerges in the concept of a relationship portfolio. Even more so than the marketing mix, relationship portfolios are not selected at a point in time, but developed *through* time. Indeed, good relationships take time to develop (Lambe, Spekman, and Hunt 2002). Therefore, though it is important to develop a relationship portfolio that complements existing organizational competences in an optimal manner, and it is important to strategically plan for such relationships, the relationships that make up the relationship portfolio can only be developed through time. Though both are portfolios, the relationship portfolio differs dramatically from a portfolio of stocks, for it is at least possible to select a portfolio of stocks at a single point in time. Consequently, a relationship marketing strategy will be more successful when it is a long-term strategy.

CONCLUSION

The S-D logic of marketing has great promise. This chapter shows how R-A theory provides a theoretical foundation for the S-D logic. It also shows how R-A theory provides an integrative tool for teaching business and marketing strategy within the S-D logic. Competition is an evolutionary, disequilibrating, dynamic process that involves firms using operand and operant resources in their search for competitive advantages and superior financial performance. As it is in competition, so it should be in marketing.

NOTES

This chapter draws extensively from Hunt and Derozier (2004), chapter 9 of Hunt (2002a), and Hunt (2004a).

1. Note that the claim is that R-A competition will allocate resources in an *efficient* manner. No claim is made that it will be an *optimally* efficient manner. The concept "optimal" is not a part of the lexicon of R-A theory.

REFERENCES

Aaker, David A. (1995), *Strategic Market Management*. New York: John Wiley & Sons.
Andrews, Kenneth R. (1971/1980/1987), *The Concept of Corporate Strategy*. Homewood, IL: Richard D. Irwin.

Arnett, Dennis B. and Shelby D. Hunt (2002), "Competitive Irrationality: The Influence of Moral Philosophy," *Business Ethics Quarterly*, 12 (3), 279–303.

Axelsson, B. and G. Easton (1992), *Industrial Networks: A New View of Reality*. London: Gower.

Baker, Michael J., C.D. Black, and S.J. Hart (1994), "Competitive Success in Sunrise and Sunset Industries," in *The Marketing Initiative*, J. Saunders, ed. London: Prentice Hall, 58–71.

Barney, Jay (1991), "Firm Resources and Sustained Competitive Advantage," *Journal of Management*, 17 (1), 99–120.

——— (1992). "Integrating Organizational Behavior and Strategy Formulation Research: A Resource-Based Analysis," in *Advances in Strategic Management*, P. Shrivastava, A.S. Hugg, and J.E. Dutton, eds. Greenwich, CT: JAI Press, 39–61.

——— (2001), "Is the Resource-Based View a Useful Perspective for Strategic Management Research? Yes," *Academy of Management Review*, 26 (1), 41–56.

Berry, L.L. (1983), "Relationship Marketing," in *Emerging Perspectives on Services Marketing*, in L. Berry, G.L. Shostock, and G.D. Upah, eds. Chicago: American Marketing Association, 25–28.

——— and A. Parasuraman (1991), *Marketing Services*. New York: The Free Press.

Bharadwaj, Sundar, P. Rajan Varadarajan, and John Fahy (1993), "Sustainable Competitive Advantage in Service Industries: A Conceptual Model and Research Propositions," *Journal of Marketing*, 57 (4), 83–99.

Chandler, Alfred D. (1990), *Scale and Scope: The Dynamics of Industrial Capitalism*. Cambridge, MA: Harvard University Press.

Conant, Jeffery S., Michael P. Mokwa, and P. Rajan Varadarajan (1990), "Strategic Types, Distinctive Marketing Competencies, and Organizational Performance," *Strategic Marketing Journal*, 11 (September), 365–83.

Conner, Kathleen (1991), "A Historical Comparison of Resource-Based Theory and Five Schools of Thought within Industrial-Organization Economics: Do We Have a New Theory of the Firm?" *Journal of Management*, 17 (March), 121–54.

Day, George S. (1992), "Marketing's Contribution to the Strategy Dialogue." *Journal of the Academy of Marketing Science*, 20 (Fall), 323–30.

——— and Prakash Nedungadi (1994), "Managerial Representations of Competitive Advantage," *Journal of Marketing*, 58 (April), 31–44.

Deshpandé, Rohit and Frederick E. Webster, Jr. (1989), "Organizational Culture and Marketing: Defining the Research Agenda," *Journal of Marketing*, 53 (January), 3–15.

Dickson, Peter R. (1996), "The Static and Dynamic Mechanics of Competitive Theory," *Journal of Marketing*, 60 (October), 102–6.

Dierickx, Ingemar and Karel Cool (1989), "Asset Stock Accumulation and Sustainability of Competitive Advantage," *Management Science*, 35 (December), 1504–11.

Falkenberg, Andreas W. (2000), "Competition and Markets," *Journal of Macromarketing*, 20 (June), 8–9.

Ford, D. (1990), *Understanding Business Markets: Interaction, Relationships, and Networks*. London: Academic Press.

Foss, Nicolai (1993), "Theories of the Firm: Contractual and Competence Perspectives," *Journal of Evolutionary Economics*, 3, 127–44.

——— (2000), "The Dangers and Attractions of Theoretical Eclecticism," *Journal of Macromarketing*, 20 (June), 65–7.

Garda, Robert A. (1988), "Comment on the AMA Task Force Study," *Journal of Marketing*, 52 (October), 32–41.

Grönroos, Christian (1996), "Relationship Marketing: Strategic and Tactical Implications," *Management Decision*, 34 (3), 5–14.

——— (2000), *Service Management and Marketing: A Customer Relationship Management Approach*. New York: John Wiley & Sons.

——— and Evert Gummesson, eds., (1985), *Service Marketing-Nordic School Perspectives*. Stockholm, Sweden: University of Stockholm, Department of Business Administration, Research Report 2..

Gummesson, Evert (1994), "Making Relationship Marketing Operational," *International Journal of Service Industry Management*, 5 (5), 5–20.

——— (1999), *Total Relationship Marketing; Rethinking Marketing Management: From 4Ps to 30Rs*. Woburn, MA: Butterworth-Heinemann.

Hakansson, H., ed., (1982), *International Marketing and Purchasing of Industrial Goods: An Interaction Approach*. Chichester, UK: John Wiley and Sons, Ltd.

Hamel, Gary and Aime Heene (1994), *Competence-Based Competition*. New York: John Wiley & Sons.

———— and C.K. Prahalad (1989), "Strategic Intent," *Harvard Business Review*, 67 (May–June), 63–76.

———— and ———— (1994a), *Competing for the Future*. Cambridge, MA: Harvard Business School Press.

———— and ———— (1994b), "Competing for the Future," *Harvard Business Review*, 72 (July–August), 122–28.

Heene, Aime and Ron Sanchez (1997), *Competence-Based Strategic Management*. New York: John Wiley & Sons.

Hodgson, Geoffrey M. (1993), *Economics and Evolution*. Ann Arbor, MI: University of Michigan Press.

———— (2000), "The Marketing of Wisdom: Resource-Advantage Theory," *Journal of Macromarketing,* 20 (June), 68–72.

Houston, Franklin (1986), "The Marketing Concept: What It Is and What It Is Not," *Journal of Marketing*, 50 (April), 81–7.

Hunt, Shelby D. (1992), "Marketing Is . . . ," *Journal of the Academy of Marketing Science*, 20 (4), 301–11.

———— (1995), "The Resource-Advantage Theory of Competition: Toward Explaining Productivity and Economic Growth," *Journal of Management Inquiry,* 4 (December), 317–32.

———— (1997a), "Competing through Relationships: Grounding Relationship Marketing in Resource Advantage Theory," *Journal of Marketing Management,* 13, 431–45.

———— (1997b), "Evolutionary Economics, Endogenous Growth Models, and Resource-Advantage Theory," *Eastern Economic Journal*, 23 (4), 425–39.

———— (1997c), "Resource-Advantage Theory: An Evolutionary Theory of Competitive Firm Behavior?" *The Journal of Economic Issues,* 31 (March), 59–77.

———— (1997d), "Resource-Advantage Theory and the Wealth of Nations," *The Journal of Socio-Economics,* 26 (4), 335–57.

———— (1998), "Productivity, Economic Growth, and Competition: Resource Allocation or Resource Creation?" *Business and the Contemporary World*, 10 (3), 367–94.

———— (1999), "The Strategic Imperative and Sustainable Competitive Advantage: Public Policy and Resource Advantage Theory," *Journal of Academy of Marketing Science,* 27 (2), 144–59.

———— (2000a), "The Competence-Based, Resource-Advantage, and Neoclassical Theories of Competition: Toward a Synthesis." In R. Sanchez and A. Heene, eds., *Theory Development for Competence-Based Management*. Vol. 6(a), in Advances in Applied Business Strategy Series. Greenwich, CT: JAI Press, 177–209.

———— (2000b), *A General Theory of Competition: Resources, Competences, Productivity, Economic Growth*. Thousand Oaks, CA: Sage Publications.

———— (2000c), "A General Theory of Competition: Too Eclectic or Not Eclectic Enough? Too Incremental or Not Incremental Enough? Too Neoclassical or Not Neoclassical Enough?" *Journal of Macromarketing,* 20 (1), 77–81.

———— (2000d), "Synthesizing Resource-Based, Evolutionary and Neoclassical Thought: Resource-Advantage Theory as a General Theory of Competition," in *Resources, Technology, and Strategy*, N.J. Foss and P. Robertson, eds. London: Routledge, 53–79.

———— (2001), "A General Theory of Competition: Issues, Answers, and an Invitation," *European Journal of* Marketing, 35 (5/6), 524–48.

———— (2002a), *Foundations of Marketing Theory: Toward a General Theory of Marketing*. Armonk, NY: M.E. Sharpe.

———— (2002b), "Marketing and a General Theory of Competition," *Journal of Marketing Management*, 18 (1–2), 239–47.

———— (2002c), "Resource-Advantage Theory and Austrian Economics." in *Entrepreneurship and the Firm: Austrian Perspectives on Economic Organization*, N.J. Foss and P. Klein, eds. Cheltenham, UK: Edward Elgar Publishing, Inc, 248–72.

———— (2004), "On the Service-Centered Dominant Logic for Marketing," *Journal of Marketing*, 68 (January), 21–2.

———— and Dennis B. Arnett (2001), "Competition as an Evolutionary Process and Antitrust Policy," *Journal of Public Policy and Marketing*, 20 (1), 15–25.

———— and ———— (2003), "Resource-Advantage Theory and Embeddedness: Explaining R-A Theory's Explanatory Success," *Journal of Marketing Theory and Practice* (Winter), 1–16.

———— and ———— (2004), "Market Segmentation Strategy, Competitive Advantage, and Public Policy: Grounding Segmentation Strategy in Resource-Advantage Theory," *Australasian Marketing Journal*, 12 (1), 7–25.

———— and Caroline Derozier (2004), "The Normative Imperatives of Business and Marketing Strategy: Grounding Strategy in Resource-Advantage Theory," *Journal of Business & Industrial Marketing*, 19 (1), 5–22.

———— and Dale F. Duhan (2002), "Competition in the Third Millennium: Efficiency or Effectiveness?" *Journal of Business Research*, 55 (2), 97–102.

———— and C. Jay Lambe (2000), "Marketing's Contribution to Business Strategy: Market Orientation, Relationship Marketing, and Resource-Advantage Theory," *International Journal of Management Reviews*, 2 (1), 17–44.

————, C. Jay Lambe, and C. Michael Wittman, (2002), "A Theory and Model of Business Alliance Success," *Journal of Relationship Marketing*, 1 (1), 17–36.

———— and Robert M. Morgan (1994), "Relationship Marketing in the Era of Network Competition," *Marketing Management*, 3 (1), 19–28.

———— and ———— (1995), "The Comparative Advantage Theory of Competition," *Journal of Marketing*, 59 (April), 1–15.

———— and ———— (1996), "The Resource-Advantage Theory of Competition: Dynamics, Path Dependencies, and Evolutionary Dimensions," *Journal of Marketing*, 60 (October), 107–114.

———— and ———— (1997), "Resource-Advantage Theory: A Snake Swallowing its Tail or a General Theory of Competition?" *Journal of Marketing*, 61 (October), 74–82.

Kohli, A.K. and Bernard Jaworski (1990), "Market Orientation: The Construct, Research Propositions, and Managerial Implications," *Journal of Marketing*, 54 (April), 1–18.

Lado, Augustine, Nancy Boyd, and P. Wright (1992), "A Competency-Based Model of Sustainable Competitive Advantage," *Journal of Management*, 18 (1), 77–91.

Lambe, C. Jay, Robert N. Spekman, and Shelby D. Hunt (2002), "Alliance Competence, Resources, and Alliance Success: Conceptualization, Measurement, and Initial Test," *Journal of the Academy of Marketing Science*, 30 (2), 141–58.

Langlois, Richard N. and P.L. Robertson (1995), *Firms, Markets and Economic Change: A Dynamic Theory of Business Institutions*. London: Routledge.

Lippman, S.A. and R.P. Rumelt (1982), "Uncertain Imitability," *Bell Journal of Economics*, 13, 418–38.

Morgan, R.E. and Shelby D. Hunt (2002), "Determining Marketing Strategy: A Cybernetic Systems Approach to Scenario Planning," *European Journal of Marketing*, 36 (4), 450–78.

Morgan, Robert M. and Shelby D. Hunt (1994), "The Commitment-Trust Theory of Relationship Marketing," *Journal of Marketing*, 58 (July), 20–38.

Narver, John C. and Stanley F. Slater (1990), "The Effect of Market Orientation on Business Profitability," *Journal of Marketing*, 54 (October), 20–35.

Nayyan, Praveen and Karen Bantel (1994), "Competitive Agility = A Source of Competitive Advantage Based on Speed and Variety," *Advances in Strategic Management*, 10A, 193–222.

North, Douglass C. (1981), *Institutions, Institutional Change, and Economic Performance*. Cambridge, UK: University of Cambridge Press.

Penrose, Edith T. (1959), *The Theory of the Growth of the Firm*. London: Basil Blackwell and Mott.

Prahalad, C.K. and Gary Hamel (1990), "The Core Competence of the Corporation," *Harvard Business Review*, 68 (May–June), 79–91.

———— and ———— (1993), "Strategy as Stretch and Leverage," *Harvard Business Review*, 71 (March/April), 63–76.

Priem, R.L. and Butler, J.E. (2001), "Is the Resource-Based 'View' a Useful Perspective for Strategic Management Research?" *Academy of Management Review*, 26 (1), 22–40.

Reed, Richard and Robert J. De Fillippi (1990), "Causal Ambiguity, Barriers to Imitation, and Sustainable Competitive Advantage," *Academy of Management Review*, 15 (January), 88–117.

Roehl, Tom (1996), "The Role of International R&D in the Competence-Building Strategies of Japanese Pharmaceutical Firms," in *Dynamics of Competence-Based Competition*, R. Sanchez, A. Heene, and H. Thomas, eds. New York: Elsevier Science, 377–96.

Rumelt, Richard P. (1984), "Toward a Strategic Theory of the Firm," in *Competitive Strategic Management*, R. Lamb, ed. Englewood Cliffs, NJ: Prentice Hall, 556–70.

Sanchez, Ron and Aime Heene (1997), *Strategic Learning and Knowledge Management*. New York: John Wiley & Sons.

———— and ————, eds. (2000), *Theory Development for Competence-Based Management*, Vol. 6(A) in Advances in Applied Business Strategy Series. Greenwich, CT: JAI Press, 177–209.

————, Aime Heene, and Howard Thomas (1996), *Dynamics of Competence-Based Competition*. New York: John Wiley & Sons.

Schulze, William S. (1994), "The Two Schools of Thought in Resource-Based Theory," in *Advances in Strategic Management*, Vol. 10A, P. Shrivastava, A.S. Huff, and J.E. Dutton, eds. Greenwich, CT: JAI Press, 127–51.

Schumpeter, Joseph A. (1950), *Capitalism, Socialism, and Democracy*. New York: Harper and Row.

Selznick, P. (1957), *Leadership in Administration*. New York: Harper and Row.

Sheth, Jagdish N. (1994), "The Domain of Relationship Marketing," handout at the *Second Research Conference on Relationship Marketing*, Center for Relationship Marketing, Emory University, Atlanta, GA, June 9–11.

———— and A. Parvatiyar (1995), "The Evolution of Relationship Marketing," *International Business Review*, 4 (1), 397–418.

Shugan, Steven M. (2004), "Finance, Operations, and Marketing Conflicts in Service Firms," *Journal of Marketing*, 68 (January), 24–26.

Slater, Stanley F. and John C. Narver (1994), "Does Competitive Environment Moderate the Market Orientation Performance Relationship?" *Journal of Marketing*, 58 (January), 46–55.

Teece, David and Gary Pisano (1994), "The Dynamic Capabilities of Firms: An Introduction," *Industrial and Corporate Change*, 3 (3), 537–56.

————, ————, and Amy Shuen (1997), "Dynamic Capabilities and Strategic Management," *Strategic Management Journal*, 18 (7), 509–33.

Vargo, Stephen L. and Robert F. Lusch (2004), "Evolving to a New Dominant Logic for Marketing," *Journal of Marketing*, 68 (January), 1–17.

Webster, Frederick E., Jr. (1994), "Executing the Marketing Concept," *Marketing Management*, 3 (1), 9–16.

Wernerfelt, Birger (1984), "A Resource-Based View of the Firm," *Strategic Management Journal*, 5 (2), 171–80.

Wong, V. and J. Saunders (1993), "Business Organization and Corporate Success," *Journal of Strategic Marketing*, 1 (March), 20–24.

6

ACHIEVING ADVANTAGE WITH
A SERVICE-DOMINANT LOGIC

GEORGE DAY

Dominant logics and disruptive technologies apparently evolve in the same way. There is a convergence of a stream of contributing technologies, methods, concepts, and theories that crystallize to form something new. This is not an abrupt emergence because the underlying elements change gradually. Instead there is usually a "tipping point" that signals and validates a seemingly radical shift. Thus, the key elements of wireless communication technologies were largely in place four decades before the "cellular revolution" took place (Adner and Levinthal 1999).

Vargo and Lusch (2004) believe we have passed the tipping point in the transition from a goods-centered to a service-dominant (S-D) logic for marketing. My purpose is to stress test their proposition with two questions. First, what are the underlying reasons for this transition? If these enablers have endurance, then this new dominant logic will likely be sustained and advanced. Second, will it change our view of how marketing resources are converted into competitive advantage? If an S-D logic prevails, then it should fundamentally change the mind-sets, schemas, and mental models of managers and researchers that determine how competitive advantage is conceptualized and resources are allocated (Bettis and Prahalad 1995; Prahalad and Bettis 1986).

ENABLING A NEW DOMINANT LOGIC

Many tributaries are feeding the "new" dominant logic, including services marketing, market orientation, customer relationship management, networked markets, mass customization, and interactivity. Each has been a high-profile part of the marketing terrain for at least a decade. Why have they converged now? One common denominator is that each draws on information technology advances that enable the universal connection to knowledge that was once dispersed and hard to reach. The drivers are the acceptance of compatibility standards that enable computer systems to converse, combined with escalating broadband communications and economical computing power.

This connected knowledge system enables the real-time coordination of dispersed organizational activities and groups, the management of cross-functional processes, and the synchronization of the myriad points of customer contact that are integral to the new dominant logic. Yet most firms are far from capitalizing on the possibilities. This means we are still in the early stages of the transition to an S-D logic. Indeed, the tipping point argument readily leads to the conclusion that the rate of transition is likely to accelerate. By facilitating information flows, and the concomitant knowledge sharing and utilization, these enablers will also speed acceptance of the premise that "knowledge is the fundamental source of competitive advantage" (Vargo and Lusch 2004, p. 9). This raises the question of who will be advantaged versus disadvantaged as the competitive landscape changes and whether these enablers will put limits on where and how an S-D logic is applied.

COMPETING WHEN THE DOMINANT LOGIC CHANGES

An S-D logic implies that firms will increasingly compete with customized solutions, realized through interactions and relationships, and involving the customer as co-producer of the relational value that is created. Although the enabling conditions are converging to encourage wider acceptance of this logic, many firms will not absorb it into their strategy. To understand the conditions in which the shift in dominant logic will lead to changes in the strategy game board, we will assign the relevant foundational premises according to whether they influence the sources of advantages or the positional advantages realized in the market.

The sources —>positions —>performance framework (Day and Wensley 1988) distinguishes between the resources that are the source of a competitive advantage, and the consequent positional advantages and relative performance outcomes, as shown in Figure 6.1. This is a cyclical process that relies on the consistency and alignment of the elements to achieve advantage, and continuous reinvestment and learning to sustain the advantage. This framework has been applied in the general theory of marketing within resource-advantage theory (Hunt 2000).

Sources of Advantage

Sources of advantage are the operant resources the firm deploys, comprising the assets such as networks, patents, and facilities that can be valued and traded, and the capabilities that enable these assets to be deployed advantageously. These capabilities apply the firm's knowledge and skills to the core processes of the business. All organizational capabilities must be aligned with a strategic theme that gives direction to the firm and sets strategic priorities so they work in concert to deliver superior relational value. This emphasis on knowledge exercised through core processes is the essence of Vargo and Lusch's (2004) premise of knowledge as the fundamental source of competitive advantage.

The market-driven capabilities of market sensing and customer relating are the pivotal operant resources to master, if the firm is to be able to identify solutions opportunities and work with target customers to co-create the solution (Day 1994). These two capabilities are nested within a complex network with many direct and indirect links to other resources. Sometimes the valuable resource is an adroit combination of capabilities, none of which is superior on its own, but when taken together makes a better package. Then competitive superiority is due to a mixture of (1) the weighted average efforts—where the business does not rank first on any asset or capability but is better on average that any of its rivals, (2) the firm's superior system integration capabilities, so that all the capabilities are self-reinforcing, or (3) the superior clarity and focus of the strategic thrust that mobilizes the resources.

The emphasis on operant resources within the new dominant logic is well grounded in the resource-based view of the firm. The immediate implication of this theory is that many firms will find it hard to gain and sustain a relational advantage through superior solutions and closer relationships.

A key premise of the resource-based view is that resource and capability development is a selective and path-dependent process. The need for *selectivity* requires an organization to con-

Figure 6.1 **Achieving Advantage**

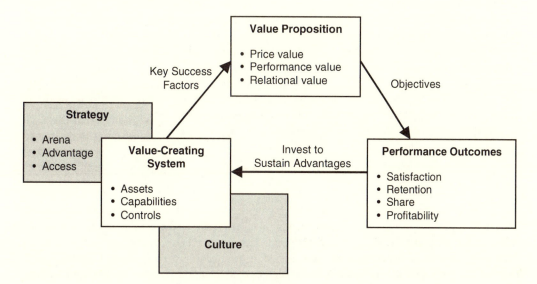

centrate attention on a few capabilities that correspond to the key success factors in the target market. Thus, firms must select whether to make relationship building and superior solutions a central versus a supportive element of their strategy.

Many firms will be unable or unwilling to follow the strategic prescriptions of an S-D logic and will choose a more product-centered transactional approach. Managers may feel they have been preempted by better-qualified rivals, that they lack the financial and organizational resources to undertake the shift, that the promised returns are too distant or uncertain, or that they have a superior opportunity with a price value strategy. This strategy caters to the (often-growing) price-sensitive segment that simply wants the best price for an acceptable quality and puts a premium on reducing cost, through the simplification of operations and offerings, and achieving economies of scale. Such a strategy may also be narrower in scope than a relational value emphasis, since it doesn't entail bundling complementary products and services and orchestrating complex partnerships.

There is path dependency in the choice of resources to develop in that the sense that firms build on what they know (Cohen and Levinthal 1990). Behind the immediate choices are histories of prior choices that sensitize them to certain issues, create a knowledge platform on which they can keep building and constrain or "lock in" the firm to a particular path.

The choice of a new strategic direction derived from the new dominant logic must overcome the inertia from this path dependency. But an entrenched logic that is built into the mind-set and mental models of managers is hard to change. First, the old logic must be unlearned (Bettis and Prahalad 1995). This can be a slow process because the prevailing dominant logic both supports and is reinforced by the current strategy and structure.

Those firms whose cultural DNA and resource heritage are congruent with a relational value strategy won't have to overcome inertia. But what could motivate a firm starting with a different legacy to overcome their momentum and follow the prescriptions of the S-D logic? Perhaps they anticipate a strategic opportunity and want to pursue it before they are locked out by present or prospective competitors. This is especially likely when a relational value strategy creates high customer-switching costs. Alternatively, they may be energized by the threat that their rivals are maneuvering to get ahead by aligning themselves to meet emerging customer requirements for greater relational value, and they fear that if they do not move quickly, they may not be able to overcome the disadvantage of being a follower.

Both these motives for pursuing the implications of the new dominant logic of competition are given further impetus by the sustainability premise of the resource-based view. According to this premise, key resources keep their value when they are protected from imitation by causal ambiguity. There is causal ambiguity when it is unclear to competitors how the source of advantage works. Causal ambiguity deepens when the resource is based on a complex pattern of coordination in a process. The complexities of a solutions strategy enabled by the new dominant logic will be hard to master—but even harder to copy.

Positions of Advantage

What we see in the market—from the vantage point of the customer or competitor—is the positional superiority achieved with superior capability. This requires the reliable provision of superior value to customers on the attributes they judge important when they make a choice. Whether there is a relational advantage per se depends first on the customer's judgment that having a close relationship with a supplier confers benefits that exceed the costs. Typical benefits include time savings, technical assistance, assurance of performance, access to latest developments (e.g., in software and technology), superior responsiveness to service requests or problems, and superior fit to the customer's needs because of personalized solutions. Of course, the customer must feel these benefits outweigh any costs due to loss of flexibility and the restricted ability to play one supplier against another.

The strongest positional advantages are gained when customers are willing to make mutual commitments through their engagement in the value-creation process. This is consistent with the sixth and seventh foundational premises that "the enterprise can only offer value propositions; the consumer must determine value and participate in creating it through the process of co-production (Vargo and Lusch 2004, p. 11).

The crux of Vargo and Lusch's argument is that a service perspective is superior to a goods-centered view because it emphasizes solutions and "points toward opportunities for expanding the market through assisting the consumer in the process of specialization and value creation" (Vargo and Lusch 2004, p. 12). This is not a new insight. Fully 63 percent of the Fortune 100 already claim to offer solutions (Sharma, Lucier, and Molloy 2002). But have these firms really encoded the concept of solutions in their dominant logic or is it merely a fashionable statement of intent?

It is unlikely that most firms are pursuing a true solutions strategy as advocated by Vargo and Lusch (2004). This would mean satisfying the following five criteria for a deep relationship that transfers a supplier's skills and knowledge to a customer who lacks them: First, it requires the *integration* of products with services to offer a complete bundle of benefits. Second there is a two-way *interaction* that results in mutual commitments ranging from information exchanges to cross-firm coordination and even relation-specific investments. This implies two further criteria: that the solution is *co-produced* by the customer and supplier and is *tailored* to each customer. Finally, the solution might also mean some absorption of the *customer's risk.* In light of these stringent criteria, arm's length referrals, one-stop shopping, or even tailoring a personal computer to suit a customer's desired configuration don't qualify as services-centered solutions.

An important caution is that many customers may only willingly enter into a few close and committed relationships. They may resist the kind of operational entanglements based on relationship-specific assets that create switching costs (Dyer and Singh 1998), such as (1) location of assets in close proximity, (2) tailoring of physical assets, or (3) human asset specificity achieved through co-specialization and shared knowledge. For example, GE Plastics installs sensors in the storage silos of injection molder customers to signal an automatic reorder when volume gets low. It takes a lot of iterative learning to make this work, which underscores the participatory and dynamic nature of the new dominant logic. But not every customer may want to subordinate their ability to bargain with suppliers or expose themselves to the risk of a single source. Thus, both product-centered and S-D logics will coexist in most markets.

Performance Outcomes

We would expect a relationship advantage to be rewarded with lower rates of defection (churn), greater loyalty and retention, and higher profit margins than the competitors. But the linkage from positional to performance outcome has proven troublesome to understand because of confounding effects, and a relationship advantage is no exception. First, customers buy a complete package of benefits, so it may be difficult to untangle the contribution made by the relationship itself. Second, the construct of loyalty is itself difficult to study. Much of the attention has focused on proxy measures such as satisfaction, which have a complex, asymmetric relationship to loyalty. Whereas loyal customers are likely to be satisfied customers, all satisfied customers will not be loyal (Oliver 1999). Loyalty is gained with a combination of performance superiority that ensures high satisfaction, plus trust and mutual commitments.

WHAT ROLE FOR MARKETING?

The emerging dominant logic has many implications, but they are not entirely what Vargo and Lusch have in mind. They believe marketing should be at the center of the integration and coordination of the cross-functional processes of a service-dominant business model. But this depends on what is meant by *marketing*. It will probably not be the marketing function or group that is found in most firms. Instead, it will be marketing as a general management responsibility of the top team that will play the crucial roles of:

- *Navigation* through effective market sensing and sharing of information, and early anticipation of market opportunities and competitive moves.
- *Articulation* by designing and refining the new value proposition in light of the prospects of gaining a competitive advantage through relational value.
- *Orchestration* by providing the essential "glue" that ensures there is alignment of all the sources of advantage toward the strategy or superior relational value, and adapted to shifting customer requirements and competitive moves.

These three roles will be played most effectively in a market-driven organization that has superior skills in understanding, attracting, and keeping the most valuable of their customers (Day 1999). This is another validation of the conclusion by Vargo and Lusch that the new dominant logic is inherently customer centered and market driven.

However, marketing plays different roles within the firm—depending on the choice of customers and value proposition, the dynamics of competition, whether the relational value position has been preempted, and the potential for solutions and service differentiation. For the same reasons, we do not expect the S-D logic to apply in all situations or in all companies. The range of application of this emerging logic is continually expanding, as companies see new possibilities for advantage and the enabling conditions continue to be nourished.

REFERENCES

Adner, Ron and Daniel A. Levinthal (1999), "Technology Speciation and the Path of Emerging Technologies," in *Wharton on Managing Emerging Technologies,* George S. Day and Paul Schoemaker, eds. New York: John Wiley & Sons, 57–74.

Bettis, Richard A. and C. K. Prahalad (1995), "The Dominant Logic: Retrospective and Extensions" *Strategic Management Journal,* 16, 5–14.

Cohen, William and Daniel Levinthal (1990), "Absorptive Capacity: A New Perspective on Learning and Innovation," *Administration Science Quarterly,* 35, 128–52.

Day, George S. and Robin Wensley (1988), "Assessing Advantage: A Framework for Diagnosing Competitive Advantage," *Journal of Marketing*, 52 (April), 1–20.

Day, George S. (1994), "The Capabilities of Market-Driven Organizations," *Journal of Marketing*, 58 (October), 37–52.

——— (1999), *The Market-Driven Organization.* New York: The Free Press.

Dyer, Jeff H. and Harbir Singh (1998), "The Relational View: Cooperative Strategy and Sources of Interorganizational Competitive Advantage," *Academy of Management Review,* 23 (4), 660–79.

Hunt, Shelby D. (2000), *A General Theory of Competition: Resources, Competences, Productivity, Economic Growth.* Thousand Oaks, CA: Sage Publications.

Oliver, Richard L. (1999), "Whence Consumer Loyalty," *Journal of Marketing,* 63, 33–44.

Prahalad, C.K. and Richard A. Bettis (1986), "The Dominant Logic: A New Linkage between Diversity and Performance," *Strategic Management Journal,* 7 (6), 485–501.

Sharma, Deven, Chuck Lucier, and Richard Molloy (2002), "From Solutions to Symbiosis: Blending with Your Customers," *Strategy and Business* (Second Quarter), 38–43.

Vargo, Stephen L. and Robert F. Lusch (2004), "Evolving to a New Dominant Logic for Marketing," *Journal of Marketing,* 68 (1), 1–17.

7

TOWARD A CULTURAL RESOURCE-BASED THEORY OF THE CUSTOMER

Eric J. Arnould, Linda L. Price, and Avinash Malshe

The dominant logic of marketing is shifting from a firm-centric view of value creation to one that examines how customers engage themselves in the value-creation process (Prahalad and Ramaswamy 2003; Vargo and Lusch 2004). The goal of this chapter is to advance a model that is better suited to dialectical value creation and a customer-centric orientation of the firm. In so doing we hope to bridge the gap between the forward-thinking managerial literature that calls for co-creation of value but falls short in its conceptualization of consumers' rich value-creative competencies, and recent consumer research produced by the Consumer Culture Theory school of thought (Arnould and Thompson 2005), which articulates an emergent theory of consumers' co-creative competence but is only erratically tied to managerial models.[1]

Vargo and Lusch (2004) argue that the new dominant logic for marketing is focused more on operant than operand resources. Briefly, operant resources are employed to act on operand resources and other operant resources. Operant resources are often invisible and intangible; at the firm level they include core competencies (knowledge and skills) or dynamic capabilities. Operand resources are tangible resources, especially goods or raw materials, over which a consumer or a firm has allocative capabilities to act in order to carry out a behavioral performance. In the managerial framework, this evolving perspective views the customer primarily as a source of operant resources for the firm, co-producing the value derived from exchanges with the firm.

The specific purpose of this chapter is to complement Vargo and Lusch's thinking by focusing on consumers' operant and operand resources. First we overview and define consumers' resources. Next we depict how operant resources of customers and firms come together to co-create value through patterns of experiences and meanings embedded in the cultural life-worlds of consumers. This analysis is then extended to illustrate new sets of problems brought into relief by the interaction of consumer and firm operant resources. Finally, we outline opportunities for new firm value propositions through improved links to consumers' operant resources. As part of this analysis we envision extensions to definitions of customer equity focused on *both* consumer operand and operant resources, in contrast to a conventional focus on consumers' operand resources alone.

CONSUMERS' OPERANT AND OPERAND RESOURCES

Figure 7.1 suggests a way to think about consumers from the vantage point of marketing's evolving logic. At the center of the figure is the consumer who actively juggles an evolving set of roles over

Figure 7.1 **The Consumer's Operant and Operand Resources**

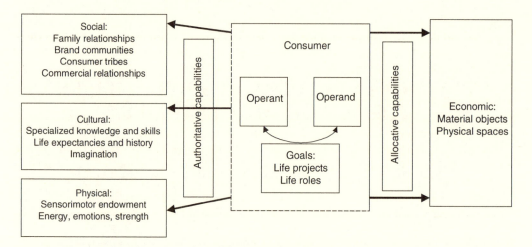

the life cycle and across social contexts. At the same time, the consumer also pursues a set of life projects or enacts a life narrative that may vary in complexity (Arnould and Price 2000). To enact these roles and to pursue these projects, the consumer deploys both operant and operand resources.

On the right side of Figure 7.1 we show the consumer's stock of operand resources. Operand resources are tangible resources, especially various culturally constituted economic resources (e.g., income, inherited wealth, food stamps, vouchers, credit), and goods or raw materials over which the consumer has allocative capabilities to carry out behavioral performances including social roles or life projects.

The consumer's operand resources include a complement of material objects that vary in quantity and quality. Many will be objects acquired from exchanges with marketers; others include gifts, inherited special possessions, found objects, and self-created ones. The consumer will also control some physical spaces such as a dwelling, workstation, or garden. Subject to social norms and legal restrictions, consumers exert partial or full allocative authority over these objects or spaces. Consumers' stock of operand resources affects their exchange behaviors with firms, but research could provide greater insight into consumers' goal-oriented use of operand resources. For example, we know homeless or impoverished consumers' life roles and life projects differ qualitatively from those with stable dwellings and average incomes, and this in turn affects how they allocate their operand resources.

Consumers' operand resources enable them to achieve goals based on distinctive deployments of firms' operant resources. Thus, some lower-income immigrant consumers favor the use of check-cashing and money-transferring services because these enable them to achieve their focused economic goals of transferring maximal remittances to stay-behind family members (Neyapti 2004). Embedded in this preference is the goal of sustaining family support networks across geographic space (Poirine 1997). Wealthy consumers, in contrast, might develop a preferred customer relationship with a bank because it allows them access to a multitude of services that facilitate their personal financial projects, for example, to move high-cost credit card debt to low-cost home equity debt. High-income consumers may mobilize multiple operand resources provided by the bank such as Internet-based and interpersonal communication channels in achieving their goals.

Consistent with recent theory on social structuration, operant and operand resources closely interact with one another, and shape both consumers' life projects and goals (Sewell 1992; Swidler 1986). The configuration of operant resources influences how consumers employ their operand resources and their use of firms' operand and operant resources. Therefore, instead of focusing purely on customers' operand resources such as how much economic power the consumer has, firms must be mindful about the operant resources consumers possess and bring to the exchange process. These resources determine which firm resources customers are going to draw on and how they will deploy firms' operand resources in value creation. Since customers' life projects/ goals are a configuration of operant resources, focus on these operant resources will enable firms to anticipate customers' desired values and help them create value in use.

The left side of Figure 7.1 shows the consumer's stock of operant resources, including physical, social, and cultural ones. Each type of operant resource is linked to cultural schemas—that is, "generalized procedures applied in the enactment of social life" (Giddens 1984, p. 21) including conventions, traditions, recipes, habits of speech and gesture, and so on; in other words, they are virtual resources. Like core competencies, they can be applied in or extended to a variety of contexts or transposed to new situations when the opportunity arises (Sewell 1992). For example, physical skills are contextualized within cultural templates for playing cricket, musical instruments, and so on, but these skills can be transposed to new contexts, as when cricket players adapt to baseball.

Whereas from the perspective of the firm, the customer is primarily an operant resource, we argue the reverse is also true from the perspective of the customer. That is, the firm figures primarily as one of many sources of operant resources customers draw on in achieving their life projects and performing their life roles (Huffman, Ratneshwar, and Mick 1999). Consumers act upon firm-produced resources to perform, recover, or even create preferred cultural schemas— some firm driven, others customer driven. For example, consumers may draw on a variety of firm-produced resources to co-create a "cozy home" or a "traditional holiday feast" as part of a bigger project of creating "a happy family" (Wallendorf and Arnould 1991).

In consumer research, a neglected element of operant resources consists of physical resources. Consumers vary in their physical and mental endowments. This affects their life roles and projects; for example, low literate and physically challenged consumers' life roles and life projects appear to differ qualitatively from those with average physical resource endowments. The low stock of physical resources and the consequentially different life goals may prompt the consumer to adopt different strategies in employing their own and the firms' operant and operand resources. For example, consumers who are legally blind employ other operant physical resources, such as other senses, and effort to a greater degree in order to compensate for the lack of vision. They might also exert authority over social operant resources during the exchange process—asking a friend or family member to accompany them and offer assistance and opinions (Baker, Stephens, and Hill 2001). Through understanding customers' operant physical resources, firms can tailor their offerings including virtual environments that relieve physical constraints, or in the case of blind consumers, ways to identify colors and various food packages through a labeling system or by location.

Marketing management scholars often propound an implicit theory of consumers as asocial isolates. However, recent research in consumer culture theory shows that customers deploy a second type of operant resources: social operant resources. Social operant resources are networks of relationships with others including traditional demographic groupings (families, ethnic groups, social class) and emergent groupings (brand communities, consumer tribes and subcultures, friendship groups) over which consumers exert varying degrees of command (Giddens 1979). If people exert allocative capabilities over operand resources, we may say they exert authoritative capabilities over social operant resources.

Some research already recognizes social connections as a consumer operant resource. A series of studies show that while making a brand choice, consumers heavily draw on their social connections. Brand choice depends upon a complex mix of type of product, type of social relations the consumer possesses, and the type of social structural unit the consumer belongs to. This research demonstrates that customers differentially deploy their strong and weak social ties with others, affecting both macro- and micro-level word-of-mouth processes. This research also shows that mobilizing social operant resources affects cultural schema and outcomes of interest to firms such as brand choices (Sirsi, Ward, and Reingen 1996; Ward and Reingen 1990).

Research has clearly delineated the value of other co-consumers for consumers. First, co-consuming groups represent a form of consumer agency. Enhanced by computer-mediated communication (everything from chat rooms, sponsored Web sites, and consumer-to-consumer marketing networks to new things like the Dodgeball program for cell phones), consumer groups have a greater voice in the co-creation of value than in the more atomistic situations that prevailed in the recent past. Second, co-consuming communities represent an important information resource for participants. Co-consumer participants in brand fests and other such manifestations can not only easily turn to one another for information about products and brand, but share cultural schema nuances associated with how to consume the product or brand creatively, and interpret these experiences "properly" (Cova and Cova 2001). Co-creative experience of the product or brand is enhanced, but—of equal significance—schemas are sustained and or reproduced over time through operant resources that accumulate through these enactments (Sewell 1992, p. 16). Third, co-consuming groups often exhibit a sense of moral responsibility that translates to socialization of other co-consumers. In particular, building on the interconnected structure of relationships and sentiments, ritual activities in consumption-oriented groupings facilitate, create, and reproduce community. Fourth, co-consuming groups tend to bring a relatively celebratory ethos to the consumption context. In short, participation in co-consuming groups provides and reinforces consumers' operant resources.

A final element of Figure 7.1 is the consumer's cultural operant resources. Consumer culture theorists conceive of cultural operant resources as varying amounts and kinds of knowledge of cultural schemas, including specialized cultural capital, skills, and goals. Holt (1998) systematically explored cultural operant resources' relationship to taste and consumption. With regard to homes, food, and fashion, he demonstrates how the consumption practices of those with large endowments of cultural operant resources tend to be oriented around abstraction, subjectivity, and self-expression; in contrast, the consumption practices of those with smaller stores of cultural operant resources tend to be oriented around mastering material constraints on consumption aspirations, functionality, and tradition.

In a study of consumers' decisions to attend a two-year technical commercial school, Allen (2002) shows that consumers with low cultural operant resources treat an embodied experience of comfort and fit as the sole basis of their choice of economical, quick, applied, clerical training. Criteria such as possibilities for personal growth, career choice, or the realization of abstract life projects do not inform their choices, and they express distaste for the attitudes and behaviors of consumers high in operant cultural resources (e.g., theoretical knowledge). Similarly, in a study of members of Winnebago-Itasca Travelers' Clubs, Peters (2004) showed that a restricted conceptual vocabulary of motive, emphasizing technical problem solving, and simple fun, friendship, and fellowship appealed to potential members.

Consumers' endowments of cultural operant resources vary not only in quantity, but also in quality. For example, Schouten and McAlexander (1995) show that subsegments of Harley-

Davidson owners deployed distinctive cultural operant resources. And Arnould, Price, and Tierney (1998) show that consumers' experiences of commercial wilderness adventures tend to divide into four narrative themes. Far from being unique to this commercial context, these narrative themes instead reflect four long-standing American cultural schemas regarding the wilderness.

The type, quantity, and quality of consumer operant resources brought to an exchange process affect the value consumers seek from exchange and the roles they expect themselves and firms to play in exchange. Much remains to be done to systematize our understanding of consumers' operant resources. As the preceding discussion suggests, firms must understand how consumers juggle their own and firm resources in order to compensate for specific types of operant resource deficits. Firms must have a clear understanding of the kinds of cultural operant resources consumers bring to an exchange process and how they use these resources, because these dynamics determine the choice criteria employed by the customer, the value they seek from the "appliances" firms provide, and their subsequent interactions with them.

FIRM AND CUSTOMER RESOURCE INTERACTION

Consumer research demonstrates consumers' experiences with brands/organizations are deeply context dependent and vary with sociocultural settings (Coulter, Price, and Feick 2003). Ample evidence affirms that through the deployment of consumer operant resources, consumers engage brands and organizations to co-create value in interactive and sometimes unanticipated ways. Consumers' imaginative transposition of schema, reinterpretation of resources in terms of alternate schema, and unexpected accumulations of resources enliven and alter firms' value propositions. Figure 7.2 suggests a way to think about the value-creation process from a resource interaction perspective. The focal element of this figure is the central portion in which consumer experience unfolds. As suggested in the figure, firms deploy operant resources to mold firm operand resources. Through these processes they present a package of elements—"appliances" in Vargo and Lusch's (2004, p. 7) terminology—to the market that takes the form of a value proposition. Consumers are invited to derive benefit through value-creation processes.

Marketing as a managerial practice has made almost all operant resources potentially available as consumables, organizing a virtually inexhaustible intersection of operant and operand resources and preexisting cultural schemas (Sewell 1992, p. 26). Some marketers' value propositions provide operant resources such as images, symbols, and myths that inspire the imagination of individuals and entire consumption communities. For example, Nike is the Greek goddess of victory, an appropriate symbol for a firm committed to performance, and one appropriated by at least some lifestyle groups (Segalen and Frère-Michelat 1994). In the Harley brand community, key consumer images form as new bikers engage with mass media images of outlaw bikers as well as other archetypes such as the cowboy, partaking in cultural constructions of masculinity inscribed in Harleys through intertextual linkages to film, pulp fiction, and television (Schouten and McAlexander 1995). Members of the X-Philes culture derive values of the deeply rooted Western quest myth, often connected to the widespread American belief in UFOs (Kozinets 1997). And *Star Trek* fans draw on utopian ideals and aspirational visions reproduced across the five television series and seven commercial films produced (Kozinets 2001).

In some cases, consumers may use firm-produced packages precisely as imagined by firms to derive more or less the value firms invest in their packages, wearing Nike shoes as a vehicle to "just do it," or using OnStar navigation systems to find their way around, for example. In this case, the firm provides the lion's share of the value-in-use. Commonly, however, consumers deploy operant resources in creative ways and derive value-in-use from the firms' package of

Figure 7.2 **Firm and Consumer Resource Interaction**

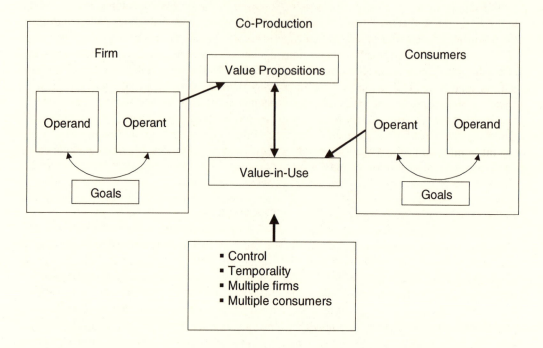

services in ways that vary from firm intent. For instance, consumers of American Girl dolls contribute imaginative resources by incorporating the dolls into individual life narratives, family history, and the teaching of American history (Kozinets, Sherry, and Diamond 2003).

Research on brand icons and the design and management of servicescapes (both built and natural) and the systematic effects they exert over consumer experiences has contributed significantly to theoretical understanding of how firms can predispose consumers to deploy operant cultural resources. These studies highlight how iconic brands and servicescapes transform imaginative resources into material realities and, furthermore, how treasured mythic resources (e.g., the Outsider, the Wild West, Horatio Alger tales of athletic achievement, or revitalization through nature) are reworked to serve commercial aims and to channel consumer experiences in certain ways (Holt 2004; Peñaloza 2000, 2001; Price, Arnould, and Tierney 1995: Sherry 1998). Just as a store layout can direct consumers' physical movements through retail space, the design of brand images and servicescapes can activate cultural operant resources in ways that direct the course of consumers' mental attention, experiences, and related practices of self-narration (Kozinets et al. 2004), enabling them to experience self-authentication or authoritative linkage to valued others (Arnould and Price 2000).

In some cases, the consumers' contributions of operant resources may outweigh the firm's contribution of operant resources. When a product becomes the focus of a brand community or consumer subculture, the consuming community could take over the value proposition in ways that are discrepant from firm intentions. This happened to the clothing brand Tommy Hilfiger that briefly became emblematic of membership in hip-hop culture. In an extreme case, Apple Newton consumers actually assumed control of the brand, taking over core marketing functions including sales and service from Apple, which abandoned the brand due to disappointing initial sales and bad public relations. Because of perceived betrayal by the brand, many Newton consumers have become fervent and vocal critics of Apple (Muñiz and O'Guinn 2001; Muñiz and Schau 2005).

Firms and consumers can provide discrepant contributions to the co-productive process. Thus, secondhand stores such as Goodwill or Salvation Army outlets provide a very basic price- and function-based assortment and value proposition. Some consumers, however, engage in luxury shopping, the purchase of excess, self-gifting, and deriving "pleasures of the hunt" through the deployment of imaginative cultural schema in identifying high-end brands, antiques, and collectibles from the firm-supplied operand resources. Thus, consumers layer discrepant schema on the baseline frugality value proposition offered by these secondhand stores (Bardhi and Arnould, forthcoming). Something like the opposite case happened with Benetton, whose controversial socially progressive advertisements led to a major clash with retailers, who blamed declining retail sales on the weight of discrepant meanings heaped on the sportswear label (Barela 2003). Such cases suggest the importance of attending to customers' value-in-use and co-opting consumers' competencies to modify or extend the firm's offerings.

One of the key benefits of adopting the resource interaction perspective is that it draws attention to the fact that co-production does not take place in a vacuum. Four elements condition the co-production process between consumer and firm. One important conditioning element is control (Meuter and Bitner 1998). The domain of experience varies in locus of control from those that are heavily under the firm's control, such as themed retail environments or corporate sporting events, to those that are under joint control such as the Denver stock show (Peñaloza 2001), to those heavily under consumers' control such as consumption festivals organized and controlled by consumers. Some of these are brand centered, such as Winnie Weekends (Winnebago Itasca Travelers' Club rallies) (Peters 2004) and Star Trek conventions (Kozinets 2002), whereas others are more loosely construed around consumer-to-consumer markets like swap meets, farmers' markets, garage sales, or performative happenings (Belk, Wallendorf, and Sherry 1989; Cova and Cova 2001). Even ephemeral groups mobilized through the deployment of firm resources might cooperate to produce shared consumption outcomes such as an old-fashioned periodic farmers' market (McGrath, Sherry, and Heisley 1993). Celsi, Rose, and Leigh (1993) note that skydivers share a powerful communal bond that greatly increases their commitment to this activity. Schouten and McAlexander (1995) demonstrate how Harley-Davidson riders derive an important part of their understanding of the brand from the connection they share with one another. Yet this understanding goes much further, to an actual way of life (Muniz and O'Guinn 2001, p. 414).

What is the bottom-line value of shifting control from firm to consumers? In exploratory work, Bendapudi and Leone (2003) show that consumer control over the service production process decreases dissatisfaction with negative outcomes and increases satisfaction with positive service outcomes. Consumer communities that form around firms' value propositions are of evident importance to managers. Communities that form around firm-produced operand resources might influence all the components of brand equity: perceived quality, brand loyalty, brand awareness, and brand associations. As noted previously, such communities carry out important functions on behalf of the brand, such as sharing information, and exerting pressure on members to remain loyal to it.

A second important conditioning element is temporality. The meaning and value of brands change over time in response to changes in ambient cultural environment and to the evolution of consumer goals. Consumers' interpretations of the value of retro brands draw on cultural schema of allegory, arcadia (utopia), authenticity, and paradox (Brown, Sherry, and Kozinets 2003). From the perspective of an individual consumer, temporality plays an important role in the emergent relationship between a customer and service provider (Price and Arnould 1999), and between customers and brands (Aaker, Fournier, and Brasel 2004). In some intergenerational contexts, researchers have shown that brands' value propositions can become emblematic signs of family continuity (Moore, Wilkie, and Lutz 2002; Olsen 1995).

At a more micro level, firms can draw on consumers' operant resources to evolve the relationship and change meanings in different ways. They can invoke consumers' repertoires of memories through their brand communication to imbue their consumption with a sense of continuity and connection to the past. They can also invest their operant resources in building and sustaining brand communities, thus ensuring longevity of consumption meanings through generations of consumers. Firms, over time, might also seek input from consumers, thus co-opting their resources in strategic decisions such as changes in product features, pricing, or product positioning.

A third important conditioning element is the competitive environment created by market offerings from multiple firms. For example, consumers create certain effects in their home environments through combining different branded consumer products (Coupland 2005). Thus, store brands help one informant family create a domestic image of value and tradition, although it is not clear that the firm encodes these meanings into its store brands. Kates (2004) shows across a range of product categories consumers exert imaginative effort to create an environment of preferred "gay friendly" brands, although the firms' brands vary in the degree to which they encode gay friendliness.

A fourth important conditioning element is the existence of multiple customers. Firms compete for customer loyalties, but their relationships with customers are often mediated through customers' social operant resources. That is, consumers might be linked to brands predominantly or only through their links to other people. Mediating social resources could take the form of institutionalized fan or brand communities, families and households, and more ephemeral consumer tribes or virtual gathering points. Brand preferences formed through intergenerational influence within the family contribute to personal identity projects, including protection of identity in transition periods, providing a safe harbor, and risk reduction (Moore, Wilkie, and Lutz 2002).

RESEARCH PROBLEMS AND OPPORTUNITIES

Recognizing consumer operant and operand resources, in the context of consumer life projects and life roles as an organizing framework, throws into relief a variety of research opportunities that go beyond the traditional theoretical foci for consumer research. Some research opportunities flow predominantly from the desire to better understand consumers' operant and operand resources (Figure 7.1). We know from a huge literature that the interplay between consumers' operant and operand resources is significant in the forging and maintenance of consumer identities, and in communicating those identities to others (Kleine and Baker 2004). However, we know relatively little about the interaction among various types of consumer operant resources. Furthermore, we do not know much about how consumers selectively manage expenditures of various types of operant resources. In other words, in what contexts do consumers expend relatively greater operant resources and on what do they expend them? How do consumers convert among operant resources and between operant and operand resources? What is the managerial relevance of this question? If the firm presumes that the consumer is drawing on cultural operant resources (e.g., taste-based preferences), but the consumer is in fact drawing on social operant resources (e.g., social connections to communities or opinion leaders), then communication strategies could be misguided, (Gladwell 2000; Surowiecki 2004).

Other research opportunities flow from the desire to better understand the interplay of consumers' and firms' operant and operand resources (Figure 7.2). Making no claim to exhaust the possibilities, Table 7.1 posits some of these research opportunities.

Table 7.1

Opportunities for Further Research Based on Consumers' Operant Resources

Theory	Traditional theoretical focus	Research opportunity
Brand equity	Product and brand management as an organizing principle; overall goodwill associated with a brand that reflects past marketing performance and predicts future sales and profit	Focus on consumer equity, but also recognize both consumer operant and operand resources contribute to the customer equity of the firm
Branding	A unified communication strategy to convey a strong, consistent, unified value proposition	Encourages consumers' value enrichment through customized links to operant and operand resources, life projects, and roles
Consumer ethnicity	Ethnic group traits, mediated by self-identification and moderated by situation, lead to ethnic consumer behaviors	Consumer ethnicity is dynamic; the interaction of dominant and dominated group operant and operand resources structure consumption behaviors
Consumer knowledge	Cognitive processes, especially memory and meta-memory and their influence on consumer decision making	Ability to activate knowledge stores through operand and operant resources knowledgeably applied but seldom understood reflexively
Consumer lifestyle	Activities, Interests, Opinions (AIO), values, and demographics; linear model from properties of mind to patterned behavioral outcomes	Redefine lifestyles in terms of the coconstitutive relationships between consumers' operant and operand resources in the context of life projects and roles
Consumer motives	Cognitivist theories of planned behavior and goal striving	Examine the interplay among life projects, narratives and roles, and consumers' operant and operand resources
Loyalty	Dyadic focus, usually one-way: "How loyal is the consumer to the firm?"	Distributed loyalties and links between loyalties in a network
Marketing communications	Communicate value propositions of the firm	Engage and direct consumer operant and operand resources (semiotic degrees of freedom associated with the value propositions of the firm and institutionalized meanings)
Satisfaction	Consumer expectancy/disconfirmation framework; "How full is your bucket?" notion	Interplay of firm and consumer operant resources with unlimited potentialities for mutual value enrichment
Servicescapes	Communicative and substantive staging of the servicescape by the service provider	Engage consumers' operant resources to enrich the communicative staging and their operand resources to enrich the substantive staging of the service/servicescape

The domain of branding and brand equity seems ripe for revision. Some work has refocused our attention from brand equity to consumer equity (Blattberg and Deighton 2000; Rust, Lemon, and Zeithaml 2004). The thrust of this research is to build brands and relationships around customer rather than firm requirements. Some research has begun to move researchers toward a co-productive model of the brand (Holt 2004). But devising strategies to figure out how to tap into consumer operant resources to build new brands or to tweak established ones is a work in progress. Some recommend focusing branding strategy on narrow niches to enhance clarity and value in the customers eyes (Rust, Lemon, and Zeithaml 2004), whereas others suggest that brands should be built about broad and deep tensions in consumers cultural operant resources (Holt 2004). Both approaches recognize that brands' values are highly particular. But the former puts control of brand customization in the firms' operant resource endowments, the latter in customers' operant resource endowments. It is likely both strategies are appropriate under certain conditions and fundamentally depend on the interplay of firm and consumer operant resources.

Relatedly, branding strategies have focused on marketing communications that convey a consistent core value proposition to the customer. We view consumers' goals, operant resources, and operand resources as touch points for consumers' value enrichment. Rather than offering a consistent core value proposition, this perspective endorses engaging and enabling customized links that induce an explosion of meanings. An excellent example, mentioned previously, is the American Girl doll, which enlists consumers' imaginative resources to strengthen links between generations, create narrations about family history, facilitate identity work, and reinforce particular values. We might posit that so-called power brands are brands that are linked to multiple operant resources, life projects, and life roles that thereby create multiple strands of meaning connecting consumers to the brand. Instead of focusing on the dyadic relationship between the consumer and the brand, as in traditional research on brand loyalty, attention shifts to how brand meanings are distributed among operant consumer resources, life projects, and life roles.

The focus on operant and operand resources promises to breathe new life into traditional foci for market segmentation. For example, in the domain of lifestyle and ethnic consumer behavior, some researchers question the adequacy of structural models of both concepts. They offer dynamic models that see both ethnicity and lifestyle as co-constitutive relationships between consumers' operant and operand resources in the contexts of mainstream and dominated group operant and operand resources, and the evolution of individual life projects and roles (Askegaard, Arnould, and Kjeldgaard, 2005; Holt 1994, 1998). Indeed, we can envision ethnic categories as co-constructed from firm and consumer operant and operand resources (Wilk 1995).

The idea of segmenting consumers around their operant resources is in its infancy. We can envision the possibility of segmenting around consumers who bring a wealth of cultural and social operant resources to a value proposition in some instances and around those who bring a paucity of resources to their relationship with the brand or firm in others. Such a strategy could be critical to successful co-production of value (Fournier et al. 2000; Kates 2004). Segmentation strategies that are based on particular operant resources would also be available to the firm. For example, such an approach to segmentation could be based on the scope and heterogeneity of consumers' imaginative resources (Chronis, Hampton, and Arnould 2004; Martin 2004). Experiential marketing sometimes promotes the value of customization without recognition of variations in the scope and nature of consumers' operant resources brought to bear on experiences, and pays little attention to the life goals and narratives into which consumers fit their experiences (Bateson 2002). Hence, a resource-based theory of the consumer could contribute to segmentation for experiential marketing.

Behaviorist and rationalist perspectives, both of which situate motivation as purely interior processes, dominate motivational research in consumer behavior (Kernan 2000). A resource-based theory of consumer motive offers a complementary theory pursued through an exploration of the interplay among life projects, narratives, and roles. Resource theory recognizes the richness of consumers' operant cultural resources and attendant projects, including their context ladenness, without overemphasizing their self-knowledge. Resource theory argues that individual motivational resources are always brought to bear in social contexts and are always informed by social templates for the imagination (Belk, Ger, and Askegaard 2003). Resource theory identifies crosscutting motivational projects (Arnould and Price 2000), modernist entrenchments (Arnould and Tissiers-Desbordes, forthcoming), and ironic goal structures (Thompson 2000).

An important implication of our perspective is that the interplay of firm and consumer operant resources should become a central focus for research inquiry. Research on the servicescape is relatively sparse, but of value in beginning to understand this domain. There are ample opportunities to consider how principles related to servicescape management map to interplays of firm and consumer resources outside the conventional boundaries of servicescapes, for example, in the consumers' homes, cars, and so on. Most servicescape research focuses on the substantive staging of the service through management of the firm's operand resources. In discussing dramaturgy and communicative staging of the servicescape, other research has moved more toward an appreciation of the role of firm operant resources in servicescape management (Arnould, Price, and Tierney 1998). However, both the dramaturgical perspective and the more conventional view of consumer participation in service delivery emphasize managerial control at the expense of the engagement of consumers' operant resources. Indeed, as Aubert-Gamet (1997) points out, firms conventionally resist consumers' attempts to exert influence over servicescapes instead of welcoming and guiding their co-creation of value.

CONCLUSION

The aim of our chapter is to begin to bridge the gap between the forward-thinking managerial literature reflected in Vargo and Lusch (2004) and commentaries on their article, and recent consumer research, especially that produced by the Consumer Culture Theory (CCT) school of thought (Arnould and Thompson 2005). The former calls for a new S-D logic that focuses on the co-creation of value but has underconceptualized consumers' rich value-creative competencies. The latter has produced rich insight into consumers' value-creative competencies but is only erratically tied to managerial models. Toward this goal, we first summarized research on consumer operant and operand resources. We then presented a conceptual model of the co-creative process and explored research that provides insight into that model. Finally, we discussed some new research directions opened up by adopting the evolving logic of firm-consumer value creation.

NOTE

1. We draw extensively on the body of research organized under the rubric of consumer culture theory in this chapter (Arnould and Thompson 2005). Rather than provide a complete compendium of references here, we encourage interested readers to refer to Arnould and Thompson (2005).

REFERENCES

Aaker, Jennifer, Susan Fournier, and Adam S. Brasel (2004), "When Good Brands Do Bad," *Journal of Consumer Research*, 31 (June), 1–16.
Allen, Douglas E. (2002), "Toward a Theory of Consumer Choice as Sociohistorically Shaped Practical

Experience: The Fits-Like-a-Glove (FLAG) Framework," *Journal of Consumer Research*, 28 (March), 515–32.

Arnould, Eric J. and Linda L. Price (2000), "Authenticating Acts and Authoritative Performances: Questing for Self and Community," in *The Why of Consumption,* S. Ratneshwar, David Glen Mick, and Cynthia Huffman, eds. New York: Routledge, 140–63.

———, ———, and Patrick Tierney (1998), "Communicative Staging of the Wilderness Servicescape," *Service Industries Journal*, 18 (3), 90–115.

——— and Craig J. Thompson (2005), "Consumer Culture Theory (CCT): Twenty Years of Research, *Journal of Consumer Research,* 31 (March), 868–882.

——— and Elisabeth Tissiers-Desbordes (forthcoming), "Hypermodernity and the New Millennium: Scientific Language as a Tool for Marketing Communications," in *Marketing Communication: Emerging Trends and Developments*, Allan J. Kimmel, ed. Cambridge: Oxford University Press.

Askegaard, Soren, Eric J. Arnould, and Dannie Kjeldgaard (2005), "Post-Assimilationist Ethnic Consumer Research: Qualifications and Extensions," *Journal of Consumer Research*, 31 (March), 160–171.

Aubert-Gamet, Veronique (1997), "Twisting Servicescapes: Diversion of The Physical Environment in a Re-Appropriation Process," *International Journal of Service Industry Management*, 8 (1), 26–41.

Baker, Stacey Menzel, Debra Lynn Stephens, and Ronald Paul Hill (2001), "Marketplace Experiences of Consumers with Visual Impairments: Beyond the Americans with Disabilities Act," *Journal of Public Policy & Marketing*, 20 (Fall), 215–24.

Bardhi, Fleura and Eric J. Arnould (forthcoming), "Thrift Shopping: Combining Utilitarian Thrift and Hedonic Treat Benefits," *Journal of Consumer Behaviour*, 4 (June), 223–234.

Barela, Mark J. (2003), "Executive Insights: United Colors of Benetton—From Sweaters to Success: An Examination of the Triumphs and Controversies of a Multinational Clothing Company," *Journal of International Marketing*, 11 (4), 113–28.

Bateson, John (2002), "Are Your Customers Good Enough for Your Service Business?" *Academy of Management Executive*, 16 (November), 110–20.

Belk, Russell W., Güliz Ger, and Soren Askegaard (2003), "The Fire of Desire: A Multisited Inquiry into Consumer Passion," *Journal of Consumer Research*, 30 (December), 326–52.

———, Melanie Wallendorf, and John F. Sherry, Jr. (1989), "The Sacred and the Profane in Consumer Behavior: Theodicy on the Odyssey," *Journal of Consumer Research*, 16 (June), 1–38.

Bendapudi, Neeli and Robert P. Leone (2003), "Psychological Implications of Customer Participation in Co-Production," *Journal of Marketing*, 67 (January), 14–29.

Blattberg, Robert C. and John Deighton (2000), "Manage Marketing by the Customer Equity Test," *Harvard Business Review* (July–August), 136–44.

Brown, Stephen, John F. Sherry, Jr., and Robert V. Kozinets (2003), "Teaching Old Brands New Tricks: Retro Branding and the Revival of Brand Meaning," *Journal of Marketing*, 67 (July), 19–33.

Celsi, Richard L., Randall L. Rose, and Thomas W. Leigh (1993), "An Exploration of High-Risk Leisure Consumption through Skydiving," *Journal of Consumer Research*, 20 (June), 1–23.

Chronis, Theodorakis, Ronald D. Hampton, and Eric J. Arnould (2004), "Gettysburg Re-Imagined: The Role of Narrative Imagination in Consumption Experience," working paper, Department of Marketing, University of Nebraska.

Coupland, Jennifer Chang (2005), "Invisible Brands: An Ethnography of Households and the Brands in their Kitchen Pantries," *Journal of Consumer Research,* 32 (June). 106–119.

Coulter, Robin Higie, Linda L. Price, and Lawrence Feick (2003), "Rethinking the Origins of Involvement and Brand Commitment: Insights from Postsocialist Central Europe," *Journal of Consumer Research*, 30 (September), 151–70.

Cova, Bernard and Veronique Cova (2001), "Tribal Aspects of Postmodern Consumption Research: The Case of French In-Line Roller Skates," *Journal of Consumer Behaviour*, 1 (June), 67–76.

Fournier, Susan, Sylvia Sensiper, James McAlexander, and John Schouten (2000), *Building Brand Community on the Harley-Davidson Posse Ride, Multimedia Case*. Cambridge, MA: Harvard Business School.

Giddens, Anthony (1979), *Central Problems in Social Theory: Action, Structure and Contradiction in Social Analysis*. London: Macmillan.

——— (1984), *The Constitution of Society: Introduction of the Theory of Structuration*. Berkeley: University of California Press.

Gladwell, Malcolm (2000), *The Tipping Point: How Little Things Can Make a Big Difference*. Boston: Little, Brown.

Holt, Douglas B. (1994), "Consumers' Cultural Differences as Local Systems of Tastes: A Critique of the Personality/Values Approach and an Alternative Framework," in *Asia Pacific Advances in Consumer Research*, 1, Joseph A. Cote and Siew Meng Leong, eds. Provo, UT: Association for Consumer Research, 178–84.

——— (1998), "Does Cultural Capital Structure American Consumption?" *Journal of Consumer Research*, 25 (June), 1–26.

——— (2004), *How Brands Become Icons: The Principles of Cultural Branding*. Cambridge, MA: Harvard Business School Publications.

Huffman, Cynthia, S. Ratneshwar, and David Glen Mick (1999), "Consumer Goal Structures and Goal Determination Processes: An Integrative Framework," in *The Why of Consumption*, S. Ratneshwar, David Glen Mick, and Cynthia Huffman, eds. New York: Routledge, 9–35.

Kates, Steven M. (2004), "The Dynamics of Brand Legitimacy: An Interpretive Study in the Gay Men's Community," *Journal of Consumer Research*, 31 (September), 455–65.

Kernan, Jerome B. (2000), "More than a Rat, Less than God, Staying Alive," in *The Why of Consumption*, S. Ratneshwar, David Glen Mick, and Cynthia Huffman, eds. New York: Routledge, 304–12.

Kleine, Susan Schultz and Stacey Menzel Baker (2004), "An Integrative Review of Material Possession Attachment," *Academy of Marketing Science Review* (1), [available at: http://www.amsreview.org/articles/kleine01-2004.pdf] (accessed May 5, 2005).

Kozinets, Robert V. (1997), "'I Want To Believe': A Netnography of The X-Philes' Subculture of Consumption," *Advances in Consumer Research*, 24, Merrie Brucks and Debbie MacInnis, eds. Provo, UT: Association for Consumer Research, 470–75.

——— (2001), "Utopian Enterprise: Articulating the Meaning of Star Trek's Culture of Consumption," *Journal of Consumer Research*, 28 (June), 67–89.

——— (2002) "Can Consumers Escape the Market? Emancipatory Illuminations from Burning Man," *Journal of Consumer Research*, 29 (June), 20–38.

———, John F. Sherry, Jr., and Nina Diamond (2003), "American Girl Doll," video presented at the Annual Conference of the Association for Consumer Research, October 9–12, Toronto, Canada.

———, ———, Diana Storm, Adam Duhachek, Krittinee Nuttavuthist, and Benet DeBerry-Spence (2004), "Ludic Agency and Retail Spectacle," *Journal of Consumer Research*, 31 (December), 658–72.

Martin, Brett A.S. (2004), "Using the Imagination: Consumer Evoking and Thematizing of the Fantastic Imaginary," *Journal of Consumer Research*, 31 (June), 136–49.

McGrath, Mary Ann, John F. Sherry, Jr, and Deborah D. Heisley (1993), "An Ethnographic Study of an Urban Periodic Marketplace: Lessons from the Midville Farmers' Market," *Journal of Retailing*, 69 (Fall), 280–320.

Meuter, Matthew L. and Mary Jo Bitner (1998), "Self-Service Technologies: Extending Service Frameworks and Identifying Issues for Research," in *AMA Winter Educator's Conference*, Dhruv Grewal and Connie Pechman, eds. Chicago: American Marketing Association, 12–19.

Moore, Elizabeth S., William L. Wilkie, and Richard J. Lutz (2002), "Passing the Torch: Intergenerational Influences as a Source of Brand Equity," *Journal of Marketing*, 66 (April), 17–37.

Muñiz, Albert M., Jr. and Thomas C. O'Guinn (2001), "Brand Community," *Journal of Consumer Research*, 27 (March), 412–32.

Muñiz, Albert M., Jr. and Hope Jensen Schau (2005), "Religiosity in the Abandoned Apple Newton Brand Community," *Journal of Consumer Research*, 31(March), 737–748.

Neyapti, Bilin (2004), "Trends in Workers' Remittances: A Worldwide Overview," *Emerging Markets Finance and Trade*, 40, (March–April), 83–90.

Olsen, Barbara (1995), "Brand Loyalty and Consumption Patterns: The Lineage Factor," in *Contemporary Marketing and Consumer Behavior*, John F. Sherry, Jr., ed. Thousand Oaks, CA: Sage, 245–81.

Peñaloza, Lisa (2000), "The Commodification of the American West: Marketers' Production of Cultural Meanings at a Trade Show," *Journal of Marketing*, 64 (October), 82–109.

——— (2001), "Consuming the American West: Animating Cultural Meaning at a Stock Show and Rodeo," *Journal of Consumer Research*, 28 (December), 369–98.

Peters, Cara Lee Okleshen (2004), "Using Vocabularies of Motives to Facilitate Relationship Marketing: The Context of the Winnebago Itasca Travelers Club," *Journal of Vacation Marketing*, 10 (June), 209–23.

Poirine, Bernard (1997), "A Theory of Remittances as an Implicit Family Loan Agreement," *World Development* 25, (4), 589–611.

Prahalad, C. K. and Venkatram Ramaswamy (2003), "The New Frontier of Experience Innovation," *MIT Sloan Management Review* (Summer), 12–18.

Price, Linda L. and Eric J. Arnould (1999), "Commercial Friendships: Service Provider-Client Relationships in Social Context," *Journal of Marketing,* 63 (October), 38–56.

Price, Linda L., Eric J. Arnould, and Patrick Tierney (1995), "Going to Extremes: Managing Service Encounters and Assessing Provider Performance," *Journal of Marketing,* 59 (April), 83–97.

Rust, Roland T., Katherine N. Lemon, and Valarie A. Zeithaml (2004), "Return on Marketing: Using Customer Equity to Focus Marketing Strategy," *Journal of Marketing*, 68 (January), 109–27.

Schouten, John W. and James H. McAlexander (1995), "Subcultures of Consumption: An Enthnography of the New Biker," *Journal of Consumer Research*, 22 (June), 43–62.

Segalen, Martine and Claude Frère-Michelat (1994), *Les Enfants d'Achille et de Nike: Une Ethnologie de la Course à Pied Ordinaire*. Paris: Editions Métailié/Seuil.

Sewell, William H. Jr. (1992), "A Theory of Structure: Duality, Agency, and Transformation," *American Journal of Sociology*, 98 (July), 1–29.

Sherry, John F. Jr. (1998), "The Soul of the Company Store: Nike Town Chicago and the Emplaced Brandscape," in *Servicescapes. The Concept of Place in Contemporary Markets*, John F. Sherry, Jr., ed. Chicago: NTC Business Books, 109–46.

Sirsi, Ajay K., James C. Ward, and Peter H. Reingen (1996), "Microcultural Analysis of Variation in Sharing of Causal Reasoning about Behavior," *Journal of Consumer Research*, 22 (March), 345–73.

Surowiecki, James (2004), *The Wisdom of Crowds: Why the Many Are Smarter Than the Few and How Collective Wisdom Shapes Business, Economies, Societies and Nations*. New York: Doubleday.

Swidler, Ann (1986), "Culture in Action: Symbols and Strategies," *American Sociological Review,* 52 (2), 273–286.

Thompson, Craig J. (2000), "Postmodern Consumer Goals Made Easy!" in *The Why of Consumption,* S. Ratneshwar, David Glen Mick, and Cynthia Huffman, eds. New York: Routledge, 120–39.

Vargo, Stephen L. and Robert F. Lusch (2004), "Evolving to a New Dominant Logic for Marketing," *Journal of Marketing*, 68 (January), 1–17.

Wallendorf, Melanie and Eric J. Arnould (1991), "'We Gather Together': The Consumption Rituals of Thanksgiving Day," *Journal of Consumer Research*, 18 (June), 13-31.

Ward, James C. and Peter H. Reingen (1990), "Sociocognitive Analysis of Group Decision Making among Consumers," *Journal of Consumer Research*, 17 (December), 245–62.

Wilk, Richard R. (1995), "Learning to be Local in Belize: Global Systems of Common Difference," in *Worlds Apart: Modernity through the Prism of the Local*, Daniel Miller, ed. New York: Routledge, 110–33.

PART III

CO-PRODUCTION, COLLABORATION, AND OTHER VALUE-CREATING PROCESSES

In Part III, a variety of authors share ideas about the centrality in service-dominant (S-D) logic of co-production, collaboration, and value-creating processes. Given that S-D logic views marketing as a continuous series of social and economic processes, largely focused on operant resources, it is not surprising that the performance of business processes both within the firm and across the supply and value networks is pivotal. Since no entity has the expertise or relative advantage in terms of competences to perform all of these processes, the importance of collaboration and value co-creation becomes evident.

Jaworski and Kohli (chapter 8), two authors that pioneered the conceptualization and measurement of market orientation, suggest that co-production should be brought to the "front-end process of identifying customer needs/wants" in their essay, "Co-creating the Voice of the Customer." Bringing the customer to the center of the value-creation network is quite different from the common approach of the firm trying to learn about customer needs that exist "out there." In contrast, Jaworski and Kohli suggest that the firm and the customer can learn together about each other's needs and wants, and then the firm and customers "figure out the goods and services that will be developed (or performed) by the firm and those that will be developed (or performed) by the customers." Co-creation must rely on an open dialog between the customer and firm. Jaworski and Kohli compare this to a "wonderful coauthor relationship." Not only do they provide prescriptions for how to engage in successfully co-creating the voice of the customer, they also suggest when not to co-create the voice of the customer. Much is to be learned by reading and studying their very thoughtful essay. In fact, as we read their essay, we kept thinking about the question of why the customer should not also be considered the co-creator of the whole marketing mix, broadly conceived. Why not explore the role of the customer in co-creating the pricing, distribution, promotion, and brand and experience components of value?

Perhaps challenging the central tenants of marketing even more provocatively, Oliver explores the notion of mutual satisfaction for both customers and firms in chapter 9, "Co-producers and Co-participants in the Satisfaction Process: Mutually Satisfying Consumption." Traditionally, marketing scholarship and writing has focused on consumer satisfaction and loyalty and has ignored firm satisfaction and the loyalty of the firm to the customer. Oliver argues that if co-production and co-participation are to achieve their full potential in an S-D logic of marketing, then there must be a reciprocation process between firm and consumer. Not only should customers be loyal to firms, but firms should be loyal to customers; and not only is customer satisfaction important, but so is firm satisfaction. Exchange must be symbiotic, and loyalty and satisfaction must be mutually beneficial. Oliver stretches researchers to think and to consider if making a value proposition is insufficient; he argues for firms also making loyalty propositions, whereby they display and deliver loyalty to their customers. However, for value to be optimized the consumer needs to reciprocate and, as Oliver mentions, "unlike the pursuits of charity giving and volunteerism, consumers are not accustomed and have not been socialized to the consideration of a provider's needs in the marketplace." Clearly, such a radical paradigm shift in the consumer satisfaction and *loyalty-dominant* logic will require marketing scholars to devote significant effort to theory development and empirical research in this arena.

Modeling how consumers can optimize their level of co-production is the focus of chapter 10, "Co-production of Services: A Managerial Extension," by Michael Etgar. Framing his premise as an economic optimization problem, Etgar demonstrates how a household can use household resources to perform activities and render service, rather than going to the market and hiring specialists to perform these activities and service. The household faced with resource constraints evaluates options in order to minimize total costs of performing activities internally and seeking these activities externally. Etgar's model recognizes, as does S-D logic, that production and consumption are not distinct activities in which consumers receive a completed output but rather ones in which consumers are involved in the complete value-creation process both producing and consuming.

Chapter 11, by Daniel J. Flint and John T. Mentzer, "Striving for Integrated Value Chain Management Given a Service-Dominant Logic for Marketing," urges researchers to consider the central role of S-D logic in supply and value chain management. Not surprisingly, S-D logic, with its emphasis on continuous processes, is a welcome philosophy in the field of supply and value chain management, in which, in a business-to-business context, co-production between customers and suppliers is pervasive.

As the functional school of marketing thought held, marketing functions are pervasive; however, they can be divided among the marketing institutions and are most often shared. When several members of a supply and value chain share the performance of a marketing function, such as promotion, transportation, storage, or risk taking, they are involved in value co-creation; thus, collaboration and coordination are the backbones of success. S-D logic embraces the learning that occurs through the continuous social and economic exchanges that make up marketing. When one couples this idea with the notion of collaboration or co-creation in the value and supply chain, one begins to recognize, as Flint and Mentzer suggest, "knowledge is co-produced in integrated value-chain management because multiple minds across several firms exchange perspectives and share skills." However, for S-D logic to be fully embraced, barriers must be overcome. Some of the barriers that Flint and Mentzer believe are most challenging include building trust in supply chain relationships, facilitating the exchange of safely guarded information, confronting the financial challenges of supply chain management, and changing the face, focus, and incentive systems of account management teams. All of these barriers relate to corporate and/or industry culture. Given the preponderance of publicly traded firms, researchers cannot ignore the impressions of shareholders and other stakeholders, for they are also seeking their own value proposition. In fact, Flint and Mentzer ask, "Because of the pressure of Wall Street for immediate returns, is it easier for private companies to implement a service-dominant logic?" We hope this research question is addressed.

Also embracing an integrated value network mentality, Lambert and García-Dastugue, in chapter 12, "Cross-Functional Business Processes for the Implementation of Service-Dominant Logic," provide a framework that can help implement S-D logic. They describe how eight processes used to integrate effort within the firm and across the entire supply chain can be supported by fundamental premises of S-D logic: customer relationship management, customer service management, demand management, order fulfillment, manufacturing flow management, supplier relationship management, product development and commercialization, and returns management. Importantly, Lambert and García-Dastugue recognize that implementing supply-chain management (and, in our opinion, S-D logic) requires a move away from managing functions (which were historically managed from an output perspective) and toward a focus on processes. They suggest that all of the corporate functions need to participate in all-process teams in order to develop value propositions for the customer. Functional silos need to be overcome but, as Lambert and García-Dastugue recognize, functional structures will not be eliminated. Firms still need deep expertise that is represented by marketing, finance, production, and information systems departments, to name a few.

This brings forth a point that we repeatedly emphasize when discussing S-D logic: S-D logic will not result in old jobs (e.g., those in marketing and sales, research and development, logistics, production, purchasing, finance) being eliminated and replaced with people that perform only cross-functional processes. The work is done at the functional level; however, cross-functional processes are key to delivering compelling value propositions. All cross-functional processes will be managed by teams, but as Lambert and García-Dastugue mention, skills and knowledge required to maintain relationships reside in the function. In this regard, they argue not only for the customer being a co-producer, but also for the supplier being a co-producer. Given this perspective, it will be important for the cross-functional business processes to be managed across the entire supply chain (see chapter 11, Flint and Mentzer). This is because no entity will perform all functions and will, as suggested by S-D logic, focus on those competences it does best.

Part III concludes with chapter 13, "Customers as Co-producers: Implications for Marketing Strategy Effectiveness and Marketing Operations Efficiency," by Kalaignanam and Varadarajan. In this chapter, the authors develop a model of the participation of customers as co-producers in a firm's value chain. They view this participation as being dependent on product characteristics, market and customer characteristics, and firm characteristics. Macroenvironmental trends and developments—especially in information, communication, and manufacturing technology—are viewed as positive moderators of the intensity of customer participation. As with all models or theories, only empirical testing will allow researchers to assess validity.

Some of the issues that the Kalaignanam and Varadarajan raise regarding the potential adverse supply- and demand-side outcomes of increased customer participation are quite interesting and insightful. For instance, as consumer communities grow, due to more co-production activities with firms, these communities could challenge the firm or even become a competitor to the firm. Also, the authors suggest that increased customer participation in co-production could have negative psychological outcomes for customers if the offering does not adequately address the customers' problems.

8

CO-CREATING THE VOICE OF THE CUSTOMER

BERNIE JAWORSKI AND AJAY K. KOHLI

INTRODUCTION

The role of a producer traditionally has been viewed as the development and delivery of goods and services, and the role of customers has been viewed as the consumption of those goods and services. The two roles have been viewed as being distinct and separate. Vargo and Lusch (2004) argue that such separation leads to lower marketing efficiency and effectiveness. They argue the role of a customer should be viewed as that of a "co-producer" of goods and services in addition to that of a consumer of those goods and services.

This brings up a central question: What does it mean for a customer to "co-produce"? *Co-production* is commonly thought of as the customer performing some of the work traditionally done by a producer. For example, a customer may engage in self-service at gas stations, navigate a firm's automated call centers, or co-design next-generation products and services (Prahalad and Ramaswamy 2004). In this essay, we extend the idea of co-production to the front end of the value-creation chain: the customer-needs identification process.

Traditionally, the customer-needs identification process has been approached from the perspective of a firm undertaking a variety of approaches to "hear" the voice of the customer (see Griffin and Hauser 1993). Thus, the firm tries to "identify" known or latent needs/wants of customers through a variety of mechanisms such as interviews, surveys, observational techniques, and so forth. In every one of these approaches, the perspective adopted is one of a firm wanting to learn about customer needs "out there." The firm does the asking, listening, observing, experimenting, learning; customer needs/wants are the objects of study. After the firm learns about customer needs/wants (i.e., hears the customer's voice), it develops and delivers goods and services that provide value to customers.

In this essay, we discuss an alternative needs-identification process in which a firm and its customers "co-create" the voice of customers as contrasted with the more traditional process in which a firm "hears" the voice of customers. In this co-creation process, the firm *and* the customers do the asking, listening, observing, and experimenting; that is, the firm *and* the customers engage in learning. The subject of study is customer needs/wants *and* firm needs/wants. The process results in the firm and customers knowing more about the needs/wants of the customer *and* the firm. Finally, after the process is complete, the firm and the customers figure out the goods and services that will be developed (or performed) by the firm and those that will be developed (or performed) by the customers.

The co-creation process differs significantly from the process designed to hear the voice of the customer. In addition, it requires a very different mindset on the part of the firm and the customers, and calls for a different set of behaviors. Importantly, we do not suggest this process is appropriate or even desirable in all cases; rather, it is a powerful tool in certain contexts but not others. For example, it is particularly useful when customer needs are relatively undefined, and customers possess the capability to produce some goods or services for their own consumption.

The rest of this essay is organized as follows. We first discuss the traditional process by which a firm hears the voice of customers. Next, we discuss the process of co-creating the voice of customers, and compare and contrast key perspectives embedded in the two approaches. We then discuss key requirements for co-creating the voice of the customer—characteristics of a dialog between a firm and its customers. We conclude with a discussion of the conditions under which co-creation of the voice of the customer particularly desirable.

HEARING THE VOICE OF THE CUSTOMER

A common premise underlying many approaches to uncovering needs/wants of customers is that they know what they need or want. For example, a firm might do an open-ended interview with a sample of customers to elicit attributes of a hospital considered by customers in making their health care choices. Next, the firm might carry out a mail survey of a larger sample of customers asking them to rate each of the attributes identified in the first step. The firm can then analyze these data and decide what products or services it should offer those customers.

In recent years, firms have recognized that sometimes customers may not know what they want or what would satisfy their needs/wants. Or, they may have some idea of what they might like but are unable to articulate it in a meaningful way to firms. In response to this realization, firms have turned to ethnographic and anthropological approaches, often used in conjunction with more traditional approaches such as the survey or the interview method (e.g., the ZMET technique developed by Jerry Zaltman 1997). These approaches often rely on observing customers interacting with products and services, and examining personal and contextual artifacts that provide insights into customers' values and motivations. Such approaches help firms develop a richer feel for the kinds of products and services customers would really like even though customers might find it difficult to articulate their needs/wants or visualize product/service concepts that would appeal to them.

Regardless of the specific approach adopted, three perspectives are common to interviews, surveys, experiments, and observational techniques used in hearing the voice of the customer:

1. The firm undertakes actions to learn about customer needs/wants.
2. The customer needs/wants are the subject of learning.
3. After the firm learns customer needs/wants, it figures out what value (goods and services) it should provide to customers.

A foundational premise of the service-dominant logic advocated by Vargo and Lusch (2004) is that the customer is always a co-producer. Their reasoning is quite straightforward: In service-oriented settings the customer is an active participant in the service encounter. Indeed, the quality of the service offering is a delicate interplay of the service itself as well as the interactions between the focal firm and its customers. It is possible to argue that this proposition might not hold in certain situations. Even so, the proposition clearly holds in a large number of cases such as service encounters, business-to-business settings, and many business-to-consumer settings. It is therefore important to explore implications of this fundamental proposition for the firm and the customer.

A major implication of the idea that a customer is often, if not always, a co-producer is that the firm performs some aspects of the value-creating activities and that the customer performs others. For example, a grocery retailer might set up self-serve checkout lanes in which the customer does the checking out of groceries. If tasks are to be divided between a firm and a customer, how should this division be determined? We argue that the firm and the customer must decide upon this division of tasks jointly. In turn, this requires that the firm and the customer both must develop a thorough understanding of each other's needs, wants, and requirements as well as respective competences.

It is possible, of course, for a firm to unilaterally decide on this division of tasks based on its abilities/priorities and its knowledge of the customer's needs, wants, and capabilities. However, this would be suboptimal for at least two reasons. First, it would be based on a limited number of firm-initiated ideas for the division of production tasks, and a limited understanding of customers' capability to "produce" their portion of the value-creating good or service. Second, such an approach would be harder to implement because it would lack the buy-in from the customer, particularly if it is large and powerful—as is frequently the case in business-to-business settings. It therefore is critical for both the firm and customers to learn each other's needs, wants, capabilities, and priorities, and then jointly apportion the value-creation activities across the two. In other words, the voice of the customer (what the customer would like the firm to do) must be co-created.

CO-CREATING THE VOICE OF THE CUSTOMER

As noted previously, co-creating the voice of the customer entails three points of departure from the more typical hearing the voice of the customer:

1. Both the firm and the customer are engaged in the learning effort (as opposed to just the firm).
2. The needs, wants, capabilities, and priorities of the customer as well as those of the firm are the subject of learning (as opposed to just the needs, wants, capabilities, and priorities of the customer).
3. The firm and the customer jointly decide what part of the production process each will participate in, and what the design or configuration of the product or services each will produce (as opposed to the firm deciding the design of the product or service it will produce).

Co-creating the voice of the customer requires an open dialog between the firm and the customer. It requires a conversation over many periods of time, each time adjusting both the focus and mode of inquiry as the firm and the customer learn more about each other's requirements and capabilities. One way to think about such a co-creation dialog is to compare it to a wonderful co-author relationship. In such a relationship there is no dominant researcher: All decisions about the research topic, the research methods, and the writing are considered jointly. One may know the rough direction of a research project; however, the project is really a journey. It is shaped over time based on the learning, problems, and opportunities that present themselves. There is some broad focus of the effort, but mostly things get figured out along the way.

For example, in course of its dialog with a customer, a firm might learn that its customer is better situated to manufacturing some of the parts needed to construct a solution that the firm was originally planning to produce for the customer. In this instance, the conversation between the firm and the customer would change in that it would no longer focus on the firm trying to learn more about the customer's requirements for those parts that the customer could better make on his own. Alternatively, in course of the conversation, the firm may learn that the customer currently is doing certain activities in-house that may be better performed by the firm. In this case, the conversation between the firm and the customer would shift to the firm trying to learn more about the customer's requirements for those specific activities. Both the firm and the customer "co-determine" the shape of the conversation, the time frame, the topics, the "rules of the conversation," and the potential destination. Such a dialog is flexible, exploratory, and adaptive.

Thus, in these customer conversations, the firm must relinquish a great deal of control with respect to the topics of focus and be prepared to disband the linearity of the typical market research approach. Conversations are likely to be nonlinear and even "double back" to previous points of common interests. Thus, these conversations often are not useful for refining current services or testing new features for next-generation products; rather, they are best used to explore —in the words of Hamel and Prahalad (1994)—how to compete for the future. Such conversations are not easy, and a strong relationship between the firm and customer is a virtual prerequisite for these conversations.

INDICATORS OF A CO-CREATION DIALOG

In the following sections, we describe several indicators or characteristics of a co-creation dialog. The likelihood of having a productive co-creation conversation is higher if both the firm and the customer agree upon these "rules of engagement" prior to commencing the conversation and periodically remind themselves of their agreement in course of the conversation. It is easy to say whether a firm and a customer are having a co-creation dialog by examining the following questions.

Is the Conversation End Point Clear or Unclear?

In a co-creation dialog, the end point of the conversation is relatively unclear. It is not clear at the start as to the products or services that will be produced by the firm and those that will be produced by its customer. In contrast, in a more typical market research effort, it is relatively clear what products and services the firm will produce. Furthermore, in a co-creation dialog, the form of the product or service might also be unclear until after the conversation. For example, a firm and a customer might engage in a dialog to identify a solution for enhancing the customer's productivity and have little idea at the start as to whether this would require education seminars, different equipment, or better negotiations with the customer's suppliers. Thus, the end point of the dialog is co-created rather than elicited or surfaced from the customer.

Do the Comments Build on Those That Came Before Them?

A critical ingredient of conversation is that each party listens carefully to what the other party says and does. A true dialog requires going beyond merely listening to the other party. It requires building upon the comments of the other party. It is not enough to merely understand what a dialog partner says; it is critical to be responsive to what the partner says. Thus, one party might build on an idea suggested by the other, propose another idea that serves the same function, relate it to something else, consciously hold it for comment later, ask for a clarification, and so on. Often, great ideas develop when one partner says something that triggers another idea in the other partner's mind, and so on. In other words, a dialog is not merely an exchange of information; it is the exploration and joint creation of new ideas.

Is There a Willingness to Explore Assumptions That Underlie the Dialog?

A conversation between two parties can get bogged down if the two parties hold erroneous assumptions about each other's beliefs and motives. A productive dialog is marked by occasional attempts by the two parties to test their assumptions about each other's situation, beliefs, and motives. Productive dialogs are marked by occasional queries such as "Could you give me a better feel for why that is important to you?" or "Has your perspective on this issue changed since the last time we performed these services for you?" Ellinor and Gerard (1998) suggest that while it is not possible to give up one's assumptions, a conversation can become much more meaningful if both parties identify and suspend their assumptions in the course of their dialog. Such suspension opens up a party's mind, and helps it absorb more from the information being provided by the other party.

Is the Conversation Exploratory: No Topic Is "Off-Limits?"

In a productive dialog, relatively few topics should be off-limits to start with. Moreover, as a dialog proceeds, new issues, concerns, and opportunities inevitably emerge. As this happens, both parties determine if any or all of these should be pursued. This does not mean that the firm and the customer cannot place a topic off-limits to narrow the scope of their conversation; however, the key point is that each party feels free to raise any issue or idea, and a decision to pursue it or not is taken jointly by the two parties once the dialog is in play.

It might even be important to have what Ellinor and Gerard (1998) call "divergent conversations" during the early part of the dialog. Divergent conversations take a dialog in different and potentially conflicting directions. For example, the firm and the customer might each raise competing ideas for solving a particular need of the customer. Although this delays closure, the active debate and breadth of ideas generated increase the odds of identifying the best course of action for the firm and the customer.

Is There an Eagerness for New Ideas?

In a productive dialog, both the firm and the customer are eager to learn of new ideas and possibilities through the dialog. They are not just open to new ideas, but hungry for them. This is different from many conversations in which a firm engages with customers myopically—validating its existing ideas or approaches, or identifying which of a convenient set of alternatives might work for the customer. In contrast, a productive dialog entails an extreme openness to explore new topics—regardless of the competition, the customer needs, or even the capabilities of the focal firm.

Do the Firm and the Customer Each Shape the Structure and Content of the Conversation?

In a true dialog, both the firm and the customer shape the structure and content of the conversation. It is critical for both to be contributing ideas as well as jointly discussing the issues and ideas to focus on and those that should be skipped. If one of the parties dominates, the dialog tends to lapse into a one-way transmission of information. It is helpful for the parties involved to explicitly raise "process checks" to identify any such unevenness that might arise in course of the dialog. Of course, this requires that both parties have something to contribute to the dialog in the first place and be willing to do so. For this reason, it is neither possible nor desirable for a firm to have a dialog with all customers.

FACTORS THAT LEAD TO SUCCESSFUL CO-CREATION DIALOGS

In the previous section, we discussed the characteristics that indicate whether a firm and a customer are having a productive dialog. In this section, we consider factors that facilitate or hinder the dialog. In addition to considering these potential antecedents of a successful dialog, one might also consider these potential selection factors for the choice of a dialog partner.

Trust

Trust is a well-explored topic in the marketing literature. It is central to much of the literature on marketing channels and customer relationship management. For a dialog to be successful, it is critical that each party trust the other, that is, be willing to rely on the other party for the soundness of its statements and ideas, and that each party's desire be to work toward a mutually beneficial end point. If trust is lacking, it is hard to expect a party to build on the comments and ideas of the other party. Moreover, in the present context, Ballantyne (2004) notes that mutual trust is not simply an "exogenous" factor that affects the quality of a dialog; rather, dialog-based interactions can engender and further strengthen trust in a firm and customer.

Value Placed on the Other's Insights

As noted previously, the true power of a dialog is realized when one party builds on the ideas of the other party in a series of back-and-forth processes that eventually lead to a co-created end point. For this to happen, it is essential that each party truly value the other's insights and perspectives. In its absence, the conversation lapses into a desire to force one's thoughts onto the other rather than listen and build off the other's thoughts. It is important to note that each party is likely to value the other's insights, provided it sees economic and other benefits that it is likely to realize by incorporating or building upon the other's ideas. In turn, this depends on the perceived capability of the other party and past experience with the party.

Complementary Skills and Perspectives

A party is likely to see far greater value from a dialog with another party if it sees the latter as being competent and having a somewhat different set of skills, capabilities, and perspectives. Diversity in knowledge and perspectives surfaces a broader range of options. This in turn increases the odds of identifying an optimal solution. However, it is important to note that if the diversity is too great, it can make reaching mutually beneficial closure difficult. Thus, a moderate amount of diversity would appear to be most desirable.

Depth of Knowledge and Experience

In addition to complementary skills, it is important that each party have a deep knowledge of select domains or areas (e.g., technology, markets, operations). If such depth is lacking, it is hard for a party to rely on input provided by the other party. Also, good ideas often lie dormant in the folds of the depth of one's knowledge and are triggered by input from other persons. Thus, depth of knowledge in one or more domains is a critical factor for a productive dialog.

Adventure Seeking

An open dialog is a little like an expedition in which one does not know what one will find. It is therefore important that the participants in a dialog enjoy the thrill that comes from exploring uncharted ideas and opportunities. Parties that are afraid of the unknown are unlikely to explore or seriously consider new ideas and opportunities likely to arise in the course of a deep give-and-take conversation. The idea is that the adventure seeker will thrive in a conversation in which the topics might be unexpected or surprising and the journey is as important as the end point. Related to this, the two parties must have a high tolerance for ambiguity. In a discourse that leads to new ideas, a tendency to summarily dismiss an ambiguous new idea as "ill conceived" or "unworkable" can lead to premature closure.

Setting of the Conversation

The setting for a dialog can also influence the quality of the dialog. It requires that the parties plan for concentrated blocks of disruption-free times. These need not be very long individually but must be planned for carefully. Note that a dialog is not just one meeting; rather, it is an ongoing set of conversations that start with the very vague and ambiguous statements of problems and possible solutions, and move on to become more specific as good ideas are developed and others discarded. Not all of the work happens in the course of each conversation; rather, considerable investigation and fact finding is done between conversations. The choice of participants from the firm and customers is critically important. Participants must be selected for their ability to listen, build, and create rather than merely sell their pet ideas.

WHEN NOT TO CO-CREATE THE VOICE OF THE CUSTOMER

As suggested previously, it would not make sense to try to engage a party that could not be trusted, didn't see value in a dialog, lacked deep knowledge, and so on. Furthermore, it is important to stress that because of the exploratory nature of the co-creation conversations, these should be pursued primarily in certain situations: when the time horizon is long, there is relatively little pressure to "get closure" on selected product or market choices, and both parties recognize that the conversations might not produce useful intelligence. In this section, we describe certain conditions when the co-creation process probably should not be employed.

Time-to-Market Cost

If a firm is under pressure to enter a market with a product or service quickly, co-creation of the voice of the customer might not be a good idea. As noted previously, the co-creation process is long and hence best used when time to market is not a consideration.

Organizational Alignment Cost

If the costs of gaining organizational alignment (i.e., sharing the key co-creation findings both horizontally and vertically in the organization and getting agreement around next steps) outweigh the potential insights to be gained from the effort, then the co-creation process should not be pursued. Note that organizational alignment costs are likely to vary from one firm to another. Firms that have a top-down culture or, alternatively, are experiencing weakness in performance often can be aligned more easily to a new way of doing business.

Opportunity Cost

The out-of-pocket costs of conducting a co-creation conversation with key thought partners over a period of time is likely to be minimal. In contrast, the opportunity costs in the short run are likely to be higher. Opportunity costs refer to lost revenues and profits (in the short run) due to a firm focusing on co-creating the voice of the customer as opposed to doing a relatively quick and dirty market research project and getting a product or service to market quickly.

CONCLUSION

Vargo and Lusch (2004) propose that the customer is always a co-producer. Furthermore, the authors argue that a firm must consider building its competitive advantage around this (and other) fundamental propositions offered in their article. In this essay, we extend the idea of a co-producer to the front end of the value-creation process: the customer-needs identification process. We attempt to provide a deeper insight into methods of dialog that firms can follow to build a stronger capability in co-producing with customers. We describe the characteristics of dialogs that can increase the ability to "co-create the future" of what a particular service encounter could entail.

There are several areas for further research on the co-creation process. First, it would be useful to develop new methods, techniques, and even tactics for engaging in productive dialogs. A useful starting point might be the counseling and clinical psychology literatures in which conversations are the cornerstone of their approaches. Second, it would be interesting to explore the psychology of the co-creation process. For example, how are decisions reached? How does one continue to motivate the co-creation process? Is this decision process similar to or different from the group decision process that is reflected in the consumer behavior literature? It would be useful to explore the structure, content, and flow of these conversations.

A third area could be termed the sociology of co-creation. Prahalad and Ramaswamy (2004) note that many conversations can unfold in communities of interest (e.g., customer communities). Thus, using the Internet or other community-oriented approaches, one can conceive of a co-creation process that is really a "multiparty co-creation process." It is possible that research in this area could be facilitated by the advent of ready-made communities on the Web. Some of the issues worthy of examination include how and why parties are included or excluded in multiparty co-creation processes, advantages and disadvantages of a multiparty co-creation process, and factors that help or hinder the multiparty co-creation process.

From a managerial standpoint, it is quite interesting to note that co-creating the voice of the customer is likely to result in deeper bonds with customers—more trust, more commitment, and more loyalty—for two reasons. First, because a customer is involved in the process, the customer builds commitment to the resultant offering by the firm. Second, because of the offering is co-developed, it has a higher probability of accurately meeting the customer needs. Finally, co-creating the voice of the customer provides a firm asymmetric information about the marketplace; that is, it provides the firm with insights that are not easily available to competitors. As such, co-creating the voice of the customer can represent a source of significant competitive advantage.

REFERENCES

Ballantyne, David (2004), "Dialogue and Its Role in the Development of Relationship Specific Knowledge," *Journal of Business and Industrial Marketing,* (19), 114–23.

Ellinor, Linda and Glenna Gerard (1998), *Dialogue: Rediscover the Transforming Power of Conversation.* New York: John Wiley & Sons.

Griffin, Abbie and John R. Hauser (1993), "The Voice of the Customer," *Marketing Science,* 12 (Winter), 1–27.

Hamel, Gary and C. K. Prahalad (1994), *Competing for the Future.* Boston, MA: Harvard Business School Press.

Prahalad, C.K. and Venkat Ramaswamy (2004), *The Future of Competition: Co-creating Unique Value with Customers.* Boston: Harvard Business School Press.

Vargo, Stephen L. and Robert F. Lusch (2004), "Evolving to a New Dominant Logic for Marketing," *Journal of Marketing,* 68 (January), 1–17.

Zaltman, Gerald (1997), "Rethinking Marketing Research: Putting People Back In," *Journal of Marketing Research,* 34 (November) 424–37.

9

CO-PRODUCERS AND CO-PARTICIPANTS IN THE SATISFACTION PROCESS

Mutually Satisfying Consumption

RICHARD L. OLIVER

> "Ask not what your country can do for you—ask what you can do for your country."
> —*John F. Kennedy, Inaugural Address, January 20, 1961*

This inspirational quote from many years past reflects the central thesis of this chapter. In most marketplace societies, consumers have become accustomed to need gratification through consumption. That is, they ask the marketer to "do for them," assuming that the revenue and profit generated by a single purchase or revenue stream generated by repeat purchases is what they do for the merchant. Here I question whether this traditional model of exchange is truly optimal from the standpoint of continued relational exchange in postmodern economies. I begin with a background to this thesis and then provide a satisfaction framework within which to work.

Recently, Vargo and Lusch (2004; hereafter V&L) have proposed a new paradigm in marketing, which they have referred to as the service-dominant logic (S-D logic). Their central proposition is that goods have become mere instruments in service delivery so that services are now exchanged for services. That is, markets are emerging into co-production entities whereby services rendered by the firm are matched by services consumers provide to the firm. One current example is Internet purchasing, in which consumers, with and without their knowledge, provide the Web vendor with information on purchasing habits.

The intent of this chapter is to more fully explore the behavioral dynamics underlying this symbiosis. This requires that the notion of mutual satisfaction be described; in other words, the now generally accepted consumer satisfaction construct must be paired with firm satisfaction as if the firm had a persona of its own. In doing so, I also explore mutually beneficial loyalty, as loyalty is now thought to be a superordinate goal of the firm (Reichheld 1996).

SATISFACTION AND LOYALTY BASICS

As described in Oliver (1997), *satisfaction* is pleasurable fulfillment. That is, some need, goal, or desire is fulfilled, and the consumer finds this level of fulfillment pleasurable in some sense. For the firm, some translation would be required so that pleasurable fulfillment could mean attainment of sales, profit, or share goals that are acceptable to the firm; the basic concept, however, remains the same.

In contrast, *loyalty* is described as a deeply held commitment to repatronize a provider despite switching incentives that might be situational or driven by competitive forces (Oliver 1997). The analogous situation from the firm's viewpoint would be a desire to serve the current customer base at all costs. That is, the firm views the consumer (or market) as so valuable to its mission that it will pass up opportunities to garner greater sales, profits, and the like from another consumer base, possibly abandoning consumers previously served. Examples of abandonment might include retailers moving upscale in merchandise, those who no longer extend credit to the poor, or those who sell out to a large conglomerate with the goal of upgrading the merchandise and/or clientele. And, in political climates, it should come as no surprise that candidates might wish to shift their positions on issues to attract more valuable voters in areas with greater political weight. In contrast, consumer-loyal firms would find a way to continue to serve their loyal customer base while extending their services to more valuable clientele. Health care services could qualify in this case.

This discussion is a prelude to the central thesis of this chapter: that, in the same way consumers can be satisfied and show loyalty to firms, satisfied firms can display loyalty to their constituencies. This symbiosis is the crux of value exchange in the context of services exchanged for services. In this sense, I disagree with V&L's foundational premise 7, which states that enterprises can only make value propositions. They can do more; they can make loyalty propositions. This is not to say that they can design so-called loyalty programs; most firms are able to accomplish this task. Rather, it is required under S-D logic that they display and deliver loyalty to their customers.

The Role of the Firm in Satisfaction

Traditionally and historically, firms provided "performance" to their customers. That is, it had been assumed that quality, as defined by the firm, would almost certainly satisfy consumers. The flaw in this position was (and is) that it ignored not only the expectations held by consumers, but also changes in these expectations. Expectations are now thought to be central to satisfaction formation, as in the generally accepted expectancy disconfirmation model (see Oliver 1997).

This model, in essence, states that expectations set a baseline around which performance is judged. Performance above expectations generally contributes to satisfaction, and performance below expectations generally contributes to dissatisfaction. Thus, performance above expectations (positive disconfirmation) results in or enhances satisfaction or makes dissatisfaction less so, while performance below expectations (negative disconfirmation) results in or exacerbates dissatisfaction or makes satisfaction less so. This, again, is from the consumer's point of view. The role of the firm, then, is not to deliver its version of performance, but to deliver a level of performance exceeding the expectations of consumers.

In an analogous manner, under S-D logic, consumers are obligated to exceed the firm's expectations for them. This will not come naturally because consumers have come to expect greater and greater service for the same dollar. Nonetheless, if the new logic is to take hold, firms and other agencies (e.g., governments) will expect more as well. This greater sacrifice might be (and has been) a theme prevalent in governments for some time. It manifests in the form of higher taxes (and concomitant willingness to pay); greater participation in the form of, for example, voting; and other supportive activities. As stated succinctly in the opening quote, "Ask not what your country can do for you."

The Role of the Firm's Providers in Satisfaction

Few firms interact directly with their customers, although Internet vendors are proving to be an exception. Most still use intermediaries or agents for customer contact, the most common perhaps being salespeople or service representatives. Recently, attention has begun to focus on the role of such providers in satisfaction, and the results, initially uninformative, are now essentially in concert. It appears that the firm's customer contact personnel, whether they are sales or service representatives, can mediate the relation between the firm and its customer base.

There are two relations of note in this sequence of communication and contact, that between the firm and its employees and that between the employees and the customer. The lay logic of these relationships is described as follows (see Heskett, Sasser, and Schlesinger 1997). If a firm cannot satisfy its customer contact employees, then it would be difficult for these contact persons to "put on a happy face." This could possibly be reflected in the manner in which the employee interacts with the consumer. The consumer, in many cases, will not distinguish the employee from the firm; thus it could become difficult for the consumer to react positively toward the firm despite the fact that the offering may be satisfactory. This has been shown in both macro studies, whereby employee satisfaction has been found to be positively correlated with customer satisfaction (e.g., Bernhart, Donthu, and Kennett 2000; Rucci, Kirn, and Quinn 1998), and in numerous micro studies, in which poor service is correlated with an unwillingness to repatronize.

The preceding discussion emphasizes the importance of factoring in the role of the service provider in the mutual satisfaction equation. In a sense, this role is nothing more than a performance variable, but a very critical one at that. V&L have referred to goods as "appliances" or an operand—a firm resource to be operated on. In contrast, an operant is an operator. Contact personnel would appear to be both an operant and an operand: They are an entity that operates on firm resources and its customers; at the same time, these personnel are resources that can be operated on. This dual role emphasizes the importance of firm contact employees in the overall satisfaction picture; further discussion will be elaborated in subsequent sections.

RELATIONSHIP MARKETING: THE EMERGENCE OF BIDIRECTIONAL THINKING

The earliest of relationship marketing writings were largely unidirectional. (See V&L 2004 and Lovelock and Gummesson 2004 for historical perspectives on this and many other themes in marketing thought.) The firm was instructed to build relationships with its customers, thereby creating satisfaction and engendering loyalty. The onus, therefore, was on the firm, and many service marketing texts adhered to this agenda. In fact, entire satisfaction or quality assessment devices used this logic in scale development; in other words, quality was assessed in terms of what the company could do for the customer.

Bidirectionality in relationships was not suggested in writings until the 1980s; its origin is briefly traced in Brownstein (1997). Couched in terms of interfirm relations, and primarily supplier and manufacturer in the venue of channel relationships (e.g., Dwyer, Schurr, and Oh 1987), this research program has now reached full tilt. It is important to note, however, that the literature continues to address the manufacturer–supplier dyad and does not generally speak to the provider–consumer relationships explored here. Another point of departure is that the interfirm literature places a premium on the criteria of mutual commitment and trust, whereas the focus here is on satisfaction and loyalty. The differences are subtle but important, because suppliers and manufacturers have profit as a major driving force, whereas this chapter targets need fulfillment. Profit is "in the equation" for firm-to-firm relations, but not for consumer relations, in which need gratification proliferates.

An example of the latter phenomenon (more on this subsequently) is the performing arts industry (e.g., Jaworski, Kohli, and Sahay 2000; Minor et al. 2004). In the arts, studios, artists, and arts houses deliver performances to audiences that are appreciated (i.e., gratifying). In turn, the audiences give back to the artists and their sponsors needed appreciations such as adoration, fan clubs, donations, patronage, and the like. But, even within this general consumption category, many firm–consumer relationships tend to be unidirectional in that providers, even after assessing needs, attempt to deliver these needs expecting only that they receive remunerations in the form of payments and revenues. The moving picture industry is a case in point in that production companies desire only top-tier box office receipts (and Oscars).

NEW BIDIRECTIONALITY: MUTUAL SATISFACTION

The central thesis in this chapter can now be stated more formally. In doing so, it can be assumed that the firms' needs assessment and service delivery mechanisms for their consumers have been adequately described in the extant literatures. To complete the mutual satisfaction requirement for true bidirectionality, focus now extends to the consumer's obligation to assess the needs of the provider and the means to deliver these needs. This would appear to be a natural transition from the production-oriented beginnings of commerce, through various consumerism movements, to mutual satisfaction. One can view this in the context of a marriage, in which harmony is thought to exist only when the needs of both parties are fulfilled.

Under interpretation of S-D logic, the consumer must sense the obligation to fulfill the needs of his or her provider in return for the provider's need-fulfilling renderings. This requires "reverse-engineering" in some sense as, presently, consumers are not accustomed to engaging in this practice. Consider the basic satisfaction model described previously for the mechanisms involved: Essentially, the provider would have expectations for its customers, and customers would be expected to meet those expectations. Under the model, customers could engender greater loyalty from the provider if they exceeded those expectations, but meeting expectations will be satisfactory for now.

Relative Power Considerations

Fortunately or unfortunately, no relationship is built on equal pillars, and some asymmetry is likely in any partnership. Thus, for simplicity, one can consider power asymmetries whereby the firm has greater power, the consumer has greater power, and the "middle ground" of equal but unequal power.

Under strong firm-relative power, such as would exist in a public utility, the expectations the firm has for its customers are oftentimes dictated; consumers can only abide "by the rules." In this case, customer assessment of a firm's needs is, at most, trivial. The firm expects prompt payment of bills and little more. It might also expect unobstructed access to the monitoring meter and that the metering equipment will not be compromised. At the other extreme, in which consumer-relative power is greatest, consumers operating under S-D logic should still respectfully consider the needs of the provider and fulfill them to honor the relationship. Local politicians with short terms might fit this latter description, and one wonders how many might have held their offices if the citizenry understood that a proposed tax increase, for example, needed support.

In the middle ground are myriads of relationships of slightly uneven power dependencies in which consumers must come to understand that a needs assessment of their suppliers would assist in maintaining the relationship. Using a commonplace example, fast food outlets, coffee shops, and other like merchants ask customers to deposit their trash in receptacles before exiting. This expectation, when fulfilled, aids the merchant by assisting in having a clean table for the next patron.

The Nature of the Consumer Market

The mutual satisfaction framework is complicated by the nature of the consumer (and merchant) market. In many or most cases, individual consumers are acting as independent agents. In others, they are acting as a collective. The purpose of this section is to illustrate the potential difficulties in relying on consumer assessments of provider needs. In part, this is a historical problem in that consumers are not accustomed to this task. But, of more importance, it illustrates the difficulties of two tasks, not one: that of consumer assessment of firm needs and subsequent fulfillment of firm needs by this same consumer. At the individual provider to individual consumer level, personal communication from the firm or its agent might be sufficient, as in the case of personal services or small businesses (e.g., "corner" stores). And at the firm or organizational level, the organization might have expectations of its customers that are quite specific and are intended to engender satisfaction. An apt example of the latter is the medical community. Doctors, acting as agents, have expectations that outpatients will adhere to a medication program and the doctors convey these expectations to the individual.

Another situation applies when consumers, acting as individual agents, must come to nearly identical conclusions as to what a provider's needs are and act in concert (as strangers) to fulfill these needs. This discussion is facilitated if I can, again, refer to the public domain. Paying one's fair share of taxes fulfills the needs of government to provide services to its constituents; acting lawfully fulfills the needs of society to maintain the public welfare; and volunteering, charity work, donating blood, and the like all serve to fulfill the social expectations that those more fortunate should aid the less fortunate. Interestingly, obeying traffic laws (e.g., stop lights) is now almost ingrained in society as a fulfillment response.

When consumers act as a collective—perhaps known to one another or perhaps unknown but bound by a common cause, such as in political partisanship—this analysis changes only slightly. Now agreement on need assessment comes more easily, as does fulfillment. The primary needs are party needs (votes), and basic fulfillment is essentially a vote for the party's candidate. But the analysis does not stop there. Attending political rallies, canvassing, encouraging others to vote, and especially donating to the campaign are related additional fulfillments.

The Nature of the Provider: The Firm's Persona

As noted previously, consumer assessment of a firm's expectations for its customers is a relatively new concept. The obvious criteria of repeat purchasing, cross-product-line purchasing, and adhering to proper usage instructions need no elaboration. Nor is the firm's reputation in the market an issue in this context. Rather, one must now view a firm (or agency, government, or country) as a human persona, having expectations for its customers or constituency and fulfillment criteria that are visible to the firm so that the performance of customers can be measured.

For example, in an omnibus survey of 205 commercial service providers, Claycomb and Martin (2002) asked individual firms what their priorities were in building relationships. I cite this study because it was the only one discovered that specifically listed firm goals in their relations with customers (not intermediaries or salespeople). Of the list of forty-two objectives revealed by methodology, most were "wishes" in the sense that firms desired specific objectives but gave no details on how to obtain them. Nonetheless, the top four are informative. The first was encouraging customers to think of the firm first when considering a purchase, followed by providing better service, encouraging customers to speak favorably about the firm, and encouraging customers to trust the firm. The provision of better service is the goal of most providers, and encouraging trust is part of the persona alluded to previously. It is also strategically nebulous. Rounding out the top ten were operational goals (adding value), consumer behavior goals (referrals, cross-buying), and affective or persona goals (enjoyment, feeling appreciated, being honest). The authors go on to say that the goals varied widely across firms and that even the nature of what a relationship meant was highly variable. Clearly, firms desire that customers have expectations of what the firm desires of them.

The Role of Intermediaries

At this point, the importance of the firm's intermediaries (customer service representatives, salespeople) becomes paramount to the mutual satisfaction endeavor. These are people who provide more direct signals to the customer as to what is expected from the viewpoint of the firm. The example of a customer service representative is a good starting point, although similar examples with salespeople as intermediaries easily come to mind.

In Maxham and Netemeyer (2003), the authors show that consumer expectations of the outcomes of complaining (i.e., the firm's response) result from *shared values* of complaint management. That is, there appears to be a bidirectional understanding of what constitutes a legitimate complaint (the firm's expectation of the behavior of its customers) and a similar understanding on the part of the consumer. Shared values were shown to enhance redress satisfaction, satisfaction with the firm, and recommendations. This redress satisfaction result has frequently been found in prior studies; the shared values issue is a nuance in this regard. Similar findings were reported by DeWitt and Brady (2003), who showed that *existing rapport* between the customer and the service provider (not intermediary) resulted in greater postfailure customer satisfaction, intention, and decrease in negative word-of-mouth (w-o-m). In the same context, *relationship continuity* can foster mutual expectations of service recovery (Hess, Ganesan, and Klein 2003). These findings, although bidirectional, all attest to the fact that firms hold expectations for their customers that are acknowledged by these customers. Thus, clear mutual expectations of appropriate requests communicated verbally or nonverbally by the firm and/or its representatives to the consumer appear to enhance firm outcomes.

One very good example of a firm wishing to instill its value system in its customer base is Harley-Davidson. The company has very specific expectations of its customers, especially of its Harley Owners Group members, and communicates these directly (see Harley-Davidson 2004). Members are expected to keep their riding skills honed through sanctioned rider skills classes, keep their bikes in safe condition, participate in charity and benefit rides, participate in rallies, and generally present a favorable image to the public. Members of the Harley Owners Group (but not necessarily other Harley-Davidson riders) generally do so. Of interest is the fact that without being nudged by the firm to comply, Harley owners are loathe to ride a bike that hasn't been kept clean and polished.

Other not-so-obvious firm expectations of customers are less easily demonstrated but exist nonetheless. For example, many firms expect that their good efforts will be rewarded by customers in the form of favorable recommendations and referrals. For example, Swan and Oliver (1989) measured postpurchase communications of many varieties in automobile purchasing. Although they did not ascertain whether dealers expected their clients to praise (or damn) them to others, anecdotal evidence of the "tell others about us" is legion. And I would be remiss if I did not mention the proselytization efforts of many sectarian faiths asking their congregations to recruit potential converts.

Methods by which this can be accomplished are not well studied in the literature. In fact, Rosen (2000, p. xiii) begins his popular press book by stating that "there isn't much formal research on buzz" and goes on to say that the Internet is one of the most formidable media for this phenomenon. Two academic examples of strategies can be cited, however. In a study by Derbaix and Vanhamme (2003), the authors show that the elicitation of surprise (deliberately exceeding expectations—see the preceding discussion) is one method of generating w-o-m. Yet another technique is similar to that described under complaint redress. Gremler, Gwinner, and Brown (2001) describe how favorable interpersonal relationships between customers and service providers' employees foster positive w-o-m behaviors. Again, it appears that firm intermediaries can be instrumental in translating company expectations of its customers to its customers.

At this point the data available to this author is mute. Aside from institutional entities such as government, political and religious organizations, close individual relationship bonds, and collective bonds, little is available to suggest that firms communicate their expectations to their customers or that customers attempt to assess firms' expectations of them. This situation heralds back to the early days of commerce where "arm's-length" transactions were (and are) prevalent. In this scenario, the merchant advertises through print, display, or other device; then a sale ensues; some form of currency or barter takes place; and the two entities part. This, referred to as a transactional exchange, is to be contrasted to the relational exchange that current marketers have espoused for some time.

In fact, Sheth and Shah (2003) suggest that many buyers actually prefer transactional exchange so that they do not feel committed or that, at some point, relational exchange may somewhat naturally degrade into transaction-based exchange because of the effort required in maintaining relations. This suggests that, for many industries, firms, and consumers, mutual satisfaction will be an infrequent, if not undesired, outcome. Thus, mutually satisfying consumption is most unlikely to become a universal phenomenon—but remains a worthy goal nonetheless.

MORE ON FIRM LOYALTY TO CUSTOMERS

In the same manner that customers can become loyal to firms and/or their products, it might be expected that firms can become loyal to customers at the individual or collective levels. In some sense, firms might take an advocacy position toward their constituents. This phenomenon can be observed in politics (the pork barrel effect); in sports, in which players "coddle" fans with autographs and the like; in popular music, in which events are performed for free (fan fares); and especially in casinos, where "high rollers" are given perquisites of all sorts, including rooms, food, drinks, and shows. One might question, however, whether these amenities constitute firm loyalty or are simply a mechanical strategy of retaining one's most profitable customers.

Displaying loyalty to customers in more traditional channels is somewhat more difficult if not more vaguely understood. Typically, this strategy relies on loyalty programs, whereby customers earn points or credits toward similar or more varied merchandise or service. The evidence on strategies of this nature is mixed, however (see Dowling and Uncles 1997), because the nature of true loyalty is not typically addressed. More generally, I have made an effort to provide a psychological basis for the loyalty response and argue that it is multifaceted with elements of product superiority perceptions and a sense of shared community with other buyers (Oliver 1999).

With these elements in mind, I will now attempt to describe a firm's sense of commitment to its constituents. No clear exposition exists to my knowledge. What does it mean when a firm "in persona" is committed to its markets in the same manner in which consumers are committed to firms or their products? One helpful indicator would be that the firm believes that its constituents are superior to those of its competitors and, in addition, might share a sense of community with its constituents. Thus, a firm's loyalty to its market should reside in a belief that its customers are special in some manner, and this superiority should be reflected in a certain pride that it is serving this market base. These thoughts arise from the examples given previously in the areas of politics, sports, and entertainment.

As said previously, it is not clear that casinos (or other firms relying heavily on loyalty programs) qualify in a pure sense. Harrah's (see Loveman 2003) might come closest to this model because of its unique approach to customer retention whereby customers are categorized into three levels (gold, platinum, diamond) based on their potential for play. Diamond players are courted and lavishly entertained whether they win or lose. It is not known, however, whether a psychological bond has been established with these players, a criterion set forth here if mutual loyalty is to be established.

CONCLUSION AND RESEARCH DIRECTIONS

The thesis proposed here, that both consumers and firms will increase their mutually dependent outcomes if they understand and satisfy the expectations each has for one another, deserves increasing attention at both the theoretical and practical levels. Unlike the pursuits of charity giving and volunteerism, consumers are not accustomed and have not been socialized to the consideration of a provider's needs in the marketplace. Rather, an adversarial stance or, at best, a psychologically distant, dispassionate exchange appears to be the norm whereby consumers "get what they paid for." At the limiting polar extreme are those exchanges in which the two parties knowingly "do battle" with one another in the culmination of an exchange. The used car market would be one example of this phenomenon: Buyers expect to be disadvantaged, and sellers believe buyers will say or do anything to drive down the price. Individual personal experiences and those of acquaintances, consumer publications, price comparison Web sites, and television exposés all serve to reinforce this perception. This has prompted a small number of automakers (e.g., Saturn) and auto resellers (e.g., CarMax) to move to a one-price, no-haggle strategy.

Consider the opposite, idyllic situation in which consumers were of the mind-set to support their providers with no-hassle fair profits, courteous dealings, complete honesty in returns, and deservedly positive w-o-m. This strategy could engender trust between partners, a key ingredient in successful relationships. At the collective level, even when consumers are unknown to one another, a sense of general trust could be instilled, recognizing that not all members of society "play by the rules." I recognize that a utopia of this sort is unlikely; it remains as a worthy goal perhaps never to be achieved. Nonetheless, institutions and marketers can use this as a template for business planning going forward.

The research issues here are straightforward. As the satisfaction of consumers has been studied aggressively, focus would need to shift to satisfying the expectations the firm has of its consumers beyond the mere return of revenues and profits. This will require internal work on the part of the firm as to what its goals are as translated to consumers. After the list is established, the next requirement would be to determine the extent to which consumers understand these needs. Given some level of understanding, the firm would need to design strategy to communicate poorly understood needs or to modify those that are not accurately held. The next step would be to determine the extent to which consumers would wish to comply or entertain complying with each. At this point, the firm might find that procedures to initiate or enhance the desire to comply are needed.

These tasks are not as difficult as they might at first seem. In a study by Oliver and Swan (1989), auto buyers were asked to rate their perceived inputs to and outcomes from the purchase. This was performed with reference to the salesperson, the dealership, and themselves for use in a test of equity theory. Although the results are not of particular relevance here, the methods employed in the study are. They resulted in little confusion on the part of the respondent as well as an adequate response rate with very little missing data. The point of this discussion is that consumers do have perceptions, however inaccurate, of "behind the scenes" data such as the fairness of a deal and even the subjective nature of a "good commission." Although neither salespersons' nor dealers' perceptions of inputs and outcomes were measured, these would have been internal metrics from the standpoint of the firm and more easily accomplished.

It is hoped that this chapter will stimulate others to begin consideration of this "radical" paradigm shift of mutual satisfaction in consumption. By modeling the activities of those institutions that must communicate their needs (charities, congregations, political organizations), to those that communicate with some measure of authority (government), to those that share belief systems (fan clubs, consumer clubs such as the Harley Owners Group), and, finally, to those that can only model or suggest needs requiring fulfillment (most retailers), an economy at least partially built on mutual trust and dependence may emerge.

REFERENCES

Bernhart, Kenneth L., Naveen Donthu, and Pamela A. Kennett (2000), "A Longitudinal Analysis of Satisfaction and Profitability," *Journal of Business Research,* 47 (February), 161–71.

Brownstein, Deborah (1997), "Commitment in Interfirm Relationships: Conceptual Roots and Research Implications," in *Research in Marketing,* vol. 13, Jagdish Sheth and Atul Parvatiyar, eds. Greenwich, CT: JAI Press, 1–17.

Claycomb, Cindy and Charles L. Martin (2002), "Building Customer Relationships: An Inventory of Service Providers' Objectives and Practices," *Journal of Services Marketing,* 16 (7), 615–35.

Derbaix, Christian and Joëlle Vanhamme (2003), "Inducing Word-of-Mouth by Eliciting Surprise—A Pilot Investigation," *Journal of Economic Psychology,* 24 (February), 99–116.

DeWitt, Tom and Michael K. Brady (2003), "Rethinking Service Recovery Strategies: The Effect of Rapport on Consumer Responses to Service Failure," *Journal of Service Research,* 6 (November), 193–207.

Dowling, Grahame R. and Mark Uncles (1997), "Do Customer Loyalty Programs Really Work?" *Sloan Management Review,* 38 (Summer), 71–82.

Dwyer, F. Robert, Paul H. Schurr, and Sejo Oh (1987), "Developing Buyer-Seller Relationships," *Journal of Marketing,* 51 (April), 11–27.

Gremler, Dwayne D., Kevin P. Gwinner, and Stephan W. Brown (2001), "Generating Positive Word-of-Mouth Communication Through Customer-Employee Relationships," *International Journal of Service Industry Management,* 12 (No. 1), 44–59.

Harley-Davidson (2004), *Harley Owners Group® Membership Manual.* Milwaukee, WI: Harley-Davidson Motor Company.

Heskett, James L., W. Earl Sasser, Jr., and Leonard A Schlesinger (1997), *The Service Profit Chain: How Leading Companies Link Profit and Growth to Loyalty, Satisfaction, and Value.* New York: The Free Press.

Hess, Ronald L., Jr., Shankar Ganesan, and Noreen M. Klein (2003), "Service Failure and Recovery: The Impact of Relationship Factors on Customer Satisfaction," *Journal of the Academy of Marketing Science,* 31 (Spring), 127–45.

Jaworski, Bernard, Ajay K. Kohli, and Arvind Sahay (2000), "Market-Driven Versus Driving Markets," *Journal of the Academy of Marketing Science,* 28 (Winter), 45–54.

Lovelock, Christopher and Evert Gummesson (2004), "Whither Services Marketing? In Search of a New Paradigm and Fresh Perspectives," *Journal of Service Research,* 7 (August), 20–41.

Loveman, Gary (2003), "Diamonds in the Data Mine," *Harvard Business Review,* 31 (May), 109–15.

Maxham, James G., III and Richard G. Netemeyer (2003), "Firms Reap What They Sow: The Effects of Shared Values and Perceived Organizational Justice on Customers' Evaluations of Complaint Handling," *Journal of Marketing,* 67 (January), 46–62.

Minor, Michael S., Tillman Wagner, F.J. Brewerton, and Angela Hausman (2004), "Rock On! An Elementary Model of Customer Satisfaction with Musical Performances," *Journal of Services Marketing,* 18 (No. 1), 7–18.

Oliver, Richard L. (1997), *Satisfaction: A Behavioral Perspective on the Consumer.* New York: Irwin/McGraw-Hill.

——— (1999), "Whence Consumer Loyalty?" *Journal of Marketing,* 63 (Special Issue), 33–44.

——— and John E. Swan (1989), "Equity and Disconfirmation Perceptions as Influences on Merchant and Product Satisfaction," *Journal of Consumer Research,* 16 (December), 372–83.

Reichheld, Frederick F. (1996), *The Loyalty Effect.* Boston: Harvard Business School Press.

Rosen, Emanuel (2000), *The Anatomy of Buzz: How to Create Word-of-Mouth Marketing.* New York: Doubleday.

Rucci, Anthony J., Steven P. Kirn, and Richard T. Quinn (1998), "The Employee-Customer-Profit Chain at Sears," *Harvard Business Review,* 26 (January–February), 82–97.

Sheth, Jagdish N. and Reshma H. Shah (2003), "Till Death Do Us Part . . . But Not Always: Six Antecedents to a Customer's Relational Preference in Buyer–Seller Exchanges," *Industrial Marketing Management,* 32 (November), 627–31.

Swan, John E. and Richard L. Oliver (1989), "Postpurchase Communications by Consumers," *Journal of Retailing,* 65 (Winter), 516–33.

Vargo, Stephen L. and Robert F. Lusch (2004), "Evolving to a New Dominant Logic for Marketing," *Journal of Marketing,* 68 (January), 1–17.

10

CO-PRODUCTION OF SERVICES

A Managerial Extension

MICHAEL ETGAR

INTRODUCTION

In their 2004 article, Vargo and Lusch (hereafter V&L) present a new viewpoint on marketing that they define as service-dominant logic (S-D logic). V&L maintain that value is created by use. As the consumer is the one who consumes and thus experiences the use, he or she participates in the performance of the value-creation activities. Therefore, the S-D logic suggests that production and consumption are not two separate activities but one continuous whole, and consumers are not recipients of a completed output but are involved in the whole value-creation process.

Value Creation and Activity Performance

To create value-in-use, various activities must be performed. For example, in their discussion of the services provided by appliances, V&L suggest that

> Goods are appliances that provide services for and in conjunction with the consumer. How-ever, for these services to be delivered, the consumers still must learn to use, maintain, repair and adapt the appliance to his or hers unique needs, usage situation and behavior (Vargo and Lusch, 2004, p. 11).

In this example, value creation requires the performance of maintenance activities, repair activities, and activities of adapting the working of the appliance to the needs of a particular household (e.g., redesigning a house). On top of it, V&L argue that consumers also must "learn"—that is, devote resources to understanding and practicing all these activities.

But consider even such a service event as going to see a movie. A consumer who wants to go to see a movie must select one, order tickets to a particular theater, pay for them, physically acquire the tickets, arrange transportation to the movie theater, enter the theater, purchase popcorn, view the movie, leave the theater, get rid of waste, and convey oneself and possibly one's family back home. We have here a string of value-generating activities or of support activities of various kinds that need to be completed before the total value of "going to the movies" is created.

The Consumer as a Decision Maker

The issue of consumers performing activities in-house instead of purchasing their performance in the marketplace has been addressed by Lusch, Brown, and Brunswick (1992). However, this chapter presents a somewhat different approach. Its focus is not descriptive but more oriented toward decision making. It focuses on the notion of consumers–producers and their need to make economic decisions similar to those used by managers in firms that produce various goods. I do use some of the constructs presented by Lusch, Brown, and Brunswick (1992) but integrate them in my decision-making model.

According to the economic theory, producers strive to perform given activities in a format that enables them to minimize their total costs (McLellan 1973). Therefore, the consumer who is a producer should behave in a similar way.

THE MODEL

This chapter presents a model that shows how consumers make strategic decisions to minimize the costs of performing value-creating activities. First, I present the assumptions of the model; then I explain its mechanism; and I conclude with a discussion of some of its implications.

Assumptions

The model is based on several assumptions as to the characteristics of the value-generating process as well as to the characteristics of the pertinent consumer decision-making process. The assumptions are as follows:

1. The value-chain-creation process is composed of distinct activities that must be performed in order to generate value that can be separated from each other.
2. The performance of these activities requires the use of various resources, especially human labor, machines, equipment, and supplies. All these bear costs for their use.
3. The consumer is aware of his or her role as a manager in the production–consumption process; this means that he or she must decide how to optimize the performance of the required activities.
4. Value-creating activities are divisible. In other words, they can be divided along a time range or along some other measuring attribute.
5. The consumer manager can use two kinds of activity performers: members of his or her household and/or specialist firms in the market. Naturally, the consumer can use both and have different mixes of household member performers and market specialist performers.
6. These activities can be moved from one type of performer to another without transfer costs.
7. One must bear in mind that it is the consumer who eventually bears all the costs of performing the relevant activities, whether performed by the household members or by the market specialists.

The Mechanism

The model proposes that to perform relevant value-creating activities, consumers–managers use a mix of performers (household members and market specialists). Consumers–producers will strive

Figure 10.1 **The Household Production Cost Function Model**

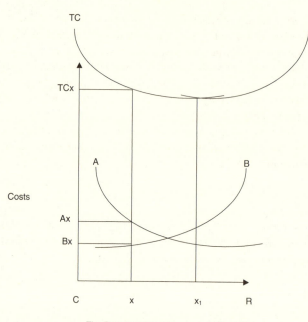

The Required Maintenance Activities Effort

A   = Household production cost function curve
B   = The curve of total expenditure for fees of specialists
TC = Total costs curve
Ax   = Household production costs when using X performer's mix
Bx   = Total expenditure on specialist fees when using X performers' mix
TCx = Total consumers' expenses for using the X performers' mix

to minimize the total costs of the performance of each activity by choosing the most efficient mix of such activity performers.

The consumer calculus works in the following way: For each activity consumers consider all the potential mixes of performers. For each mix, the consumer calculates its total production costs. Those include the costs of employing the household members and the cost of fees paid to specialists.

Figure 10.1 presents the model. The activity used (as an example only) is maintenance of an electric appliance. Usually, maintenance needs are defined by years or months, so I chose to define this activity in terms of maintenance for one year.

The horizontal axis in Figure 10.1 presents the continuum of the potential mixes of performers the consumer might use for the performance of this activity. On one extreme, on the left side, defined by point C, the performers' mix includes only the household members. In this case, maintenance of the appliance is performed by the consumer and/or other members of the consumer's household.

As we move along this continuum from point C to point R, the mix changes: The share of the contribution of the household members to the performance of the particular activity declines, and the share of the contribution of the market specialists increases. At the other extreme, on the right side, defined as point R, the performers' mix includes only the market specialists without any input from household members. Here, the consumer purchases the performance of all the pertinent activity from market specialists.

The vertical axis marks costs and presents three cost curves. Curve A represents the cumulative costs of performing the relevant activities or parts of them by the household members. Following Etgar (1978), I define this curve as the *household production cost function*. The curve is at its highest at point C when the household members are the only performers and is at its lowest level at point R when the specialists are the only performers.

Curve B indicates the cumulative expenditures facing the same consumer when he or she purchases the same service from a market specialist. It is positioned exactly opposite to curve A. Its highest level is at point R (the specialist is responsible for all the maintenance) and its lowest is at point C (household members do all the maintenance). To simplify the argument at this point, let us assume that both costs curves are curvilinear to indicate economies of scale in activity performance.

The TC curve shows the total expenditures for all the potential mixes of performers. TC is constructed for each producer's mix by adding the internal household costs as presented by curve A with the specialist fees as presented along curve B. Consider a hypothetical mix presented by the point X. At this level, the total expenditure that a consumer will bear will be

$$Ax + Bx = TCx$$

and it is indicated on the TC curve.

The consumer then scans the TC curve and chooses the mix of performers that offers the minimum total cost. This point is presented at Figure 10.1 by the point X1.

A shift of X1 to the right implies that optimal mix will include more work done by the market specialists and less done by the household members. A shift to the left implies the opposite.

Shifts of the Household Production Cost Function

Consumers–managers will change their optimal performers' mix due to exogenous changes that result in corresponding shifts of curves A or B. A downward shift of curve A implies that for each mix of performers, costs of performing the pertinent activity by the household members has gone down. An upward shift of this curve implies the opposite.

Similar changes could happen to curve B. A downward shift to the right implies lower specialist fees. An upward shift to the left implies higher specialist fees. However, an individual consumer takes these fees as given in his or her decision making, and therefore I do not discuss those fees in this chapter.

The Determinants of the Household Production Cost Function

The economic theory suggests that overall costs of production of any good are affected by the costs of various inputs used in the production process, by the technology used, and the relative efficiency of using these resources (McLellan 1973). A household production cost function (curve A) is determined by the same cost factors. Those include the following:

1. *Labor costs.* Labor costs reflect, first, the amount of time members of a specific household spend on performing the specified activities. The amount of time required reflects the skills members of the household might possess as a result of natural inclinations, skills, and previous expe-

rience. Thus a retired electrician will be probably handier at appliance repairs than a retired university professor.

2. *Price (value) of the time used for activity performance.* This primarily reflects the economic value of the time unit a member of the household spends participating in the performance of the required task. This can be calculated as the income forgone that this member of the household could earn in the marketplace outside the household at the same time.

These revenues reflect the skills and the abilities of each household member to command a salary at the marketplace. It also incorporates "social" costs or values that consumer puts on time not spent with relatives and friends. Finally, there are also psychological costs of "wasting" one's time on activities less preferred.

In some cases, social and personal costs could be offset by positive values that certain activities might provide to particular consumers. Home bread baking takes time that could be used for socializing with friends and therefore has some "costs," but it also has a "fun" value. In such cases the costs to the consumer of such an activity are reduced.

Multiplying the amount of time used times its value provides the consumer with the evaluation of the inherent costs of labor used.

3. *Costs of use of equipment.* The consumption–production process requires use of equipment such as cars (for deliveries), refrigerators (for storage), electricity, housing space (for in-house storage), and so on. Purchasing such equipment pieces involves capital outlay and forces the consumer–producer to invest accordingly.

4. *Risks of learning unique skills* that might not be applicable for other activities. Examples are the skills to repair a specific model of a television set or learning how to use a given version of a computer program. The more service specific are the skills, the more they imply the risk of losing the investment if the relevant service becomes obsolete or unnecessary. For example, consider the problems of relearning the details of each new version of Microsoft Office.

5. *Costs of renting or buying specific equipment* needed for the performance of such activities.

The Effect of Changes in the Cost Components on Consumer Strategies

Changes in any of these cost components affect the household production cost function. Figure 10.2 shows graphically the effect of potential reduction in any of the previously mentioned cost components. A decline in any of these household production cost components causes curve A to move down to the position of A2. Consequently, the initial total costs curve—TC1—is replaced by a new one—TC2, which is located to the left of the first one. The impact of this shift is that the minimum cost point moves to the left as well. As a result, the consumer changes his or her mix of performers. The share of the household effort in the performers' mix increases and that of the specialists decrease.

An increase in any of these cost factors has the opposite effect on the household production cost function. It raises curve A to the right, and the optimal performers' mix will include more specialists and fewer inputs from the consumer's household.

The increase or decrease in the fees specialists charge has obvious effects on the performers' mix. But regular consumers cannot change these fees and must consider it as a given.

IMPLICATIONS AND EXTENSIONS OF THE MODEL

The costs of performing activities by household members differ across consumers and can vary also from one activity to another.

Figure 10.2 **The Effects of Change on the Household Production Cost Function**

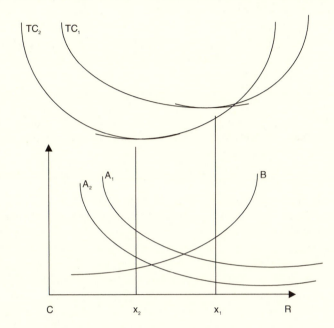

The Required Maintenance Activities Effort

A_1 = Initial household production cost function curve
A_2 = Household production cost function curve after decrease in household costs
TC_1 = Total costs curve before the change
TC_2 = Total costs curve after the change
X_1 = The optimal performers' mix before the change
X_2 = The optimal performers' mix after the change

Differences among Consumers

The household production cost function is affected by several household characteristics. The most important are those that affect the value (price) of time used by household members.

Age

Younger consumers usually earn less but have more free time and more energy. Therefore, on the average their time has less economic value than that of a person 40 or 50 years of age. As consumers grow up and change, time becomes more valuable. As consumers reach the retirement age, the economic value of their time declines again. Therefore, one might find that among older consumers there is a higher tendency to engage in in-house production.

Income Differentials

On the one hand, households with higher incomes reflect the higher earning capabilities of their members. This implies higher "costs" of forgoing these incomes for using the time of these members for internal production.

On the other hand, however, more affluent households can find it easier to "invest" in equipment necessary for performance of capital intensive activities (e.g., refrigerators, large freezers, large storage facilities) and "invest" time in learning advanced skills such as gourmet cooking. Therefore, the overall effect of the income variable on consumers' selection of the performers' mix is not clear.

Cultural Differences

Cultures affect the social norms as to the roles of various household members and especially those of women and children (Usunier 2000). In some cultures, women are expected to stay at home and cannot work outside the household. This in turn lowers the economic value of their time. These households will therefore tend to entrust more value-creating activities to their household members, namely to the women.

Cultures with norms that accept women's participation in the workforce and that expect children go to school rather than work in the household will generate an opposite trend. In such cultures women's time has market value, and therefore, the "indirect" costs of internal household production are higher.

As a result, these households will be less inclined to forgo such income in order to perform value-creating activities within the household. Therefore, these households will prefer to employ specialists to perform the necessary value-creating activities.

In some ethnic groups, the performance of various value-creating activities by members of the household carry important symbolic meaning or are designed as taboos and are forbidden. Thus, for example, among members of some castes in India, handling garbage or washing dirty linen is deemed to be impure. This implies prohibitive costs for their performance within one's household, and such households will use more specialists for their performance.

When two or more of these factors appear simultaneously in the same households, the total effect is not clear beforehand.

Differences among Activities

Besides the differences among consumers, one might find also that different activities will have different resource requirements and therefore might affect the internal costs of a household in a somewhat different format. Some activities are more time-consuming than others. Irrespective of the effect of household characteristics described previously, more time for performance implies higher costs for in-house production.

Therefore, consumers will prefer to use more market specialists for their performance. Similarly, activities that demand more specialized equipment and unique skills will also be considered too risky for in-house performance.

The following sections detail other potential differentiating factors among activities.

Complexity

Some activities are more complex and complicated than others. Complexity increases the costs of internal performance because consumers need to learn more and run the risk of wasted know-how. Therefore, for example, consumers will tend to purchase more mechanical car repairs from specialists than services involving general care of homes.

Technological Innovations

The level of knowledge required for the performance of various activities might decline due to technological innovations. Thus, for example, complicated repairs of household appliances are replaced today by "unplug and replace," which requires no knowledge in electronics. This trend should increase the tendency of consumers to replace the work of specialists by their own effort.

Specific Equipment and Knowledge

Some activities demand the use of specific equipment and unique know-how. Others do not. The more specific the equipment used or the knowledge needed, the higher the costs of performing such an activity by household members. Consumers will be more likely to use specialists for the performance of the major part of such activities.

The Dynamic Changes

Consumer characteristics and activity attributes do change over time, though slowly. This in turn leads consumers eventually to change their performers' mix. Consumer behavior might change from one generation to another, following changes in the business environment. In the following section I first outline several macro changes that lead to an increase in the costs of in-house performance, and then I map out the changes that have the opposite effects.

Changes That Increase Costs

Social and Cultural Changes. Today, cultural changes motivate more and more consumers to use their free time for entertainment, sports, or education. This trend increases the social and the psychological costs of time household members spend on the performance of the value-creating activities associated with regular consumption activities such as food consumption. Consumers therefore will tend to increase the share of the specialists in the mix of performers. One result is the growing popularity of out-of-home eating and entertaining.

Demographics. A major demographic change in the mature economies of the United States, Western Europe, and Japan is the growth in the number of smaller families and of more single-person households. In such households less time is available and the corresponding costs of using one's time for the performance of consumption-related activities have increased sharply. This raises the costs of household production with the corresponding increase in the share of the specialists in the performers' mix. Here one can see the corresponding effect in the growth of semi-prepared foods and dishes, greater reliance on home delivery of foods, and increased outsourcing of various home maintenance activities.

Entry of Women into the Workforce. The twentieth century has seen a sharp increase in the share of women joining the workforce. Traditionally, women were the buying agents and were responsible for household operation in many households in the United States and Europe. In the modern era, many women gain education and join the workforce. This reduces the amount of women's time that households can use for in-house performance of consumption-related activities. The effect on the mix of performers is similar: lower share of household inputs and higher share of specialists in the performers' mix. Growth of telemarketing and Internet-based shopping are two examples of the possible effects of this trend.

Globalization. The globalization trend integrates more and more economies together. But it also brings more and more people in the fast-growing economies to adopt Western-like employment, demographic, and consumption patterns. This in turn tends to spread the effects depicted in the preceding sections into more and more countries.

Technology. The development of the Internet as a tool for interaction between buyers and sellers has greatly reduced the costs of purchasing and therefore reduced the total costs of performance of consumption-related activities by consumers, their spouses, and their children.

Changes That Lower Costs of Household Production

Whereas some dynamic forces tend to raise the costs of performing value-generating activities by the household members, other forces have the opposite effect.

Recession

Economic recession and the bursting of the high-tech bubble have increased the number of unemployed and the amount of time people stayed between jobs. This has reduced the market value of time for many consumers and thus lowered the "costs" of internal production.

Cultural Changes

Some cultural changes such as New Age beliefs and behavior, and the search for self-fulfillment are upgrading the status of many basic activities associated with consumption and home maintenance (e.g., bread baking). Similarly, the novel trend of cooking and self-preparing of foods might have upgraded the status of all food-preparation activities. This again offsets the cost of their internal production.

Another important change is that in many places, shopping has become involved with entertainment. This has made purchasing less of a cost factor and more of a value-producing factor in itself. Again, this might offset some of the regular costs of performing consumption-related activities. All these induce households to increase the share of activity performance by their households

Increased Efficiency of the Consumer as a Producer

The quality of the household refers to its efficiency as consumers (Xue and Harker 2002). Consumer efficiency refers to the speed with which he or she can complete the required process for delivering the service. An increase in the general level of education in a market can lead to more efficient consumption. This in turn implies that consumers need less time for the in-house performance of the various activities. This lowers costs of in-house production and could lead consumers to entrust more activities to their household members and buy less from specialists.

Major Issues

The basic assumptions of the model are also the sources of its major problems. First, one might argue with the basic notion that consumers behave like optimizing machines. Critics might propose that consumers take into consideration other aspects of behavior besides the wish to reduce costs, such as the need for control. Yet, any in-depth analysis will reveal that in a world of scarce resources, households must make economic decisions as to the use of their scarce household resources, be they time, financial resources, or household equipment. Therefore, a model such as the one presented here makes sense.

Second, the model assumes that consumers have all the relevant cost information. In reality, some consumers might not have it or might not know how to use it to make the relevant conclusions. When consumers underestimate the time they need for the performance of a particular activity, they might prefer to use more of their in-household resources than they should, and vice versa, when they overestimate the time or the complexity demanded for the activity performance. Consumers therefore could use risk-reducing techniques to make decisions with only partial information.

Third, the model assumes that there are no transfer costs for moving activities from household members to specialists and vice versa, but that might not be the case. When activities are moved from the household to market specialists, the consumer might incur such costs as specification of instructions to market specialists (extra time and effort), chances of misunderstanding, need to haggle over the fees involved, selection of appropriate specialists, and costs of policing execution. When activities are moved from a market specialist to a household member, one might consider such costs as lack of specialized knowledge, which could lead to poor or mediocre performances.

Fourth, the model assumes perfect divisibility of the activities among the various performers. In reality, some activities might not be so easily divided, forcing the consumer to make either-or kinds of decisions. All these imply corresponding adjustments in the model.

DISCUSSION

This chapter takes us some steps further from the basic notion of consumer as a co-producer. It expands our understanding of consumer co-production decisions and behavior and, as such, contributes to the understanding of how consumers actually cope with their role as producers. Based on economic assumptions, it presents a model of a consumer–producer. This consumer must make managerial decisions as to how to perform the necessary value-creating activities at the lowest costs possible. One of the most important ways to achieve that is by choosing the optimal mix of performers of the various value-creating activities.

An important implication of the model presented in this chapter is that consumers–producers might decide to apply their decision-making calculus to a wide array of additional activities performed along the production–consumption value chain. They might evaluate the costs of such activities as product delivery, or even new product development or design, and decide to what extent they themselves should become involved in their performance.

Thus, the role of the consumer/user in the e-business exchange extends beyond that of a consumer in a typical retailer–consumer transaction. The consumer provides information (about both his or her needs as well as how well the product actually works), makes the necessary choice of books or computer components, and even decides about the supplier—deciding whether to get a new book versus a used one for a lower price, for example (Xue and Harker 2002).

The model can also expand our current knowledge of retailing change and serve as a basis for a new version of the wheel of retailing theory. It can explain how, why, and when new retailing formats are developed and when and why old retailing formats die. New formats develop when consumers want to change their mix of performers of value-creating activities, hence the growth of home delivery, use of interior designers, and use of professional organizers for children's birthday parties to replace the time and energies of busy moms.

The household production cost function is dynamic, and it changes from one consumer segment to another. Different household traits can help identify appropriate consumer segments that will rely more on internal production and those that will rely more on specialists. Analyzing future trends in population growth, economics, and cultural changes can help scholars and managers to predict the future trends in this topic.

FURTHER RESEARCH

Further research should test some of the proposals developed in this chapter. There is also a need to quantify the model and suggest a measurable costing system for in-house activities. Case studies of novel retailing formats and novel products should be explored to see how they fit into the proposed model.

A potential avenue of research is to expand the theoretical model presented by relaxing the assumption of smooth transfer of activities between performers. When such transfers are not smooth and involve costs of their own, these costs must be integrated in the model. We know from channel theory that when transactions are not costless, diverse governance structures are developed (Heide 1994). Researchers should explore the application of these ideas into the co-production model.

ACKNOWLEDGMENT

The author acknowledges the assistance of the research unit of the School of Business Administration at the College of Management in the writing of this chapter.

REFERENCES

Etgar, M. (1978), "The Household as a Production Function," in *Research in Marketing,* Vol. 1, J. Sheth, ed. Greenwich, CT: JAI Press, 75–98.
Heide, J. (1994), "Interorganizational Governance in Marketing Channels," *Journal of Marketing,* 55 (April), 29–37.
Lusch, R.F., S. Brown, and G. Brunswick (1992), "A General Framework for Explaining Internal vs. External Exchange," *Journal of the Academy of Marketing Science* 20 (2), 119–34.
McLellan J.D. (1973), *Production Decisions and Control.* New York: Hamilton Institute.
Usunier, J.C. (2000), *Marketing Across Cultures, 3d Ed.* Upper Saddle River, NJ: Prentice Hall, Financial Times.
Vargo, S.L. and R. Lusch (2004), "Evolving to a New Dominant Logic for Marketing," *Journal of Marketing,* 68 (January), 1–17.
Xue, M. and P. Harker (2002), "Customer Efficiency: Concept and Its Impact on E-business Management," *Journal of Service Research* 4 (4), 253–61.

11

STRIVING FOR INTEGRATED VALUE CHAIN MANAGEMENT GIVEN A SERVICE-DOMINANT LOGIC FOR MARKETING

DANIEL J. FLINT AND JOHN T. MENTZER

INTRODUCTION

In this chapter, we expand on the initial points made in three foundational premises in Vargo and Lusch's (2004) service-dominant (S-D) logic for marketing that have particular relevance for integrated value chain management—specifically foundational premises 6 (i.e., the customer is always a co-producer), 7 (i.e., the enterprise can only make value propositions), and 4 (i.e., knowledge as the fundamental source of competitive advantage). We highlight challenges and current business practices emerging from corporate concern for value management within integrated global supply chains that support these three premises. Integrated value chain management is distinguished as the most effective and efficient operation of supply chain management. *Integrated value chain management* refers to fully interconnected and smoothly operating supply chains. Now that supply chain management has moved toward the center stage of enterprise management, organizations are trying to determine opportunities to improve the state of the art. The term *integrated value chain management* is used to clearly reflect the goal for which supply chain management now strives: a service orientation to multiple enterprise management.

Within this context, the critical differentiating roles knowledge, supply chain partnerships (which involve co-production), and services play within global value chains are emphasized. What is changing is a shift toward a process orientation in which differentiation and resultant revenue generation (key marketing objectives) come from knowledge about processes such as co-production and innovation with business customers, knowledge about both similarities and differences among a wide variety of cultures and subcultures, knowledge about processes for customer learning and translation of that knowledge into marketing strategies, and knowledge about processes for linking firms together around the globe to develop efficient and effective supply chains. Thus, value propositions now involve products, services, processes, experience (history), and networks of relationships, all aimed at superior value creation. In many cases customers are partners as well as suppliers, exchanging and modifying value propositions within a dynamic web of constantly changing needs. This chapter draws primarily on business customer value and supply chain management domains.

Figure 11.1 presents an S-D logic for integrated value chain management with respect to co-production, value propositions, and knowledge management.

Figure 11.1 **Service-Dominant Logic for Integrated Value Chain Management**

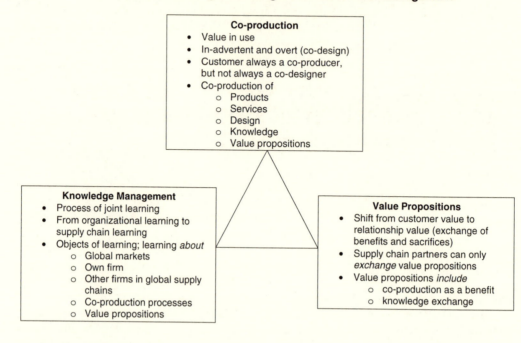

CO-PRODUCTION

Vargo and Lusch (2004) contend that an S-D logic for marketing recognizes that customers are significant participants in the creation of value and state in foundational premise 6 that the customer is always a co-producer. Much of Vargo and Lusch's (2004) discussion focuses on end-use consumers; however, if anywhere there exists co-production between customers and suppliers, it is in the business-to-business (B2B) relationships that exist upstream from the end-use consumer. Within business-to-business relationships themselves, supply chain management has attracted a great deal of attention in both practice and scholastic research due to the significant cost management and competitive advantage potential that reside in superior management of supply chain processes. Superior integrated value chain management demands close after-the-sale interaction among many parties that manifests co-production in many forms.

Supply chain management has been defined as "the strategic management of all the traditional business functions that are involved in any flows, upstream or downstream, across any aspect of the supply chain system" (Mentzer 2004, p. 5). It involves coordination and cooperation across functions for at least three organizations. Such integration requires extensive exchange of information, products, services, finances, and risk. Here we wish to emphasize the concepts of value-in-use, inadvertent versus overt co-production, and objects of co-production.

Value-in-Use

Value is created for business customers when suppliers' products, information, support personnel (e.g., account managers, logistics managers, design engineers, field service technicians, account-specific financial analysts, customer service representatives), logistics services, and other services are incorporated into specific customer processes, operations, and facilities that constitute varied use situations (Woodruff and Gardial 1996). Customers operate in many different situations, as reflected by multiple receiving facilities, launch of new facilities, crises in overburdened facilities, and changes in market demand, to name a few. Customers value different components of suppliers' value propositions in each of their different use situations. Thus, suppliers must anticipate or respond to varying value perceptions and desires associated with different customer use situations.

Customer value research, although still in the embryonic stage, finds that business customers interact with suppliers in attempts to achieve certain functional and relationship goals. Due to the variety of use situations in continual flux, suppliers find they need ever deeper and timelier information from customers to create value continuously. Customers are finding that ensuring supplier agility and responsiveness to their changing demands requires deeper and timelier information from suppliers. These two emergent deeper-understanding realizations by suppliers and customers give rise to the joint goal of integrated value chain management. In this sense, customers are always co-producers of value, and value is never simply embedded in the product or service itself.

Integrated value chain management deals with the *use* of information *about* and *by* all business functions to facilitate the flow of goods and services through the supply chain. Customers value transportation information, inventory information, security and risk information, storage facility network design, forecasting information, and financial information differently depending on specific use situations. In *utilizing* this information and helping to ensure its accuracy and form, customers co-produce value with suppliers. This kind of co-production represents co-production through consumption.

Inadvertent versus Overt Co-production

There are two ways customer organizations become involved in co-production, and creating value through consumption is only one of them. The other is through co-design. Through direct feedback (e.g., satisfaction surveys, direct comments to supplier account management teams) and indirect feedback (e.g., reducing, canceling, increasing orders), customers influence development and modification of those products and services offered by suppliers, and as such *inadvertently* influence product and service design. More overtly, customers become directly involved with suppliers to specifically develop and modify products and services. Many strategically important suppliers have co-located personnel and resources within customers' premises to improve the effectiveness and efficiency with which product design, manufacturing, and delivery decisions are made.

However, integrated value chain management must recognize that although customers are always value co-producers, they are not always co-designers. Lack of feedback from customers, whether instigated by the supplier or the customer, leaves important value-creation design ideas out of the supply chain.

Objects of Co-production

What exactly is co-produced in integrated value chain management? For starters, co-production and co-design are particularly noticeable in the design and execution of logistics processes within integrated value chain management. *Logistics* has been defined as "that part of the supply chain processes that plans, implements, and controls the efficient, effective forward and reverse flow and storage of goods, services, and related information between the point of origin and the point of consumption in order to meet customers' requirements" (Council of Logistics Management 2003). Logistics as an industrial marketing service can be executed by a third party or executed internally. Because logistical needs vary widely across firms within supply chains, often the logistics services are custom designed with significant input from multiple shippers and receivers. Clearly services are co-designed in many ways. Integrated value chain management services include at least transportation, inventory management (e.g., vendor management of inventory, physical storage of inventory, consignment agreements), assembly/contract manufacturing within storage facilities, information technology system design, forecasting management, material requirements planning, and dedicated supply chain experts on account management teams. Pulling together this bundle of support services provided to partner firms throughout the supply chain requires direct and continual input from each of the other organizations, but most importantly from downstream customers. The most strategic customers in supply chains become involved in the co-design of these services. The less strategic customers are not always involved in co-design efforts, but certainly serve as co-producers as they interact with supplier personnel in the performance of these services.

Through continual relationship management across functions and firms, knowledge is generated about markets, systems, processes, and operations. This knowledge is co-produced in integrated value chain management because multiple minds across several firms exchange perspectives and share skills. Integrated value chain management organizational learning, which is the co-production of knowledge within and across a firm, expands to supply chain learning.

Finally, value propositions are co-produced. Businesses rarely prepackage value propositions that are delivered to business customers. Instead, they work and engage in dialogue with customers as components of value propositions, which are then considered and modified to the satisfaction of both parties. Integrated value chain management strives for this mutual understanding of an exchange of mutually developed value propositions.

We argue that services, knowledge, and value propositions are always co-produced, and often co-designed (sometimes inadvertently and sometimes overtly) within integrated value chain management. Thus, we extend foundational premise 6 to *supply chain partners* are always co-producers of *value for each other* within integrated value chain management.

VALUE PROPOSITIONS

Foundational premise 7 states that the enterprise can only make value propositions (Vargo and Lusch 2004). This premise recognizes that value is not embedded in products but is created by customers as they interact with suppliers' products and services. To take this further, the "proposition" is that particular products and services *potentially* could be of value if the customer finds a way to utilize them toward goal achievement; that is, it is *proposed* that the products and services could help the customer create value for himself or herself.

Supply chain management, business customer value, and relationship marketing research emphasize the perspective that value is *exchanged* between supply chain partners—not merely delivered from supplier to customer. For example, business customer value research is beginning to explore the notion of relationship value (Ulaga 2003). Looking at business customer value research specifically, one finds that customer value can be viewed in several ways. First, value can be viewed as a trade-off between what is received and what is given up (Zeithaml 1988). Second, business customers value functional benefits, service benefits, and relationship benefits, and tolerate certain monetary and nonmonetary sacrifices (Lapierre 2000; Ulaga 2003). Often changes in nonmonetary sacrifices significantly affect the strength of supply chain relationships. Third, value can be viewed in terms of a hierarchy of goals or desired consequences whereby supplier attributes are viewed as valuable because they facilitate goal attainment and minimize sacrifices incurred along the way (Bagozzi and Dholakia 1999; Woodruff 1997). Fourth, value can be viewed in terms of the interaction between suppliers' products/services, customers' use situations, and customers' desired goals and end states (Woodruff 1997). These categorizations simply help us understand what is meant by *value* and as such how perceptions of value propositions might vary.

We also know that business buying decisions often involve numerous members of the customer organization—that is, the buying center. Therefore, integrated value chain management demands a solid understanding of supply chain management–relevant value perceptions for each of these individuals. Specifically, suppliers must understand goals and end states for desired functional, relational, and service benefits, desired monetary and nonmonetary sacrifices, acceptable trade-offs among these benefits and sacrifices, and various relevant use situations for each member of the buying center—members who often change as contracts and use situations change. The resources to gain this level of understanding are significant but are required for the development of solid value propositions. Similarly, account management has moved continuously toward cross-functional teams, meaning that what selling center members value from customers varies as well. Since supplier value involves similar categories of benefits and sacrifices as customer value, there is quite a lot that customers should understand about suppliers' desires as well. So both parties are *exchanging* value propositions, and those propositions include co-production opportunities and knowledge as key benefits.

Thus, we extend foundational premise 7 as follows: *Integrated value chain partners* can only *exchange* value propositions.

KNOWLEDGE MANAGEMENT

The third foundational premise to address here is premise 4 (knowledge as the fundamental source of competitive advantage). Effective integrated value chain management demands knowledge about global markets, multiple relevant supply chain member firms, and processes. Concerning global market knowledge, supply chains must generate knowledge about targeted end-use customer desires and demand levels in numerous countries and cultures, as well as the desires and demand levels for firms throughout the supply chains serving these countries. Concerning knowledge about supply chain member firms, members must generate knowledge about each firm's culture, strategies, processes, and operations—planned and current. Concerning processes, supply chain members must generate knowledge about processes for integrating across functions and firms. Note that we specifically use the term *generate* as opposed to *share* or *exchange*, because integrated value chains co-produce (foundational premise 6) knowledge about markets and operations. They also co-produce knowledge about knowledge generation; that is, they learn *how to learn* together. Because individual skill levels, knowledge levels, and ways of learning vary so widely, any partnership involving many people from several organizations quite naturally requires a great deal of management of the process of learning itself in order for knowledge to be generated about other aspects of integrated value chain management.

If knowledge is a fundamental competitive advantage, then at the heart of integrated value chain knowledge management is global supply chain learning—specifically, multiple organizations across the globe knowing how to generate knowledge about global markets, global customers, and global supply chains. As such we expand organizational learning to supply chain learning and by extension, knowledge as the fundamental source of competitive advantage to supply chain learning processes as the key source of competitive advantage in integrated value chain management.

CHALLENGES THAT LIE AHEAD

Numerous challenges exist for both academics and practitioners in moving supply chain management toward integrated value chain management given the S-D logic emerging in supply chain management thinking. The first step lies in recognizing that an S-D logic can serve to orient thinking and bring into the foreground those issues that are important across industries and continents when addressing supply chain challenges. Beyond defining terms such as *trust* and *value*, we must move toward learning better ways to make happen what we know must be done. This requires full and open recognition of barriers to our march toward integrated value chain management and confrontation of those barriers head on. Some of the most pressing issues include building trust within supply chain relationships, facilitating the exchange of safely guarded information, facing the financial challenges of supply chain management, and changing the face, focus, and incentive systems of account management teams.

Building Trust within Supply Chain Relationships

Trust is a core enabler of sustainable supply chain relationships. It is important to note that trust needs to go beyond the individual. It must extend to the organization and be present in dealings at every management level and functional area—be it purchasing, logistics, engineering, sales, marketing, or any other function—to create value among supply chain partners. Given the necessity for co-production of knowledge and value propositions and the exchange of value within integrated value chain management, trust among supply chain partners will become more critical in creating value for end-use consumers. Traditionally, organizations have been reluctant to share strategy, process, and operational information with supply chain partners and often find it difficult to do so within their own firms. However, co-production of service, knowledge, and value propositions demands refinement of processes aimed specifically at building and maintaining trust among supply chain partners. Research suggests that integrated supply chain relationships depend on trust, commitment, mutual dependence, organizational compatibility, shared visions, leadership, top management support, and frequent interaction (Ganesan 1994; Geyskens et al. 1996; Gundlach, Achrol, and Mentzer 1995; Gundlach and Cadotte 1994; Mentzer, Min, and Zacharia 2000; Mentzer et al. 2001; Morgan and Hunt 1994; Rinehart et al. 2004; Thibaut and Kelley 1959; Wilson 1995). Without the relationship management cornerstones of trust, commitment, and dependence, supply chain partners cannot develop the close, coordinated ties that lead to effective and efficient value co-production. To carry this further, an S-D logic for integrated value chain management hinges on the exchange of closely guarded information.

To address this challenge, we propose two research questions:

1. What supply chain relationship factors place pressure on, inhibit, or damage trust in supply chains?
2. What roles do organizational culture and organizational culture fit across organizations play in helping to build trust?

Facilitating the Exchange of Safely Guarded Real Time Information

Mentzer, Foggin, and Golicic (2000) found one of the primary impediments to supply collaboration was a lack of trust in sharing critical information with potential supply chain partners. Without such information as point-of-sale demand, inventory levels, supply chain costs, advertising/ promotion/merchandising plans, and strategic goals, supply chain partners will continually inadvertently act at cross purposes in the effort to produce value. Without such information, it might be impossible to understand what supply chain partners truly value and of what they are truly capable, thus circumventing integrated value chain management efforts.

One piece of information that has become extremely critical as well as sensitive is that of forecast data. However, joint forecasting not only improves individual firm performance within supply chains, it also facilitates co-production of value. Yet, relatively little attention has been paid to the role of sales forecasting and demand management in the supply chain, or how that role might change depending on the position in the supply chain that a company occupies. From an integrated value chain management perspective, the question arises, "Do all members of the supply chain need to forecast demand?" In fact, taking an integrated value chain management perspective reveals that any supply chain has only one point of independent demand—or the amount of product demanded (by time and location) by the end-use customer of the supply chain (Mentzer and Moon 2004). Whether this end-use customer is a consumer shopping in a retail establishment or online (business to consumer, or B2C), or a business buying products and services for consumption in the process of conducting their business operations (B2B), the demand of these end-use customers determines the true demand that will flow through the supply chain. In a new S-D logic, the value being exchanged through the supply chain lies within modifying forecasting management processes such that joint forecasting can be accomplished.

The company in the supply chain that directly serves this end-use customer directly experiences this independent demand. All subsequent companies in the supply chain experience a demand that is tempered by the order fulfillment and purchasing policies of other companies in the supply chain. This second type of supply chain demand is called *derived demand*, because it is not the independent demand of the end-use customer, but rather a demand that is derived from what other companies in the supply chain do to meet their demand from their immediate customer (i.e., the company that orders from them) (Mentzer and Moon 2004). It is important to note that only one company in any given supply chain is affected by independent demand. The rest are affected by derived demand. Equally important, the techniques, systems, and processes necessary to deal with derived demand are quite different from those of independent demand. In fact, many companies develop elaborate sales forecasting techniques, systems, and processes when, in fact, they do not even need to forecast.

Recognizing the differences between independent and derived demand, recognizing which type of demand affects a particular company, and developing techniques, systems, and processes to jointly deal with each company's particular type of demand can have a profound impact on supply chain costs, customer service levels, and the value each company brings to supply chain value co-production processes. As such, the service each supply chain partner brings to the table is providing the most appropriate knowledge, techniques, process, and systems to enhance forecasting management at the entire supply chain level.

Certain research opportunities exist concerning the sharing of critical information:

1. How does a service-dominant orientation among supply chain partners affect the exchange of critical market and supply chain information?
2. How does a service-dominant orientation among supply chain partners affect the co-production of demand throughout the supply chain?

Facing Financial Challenges of Integrated Value Chain Management

One critical challenge inherent in moving toward an S-D logic for integrated value chain management involves convincing both supply chain partners and Wall Street of the importance in recognizing individual firm–level transaction losses for the good of long-term supply chain success. Wall Street wants to see immediate positive results. Efforts to improve the long-term profitability of the company and/or the supply chain, at the expense of profits next quarter, are met with skepticism at best from Wall Street. More likely, such a move is met by a "sell" recommendation that drives down the stock price. Because senior management spends much of its time worrying (appropriately) about shareholder value, much of their concern is focused on the day-to-day stock price. Thus, publicly traded companies can easily become driven by what Wall Street wants to hear, rather than by what is best for the long-term competitive advantage of the company and the supply chain. This orientation can conflict with an integrated value chain management goal.

Unfortunately, many of the integrated value chain management strategies discussed in this chapter fall into this category of investments that might not make the company "look good" in the next quarter but pay off in the long run. When companies implement an integrated value chain management strategy, the first thing that happens is a considerable investment in systems, personnel, and training to realize the level of information/knowledge sharing and value co-production collaboration with supply chain partners to make the strategy work. These events have a substantial negative effect on earnings for the initial quarters in which the strategy is implemented—a fact that invariably drives down the stock price. (After all, the company shows an initial decrease in earnings per share.) The fact that this strategy has a considerable long-term positive effect on earnings does not get factored into the stock price for the first quarter.

The challenge is to convince Wall Street that these moves are positive. In many ways, implementing what has been discussed here is easier for privately held companies. When the chief executive officer (CEO) of a privately held company is presented with an integrated value chain management strategy that will hurt earnings for one quarter but make considerable improvement in earnings over the long run, he or she does not have to worry about what Wall Street will do to the stock for one quarter. Rather, the CEO simply decides if the return on investment (i.e., the cost/benefit analysis necessary for value analysis) is appropriate for the company and makes a decision. Unfortunately, the CEO of a publicly traded company spends much less time on the return-on-investment decision, and much more time than their privately held company counterpart worrying about what Wall Street (and, subsequently, their stockholders) will think next week. In other words, shareholder impressions (not necessarily long-term shareholder value) are a major component of the value proposition of publicly traded company CEOs.

We see many examples of this phenomenon in business. Salespeople are pushed to generate additional sales at the end the quarter to make the quarterly numbers, even if such pushing hurts their relationships with customers. One company discovered its salespeople were going to customers at the end of the quarter and asking them to place orders for products they could not use. The reason? The salesperson told the customer, "It would really help me if you placed this order this week, so we could make our sales numbers, and you can cancel the order next week." Of course, what was happening was the company was preoccupied with "making the numbers" it had promised to Wall Street. The accounting system recorded the sales in the quarter when they were needed and recorded negative sales (the cancellation) in the next quarter. This tactic met the short-term (this quarter) goals of the company but ignored the negative strategic impacts: The negative sales would have to be made up next quarter, salespeople were spending time "meeting the numbers" instead of actually building value-based relationships with customers and making real sales, artificial sales followed by cancellations were wreaking havoc on supply chain operations, and perhaps most importantly everyone involved was encouraged to "massage the numbers" rather than co-produce value in the supply chain.

Many companies hurt their long-term strategic value propositions (not the least of which is profitability) by playing such games. What happens when customers realize that, each quarter, if a company is not making its sales numbers, the company will drastically reduce prices to get more sales before the quarter is over? If they are smart, they will wait for the end-of -quarter "sale" and then buy enough product at the reduced price to last them for the next three months. The result is they have enough inventory to see them through the last month of the quarter, plus enough inventory to see them through the first two months of the next quarter—just enough to keep from buying long enough in the next quarter to get the supplier to panic again and lower prices. In fact, customers can work out a mathematical model that includes the amount of the end-of-quarter discounts and their own cost of carrying the extra inventory and determine their optimal forward-buying amount. The result, of course, is customers come to expect to never buy at the "regular" price, thus taking away supplier margins.

This is good for the tactics of the customer, but what does it do to sales patterns of the supplying company? It creates repeating patterns of demand in which derived demand is very low for the two months (causing inventory buildup) when margins (prices) are higher, and one month of high derived demand (causing higher production costs) in which margins (prices) are lower. Thus, the tactic of "making the quarterly numbers" is detrimental to the strategic success of the company—in effect, encouraging customers to take away supplier margins and disrupt smooth supply chain operations flows (both elements of supplier value). Perhaps most importantly, it encourages customers to take an adversarial position, rather than a mutual, value–co-producing position with their suppliers.

Research questions that emerge from a financial focus of supply chain management might include the following:

1.   Are firms that adopt an S-D logic to supply chain management able to create more value for buyers and sellers?
2.   Are firms that adopt an S-D logic able to convince Wall Street of the long-term benefits of this logic?
3.   Because of the pressures of Wall Street for immediate returns, is it easier for private companies to implement an S-D logic?

Changing the Face, Focus, and Incentive Systems of Account Management Teams

We need to move more rapidly away from traditional account management, to account management teams such as core teams and selling centers (Moon and Armstrong 1994), and specifically to account management teams that include supply chain and logistics expertise (Flint and Mentzer 2000). Far too few organizations incorporate supply chain management experts in daily account management. Of those that do, most do so primarily for strategic and national accounts due to resource constraints of assigning such teams to all accounts. Supply chain experts add value by seeing opportunities that traditional sales managers do not see, which enables supply chain management knowledge and expertise to become a differential advantage and not merely a cost and operational management domain. Incentive systems become an important challenge in the management of such teams. More important is the challenge of finding the right supply chain experts who are also good marketers (i.e., good listeners and communicators to customers). Some researcher challenges lie in determining the conditions under which such teams generate the most profits for supply chain partners, identifying the best kind of person for the supply chain marketer role (e.g., a marketer then trained in supply chain management or a supply chain management expert then trained in marketing), and the design of account management incentive systems. Clearly, integrated value chain management and long-term financial goals motivate a move away from traditional quota- and commission-based incentive systems that could inhibit value co-production.

The focus of these cross-functional account management teams needs to shift toward a process mentality in an S-D logic. Value propositions and knowledge generation will become more long-term in orientation in integrated value chain management and, as such, focused on determining how firms will interact with each other through an integration of processes. Selling process integration represents a shift away from selling products, but it also involves tolerance for value chain system changes.

If management is largely about the development and execution of processes that span functions, then supply chain management extends this process focus to multiple organizations. The problem is that many firms still hold to the idea of functional management, which can be seen in organizational structures and incentive systems. A process mentality highlights operations within the value chain and forces personnel and even individual supply chain partners to the background, thus enabling the system to evolve and morph as the changing values of the market environment dictate.

Similarly, account management teams with an integrated value chain process focus need different incentive systems than traditional account management teams. If performance is important, then measurement is important. Organizations, to a great degree, are not measuring key supply chain processes, activities, or outcomes that co-produce value and, as a result, often have reward systems that are not aligned with their integrated value chain management strategies. Linking measures and rewards to integrated value chain management strategies is necessary to ensure alignment and focus. Performance measurement systems should be formally evaluated and managed. Otherwise, the result is a performance measurement "system" in which the interrelations between the measures are not known, duplication is frequent, omissions are undetectable, and many misalignments result. As a consequence, companies inadvertently reward their personnel for not co-producing value propositions for their customers.

This discussion of account management teams leads to several proposed research questions:

1. Under what conditions do account management teams that include a supply chain management focus enhance value co-production within the supply chain?
2. On what processes should account management teams focus as they shift toward an integrated value chain perspective from a contract negotiation perspective?
3. What account management team incentive systems are best suited for an S-D logic–oriented, cross-functional account management team?
4. Do such incentive systems drive increased firm profitability?

CONCLUDING COMMENT

Clearly for supply chain management to move toward integrated value chain management, stronger supply chain partnerships must develop. Doing so requires overcoming a host of challenges, some of which we have highlighted here. Similarly, research needs to develop a much deeper understanding of valuing co-production related phenomena. The S-D logic implies that the process of overcoming these obstacles to integrated value chain management can itself serve as a way for supply chain partners to create value for each other. Specifically, as partners co-produce knowledge and value propositions, they ought to form stronger bonds and deeper understandings of each other, enabling specific integrated value chains to exist as a competitive entity for longer periods of time.

REFERENCES

Bagozzi, Richard P. and Utpal Dholakia (1999), "Goal Setting and Goal Striving in Consumer Behavior," *Journal of Marketing,* 63 (special issue), 19–32.

Council of Logistics Management (2003), www.clm1.org. Accessed October 25, 2003.

Flint, Daniel J. and John T. Mentzer (2000), "Logisticians as Marketers: Their Role When Customers' Desired Value Changes," *Journal of Business Logistics,* 21 (2), 19–45.

Ganesan, Shankar (1994), "Determinants of Long-Term Orientation in Buyer-Seller Relationships," *Journal of Marketing,* 58 (April), 1–19.

Geyskens, Inge, Jan-Benedict E. M. Steenkamp, Lisa K. Scheer, and Nirmalya Kumar (1996), "The Effects of Trust and Interdependence on Relationship Commitment: A Trans-Atlantic Study," *International Journal of Research in Marketing,* 13 (October), 303–17.

Gundlach, Gregory T., Ravi S. Achrol, and John T. Mentzer (1995), "The Structure of Commitment in Exchange," *Journal of Marketing,* 59 (January), 78–92.

——— and Ernest R. Cadotte (1994), "Exchange Interdependence and Interfirm Interaction: Research in a Simulated Channel Setting," *Journal of Marketing Research,* 31 (November), 516–32.

Lapierre, Jozee (2000), "Development of Measures to Assess Customer Perceived Value in a Business-to-Business Context," in *Advances in Business Marketing and Purchasing,* Vol. 9, Arch G. Woodside, ed. Greenwich, CT: JAI Press, Inc., 243–86.

Mentzer, John T. (2004), *Fundamentals of Supply Chain Management: Twelve Drivers of Competitive Advantage.* Thousand Oaks, CA: Sage Publications.

———, William DeWitt, James S. Keebler, Soonhong Min, Nancy W. Nix, Carlo D. Smith, and Zach G. Zacharia (2001), "Defining Supply Chain Management," *Journal of Business Logistics,* 22 (2), 1–26.

———, James H. Foggin, and Susan L. Golicic (2000), "Collaboration: The Enablers, Impediments, and Benefits," *Supply Chain Management Review,* 4 (September/October), 52–58.

———, Soonhong Min, and Zach G. Zacharia (2000), "The Nature of Interfirm Partnering in Supply Chain Management," *Journal of Retailing,* 76 (4), 1–20.

——— and Mark A. Moon (2004), "Understanding Demand," *Supply Chain Management Review,* 8 (May/June), 38–45.

Moon, Mark A. and Gary M. Armstrong (1994), "Selling Teams: A Conceptual Framework and Research Agenda," *Journal of Personal Selling and Sales Management,* 14 (1), 17–30.

Morgan, Robert M. and Shelby D. Hunt (1994), "The Commitment-Trust Theory of Relationship Marketing," *Journal of Marketing,* 58 (July), 20–38.

Rinehart, Lloyd M., James A. Eckert, Robert B. Hanfield, Thomas J. Page, and Thomas Atkin (2004), "Structuring Supplier-Customer Relationships," *Journal of Business Logistics,* 25 (1), 25–62.

Thibaut, John W. and Harold H. Kelley (1959), *The Social Psychology of Groups.* New York: John Wiley & Sons.

Ulaga, Wolfgang (2003), "Capturing Value Creation in Business Relationships: A Customer Perspective," *Industrial Marketing Management* 32 (8): 677–93.

Vargo, Stephen L. and Robert F. Lusch (2004), "Evolving to a New Dominant Logic for Marketing," *Journal of Marketing,* 68 (January), 1–17.

Wilson, David T. (1995), "An Integrated Model of Buyer-Seller Relationships," *Journal of the Academy of Marketing Science,* 23 (4), 335–45.

Woodruff, Robert B. (1997), "Customer Value: The Next Source for Competitive Advantage," *Journal of the Academy of Marketing Science,* 25 (Spring), 139–53.

——— and Sarah Fisher Gardial (1996), *Know Your Customer: New Approaches to Customer Value and Satisfaction.* Cambridge, MA: Blackwell Publishers.

Zeithaml, Valarie A. (1988), "Consumer Perceptions of Price, Quality, and Value: A Means-End Model and Synthesis of Evidence," *Journal of Marketing,* 52 (July), 2–22.

12

CROSS-FUNCTIONAL BUSINESS PROCESSES FOR THE IMPLEMENTATION OF SERVICE-DOMINANT LOGIC

Douglas M. Lambert and Sebastián J. García-Dastugue

To implement the service-dominant (S-D) logic within an organization, management must identify the core competencies that make the customer choose the firm over its competitors and those services for which customers will pay a premium price. These core competencies are derived from the application of specialized skills and knowledge, and form the basis of a firm's competitive advantage (Vargo and Lusch 2004). A market orientation and long-term relationships are necessary for the development of an organization's competitive advantage. Management must identify the relationships that are critical for the firm's success now and in the future, and integrate activities with key customers and suppliers who are co-producers of the value proposition for the end-customer/consumer.

Management must not only develop knowledge of the customer, but also develop market intelligence that includes the ongoing evaluation of environmental factors that might affect the firm's business or that of its customers. To be effective, market intelligence needs to be disseminated throughout the organization, and the organization needs to be responsive to this knowledge of the customer (Kohli and Jaworski 1990). The integration of activities across the firm's corporate functions is a requirement for the successful adoption of a market orientation (Kohli and Jaworski 1990; Narver and Slater 1990). Failure to integrate activities effectively will hinder management's ability to make the entire value system work (Normann and Ramírez 1993). The integration of activities across multiple corporate functions is implemented using cross-functional teams and cross-functional business processes (Day 1997; Srivastava, Shervani, and Fahey 1999; Vargo and Lusch 2004). The implementation of cross-functional business processes changes the role of the corporate functions in the organization (Achrol 1991; Homburg 2000; Homburg, Workman, and Krohmer 1999). The role of the function in the firm depends on the contribution of each function to the direction and integration of the cross-functional business processes (Day 1997).

Close relationships are supported by in-depth and integrated customer knowledge (Parvatiyar and Sheth 2001). As marketing proceeds toward a service-oriented, relationship-based paradigm, many existing models and concepts must be updated to include what ultimately matters: lifetime value of the customer relationship (Rust 2004). When transactions in a relationship are driven by choice elements other than brand and value, elements such as switching costs should be considered. Switching costs sufficiently high to lock a customer in a relationship with a supplier might be based on competencies developed in any corporate function. For example, a customer might

become locked in a relationship with a supplier that has demonstrated superior product development capabilities because it is possible to leverage the supplier's capability to introduce novel
products more frequently and on a timelier basis. The choice elements might not be identified at
the beginning of a relationship but rather evolve over time (Rust 2004).

Our goal is to present a framework to assist management in the successful adoption of the S-D
logic through the implementation of cross-functional business processes. We begin this chapter
with a section that describes business process management. Then, we present a framework comprising eight business processes that, when implemented, will integrate activities within a firm
and across firms in the supply chain. Next, we describe how the cross-functional business processes are supported by the fundamental premises of S-D logic (Vargo and Lusch 2004). Finally,
we present conclusions.

BUSINESS PROCESS MANAGEMENT

A *business process* is a structured set of activities with specified business outcomes for customers
(Davenport and Beers 1995).[1] Initially, business processes were viewed as a means to integrate
corporate functions within the firm. Now business processes are used to structure the activities
between members of a supply chain. Hammer (2001) points out that it is in the integration of
business processes across firms in the supply chain where the real "gold" can be found.

The concept of organizing activities as business processes was introduced in the late 1980s and
became popular in the early 1990s, after the publication of books by Hammer and Champy (1993)
and Davenport (1993). The motivation for implementing business processes within and across members of the supply chain might be to make transactions efficient and effective or to structure interfirm
relationships in the supply chain. The first motivation focuses on meeting the customer's expectations for each transaction; the second on achieving long-term mutual fulfillment of promises.

The transactional view of business process management is rooted in advances in information
and communication technology that enable time compression and availability of information
throughout the organization (Hammer and Mangurian 1987). This transactional approach to redesigning business processes is based on Taylor's principles of scientific management, which
aim to increase organizational efficiency and effectiveness using engineering principles from
manufacturing operations (Taylor 1911). In this case, business process redesign is based on standardizing transactions and the transfer of information (Davenport and Short 1990). The goal is to
improve outcomes for customers by making transactions more efficient and accurate.

The second view of business process management focuses on managing relationships in the
supply chain and is based on an evolving view of relationship marketing. A significant amount of
the marketing literature is concerned with market transactions (business transactions with customers) and the fulfillment of orders. Rooted in economic theory, researchers studied the efficiency of transactions with the customers, which raised awareness about the importance of customer
retention (Webster 1992). Obtaining repeat business—that is, conducting multiple transactions
with the same customer—is more cost efficient than obtaining a new customer (Kotler 1997).

The concept of relationship management in the context of network organizations was introduced
by early marketing channels researchers such as Alderson (1950) and Bucklin (1966), who conceptualized why and how channels are created and structured. From a supply chain standpoint, these
researchers were on the right track in terms of (1) identifying who should be a member of the
marketing channel, (2) describing the need for channel coordination, and (3) mapping the structure
of marketing channels. However, for the past thirty-five years, most marketing channels researchers
ignored two critical issues. First, they did not have a total supply chain perspective. Second, market-

ing channels researchers focused on marketing activities and flows across the channel and overlooked the need to integrate and manage multiple key processes within and across companies. Webster
(1992) challenged marketers and marketing researchers to consider relationships with multiple firms.
He also called for cross-functional consideration in strategy formulation.

Relationship marketing is about establishing, maintaining, and enhancing relationships with
customers in order to meet the objectives of both parties to the exchange at a profit, which is
accomplished by the fulfillment of promises (Grönroos 1990). Thus, the focus of developing and
maintaining relationships in the supply chain is beyond the fulfillment of one or a set of transactions. In this environment, managers need to focus on helping customers achieve their objectives,
which requires an S-D logic.

The field of relationship marketing is focused on the customer side, looking downstream in the
supply chain. However, the development and maintenance of relationships with key suppliers
should be based on the same pillars—mutuality and fulfillment of promises—in order for suppliers to be profitable. Management needs the support of the firm's key suppliers to fulfill the promises made to customers and meet financial goals. In other words, corporate success is based on
relationship management with both suppliers and customers.

Both the transactional and the relationship approaches to implementing business processes
have benefits. Simply making transactions more efficient has limited value in terms of creating a
competitive advantage. Although transactional efficiency requires information technology (IT),
IT is a necessary but not sufficient element to enable the adoption of a marketing orientation (Day
2003). Top performers change the way they do business and adapt their organizations to the new
environment (Day 1999). IT provides up-to-date information to geographically dispersed managers, working in different functions. Consequently, IT facilitates the implementation of cross-
functional teams and can be used to support relationships with key members of the supply chain.

The management of interorganizational relationships with members of the supply chain involves people, organizations, and processes (Webster 1992). The ability to manage
interorganizational relationships "may define the core competence of some organizations as links
between their vendors and customers in the value chain" (Webster 1992, p. 14). This is a foundational premise of the S-D logic (Vargo and Lusch 2004). Several authors have suggested implementing business processes in the context of supply chain management, but there is not yet an
"industry standard" on what these processes should be. The value of having standard business
processes in place is that managers from organizations in the supply chain can use a common
language and can link up their firms' processes with other members of the supply chain, as appropriate. "Regardless of the type of organization, the fundamental process does not change; people
still exchange their often collective and distributed specialized skills for the individual and collective skills of others" (Vargo and Lusch 2004, p. 8).

Executives involved in our research believed that in order to increase competitiveness and
profitability, internal activities and business processes should be linked across multiple companies. Our research also shows that in some cases, customers and suppliers were using different
names to describe similar processes and, in other cases, were using the same name to describe
different processes. To facilitate communication across corporate functions and across members
of the supply chain, a standard set of business processes is needed.

A FRAMEWORK FOR SUPPLY CHAIN MANAGEMENT

The supply chain is a network of organizations. Increasingly, the management of relationships
across the organizations that make up the supply chain is being referred to as *supply chain man-*

agement. Supply chain management offers the opportunity to capture the synergy of intra- and interorganizational integration and management.

Before proceeding, it is important to define *supply chain management* because there is still a great deal of confusion over the term. Frequently, it is seen as a synonym for *logistics* (Simchi-Levi, Kaminsky, and Simchi-Levi 2000), *operations management* (APICS 2001), *procurement* (Monczka, Trent, and Handfield 1998), or a combination of the three (Wisner, Keong Leong, and Tan 2004). Many regard the supply chain as being composed of inbound materials, raw material inventories, manufacturing, finished goods inventories, and distribution, and view supply chain management as the management of these activities within the purview of a single firm. Others view the supply chain as these activities from point of origin to point of consumption. Another perspective of supply chain management is based on the management of relationships with key customers and suppliers, and communication among business functions (Ellram and Cooper 1993).

A major weakness of much of the supply chain management literature is that most authors appear to assume that everyone knows what a supply chain is and who the members are. Few researchers have dedicated effort to identify specific supply chain members, key processes that require integration, or what management must do to manage the supply chain successfully.

In this section, we present the supply chain management framework developed by the Global Supply Chain Forum (GSCF). In 1992, researchers and executives from a group of companies with international operations, later to become the GSCF, began the development of a relationship-oriented and process-based supply chain management framework. The GSCF defines supply chain management as follows:

> Supply chain management is the integration of key business processes from end user through original supplier that provides products, services, and information that add value for customer and other stakeholders (Lambert 2004, p. 2).

The GSCF view of supply chain management is illustrated in Figure 12.1, which depicts a simplified supply chain network structure, the related information and product flows, and the eight supply chain management processes that must be implemented across corporate functions and across organizations in the supply chain. Thus, business processes become supply chain management processes to manage the links across intra- and intercompany boundaries. The customer relationship management process of the seller and the supplier relationship management process of the buyer form the links in the supply chain, and the other six supply chain management processes are coordinated through these two (for more information about the GSCF framework, see www.scm-institute.org).

Managing the entire supply chain is a very difficult and challenging task, as illustrated in Figure 12.2, because of the complexity required to manage all suppliers back to the point of origin and all products/services out to the point of consumption. Typically, executives have been more likely to manage their supply chains to the point of consumption than back to the point of original supply, because whoever has the relationship with the end user has the power in the supply chain. Intel created a relationship with the end user by having computer manufacturers place an "Intel inside" label on their computers. This affects the computer manufacturers' ability to switch microprocessor suppliers.

The implementation of the GSCF framework involves three steps: mapping the network structure; deciding which customers and suppliers with whom to link business processes and which of the eight processes will be involved; and deciding the level of management to dedicate to each relationship. In the next section, we describe the eight supply chain management processes.

Figure 12.1 **Supply Chain Management: Integrating and Managing Business Processes across the Supply Chain**

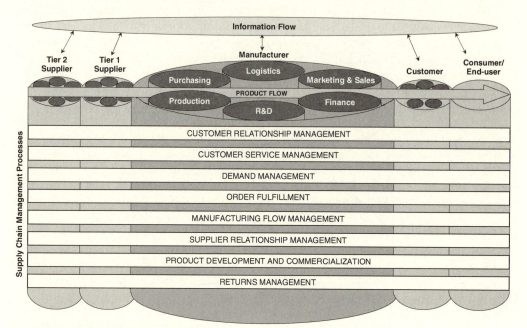

Source: Lambert (2006), p. 3.

Supply Chain Management Processes

Successful supply chain management requires a change from managing individual functions to integrating activities into key supply chain management processes. In many major corporations, such as 3M, management has reached the conclusion that meeting business goals and providing value to customers cannot be accomplished without implementing cross-functional business processes. The supply chain management processes identified by members of the GSCF follow:

- customer relationship management
- customer service management
- demand management
- order fulfillment
- manufacturing flow management
- supplier relationship management
- product development and commercialization
- returns management

A description of each of the eight processes follows (Lambert 2004).

Customer Relationship Management

Customer relationship management provides the structure for how the relationships with customers will be developed and maintained. Management identifies key customers and customer

Figure 12.2 **Supply Chain Network Structure**

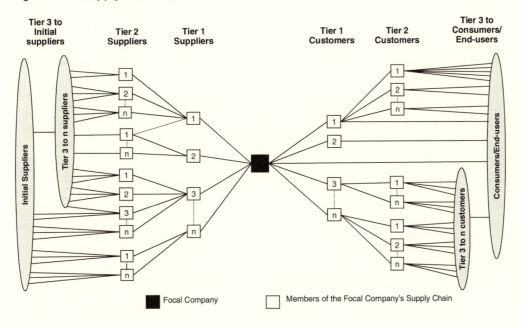

Source: Lambert (2006), p. 53.

groups to be targeted as part of the firm's business mission. The goal is to segment customers on the basis of their value over time and increase customer loyalty by providing customized products and services. Cross-functional customer teams tailor product and service agreements (PSAs) to meet the needs of key accounts and for segments of other customers. The PSAs specify levels of performance. The teams work with key customers to improve processes and eliminate non–value-added activities. Performance reports are designed to measure the profitability of individual customers as well as the financial impact of the firm's business on the customer (Lambert and Pohlen 2001).

Customer Service Management

Customer service management provides the key point of contact for administering the PSAs developed by customer teams as part of the customer relationship management process. Customer service managers are internal advocates for customers and proactively identify potential problems in fulfilling the organization's promises as contained in the PSA. The customer service management process might also include assisting customers with product applications, order management, or any other request.

Demand Management

Demand management is the supply chain management process that balances the customers' requirements with the capabilities of the supply chain. With the right process in place, management can match supply with demand proactively and execute the plan with minimal disruptions. The process is not limited to forecasting. It includes synchronizing supply and demand, increasing flexibility, and reducing variability. A good demand management system uses point-of-sale and key customer data to reduce uncertainty and provide efficient flows throughout the supply chain. Marketing requirements and production plans should be coordinated on an enterprisewide basis. Thus, multiple sourcing and routing options are considered at the time of order receipt, which allows market requirements and production plans to be coordinated on an organizationwide basis. In advanced applications customer demand and production rates are synchronized to manage inventories globally.

Order Fulfillment

The order fulfillment process involves more than just filling orders. It includes all activities necessary to define customer requirements and to design a network and a process that permits a firm to meet customer requests while minimizing the total delivered cost as well as filling customer orders. This is not just the logistics function; it must be implemented cross-functionally and with the coordination of key suppliers and customers. The objective is to develop a seamless process from the supplier to the organization and then on to its various customer segments.

Manufacturing Flow Management

Manufacturing flow management is the supply chain management process that includes all activities necessary to obtain, implement, and manage manufacturing flexibility in the supply chain and to move products through the plants. Manufacturing flexibility reflects the ability to make a wide variety of products in a timely manner at the lowest possible cost. To achieve the desired level of manufacturing flexibility, planning and execution must extend beyond the four walls of the manufacturer in the supply chain to include key customers and suppliers.

Supplier Relationship Management

Supplier relationship management is the process that defines how a company interacts with its suppliers. As the name suggests, this is a mirror image of customer relationship management. Just as a company needs to develop relationships with its customers, it also needs to foster relationships with its suppliers. As in the case of customer relationship management, a company will forge close relationships with a small subset of its suppliers and manage arm's-length relationships with others. A PSA is negotiated with each key supplier that defines the terms of the relationship. For segments of less critical suppliers, the PSA is not negotiable. Supplier relationship management is about defining and managing these PSAs. Long-term relationships are developed with a small core group of suppliers. The desired outcome is a win-win relationship in which both parties benefit.

Product Development and Commercialization

Product development and commercialization is the supply chain management process that provides the structure for developing and bringing to market products jointly with customers and suppliers. The product development and commercialization process team must coordinate with customer relationship management to identify customer articulated and unarticulated needs; select materials and identify supplier capabilities in conjunction with the supplier relationship management process; and interact with the manufacturing flow management process team to identify the appropriate manufacturing technology for manufacturing for the product/market combination.

Returns Management

Returns management is the supply chain management process by which activities associated with returns, reverse logistics, gatekeeping, and avoidance are managed within the firm and across key members of the supply chain. The correct implementation of this process enables management not only to manage the reverse product flow efficiently, but to identify opportunities to reduce unwanted returns and to control reusable assets such as containers. Effective returns management is an important part of supply chain management and provides an opportunity to achieve a sustainable competitive advantage.

Each of the eight processes is cross-functional and cross-firm, and can be broken down into a sequence of strategic subprocesses, in which the blueprint for managing the process is defined, and a sequence of operational subprocesses, in which the process is actualized. Each subprocess is described by a set of activities. Cross-functional teams are used to define the structure for managing the process at the strategic level and implementation at the operational level. These processes are shown in Figure 12.1. The appendix (pp. 164–165) shows each of the eight processes with its corresponding subprocesses at both strategic and operational levels.

Functional Involvement in the Supply Chain Management Processes

The successful implementation of the supply chain management processes requires the involvement of all functions. Functional involvement can be defined as "formal and informal direct contact among employees across departments" (Jaworski and Kohli 1993, p. 56). There is agreement that corporate functions need to be connected (Kahn and Mentzer 1998; Krohmer, Homburg, and Workman 2002), and the integration of corporate functions is necessary for the successful implementation of business processes (Day 1997; Gunasekaran and Nath 1997).

As business-to-business relationships develop and become tighter, more cross-functional involvement is required (Lambert, Emmelhainz, and Gardner 1996). The management of close business relationships becomes the management of the multiple points of contact between the functions of the organizations involved. Not only is high-level executive involvement necessary, but multiple levels within each function should be interacting on a regular basis (Lambert and Knemeyer 2004). The type of relationship that management in both organizations wants to achieve will determine the degree of intracompany integration that is necessary.

The implementation of each process should be led by a cross-functional management team. The teams are responsible for the design and implementation of the processes. All incumbent functions including, but not limited to, marketing and sales,[2] production, finance, research and development, purchasing, and logistics should participate in the process teams. The members of the cross-functional teams provide their functional expertise and ensure that the decisions are the right ones for the whole firm.

Failure to involve all functions can yield subpar performance or even result in failed initiatives. For example, a manufacturer of consumer durable goods implemented a rapid delivery system that provided retailers with deliveries in twenty-four to forty-eight hours anywhere in the United States. The rapid delivery system was designed to enable the retailers to improve product availability while holding less inventory. Six years later, after the manufacturer's finance function adopted economic-value-added (EVA) measures, the customers had not seen the inventory reductions, and top management increased the delivery time from forty-eight to seventy-two hours. The rapid delivery system never achieved its full potential as a service because the marketing organization still provided the customers with incentives to buy in large volumes (Lambert and Burduroglu 2000). This example should make it clear that failure to manage all of the touches will diminish the impact of initiatives in the supply chain. Using the framework presented in this chapter will increase the likelihood of success because all functions are involved in the planning and implementation of initiatives with key customers and suppliers.

All corporate functions are involved in all process teams in order to ensure that the knowledge and skills of each function is considered in the development of the value proposition for the customer. For example, in the customer relationship management process, sales provides the account management expertise, marketing provides the marketing plan and resources, research and development provides technological capabilities of the firm, logistics provides knowledge of customer service requirements and logistics capabilities, manufacturing provides the manufacturing capabilities, purchasing provides the sourcing capabilities, and finance provides customer profitability reports and financing capabilities.

In a service-centered organization, the customer requirements must be used as input to the functional strategies. Furthermore, all corporate functions may provide input with respect to how best to add value for customers. The fundamental unit of exchange is service (Vargo and Lusch 2004), and the service will be provided by the function or functions where the specialized skills and knowledge to produce the service reside. For example, manufacturing flexibility requires better planning capability and might require increased flexibility from suppliers. Flexibility is expensive and cannot be offered to all customers equally. However, flexibility can be offered to key customers, to those who are willing to reward the organization for the higher level of flexibility.

If the proper coordination mechanisms are not in place across the various functions, the process will be neither effective nor efficient. For example, purchasing depends on sales/marketing data fed through a production schedule to assess specific order levels and timing of requirements. These orders drive production requirements, which in turn are transmitted upstream to suppliers.

Typically, firms will have their own functional silos that must be overcome, and a process approach must be accepted in order to successfully implement supply chain management. However, the functional structure will not be replaced by processes because functional expertise is necessary, and the activities required to operate the business are performed within the functions. In addition, not all functional activities will be performed in cross-functional processes. For example, the timing of an advertising campaign needs to be coordinated through the cross-functional processes because advertising is designed to lift demand and resources need to be aligned in order effectively respond to the increased demand. However, the specifics of the advertising campaign such as media selection and the evaluation of how effective the advertising has been in attracting end customers will continue to be performed within the marketing function, where the required functional expertise resides. In the same vein, the decision on lead times, picking accuracy, fill rates each customer gets, and what plants will produce what products is performed by a cross-functional team in which marketing is involved. The actual picking of the order and shipping of the product is done within the firm's logistics organization.

As cross-functional processes are adopted, the relative strength of each corporate function will be diminished (Day 1997); however, gaining involvement of other functions in marketing decisions should result in better bottom-line results (Krohmer, Homburg, and Workman 2002). The business processes described in this chapter represent a framework for the integration of activities that traditionally are performed within a corporate function but for maximum efficiency and effectiveness must be coordinated or performed cross-functionally. The business processes also facilitate the alignment of functional performance measures with corporate goals and profitability.

SERVICE-DOMINANT LOGIC AND SUPPLY CHAIN MANAGEMENT PROCESSES

The eight foundational premises described by Vargo and Lusch (2004) provide a starting point for the evaluation of service-centered business opportunities. The supply chain management processes provide managers who want to implement the S-D logic with a framework that is being used in a number of major corporations.

Foundational premise 1 states that the application of specialized skills and knowledge is the fundamental unit of exchange. To base the exchange on a broader set of skills and knowledge, functional activities must be integrated. Furthermore, multiple activities must be integrated with key customers and suppliers. The supply chain management processes are cross-functional and cross-firm, which enables the exchange of a broad set of skills and knowledge. Our research findings show that as relationships become closer and more developed, more corporate functions participate in each relationship because the skills and knowledge required to maintain the relationship reside in multiple functions (Lambert 2004; Lambert and Knemeyer 2004).

Foundational premise 2 indicates that indirect exchanges mask the fundamental unit of exchange. The fundamental unit of exchange requires a bundle of skills and knowledge that reside in the corporate functions. In many cases, executives leading the corporate functions lose their focus on customers and turn their attention to the achievement of functional objectives, such as minimizing unit manufacturing cost for the production function. Minimizing the unit manufacturing cost might lead to increasing batch sizes in order to enjoy bigger economies of scale, which could result in a loss of responsiveness. To align resources and objectives across multiple functions, cross-functional business processes that are customer focused must be implemented.

Foundational premise 3 is that goods are distribution mechanisms for service provision. In business-to-business relationships, choice elements evolve over time. As the focus moves from individual business transactions to long-term relationships, choice elements include reliability, flexibility, and/or adaptability of operations and systems, which requires the management of all the touches between the two organizations involved in the relationship. For example, a quick-service restaurant chain operator buys the sauces for the promotional sandwiches from a supplier who uses the product development capability as a competitive advantage. Although product flows in the supply chain, the customer actually buys the supplier's capability to transform a market trend in consumers' taste into a sauce for a promotional sandwich that will provide a competitive advantage for the quick-service restaurant operator. For the supplier to successfully provide this product development capability, the cross-functional coordination achieved by implementing the supply chain management processes is necessary.

This example leads to the fourth foundational premise, which states that knowledge is the source of competitive advantage. To develop a competitive advantage, an organization must gain in-depth knowledge about the customer from a cross-functional perspective because the necessary service provision might require skills from any corporate function. The supply chain is managed link by link, relationship by relationship. Each link is managed by cross-functional teams through the customer relationship management and supplier relationship management processes. These processes facilitate information flow to all corporate functions involved in the relationship and enable the value proposition to include aspects from multiple functions.

As products commoditize, it is necessary to differentiate the offering from those of competitors by focusing on service. The result is that, in the end, all economies are service economies, which is foundational premise 5 of the S-D logic. Focusing on service requires developing intimacy between customer and supplier. The successful implementation of cross-functional teams is required to achieve sufficient intimacy with the customer to identify the choice elements that make the difference.

Foundational premise 6 asserts that the customer is always a co-producer. We believe that both the customer and the supplier are co-producers, because activities are integrated through the implementation of cross-functional business processes. Customer and supplier involvement are required for the successful implementation of the supply chain management processes. The extent of involvement in a relationship will depend largely on the value proposition made by each customer and supplier and the closeness of the relationship. In the closest type of relationships, the level of integration is such that the organizations work as extensions of each other.

Foundational premise 7 is that each organization can only make value propositions. Management must measure the value provided from the customer's perspective and measure performance over time. The cross-functional business processes are focused on providing value for the customer, the supplier, and the firm. Successful implementation of the processes will add value to both organizations in the relationship. Managers should evaluate relationship by relationship the value proposition for key customers and suppliers from an internal perspective as well as from the other's point of view. Estimating the value that the firm provided becomes a powerful negotiation tool to stop using price as the single criterion. A seller must estimate the contribution to its customer's profitability as well as understand the contribution of each customer to the organization's profitability. Similarly, management must understand the contribution of key suppliers to the profitability of the organization as well as its contribution to the profitability of suppliers.

Foundational premise 8 states that an S-D logic is customer-oriented and relational. The supply chain management processes have been designed to achieve customer orientation on all activities performed in all corporate functions. As functions become customer oriented, more functional participation in key relationships will occur. Increased functional involvement in a relationship will lead to the development of choice elements based on knowledge and skills that have the potential to become a competitive advantage for the organization.

See Table 12.1 for a summary of the relationship between each foundational premise of S-D logic and the cross-functional processes of the GSCF supply chain management framework.

CONCLUSIONS

Executives are becoming aware of the emerging paradigm of inter-network competition, and that the successful integration and management of supply chain management processes across members of the supply chain will determine the ultimate success of the single enterprise. Managing the supply chain cannot be left to chance. For this reason, executives are striving to interpret and determine how to manage the company's supply chain network, thus achieving the potential of supply chain management.

Research with member firms of GSCF has found that successful supply chain management involves the implementation of eight cross-functional processes across firms in the supply chain. Much friction, and thus waste of valuable resources, results when supply chains are not integrated, appropriately streamlined, and managed. A prerequisite for successful supply chain management is to coordinate activities within the firm.

The successful implementation of cross-functional, cross-firm business processes is required for the adoption of S-D logic, which is relational and customer-oriented, and in which the customer is always a co-producer (Vargo and Lusch 2004). Research efforts of GSCF show that the main reason why close business-to-business relationships fail is due to unrealistic expectations on the part of one or both of the parties involved. As closer relationships are developed, functional involvement at

Table 12.1

Service-Dominant Logic Foundational Premises and the GSCF Supply Chain Management Framework

Foundational premises of S-D logic	How the GSCF supply chain management framework supports S-D logic
FP_1: The application of specialized skills and knowledge is the fundamental unit of exchange.	Because all processes are cross-functional and cross-firm, more broad-based skills and knowledge are brought to the exchange.
FP_2: Indirect exchange masks the fundamental unit of exchange.	The fundamental unit of exchange requires a bundle of skills and knowledge that reside in multiple function, but functions traditionally are not customer focused which is why it is necessary to implement cross-functional business processes that are customer-focused.
FP_3: Goods are distribution mechanisms for service provision.	In business-to-business relationships, key choice elements are service-based, such as the way activities are executed including reliability, flexibility, and adaptability. Service provision requires the cross-functional coordination of skills and knowledge through business processes.
FP_4: Knowledge is the fundamental source of competitive advantage.	The supply chain is managed link by link, relationship by relationship, and the customer relationship management and supplier relationship management processes form the critical cross-functional linkages that facilitate the information flows and enable the firm to make value propositions to the customer and gain competitive advantage.
FP_5: All economies are service economies.	Increasingly, every organization is selling commodities, and what differentiates one from another are the relationships that are developed with customers and suppliers through the implementation of cross-functional teams.
FP_6: The customer is always a co-producer.	None of the supply chain management processes can be successfully implemented without customer involvement. Suppliers also need to be involved. Thus, customers and suppliers are co-producers.
FP_7: The enterprise can only make value propositions.	The cross-functional processes are focused on providing value for the customer, the supplier, and the firm. Thus, cross-functional business processes can be used to assess the value propositions for each organization engaged in a relationship.
FP_8: A service-centered view is customer oriented and relational.	The cross-functional processes enable firms to get close to customers in an integrated format that enables the customization of services.

multiple levels of each organization is required. The business processes described in this chapter can be used to successfully manage business relationships in the context of S-D logic.

The GSCF framework supports the adoption of the customer orientation of the firm because the supply chain management processes are designed to align organizational knowledge and skills to customers' needs. The processes are designed to assist corporate functions in focusing on the customer by identifying the role of each corporate function in each process. Adopting the processes enables the organization to overcome barriers that stem from conflicting functional objectives. Because the required activities in the processes are integrated with those of key customers and suppliers, by design, the GSCF framework regards the customer and the supplier as coproducers. The approach to supply chain management described in this chapter is about the management of relationships with suppliers and customers. Although marketing strategy formulation has always considered internal and external constraints, supply chain management makes explicit the evaluation of present and future needs from the perspective of all functions. The successful implementation of supply chain management enables the identification of the skills and knowledge required to create competitive advantage. Cross-functional teams and integration of activities with key members of the supply chain are becoming a requirement for developing and fulfilling the promise to customers.

Over the past fifty years, there has been a trend away from focusing on independent business transactions to focusing on long-term relationships. In many fields of study, there have been advocates for the development of the long-term relationships that are required to adopt S-D logic (Vargo and Lusch 2004). However, there has not been a comprehensive framework that management can use to align successfully corporate resources to business relationships that contribute the most to present and future corporate success.

NOTES

1. This section is based on Lambert (2006), pp. 17–18.
2. In many organizations, marketing and sales are viewed as separate corporate functions.

REFERENCES

Achrol, Ravi S. (1991), "Evolution of the Marketing Organization: New Forms for Turbulent Environments," *Journal of Marketing,* 55 (4), 77–93.
Alderson, Wroe (1950), "Marketing Efficiency and the Principle of Postponement," in *Cost and Profit Outlook,* September (3) 15–18.
APICS (2001), *Basics of Supply Chain Management, CPIM Certification Review Course, Participant Guide. Version 2.1,* Alexandria, VA: APICS, The Educational Society for Resource Management.
Bucklin, Louis P. (1966), *A Theory of Distribution Channel Structure.* Berkeley, CA: IBER.
Davenport, Thomas H. (1993), *Process Innovation: Reengineering Work through Information Technology.* Boston: Harvard Business School Press.
——— and Michael C. Beers (1995), "Managing Information about Processes," *Journal of Management Information Systems,* 12 (1), 57–80.
——— and James E. Short (1990), "The New Industrial Engineering: Information Technology and Business Process Redesign," *Sloan Management Review,* 31 (4), 11–27.
Day, George S. (1997), "Aligning the Organization to the Market," in *Reflections on the Futures of Marketing,* Donald R. Lehmann and Katherine E. Jocz, eds. Cambridge, MA: Marketing Science Institute, 67–93.
——— (1999), *The Market Driven Organization: Understanding, Attracting, and Keeping Valuable Customers.* New York: The Free Press.
——— (2003), "Creating a Superior Customer-Relating Capability," *Sloan Management Review,* 44 (3), 77–82.
Ellram, Lisa M. and Martha C. Cooper (1993), "The Relationship between Supply Chain Management and Keiretsu," *The International Journal of Logistics Management,* 4 (1), 1–12.
Grönroos, Christian (1990), *Service Management and Marketing: Managing the Moments of Truth in the Service Competition.* Lexington, MA: Free Press/Lexington Books.
Gunasekaran, A. and B. Nath (1997), "The Role of Information Technology in Business Process Reengineering," *International Journal of Production Economics,* 50 (2, 3), 91–104.
Hammer, Michael (2001), "The Superefficient Company," *Harvard Business Review,* 79 (8), 82–91.

———— and James Champy (1993), *Reengineering the Corporation: A Manifesto for Business Revolution,* 1st ed. New York: Harper Business.

———— and Glenn E. Mangurian (1987), "The Changing Value of Communications Technology," *Sloan Management Review,* 28 (2), 65–71.

Homburg, Christian (2000), "Fundamental Changes in Marketing Organization: The Movement toward a Customer-Focused Organizational Structure," *Journal of the Academy of Marketing Science,* 28 (4), 459.

————, John P. Workman, Jr., and Harley Krohmer (1999), "Marketing's Influence within the Firm," *Journal of Marketing,* 63 (2), 1–17.

Jaworski, Bernard J. and Ajay K. Kohli (1993), "Market Orientation: Antecedents and Consequences," *Journal of Marketing,* 57 (3), 53–70.

Kahn, Kenneth B. and John T. Mentzer (1998), "Marketing's Integration with Other Departments," *Journal of Business Research,* 42 (1), 53–62.

Kohli, Ajay K. and Bernard J. Jaworski (1990), "Marketing Orientation: The Construct, Research Propositions, and Managerial Implications," *Journal of Marketing* 54 (April), 1–80.

Kotler, Philip (1997), *Marketing Management: Analysis, Planning, Implementation, and Control,* 7th ed. Englewood Cliffs, NJ: Prentice-Hall.

Krohmer, Harley, Christian Homburg, and John P. Workman (2002), "Should Marketing Be Cross-Functional? Conceptual Development and International Empirical Evidence," *Journal of Business Research,* 55 (6), 451–65.

Lambert, Douglas M. (ed.). (2004), *Supply Chain Management: Partnership, Process, Performance.* Sarasota, FL: Supply Chain Management Institute.

———— (ed.) (2006), *Supply Chain Management: Partnership, Processes, Performance,* 2d ed. Sarasota, FL: Supply Chain Management Institute.

———— and Renan Burduroglu (2000), "Measuring and Selling the Value of Logistics," *The International Journal of Logistics Management,* 11 (1), 1–17.

————, Margaret A Emmelhainz, and John T. Gardner (1996), "Developing and Implementing Supply Chain Partnerships," *The International Journal of Logistics Management,* 7 (2), 1–18.

———— and A. Michael Knemeyer (2004), "We're in This Together," *Harvard Business Review,* 82 (12), 55–64.

———— and Terrance L. Pohlen (2001), "Supply Chain Metrics," *The International Journal of Logistics Management,* 12 (1), 1–19.

Monczka, Robert M., Robert J. Trent, and Robert B. Handfield (1998), *Purchasing and Supply Chain Management.* Cincinnati, OH: South-Western College Publishing.

Narver, John C. and Stanley F. Slater (1990), "The Effect of a Market Orientation on Business Profitability," *Journal of Marketing,* 54 (4), 20–35.

Normann, Richard and Rafael Ramírez (1993), "From Value Chain to Value Constellation: Designing Interactive Strategy.," *Harvard Business Review,* 71 (4), 65–77.

Parvatiyar, Atul and Jagdish N. Sheth (2001), "Customer Relationship Management: Emerging Practice, Process, and Discipline," *Journal of Economic and Social Research,* 3 (2), 1–34.

Rust, Roland T. in Bolton, Ruth N., George S. Day, John Deighton, Das Narayandas, Evert Gummesson, Shelby D. Hunt, C. K. Prahalad, Roland T. Rust, and Steven M. Shugan (2004), "Invited Commentaries on 'Evolving to a New Dominant Logic for Marketing,'" *Journal of Marketing,* 68 (1), 18–27.

Simchi-Levi, David, Philip Kaminsky, and Edith Simchi-Levi (2000), *Designing and Managing the Supply Chain: Concepts, Strategies, and Case Studies.* Boston. MA: Irwin/McGraw-Hill.

Srivastava, Rajendra K., Tasadduq A. Shervani, and Liam Fahey (1999), "Marketing, Business Processes, and Shareholder Value: An Organizationally Embedded View of Marketing Activities and the Discipline of Marketing.," *Journal of Marketing,* 63 (4), 168–79.

Taylor, Frederick Winslow (1911), *The Principles of Scientific Management.* New York: Harper & Bros.

Vargo, Stephen L. and Robert F. Lusch (2004), "Evolving to a New Dominant Logic for Marketing," *Journal of Marketing,* 68 (1), 1–17.

Webster Jr., Frederick E. (1992), "The Changing Role of Marketing in the Corporation," *Journal of Marketing,* 56 (4), 1–17.

Wisner, Joel D., G. Keong Leong, and Keah Choon Tan (2004), *Supply Chain Management: A Balanced Approach.* Mason, OH: Thomson South-Western.

Appendix

SUPPLY CHAIN MANAGEMENT: Processes, and Strategic and Operational Subprocesses

Processes	Strategic Subprocesses	Operational Subprocesses
Customer Relationship Management	1. Review Corporate and Marketing Strategy 2. Identify Criteria for Categorizing Customers 3. Provide Guidelines for the Degree of Differentiation in the Product/Service Agreement 4. Develop Framework of Metrics 5. Develop Guidelines for Sharing Process-Improvement Benefits with Customers	1. Differentiate Customers 2. Prepare the Account/Segment Management Team 3. Internally Review the Accounts 4. Identify Opportunities with the Accounts 5. Develop the Product/Service Agreement 6. Implement the Product/Service Agreement 7. Measure Performance and Generate Profitability Reports
Customer Service Management	1. Develop Customer Service Strategy 2. Develop Response Procedures 3. Develop Infrastructure for Implementing Responses Procedures 4. Develop Framework for Metrics	1. Recognize Event 2. Evaluate Situation and Alternatives 3. Implement Solution 4. Monitor and Report
Demand Management	1. Determine Demand Management Goals and Strategy 2. Determine Forecasting Procedures 3. Plan Information Flow 4. Determine Synchronization Procedures 5. Develop Contingency Management System 6. Develop Framework of Metrics	1. Collect Data/Information 2. Forecast 3. Synchronize 4. Reduce Variability and Increase Flexibility 5. Measure Performance
Order Fulfillment	1. Review Marketing Strategy, Supply Chain Structure & Customer Service Goals 2. Define Requirements for Order Fulfillment 3. Evaluate Logistics Network 4. Define Plan for Order Fulfillment 5. Development Framework of Metrics	1. Generate and Communicate Order 2. Enter Order 3. Process Order 4. Handle Documentation 5. Fill Order 6. Deliver Order 7. Perform Post Delivery Activities and Measure Performance

Appendix

SUPPLY CHAIN MANAGEMENT: Processes, and Strategic and Operational Subprocesses (cont.)

Processes	Strategic Sub-Processes	Operational Sub-Processes
Manufacturing Flow Management	1. Review Manufacturing, Sourcing, Marketing, and Logistics Strategies 2. Determine Degree of Manufacturing Flexibility Requirement 3. Determine Push/Pull Boundaries 4. Identify Manufacturing Constraints and Determine Capabilities 5. Develop Framework of Metrics	1. Determine Routing and Velocity through Manufacturing 2. Perform Manufacturing and Materials Planning 3. Execute Capacity and Demand 4. Measure Performance
Supplier Relationship Management	1. Review Corporate, Marketing, Manufacturing, and Sourcing Strategies 2. Identify Criteria for Categorizing Suppliers 3. Provide Guidelines for the Degree of Customization in the Product/Service Agreement 4. Develop Framework of Metrics 5. Develop Guidelines for Sharing Process-Improvement Benefits with Suppliers	1. Differentiate Customers 2. Prepare the Supplier/Segment Management Team 3. Internally Review the Supplier/Supplier Segment 4. Identify Opportunities with the Suppliers 5. Develop the Product/Service Agreement and Communication Plan 6. Implement the Product/Service Agreement 7. Measure Performance and Generate Supplier Cost/Profitability Reports
Products Development and Commercialization	1. Review Corporate, Marketing, Manufacturing, and Sourcing Strategies 2. Develop Idea Generation and Screening Processes 3. Establish Guidelines for Cross-functional Product Development Team Membership 4. Identify Product Rollout Issues and Constraints 5. Establish New Product Project Guidelines 6. Develop Framework of Metrics	1. Define New Products and Assess Fit 2. Establish Cross-functional Product Development Team 3. Formalize New Product Development Project 4. Design and Build Prototypes 5. Make/Buy Decision 6. Determine Channels 7. Perform Product Rollout 8. Measure Process Performance
Return Management	1. Determine Returns Management Goals and Strategy 2. Develop Avoidance, Gatekeeping, and Disposition Guidelines 3. Develop Returns Network and Flow Options 4. Develop Credit Rules 5. Determine Secondary Markets 6. Develop Framework of Metrics	1. Receive Return Request 2. Determine Routing 3. Receive Returns 4. Select Disposition 5. Credit Consumer/Supplier 6. Analyze Returns and Measure Performance

Source: Adapted from Lambert, Douglas M. (*ed*) *Supply Chain Management: Partnerships, Processes, Performance,* 2nd. Edition, Sarasota, FL: Supply Chain Management Institute, 2006.

13

CUSTOMERS AS CO-PRODUCERS

Implications for Marketing Strategy Effectiveness and Marketing Operations Efficiency

KARTIK KALAIGNANAM AND RAJAN VARADARAJAN

"The customer is always a co-producer" is one of the eight foundational premises of marketing advanced by Vargo and Lusch (2004a; hereafter V&L 2004a). Indeed, the outlook as well as the manner in which firms relate to their customers and suppliers has undergone a metamorphosis in recent years. Furthermore, the view that the role of the firm, its customers, and its suppliers are distinct and delineable has given way to the view that their roles are interchangeable. The following examples are instructive in regard to the role of customers as co-producers:

> SBC Communications, a telecommunications firm, has achieved considerable success in motivating its residential customers to migrate to the Internet and sign-up for online billing and payment in place of paper based bills being mailed to the customer's home address. In an attempt to promote customer migration to the Internet, SBC offers its customers financial incentives such as a dollar off on their monthly telephone bills and non-financial incentives such as free services (e.g., reverse number look up directory) and enhancements (e.g., the ability to view past bills). Northwest Airlines offers customers in its frequent flyer program a discount of 1000 frequent flyer miles for redeeming frequent flyer miles for travel awards on its web site rather than calling a reservation agent via its toll free number. After the expiration of the one-year warranty period, Hewlett Packard charges its customers $25 to $30 for providing customer support for its hardware products over the telephone. However, its Internet based self-service customer support system is priced considerably lower (New York Times 2003, p. 5).

> Paris Miki, a Japanese eyewear retailer, has developed a business environment that fosters dialogue and collaboration with its customers. The Mikissimes design system eliminates the need for customers to review myriad choices in order to select eyeglasses. First, the system takes a digital picture of the customer. Next, the system thoroughly analyzes the attributes of the customer and stated preferences regarding the kind of look they would prefer. In collaboration with the customer, the retailer works on adjusting the shape and size of the lens in order to achieve a perfect match. Finally, customers complete the design by selecting from a number of options for the nose bridge, hinges and arms (Gilmore and Pine 1997, p. 92).

An example that elevates the concept of the customer as a co-producer, to an even higher level, is a Microsoft initiative in the works that entails the use of the human body as a computer bus to communicate with various devices. For example, the initiative entails the use of physical resistance offered by the human body to input from a keypad or other input device. Complementing this initiative are efforts to use the human body to generate power for the network. For instance, a "kinetic power converter" in the wearer's shoe or wristwatch being used to produce electricity, much in the same way that an old fashioned self winding watch extracted energy from its owner's normal movements (The Economist 2004, p. 66).

As evidenced by the foregoing examples, the *motives, mechanics, nature,* and *extent* of customer involvement in co-production appears to be contingent on a host of factors. Collectively, in the first set of examples (SBC Communications, Northwest Airlines, and Hewlett-Packard), the mechanics employed to increase customer involvement in the co-production of service (by motivating customers to migrate to the online channel) encompass the use of monetary and nonmonetary incentives and disincentives. The overarching objective in all of these instances seems to be enhancing the efficiency of marketing operations, while ensuring that the effectiveness of the underlying marketing strategy is not compromised. In other words, customer resources are leveraged to increase customer involvement in co-production in order to lower costs (i.e., to enhance marketing operations efficiency). The Paris Miki example is illustrative of a business leveraging advances in technology to involve customers as co-producers in order to customize the product and achieve a closer fit with the unique preferences of individual customers (i.e., to enhance the effectiveness of marketing strategy). Here, *marketing strategy effectiveness* refers to the appropriateness of a business's decisions relating to the total amount of marketing resources deployed, types of marketing resources deployed, and pattern of deployment of marketing resources across resource types deployed to facilitate the achievement of competitive positional advantage(s) in the marketplace. *Marketing operations efficiency* refers to the minimization of costs incurred in implementing the chosen marketing strategy.

In reference to their foundational premise, "the customer is always a co- producer," V&L (2004a) note that the customer becomes primarily an *operant resource* (co-producer) rather than an *operand resource* (target) and can be involved in the entire value and service chain in acting on operand resources. Against this backdrop, this chapter explores how product characteristics, market and customer characteristics, and firm characteristics affect the extent of customer involvement with the firm in various activities spanning the value chain such as innovation and new product development, co-production, supply chain management, and customer relationship management. The catalytic effects of recent developments in the fields of communication technology, information technology, and self-service technology on these linkages are also explored. We then highlight the implications of customer involvement with the firm in various activities transcending the value chain from the standpoint of marketing strategy effectiveness and marketing operations efficiency.

The remainder of the chapter is organized as follows. First, we provide a brief overview of marketing strategy effectiveness and marketing operations efficiency. Next, we highlight the linkages between mass production and mass customization and customers as service recipients and customers as service co-producers. Third, we propose a conceptual model delineating factors affecting the intensity of customer involvement with the firm. We conclude the chapter with a brief discussion on directions for further research.

MARKETING STRATEGY EFFECTIVENESS AND MARKETING OPERATIONS EFFICIENCY

Strategy exists at multiple levels in an organization, chief among them being strategy at the corporate, business unit, and functional levels. *Corporate strategy* refers to a firm's decisions pertaining to the business arenas in which it chooses to compete. A firm's corporate-strategy decisions manifest as its business portfolio and pattern of allocation of resources across businesses. *Competitive strategy* refers to strategy at the business-unit level and is concerned with where and how individual businesses in the firm's portfolio should compete in order to achieve and maintain defensible competitive positional advantage(s) in the marketplace. Cost leadership, differentiation, focused cost leadership, and focused differentiation constitute the broad generic competitive strategies that businesses can pursue. *Cost leadership strategy* refers to a business leveraging its skills and resources to achieve a defensible position of competitive cost advantage in the marketplace (i.e., being the lowest cost producer). *Differentiation strategy* refers to a business leveraging its skills and resources to differentiate its product offering from its competitors' product offerings to achieve a defensible position of competitive differentiation advantage in the marketplace (see Porter 1980, 1985). *Marketing strategy* refers to a business's decisions and actions relating to where to compete at a greater level of specificity (e.g., country markets, market types—business-to-business versus business-to-consumer—and market segments) and how to compete utilizing resources entrusted to the marketing function (e.g., market-based assets). Decisions relating to how to compete manifest as types of marketing resources to deploy, total amount of marketing resources to deploy, and pattern of deployment of marketing resources to facilitate the achievement of competitive positional advantage(s) in the marketplace.

Pursuit of a cost leadership strategy does not necessarily mean an intention on the part of a business to sell its product offering at the lowest price relative to competitors. It could well be a deterrent to competitors' using price as a tool to attract the business's customers. A competitive imperative for businesses pursuing a differentiation strategy is to make salient the nonprice attributes of their offerings to buyers. Toward this end, businesses segment the market into homogenous groups and offer unique value propositions to each group such that heterogeneity in customer preferences is adequately met.

On one hand, the importance of achieving a sustainable competitive advantage as a means to achieving superior marketplace performance and financial performance seems to be widely underscored in the strategy literature. On the other hand, however, there seems to be a dearth of research focusing on business operations efficiency–related issues as well as a lack of appreciation of the importance of efficiently implementing a chosen strategy. As pointed out by Schendel (1985), a business, regardless of the strategy it pursues (i.e., cost leadership or differentiation), must strive to achieve a competitive advantage in an efficient manner.

All else being equal, a business pursuing a differentiation strategy will incur higher *manufacturing* costs relative to a business pursuing a cost leadership strategy. In addition, the former business is also likely to incur higher marketing costs as a consequence of the need to communicate effectively to customers the benefits associated with the unique and differentiating features of its offering. Efficiency in marketing operations can enable a business pursuing a differentiation strategy to be *price competitive* and less severely affected by rising factor costs associated with an inflationary environment (Miller 1984).

FROM MASS PRODUCTION TO MASS CUSTOMIZATION AND
SERVICE RECIPIENTS TO SERVICE CO-PRODUCERS:
AN OVERVIEW

Over the past two decades, there has been a growing interest in distinguishing between mass production and mass customization as distinct ways of competing in the marketplace. In this genre, Hayes and Wheelwright (1979) offer a framework that matches the firm's product-market characteristics with the manufacturing process characteristics. They note that standardized products are best manufactured in assembly-line types of operations, whereas custom-made products are best manufactured in job shops. The reasons underlying such normative assertions stem from considerations of economies of scale and capital investments needed to produce goods in high volumes.

The success of firms such as Ford and Sears during the twentieth century is, in part, attributable to their pursuit of an undifferentiated marketing strategy—offering a standardized product, notwithstanding heterogeneity in customers' preferences. It is worth noting that the pursuit of an undifferentiated marketing strategy by large corporations gained primacy in the post–World War II era, more so due to the prevailing market conditions rather than businesses considering customers as objects of their action. That every customer is unique is a fact that long has been recognized by producers as well as marketing intermediaries. However, technology (information and manufacturing technology) that firms could employ to offer customized products to the specifications of individual customers at an affordable price was nonexistent. This, along with the need to make available low-priced goods in the post–World War II era forced firms to rely on economies of scale in manufacturing and distribution. Furthermore, customers seemed to be willing to trade off products customized to their unique needs for lower prices.

The issue of whether businesses could simultaneously pursue a strategy of differentiation and cost leadership has been actively debated for a long time. The success of mass customization strategy was impeded by the absence of mechanisms for interacting with customers and obtaining information about their specific needs and of flexibility (e.g., production processes) to alter the product in accord with the information pertaining to the preferences of individual customers. The significant progress in manufacturing technologies (e.g., flexible manufacturing systems, computer-aided design, computer-aided engineering) in the recent past implies that the factory is no longer a bottleneck to producing a variety of products. Likewise, developments in information technology (i.e., communication technology, database technology, and computing technology) enable customers to create value by collaborating with the firm. Consider the following case in point:

> [General Electric's] plastics division recently launched a web-based initiative that shifted significant aspects of the innovation process to customers. This initiative forced GE to change the ways in which sales and marketing acquired information about and served its customers. GE does not design or manufacture plastics but instead provides resins that must match the end product as well as the manufacturing process employed. Since 1998, GE Plastics has enabled its customers to order plastics online and access its 30 years of proprietary knowledge through its website. Registered users are provided access to company data, engineering expertise and simulation software. By leveraging the available knowledge and technology to conduct trial and error experiments, customers are able to ascertain how a certain grade of plastic with a specific type of reinforcement would flow into and fill a

mold. The rationale for this initiative, which cost GE $5 million, was the huge potential for cost savings, more so than the expertise of customers in this process. GE leverages the website to track prospects and transmit such information to the marketing staff. Fueling much of the growth of GE's plastics division are the one million visitors per year who are screened for potential sales which is approximately one-third of all new customer leads. The on-line tools have also enabled GE to enhance customer satisfaction at considerably lower costs (Thomke and von Hippel 2002, p. 79).

As can be inferred from the preceding example, the transition of manufacturing from a mass-production to a mass-customization environment and the transition of customers from being service recipients to service co-producers are closely intertwined. In the wake of increasing intensity of competition, in a growing number of industries, the viability of a strategy of cost leadership in the context of standardized products (coupled with the lowest price) is suspect. Needless to say, in certain industries and/or market segments in an industry, a standardized product offering at the lowest price (based on a strategy of cost leadership) might be viable. A more realistic scenario appears to be one in which mass-production and mass-customization strategies continue to coexist, thus providing businesses with flexibility in catering to a changing marketplace. A similar trend can be sensed from a demand-side perspective. It is conceivable that customers would choose to actively participate with the firm in co-creating value under certain contingencies and prefer to passively appropriate value in other situations. A detailed discussion of the factors influencing the intensity of customer participation with the firm follows.

INTENSITY OF CUSTOMER PARTICIPATION WITH FIRMS: A CONCEPTUAL MODEL

Figure 13.1 presents a conceptual model delineating the determinants of the intensity of customer participation with firms. A firm's value chain can be conceptualized in terms of primary activities necessary to physically create the product, market and deliver to buyers, and support and service after the sale is consummated, and support activities that provide the requisite inputs and infrastructure to perform the primary activities (Porter 1985). In reference to the value chain, *intensity of customer participation* with the firm can be conceptualized as the ratio of mental and physical resources contributed by the customer to that by the firm in the context of specific activities such as idea generation, product development, production, distribution, and postsale.

Alternatively, the intensity of customer participation with the producer firm can be conceptualized in terms of core business processes that are critical to the achievement of the organization's goals. Srivastava, Shervani, and Fahey (1999) conceptualize the creation of customer value in terms of development of new products (i.e., product development management process), acquisition and conversion of inputs into desired customer outcomes (i.e., supply chain management process), and development and maintenance of relationships with channel partners and end users (i.e., customer relationship management process). Each of these processes can be further disaggregated into subprocesses. For instance, the customer relationship management process can be disaggregated into customer acquisition, development and retention, and termination processes. The subprocesses can be further subdivided into specific activities and programs such as lead generation, lead qualification and customer referral (customer acquisition process), and cross-selling and customer loyalty programs (customer development and retention process). In summary, the foregoing conceptualizations highlight the broad scope of opportunities available to producer firms to co-opt customers in co-creating value.

Figure 13.1 Participation of Customers as Co-producers in the Firm's Value Chain: A Conceptual Model

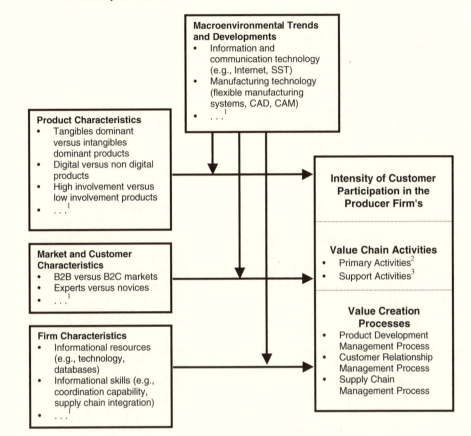

Note: Participation of customers as co-producers can be construed in the context of either value chain activities or value creation processes.

[1]The items listed in the boxes are intended to be illustrative and not exhaustive.

[2]Inbound logistics, operations, outbound logistics, marketing and sales, and service.

[3]Firm infrastructure, technology development, and procurement (see Porter 1985).

The intensity of customer participation with the firm is modeled in Figure 13.1 as a function of (1) product characteristics, (2) market and customer characteristics, and (3) firm characteristics. In the interest of ease of exposition, although intrinsically continuous, a number of characteristics are shown in Figure 13.1 as dichotomous. The dotted line in each of the boxes serves to denote that the characteristics delineated constitute only a partial list and are intended to be representative rather than exhaustive. The model also explicates the positive effects of macroenvironmental trends in areas such as information technology, communication technology, and manufacturing technology on these linkages. That is, leveraging the potential of these technologies can enable firms to involve customer participation in various processes and activities to an even greater extent.

Consider for instance, the ability of customers these days to schedule the shipment of a package through a carrier such as United Parcel Service (UPS). At UPS's Web site, the customer can schedule a time for the package to be picked up from a prespecified location, prepay with a credit card the cost of shipping, and print the shipping label for affixing on the package. After the package has been picked up, the customer can track the status of the package in transit and date and time of delivery by accessing UPS's Web site.

A detailed discussion of the rationale underlying the linkages explicated in Figure 13.1 follows.

Product Characteristics

Product characteristics such as tangibles versus intangibles dominant, digital versus nondigital, and high versus low involvement can affect the intensity of customer participation with the firm in specific activities as well in the aggregate.

Tangibles- versus Intangibles-Dominant Products

The need to differentiate between goods and services in the context of marketing strategy was explicated almost three decades ago in a seminal piece by Shostack (1977). A key difference centers on the fact that whereas generally goods are first produced and then consumed, many services are characterized by the simultaneity of production and consumption. V&L (2004a, 2004b) note that such differences between goods and services are derived from a manufacturer's perspective and not from the customer's perspective. At a high level of abstraction, it can be argued that because both goods and services offer bundles of intangible benefits to customers; they are similar in nature. However, there are fundamental differences between goods and services even from a customer's standpoint that need further elaboration. Service-based solutions entail customers paying for temporary access, whereas goods-based solutions entail customers paying for ownership.

This is a nontrivial difference from the standpoint of both the firm and the customer. Consider for instance, a customer wanting to purchase (i.e., own) an automobile versus renting an automobile. Regardless, the automobile per se does not become more or less tangible. Although the core benefit derived in both of these situations is transportation, the customer is likely to evaluate these experiences differently. Whereas in the former, the customer is likely to place greater emphasis on tangible elements of the exchange (e.g., automobile features), in the latter he or she is likely to place greater emphasis on the intangible elements (e.g., ease of vehicle pickup and drop-off) of the exchange.

Similarly, consider for instance, a customer faced with the need to file his or her annual personal income tax returns. In this context, the choices of buying software (i.e., good) for income tax preparation versus buying the expertise of a tax consultant (i.e., service) might be viewed as substitutes. However, a closer examination reveals that using the tax preparation software provides the customer time utility (i.e., the ability to use it anytime), place utility (i.e., the ability to use it anywhere), and possession utility (i.e., the ability to reuse it a number of times). All else equal, leveraging the expertise of the tax consultant would require a greater amount of customer inputs (i.e., effort and time) in co-producing the outcome (i.e., tax returns), in light of the need for the customer to physically interact with the tax consultant to explain his or her tax history. Although use of the tax preparation software also entails customer participation in the co-production of the product, the extent of customer participation is relatively less because of the ability to preprogram the software to perform the bulk of the tasks entailed in co-producing the product.

In the context of health care, a credence good (Darby and Karni 1973), considerable information asymmetry exists between the health care service provider (the physician) and the consumer (patient). Nevertheless, the consumer is a participant in this service experience in that he or she is the object on which the service is performed. With the growth of the Internet, the diminishing information asymmetry between the health care service provider and consumer offers the potential for better experiences for the consumer. Consider the following case in point:

> News relating to the announcement of clinical trials for Gleevec, a promising leukemia drug by Novartis AG, diffused rapidly through patient communities resulting in thousands of patients wanting to participate in the trial. Furthermore, extensive activism by leukemia patients who were on early trials of this drug led to a speeding up of its production and the Food and Drug Administration (FDA) expediting its approval (Prahalad and Ramaswamy 2002, p. 4).

Digital versus Nondigital Products

Sellers are generally faced with the dilemma of how best to respond to the heterogeneous needs of the marketplace. For example, should they modify the product, engage in persuasive communication (advertising), or offer incentives to align the market's preferences with its offerings? Among other factors, the cost implications of these alternatives are a function of the complexity of the product in question. However, for the most part, the cost implications are irrelevant in the context of customization of digital products distributed through the Internet. *Digital products* refer to products whose core benefits can be digitized. Newspapers, books, software, and music are examples of digital products. A fundamental difference between digital and nondigital products is the degree to which customers can potentially participate in creating value. Relative to nondigital products, digital products offer a broader range of opportunities for firms to engage customers to enhance the efficiency of marketing operations as well as the effectiveness of the underlying marketing strategy. Facilitating customers to access their Web site for purposes such as downloading software upgrades and patches and resolution of technical problems enables firms to lower the costs of their business operations without compromising the effectiveness of the strategy pursued. Case in point:

> Claris, a spin-off of Apple Computer, in addition to employing web servers for external communication and dedicated servers for internal communication, employs bulletin board services (BBS) to communicate with its customers segments. The BBS serves as a central location for sharing of software files between the firm and its customers. During the launch of its first software, Claris leveraged customers as a resource to "debug" technical problems in the software by asking customers to download patches (i.e., software bug fixes) from its web server (Settles 1995).

The greater scope for customization of digital products also stems from the ability to aggregate (e.g., enabling a buyer to download a customized CD album that is a compilation of individual pieces selected by the buyer) and disaggregate (e.g., enabling a buyer to download a single song contained in an album rather than the entire album) at relatively lower costs. Similarly, a customer can create a customized electronic newspaper by requesting news alerts pertaining to mergers and acquisitions–related events, games featuring a favorite sports team, weather in specific cities, and reviews of new movies with favorite actors. Although, there is a nontrivial fixed cost associated with customization of digital products, the variable cost associated with customization is near zero.

High- versus Low-Involvement Products

Involvement in a product category refers to a consumer's enduring perceptions of the importance of the product category based on his or her needs and values. A body of literature in consumer behavior draws attention to the importance of this key product characteristic (high- versus low-involvement products) in reference to intensity of customer involvement with the firm (Bettman 1979; Petty and Cacioppo 1986). Realistically, the extent of customer involvement in the purchase and use of a product such as a house will be much greater relative to purchase and use of a product such as toothpaste. Customers are likely to be relatively unwilling to exert effort in the buying of low-involvement products because failure to exert effort is unlikely to have adverse consequences. V&L (2004a) note that regardless of whether the product in question is a good or a service, benefits cannot be realized without the involvement of the customer. Although consumption cannot happen without the involvement of the consumer, the resources expended by customers (i.e., cognitive and affective) will vary with the level of involvement in the product. Furthermore, the feasibility of involving customers in co-production and the potential for enhancing the efficiency of marketing operations through greater involvement of customers is greater for low-involvement, intangibles-dominant products than for low-involvement, tangibles-dominant products. Consider, for instance, a low-involvement, intangibles-dominant product such as air travel, and contrast it with a low-involvement tangible-dominant product such as toothpaste. In regard to the former, recent technological advances are conducive to greater customer involvement in co-production at multiple stages such as making flight reservations over the Internet, and checking in and printing of boarding passes at kiosks in the airport. In fact, as an alternative to printing of boarding passes at an airport self-service kiosk, several airlines allow customers to print their boarding passes at home, up to twenty-four hours prior to the scheduled departure time, using the customer's personal resources such as computer, printer, and paper.

Market and Customer Characteristics

Business-to-Business versus Business-to-Consumer Markets

A key difference between business-to-business (B2B) and business-to-consumer markets (B2C) is the greater degree of interdependence between buyers and sellers in the former. The number of buyers in B2B markets being fewer compared with B2C markets makes sellers more dependent on buyers. Likewise, buyers are dependent on suppliers for a continued and stable supply of raw materials, components, or subassemblies that are essential for their business operations. In B2B markets, the product is an array of economic, technical, and personal relationships between buyers and sellers.

Along similar lines, von Hippel (1978) distinguishes between the *manufacturer active paradigm* (MAP) in B2C settings and the *customer active paradigm* (CAP) in B2B settings. In the former, the role of the customer is relatively passive, such as responding to questions posed by the manufacturer about needs for new products. In the latter, it is not uncommon for the customer to develop the entire product or solution and then approach the supplier to produce and commercialize the product. Specifically, customers provide product design data to the supplier along with information about the need for a new product. Consider the following case in point:

> The "Solderless Wrapped Connection," a means for making a reliable, gas-tight electrical connection by wrapping a wire around a special terminal, was conceptualized and tested at Bell Labs. After years of testing, the hand tool portion of the system was built by Keller Tool, an independent supplier. Realizing the potential for marketing the solderless wrapped connection to some of its other customers, Keller requested and obtained a license to sell the hand tools in the open market. Currently, Keller is the major supplier of solderless wrapped connection equipment (von Hippel 1978, p. 41).

The growth of the Internet is enabling suppliers to serve clients *efficiently and effectively* in business markets by providing end-to-end solutions as opposed to being transaction oriented. Consider the following case in point:

> Milpro.com is the website of Milacron Inc., an Ohio-based small machine tool manufac-turer. Through Milpro.com, the firm sells high margin coolants, cutting wheels, and drill bits directly to small machine shops. In addition, the website also assists customers with a broad array of related *business* challenges, such as buying and selling used equipment, identifying new *business* opportunities, and troubleshooting problems. For example, the site includes a software wizard that guides customers through a set of questions about a process (e.g., grinding) and related problems (e.g., chatter marks) and then recommends particular products, much as an experienced sales representative would. Through such *ser-vices,* Milacron has been able to attract the attention and the *business* of small machine shops, a group that's difficult and expensive to reach through traditional channels. These shops, in turn, gain access to expertise that they could not otherwise afford and would not be available through a transaction-focused exchange (Wise and Morrison 2000, p. 92, em-phasis added).

Experts versus Novices

A firm's motivation to enhance customer participation notwithstanding, the idiosyncrasies of cus-tomers, such as their knowledge structures and receptivity toward the firm, affects their ability to contribute to the value-creation process. It has been observed that consumers generally have a disutility for cognitive effort; in other words, they tend to be "cognitive misers." The consumer behavior and psychology literature point out that expert consumers tend to have superior product category knowl-edge compared with novices. An implication of this difference is that expert consumers process information at levels above and below the basic level, allowing finer levels of discrimination. In contrast, novices process information at the basic level determined by concrete perceptual attributes (Alba and Hutchinson 1987). Along similar lines, research in new product development suggests that certain users face needs in the marketplace long before others (von Hippel 1986). As a result, there has been a tendency among firms in certain industries to involve lead users in developing and testing new product concepts. Consider, for instance, the development of Linux. A rudimentary version of the operating system was developed and posted on the Web by a student from the Univer-sity of Helsinki. However, the credit for improving it significantly belongs to several expert users from all over the world who were able to download the software for free, test it for bugs, and modify it by adding new features. In such interactive product development situations, it is conceivable that users contribute more to value creation than the producer.

Firm Characteristics

Information Resources and Skills

Competitive business strategy entails leveraging a firm's unique skills and resources to perform activities in the value chain better than competitors. Compared to the industrial era, during which a business's value chain was predominantly characterized by flow of physical goods and ser-vices, in the present, increasingly, the value chain is characterized by greater informational flows. In any industry, some firms are likely to be better at acquiring, disseminating, and utilizing information than their competitors. The efficacy of a mass customization strategy depends on the technological skills and resources at the disposal of the firm to harness a vast amount of information about customers, tailor the product to the needs of individual customers, and deliver customized products. Consider for instance, the prevalence of recommendation agents in the electronic marketplace. Amazon.com recommends books by leveraging other customer's purchase data to create personalized shopping experiences. General Motors's Web-based virtual advisor provides recommendations based on information provided by customers about preferred attributes. Information and news delivered over the Internet to individuals' desktops are customized in accord with stated preferences.

Dell Inc.'s mass-customization strategy has received considerable attention in the business press. Dell's intranet sites, referred to as "Premier Pages," are customized to the requirements of more than 200 global customers and provide direct access to purchasing-related and technical information about specific configurations of its products such as desktop and laptop computers and servers. The Web site offers an interactive choice board that enables individual customers to customize their desktop or laptop computer based on the available alternatives. A problem that plagues and severely impairs the profitability of manufacturers of personal computers marketed through retail outlets is the obsolescence of the finished goods inventory at the retail level. By interacting directly with customers, PC manufacturers such as Dell are able to circumvent this problem as well as increase their inventory turnover as a result of being able to more accurately estimate demand. Real-time information about demand, in turn, allows providers of logistics services to better coordinate the transportation of the requisite number of components and subassemblies from the warehouses of vendors to the facilities of the PC manufacturer. Real-time information about demand also enables providers of transportation and logistics services to assemble related shipments from different facilities (e.g., the computer and monitor) and deliver them together to the customer (Magretta 1998).

The effectiveness of a firm's pricing strategy is also increasingly dependent on its skills at leveraging information about customers and bringing them to bear on its decisions in a timely manner. In the past, the absence of mechanisms to determine the reservation prices of customers implied that a firm's pricing strategy was frequently suboptimal, resulting in either loss of revenues due to low prices or lost sales due to high prices. With the information asymmetry that existed between firms and customers diminishing in an Internet environment, buyers are beginning to participate in the pricing process. The dynamic pricing strategy pursued by Priceline.com is illustrative in this regard. Instead of being passive recipients, customers indicate their initial reservation price and thereafter increase the price iteratively until the firm accepts the customer's stated price. Whereas the motivation for customers to *co-produce* stems from the desire to get the best price, the motivation for firms to enable customer involvement is to optimize the revenue realized.

In summary, it can be argued that underlying the ability of firms to increase customer participation in various stages of the value chain (e.g., inbound and outbound logistics, marketing and sales/service, operations) or in the core business processes (i.e., product development management, supply chain management, and customer relationship management) are its resources and skills that enable exchange of information, co-ordination with value chain partners (e.g., customers and suppliers), and delivery of the customized product to customers.

FUTURE RESEARCH DIRECTIONS

This chapter highlights the nature and magnitude of customer participation in various activities spanning from idea generation to after-sale service with firms and its implications for marketing strategy and marketing operations management. The increasing prevalence of customers as co-producers highlighted in this chapter raises several interesting research questions, most importantly, the likely adverse supply-side and demand-side outcomes of increased customer participation.

Supply Side Issues

In general, increased customer participation in co-production has the benefit of enhancing the effectiveness of marketing strategy and/or enhancing the efficiency of marketing operations. However, managers must be cognizant of likely unintended consequences. For instance, the rapid proliferation of online customer communities has also resulted in customers actively interacting among themselves as well as being increasingly vocal in regard to their relationships with firms. The presence of consumer activist groups on the Internet poses unique challenges to managers in developing their public relations program. For instance, Markus Noga, a Lego Mindstorms customer, developed an unauthorized operating system for one of its microcomputers. By naming it LegOS, the ardent fan of the company made it available to everybody through online communities. The firm was faced with the challenge of how to respond to this initiative. On one hand, allowing customers to download this operating system could potentially damage the microprocessor in Lego Mindstorms's system. On the other hand, not responding raises the question of whether the firm should allow customers to override its code and claim intellectual property rights to their creation (Prahalad and Ramaswamy 2002). Amazon.com faced a similar public relations challenge when customers in online communities expressed their displeasure over being charged differential prices for identical products. While it is clear that the emergence of consumer advocacy groups in online communities is inevitable, explicating the mechanics for firms to engage with such online communities could benefit from further research.

Firms and customers relate to each other in several ways. In addition to being co-producers, customers could also relate to firms as competitors in either the same market or in a different market. For example, American Express and AT&T shared a buyer–seller relationship, in which American Express supplied AT&T with travel services for a long time. However, this situation changed dramatically when AT&T entered the credit card industry with its Universal Card in March 1990 (Carlin et al. 1994). Jack Welch, the former chairman and CEO of General Electric, rephrases the "Riddle of the Sphinx" and asks, "Who is my customer in the morning, my rival in the afternoon and my supplier in the evening?" (Bradley 1993). Hence, the need for research explicating the contingencies when engaging with customers rather than assuming that greater customer participation in co-production–related activities is always desirable.

Demand-Side Issues

It has been pointed out that increased customer participation in co-production could have negative psychological outcomes for customers (Bendapudi and Leone 2003). Specifically, the self-serving-bias literature has been invoked to argue that situations in which the outcomes are jointly produced could have a detrimental effect on customer satisfaction. This is because of the tendency of customers to give themselves credit for positive outcomes but blaming the partner in the case of negative outcomes. Likewise, Dabholkar and Bagozzi (2002) note that consumer traits such as self-efficacy and need for interaction influence the degree to which customers are motivated to perform certain tasks in a dyad. There is a need for exploring the psychological processes affecting customers when they contribute in greater amounts to the value-creation process.

Locus of Innovation

There is growing recognition that the knowledge required for generating breakthrough ideas in a number of industries no longer resides within a single firm. It is common in the field of biotechnology to find a single publication (e.g., identifying a candidate for the gene determining susceptibility to breast and ovarian cancer) involving researchers from varied fields such as medical schools, pharmaceutical companies, and government research laboratories. Producers of information products frequently rely on customers to beta-test new products. For instance, whereas Stata, the maker of statistical software packages, enlists the help of customers in writing software add-on modules for doing the latest statistical techniques, Bush Boake Allen (BBA) provides a tool kit to customers to develop their own flavors (Thomke and von Hippel 2002). According to the manager of Hallmark's knowledge leadership program, leveraging user communities helps it to "get out of the building and connect to the marketplace. The principles of innovation are based on the belief that innovation occurs out there just as much as it occurs in here" (Banks and Daus 2002, p. 184). The shift in the locus of innovation from firm-centric networks to user-centric networks (e.g., customer-initiated thematic communities) in certain industries (e.g., software, medicine, financial services, pharmaceuticals) constitutes an area for further research.

CONCLUSION

The growing interest in the role of customers as co-producers is a consequence of the emergence of standardized and inexpensive communication networks (e.g., the Internet). Such macroenvironmental trends notwithstanding, the extent to which customers participate with the firm in co-creating value depends, as outlined in this chapter, on a host of factors. Whereas customer participation in the case of a live music concert is limited to the extent of the customer being present to experience the performance, a personal fitness program would entail greater customer participation in co-producing the desired outcome. This chapter highlights the extent of customer participation in a firm's core business processes and/or value chain activities and their implications for enhancing the effectiveness of marketing strategy and efficiency of marketing operations. We hope that the issues highlighted here also provide the impetus for further debate and discussion.

REFERENCES

Alba, Joseph W. and Wesley J. Hutchinson (1987), "Dimensions of Consumer Expertise," *Journal of Consumer Research,* 13 (March), 411–54.

Bendapudi, Neeli and Robert P. Leone (2003), "Psychological Implications of Customer Participation in Co-Production," *Journal of Marketing,* 67 (January), 14–29.

Bettman, James R. (1979), *An Information Processing Theory of Consumer Choice.* Reading, MA: Addison-Wesley Publishing Company.

Banks, Drew and Kim Daus (2002), *Customer Community.* San Francisco, CA: John Wiley & Sons.

Bradley, Stephen (1993), "The Role of IT Networking in Sustaining Competitive Advantage," in *Globalization, Technology, and Competition,* Bradley et al. eds. Cambridge, MA: Harvard Business School Press.

Carlin, Barbara A., Michael J. Dowling, William D. Roering, John Wyman, John Kalinoglou, and Greg Clyburn (1994), "Sleeping with the Enemy: Doing Business with a Competitor," *Business Horizons,* 37 (September/October), 9–15.

Dabholkar, Pratibha A. and Richard P. Bagozzi (2002), "An Attitudinal Model of Technology Based Self-Service: Moderating Effects of Consumer Traits and Situational Factors," *Journal of the Academy of Marketing Science,* 30 (Summer), 184–201.

Darby, Michael R. and Edi Karni (1973), "Free Competition and the Optimal Amount of Fraud," *Journal of Law and Economics,* 16 (April), 67–88.

The Economist (2004), "The Skinny on IT," 372 (8382), 66–68.

Gilmore, James H. and Joseph B. Pine II (1997), "The Four Faces of Mass Customization," *Harvard Business Review,* 75 (January/February), 91–102.

Hayes, Robert H. and Steven G. Wheelwright (1979), "The Dynamics of Product-Process Lifecycles," *Harvard Business Review,* 57 (March/April), 127–37.

Magretta, Joan (1998), "The Power of Virtual Integration: An Interview with Dell Computer's Michael Dell," *Harvard Business Review,* 76 (March/April), 72–84.

Miller, David M. (1984), "Profitability = Productivity + Price Recovery," *Harvard Business Review,* 62 (May/June), 145–53.

New York Times (2003), "Customer Service at a Price" (February 24), 5.

Petty, Richard E. and John T. Cacioppo (1986), *Communication and Persuasion.* New York: Springer-Verlag.

Porter, Michael E. *(1980), Competitive Strategy.* New York: The Free Press.

——— (1985), *Competitive Advantage: Creating and Sustaining Superior Performance.* New York: The Free Press.

Prahalad, C.K. and Venkatram Ramaswamy (2002), *The Future of Competition: Co-Creating Unique Value with Customers.* Cambridge, MA: Harvard Business School Press.

Schendel, Dan (1985), "Strategic Management and Strategic Marketing: What Is Strategic About Either One?" in *Strategic Marketing and Management,* H. Thomas and D. Gardner, eds. New York: John Wiley & Sons, 41–63.

Settles, Craig (1995), *Cybermarketing: Essentials for Success.* New York: Ziff-Davis Press.

Shostack, Lynn G. (1977), "Breaking Free from Product Marketing," *Journal of Marketing,* 41 (April), 73–80.

Srivastava, Rajendra K., Tasadduq A. Shervani, and Liam Fahey (1999), "Marketing, Business Processes, and Shareholder Value: An Organizationally Embedded View of Marketing Activities and the Discipline of Marketing," *Journal of Marketing,* 63 (Special Issue), 168–79.

Thomke, Stefan and Eric von Hippel (2002), "Customers as Innovators: A New Way to Create Value," *Harvard Business Review,* 80 (April), 74–81.

Vargo, Stephen L. and Robert F. Lusch (2004a), "Evolving to a New Dominant Logic for Marketing," *Journal of Marketing,* 68 (January), 1–17.

——— and ——— (2004b), "The Four Service Marketing Myths: Remnants of a Goods-Based Manufacturing Model," *Journal of Service Research,* 6 (May), 324–35.

von Hippel, Eric (1978), "Successful Industrial Products from Customer Ideas," *Journal of Marketing,* 42 (January), 39–49.

——— (1986), "Lead Users: A Source of Novel Product Concepts," *Management Science,* 32 (July), 791–805.

Wise, Richard and David Morrison (2000), "Beyond the Exchange: The Future of B2B," *Harvard Business Review,* 78 (November/December), 86–97.

PART IV

LIBERATING VIEWS ON VALUE AND MARKETING COMMUNICATION

At the center of S-D logic is a focus on a value-creation process that occurs when a customer consumes, rather than when output is produced through manufacturing. Unsold goods might have costs, and goods sold might have value-in-exchange, but from the customer's perspective, they are transmitters of value only when they are employed as appliances to fill functional and higher-order needs. Marketing should therefore focus on value-creating processes that involve the customer as a co-creator of value. In short, the firm can only make value propositions; it cannot create and/or deliver customer value. For this co-creation to occur, marketing communication is central, but it is not the type of marketing communication we have focused on in the past, which is heavily promotion oriented and directed at getting customers to do what we want them to do. S-D logic argues for communication centered on conversation and dialogue in which customers are *communicated with,* rather than *promoted to.* Thus, in a real sense, one could ultimately view the customer as not only the co-creator of the offering but also a co-creator of the entire marketing strategy.

Woodruff and Flint in chapter 14, "Marketing's Service-Dominant Logic and Customer Value," remind us of a very salient point. That is, co-producing actually "clouds who is seller and who is customer, since each is involved in creating value for the other." We have a tendency to view the firm as the seller and the customer as the buyer. In economic theory the firm is captured in the supply function and the customer in the demand function. Woodruff and Flint suggest that if the exchange is relational, which S-D logic assumes, both customer and firm are a customer and a seller. Thus value-creation research should not be one-sided and only consider the down-line customer.

Supportive of S-D logic's emphasis on value being a customer-experiential phenomenon, Woodruff and Flint suggest we do research to understand better customer value processes. For instance, they see a need for research about (1) how customer value judgments change over time, (2) how customer value judgments become more negative over time, (3) how customer value judgments change with context, and (4) how the components of an offering can be valued differently. They further elaborate a research agenda for customer-value theory.

Customer and firm interactions are the central topic of Berthon and John's provocative writing in chapter 15, "From Entities to Interfaces: Delineating Value in Customer-Firm Interactions," and, as they suggest, central to S-D logic. They view a firm's offering as comprising interactive and noninteractive components, with the latter becoming increasingly commodity-like and most firms competing for differential advantage on the interaction component. This chapter helps the reader recognize that with the standard goods-dominant paradigm, it would be virtually impossible to model the spontaneous, creative, and uncertain processes of firm–customer interaction.

"I Can Get It for You Wholesale" is the subtitle of Morris Holbrook's chapter 16, "ROSEPEKICECIVECI vs. CCV: The Resource-Operant, Skills-Exchanging, Performance-Experiencing, Knowledge-Informed, Competence-Enacting, Co-producer–Involved, Value-Emerging, Customer-Interactive View of Marketing versus the Concept of Customer Value." Holbrook suggests he can get S-D logic for you wholesale because the fundamental propositions of S-D logic are essentially captured in an eight-cell matrix that presents a typology of customer values. Holbrook's typology of customer value has much to recommend it and requires careful study. S-D logic also has a very central and strongly emphasized value-creation focus, as captured in foundational premises 6 and 7 (Vargo and Lusch, chapter 1). However, S-D logic also has a "wholesale form"—"service is exchanged for service"—that is considerably easier to grasp than Holbrook's "ROSEPEKICECIVECI" and more informative than the "Concept of Customer Value."

In addition, S-D logic is more than a theory about customer value; it is also a theory about firm behavior and, as we suggest elsewhere in this book, also rich in macromarketing and public policy implications. We also believe that S-D logic is a potential foundation for a general theory of marketing (chapter 32). In brief, what Holbrook can get for you wholesale is different from, and we would argue somewhat less rich and robust, than what S-D logic offers.

Marketing communication is not broad enough, according to Ballantyne and Varey. In chapter 17, "Introducing a Dialogical Orientation to the Service-Dominant Logic of Marketing," these authors argue that S-D logic needs a dialogical orientation so that value can be co-created via dialogue and learning. They introduce dialogue as a preferred form of communicative interaction, rather than marketing's monological approach, which stifles innovation and is largely message making. The dialogical approach to human interaction, in contrast, stimulates learning together and relationship development. Ballantyne and Varey further argue that the tripartite fundamentals of S-D logic are communicative interaction, knowledge application, and relationship development. We believe the ideas they present help advance S-D logic.

One of the few contributions in this book of essays that focuses on operationalizing S-D logic is presented by Tom Duncan and Sandra Moriarty in chapter 18, "How Integrated Marketing Communication's 'Touchpoints' Can Operationalize the Service-Dominant Logic." Viewing service as a communicative experience complements S-D logic, and we think this is a valuable addition. Duncan and Moriarty coach us that IMC's touch point branding is "an intangible resource that uses interactivity for the co-creation of value that drives customer and other stakeholder relationships." Touch points are operant resources and involve the branded product/company and the customer or prospect as jointly acting parties to co-create meaning and value. It is the experience of the touch point that results in value. And in the meantime, it is an opportunity to gather feedback or engage in conversation with the customer, reinforce brand promises, and increase customer involvement with the brand.

14

MARKETING'S SERVICE-DOMINANT LOGIC AND CUSTOMER VALUE

ROBERT B. WOODRUFF AND DANIEL J. FLINT

INTRODUCTION

In a recent *Journal of Marketing* article, Vargo and Lusch (2004) present a strong case for re-thinking the nature of marketing. They argue that an emerging paradigm shift moves us toward a service-dominant (S-D) logic as the foundation for marketing thought and practice. Interestingly, Vargo and Lusch (2004) refer to *value* and related terms (e.g., *value-added*, *value creation*, *value-in-use*, *value-in-exchange*, *customer-perceived value*) well over fifty times. Clearly, their proposed paradigm shift places great emphasis on customer value. This is understandable because service relationships depend on the ongoing exchange of value. In this chapter, we extend the value theme. We believe that for the S-D logic to succeed as a paradigm shift, marketing thought and practice must be founded on greater in-depth understanding of customer value phenomena.

Foundational Premises Involving Value

Vargo and Lusch (2004) discuss eight foundational premises underlying the S-D logic. In at least three of these premises, value plays a central role. For instance, foundational premise 1 considers the value of specialized skills and knowledge being exchanged by relational partners. Correspondingly, marketing thought and practice should focus on the processes by which partners create and exchange value derived from skills and knowledge.

Later in the article, these authors argue that customers co-produce value with the seller (foundational premise 6). In the course of using a product or service, a customer performs certain activities that create value. Though intriguing, we know little about how and why customers engage in co-producing value. In addition, co-producing clouds who is seller and who is customer, because each is involved in creating value for the other.

Finally, Vargo and Lusch (2004) believe that a service orientation requires that customers and sellers build relationships with each other (foundational premise 8). The seller is "doing things, not just for the customer but also in concert with the customer" (p. 11). Relational exchange suggests that interactions between partners occur over time and likely have social as well as economic aspects to value.

Foundational premises 1, 6, and 8 are highly interrelated premises. The parties exchange skills and knowledge needed by the other. Both parties' skills and knowledge co-produce value that makes exchange viable. The relational nature of exchange means that both parties must understand and be sensitive to the nature of value desired by the other. Furthermore, value takes on a temporally oriented process nature that shifts over time as exchange partners experience and reflect on their relationship.

Purpose of the Chapter

We believe that marketing thought is seriously deficient in its understanding of customer value-related phenomena. Consequently, we devote this chapter to building a case for increased attention to improving this understanding through more description and theory construction regarding value phenomena. In the next section, we critique the existing state of customer value knowledge. We show that marketing has focused primarily on definitions and categorizing value types. Though useful, this knowledge base is not adequate. Our knowledge of customer value has not progressed to the level needed to support Vargo and Lusch's (2004) S-D logic for marketing. We follow this critique by discussing the phenomenological nature of customer value and propose specific value phenomena for study. Finally, we offer a research agenda that can lead to improved understanding of value phenomena, and we discuss selected implications for marketing.

THE STATE OF CUSTOMER VALUE

Coinciding with marketing's growing interest in a customer orientation, customer value research offers important insights into its nature. Discussions of alternative concept definitions have expanded our understanding of value perceptions. Moreover, we know more about the different types of value that customers seek. We comment on each of these contributions and relate them to value knowledge development.

Customer Value Definitions

Marketing literature frequently refers to customer value. Often, these references take a seller's perspective, such as in discussing their need to create and deliver value to targeted customers. For example, the popular business press churned out several books on the wisdom of creating value-based strategies (e.g., Band 1991; Gale 1994; Naumann 1995; Slywotzky 1996). Similarly, books, articles, and papers by academics discuss customer value, particularly as it helps to explain some other behavior. For example, some focus on sellers' design of marketing strategy (e.g., Day 1990; van der Haar, Kemp, and Omata 2001; Vargo and Lusch 2004; Woodruff 1997), whereas others use value to explain some aspect of customer behavior (Lam et al. 2004). Perhaps this explains why much of the customer value literature is concerned with concept definitions, which tend to position value as a variable or state of being.

Definitions of Value

As Vargo and Lusch (2004) note (pp. 5, 9), the marketing literature offers quite different conceptual definitions of customer value. We briefly review four of them. One long-held view, the *value-added* concept, takes a seller's perspective. Using a container analogy, a product or service is a vessel in which a seller places transformed operand resources. As such, value is something created, originally owned, and offered for sale by a seller. In this sense, a product or service has value, independent from customers' perceptions (Holbrook 1994). Marketing's concern for product/service value-added aspects comes in designing offers that targeted consumers likely will purchase. An offer must meet consumer needs. Consequently, whereas the value-added concept focuses on what the seller has contributed to a product/service offering, customer perceptions of those offers likely influence marketing decisions.

The value-added concept has operational appeal for sellers. By thinking about product/service offers as "bundles of attributes," managers position customer value in terms of seller-controlled variables. Using market research and/or other sources, managers explore likely consumer response to variations in offers comprising different attribute combinations (Griffin and Hauser 1993). Although it makes sense to study customer response to attribute bundles, the value-added concept's major limitation comes from underemphasizing the customer's world. Managers might get caught up with the value of materials, labor, and services contributed to a product/service offering and overestimate how well they understand how customers view that offering relative to their needs and use situations.

Second, customer value, again taking a seller's perspective, has been defined as the *economic worth of a customer*. Much of customer relationship management (CRM) adopts this notion (e.g., Gupta and Lehmann 2004; Ryals and Payne 2001), in which a seller's concern is to extract more value from existing customers and to segment customers according to the value potential they represent for the seller. Also, CRM differentiates marketing strategy for customers possessing high versus low value. Interestingly, this concept has relevance for relational exchange because it indicates that sellers seek value from customers as well as vice versa.

Third, value also has been defined as the *economic worth of a seller's product/service offerings* to customers. This notion suggests that customers translate value into monetary equivalence. Sometimes customers think of value in terms of getting a "deal," whereby value is equated to low price (Zeithaml 1988). This concept might also be implied in calculations common to some business-to-business (B2B) transactions in which customers explicitly consider the economic impact of a seller's offer on their business operations. However, as a general definition of customer value, this concept is too limiting. Richins (1994b) discusses several convincing reasons for this observation. For example, some things that people might value are not economic products or services (e.g., memories of a loved one, psychic benefit of owning a name brand). Furthermore, customers themselves might not think about value in economic terms.

Fourth, Vargo and Lusch (2004) refer to *value-in-use*, which conceptualizes value as a phenomenological experience perceived by a customer interacting with products/services bundles in use situations. Rather than the value contained in the product, here *value* refers to a customer's meaning attached to product/service bundles relative to a use context. Support for this phenomenological-oriented concept comes from means-end theory, as Vargo and Lusch (2004) note (p. 9). In particular, the notion of consequences in a means-end hierarchy indicates that valuation of products/services depends on customers' experiences with their use in situations of importance to them. Unfortunately, means-end theory is not well developed or widely applied in marketing thought, though some movement in that direction has occurred (e.g., Gardial et al. 1994; Gutman 1982; Holbrook 1994; Overby, Gardial, and Woodruff 2004; Richins 1994b; Woodruff 1997; Zeithaml 1988).

Summary

Although each of these definitions has merit, writers are not always clear as to which one is being used, creating confusion about the nature of customer value. We believe that none of the preceding definitions capture the complex nature of customer value. Although each concept might describe a part of its nature, each leaves out other parts. For the S-D logic to progress toward becoming a paradigm, marketing should strive for a more comprehensive, in-depth understanding of this foundational concept. In part, greater insight might come from reassessing and integrating the various existing definitions. More likely, however, new research on the nature of customer value should play a role in better understanding its nature.

Customer Value Types

Several writers extend the customer value-in-use definition by discussing types of value. The classifications and typologies are different, and we are not aware of any research that has resolved these differences. For example, Sheth, Newman, and Gross (1991) differentiate five different types of customer value: functional value, social value, emotional value, epistemic value, and conditional value. Lai (1995, p. 383) proposes eight "generic product benefits" types: functional, social, affective, epistemic, aesthetic, hedonic, situational, and holistic. Holbrook (1994) presents a typology of customer value using three dimensions of value: intrinsic/extrinsic, self-oriented/other-oriented, and active/passive. These dimensions result in eight different kinds of customer value: efficiency, excellence (quality), politics (success), esteem, play, esthetics, morality, and spirituality. In a B2B context, Gassenheimer, Houston, and Davis (1998) distinguish between economic value and social/relationship value of business relationships, as have others (Lapierre 2000; Ulaga 2003).

These classifications implicitly consider customer value as a customer's judgment about the goodness or badness of an experience, a perceptual state of being. For example, Holbrook (1994, p. 27) refers to customer value as preference or "favorable disposition, general liking, positive affect, judgment as being good." However, Woodruff (1997) suggests a broader classification when he notes that consumers form judgments about both desired value (e.g., the types of value wanted from using a product or service offering) and received value experienced from actual use (i.e., the goodness or badness judgment of an actual purchase or use experience). Consistent with the notion of goal-oriented customers, their judgments of goodness and badness of a product/service offering experience likely reflect some goal or desired value.

Such classifications are helpful in understanding the complexity of customer value perceptions. Quite likely, customers could hold multiple judgments of value regarding a product/service offering, simultaneously. The literature recognizes this possibility by referring to value trade-offs that customers make between positive (i.e., benefits) versus negative (i.e., sacrifices) value judgments (e.g., Zeithaml 1988).

Customer Value Processes

Neither definitions nor classifications say much about how or why customers form the value judgments they do. It is one thing to know that customers value fun, for example, but quite something else to understand how and why that valuation occurs. Philosophizing about values has been going on for a long time (e.g., Holbrook 1994; Munsterberg 1909), but little has been done to build customer-value-process descriptions or theory empirically. Perhaps this deficiency occurs because of marketing's tendency to overemphasize customer value as a perceptual state and underemphasize its process nature. There are exceptions, of course. For example, Day (2002) and Day and Crask (2000) integrate valuation and satisfaction processes. Richins (1994b) conducted research on "valuing things," suggesting that value states result from processes in which consumers attach meaning to objects. Flint, Woodruff, and Gardial (2002) report on research describing customer value change processes. In the next section, we build on these initial attempts at shifting customer value research from state to process.

TOWARD UNDERSTANDING CUSTOMER VALUE PHENOMENA

In this section, we explore the foundational elements for research intended to study customer value as process. We explore the phenomenological nature of customer valuation and suggest different types of value phenomena that should be of interest to marketing thought and practice.

The Phenomenological Nature of Customer Value

Description and/or theory construction starts when one selects a phenomenon for study. We believe that customer value should attain the status of a critical phenomenon about which marketing thought should have much to say. Vargo and Lusch (2004) make this case by describing the central role that value plays in a service-dominated economy. Furthermore, by recommending that marketing pay more attention to the value-in-use concept, they implicitly recognize the phenomenological, experiential nature of value. This view raises challenging questions of how and why customer value judgments occur. For instance, who is the customer in a relational exchange? On the surface, it might seem obvious who is customer and who is seller. But, as noted previously, relational exchange clouds this distinction. Moreover, what is customer value as a phenomenon like? We briefly address each of these questions.

Who Is the Customer in Relational Exchange?

Determining who the seller and the customer are might have merit within transactional exchange in a monetary-based system. However, the S-D logic advocates more attention to relational exchange (Vargo and Lusch 2004). Services are purchased and consumed over time and in cooperation between both exchange partners. When both partners are co-producing value, their roles overlap. For relationships to form and grow, each exchange partner must create and deliver value for the other. Consequently, both partners in relational exchange could at times act like either customer or seller.

Although we do not advocate giving up the conceptual distinction between customer and seller, relational exchange has an important implication for customer value phenomena. These phenomena can be experienced by both partners in relational exchange. Customer value research should explore this possibility.

What Is Customer Value as a Phenomenon Like?

To answer this question, we draw on excellent discussions of value in Holbrook (1994) and Richins (1994a, b). Holbrook (1994) adopts a phenomenological definition of value when he says it is "an interactive relativistic preference experience." He believes that something has value when a customer attaches preference to it. Value-as-preference is a judgment occurring as an outcome of a customer's "experience of interacting with some object" (p. 27). Note that in relational exchange, "interacting" extends beyond a physical product or service to the social process of engaging in service use with an exchange partner.

Holbrook (1994) further argues that a preference judgment involves comparison. That is, preference is relative to something else, such as desired value in situational context. It is important to note that means-end theory indicates that comparison occurs within a customer's use/situational contexts (Gutman 1982). Customers attach preference to consequences they experience within the particular situation in which a product/service offering is used or intended to be used.

The comparative nature of customer value suggests that customers are likely reflexive when engaged in making value judgments. They can think about themselves relative to the product/ service offering in the use situation context. Part of this reflexivity might involve visioning. That is, customers might envision what they want to be or to experience in the use situation or as a result of the use situation. Furthermore, a customer might attach value to this vision, as suggested by the concept of desired value discussed earlier.

Richins (1994a, b) focuses on the role of meaning in the attachment of value to objects. In her view, meaning arises from persons interacting with possessions, and "a possession's value derives from its meaning" (1994b, p. 505). Meanings can be public in the sense of being assigned by others, such as members of a social group or a culture. Such meanings suggest that an object has value independent from the perceptions of a customer, consistent with the value-added notion (e.g., gems are valuable because they are widely judged to be expensive). Meanings also might be private and composed of the "sum of the subjective meanings that object holds for a particular individual" (1994b, p. 506). Consequently, a person might attach value to an object because of what it means to him or her, personally, such as the sentimental value of a photograph. Richins (1994b) uses the possible relationships of meanings to possessions to identify categories of value: utilitarian value, enjoyment, representations of interpersonal ties, and identity and self-expression, though her research is more concerned with the nature of meanings.

Although both Holbrook (1994) and Richins (1994a, b) tend to define value as a judgment state, they occasionally refer to value-related processes. For example, Richins (1994b) discusses "the creation of meaning" (p. 517), and in the course of discussing value judgments, Holbrook (1994) occasionally mentions valuation and preference formation. These references suggest underlying processes occurring in conjunction with value judgments. Such phenomena suggest new research directions.

Customer Value–Related Phenomena

Far too little research has been done to even suggest either description or theory about valuation processes. However, past research could help researchers think about customer value–related phenomena of a process nature important to marketing thought. To illustrate, we briefly discuss four such experiential phenomena. Our intent is not to be all inclusive, but rather to speculate on the variety of process-related phenomena for which further research can add to our understanding of the nature of customer value.

Customer Value Change

We know that customer value judgments change over time. However, what is this change process like? Flint and colleagues (Flint and Woodruff 2001; Flint, Woodruff, and Gardial 2002) have begun to provide insight into this question in a B2B context. Focusing on customer desired value, they discovered several intriguing aspects about change processes. First, customer desired value change coincides with events both internal and external to the customer organization. Although the role of external events is not a surprise, the literature has not said much about the role of internal events. For example, hiring a new purchasing manager, restructuring, and lost business apparently can trigger significant change in what a customer desires from its suppliers.

Second, customer desired value change is associated with emotion among managers in an organization. Flint, Woodruff, and Gardial (2002) called this emotion "tension." We do not know enough about the nature of the influence that tension plays in customer value change processes. Nor do we know much about any other possible emotions involved in value change processes. Third, in periods of desired value change, managers adopt change strategies directed toward suppliers to get them to comply with new desired value. Apparently, customer valuing is a much larger process than just the events and activities leading up to a change in a customer value state.

The dynamic nature of customer value change provides a rich direction for research. Marketing needs to know more about how initial value judgments take shape and how these early judgments might affect change processes. Furthermore, in an ongoing service-dominated relationship, there might be many opportunities for value judgments to change periodically. Marketing needs to know if the change process itself takes on different characteristics as more and more of these opportunities are experienced. It would be interesting to compare the nature of change process at various points in time over the life of a seller–customer relationship to see what differences arise.

Using the Woodruff (1997) distinction between desired and received customer value judgments, we should not assume that the formation and change processes are the same for each type of judgment. For example, we do not yet know enough about how perceptions/reflections of past value received changes in light of recent experiences. Consequently, we need to know more about how desired and received value judgments arise and then change over time. Moreover, we are intrigued by the possibility that the desired value and received value change processes interact. It could be that customer perceptions of one might color perceptions of the other.

The Nature of Devaluing

Customers might migrate toward stronger and more positive evaluations of product/service offerings, but that is not the only possibility. An interesting aspect of value change involves devaluing, in which judgments become more negative. Several writers discuss the potential for devaluing to occur (e.g., Brendl, Markman, and Messner 2003; Schwartz 1990; Woodruff and Gardial 1996). This phenomenon could show up in desired value over time as a decline in the importance of certain needs. Customers also might devalue received value by denigrating certain features of a product/service offering. Devaluing raises many questions. For instance, do customers form new value desires first and then actively find fault with (devalue) current products/services in order to justify the new desired value? Or do they find fault with current products/services first and then seek out new value propositions? How is devaluing of product/service offerings different from devaluing relationships? These questions indicate the enormous opportunity to learn more about how and why devaluing occurs.

Context Influence on Value Judgments

The everyday nature of customer value phenomena emphasizes the importance of better understanding the interaction between valuation and context. Many questions come to mind: What are the circumstances like in which customer value processes are embedded? How does this context influence the valuation processes and their outcomes? Furthermore, some types of context might be particularly worth studying. The nature of a relationship between supplier and customer likely provides a critical context for customer valuation. For example, do strong relationships inhibit devaluing from occurring? Is value change more likely to have variation early in a relationship when compared to later in a growing relationship?

Means-end theory points to use situations' contexts for valuation. There are many aspects of use situations that could interrelate with formation and change of value judgments, both desired and received. We are especially intrigued by the use situation in which a product offering is first experienced. Characteristics of this early context could affect the likelihood of later value change. Consider an athlete in an especially important game who drinks Gatorade for the first time while defeating a key opponent. The warm feelings from the game could carry over to the judgment about that product, making these judgments resistant to change in the future. Other special contexts might be equally intriguing to understand.

Valuation for Non–Product Offer Components

There are many components to a product/service offering, and valuation might not occur in the same way for each one. By breaking out these components, we can study the nature of valuation for different ones. Vargo and Lusch (2004), in their service-centered view of marketing, emphasize an especially important one—a relationships between a seller and a customer. Relationships raise important customer value and valuation questions. For instance, how do customers perceive the value of a relationship with a supplier? How does this value judgment arise and then change? How are the value and valuation of a relationship similar to or different from the value and valuation of the product or other service component of an offering? Intriguingly, in a supply chain in which innovation is common, it might be okay, even encouraged, for customers to devalue specific supplier products and services as long as they do not devalue the supply relationship. Stewart (2004) explores these kinds of questions from both a customer's and a seller's point of view. More is needed.

Co-producing Value

Vargo and Lusch's (2004) co-producing notion suggests that valuation might coincide with processes in which both customers and suppliers are actively engaged. However, we know very little about whether customers see themselves as playing this role or what the nature of co-producing is like. For instance, are customers co-producing on their own, in cooperation with suppliers, or sometimes both? Where in supply chains is value co-produced? When customers co-produce value, who benefits from or receives this value (e.g., customers themselves, suppliers, both customers and suppliers)? What goes on during co-producing and what would compel customers to engage in this activity?

Summary

By laying out valuation phenomena, we want to encourage positioning customer value as much more than a cognitive state reflected in static value judgments. Customer value also includes a host of related, dynamic phenomena that center on important everyday activities of customers interacting with product/service offerings of sellers. We know very little about these process aspects of customer value, and that creates an enormous opportunity for further research. In the next section, we propose a customer value research agenda for marketing, one that takes on added urgency by the shift in marketing toward an S-D logic.

PROPOSED CUSTOMER VALUE THEORY RESEARCH AGENDA

Because we believe that marketing thought is at a very early stage of understanding customer value phenomena, we oriented a proposed research agenda toward description and theory construction. In the following sections, we briefly discuss three phases of recommended research on customer value.

Phase I: Understand Customer Value Phenomena

The four different kinds of customer value experiential phenomena highlight the variety of directions which customer value research might take. All of these phenomena are interrelated in the sense of occurring in a larger dynamic customer value change process. For example, devaluing will likely occur at some point over the life of a customer's interest in a particular product/service offering, or in a whole product/service category. It might represent a step in the progression of customer value judgments arising under new situational circumstances. Consequently, research on customer value change might discover new knowledge about devaluing, even if that was not the intended research objective at the outset. Similarly, drilling down for in-depth understanding of customer value change could yield insights into the nature of value for customer relationships with suppliers and how these perceptions might differ from the nature of value for product, delivery, and price aspects of supplier offerings. For instance, devaluing of specific products/services could be initial symptoms of devaluing of the supply relationship as a whole. Devaluing also could be a precursor to new emergent desired value or evidence that new value desires are emerging.

This phase is crucial to redirect customer value research beyond current emphasis on definitions and typologies. This chapter only begins to lay out the many opportunities to more fully understand the processes by which value judgments, both desired and received, arise, change, and presumably eventually decline. If we are in a transition to a new S-D logic, a highly customer-centric paradigm, this phenomenological research takes on new urgency.

Methodologically, we believe that this phase should rely heavily on qualitative research. Marketing needs a richer base of knowledge exploring how customers perceive, think about, and engage in customer value processes. Qualitative research is well suited to provide these insights.

Phase II: Understand Seller Value Phenomena

Previously, we noted that relational exchange clouds the distinction between customer and seller. To use Vargo and Lusch's (2004) terms, relationship partners co-produce value for themselves and each other. For this reason, customer value studies should not be limited to just customers in the traditional sense. Sellers also experience valuation processes, and marketing should have an equally in-depth understanding of their nature. Many of the research questions are the same as those that we discussed in the previous section on the phenomenological nature of customer value. We just substitute "seller" for "customer."

Methodologically, this phase is similar to the previous one in benefiting most from qualitative research. The focus should be on generating rich understanding of sellers' perceptions of value processes. However, to fully understand the nature of co-producing, sampling eventually might have to shift to relational dyads because the point of view of either customer or seller alone might not be adequate.

Phase III: Theory Testing across Contexts

Some researchers might be interested in expanding substantive findings from research in phases I and II toward more formal theory applicable to a wider variety of contexts. Perhaps the most important context concern could be culture. Much of the limited understanding that we have about customer value phenomena comes from research conducted in the United States, Western Europe, and Great Britain. We cannot say that these findings will hold up in other, very different cultures. For example, Broyles, Schumann, and Woodruff (2004) question whether the disconfirmation model, the most common theoretical foundation for consumer satisfaction, will hold up in non-Western cultures such as China. Their arguments could just as well apply to customer value description or theory.

Other contexts are related to the S-D logic as well. This logic encourages thinking of value within an overall supply chain. Interestingly, there might be differences in customer value processes at different places in a network of organizations. For instance, is B2B relational valuation similar to or different from business-to-consumer (B2C) valuation? How does co-producing work at different places in a supply chain?

Methodologically, this phase could benefit from quantitative research as well. Taking direction from categories and processes revealed by phases I and II, surveys and experiments could shed light on how well emerging theory holds across different contexts. Moreover, quantitative research might be used to better understand some aspects of customer value such as the extent, rate, and magnitude of value change occurring in particular contexts.

Summary Observations

Although we presented our proposed research agenda in phases, we did not intend to suggest a linear order to them. Clearly, research in phases I and II easily could be conducted concurrently. Later, sequential efficiency might come from letting phases I and II research guide phase III research. We need to know much more about customer valuation before engaging in theory-testing research. However, recycling back and forth between the phases likely will happen.

In an applied field, further research on customer value phenomena should be guided by the problems and issues critical to both academics and practitioners. Vargo and Lusch (2004) provide a much-needed applied rationale for expanding research on customer value. Their notions of value from services, co-producing value, and the relational nature of service exchange in particular suggest applied problems and issues that almost demand a rich descriptive and/or theoretical foundation on customer valuation processes. We need not go further than their arguments to justify our research recommendations.

IMPLICATIONS FOR S-D MARKETING

In this section, we take the point of view of a seller in suggesting illustrative implications of customer value research needs. This coincides with marketing thought's tendency to take the seller's perspective when discussing marketing application by managers. We very briefly discuss application needs in three areas of marketing mentioned by Vargo and Lusch (2004): market sensing, value propositions, and relationship management.

Market Sensing

Marketing relies on market sensing to bring market and customer knowledge into an organization's decisions (Day 1990; Day et al. 2004). In particular, this skill should enable managers to understand key aspects of their customers' valuation processes. Many market re-search techniques are available for this purpose, along with many highly skilled professional research people who know how to use them. Yet, we see at least two major deficiencies in these skills related to customer value.

First, we believe that the value-added concept tends to dominate organizations' thinking about customers. Ironically, the marketing literature often advocates doing otherwise (Lai 1995). It is almost an axiom in marketing thought that customers buy what product/service offerings can do for them and not the attributes of the offering itself. However, how often is this axiom really applied in business practice, particularly beyond advertising? We frequently see market research being used to find out what attributes that customers feel should be designed into offerings or with which they are satisfied, which implicitly reinforces managers who think "value-added." Too infrequently do we see managers request or have access to market research that truly helps them understand the higher-order consequences that customers seek in specific use situations.

This deficiency is particularly surprising because customer value knowledge already exists that could guide different applications of market research tools. For example, means-end theory has been around for more than two decades and it places great emphasis on the consequences that customers seek (i.e., use benefits) or want to avoid (i.e., use sacrifices) in their own use situations. We just do not see this framework being applied often enough in marketing practice. Perhaps the theory has not been sufficiently developed for wide application.

The second deficiency is more understandable given the state of the art of marketing knowl-edge. The dynamic nature of customer value judgments and valuation places a premium on sup-pliers anticipating value change. Suppliers who are first to understand that their customers want new and different value from them have more lead time to respond than competitors who do not. Yet, marketing research has limited ability to anticipate change quickly, in no small part due to very little understanding of what value change processes are like. More advanced understanding of these processes likely will pay off for managers, such as by identifying leading indicators of value change that could be incorporated into market-sensing activities. Our proposed research agenda considers this goal.

Value Propositions

Value propositions should help managers implement marketing strategies by enabling them to verbalize the value characteristics of their offer. Yet, value propositions too often take a value-added perspective by articulating what value a seller has designed into its offer. This perspective might be adequate when value propositions serve as a guide for internal organization customers but are less adequate when used to communicate with external customers. These customers likely think more about value-in-use than the value-added concept. We believe that more focused appli-cation of means-end theory, particularly as expanded by more valuation research, could help managers create more customer-sensitive value propositions.

Value propositions typically address the creation of value to customers who are presumed to be formulating positive value judgments. We know less about how value propositions might deal with customers who are engaged in devaluing processes. If devaluing stems from noncontrollable cir-cumstances, there might not be anything that a seller can do. For example, a customer who recently has relocated might devalue a service provider because it is no longer convenient to use. In contrast, suppose the devaluing happens because a customer had a very bad incident involving poor service from the provider. In this case, value propositions might be developed and used to convey service recovery actions that will alleviate such performance problems in the future (e.g., Bolton and Drew 1991). More research on devaluing processes should help further this kind of application.

Relationship Management

In relational exchange, value likely flows back and forth between the exchange partners. Each partner periodically makes value judgments, both about desired and received value, which are subject to change. Some aspects of this value might be economic (similar to the economic worth notions discussed previously), but other aspects likely will be noneconomic. Relationship value could be like that. It is difficult to economically quantify such value aspects of relationships as trust, similarity of values, and supportive dispositions. Managers in organizations will have to become skilled at managing all value aspects of relationships, not just the economic ones.

Relationship value likely will have different properties depending on whose perspective in the exchange is taken. For example, each partner might not want exactly the same kinds of value from the other. The customer might place a premium on the seller's ability to help the organization look good to their customers, whereas the seller wants the customer to be loyal in the face of competitor appeals. Consequently, research on managing relationships must consider the two-way flow of dissimilar value between the exchange partners.

Finally, at least some of this relationship value results from co-producing activities. These activities likely change the way relationship partners think about value. Relationship partners might need new metrics to assess the overall value of the relationship shared by the partners, including both economic and noneconomic aspects.

CONCLUDING COMMENT

In this chapter, we argue for much greater focus on experiential customer value phenomena. We believe that it is time to move beyond discussions of the definition of customer value and classifications of types of value. Marketing's greatest need for customer value knowledge concerns valuation process phenomena. By shifting customer value thought beyond a state variable to include interrelated experiential processes, we open the door for new research to better understand its dynamic nature. We believe that marketing thought's movement toward a service-dominated, customer-oriented, and relational paradigm places increasing urgency on conducting such research.

REFERENCES

Band, William A. (1991), *Creating Value for Customers.* New York: John Wiley & Sons.

Bolton, Ruth N. and James H. Drew (1991), "A Multistage Model of Customers' Assessments of Service Quality and Value," *Journal of Consumer Research,* 17 (March), 375–84.

Brendl, C. Miguel, Arthur B. Markman, and Claude Messner (2003), "The Devaluation Effect: Activating a Need Devalues Unrelated Objects," *Journal of Consumer Research* 29 (March), 463–73.

Broyles, S. Allen, David W. Schumann, and Robert B. Woodruff (2004), "Questioning the Applicability of the Consumer Disconfirmation Model Beyond Western Culture: Cultural Differences in Modes of Thought," working paper, The University of Tennessee.

Day, Ellen (2002), "The Role of Value in Consumer Satisfaction," *Journal of Consumer Satisfaction, Dissatisfaction and Complaining Behavior* 15, 22–32.

——— and Melvin R. Crask (2000), "Value Assessment: The Antecedent of Customer Satisfaction," *Journal of Consumer Satisfaction, Dissatisfaction and Complaining Behavior* 13, 52–60.

Day, George S. (1990), *Market Driven Strategy: Processes for Creating Value.* New York: The Free Press.

———, John Deighton, Das Narayandas, Evert Gummesson, Shelby D. Hunt, C.K. Prahalad, Roland T. Rust, and Steven M. Shugan (2004), "Invited Commentaries on 'Evolving to a New Dominant Logic for Marketing,'" *Journal of Marketing* 68 (January), 18–27.

Flint, Daniel J. and Robert B. Woodruff (2001) "The Initiators of Changes in Customers' Desired Value: Results from a Theory Building Study," *Industrial Marketing Management* 30 (4), 321–37.

———, ———, and Sarah Fisher Gardial (2002), "Exploring the Customer Value Change Phenomenon in a Business-to-Business Context," *Journal of Marketing* 66 (October), 102–17.

Gale, Bradley T. (1994), *Managing Customer Value.* New York: The Free Press.

Gardial, Sarah Fisher, D. Scott Clemons, Robert B. Woodruff, David W. Schumann, and Mary Jane Burns (1994), "Comparing Consumers' Recall of Prepurchase and Postpurchase Evaluation Experiences," *Journal of Consumer Research,* 20 (March), 548–60.

Gassenheimer, Jule B., Franklin S. Houston, and J. Charlene Davis (1998), "The Role of Economic Value, Social Value, and Perceptions of Fairness in Interorganizational Relationship Retention Decisions," *Journal of the Academy of Marketing Science,* 26 (Fall), 322–37.

Griffin, Abbie and John R. Hauser (1993), "The Voice of the Customer," *Marketing Science,* 12 (Winter), 1–27.

Gupta, Sunil and Donald R. Lehmann (2004), "What Are Your Customers Worth?" online *Newsletter of the Center on Global Brand Leadership,* sponsored by Columbia Business School, University of Munich, ESADE, Hong Kong University, and Yonsei University. www.globalbrands.org/resources/cbgl online july04.htm. Accessed July 25, 2004.

Gutman, Jonathan (1982), "A Means-End Chain Model Based on Consumer Categorization Processes," *Journal of Marketing,* 46 (Spring), 60–72.

Holbrook, Morris B. (1994), "The Nature of Customer Value: An Axiology of Services in the Consumption Experience," in *Service Quality: New Directions in Theory and Practice,* Roland Rust and Richard L. Oliver, eds. Thousand Oaks, CA: Sage Publications, 21–71.

Lai, Albert Wenben (1995), "Consumer Values, Product Benefits and Customer Value: A Consumption Behavior Approach," in *Advances in Consumer Research,* Frank R. Kardes and Mita Sujan, eds. Provo, UT: Association for Consumer Research, 22, 381–88.

Lam, Shun Yin, Venkatesh Shankar, M. Krishna Erramilli, and Bvsan Murthy (2004), "Customer Value, Satisfaction, Loyalty, and Switching Costs: An Illustration from a Business-to-Business Service Context," *Journal of the Academy of Marketing Science* 32 (Summer), 293–311.

Lapierre, Jozee (2000), "Development of Measures to Assess Customer Perceived Value in a Business-to-Business Context," in *Advances in Business Marketing and Purchasing,* Vol. 9, Arch G. Woodside, ed. Greenwich, CT: JAI Press, Inc., 243–86.

Munsterberg, Hugo (1909), *The Eternal Values.* New York: The Houghton Mifflin Company.

Naumann, Earl (1995), *Creating Customer Value.* Cincinnati, OH: Thompson Executive Press.

Overby, Jeff W., Sarah Fisher Gardial, and Robert B. Woodruff (2004), "French versus American Consumers' Attachment of Value to a Product in a Common Consumption Context: A Cross-National Comparison," *Journal of the Academy of Marketing Science* 32 (Fall), 437–460.

Richins, Marsha L. (1994a), "Special Possessions and the Expression of Material Values," *Journal of Consumer Research,* 21 (December), 522–33.

——— (1994b), "Valuing Things: The Public and Private Meanings of Possessions," *Journal of Consumer Research,* 21 (December), 504–521.

Ryals, Lynette and Adrian Payne (2001), "Customer Relationship Management in Financial Services: Towards Information-Enabled Relationship Marketing," *Journal of Strategic Marketing* 9 (March), 3–28.

Schwartz, Barry (1990), "The Creation and Destruction of Value," *American Psychologist,* 45 (1), 7–15.

Sheth, Jagdish N., Bruce I. Newman, and Barbara L. Gross (1991), *Consumption Values and Market Choices: Theory and Applications.* Cincinnati, OH: Southwestern Publishing Company.

Slywotzky, Adrian J. (1996), *Value Migration.* Boston: Harvard Business School Press.

Stewart, Geoffrey T. (2004), "Relational Value Exchange: A Grounded Theory Study of Buyers' and Sellers' Approaches to Building, Maintaining, and/or Dissolving Interorganizational Relationships," dissertation draft, The University of Tennessee.

Ulaga, Wolfgang (2003), "Capturing Value Creation in Business Relationships: A Customer Perspective," *Industrial Marketing Management* 32(8), 677–93.

van der Haar, Jeanke W., Ron G.M. Kemp, and Onno Omata (2001), "Creating Value that Cannot Be Copied," *Industrial Marketing Management,* 30, 627–36.

Vargo, Stephen L. and Robert F. Lusch (2004), "Evolving to a New Dominant Logic for Marketing," *Journal of Marketing,* 68 (January), 1–17.

Woodruff, Robert B. (1997), "Customer Value: The Next Source for Competitive Advantage," *Journal of the Academy of Marketing Science,* 25 (Spring), 139–53.

——— and Sarah Fisher Gardial (1996), *Know Your Customer: New Approaches to Customer Value and Satisfaction.* Cambridge, MA: Blackwell Publishers.

Zeithaml, Valarie A. (1988), "Consumer Perceptions of Price, Quality, and Value: A Means-End Model and Synthesis of Evidence," *Journal of Marketing,* 52 (July), 2–22.

15

FROM ENTITIES TO INTERFACES

Delineating Value in Customer–Firm Interactions

PIERRE BERTHON AND JOBY JOHN

INTRODUCTION

Scholars have argued that the locus of economic value is increasingly shifting from tangible resources to intangible resources such as information and knowledge (e.g., Day 1992; Glazer 1991), and from transactions to relationships (e.g., Berry 1983; Gummesson 1995). This shift has recently been formalized into an emerging dominant logic for marketing (Vargo and Lusch 2004), wherein services rather than goods make up the fundamental unit of economic exchange. We propose that at the root of this dominant logic of marketing lies the notion of interaction (cf. Czepiel et al. 1985). It is through interactions that information is exchanged and knowledge generated, and it is through interactions that services are co-designed, co-created, and consumed. We propose a shift in focus from the *entities* in an exchange (i.e., customer and firm) to the *interactions* between the entities, for interactions constitute the very fabric of an exchange. Indeed, interactions constitute the building blocks of all marketing relationships, and it is increasingly through interaction that *value* is co-created by the entities.

We propose that it is useful to think of offerings as having an interactive value component and a noninteractive value component. Indeed, it can be observed that the proportion of value realized through direct customer–firm interaction has increased in recent years. Indeed, we project that in the future firms will increasingly be forced to compete on the interactive component of their offerings, as the noninteractive component becomes a commodity.

We argue that the basic unit of offerings will increasingly become discrete customer–firm interactions. Thus, there is an imperative to understand the value dimensions of interactions and the elements of their provision to ensure the delivery of high-value interactions. What brings this imperative to the fore is that in today's marketplace, the pervasive incorporation of information technology (IT) applications has dramatically changed the nature, scope, and frequency of customer–firm interactions. The benefits of IT have often been framed in terms of information intensity—the extent to which value is created through information processing. What tends to be overlooked is that information can be produced and consumed (thereby creating value) only through *interactions*. Thus, we argue that any claim to a new dominant logic for marketing must include the role of customer–firm interactions in the value-creation process and consequently the realization of competitive advantage.

In this chapter, we introduce a new concept we call "interaction intensity" and delineate a framework for understanding and managing customer–firm interactions. We focus our discussion on the customer–firm dyad and illustrate the ideas in this context. However, the insights are more generally applicable along the entire value chain. This chapter is set out as follows. First, we articulate our view of "offering" in terms of interactive value and define the construct *interaction intensity*. Second, we outline the provider's perspective to a firm's value creation and delivery in terms of the content and process, and structure and sequence, of interactions. Third, we specify key interaction value dimensions from the customer's perspective. Finally, we present the challenges for practitioners and scholars.

INTERACTION INTENSITY

Building on Vargo and Lusch's (2004) "service-centered" dominant logic, we suggest that the new paradigm of marketing needs to focus on interactions rather than entities. When offerings produce results for the customer, value is realized through customers' interaction experience with the offering. Thus, what is key is the value-in-use, or experience value, of the interaction.

Interaction is defined as reciprocal action, or influence of persons or things on each other (OED 1990). At the interface of the firm with the customer or any other stakeholder, something is exchanged and value is created through interactions. Indeed, total value can be seen as being composed of an interactive component and a noninteractive component. Thus, an offering can be conceptualized as comprising two components: first, a stand-alone component that involves no interaction between the firm and customer; and second, an interactive component that is dependent on customer–firm interaction. Thus, total value in an offering equals the noninteractive value plus the interactive value:

$$V_{total} = V_{noninteraction} + V_{interaction} \text{ or } V_t = V_{ni} + V_i$$

For example, the noninteraction value component (V_{ni}) of an offering might comprise the day-to-day use of the Adobe Acrobat software, whereas the interaction value component (V_i) comprises the assistance, advice, updates, and patches of the Adobe Acrobat software that involve interactions with the firm. As the relative *ratio* or *proportion* of interaction value to noninteraction value rises, the firm can be said to be more interaction intensive. Indeed, a firm can be defined as more or less interaction intensive to the extent that the interactive value component of the offering constitutes total value.

Thus, *interaction intensity* is defined as the degree to which the total value in an offering is uniquely determined by the interactions between the customer and firm:

$$\text{Interaction intensity, } I = V_i / V_t \text{ where } 0 \le I \le 1$$

As a measure, interaction intensity thus varies between 0 and 1, where an offering with $I = 0$ is a pure noninteractive offering and an offering with $I = 1$ is a pure interactive offering. Figure 15.1 shows the spectrum of interaction intensity and maps various points on the continuum. A firm's offering can be placed on the interaction–intensive continuum on the basis of the extent to which the interaction component forms the basis of offering value. To the left of the midpoint of the continuum are products that have a lower proportion of interaction value compared to noninteraction value in the total value of the offering from a firm. Conversely, to the right of the midpoint are products that have a higher proportion of interaction value compared to noninteraction value in the total value of the offering from a firm.

Figure 15.1   **The Interaction Intensive Continuum (V_i / V_t): Interactive Value (V_i) as a Proportion of the Total Value Offering (V_t)**

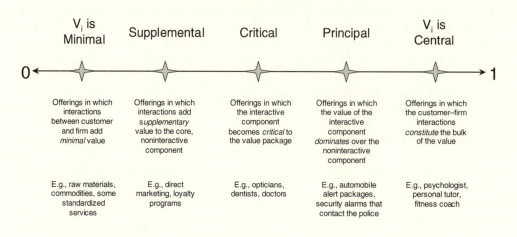

On the far left of the continuum lie offerings whose value is essentially independent of interactions with the firm: Value lies primarily with the noninteractive component. Indeed, interaction between firm and customer is typically limited to a single interaction in which a product is exchanged for money. Many traditional products such as raw materials and manufactured goods as well as some highly standardized services such as fast-food services would fit this category. Customer–firm interaction essentially adds minimal value to the core offering.

Next along the continuum, interaction value is introduced in various forms to supplement the noninteractive component. This can range from prepurchase marketing communications to postpurchase communications regarding product upgrades, updates, service opportunities, loyalty rewards, and so on. Examples include many forms of direct marketing and various loyalty programs.

The midpoint of the continuum represents a watershed—the interactive component becomes *critical* to the value offering. Indeed, it is useful to think of this point as the stage where the interactive component becomes essential to *obtaining* value from the noninteractive component. For example, a visit to an optometrist for prescription glasses entails an interaction with the optometrist who tests your eyes and develops a uniquely customized sight solution, which is then embodied in a noninteractive component in the form of a pair of spectacles. Without the interaction with the optometrist, the glasses would have little or no value. Other examples include the fitting of teeth braces by an orthodontist and the ongoing tailoring of a warfarin dosage to a person with hypercoagulation.

At the next stage of the continuum, the value of the interactive component becomes primary. At this point, the noninteractive component might still be essential or necessary, but its role is essentially as a *facilitator* for the interactive component. For example, General Motor's monthly subscription OnStar offering comprises an electronics package integrated into the automobile that allows the owner to call for remote unlocking and starting of the car, to book a service appointment, and to call for medical and or mechanical assistance. House alarms that directly alert the police in the case of break-in are another example.

Finally, on the far right of the continuum lie offerings for which interactions with the provider essentially *constitute* the offering. In this instance, value is inextricably co-created through the interaction process. Examples include therapy with a psychologist, a personal fitness coach, and some forms of personal tuition.

Having defined *interaction intensity* as the degree to which the total value in an offering is uniquely determined by customer–firm interaction, we can return to the relationship between interaction and information. In an age defined by IT, this relationship is pivotal and is most evident in marketing: the focus of customer–firm interactions. Here, IT can facilitate increasingly synchronized, memorized and individualized marketing interactions, which, if properly managed, can result in real-time, intimate conversations between parties (cf. Deighton 1996).

The concept of interaction intensity is related to Glazer's (1991) notion of information intensity, for it is *through* interactions that information is on the one hand consumed (i.e., existing information utilized) and on the other hand produced (i.e., new information created). However, the relationship runs both ways. For, as interactions migrate from the physical to the informational (i.e., from matter-intensive interactions to information-intensive interactions), the potential *cost* of each interaction falls and the potential for *automation* increases to 100 percent. When informational interactions are fully automated, cost tends to zero (cf. Bakos 1998; Malone, Yates, and Benjamin 1987). Here, we have essentially frictionless interactions, in which cost is uncoupled from frequency of interaction. Thus, we have potentially infinite scalability of interaction frequency. However, as automation is typically adopted asymmetrically between parties, costs also tend to accrue asymmetrically. For example, the cost of sending of junk e-mails is essentially zero to the firm but far from costless to the consumer. In other instances, benefits of automated interactions to the consumer can outweigh the costs. Thus, in the instance of automated update on stock prices to a trader, the cost of checking the prices is outweighed by the benefit. The point is that interaction intensity in information-intensive environments is a double-edged sword. Reduced costs of interactions for the firm has encouraged indiscriminate use of IT that could have inadvertently led to reduced benefits and increased costs to the customer.

For an understanding of where on the interactive intensity continuum the value in a firm's offering lies, it is useful to view the interactive value in an offering from both the provider's as well as the customer's perspective. The provider perspective resides in a view of the content, process, structure, and sequence of interactions. In contrast, the customer's perspective resides in parsing out the value of interactions into its constituent dimensions. In the rest of this chapter, we outline these two perspectives on the nature of interactions analyzing how value is created and delivered by the provider and how value is consumed by the customer.

INTERACTION VALUE: THE PROVIDER'S PERSPECTIVE

Content and Process

The *content* refers to the "raw materials" or operand resources (cf. Vargo and Lusch 2004) involved in interaction. It is made up of three elements: matter, energy, and information. It is important to realize two pertinent points in how these elements relate. First, there is an economic value hierarchy: Value has increasingly migrated away from matter and energy to information (Bell 1973). Second, although the focus has increasingly shifted to the information element of interactions, each interaction has a material and energy substrate on which the informational component "rides." For example, e-mail exchange between two parties depends on both physical infrastructure (matter) and electrical impulses (energy) to convey the information.

The *process* refers to what is being done to the content according to the objective of the interaction; it involves the operant resources (cf. Vargo and Lusch 2004) brought to the interaction.

Table 15.1

Content and Process Elements in Interactions

	Transport (convey)	Transform (convey)	Transpose (convey)
Matter	**Simple Transportation** Conveyor belts or pipelines transporting matter	**Manufacturing** Packaged goods manufactured from physical raw material	**Retailing** An exchange of goods for money
Energy	**Provision** Electric supply lines conveying electricity	**Conversion** Converting energy from burning gas into heat on a cooking range	**Exchange** Heat transfer processes as in an air conditioner
Information	**One-way Communication** Cables, wireless, or radio signals conveying digital data	**Data Processing** Converting digital data, text and graphics, audio and video	**Two-way Communications** Human–human conversations

The content in an interaction can be processed via three modes: by being transported, transformed, or transposed. *Transportation* comprises interaction processes in which entities are moved from one physical location to another. *Transformation* comprises interaction processes in which entities are transformed in form or function. *Transposition* comprises interaction processes in which two or more entities interact in a nonrecursive exchange. When the elements of content and process are juxtaposed, a three-by-three matrix is produced, as illustrated in Table 15.1. These elements are both independent and combinatory.

Value creation by a firm has been substantially altered with the advent of the Internet. Traditional manufacturers (e.g., packaged goods or business-to-consumer firms) can now reach their customers directly. These firms are not just involved in transport and transform processes, but also in the transpose process. Similarly, the content of value creation involves a lot more information than ever before. Recalling our conceptualization of interaction intensity, we suggest that the proportion of the interactive value component in total value created and delivered by the firm is increasing. Firms and customers as entities are interacting in a multitude of new and different ways through the convergence of multiple technologies. Hence, the interfaces between interacting entities are becoming increasingly important. Consequently, the structure and sequence of interactions comprise the next piece for analyzing value creation and delivery by the firm.

Structure and Sequence

The *structure* of an interaction is defined by the type and number of entities involved (cf. Hoffman and Novak 1996). We can specify two types of entities—person and machine—yielding three generic types of interaction: person-person, person-machine, and machine-machine. For any type of entity, we can identify structural variations of interactions on the basis of the number of entities involved in the interaction: one-to-one interactions, in which one customer interacts with one company or its representative (e.g., you and your doctor); many-to-one interactions, in which many customers interact with one another and one company or its representative (e.g., a university class and its professor); one-to-many interactions, in which many companies interact with one another and with a focal customer (e.g., a company and its computer software suppliers); and

Table 15.2

Customer–Firm Interactions Sequence in the Consumption Process

	Customer and firm role in interactions
Before Consumption	Decision, Design, Production, Marketing, and Delivery of the Offering: • Firm and/or customer directs/influences offering selection decision process • Firm performs design, production, marketing, and delivery • Firm and customer co-design, co-produce, co-market, and co-deliver the product
During Consumption	Monitoring, Directing, and Partaking of Consumption • Firm and/or customer direct access, transaction, and benefit • Monitoring Consumption—Firm (or customer) monitors consumption • Directing Consumption—Firm (or customer) directs or coordinates consumption • Co-Consumption—Firm and customer both partake of consumption
After Consumption	Monitoring, Learning, and Managing Consumption • Feedback enabling the monitoring of customer-experienced quality • Learning—Feedback enabling redesign • Managing past experiences • Managing future experiences • Managing customer termination

many-to-many interactions, in which many customers interact with one another and with many interacting companies (e.g., a stock market).

The type of interaction varies by both the stage in the value chain and by the stage in the consumer's consumption process. Therefore, the stage, or *sequence*, of interactions can be critical. In terms of flow of value along the value chain, first there are vertical interactions with suppliers and vendors upstream of the firm. Second, there are horizontal interactions with the wider environment, such as the firm's competitors, collaborators, strategic alliance partners, government, social groups, and so on. Third, there are internal interactions among department and individuals within the firm. Fourth, there are vertical interactions with the consumer downstream of the firm.

In terms of the stage in the consumption process, it has long been realized that the sequence of customer–firm interactions are critical to value. Specifically, the stage of the consumption process influences both affective and rational (goal-specific) responses of the customer (Berry, Seiders, and Grewal (2002). Following Berry, Seiders, and Grewal (2002), we break down the consumption process into three main stages: before consumption, during consumption, and after consumption. These are repeated and nested within subsequent exchange cycles. The types of interactions and the respective roles for the customer and the firm that constitute each stage are summarized in Table 15.2. The elements of value creating interactions within each of the three stages, although conceptually distinct, vary in their temporal distinction based upon the nature of the marketing exchange.

At each stage of consumption there are potentially different types of interactions between the provider and customer. Each of these interactions carries a different value configuration to both provider and customer. To understand fully the implications of the interaction-intensive context, the manager must first analyze how context affects the interaction. The role of the provider and the customer in interactions can manifest in several different ways in each stage of consumption. Identifying and analyzing the roles of either entity in an interaction is necessary to understand the value of the interaction to each party in the interaction. Understanding the value of all interactions with customers during all three stages of consumption is an imperative for the firm. Such an understanding provides the firm with direction on where the resources of the firm need to be allocated based on the interaction and noninteraction value components of value in an offering.

INTERACTION VALUE: THE CUSTOMER'S PERSPECTIVE

There is ample evidence that customer–firm interactions have a significant impact on customer value. For example, in a study of customer-initiated contacts with manufacturers, Narayandas and Bowman (2001) found that highly loyal customers value the interactions and procedures more than distributions and rewards received from manufacturers. Moorman, Zaltman, and Deshpandé (1992) found that the quality of customer–firm interactions in the market research services industry was a key variable in their model on relationships. Indeed, perceived quality of interactions was more important than trust itself because of its mediating effect on the benefits from the service. Although these and other studies clearly confirm the importance of customer–firm interactions, the question is this: What exactly is the composition of the value of interactions? As a business interaction, a customer–firm interaction is focused on a task—a focused interaction, to use Goffman's (1985) distinction. Based on our research, we propose that value in an interaction from the consumers' perspective is a function of seven dimensions: content, control, continuation, customization, currency, configuration, and contact. We now discuss each in turn.

Content Value

Fundamentally, customers derive value from the core content of the interaction in what was accomplished. Was the goal of the interaction accomplished? When conceptualized as the net benefit of customer–firm interactions for the customer, it becomes clear that customers would value reliable outcomes from interactions with firms. We label this fundamental dimension as "content," reflecting the extent to which the outcome of the interaction met the customer's goal of the interaction. For example, a telemarketing call from your phone company selling additional services that you do not need would provide no content value to you because the outcome of the interaction did not meet any need of yours.

Control Value

A customer–firm interaction inherently embodies an interdependence between the two entities in the interaction. We label this (inter)dependence dimension as *control*, reflecting the extent to which the firm enables the customer to direct the interaction. For example, you decide to go away for the weekend and contact your telephone provider to specify that you want all your phone calls diverted to your mobile phone. Web site interactivity studies (cf. Liu 2003) also confirm that individuals value their ability to control the interaction.

Continuation Value

In customer–firm interactions in which the entities involved are engaged in a relationship, there is a history of previous interactions. Firms that learn about a customer from every interaction typically do so by obtaining, recording, utilizing, and deploying information from each individual customer interaction. An expression of continuation value in an interaction refers to the idea that the marketer uses information on a customer's history to provide value evident in a subsequent interaction. We label this history dimension as *continuation*, reflecting the extent to which the firm integrates the past and the future in an interaction. For example, when booking a room at the Ritz Carlton, the staff is alerted to the fact that a regular customer who is asthmatic always requests a nonsmoking room with special pillows and bed linen.

Customization Value

This value dimension is related to the continuation value but is irrespective of chronology and history; instead, it pertains to the individual-level customization adjustments that are made by the firm in the customer–firm interaction. Customers value interactions when the firm is able to empathize or respect the customer's situation. We label this personalization dimension as *customization*, reflecting the extent to which the firm tailors the interaction to a specific customer. For example, a Web site of a firm might be designed to personalize its appearance and interface to individual customers.

Currency Value

Customers value interactions when the firm is responsive to their needs and is prompt in responding to their requests. We label this value dimension of timeliness as *currency*, reflecting the extent to which the interaction respects the temporal relevance for the customer. Interactions should be sensitive to time and timing. For example, a quote on a security carries with it the temporal relevance for a prospective investor.

Configuration Value

Similar to the temporal relevance of an interaction, there is value in the locational relevance of an interaction. We label this location value dimension as *configuration*, reflecting the extent to which the interaction respects the locational relevance for the customer. Interactions should be space sensitive. For example, you request, via mobile phone, advice on finding a vegetarian restaurant within walking distance. Using a global positioning system, your position is determined and a list of vegetarian restaurants, their ratings, distances, and directions are transferred to your phone screen.

Contact Value

Service marketers have distinguished between process and outcome in a service delivery. For example, Grönroos (1984) distinguished between technical and functional quality. In medical sociology, the distinction is made between curing and caring. We label this experience value dimension as *contact*, reflecting the extent to which the overall experience of the interaction provides value to the customer. For example, when you are finally seated at your table after a long wait at the restaurant, the manager comes over and apologizes for the wait and offers a complimentary appetizer and cocktail.

Each of these seven dimensions of value of interactions appears to capture a distinctive aspect of interactions. These dimensions are both independent and combinatory and reflect both the efficiency and the effectiveness of the interaction. Thus, it is possible to have anything from a one-way to a seven-way combination of the dimensions. The dimensions are summarized in Table 15.3.

Table 15.3

Seven Value Dimensions of Interactions

Dimension	Definition
Content	The task fulfilment, outcome quality of the interaction
Control	The extent to which the customer—in real time—directs the interaction
Continuation	Long-term/integrative learning interaction
Customization	Individual tailored interaction, over and above time and place
Currency	Time (virtual and real) sensitive interaction
Configuration	Space (virtual and real) sensitive interaction
Contact	Experiential quality of the interaction

MANAGERIAL CHALLENGES

Properly managed interactions can generate significant value to both parties in a marketing exchange. However, managers should be cognizant of several challenges in interactive intensive offerings, including an increase in consumer expectations, customer power, and interaction fatigue.

Customer Expectations

Interaction intensity can cause an increase in customer expectations. The reasons for this are two-fold: expectations of firm learning and expectations of customer compensation. First, customers might expect firms that they interact with frequently to learn from the interactions and produce market offerings of greater value. For example, a firm that is always soliciting feedback on the quality of its offering yet does nothing to improve the service will suffer as the gap between customer expectations and perceptions of the service diverges. Second, most interactions carry a cost for the customer, for which they will expect to be recompensed. For example, customers increasingly expect payment for involvement in focus groups and other market-research interactions.

Customer Power

Interaction intensity can increase customer power. As the firm increasingly involves customers to co-design and co-produce solutions, there is a concomitant increase in the customers' ability to influence the firm. For example, Boeing gave up considerable control over the 777 aircraft project when it invited the major long-haul airlines, such as United Airlines and British Airways, to become involved in the design and development of the airplane.

Customer Fatigue

Interaction intensity can result in interaction fatigue. As firms increase interactions with the consumer, there is an increasing danger of consumers becoming tired of the interaction. For example, when dining at a restaurant, a waiter's repeated question "Is everything all right?" quickly turns from helpful to tiresome interaction. However, the problem of interaction fatigue opens up the opportunity for firms to automate interactions for the consumer. For example, rather than students having to see their tutors on a regular basis, each student might have a database of their objective grades and subjective evaluation of their learning experience. When certain value thresholds are reached, an appointment could be automatically scheduled.

Design Challenges

The managerial imperative is to design and deliver a differentiated set of integrated interactions that create and capture value for both the customer and the firm. To do this, firms will need to explore several issues: First, they must understand the customer's priorities in terms of the value dimensions. Second, they should identify possible trade-offs among dimensions. Third, they should identify the resultant benefits of interactions from the firm's perspective. And finally, they must design and deliver differentiated interactions for which customers will be prepared to pay a premium.

It is entirely possible that customers could place different weights on each of the interaction value dimensions. It is also feasible that customers might employ a compensatory model to trade-off among the seven value dimensions. To complicate matters further, it is possible that these trade-offs may vary from one situation to another for the same customer. For example, how much value does the customer place on the contact value of a particular interaction? Is the customer prepared to trade off contact value for content value? Under what conditions will the trade-off vary from time to time? What value does the firm accrue if the interaction is provided? Thus, if the firm can provide an economically viable interaction in a context that adds value to the customer, the firm should consider finding ways to provide that offering. Such interactions might actually offer a revenue opportunity for the firm.

In our view, the manager must begin with the objective of the interaction and proceed to design the content, process, structure, and sequence of a set of interactions to meet that objective. Ideally this should be an iterative process, which intimately involves the customer. Very often, customer–firm interactions occur without plan or design, which results in no clear idea as to their value. Thus, objectives need to be stated in terms of the value that is created and captured for the entities involved in the interaction.

Once the value objectives are set, we suggest that managers proceed to design the content, process, structure, and sequence of a set of interactions to deliver and capture that value. An analysis of the structural configuration requires examining the interaction in terms of the individuals (or entities) involved to determine who (or what) is or should be involved in the interaction. The content and process of the interaction should be assessed against the objectives of the interactions. Depending on the stage of consumption, some interactions are transactions, whereas others might be customer support or interactions with prospective customers. Are these interactions designed appropriately for the customer for that specific objective of the interaction? This exercise necessitates an analysis of the valuation of each interaction.

The value of the interaction should be measured in terms of the costs and benefits to the firm and to the customers along the seven value dimensions and appropriate modifications must be made. Does the interaction accomplish its task? If so, do the benefits outweigh the costs? Is the ownership of control of the interaction appropriate to the customer? Is there an appropriate level of customization and continuity delivered in the interaction? How well does the value of interaction measure up in terms of currency or configuration? What is the gestalt contact experience of the customer in the interaction? To guide managers on these questions, we identify several research opportunities.

RESEARCH CHALLENGES

This chapter provides an initial definition of interaction intensity and offers a conceptual framework to guide further research into customer–firm interactions. Further research is needed to address the following areas: formalization of the value of interactions, operationalization and measurement of the value dimensions, and specification of the relationship between value and frequency of interaction.

For example, in this chapter we identify seven dimensions that customers implicitly use to assess the value they derive from interactions with firms. Subsequent research might involve the development of a scale to measure these dimensions of value and assess their relationship to firm-controlled antecedents and customer-level dependent measures such as satisfaction and loyalty.

Although we do not explicate any product/industry-related, firm-related, or individual customer factors that could moderate the effects of the customer–firm interactions on customer perceptions of value, we can expect that these factors could provide a better understanding of the effectiveness of customer–firm interactions. For example, researchers can develop methods to determine individual customer differences in each of the dimensions of value in customer–firm interactions. We can expect that the weight given to each dimension would be different from person to person and from situation to situation. The specific conditions that determine the differences would provide managerial utility to the understanding of what customers value in an interaction with the firm.

CONCLUSION

In this chapter, we propose that interactions lie at the root of the new dominant logic of marketing. It is through interactions that services are co-designed, co-created, and consumed; it is through interactions that information is exchanged and knowledge is generated; and it is through interactions that markets and marketing relationships are built and sustained.

Differentiating the interactive and noninteractive components of an offering, we suggest that value is increasingly migrating to the interactive component. We offer a new concept: *interactive intensity*, defined as the degree to which the total value in an offering is uniquely determined by the interactions between the customer and firm.

In our analysis of interactions, we discuss the provider's perspective in terms of the content, process, structure, and sequence of interactions. From the customer's perspective, we outline seven dimensions or aspects of interactions that deliver value.

We suggest that the management of interaction intensity raises various challenges, among which increases in consumer expectations, customer power, and customer interaction fatigue are perhaps primary. We conclude the chapter with a brief look at the research challenges that the notion of interaction intensity provides, including issues of operationalization and measurement.

ACKNOWLEDGMENTS

The authors acknowledge the contribution of John Deighton, Harvard University, in the development of an earlier version of this chapter.

REFERENCES

Bakos, Yannis (1998), "The Emerging Role of Electronic Marketplaces on the Internet," *Communications of the ACM,* 41 (8), 35–42.

Bell, David (1973), *The Coming of the Post-Industrial Society.* New York: Basic Books.

Berry, Leonard, L. (1983), "Relationship Marketing," in *Emerging Perspectives of Services Marketing,* Leonard L. Berry, G. Lynn Shostack, and Gregory D. Upah, eds. Chicago: American Marketing Association, 25–28.

————, Kathleen Seiders, and Dhruv Grewal (2002), "Understanding Service Convenience," *Journal of Marketing,* 66 (3), 1–17.

Czepiel, John A., Michael R. Solomon, Carol F. Surprenant, and Evelyn G. Gutman (1985), "Service Encounters: An Overview," in *The Service Encounter: Managing Employee/Customer Interaction in Service Business,* John A. Czepiel, Michael R. Solomon, and Carol F. Surprenant, eds. Lexington, MA: Lexington Books, 3–15.

Day, George S. (1992), "Continuous Learning about Markets," *Strategy and Leadership,* 20 (September-October), 47–49.

Deighton, John (1996), "The Future of Interactive Marketing," *Harvard Business Review,* (November/December), 151–62.

Glazer, Rashi (1991), "Marketing in an Information Intensive Environment: Strategic Implications of Knowledge as an Asset," *Journal of Marketing,* 55 (October), 1–19.

Goffman, Erving (1985), *Encounters: Two Studies in the Sociology of Interaction,* Robert McGinnis, ed. New York: Macmillan Publishing Company.

Grönroos, Christian (1984), "A Service Quality Model and Its Implications," *European Journal of Marketing,* 18 (4), 36–44.

Gummesson, Evert (1995), "Relationship Marketing: Its Role in the Service Economy," in *Understanding Services Management,* William J. Glynn and James G. Barnes, eds. New York: John Wiley & Sons, 244–68.

Hoffman, Donna L. and Thomas P. Novak (1996), "Marketing in Hypermedia Computer-Mediated Environments: Conceptual Foundations," *Journal of Marketing,* (July), 50–68.

Liu, Yuping (2003), "Developing a Scale to Measure the Interactivity of Websites," *Journal of Advertising Research,* 43 (June), 207–16.

Malone, Thomas W., Joanne Yates, and Robert I. Benjamin (1987), "Electronic Markets and Electronic Hierarchies," *Communications of the ACM,* 30 (6), 484–97.

Moorman, Christine, Gerald Zaltman, and Rohit Deshpandé (1992), "Relationships Between Providers and Users of Market Research: The Dynamics of Trust Within and Between Organizations," *Journal of Marketing Research,* 29 (August), 314–28.

Narayandas, Das and Douglas Bowman (2001), "Managing Customer-Initiated Contacts with Manufacturers: The Impact on Share of Category Requirements and Word-of-Mouth Behavior," *Journal of Marketing Research,* 38 (August), 281–97.

Oxford English Dictionary (1990). Oxford University Press, Oxford.

Vargo, Stephen L. and Lusch, Robert F. (2004), "Evolving to a New Dominant Logic for Marketing," *Journal of Marketing,* 68 (January) 1–17.

16

ROSEPEKICECIVECI versus CCV

The Resource-Operant, Skills-Exchanging, Performance-Experiencing, Knowledge-Informed, Competence-Enacting, Co-producer–Involved, Value-Emerging, Customer-Interactive View of Marketing versus the Concept of Customer Value: "I Can Get It for You Wholesale"

Morris B. Holbrook

A NEW LOGIC FOR MARKETING

The View According to Vargo and Lusch

In their recent lead article for the *Journal of Marketing,* Stephen L. Vargo and Robert F. Lusch (2004; hereafter V&L) offer a comprehensively well-articulated, carefully nuanced, thoroughly documented, highly provocative, and potentially influential formulation under the title "Evolving to a New Dominant Logic for Marketing." These authors summarize this new logic for marketing by means of *eight foundational premises*—in effect, replacing the familiar Four P's with Eight FP's that deserve the attention of all marketers and that beg for assimilation by every serious student of marketing-related concepts.

    According to this new logic—using my own somewhat modified but V&L–friendly terminology—the evolving paradigm for marketing increasingly displays the following eight characteristics.

1. Resource Operant (RO)

Drawing on resource-advantage theory (e.g., Hunt 2000) and core-competency theory (e.g., Day 1994; Prahalad and Hamel 1990), the firm is seen as performing services based on specialized activities that entail the application of certain skills where, recalling Fredric Bastiat (1848, 1860), "services are exchanged for services" (quoted by V&L 2004, p. 17).

2. Skills Exchanging (SE)

It follows that the fundamental basis for marketing-related transactions involves the services-for-services exchange of skills (e.g., Hamel and Prahalad 1994; Teece and Pisano 1994).

3. Performance Experiencing (PE)

In such an exchange process, goods are merely the mechanisms to perform services (e.g., Norris 1941) that provide experiences (e.g., Pine and Gilmore 1999) conducive to the satisfaction of customer needs and wants (e.g., Gutman 1982).

4. Knowledge Informed (KI)

This experience-providing performance requires the operant use of knowledge (e.g., Capon and Glazer 1987) so that the essential activity involves a flow of information (e.g., Evans and Wurster 1997).

5. Competence Enacting (CE)

Via this information flow, the firm enacts its knowledge-based competence in ways that render valued services (e.g., Quinn, Doorley, and Paquette 1990).

6. Co-producer Involved (CI)

Such a service-rendering process requires the involvement of the customer as a co-producer of the relevant need fulfillments and want satisfactions that constitute value (e.g., Normann and Ramírez 1993).

7. Value Emerging (VE)

Thus, consistent with the tenets of relationship marketing (e.g., Gummesson 1998), value emerges from the interaction between a firm and its customer or between a producer and the consumer (e.g., Grönroos 2000).

8. Customer Interactive (CI)

So the interactive nature of this consumer–producer interface establishes relationship-based marketing (e.g., Berry 1983), individually customized offerings (e.g., Davis and Manrodt 1996), and market-driven strategy (Day 1999) as the essence of a true customer-centric but enterprise-integrated and therefore mutually balanced orientation (e.g., Barabba 1995; Gummesson 2002).

What Does It All Mean?

In developing the formulation just described, V&L have created a worthwhile distillation of recent thinking in the field of marketing as this discipline gropes its way into the next millennium. As indicated by even the highly condensed cast of characters cited in the preceding briefest-of-brief summary (which mostly reflects V&L's compendious reading list, not my own more limited exposure to this particular literature), the proponents of the new logic have drawn on a diversity of influences for far-ranging sources of inspiration that include everybody from Alfred Marshall to Wroe Alderson, from Adam Smith to Philip Kotler, from Plato to Shelby Hunt. Yet the sweep of V&L's vision encompasses a purview so broad of a subject matter so inchoate that it inevitably raises the troubling question: "What does it all mean?"

    If we play a favorite pedagogical game—the age-old acronym maneuver—we arrive at the charming term that serves as the main title to this chapter: *ROSEPEKICECIVECI*. This dubiously helpful mnemonic follows from the Eight FP's just enumerated in describing the *Resource-Oper*-ant, *Skills-Exchanging, Performance-Experiencing, Knowledge-Informed, Competence-Enact*-ing, *Co-producer-Involved, Value-Emerging, Customer-Interactive* View of Marketing. ROSEPEKICECIVECI or RO-SE-PE-KI-CE-CI-VE-CI or RoSePeKiCeCiVeCi—pronounced to rhyme, for reasons that need not detain us here, with "the entelechy of Penderecki"—encapsu-lates the foundations of V&L's argument for a new paradigm. However, it embraces such a large number of disparate components, draws from so many scattered sources, and jumbles so many complementary contributions into the half-cooked conceptual pot of its eclectic ideational stew that one comes away with a rather bewildering sense of befuddlement—a nagging feeling of having missed the forest for the trees, beautiful and well-etched as those trees might be.

So what—we might wonder—is the crux, the nub, the gist, the nugget, the basis, the elusive essence of V&L's thinking? If pressed, the authors would respond—without doubt, I believe—that the key idea unifying their festival of insights concerns the *evolution of marketing thought* in the direction of a *service-centered* view of *exchange*. Indeed, the ascendance of a "service-cen-tered" focus provides the punch line for V&L's abstract when they regard the "new dominant logic for marketing" as "one in which service provision rather than goods is fundamental to economic exchange" (p. 1). The remainder of their article offers a tour de force on this theme—now referred to as the *service-dominant logic* of marketing (S-D logic).

That V&L pursue this S-D logic throughout will appear with great clarity to any reader who devotes more than the most cursory glance to their article. As one indication, consider the struc-ture of the "Discussion" section (pp. 12–14). This section contains fifteen paragraphs. Twelve of these paragraphs explicitly mention the term *service-centered* within the first few words, and three modify the wording slightly to *service-provision* or *service provision*. One would have to be pretty dense not to get the point that, according to the S-D logic, service-centered service provi-sion via the exchange of services for services lies at the heart of V&L's conceptualization.

Beyond dense, one would have to be pretty mean-spirited not to recognize the scope and power of V&L's conceptualization and presentation. Nonetheless, it strikes me that the force of their argument might have surfaced even more clearly had V&L provided some sort of diagram, picture, or other visual aid to organize the key components of their service-centered perspective. For example, such a diagrammatic representation might take the shape of the schema for an S-D logic of marketing shown in Figure 16.1.

I do not know if V&L would find this schema for an S-D logic of marketing or something like it to be a useful encapsulation of the eight fundamental premises (Eight FP's) represented by ROSEPEKICECIVECI. However, it does seem to me that we need some sort of distillation to provide an underlying structure for the Eight FP's of the S-D logic—perhaps even a reorganiza-tion of the Eight FP's to follow that supportive conceptualization more convincingly.

Further in that spirit, I might suggest that there exists an alternative summary concept capable of capturing the essence of V&L's S-D logic and that this alternative conceptualization extends our grasp beyond that permitted by ROSEPEKICECIVECI's more circumscribed service-cen-tered approach. In short, I would argue that the S-D logic is subsumed under a perspective with even greater scope and power—but one neglected by V&L (2004) and by most of the sources they cite. Specifically, I refer to a framework based on the concept of customer value.

THE CONCEPT OF CUSTOMER VALUE

Insights drawn from the concept of customer value (CCV) have fascinated me for roughly the past twenty years and have gradually coalesced into what I regard as an all-embracing view of marketing

Figure 16.1 **Schema for a Service-Dominant Logic of Marketing**

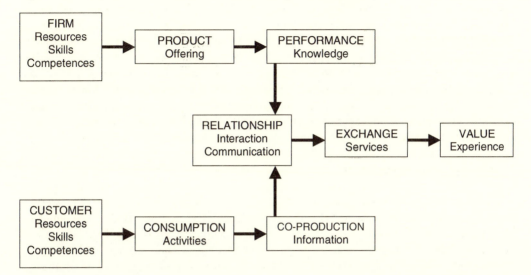

as a value-creating endeavor. This is not the place to offer a full catalog or summary of the work that has appeared in the past two decades on the topic of customer value (e.g., Holbrook 1984, 1994a, 1994b, 1995, 1996, 1999a, 1999b, 2005; Holbrook and Corfman 1985) and that—beginning in 1984 (based on Holbrook 1984)—has been presented at no fewer than twenty-five leading universities and other venues around the world: New York University (1984); University of Utah (1984); University of Michigan (1984); Ohio State University (1985); University of Quebec at Montreal (1986); Dartmouth (Tuck School, 1987); University of Illinois (School of Communication, 1987); University of Pennsylvania (Wharton, 1988); McGill University (1988); University of California in Los Angeles (1988); University of British Columbia (1989); Rutgers University at New Brunswick (1989); University of Arizona (1990); Iowa State University (1992); Baruch College (1995); Association for Consumer Research (1996); Edith Cowan University (Perth, Australia, 1996); University of Texas at Austin (1996); Japanese Marketing Association (Tokyo, 1999); Hakuhodo, Inc. (Tokyo, 1999); Diamond, Inc. (Tokyo, 1999); University of Miami (AMA Doctoral Consortium, 2001); Society for Marketing Advances (2002); University of Pennsylvania (Wharton, 2003); and, of course, Columbia University (on multiple occasions). Rather, I shall offer a very brief summary of what I take to be the nature and types of customer value, as illuminated by CCV.

What Customer Value Is Not

Before proceeding to short summaries of the nature and types of customer value, according to the CCV, I should perhaps offer a brief indication of what customer value (CV), as envisioned here, is not.

First, in my view, CV is not just one subcategory of one type of value. For example, CV is *not* just economic value to the customer (EVC) (e.g., Best 2004; Forbis and Mehta 1981). EVC does refer to one subspecies of CV, but only to those aspects that involve a dollar-based trade-off of comparative benefits versus costs. From a broader perspective, there is a lot more to the CCV than that.

Second, emphatically, CV is *not* another term for lifetime value of the customer to the firm (LVCF) (e.g., Blattberg, Getz, and Thomas 2001; Gupta and Lehmann 2003). The latter perspective —quite important to those who espouse the advantages of relationship marketing or customer-relationship management in building loyalty based on trust to encourage the retention of customers over time—focuses on the value *of* a customer to the firm as opposed to the value of a firm's offering *to* a customer. In other words, it pursues a perspective diametrically opposed to that advocated here.

Unfortunately—despite the fact that our use of the term *customer value* has earlier origins (e.g., Holbrook 1984, 1994a, 1994b; Holbrook and Corfman 1985) and follows from a long tradition of work in axiology (for reviews, see Holbrook 1994b, 1999a, 1999b)—proponents of EVC and LVCF have made free use of the term *customer value* in ways that cannot help but confuse the casual reader of the marketing literature. If I had my druthers—surely, a big "if"—I would give them EVC and LVCF and preserve CV for use in the context pursued here.

The Nature of Customer Value

The aforementioned work on the nature of CV defines it as an *interactive relativistic preference experience.* Let us examine each of these four closely interrelated terms briefly.

First, CV is *interactive* in that it involves a relationship between some subject (e.g., a consumer) and some object (e.g., a product). Here, the *consumer* refers to any type of customer—a house spouse, a business, a member of the channel of distribution. Similarly, the *product* refers to any offering by a producer—any person, place, or thing—any good, service, political candidate, celebrity, store, tourist site, recreational venue, public event, social cause, innovative idea (meme), or . . . whatever. No value exists without an interaction between some subject (consumer) and some object (product). In an analogy attributed to Alfred Marshall, the subject and object resemble the halves to a pair of scissors: You need both, working together, to get results. In other words, if a tree falls in the forest and no one hears it, it might or might not have made a sound, but without someone hearing it, that sound cannot have had any value.

Second, CV is *relativistic* in at least three senses:

1. CV is *comparative* and depends on the relative merits of one object as opposed to another. We can state the value of one thing only by comparison with something else. For example, Morris may feel that drinking Coke is good (compared with drinking, say, Pepsi) but that drinking cola is bad (compared with drinking, say, beer). Here and elsewhere, our conclusions about relative value—in this case, the goodness or badness of Coca-Cola—depend on the comparison under consideration (good compared with Pepsi, bad compared with Budweiser).
2. CV is *situational* in that it varies from one evaluative context to another. For example, Morris might prefer beer (say, Sam Adams) to cola (say, Diet Coke) at dinner but cola (say, Diet Coke) to beer (even Sam Adams) at lunchtime.
3. CV is *personal* and differs from one individual to the next. For example, whereas Morris might favor beer over cola or wine with the evening meal, his wife Sally might prefer wine to beer or cola at suppertime. The personal relativity of value is, of course, the implicit rationale behind virtually every aspect of marketing strategy—for example, the whole notion of market segmentation—a guiding assumption from which almost everything we do derives its fundamental logic. If CV did not differ among people, marketing strategy would disappear.

Third, value refers to a judgment of *preference.* From various viewpoints, we call this preference judgment by many different names: attitude (like/dislike), affect (favorable/unfavorable), valence (positive/negative), evaluation (good/bad), opinion (pro/con), satisfaction (high/low), behavioral tendency (approach/avoid), or choice (choose/reject). Each of these terms has spawned a whole field of study unto itself. Yet all share the common property that they investigate ways in which one thing is preferred to another on some relevant criteria or dimension(s).

Fourth, value resides not in an object, a product, or a possession but rather in and only in (or *inn*) a consumption *experience*. Beth Hirschman and I first advocated this perspective more than twenty years ago (e.g., Hirschman and Holbrook 1982, 1986; Holbrook 1987; Holbrook and Hirschman 1982) and it has since flowered into a virtual cottage industry in consulting circles (e.g., Pine and Gilmore 1998, 1999) and on the marketing-seminar circuit (e.g., Schmitt 1999, 2003). Latter-day authors such as Pine and Gilmore (1998, 1999) have given scant credit to the origins of this idea that CV resides *inn* a consumption *experience*. Even my friend and colleague Bernd Schmitt (2003) claims that "when I wrote *Experiential Marketing* [1999] 'experience' was a new term" (p. vi). I find this historical amnesia somewhat frustrating. But I hasten to acknowledge that Beth and I were guilty of the same sin of omission. It turns out that the experiential nature of all value is an old and venerable theme. It appeared in the work of Walter Woods (1981) and, from there, can be traced to the influence of Wroe Alderson (1957). Indeed, Stanley Lebergott (1993) has followed its trail—through Alfred Marshall—all the way back to Adam Smith. So, as usual, there is nothing new under the sun. V&L cite Ruby Turner Norris (1941)—a founder of the Consumer's Union—as one source for such insights in general and for V&L's service-centered perspective in particular. But an even more pertinent quotation comes from the midcentury work of the economist Lawrence Abbott (1955, p. 40):

> The thesis . . . may be stated quite simply. What people really desire are not products but satisfying experiences. Experiences are attained through activities. In order that activities may be carried out, physical objects or the services of human beings are usually needed. Here lies the connecting link between man's inner world and the outer world of economic activity. People want products because they want the experience-bringing services which they hope the products will render.

The Dimensions of Customer Value

In the aforementioned work on CV, the types of CV emerge from a classification scheme based on three key underlying dimensions or distinctions. (Conceptually, these dimensions are continua, but they are presented as dichotomous distinctions for ease of exposition.)

1. Extrinsic/Intrinsic

Value is *extrinsic* when some object or experience serves as the means to an end, performing a function that is instrumental or banausic in nature. By contrast, *intrinsic* value refers to the case in which an experience is prized for its own sake—that is, self-justified as an autotelic end in itself.

2. Self-Oriented/Other-Oriented

Value is *self-oriented* when some object or experience is valued for one's own sake—for how it affects "me" or for how "I" respond to it. By contrast, *other-oriented* value attaches to something prized in connection with the reactions of others—for "their" sake, for how it affects "them," or for how "they" respond to it. Here, "others" can include a wide spectrum of beings—ranging

Table 16.1

Typology of Customer Value

		Extrinsic	Intrinsic
Self-Oriented	*Active*	EFFICIENCY (O/I or O – I)	PLAY (fun)
	Reactive	EXCELLENCE (quality)	AESTHETICS (beauty)
Other-Oriented	*Active*	STATUS (fashion)	ETHICS (justice, virtue, morality)
	Reactive	ESTEEM (materialism)	SPIRITUALITY (rapture, ecstasy)

from one's immediate family, friends, or colleagues; to one's community, subculture, or country; to the world, the solar system, or the universe; to nature, the cosmos, or a deity.

3. Active/Reactive

Value is *active* when a subject manipulates some object or experience as the source of value—that is, when "I" do something to "it," when "I" act on "it," or when "I" perform an activity that shapes or changes "it." By contrast, *reactive* value occurs when a subject is manipulated by the object—that is, when "it" does something to "me," when "it" moves "me" in some way, or when "I" respond to "it."

The Types of Customer Value

Combining the three dimensions just described—still viewing them as three dichotomous distinctions—produces a typology of CV that portrays eight key types of value, as shown in Table 16.1.

As presented here, the typology of CV distinguishes eight key types of value (CAPITAL LETTERS) resulting from a combination of the three dimensions just described (*italics*) with an example provided to illustrate each category (lowercase letters in parentheses). Full accounts of these eight types have appeared in the references cited previously (e.g., Holbrook 1984, 1994a, 1994b, 1999, 2005). Here, I shall confine myself to just the briefest of summaries.

- EFFICIENCY occurs when some object or experience is actively used as a means to a self-oriented end. Often, we measure efficiency as a ratio (O/I) or a difference (O – I) between outputs (O) and inputs (I). When O and I are represented by dollar benefits ($B) and dollar costs ($C), we refer to monetary efficiency explicitly as EVC (EVC = $B–$C). If—as often happens—inputs (I) represent time (T), we refer to efficiency as convenience (B/T). Innumerable products owe their value primarily to the latter type of consideration—fast foods, convenience stores, speed dating, TiVo, credit cards (enjoy now, pay later).
- EXCELLENCE refers to the case in which some object or experience is appreciated for its capacity to function well as the means to a self-oriented end but is not necessarily used for that purpose. Its potential for instrumental functionality is reactively admired but not actually deployed. Often, we refer to this type of value as "quality"—as in the case of a high-

quality Ferrari that would easily cruise at 180 miles per hour but that we refrain from driving that fast for fear of breaking the law, getting caught, and receiving a traffic ticket.

- STATUS arises when one person's consumption is used actively as the means of influencing the responses of some relevant other. Various forms of impression management confer this type of value—as in the case of fashion, in which the style of one's clothing (e.g., Armani suit) and the cachet of other accoutrements (e.g., Rolex watch) are intended to communicate a favorable image to someone else.

- ESTEEM closely resembles status, as just described, but assumes a more reactive posture involving a sense of satisfaction in the awareness that one's possessions or other consumption habits would/could/should win approval from relevant others. Materialism in general or Veblenesque conspicuous consumption would exemplify this type of esteem-related value— as when a person derives pleasure from contemplating the prestigious associations of a fine necktie from, say, Hermés or Zegna that is too expensive to wear and is instead left hanging in the closet.

- PLAY shifts the focus to the self-justifying value of an experience enjoyed by oneself and actively pursued for its own sake. Such aspects of playfulness distinguish the fun of leisure activities (e.g., Morris playing the piano in an amateur jazz group) from the drudgery of . . . work (e.g., Vladimir Feltsman practicing scales to prepare for a well-paid concert recital at Carnegie Hall).

- AESTHETICS involves the reactive self-oriented appreciation of an experience prized for its own sake—as when admiring the beauty of an artwork or enjoying the scenic splendor of a majestic sunset. Works of art potentially contribute to this aesthetic type of value when and only when (or *whenn*) their appreciation is regarded as an end in itself. The moment we use an artwork as the means to some other end—say, deploying an Eminem CD as a coaster to prevent one's coffee cup from leaving rings on the table or regarding a gleaming sculpture by Jean Arp as a potentially effective doorstop—the resulting value stops being aesthetic and starts being something else (e.g., efficiency or excellence).

- ETHICS refers to consumption activities pursued for their own sake by virtue of the effect they have on others. This scenario would cover everything from "green" consumption to charitable donations to eating only dolphin-safe tuna. Again, actively pursued other-oriented value is ethical *whenn* it serves as an end in itself—as when we say that virtue is its own reward.

- SPIRITUALITY represents the reactive side of other-oriented experiences valued for their own sake—especially when the relevant "other" is some higher-level entity such as nature, the cosmos, or a deity. For example, meditation or prayer—putting oneself in touch with an Other in hopes of experiencing the ecstasy or rapture associated with a disappearance of the self-other dichotomy—remains spiritual *whenn* the experience is pursued for its own sake (as in a state of nirvana or beatitude) rather than as the means to some other end (as in Janis Joplin's "O, Lord, won't you buy me a Mercedes-Benz").

The Compresence of Customer Value: Meditations on a Vibraphone

Lurking beneath the surface whenever we contemplate CCV is the recognition that any one consumption experience could contribute to many or even all types of customer value. Indeed, this multivocality or compresence of multiple value types is, I believe, the norm rather than the exception. I have argued elsewhere (Holbrook 1994a, 1994b, 1999, 2005) that this value compresence appears in consumption experiences ranging all the way from the sublime (e.g., going to church)

Table 16.2

Meditations on a Vibraphone

		Extrinsic	*Intrinsic*
Self-Oriented	*Active*	EFFICIENCY (reduced price, free shipping, no taxes)	PLAY (creativity)
	Reactive	EXCELLENCE (loudness, variable speed)	AESTHETICS (appearance, musicality, A = 440)
Other-Oriented	*Active*	STATUS (decoration)	ETHICS (peace, patriotism)
	Reactive	ESTEEM (prestige, celebrity)	SPIRITUALITY (ethereal, soulful, celestial sound)

to the mundane (e.g., doing the laundry) to the ridiculous (e.g., chewing gum). As a new illustration, let us consider the *Meditations on a Vibraphone* represented by Table 16.2.

During the summer of 2002, I purchased a new Century M75 vibraphone, produced by the Musser Company in Elkhart, Indiana—a subsidiary of Ludwig (drums), which is a subsidiary of Selmer (saxophones), which is a subsidiary of Steinway (pianos). (How's that for a corporate pedigree?) For those not familiar with this particular type of musical instrument, I should perhaps explain that a vibraphone, vibraharp, or vibes—most frequently used by jazz musicians, but also ubiquitously evident in large orchestras, school bands, popular music, television commercials, and sitcom soundtracks—is a percussion instrument, played with yarn- or cord-covered mallets, something like a xylophone or a marimba. Unlike these musical cousins, however, the vibes consists of metal (not wooden) bars covering two and a half to four octaves (most commonly, three octaves). The ringing sound of these metal bars is reinforced by resonators—one hanging under each bar—and, unlike a xylophone or marimba, can be sustained for a long duration or cut off abruptly by means of a damper pedal. In further contrast to the other instruments, the top of each resonator on a vibraphone contains a fan or beater connected to a rod that runs through the resonators and turns all the fans simultaneously by means of a rubber belt driven by the pulley of a small motor whose speed might or might not be adjustable. The vibraphone produces a rather charming chime-like effect, with a great purity of tone, capable of cutting through the sound of (say) a jazz rhythm section. Over the years, the roster of great vibraphonists has included such memorable names as Red Norvo, Lionel Hampton, Milt Jackson, Dave Pike, Victor Feldman, Bobby Hutcherson, Mike Mainieri, Gary Burton, Steve Nelson, Joe Locke, and Stefon Harris— but not, I'm sorry to say, Morris Holbrook. Despite my own conspicuous absence from this list of noteworthy vibists, I do enjoy playing the instrument and—on that shaky logic, in an admittedly self-indulgent mood—decided to give myself a rather extravagant present in the form of the Musser Century M75.

In the present context, the key point of all this involves the degree to which the experience of owning and playing this instrument contributes to *all* the different types of customer value displayed in Table 16.2.

• EFFICIENCY. Thanks to the zeal of a local dealer—struggling to compete in the over-crowded New York City marketplace—I managed to negotiate a fairly high EVC. Specifically, EVC was bolstered by a generous discount off the list price and by the dealer's willingness to arrange shipping direct to me from the manufacturer in Elkhart, Indiana—thereby saving both delivery costs and tax expenses. Altogether, in terms of EVC, I acquired the ponderously expensive vibraphone at a savings of approximately 25 percent.

• EXCELLENCE. The Musser Century M75 is a big, sturdy, heavy, solid, console-like instrument with many features that bespeak quality even where they might be reactively admired more than actively used. For example, the Century potentially plays louder than most vibes, though I would not want to test this out in full for fear of disturbing the neighbors. Similarly, the adjustable motor turns the fans at speeds ranging from about 60 to about 340 beats per minute (bpm), though I would never set the tremolo much below about 100 or much above about 120 bmp. It's just nice to know that loudness and a wide range of vibrato speeds are viable options, even if you do not plan to use these features in actual practice.

• STATUS. There is, of course, some sense in which the physical appearance of the Musser M75 contributes a status-enhancing decorative element to our living space, suitable for making a favorable impression on dinner guests and other distinguished visitors. The body of the vibes is pure black with gold trim. The bars, resonators, and pedal are all bright gold. Overall, the Century presents a rather ornate appearance that creates an almost opulent match with the Art Deco style of our 1930s apartment.

• ESTEEM. Even if friends and neighbors did not come from miles around to admire the Century vibraphone, its mere possession carries a certain degree of self-gratifying cachet. The prestige of the Musser M75 is indicated by the fact that this instrument is often referred to as the "Cadillac of vibraphones." (Personally, I would prefer the Mercedes, the Lexus, or even the Jaguar of vibraphones, but that's another story.) Furthermore, personal appearances and advertising campaigns over the years have associated the Musser name with a number of illustrious celebrity endorsers such as Lionel Hampton, Milt Jackson, and Gary Burton. By playing a Century M75, one gains the vicarious sense of identifying with one's musical heroes.

• PLAY. Performing on a musical instrument for fun involves the kind of playfulness that is the essence of true creativity. That is, playing the vibraphone provides pleasure to oneself (certainly not to one's family and even less to one's neighbors) via a leisure pursuit whose hedonic aspects are enjoyed purely for their own sake (rather than to further any other conceivable goal or objective to which they might contribute). Morris playing the vibes is the epitome of an essentially useless activity pursued for its self-oriented intrinsic rewards and for no other purpose.

• AESTHETICS. Beyond the visual and sonic beauty of its appearance and its musicality—experiential aspects reactively appreciated for their own sake—the advent of the Century vibes raised a highly specific aesthetic issue in the Holbrook household. Specifically, Musser offers a variety of tunings—the two most popular being A = 440 cycles per second (like a modern piano) or A = 442 cps (like a European orchestra). After long consultations with our piano tuner and much prayerful thought, I decided to order the older A = 440 tuning on the logic that it would complement that of our Steinway baby grand in case I ever wanted to play some duets. The match/mismatch of an A440/A442 vibraphone with an A440 piano would produce a pleasant/ clashing aesthetic effect. (This is a pretty remote possibility, given the disruption it would cause in our relations with the neighbors. But you never know when, say, Keith Jarrett or Chick Corea or Makoto Ozone might drop by in search of a friendly collaboration.) Despite my ordering the A = 440 tuning from the dealer in New York City, the manufacturer in Indiana shipped the instrument with A = 442 cps. When I filled out the warranty card—under "Comments"—I mentioned my disappointment in receiving the wrong tuning. Within days if not hours, Musser had contacted me, apologized profusely, and agreed to send a new set of bars tuned at A = 440 cps, with prepaid return-addressed packaging for the A = 442 bars. After an easy self-installation, my A = 440 tuning was good to go. (I eagerly await a call from Keith, Chick, or Makoto—but, so far, not a word.)

• ETHICS. As already implied, the number-one ethical issue posed by the arrival of the Musser Century M75 vibraphone in the Holbrook household has been the challenge of keeping peace with the neighbors, who doubtless cringe in pain and indignation at the sound of every note I play. In the context of New York City—famous for its thin floors, skimpy walls, and short tempers—the problem of maintaining harmony with those in surrounding apartments constantly besets anyone wishing to lead the life of an amateur musician. Beyond that, on a more global level, the purchase of a vibraphone raises ethical questions concerning one's patriotic duty. Many years ago, the leading American vibraharp maker—Deagan in Chicago—was purchased by Yamaha, which apparently moved the production of its vibraphones to Japan and changed the name to that of its own brand. (Why Yamaha would purchase Deagan and then surrender both its brand equity and its manufacturing facilities is a mystery that I have long puzzled over and cannot explain. Maybe it was just a stratagem for taking the leading competitor off the market.) Another major American vibes maker, JeNCo, also went out of business many years ago. So, today, any U.S. citizen purchasing a vibraphone faces a potential crisis of conscience over whether to support the Japanese by choosing Yamaha or to buy American by selecting Musser, Ross, Adams, or another domestic brand. Fortunately for me, this patriotic dilemma was largely resolved by the fact that Yamaha does not make a model remotely comparable to the Musser Century M75. (Bergerault in France does make a magnificent Century-like instrument, but it is so expensive as hardly to have caused a quiver of regret.)

• SPIRITUALITY. Because the sound of a vibraphone emanates from the striking of a silver or gold bar, it possesses a purity of tone comparable to that of a tuning fork. This crystal-clear effect resembles that of ringing a set of small bells. Its aura is ethereal, soulful, and—I believe—almost celestial in spirit.

All this suggests that—like virtually any other consumption activity one might name—the experience of owning and playing a vibraphone confers a number of different types of CV. In the case of my meditations on the Musser Century M75, this multivocality of value extends to *all* types of CV. It goes without saying that anyone contemplating the design, manufacture, pricing, distribution, advertising, or selling of vibraphones would/could/should keep this compresence of value firmly in mind as the basis for negotiating a potentially rewarding interactive customer–producer relationship.

CCV AND ROSEPEKICECIVECI

Admittedly, not one of the numerous publications or presentations mentioned previously on the CCV has attained the high visibility of just one article in the *Harvard Business Review* or just one book published by The Free Press. Nonetheless, I might have hoped that my various labors on behalf of CCV might have won the attention of at least those who attended my talks or edited the volumes in which my work appeared. It seems, however, that I have had no such luck. The literature on the S-D logic (aka ROSEPEKICECIVECI) cited by V&L is virtually unanimous in its silence concerning CCV as developed by yours truly. This is a sad state of affairs—damaging to my own personal ego, of course, but also unfortunate for you too, Dear Reader, because of what I believe to be the gap that it leaves in our understanding of the S-D logic. In short, I believe that CCV potentially encompasses and subsumes virtually everything that has been said—as in the excellent work by V&L—on the subject of ROSEPEKICECIVECI.

I Can Get It for You Wholesale

I once attended a twelve-week seminar co-taught by the great sociologist and polymath Paul Lazarsfeld. Professor Lazarsfeld was a charming but intimidating personage—erudite in his reading, encyclopedic in his knowledge, voluble in his verbiage, thick in his German accent, profound in his wisdom, folksy in his manner, generous in his encouragement of work by others. And gentle, by the way, in his treatment of a reverential young doctoral student—namely, me. Beyond that, he possessed a curious or even cute little quirk. Specifically, no matter what someone else managed to accomplish analytically or empirically, Lazarsfeld always thought—most times, correctly—that he could achieve the same result with less effort or greater elegance. In his own oft-repeated words, "Hey, I can get it for you wholesale."

In some cases (though certainly not in that of Professor Lazarsfeld), this attitude might seem rather self-satisfied, smug, or even condescending. Hence, I want to be sure that my own labors on behalf of the CCV are not interpreted as reflecting those kinds of character flaws. Indeed, I make no claim that CCV demonstrates effortless elegance on my part but only that it does manage—by dint of endless labor and lengthy evolution—to embrace and even to transcend the multifarious ideas assembled by V&L in explicating the S-D logic. I shall attempt to support this point by revisiting the Eight FP's and suggesting how, I believe, each aspect of ROSEPEKICECIVECI is covered by CCV.

Covering ROSEPEKICECIVECI

1. Resource Operant (RO)

CCV regards the object—that is, the product or offering (person, place, thing, good, service, event, idea, or whatever)—as the embodiment of specialized activities and skills invested in its creation. Furthermore, and of equal importance, CCV emphasizes that—whether through active manipulation or reactive appreciation—the subject (i.e., the customer) draws upon consumption-related skills based on education, training, emulation, practice, and other sources of value-creating knowledge.

2. Skills Exchanging (SE)

As with RO, CCV recognizes that resources embodied in the offering and invested in the act of consumption perform services that create value so that, as with SE, marketing-related transactions involve the services-for-services exchange of skills.

3. Performance Experiencing (PE)

Hence, as with PE, CCV regards the object (product) as a vehicle for the performance of services that provide experiences central to the creation of value. In this connection, recall the apposite words—quoted earlier at greater length—of Lawrence Abbott (1955, p. 40): "People want products because they want the experience-bringing services which they hope the products will render." In short, products perform services that provide experiences that create value. From this, it follows—in CCV, as in ROSEPEKICECIVECI—that all products are services.

4. Knowledge Informed (KI)

To repeat—according to CCV, as with KI—the object (product) embodies an investment of knowledge that affects the informed experiences of the subject (customer) in what is fundamentally a knowledge- or information-transferring process of communication. Indeed, the features-attributes-benefits (FAB) view of value creation is essentially a special case of the more general source-message-receiver (SMR) model of communication and is therefore just one more reminder of the ways in which a flow of information underlies all human activity.

5. Competence Enacting (CE)

It follows—from CCV, as from CE—that, in producing an object (offering), the firm enacts its knowledge-based competence in ways that render potentially valued services.

6. Co-producer Involved (CI)

However, as with CI, CCV insists that the realization of this potential value requires the involvement of the customer as a co-producer of the relevant services. Indeed, this co-creation of value follows ineluctably from the basic definition of CV as an interactive relativistic preference experience. As noted previously, this subject-object interactivity implies that value resides at the interface between a customer and a product or offering.

7. Value Emerging (VE)

Thus—consistent with the implications of VE for the efficacy of relationship marketing—CCV stresses the subject–object interaction in ways that emphasize the imperative of a sustainable bond between an offering and its customer. The value that emerges from this bond goes by many names—brand equity, loyalty, trust—all conducive to a sustained preference and, therefore, implicit in CCV's notion of an interactive relativistic preference experience.

8. Customer Interactive (CI)

So the interactive nature of this subject–object or consumer–producer interface extends beyond the inherently lopsided focus of a potentially suicidal customer orientation to embrace the tenets of a more balanced perspective—one that integrates both sides of the marketplace, both the producer (object) and the consumer (subject)—what I like to call a survival orientation or what others (cited previously) have called relationship-based marketing, market-driven strategy, or a meeting of the minds.

CONCLUSION: SO WHY AIN'T I RICH?

When Neil Borden (1964) wrote the first coherent account of the elements embodied by the marketing mix, he included such a long list of items—rivaling the proverbial Chinese menu in the confusing prolixity of its multiplicitous excess—that subsequent thinkers struggled with the need to condense this profusion into something more concise and coherent. Jerome McCarthy (1968) found a magic formula in the shape of his famous Four P's (product, price, place, and promotion) —a structured condensation of the marketing mix that has informed our conceptualization of marketing management ever since.

I believe that V&L have performed a valuable service—comparable to Borden's discovery of the marketing mix—in calling attention to the multifaceted ways in which marketing could/would/ should benefit by reformulating its view of itself according to an S-D logic. Reflective of V&L's

commendably massive scholarship, they present this S-D logic in the shape of a laundry list of foundational premises—the Eight FP's, referred to here as ROSEPEKICECIVECI—that, in their eclectic sweep, cannot help but remind us of Borden's multifarious outpouring. Indeed, for my money, V&L have pushed Miller's seven-plus-or-minus-two principle past its limits. Even after laboring mightily to construct a handy acronym—ROSEPEKICECIVECI (a form of "chunking" to facilitate memory)—I find that, from one day to the next, I cannot remember V&L's Eight FP's, no matter how hard I try. Besides betraying the limitations in my own dwindling cognitive capacities, this inability results—I believe—from the lack of a clear pattern or coherent rationale underlying the rather grab-bag nature of V&L's listlike mode of organization.

V&L have effectively enunciated an S-D logic that could eventually emerge as a new paradigm of marketing thought, whereupon we shall recall V&L's work as a seminal contribution in that direction. But ROSEPEKICECIVECI does not yet constitute a systematic scheme or a focused framework for thinking. Rather, it lacks a transparent structure. If the Eight FP's are indeed foundational, the edifice that V&L have built upon them stands precariously—like a house of cards—ready to collapse at any moment. To some skeptics, the Eight FP's might look like the laundry list of a preoccupied housekeeper who has not gotten around to using the washer or dryer for quite a while. It's easy to toss another pair of socks onto the growing pile, but the unsorted heap of shirts, pants, underwear, and hankies does not constitute a convincing entity. In short, the parts do not combine to form a meaningful whole.

In a humble spirit—analogous to the efforts of McCarthy in formulating the Four P's to rescue the world from the confusions of Borden's unmanageably manifold marketing mix—I have offered the CCV as a framework for thinking that leads to insights essentially identical to those offered by the more unwieldy collection of Eight FP's, affectionately referred to as ROSEPEKICECIVECI. Please notice, Dear Reader, that CCV begins with just a simple four-word definition of CV: an interactive relativistic preference experience. From this, it extrapolates three key dimensions of CV: extrinsic/intrinsic, self-oriented/other-oriented, and active/reactive. These combine to describe eight basic types of CV. So—rather compactly, if not exactly elegantly and emphatically not effortlessly—CCV provides a structured rationale, schema, or framework that encompasses and encapsulates the epiphanies of ROSEPEKICECIVECI.

In this respect, I'm hoping, Paul Lazarsfeld would have approved. So maybe, I'm thinking, we have discovered at last, Dear Reader, why I ain't rich. The reason, I'm guessing, is that I have gone and gotten it for you wholesale.

REFERENCES

Abbott, Lawrence (1955), *Quality and Competition.* New York: Columbia University Press.

Alderson, Wroe (1957), *Marketing Behavior and Executive Action.* Homewood, IL: Richard D. Irwin.

Barabba, Vincent P. (1995), *Meeting of the Minds: Creating a Market-Based Enterprise.* Boston: Harvard Business School Press.

Bastiat, Fredric (1848, ed. 1964), *Selected Essays on Political Economy,* trans. Seymour Cain, ed. George B. de Huszar. Princeton, NJ: Van Nostrand.

——— (1860), *Harmonies of Political Economy,* trans. Patrick S. Sterling. London: J. Murray.

Berry, Leonard L. (1983), "Relationship Marketing," in *Emerging Perspectives of Services Marketing,* Leonard L. Berry, Lynn Shostack, and G.D. Upah, ed. Chicago, IL: American Marketing Association, 25–28.

Best, Roger J. (2004), "Economic Benefits and Value Creation," in *Market-Based Management: Strategies for Growing Customer Value and Profitability,* Roger J. Best, ed. Upper Saddle River, NJ: Prentice Hall, 88–91.

Blattberg, Robert C., Gary Getz, and Jacquelyn S. Thomas (2001), *Customer Equity: Building and Managing Relationships as Valuable Assets.* Boston: Harvard Business School Press.

Borden, Neil H. (1964), "The Concept of the Marketing Mix," *Journal of Advertising Research,* 4 (June), 2–7.

Capon, Noel and Rashi Glazer (1987), "Marketing and Technology: A Strategic Coalignment," *Journal of Marketing,* 51 (July), 1–14.

Davis, Frank W. and Karl B. Manrodt (1996), *Customer-Responsive Management: The Flexible Advantage.* Cambridge, MA: Blackwell.

Day, George (1994), "The Capabilities of Market-Driven Organization," *Journal of Marketing,* 58 (October), 37–52.

——— (1999), *The Market Driven Organization: Understanding, Attracting, and Keeping Valuable Customers.* New York: The Free Press.

Evans, Philip B. and Thomas S. Wurster (1997), "Strategy and the New Economics of Information," *Harvard Business Review,* 75 (September/October), 71–82.

Forbis, John L. and Nitin Mehta (1981), "Value-Based Strategies for Industrial Products," *Business Horizons,* 24 (May/June), 32–42.

Grönroos, Christian (2000), *Service Management and Marketing: A Customer Relationship Management Approach.* West Sussex, UK: John Wiley & Sons.

Gummesson, Evert (1998), "Implementation Requires a Relationship Marketing Paradigm," *Journal of the Academy of Marketing Science,* 26 (Summer), 242–49.

——— (2002), "Relationship Marketing and a New Economy: It's Time for Deprogramming," *Journal of Services Marketing,* 16 (7), 585–89.

Gupta, Sunil and Donald R. Lehmann (2003), "Customers as Assets," *Journal of Interactive Marketing,* 17 (Winter), 9–24.

Gutman, Jonathan (1982), "A Means-End Chain Model Based on Consumer Categorization Processes," *Journal of Marketing,* 46 (Spring), 60–72.

Hamel, Gary and C.K. Prahalad (1994), *Competing for the Future.* Boston: Harvard Business School Press.

Hirschman, Elizabeth C. and Morris B. Holbrook (1982), "Hedonic Consumption: Emerging Concepts, Methods and Propositions," *Journal of Marketing,* 46 (Summer), 92–101.

——— and ——— (1986), "Expanding the Ontology and Methodology of Research on the Consumption Experience," in *Perspectives on Methodology in Consumer Research,* David Brinberg and Richard J. Lutz, eds. New York: Springer-Verlag, 213–51.

Holbrook, Morris B. (1984), "Axiology in Consumer Research: The Nature of Value in the Consumption Experience," working paper, Graduate School of Business, Columbia University.

——— (1987), "O, Consumer, How You've Changed: Some Radical Reflections on the Roots of Consumption," in *Philosophical and Radical Thought in Marketing,* F. Firat, N. Dholakia, and R. Bagozzi, eds. Lexington, MA: D.C. Heath, 156–77.

——— (1994a), "Axiology, Aesthetics, and Apparel: Some Reflections on the Old School Tie," in *Aesthetics of Textiles and Clothing: Advancing Multi-Disciplinary Perspectives,* ITAA Special Publication #7, Marilyn Revell DeLong and Ann Marie Fiore, eds. Monument, CO: International Textile and Apparel Association, 131–41.

——— (1994b), "The Nature of Customer Value: An Axiology of Services in the Consumption Experience," in *Service Quality: New Directions in Theory and Practice,* Roland T. Rust and Richard L. Oliver, eds. Thousand Oaks, CA: Sage Publications, 21–71.

——— (1995), *Consumer Research: Introspective Essays on the Study of Consumption.* Thousand Oaks, CA: Sage Publications.

——— (1996), "Customer Value—A Framework For Analysis and Research," in *Advances in Consumer Research,* Vol. 23, Kim P. Corfman and John G. Lynch, Jr., eds. Provo, UT: Association for Consumer Research, 138–42.

——— (1999a), "Introduction to Consumer Value," in *Consumer Value: A Framework for Analysis and Research,* Morris B. Holbrook, ed. London: Routledge, 1–28.

——— ed. (1999b), *Consumer Value: A Framework For Analysis and Research.* London: Routledge.

——— (2005), "Customer Value and Autoethnography: Subjective Personal Introspection and the Meanings of a Photograph Collection," *Journal of Business Research,* 58 (1), 45–61.

——— and Kim P. Corfman (1985), "Quality and Value in the Consumption Experience: Phaedrus Rides Again," in *Perceived Quality: How Consumers View Stores and Merchandise,* Jacob Jacoby and Jerry C. Olson, eds. Lexington, MA: D.C. Heath, 31–57.

——— and Elizabeth C. Hirschman (1982), "The Experiential Aspects of Consumption: Consumer Fantasies, Feelings, and Fun," *Journal of Consumer Research,* 9 (September), 132–40.

Hunt, Shelby D. (2000), *A General Theory of Competition: Resources, Competences, Productivity, Economic Growth*. Thousand Oaks, CA: Sage Publications.

Lebergott, Stanley (1993), *Pursuing Happiness: American Consumers in the Twentieth Century*. Princeton, NJ: Princeton University Press.

Normann, Richard and Rafael Ramirez (1993), "From Value Chain to Value Constellation: Designing Interactive Strategy," *Harvard Business Review*, 71 (July–August), 65–77.

McCarthy, E. Jerome (1968), *Basic Marketing: A Managerial Approach*. Homewood, IL: Richard D. Irwin.

Norris, Ruby Turner (1941), *The Theory of Consumer's Demand*. New Haven, CT: Yale University Press.

Pine, B. Joseph, II and James H. Gilmore (1998), "Welcome to the Experience Economy," *Harvard Business Review* (July/August), 97–105.

——— and ——— (1999), *The Experience Economy: Work Is Theatre & Every Business a Stage*. Boston: Harvard Business School Press.

Prahalad, C.K. and Gary Hamel (1990), "The Core Competence of the Corporation," *Harvard Business Review*, 68 (May/June), 79–91.

Quinn, James Brian, Thomas L. Doorley, and Penny C. Paquette (1990), "Beyond Products: Services-Based Strategy," *Harvard Business Review*, 68 (March–April), 58–66.

Schmitt, Bernd H. (1999), *Experiential Marketing: How to Get Customers to Sense, Feel, Think, Act, and Relate to Your Company and Brands*. New York: The Free Press.

——— (2003), *Customer Experience Management: A Revolutionary Approach to Connecting with Your Customers*, Hoboken, NJ: John Wiley & Sons.

Teece, David and Gary Pisano (1994), "The Dynamic Capabilities of Firms: An Introduction," *Industrial and Corporate Change*, 3 (3), 537–56.

Vargo, Stephen L. and Robert F. Lusch (2004), "Evolving to a New Dominant Logic for Marketing," *Journal of Marketing*, 68 (January), 1–17.

Woods, Walter A. (1981), *Consumer Behavior*. New York: North Holland.

17

INTRODUCING A DIALOGICAL ORIENTATION TO THE SERVICE-DOMINANT LOGIC OF MARKETING

DAVID BALLANTYNE AND RICHARD J. VAREY

INTRODUCTION

We are very interested in the service-dominant (S-D) logic of marketing thesis. Stephen Vargo and Robert Lusch have skillfully brought together several previously disparate marketing concepts, ideas, and perspectives in a way that is likely to challenge the presumptions of mainstream theory and practice. However, it seems to us that there is still more to be done in understanding what an S-D logic of marketing might entail and shifting marketing thought in this direction. We are pleased to collaborate on this work in progress.

The S-D logic thesis gives support to much of our own work on relationship development, knowledge application, and communicative interaction in marketing (Ballantyne 2004b; Christopher, Payne, and Ballantyne 2002; Varey 2000, 2002a; Varey and Lewis 2000). We clearly see these three strands of thought intertwined in the new S-D logic. However, in this chapter we are particularly interested in exploring the role of dialogue as a form of communicative interaction. We also want to broaden the framework of marketing communication, through which buyers and suppliers make their value propositions (offerings). This is not given any depth of treatment in the S-D logic thesis, although there are supportive references (Vargo and Lusch 2004).

We see dialogical interaction as an ideal form of communication within the S-D logic because it supports the potential for co-creation of value and sustainable competitive advantage. It also makes a strong counterpoint to mainstream marketing's *monological* assumptions and the constraints on innovation that flow directly from that. First, we reflect a little on the validity of the common sense of communication. Next, we clarify our understanding of the concept of dialogue. We then consider the potential for marketing to be dialogical. Our discussion then moves on to critically discuss four of the fundamental premises of the S-D logic as set out by Vargo and Lusch (2004). We conclude with some related thoughts on communication, relationship, and knowledge.

THE COMMON SENSE OF COMMUNICATION

Several related observations are worthwhile at the outset. First, the dominant forms of marketing practice operate as one-way message-making systems. In this context, commonplace thinking has come to accept as normal the decoupling of interaction and communication. Second, in everyday use the term *dialogue* is unreflectively taken to mean an extended conversation among two or more people. In other words, confusion and detachment abound. By way of contrast, our notion of dialogue embodies a preindustrial perspective on human interaction: We see dialogue as an interactive process of learning together (Ballantyne 2004a). Third, dialogical interaction fits well with the notion of relationship development and knowledge generation in marketing, even in an epoch of e-commerce (Varey 2002b). We want to put the variety of marketing interaction back together again, but set in the context of postindustrial marketing.

Marketing communication is the underlying process through which marketing activity and resources are converted into economic outcomes. However, when we constantly emphasize outcomes, we miss the point that marketing processes are grounded in purposeful social interaction (Varey 2002a). Managers tend more to strive to control their own destiny and that of their firm, rather than anticipate and respond to service needs (including provision of serviceable goods). Ethical questions disappear in the assumed appropriateness of self-interested profit maximization. This control-driven self-interest finds expression in the monological (one-way) mode of marketing communication that is dominant today. Managers and firms gain short-run advantage from this, but it is unclear how societies or indeed any of a firm's constituent stakeholders benefit in the long run.

We need to regain the sense of marketing as a social phenomenon—as implied by the idea of relationship marketing and also evident in the S-D logic of marketing. This would require recognition of markets as comprising sellers *and* buyers, all of whom are *social actors* who interact to construct economic exchange outcomes. Such a shift in marketing theory and practice would require some rethinking of marketing's reliance on the efficacy of communicating at long distance through mediators to a homogenous mass market. In fact, this kind of communication—the act of *uttering*—is not really communication at all but simply message making. Communication only comes about when someone watches, listens, reads—and understands to the extent that further communication could follow on. The mere act of uttering does not constitute communication (Luhmann 2000).

On this basis, much so-called marketing communication comprises unopened messages, unrequited messages, and deliberate message avoidance on the part of the targeted receiver. In this, the marketer seeks to manipulate and works insincerely, assuming that this behavior is taken for granted by participants and observers. Yet, although advertising might indeed declare its motives, it refines and often conceals its methods. The intention is to control purchase and consumption by reminding people that there is something to buy and that a particular name or product deserves special attention. In other words, consumers recognize that *what* they see is advertising, but not *how* they are influenced. Ironically, we are all "free to choose" whenever we want something.

This kind of convoluted communication logic does not begin to explain the variety of ways in which we might reconnect communication with interaction, to generate and circulate information, co-create meaning, acquire knowledge, achieve flashes of inspired understanding, and make value together.

We need to escape from this twentieth-century monological communication model that converts all explanation into discrete message particles for mechanistic transmission and gives primacy to the role of sender as the dominant agent. The agent controls the mechanisms to enable the flow of information and also attempts to control the communicative event with the chosen "receiver." The problem is, of course, that the agent defeats his or her best intentions in so doing, cutting off the spontaneous nature of continuing interaction and collaboration that is implied in the term *marketing exchange*. This model remains the dominant communication logic in market-

Figure 17.1 **Marketing Communication Matrix**

ONE-WAY

The conventional managerial approaches, giving prominence to the planning and crafting of persuasive informational messages

(Many messages will remain unopened, unseen, and unheard)

TWO-WAY

Communicative interaction, both formal and informal, which might be prompted by planned messages to or for customers, as mentioned previously

(This includes more spontaneous and dialogical approaches between participants that give prominence to listening and learning)

Communication to

Planned persuasive messages aimed at securing brand awareness and loyalty

e.g., Communicating the "unique selling proposition" to the mass market in concrete and symbolic terms

Communication for

Planned persuasive messages but with augmented offerings for targeted markets

e.g., Communicating targeted customer life cycle products; product or service guarantees; loyalty programs

Communication 'with'

Integrated mix of planned messages and interactively shared knowledge

e.g., Face to face encounters

e.g., Direct (database) marketing

e.g., Call centers

e.g., Interactive business-to-business Internet portals

Communication between

Dialogue between participants based on trust, learning, and adaptation, with co-created outcomes

e.g., Key account liaison between two or more firms

e.g., Expansion of communities of common interest, often Internet based

e.g., Teamwork among staff project groups within one firm, or among firms

Mass markets → **Portfolio/Mass-Customized** → **Discrete/Networks**

Source: Ballantyne (2004a).

ing texts and in use, notwithstanding the emergence of more interactive perspectives over the past decade in direct marketing and integrated marketing communication (see also Duncan and Moriarty 1998; Grönroos and Lindberg-Repo 1998).

The potential for broadening the variety of forms of communicative interaction, from monologue to dialogue, has been developed as a communication matrix by (Ballantyne 2004a). This matrix includes one-way message making, directed to or for a firm's customers and other parties, where *to* means the basic offering, and *for* means a more value-added and targeted format. As well, there is recognition of two-way communication with customers and other parties, and also the relatively unexplored zone of potential represented by dialogical interaction, between the focal firm and its customers and other parties (see Figure 17.1).

One of the authors has recently seen a software product brochure that claims that the product "makes sure you ask the right people about the relevant issues at the right time by engaging them in one-to-one interactive dialogues at key touch points in the relationship." What does this promise mean? What would a dialogue that is not interactive be like? Furthermore, in a recent article by a leading U.S. brand consultant, it is claimed that a "marketing dialogue between brands and consumers" is replacing "the one-way conversation" of advertising. How does a collection of signs and artifacts interact with a person such that dialogue is possible? Confusion abounds. We need to return to an earlier common sense notion of what it once meant to be dialogical in communication.

CLARIFYING THE CONCEPT OF DIALOGUE

We define *dialogue* as an interactive process of learning together (Ballantyne 2004b). This is close to the original meaning, from the Greek *dialegesthai,* which was to think and speak about something in such a way that the thing the speakers were talking about was recognized as different, and, in talking together, the speakers were able to move toward a new intellectual understanding. Dialogue holds the promise of revealing something new and implies a developmental shift in the relationship between the parties involved. Dialogue is also a useful communicative approach to knowledge development within and between firms. In dialogue, the co-creation of knowledge is possible. Or a dialogical approach might well allow participants to disagree on what those new knowledge positions ought to be. It follows that dialogue cannot be reduced to one person's activity alone or reduced to one person's perspective alone; it is inherently relational. Clearly, the intention in engaging in dialogical interaction is not unidirectional, self-serving, or accomplishment by control. On the contrary, the purpose is open ended, discovery oriented, and value creating.

The first problem in using the term *dialogical interaction* is linguistic and semantic. Much so-called dialogue in practice is no more than two-way combative (dialectical) monologues, or at best, message making with feedback—the hoped-for prize is acceptance of one party's asserted claims in support of an ideological or commercial preference exclusively for self-interest. However, in dialogue participants speak and act *between* each other, not *to* each other. We take the view that all marketing outcomes are fulfilled through social processes (directly or indirectly) so there are a range of social values likely to be fulfilled as well, according to time, place, and circumstances. As long as no party is treated as a means to an exclusively private end, the process can proceed, and indeed be repeated again another time. This ethical underpinning for dialogue can best be experienced through interactions built on trust. Without receiving the trust of another, and being trustworthy, dialogue comes to an end soon enough. Dialogue, it seems to us, is an essential basis for the authentic pursuit of innovation and creativity in markets, within firms, and between firms. Yesterday, today, and tomorrow, by whatever name it travels under, it is an interactive process of learning together. It creates value in new and surprising ways, disrupts market norms, and challenges societal behaviors in the broadest sense.

CAN MARKETING REALLY BE DIALOGICAL?

Of course, marketing, in its modern principles and in practices, has not been seen as a dialogical activity. Yet, the central concept of marketing is exchange, and is not exchange a reciprocal event? What detracts from the fluidity of the twentieth-century marketing concept is the almost universal presupposition of unidirectional, goal-seeking behavior—in which marketing is seen to be successful at the point that the targeted object (buyer) yields to the persuasion of the seller. Although it is not often put like this, marketing is living a life for profit of a vastly restricted value.

The bigger picture, better understood in the relationship marketing literature, is that marketing is interactions within networks of relationships (Gummesson 1999). This redefines marketing exchange as an open-ended process in terms of time and place. Interactions over time are the enactments of the exchange process (Ballantyne 2003). Moreover, the spatial setting (or *servicescape*) in which various episodes of interactions are embedded is critical to how a seller's offer is valued by the buyer. Furthermore, these interactions can be viewed as part of a customer relationship development process, or as a process from which the customer determines what is of value. And in these interactions, it is through service that the sale takes place in a virtuous cycle of service and sales. This is not news in the relationship marketing, business-to-business marketing, or services marketing literature, but traditional consumer product–dominant marketing texts tend to footnote it because what is offered is of intangible value, of a kind that cannot be exclusively controlled by the seller through a unidirectional communication system.

Although marketing's embedded motives remain control and profit maximization, it becomes difficult to imagine how marketing interaction could also be driven by a genuine concern for customers. Yet these positions are not irreconcilable. Such reconciliation requires a longer-term view and a learning perspective in which dialogue might find a place. Any charge of naïve altruistic intent can be addressed rationally on the basis that respect for the needs of the other is a prerequisite for our own need fulfillment. In co-creating value through dialogue and learning, the reciprocal success benchmark becomes, "If it is better for us, then it becomes better for me." This involves a shift in strategic perspective to recognize a broader view of stakeholder interests, which in turn requires a shifting of mental models to accommodate the idea of a market as a socially constructed *network* of relationships in which interactions have economic consequences.

We conceive of marketing as grounded in interaction in potentially three ways: First as informational, second as communicational, and third as dialogical (see Table 17.1).

These categories are conceived of as ideal types following Weberian tradition. In other words, they are pure constructs, and some category overlap is likely in practice. We do not claim that they are moral or ethical categories. The informational mode includes all message making which has the useful intention to inform. The more manipulative practices of transactional marketing and much of what currently passes as customer relationship management (CRM) are extreme versions of this. Next, much of marketing's current relationship-oriented aspirations are grounded in the *communicational* mode, in which listening and informing are the product of interaction, especially in services marketing and B2B marketing.

Finally, our view of marketing's unrealized potential is in the *dialogical* mode. This potential is always available. However, without a legitimizing framework, perhaps only the brave will succeed. In this spirit, we hope that our classification hastens a break-free from myopic monological straitjackets. Marketing communication has been locked into a way of thinking that sees message

Table 17.1

A Classification of Interaction Modes

Mode of interaction	Underlying political and decision practices	Source of value	Form of market system coordination
Informational: Persuasive message making	Controlling and dominating	Supplied by persuasive *selling* of the benefits	Hierarchy
Communicational: Informing and listening	Integrated communicative interaction and stakeholder equity	Negotiated value co-produced through promise making and promise keeping	Interactive
Dialogical: Learning together	Finding a voice in co-determination	Emergent value co-created in *learning*	Network

making as *the* dominant mode. Working on the false notion that a message can possess a fixed meaning, marketing has focused attention and resources on the means of coding these messages and regulating their transmission. This is done for the purpose of trying to change other peoples' choices. This is how it has been in the past, and this is what has been carried forward relatively unchallenged to the present time.

DIALOGUE AS LEARNING TOGETHER

Dialogue as we have defined it brings opportunities for learning together and generating value in new ways, both within the firm and among firms, as co-created solutions for market and supply problems and opportunities. Furthermore, the particular circumstance of value creation means it is difficult for competitors to copy. Of course, there are constraints to increasing the spiral of communicative reciprocity, which have to be acknowledged as well. Dialogue in marketing is not so much a method of communication as an orientation to it. There is always potential for the frustration of intentions between buyer and seller, and indeed other stakeholders. There is the possibility of a mismatch of expectations. Or one party might attempt to control the interaction by establishing a purely informational engagement. Alternatively, one party might attempt to interact in dialogical mode but is met by an informational response. And perhaps some of the time the parties involved will understand each other quite well but just don't want to agree! Again, our test for dialogical authenticity is whether or not interaction brings opportunities for learning together. We suggest that such a test might focus on constructing understanding, creating common agreement, and disrupting assumptions.

1. Dialogue aims at developing an understanding of each participant's point of view, and interaction sets up suitable conditions for listening and learning together. Dialogue in marketing is much more than alternating monologues and covers the joint investigation of needs, wants, desires, problems, issues, and decisions to be made. To achieve this grand aspiration, at least some of the time, we have to do better than attending to service quality issues and identifying mechanistic CRM-mediated contact opportunities as touch points. Instead, we suggest that marketers might experimentally and selectively engage in dialogical inquiry (listening and learning) and so become more reflective of the consequences of past actions. Dialogical outcomes go beyond

one's own understanding, and so finding creative solutions to previously intractable problems is quite possible.

2. Dialogue could lead to common agreement on any particular issue, or perhaps a variety of different interpretations will remain in play. It is quite possible to achieve understanding even if the parties agree to differ. Dialogical interaction means becoming more aware of routine but hidden thought patterns and assumptions held by ourselves and by others. In dialogue, an attempt is made to query one's participants' assumptions and prejudices and likewise to confront one's own, some of which can be really difficult to access. We conclude that the mutual checking of assumptions is fundamental to learning together, and helpful in reaching more enlightened exchanges of mutual value.

3. Dialogue creatively disrupts the taken-for-granted and unspoken assumptions that restrict commitment and satisfaction to the ordinary. Dialogue is not simply a two-way dissemination of information for decision making and action. Any cognitive dissonance induced by dialogue can be positive if there is mutual effort and trust. We conclude that not everyone is ready for dialogue, but this can be tested in practice, interactively, and incrementally. Give or take some attempts at persuasion at the outset, and then some experience in mutual informing and listening, extraordinary exchanges can occur when the trust level is adequate to the anticipated risk involved.

REFLECTING ON THE S-D MARKETING LOGIC

So far we have reflected on the common sense of marketing communication, and also the lack of it. Then we clarified our understanding of the concept of dialogue. We then considered the potential for marketing to be dialogical. The concepts of relationship development and knowledge application are strongly featured in the original S-D logic (Vargo and Lusch 2004). There are also references in support of dialogue, which has been the platform for our discussion about the variety of communicative interaction, through which buyers and suppliers might agree on their value propositions (offerings).

Vargo and Lusch have said that the application of specialized skills and knowledge is *the* fundamental unit of exchange. However, we believe that three strands make up a fundamental conceptual unity of exchange activities: communicative interaction, relationship development, and knowledge application. This we see as the way forward for the S-D logic of marketing (see Figure 17.2).

We find it difficult to isolate one strand of exchange activity and its effects without reference to the others. We also find it reassuring that Alderson, writing at the time of the then-emerging managerial perspective of marketing, located exchange as the joint activity that identified marketing (Alderson 1957). Thus:

> Marketing is the exchange which takes place between consuming groups and supplying groups.

It is not clear to us why Vargo and Lusch (2004, p. 6) have added a unit-of-exchange perspective to the application of specialized skills and knowledge at the fundamental level. If this unitized exchange is intended for use as measurement, then we hope a new controversy can be avoided about how marketing adds value, and how much value does it add?

Taking a tripartite view of the fundamentals of S-D marketing, communicative interaction in its various forms supports learning about the customer, and this learning supports trust and the appropriate knowledge application and development of the relationship. This also prevents both

Figure 17.2 **Tripartite Fundamentals for Service-Dominant Marketing**

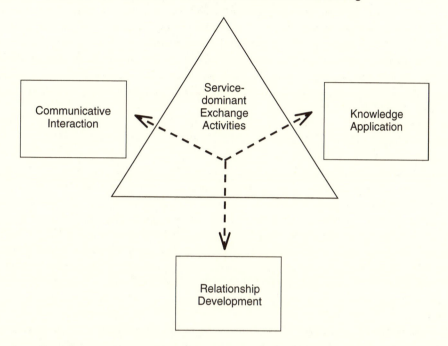

parties from having to "reinvent the wheel" of relationship-specific knowledge with every new transaction. If both parties go further and trust each other in dialogue, the co-creation of knowledge might generate value in new ways, and cost efficiencies could result through interdependencies so created. The application of knowledge can be explicit or tacit, co-produced or co-created together. Here we are making a distinction between co-production of knowledge through communicational interaction (an exchange) and co-creation through dialogical interaction (something unique and new). Customer value becomes something a seller proposes and a customer then judges in two forms: (1) Exchange value is one kind of judgment made by the customer, and (2) because a product is a store of value, judging value-in-use is its confirmation. And so the cycle of S-D logic of marketing turns.

We agree (subject to the preceding comments) on four of the foundational premises proposed by Vargo and Lusch (2004) and comment on the remaining four in the following section in terms of what we see as necessary links to communicative interaction and dialogue.

Critique on Four of the Foundational Premises of the S-D Logic

FP₄: Knowledge Is the Fundamental Source of Competitive Advantage

We would add that it is the *renewal* of knowledge that is more aptly the fundamental source of competitive advantage. Following Nonaka and Takeuchi (1995), knowledge takes two forms: tacit and explicit. Vargo and Lusch have recognized the fundamental importance of human skills, competencies, and the accumulated work experiences of employees, which is another way of saying *tacit knowledge.* Tacit knowledge operates more or less at an unconscious level of application, which means it tends to be underrecognized as a firm-based resource. However, tacit knowledge is gained through observation, imitation, and mutual experience. The second form of knowledge, *explicit knowledge,* is media based and can be digitized and circulated. Both forms of knowledge are valued as resources but are different. The first is applied directly in creating value. The second is a store of knowledge that can be usefully accessed in creating value. The first is an operant resource and the second is an operand resource, in the way that Vargo and Lusch (2004) use these terms. Many firms get sidetracked in building up explicit knowledge, using expensive data-warehousing or CRM systems, and ignore the active resource within, their operant resource, or employees' tacit knowledge.

The main point we make is this: Although competition between firms stimulates knowledge discovery at the macro level (Vargo and Lusch, 2004, p. 9), we want to give equal or more emphasis to the knowledge renewal processes operating at the micro level, because these can be activated in communicative interaction. At the level of the firm, explicit knowledge, expressible in a speech or writing, can be exchanged with fluency within networks of trust-based relationships. Skills-based tacit knowledge can also be learned or co-created to great effect through dialogue, especially when a strategic approach to *internal marketing* communication is taken allied to a process of knowledge renewal (Ballantyne 2003; Varey and Lewis 2000). Also, if we conceive of firms as networks of relationships, then the boundaries of trust between firms can be extended by mutual agreement, and we might do better to talk of clusters of collaborating firms as knowledge networks competing with knowledge networks (Normann and Ramírez 1993). We see such networks as a consequence of relationship development, whether intentional or otherwise.

What is critical for knowledge renewal is the willingness of employees to pass on what amounts to their know-how, their tacit knowledge. To do this, they must *trust* the firm's and others' motives. Many managers do not understand that the quality of the relationships among employees has a strong impact on learning and therefore on knowledge renewal within the firm. When you look at the three core knowledge exchange patterns within firms, as described in Figure 17.3, the nature of the constraints working against knowledge renewal within firms becomes clear. The hierarchical exchange pattern is so pervasive that the other two knowledge exchange modes become ineffective or are ignored.

Knowledge sharing and its application in creating customer value is a hidden source of competitive advantage—whether working together as employees across functional borders to achieve cost efficiencies or working with customers to improve customer value. The particular point of interest to us here is that a knowledge renewal strategy demands open communicative interaction and especially frequent dialogue within the firm, among firms, and among supplier firms and customers. In this way, managers and other employees can constantly reexamine what they have previously learned and now take for granted.

FP$_6$: The Customer Is Always a Co-producer

We also take the view that the customer is a co-producer of value and support the idea of value-in-use as one aspect of the determination of value by the customer postsale, as part of a continuing process within the buyer–seller relationship. We also see the co-production of value as embedded in any useful communicative interaction, prior to any sale and postsale, quite apart from any residual of value represented by the goods component of that value assessment. However, we prefer to reserve the terms *co-creation of value* and *co-creation of knowledge* for more spontaneous, generative dialogical approaches, in which putting things together that others do not think go together achieves something new and of unique value in the process. It is in

Figure 17.3 **Knowledge Exchange Patterns within Organizations**

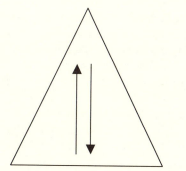

Pattern 1: Hierarchical Exchanges

Expert knowledge is exchanged and legitimized through formal hierarchical channels. The dominant distribution path is from the top of the organization to the bottom. Upward-moving knowledge claims also occur, subject to explicit rules or implicit constraints.

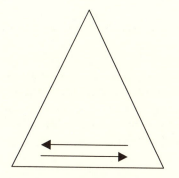

Pattern 2: Interfunctional Exchanges

Knowledge is exchanged between internal suppliers and internal customers along value chains, end to end. Knowledge claims are legitimized by reference to external customers' needs. The utility of these internal exchanges is often constrained by a lack of *customer consciousness*, producing self-serving links in the value chain.

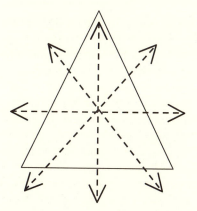

Pattern 3: Network Exchanges

Knowledge is generated and circulated by exchanges within spontaneous, internal communities. Common social or economic interest drives these voluntary employee networks. They might seek to legitimize their knowledge claims through the hierarchical organization in which they are embedded.

Source: Ballantyne (2003).

this endeavor that competitive advantage might be found. The interesting question seems to be just where to delimit marketing activity, even though the customer's value determination as a co-producer might extend beyond the point of sale, over time and place. To paraphrase McKenna (1991), marketing is everything but not everything is marketing! For example, what if we choose to boil potatoes for dinner (customer as operant resource, still in co-production mode, and potatoes as operand resource in transformation)? Is this *really* a continuous part of marketing activity? We think not.

FP₇: The Enterprise Can Only Make Value Propositions

The enterprise (firm) can only make value propositions (offerings), because it is the customer who determines value for him- or herself and co-produces it. This means that exchange value for the customer includes the estimated value-in-use of any goods exchanged. We would add that there can be no expectations of a satisfactory relationship developing unless suppliers also determine their own sense of value, which means that value propositions should be conceived, from the outset, as particular proposals to and from suppliers and customers seeking equitable exchanges of value. It is not often recognized that one value proposition is always offered for another, yet both are enjoined in exchange, or there will be no exchange! To achieve this end, a negotiated agreement might be needed, which in turn might require some depth of dialogical interaction.

Vargo and Lusch (2004, p. 12) have said:

> Even in the case when the firm does not want to extend or repeat patronage, it is not freed from the normative goal of viewing the customer relationally.

We agree. And one aspect of viewing the customer relationally is to balance the interests of the customer and the supplier over time within a relational context. Although marketing is inherently customer oriented, suppliers determine their own value in exactly the same way as customers do. These value perspectives are two sides of one coin. This point is so obvious that it can be overlooked—hence our emphasis on the reciprocity of value propositions.

FP₈: A Service-Centered View Is Customer Oriented and Relational

Service interaction and the co-production of value demand viewing the customer relationally. We agree. However, we would argue that communication is the conduit for the S-D marketing logic and within that, dialogical interaction is the fast track to learning together and hence to knowledge renewal. We would add that relationships are emergent and a consequence of learning together over time.

Instead of managing communication, knowledge, or relationships as top-down activity, as is common practice, each perhaps supported by separate enabling technologies, all three make sense enjoined within a pragmatic S-D logic, as discussed previously and shown in Figure 17.2. In this light, S-D logic can be seen as a strategy for reestablishing the centrality of interaction (or the encounter, as it was called in the services literature of the 1980s) as a grounded form of microeconomic practice. As *value* is a descriptor for the consequences of interaction between buyers and sellers, we understand this term as meaning a "preferential judgment" (Holbrook 1994), whereas *values* are the criteria, or guiding principles, by which the judgment is made. We find this distinction helpful.

POSTSCRIPT

Marketing's role as a facilitator of exchange within the S-D marketing logic becomes clear but challenging. If core competencies are to be identified, further developed, and framed as value propositions, new knowledge must be generated and applied within the firm and between the firm and its stakeholders. This means that communication will necessarily be more fluid and interactive. The whole value-creating enterprise will function only if marketing's involvement is collaborative, and seen to be so.

Thus, marketing management becomes market oriented. This agenda will be a daunting prospect for traditional marketing warriors; however, for others much of the problem will be adjusting to new language and meanings. In moving to explore the S-D logic further, issues surrounding relationships, communication, and knowledge stand out. Introducing a dialogical orientation to learning together might be a fast-track approach.

REFERENCES

Alderson, Wroe (1957), *Marketing Behavior and Executive Action.* Homewood, IL.: Richard D. Irwin.
Ballantyne, David (2003), "A Relationship Mediated Theory of Internal Marketing," *European Journal of Marketing,* 37 (9), 1242–60.
——— (2004a), "Dialogue and its role in the development of relationship specific knowledge," *Journal of Business and Industrial Marketing,* 19 (2), 114–23.
——— (2004b), *A Relationship Mediated Theory of Internal Marketing.* Helsinki: Swedish School of Economics & Business Administration.
Christopher, Martin, Adrian Payne, and David Ballantyne (2002), *Relationship Marketing: Creating Stakeholder Value.* Oxford: Butterworth-Heinemann.
Duncan, T. and S. E. Moriarty (1998), "A Communication-based Marketing Model for Managing Relationships," *Journal of Marketing,* 62 (2), 1–13.
Grönroos, C. and K. Lindberg-Repo (1998), "Integrated Marketing Communications: The Communications Aspect of Relationship Marketing," *Integrated Marketing Communications Research Journal,* 4 (1), 3–11.
Gummesson, E. (1999), *Total Relationship Marketing: Rethinking Marketing Management: From 4Ps to 30Rs.* Oxford: Butterworth-Heinemann.
Holbrook, M. B. (1994), "The Nature of Customer Value," in *Service Quality: New Directions in Theory and Practice,* Roland T. Rust and Richard L. Oliver, eds. Thousand Oaks, CA: Sage Publications, 21–71.
Luhmann, N. (2000), *The Reality of the Mass Media,* K. Cross, trans. Stanford, CA: Stanford University Press/Polity Press.
McKenna, R. (1991), *Relationship Marketing: Own the Market through Strategic Customer Relationships.* London: Century Business Books.
Nonaka, I. and H. Takeuchi (1995), *The Knowledge-Creating Company: How Japanese Companies Create the Dynamics of Innovation.* New York: Oxford University Press.
Normann, Richard and Rafael Ramírez (1993), "From Value Chain to Value Constellation: Designing Interactive Strategy," *Harvard Business Review,* 71 (July–August), 65–77.
Varey, R.J. (2000), "A Critical Review of Conceptions of Communication Evident in Contemporary Business & Management Literature," *Journal of Communication Management,* 4 (4), 328–40.
——— (2002a), *Marketing Communication: Principles and Practice.* London: Routledge.
——— (2002b), *Relationship Marketing: Dialogue and Networks in the E-Commerce Era.* Chichester, UK: John Wiley & Sons.
——— and B. R. Lewis, eds. (2000), *Internal Marketing: Directions for Management.* London: Routledge.
Vargo, Stephen L. and Robert F. Lusch (2004), "Evolving to a New Dominant Logic for Marketing," *Journal of Marketing,* 68, 1–17.

18

HOW INTEGRATED MARKETING COMMUNICATION'S "TOUCHPOINTS" CAN OPERATIONALIZE THE SERVICE-DOMINANT LOGIC

TOM DUNCAN AND SANDRA MORIARTY

Complementing how Vargo and Lusch (2004; hereafter V&L) have interpreted the market-place in terms of service, this chapter looks at "intangible resources" from a brand communication perspective. This perspective centers on brand–customer "touchpoints," which is what integrated marketing communication has been designed to manage. This chapter's discussion of integrated marketing communication's (IMC's) touchpoints offers one way to operationalize V&L's "service is everything" concept. We believe not only that the service and brand communication perspectives are related and interdependent, but that service, as defined by V&L, is to a great extent defined for customers and other stakeholders by the brand messages delivered by the many brand touchpoints. Explaining the relationship and interdependence of these two perspectives, and showing how service value can be enhanced, is the purpose of this chapter.

When most people hear "brand communication" with regard to marketing, the first thing that comes to mind is mass advertising and promotion. To see how to add value to service, however, requires a concept and process that is far more reaching and cross-functional than traditional advertising and promotion. It requires an IMC that is broad in scope and drives customer–brand relationships.

Although some define IMC very narrowly ("one voice, one look"), a broader scope definition of IMC is "an ongoing, interactive, cross-functional process of brand communication planning, execution, and evaluation that integrates all parties in the exchange process in order to maximize the mutual satisfaction of each others' wants and needs" (Duncan and Mulhern 2004, p. 9). Several elements differentiate this IMC concept from traditional advertising and promotion: (1) that IMC is an ongoing process, not just a series of ad campaigns and promotions, (2) IMC is dialogic and intensifies interactivity, (3) IMC is dependent on cross-functional organization, (4) the focus is on brand communication (rather than just advertising or marketing communication), and (5) IMC involves all stakeholders—that is, all parties in the exchange process, rather than just those in the marketing department and customers.

To better understand how these dimensions of IMC intersect with the service-dominant logic, consider the following list of postulates:

1. Brand touchpoints are operant resources (i.e., "producers of effects") and value-producing communication events/acts.
2. A service is a communication experience.
3. Interaction produces information, which is a source of added value.
4. The co-creation of positive value at touchpoints creates and strengthens relationships.
5. Varied and multiple touchpoints create a value field that can also be described, in V&L's words (p. 5), as "a continuous series of social and economic processes."
6. Cross-functional management is needed for a value field of successful interactions.
7. Consistency in brand messages (and service) anchors relationships.

Following is a discussion of each of these postulates that further explains the points of inter-section between the service paradigm and the brand communication, or IMC, perspective.

1. BRAND TOUCHPOINTS ARE OPERANT RESOURCES (I.E., PRODUCERS OF EFFECTS") AND VALUE-PRODUCING COMMUNICATION EVENTS/ACTS

A brand touchpoint is created when a customer, prospect, or other stakeholder is exposed, in some manner, to a brand and consequently has "a brand experience." Touchpoints include such incidents as using a product, discussing a brand with another person, seeing an ad, walking into a retail store (where the store is the brand), noticing a brand on display, taking a product in for repair, and discarding the product. In the V&L service approach, touchpoints are important oper-ant resources, a point where "an . . . act is performed that produces an effect" (p. 2). In this case, the act is jointly "performed," with the branded product/company as one of the actors and the customer or prospect as the other.

Although the phrase "brand touchpoint" (also "brand contact point") has been around for years, many marketing managers still think of brand touchpoints as those created by some planned marketing communication activity such as mass media advertising, sales promotion, direct-response marketing, events, and public relations. Those with this narrow view of touchpoints will have an increasingly difficult time successfully managing their brands. This is because, in most cases, non–marketing communication touchpoints, what V&L call operant resources, have much greater impact on customer relationships (and thus, brand equity) than do those created by marketing communication messages.

For example, how a product is priced (e.g., Bic pens at $.59 versus Mont Blanc pens at $2,000), where it is distributed (e.g., K-Mart or Nieman Marcus), how it performs (e.g., meets or doesn't meet expectations), how customers are treated by customer service representatives (e.g., rudely versus courteously), how a company's leaders behave (e.g., Martha Stewart versus Michael Dell), and even how a company does its accounting (e.g., Enron versus Johnson & Johnson) can send powerful brand messages that quickly overpower and negate years of advertising and promo-tional messages. In other words, not only are these marketing mix messages important contribu-tors to a brand's value proposition, they could also interact negatively with the more formal marketing communication messages.

Today's marketing is more complex than ever before because of all the different ways in which brands can and do (often unknowingly) communicate with customers and prospects. In addition to providing promotional opportunities, touchpoints should be seen as opportunities to

1. Add value to product offerings (improve the brand experience)
2. Gather feedback to monitor customer satisfaction

3. Deliver additional brand messages to increase brand knowledge, increase the brand's share of customers, and strengthen the customer–brand relationship

In other words, a *successful* brand touchpoint is at its most basic a value-producing act for both the company and the customer. Although this greater menu of communication alternatives enables a company to interact with customers on a more timely and personal level, the increased number of alternatives also provides more opportunity for communication failure, which reduces the value for customers, which in turn reduces value for a company. Although V&L do not discuss value reduction, their new service logic helps explain how perfectly good products (both goods and primary services that meet or even exceed production standards) can produce negative value in the exchange process. This can happen because the customer is participating in the creation of the "service" and thus directly affects the value received. Negative value can be the result of faulty participation and/or by misperception—a result of miscommunication.

If the profusion of touchpoints and the customer's participation in creating value are not adequately managed, they could also create confusion and contribute negatively to the brand relationship.

2. A SERVICE IS A COMMUNICATION EXPERIENCE

We believe this communication perspective, although somewhat different from a service perspective, in fact complements the service perspective. The communication perspective, as expressed through the IMC approach, can be seen to operationalize V&L's S-D logic. This is because IMC is also customer focused and provides, through brand touchpoints, the opportunity for value creation within an emotionally involving experience. Touchpoint communication transforms a transaction into a dialogic interaction that conveys personal connections and surrounds the event with an emotional halo of liking (or, negatively, of disliking) the brand experience.

As the dominant logic driving marketing moves from being goods to service based, it obviously focuses more on intangible resources, the co-creation of value, and relationships leading to enduring brand/customer relationships (V&L 2004). It is for this reason that the major portion of shareholder—and customer—value moves from being tangible to intangible.

A customer's overall brand impression (i.e., brand value) is the sum of an integrated bundle of perceptions, what Alderson (1957, p. 69) refers to as "the whole process of creating utility," and determines the strength of the brand relationship. This is important because corporate brand equity is the net sum total of all brand relationships. The bottom line is that the nature of the communication experience is indicative of the effectiveness of the service dimension of the product.

The primary value of a touchpoint is the experience it provides. Every touchpoint offers an opportunity to increase brand recall and brand knowledge. But more important from the customer's perspective is that the depth and manner of the contact contributes to the emotional value of the contact. A good example of this comes from a colleague who recently stayed for two weeks in Tokyo at a midsized hotel. When he checked out, both persons behind the desk walked with him out to the street, flagged down a taxi, loaded his luggage, and stood waving good-bye as the taxi pulled away. A friendly welcome is fairly common at most hotels but a make-you-feel-special goodbye is rare. This emotional "heat" adds warmth to the touchpoint experience. The result of a positive, emotionally engaging touchpoint experience is not only higher brand recall and loyalty, which increases the brand's own equity, but another added value for the customer.

The principles and strategies of experiential marketing (Pine and Gilmore 1999) suggest that people are searching for experiences (i.e., service benefits) and are more affected by the experience dimension of a brand than by simply acquiring and using the basic product. This is why there is such a huge range, in most product categories, of price points. It is true that products vary in quality, but often the difference between brands is based more on image, which provides these value-added emotional experiences. Touchpoints not only offer engagement and the opportunity to move from a passive to an active mind-set, they also surround the activity with an atmosphere of involvement, which is basic communication.

3. INTERACTION PRODUCES INFORMATION, WHICH IS A SOURCE OF ADDED VALUE

Most traditional marketing communication has been driven by a model of one-way targeted mass communication. In contrast, IMC is driven by a combination of one- and two-way communication models that recognize that interactivity provides feedback. This feedback, which provides customer insight, helps a brand better serve its customers by providing customer profile information so marketing communication messages can be more targeted and personalized.

This broader view of brand communication transforms the traditional concept of a marketing "exchange" from being simply a business transaction to being an interactive brand experience, a viewpoint that is consistent with V&L's idea that the revised logic focuses on the *co-creation* of value and relationships.

The idea of interaction is basic to both marketing and communication (Duncan and Moriarty 1998). In traditional marketing, an interaction is a transaction or an exchange. In communication, an interaction is a conversation or a dialogue; in marketing, an interaction sets up a collaborative relationship with a customer. In marketing communication, IMC has produced a paradigm shift, similar to the one proposed by V&L, which moves marketing from a one-way model with its focus on segmenting and targeting to a two-way model that facilitates interaction. Two-way communication is basic to V&L's customer-centric model of the service-dominant paradigm where it is seen as a basic core competence.

According to V&L, skills and knowledge are the fundamental units of exchange. In IMC, interaction is an information-producing event that makes information the fundamental unit of exchange. As Evans and Wurster (1997, p. 72) suggest, "every business is an information business." It is through the differential use of information, or knowledge, applied in concert with the knowledge of other members of the service chain that the firm is able to make value propositions to the consumer and gain competitive advantage. Because information is the content of the value exchange, it is of value for consumers in purchase situations, and of value to a company in targeting messages and when responding to customer inquires and complaints.

4. THE CO-CREATION OF POSITIVE VALUE AT TOUCHPOINTS CREATES AND STRENGTHENS RELATIONSHIPS

Most companies and marketing communication agencies know how to create touchpoints. Unfortunately, these touchpoints are often overused, misused, and misdirected, resulting in creating brand experiences that are annoying and intrusive. In other words, they sometimes show little sensitivity as to when and where to "touch" prospects and customers and thus end up creating negative value.

In planning marketing programs, attention should focus on those touchpoints that are most critical in creating and retaining relationships. The critical touchpoints are, in the words of Jan Carlson, "moments of truth." A former SAS airlines CEO, Carlson was a superb marketer who realized that certain brand–customer touchpoints could be directly related to future purchase decisions. Critical touchpoints involve more than a customer simply coming in contact with a brand message. A critical touchpoint (CTP) implies a connection. A CTP is when a brand and a customer (prospect, or other stakeholder) *connect* on an emotional level. It is an interactive brand communication experience that either strengthens or weakens a customer's relationship with the brand. Managing these critical touchpoints is what we call *critical touchpoint branding.*

When a customer and a brand connect at a brand touchpoint, the interaction is based on a symmetrical relationship, rather than an asymmetrical one with its notion of sender as source and receiver as target. In a symmetrical brand–customer relationship, the goal of communication is as much focused on responding to customer-initiated messages as it is on sending "selling" messages. The service-centered view of marketing, as well as the relationship-marketing approach, moves the marketing discipline into this more balanced view of a brand relationship.

What must not be overlooked in the holistic service concept, V&L's notion of an operant resource, is the fact that customers increasingly initiate the interaction—that is, brand communication. As V&L (p. 5) state, "The service-centered view of marketing implies that marketing is a continuous series of social and economic processes." We think a more accurate statement is that marketing is a continuous series of social and economic *interactions.* This being the case, a relationship concern is making sure company response messages are just as strategic and well executed as its initiated marketing communication messages.

Even more important is to make sure that customers have recourse when they have a problem. This is done by ensuring that customers can easily and smoothly contact a company and receive timely and knowledgeable responses from employees empowered to solve customer problems. When this is done properly, a service is performed that adds value to the brand. Research into customer-initiated contact has found that, in general, most companies do an abysmal job of handling this aspect of touchpoints. Rarely do more than 50 percent of customer-initiated contacts receive responses that customers rate as "good." (Compare that to the quality movement for production, in which a 99 percent quality performance is often demanded.)

Because critical touchpoints have a significant impact on the minds and hearts of customers, these "touching experiences" must be strategically designed and managed. Some places and times are more appropriate than others for touching, and there are different ways to touch. Consider how touching works in personal relationships: In those that are distant or impersonal, touching might not be appropriate at all beyond shaking hands, if that; in other relationships, one greets another with a hug or peck on the cheek.

With regard to commercial relationships, the appropriate closeness varies with the personality of the brand, length of the relationships, frequency of interaction, and relationship moderator. An automatic teller machine (ATM) transaction, for example, is much more distant and impersonal than a personal interaction with a bank teller. Nevertheless, some customers prefer the convenience and anonymity of the ATM, whereas others expect their bank's tellers to know them by name. A Lexus dealership might close a deal with a handshake, but a Saturn new customer might get a group serenade. The closer the customer and brand, the more willing the customer is to be touched, interact, share personal information, and introduce friends to the brand. This level of touching can be equated to the quality level of the service encounter.

As mentioned, touchpoints are operant service-related resources that can add value, which in turn creates stronger customer relationships. The end result of good touchpoint management is brand–customer closure. Brand–customer closure could be likened to a zipper or Velcro closure, in which both sides must participate equally in making a connection. The higher the quality of the zipper (or in our case, the brand experience), the stronger and more enduring bond between company and customer. Just as the closure on a coat serves to keep heat in and cold out, closure in a brand relationship keeps the relationship comfortable and protects it from mistrust and dissatisfaction.

5. VARIED AND MULTIPLE TOUCHPOINTS CREATE A VALUE FIELD

The essence and source of corporate brand equity, as mentioned previously, is the net sum total of stakeholder relationships that are the result of individualized bundles of integrated perceptions. These perceptions are created by not just marketing communication messages, but *all* messages that are sent by an organization at every touchpoint. Everything a company does, and sometimes what it doesn't do, sends a brand message.

Touchpoints are the home of a variety of communication situations and processes that create value. A brand's relationship with a customer evolves and develops across time and multiple contact points. In a service-focused marketing program, a customer becomes aware of a brand, obtains information about it, tries it, buys it, gets training, maybe returns it or complains about it and contacts customer service, comments on it to friends, gets repairs, and, the brand's company hopes, buys it again. Relationship communication, like service, is not an event, a specific time, or a specific place, but rather an ongoing process with many controlled and uncontrolled inputs.

To visualize this, think of a value field that is based on two-way, interactive communication with multiple overlapping and interacting touchpoints. This is in contrast to a marketing communication value chain, which is a succession of one-way mass-mediated messages. Creating and, more importantly, maintaining customer relationships involve a dynamic constellation of interactions at multiple touchpoints.

The traditional concept of a value chain is a linear step-by-step process that adds value to a product. Normann and Ramírez (1993, p. 69) argue that the marketing concept should move from a value chain to a value constellation. As they explain, "the only true source of competitive advantage is the ability to conceive the entire value-creating system and make it work." The value field is a useful metaphor because it effectively describes a network or system of interactions, most of which are service based and deliver information. The only problem with Normann and Ramírez's "constellation" concept is that, like previous writers on the value chain, it focuses primarily on upstream activities and actors. If their metaphor is expanded to include the variety of downstream touchpoints, then their constellation would be the same as the value field concept.

To successfully manage a value field, touchpoints beyond those created by marketing communication must be identified and appreciated for how powerful they can be. This is because, as stated before, everything sends a brand message. A benefit of recognizing touchpoints as the components of a brand value field is seeing a map of interdependencies and relationship contacts. The value field concept helps identify the links between and among the touchpoints and how the various touchpoints collectively present the brand's messages and create brand meaning.

6. CROSS-FUNCTIONAL MANAGEMENT IS NEEDED FOR A VALUE FIELD OF INTERACTIONS

Because brand communication crosses departmental lines, its management needs to be boundary spanning. The best way to achieve this is through cross-functional management. The complexity of interactions, both upstream and downstream, that are involved in the management of value creation puts stress on traditional hierarchical organizational structures. A value field of touchpoints includes both horizontal and vertical interactions. Because brand touchpoints are a result of a variety of communication sources, a cross-functional management organization must include all the departments, divisions, and management decisions that touch the customer (and other key stakeholders)—everything from traditional marketing communication managers to customer service, packaging managers, channel members, and frontline employees.

Getting cross-functional cooperation, however, can be an issue. Knocking down or linking internal silos is a challenge that still faces many companies. Managing touchpoints requires a cross-functional committee whose responsibility is to plan, prioritize, monitor, and make adjustments where necessary—in other words, manage an ongoing process that seeks to identify and leverage positive CTPs and redesign or eliminate negative CTPs.

7. CONSISTENCY ANCHORS RELATIONSHIPS

Because the messages generated at touchpoints are so varied, it stands to reason that the degree of brand impact on customer relationships and retention also varies touchpoint by touchpoint. But one thing is certain: Message consistency is an added value. Customers want a Snickers bar that tastes exactly like the Snickers bars they have been eating for years. When they go to their favorite coffee shop, they want to be able to order their favorite drink from their favorite coffeemeister. And it helps if that person shows that he or she recognizes them.

A valuable corporate core competency in service and brand communication is consistency in how the company interacts with its customers, prospects, and other stakeholders. How is this consistency achieved? In retailing, one process that has proven itself is the Nordstrom mantra: The customer is always right. In selling a blouse or set of crystal, in which the interaction is between one customer and a salesclerk, this is pretty easy to execute. However, when IBM is selling a multimillion-dollar customer relationship management (CRM) system to General Motors, things become more challenging because of the expanded number of players, the complexity of the product, and the dollars involved.

But consistency does not mean the same service and message to everyone. In IMC we talk about strategic consistency in core brand values that remain the same while the brand messages might vary by target market and the communication situation—different messages for the trade and the consumer audiences, for example. And, of course, internal marketing will have an employee-centric focus. But yet, there is consistency in theme, overall objectives, and brand mission and position. The same is true for service—the standard of service should be constant, although the specific activities may vary.

At the heart of a brand's value field should be the core values of the brand. A core value is what the brand stands for—such things as quality and sentiment (Hallmark), safety (Volvo), engineering quality (Mercedes), and performance (Nike). An effective core value is embedded deep in the corporate culture and is reflected in the attitudes and behaviors of employees. It's the foundation on which the brand is anchored and that provides the basis for employee commitment and customer brand loyalty. It is the touchstone for the touchpoints and is reflected in V&L's service concept.

A core value that anchors brand touchpoints provides strategic message consistency. An example is Apple computer. The slogan "think different" co-opted and one-upped IBM's "think" moniker. More important, it drove all of Apple's operations, activates, and interactions—the easy-to-use operating system, the distinctive design of its computers, its informal operating style and corporate culture, and its advertising, which focused on creativity and liberating people from rigid systems (Apple's *1984* commercial and its later "think different" campaign).

Table 18.1

Touchpoint Interaction Benefits

Company benefits	Customer benefits
1. Feedback to monitor customer satisfaction and provide customer insight, which enables company to better meet needs and wants of customers	1. An overall better brand experience
2. Leveraging marketing communication investment by maximizing message delivery and minimizing the negative messages that can negate marketing communication messages	2. Facilitating two-way communication, which provides recourse when something goes wrong
3. Leveraging each interactive experience to increase brand awareness, brand associations, perceived quality of the brand, and brand loyalty—the four constructs of brand equity*	3. Increasing brand trust and, in essence, provides customers with "brand insurance," which reduces or eliminates the risk in buying and using a product

*Aaker and Joachimsthaler (2000), p. 72.

CONCLUSION

Table 18.1 distills the points made here. Why bother with the intersection of service and brand touchpoints? Touchpoint interactions deliver benefits for both sides of the communication partnership. For the brand and company, touchpoints are opportunities to better gather feedback, deliver more brand messages, reinforce brand promises, and increase customer involvement with the brand. At the same time, customers should benefit from touchpoint interactions through the added experiential value, increased brand satisfaction, and needs that are better met. As in any interaction, better communication is a win/win situation.

REFERENCES

Aaker, David and Erich Joachimsthaler (2000), *Brand Leadership.* New York: The Free Press.

Alderson, Wroe (1957), *Marketing Behavior and Executive Action.* Homewood, IL: Richard D. Irwin.

Duncan, Tom and Sandra Moriarty (1998), "A Communication-Based Marketing Model for Managing Relationships," *Journal of Marketing* 62 (April), 1–13.

——— and Frank Mulhern, eds. (2004), "A White Paper on the Status, Scope, and Future of IMC," published by Daniels College of Business and Northwestern University's IMC Programs.

Evans, Philip B. and Thomas S. Wurster (1997), "Strategy and the New Economics of Information," *Harvard Business Review,* 75 (September/October), 71–82.

Normann, Richard and Rafael Ramírez (1993), "From Value Chain to Value Constellation: Designing Interactive Strategy," *Harvard Business Review,* 71 (4), 65–77.

Pine II, B. Joseph and James H. Gilmore (1999), *The Experience Economy.* Boston: Harvard Business School Press.

Vargo, Stephen and Robert, Lusch (2004), "Evolving to a New Dominate Logic for Marketing," *Journal of Marketing,* 68 (January), 1–17.

PART V

ALTERNATIVE LOGICS

Several of the thought leaders who contributed to this effort suggested additional, alternative, or perhaps multiple logics that could contribute to marketing's search for a new dominant logic. We are thankful to them for their ideas and, at times, well-thought-out critiques. Although in some cases we disagree, we feel it is helpful to marketing's charting a new course that diverse views be considered and debated. It is of course appropriate that those skeptical of service-dominant (S-D) logic propose alternative paradigms, and we applaud those who did. However, the issue of whether the specific critiques drive the alternative agenda or the alternative agenda drive the critiques is left to the reader.

Part V begins with a thoughtful and provocative essay by Venkatesh, Peñaloza, and Firat, "The Market as a Sign System and the Logic of the Market" (chapter 19), which suggests the starting point of analysis for the marketing discipline should be the market. It is important to note that they urge us to focus on the global market economy and to view it as a "sign economy." Their emphasis on macrostructures is certainly in line with the perspectives advanced in the chapters to follow by Wilkie and Moore (chapter 20) and Laczniak (chapter 21).

A focus on markets, as Venkatesh, Peñaloza, and Firat acknowledge, is not inconsistent with S-D logic. S-D logic emphasizes intangibles, co-creation of value, and relationships. The global market economy, as a macrostructure, is intangible, although grounded and linked to tangible things such as natural resources, commodity production, geography, weather patterns, and so on. Also, we should point out that markets, whether local, regional, or global, are co-created because they involve buyers and sellers interacting to determine norms, language, signs, and meanings. Finally, the S-D logic focus on relationships is supportive of global market economies in which the relationships or networks might begin at the micro level but then, layer upon layer, develop into intricate webs of relationships (via markets and signs) among countries and/or geopolitical areas.

The authors have the goal of developing a "theory of the markets" or "theories of markets." We think that the authors are correct that a general theory of markets would be a higher-order framework than a *theory of marketing,* and we look forward to their further work in this area and to seeing how it fits S-D logic. Our expectation is that S-D logic will emerge as a higher-order construct than "sign value," and thus provide a foundation for not only a theory of marketing, but also a theory of markets (see chapter 32).

Chapter 20, "Examining Marketing Scholarship and the Service-Dominant Logic" by Wilkie and Moore, provides much fodder for meaningful discussion. What will S-D logic have to say about or contribute to aggregate conceptions of marketing is a legitimate area of inquiry and discussion.

The authors conceptualize an aggregate marketing system (AGMS) as composed of marketers, consumers, and government. A primary concern they have is that there is too much attention to the firm in the S-D logic, or at least not a balanced attention on other parts of the system. A new dominant logic of marketing must be able to address the AGMS more fully. We hope that others will participate in the open-source development of S-D logic to ensure that it encompasses the nature and scope of marketing and includes both micro- and macromarketing scholarship. Perhaps a good starting point for those interested in this open-source effort is chapter 32, "Service-Dominant Logic as a Foundation for a General Theory."

Also embracing a broader view is chapter 21, "Some Societal and Ethical Dimensions of the Service-Dominant Logic Perspective of Marketing." Laczniak calls attention to broader and more macro issues. In a manner supportive of the open-source nature of S-D logic, he encourages further work that addresses (1) higher order societal benefits, (2) learning processes that involve more than financial feedback, (3) conceiving not only customers as co-participants but other stakeholders, and (4) the development of *authentic* trust between the firm and customer. We find ourselves excited about these suggestions because we believe S-D logic to be pro-society, pro-firm, dynamically adaptive (based on feedback), pro-value creation networks and other stakeholders, and supportive of the development of authentic, versus merely contractual, trust. Indeed, we find ourselves in agreement with Laczniak when he suggests that the social and ethical elements of marketing's provision of service should be important parts of future discussions.

"The New Dominant Logic of Marketing: Views of the Elephant" is the topic of chapter 22 by Ambler. Using the elephant description metaphor, he asks about whether "the 'marketing elephant' is changing or are we merely seeing the same beast from different points of view?" Ambler suggests that the new financial ecology of the firm is leading to finance providing the new dominant logic for marketing. He goes as far as to suggest that marketing should be redefined as the sourcing and harvesting of cash flow. The dominant logic he offers is one directed at "building brand equity in order to maximize long-term cash flow."

Lehmann in chapter 23, "More Dominant Logics for Marketing: Productivity and Growth," argues that for public, for-profit firms there are two firm objectives that loom large: marketing productivity and revenue growth. He argues that "firm performance is not just a reward for connecting with customers; for a publicly held for-profit firm it is the reason to connect. Satisfying/pleasing/delighting customers then is often a necessary but not sufficient condition." S-D logic suggests a different perspective. It argues that firms exist and are legitimized by society because they provide service, and firm performance helps to inform the firm if it is doing a good job of serving. Thus, a primary purpose of firm performance, such as revenue growth, is as a learning mechanism. Basic learning involves rewards and punishments, and S-D logic views firm revenue growth as a reward that reinforces behavior and revenue decline or below-par revenue growth as a punishment and also reinforcement of what is not working. We agree with Lehmann that firms have a growth imperative. However, we disagree about the role of revenue growth. It might be a dominant logic in many firms, but if the firm succeeds in the long term with revenue growth, then we believe S-D logic would argue that it is almost always tied to *serving* the customer (market). Lehmann concludes that "for better or worse, the dominant logic for a marketing profession that wants to 'matter' must be financial results in general and growth in particular oriented."

"An Economics-Based Logic for Marketing" is the theme of the chapter prepared by Thorbjørn Knudsen in chapter 24. Knudsen argues that there is a co-evolution taking place in economic thought that is entirely consistent with S-D logic. We acknowledge that we did not deal extensively with neoclassical and more contemporary economics in our original *Journal of Marketing* article on S-D logic (chapter 1)—though we did deal with it somewhat more extensively in earlier revisions—and that several contemporary economists have pointed out the limitations of the standard economic model and proposed adjustments.

However, we submit that at least some of what Knudsen sees as parallel with S-D logic is actually more parallel with arguments that we have heard that S-D logic is attacking a "straw man" because the goods-dominant (G-D) model was abandoned with the advent of the consumer orientation. As we have argued elsewhere, the consumer orientation does not represent the abandonment of G-D logic; it is an adjustment to and necessitated by G-D logic. Likewise, we suggest that at least some of the adjustments to which Knudsen refers are just that—adjustments to the underlying G-D-oriented, microeconomic model. By contrast, S-D logic represents a change to the foundation of the model of exchange, one that implies consumer centricity and value-in-use, rather than a modification of a flawed model.

Regardless, to the extent that economic scholars have already embraced their own "S-D logic," we applaud them. We find Knudsen's parallels between S-D logic and changes in economic thought as well as the overlap between some of the sources that he cites and the pedigree of S-D logic to be both confirming and encouraging.

Brodie, Pels, and Saren in their essay in chapter 25, "From Goods- toward Service-Centered Marketing: Dangerous Dichotomy or an Emerging Dominant Logic?" challenge S-D logic by reviewing the research of the Contemporary Marketing Practices (CMP) group. They see this research suggesting that there is an alternative competing logic of "goods and services." They also suggest that firms need to be flexible and adapt to opportunities in which a goods-centered logic might be best; at other times, a service-centered logic; and at still other times or in other situations, both might be required. They also argue for more empirical research to investigate if S-D logic is being adopted in industry. Our response is brief. We take exception with the implication that G-D and S-D logic are representative of the goods-versus-services dichotomy often found in the literature. In fact, we reject this notion; goods and service, as we use the terms, are not alternative categories of products—units of output. Service is an active process of using one's resources to benefit another party, rather than a type of (intangible) good. There is only a dichotomy if goods and service are viewed through the lens of G-D logic (see chapter 3)—a common error when one first encounters S-D logic (e.g., Achrol and Kotler, chapter 26; Ambler, chapter 22; Kalaignanan and Varadarajan, chapter 13; and a few others in this book).

We believe that G-D logic and S-D logic are competing philosophies about the exchange process, and although some firms might be adopting part of each, we argue in this book and elsewhere that, from a normative perspective, S-D logic is more likely to lead to value creation and should be fully embraced, rather than embracing it with remnants of G-D logic. We also argue that the fact that some firms do not embrace S-D logic does not detract from the validity of its normative prescriptions. Furthermore, because S-D logic has normative implications, it would be beneficial to learn about instances of positive outcomes for firms that do adopt its philosophy,

In concluding this part, Achrol and Kotler in chapter 26 observe, "[B]ut radical new strides for a discipline rarely come as airtight, full-blown arguments (Einsteins of the world excepted), and can be prematurely rejected or politely ignored because of too many ambiguities and vague areas, loose ends, or exaggerated claims." For this reason, Achrol and Kotler, in "The Service-Dominant Logic for Marketing: A Critique" offer a critical analysis of the S-D logic of marketing. Their critique is built around our support for Bastiat's view that "the great economic law is this: Services are exchanged for services. . . . It is trivial, very commonplace; it is, nonetheless, the beginning, the middle, and the end of economic science."

Achrol and Kotler oppose this view because, as they state, "Unfortunately the important questions of science are rarely about the obvious—that is, that which needs no explanation. Science is explanation. Where every thing is the same, or can be reduced to a common denominator, there is little to explain." Unfortunately, this is a very weak criticism that is contrary to the practice of science. For example, over the past fifty years marketers have tended to accept that marketing is centered on exchange; so everything is about exchange (regardless of whether it is the exchange of goods, ideas, causes, etc., or, as we suggest, "service"). The fact that one accepts that everything in marketing is about exchange does not mean there is nothing or little left to explain in marketing. Furthermore, virtually all sciences seek a general theory that helps to explain everything in the domain of that science.

These are not trivial pursuits. Nor should "obvious" be confused with lack of explanation. Scientific eloquence results from transforming complex phenomena into easily understandable models; explaining is the process of capturing parsimony. For both, we believe "obvious" is more of a compliment than a pejorative.

Achrol and Kotler further suggest that "despite the claim to the contrary, practically every rationale that V&L put forward is grounded in the goods versus services distinction." Not only do we not agree, we explicitly reject the goods-versus-services distinction, and we argue that this overdebated issue completely misses the point. Rather than respond in detail, we refer the reader to our article, "The Four Service Marketing Myths: Remnants of a Goods-Based, Manufacturing Model," which appeared in the May 2004 issue of the *Journal of Service Research*, and chapter 3, "Service-Dominant Logic: What It Is; What It Is Not; What It Might Be."

This well-known pair of marketing scholars, the latter whose name is almost synonymous with marketing education, suggests that the goods–service debate is not one of substance but one that is "merely stylistic and rhetorical." Actually, in part, we agree with them on this point, but we also point out that it is they who advance this debate, and that it is a debate that has nothing to do with S-D logic. Their central argument is that if you "substitute the term *services* for *goods* and vice-versa" you will find that there is no loss of meaning in the distinctions we purportedly are asserting in our discussion of the G-D logic and S-D logic. If, as is apparently the case, Achrol and Kotler view both goods and services as units of output (with the latter being characterized by intangibility), then we would have to agree with their view, and thus the argument. However, this characterization of the relationship between goods and *service* is inconsistent with our views, and their argument is orthogonal to S-D logic. Considering the fact that we cite one of these authors (Kotler) in our original *Journal of Marketing* article (reprinted as chapter 1) in his assertion that "the importance of physical products lies not so much in owning them as in obtaining the services they render"—an exceptionally S-D logic–consistent notion—we are surprised that they both advance an inconsistent goods–service definition and appear so critical of our position.

Where we believe these prominent authors go down the wrong path—and we have experienced this with others that have read, though perhaps not as carefully as might be necessary, our exposition on S-D logic—is that our summary statements on G-D logic versus S-D logic is not about goods versus services in the usual sense of these words but about drastically *different philosophies.* For this reason, in our initial *Journal of Marketing* article (reprinted as chapter 1) we urged that "the service-centered view should not be equated with (1) restricted, traditional conceptualizations that often treat services as a residual (that which is not a tangible good; e.g., Rathmell 1966); (2) something offered to enhance a good (value-added services); or (3) what have become classified as services industries, such as health care, government, and education." In fact, we forewarn that many organizations that all would agree are in the service industry (IRS, airlines, health care) have adopted a G-D logic and have focused on "units of output" and maximizing or optimizing profit or cash flow or some other measure of organizational performance based on the careful setting of decision-making variables and the standardization of production.

There are many distinctions between the G-D logic and S-D logic, and we will not dwell on these here (however, see chapter 32) except for one that is very important. In common with resource-advantage theory, the act of maximization or optimization is not in the vocabulary of S-D logic. What is in S-D logic is striving, via learning, to better serve the customer and improve organizational performance. The technique employed by Achrol and Kotler of switching the words *goods* and *service* between our descriptions of the G-D view versus the S-D view is thus a faint-hearted attempt to suggest our arguments are stylistic and rhetorical. It represents an effort to discount S-D logic by invoking G-D logic—which, arguably, serves to make our point.

We are actually very pleased that these two prominent thought leaders have made a frontal assault on S-D logic. Their criticism of S-D logic will no doubt focus more attention on it. Because we embrace the co-creation tenet of S-D logic in our scholastic philosophy and, thus, want S-D logic to be a collaborative, open-source theory of marketing, business, and potentially of society, their critique has additional benefit. Only by being fully open to dialogue and debate can the progress we envision occur.

19

THE MARKET AS A SIGN SYSTEM AND THE LOGIC OF THE MARKET

ALLADI VENKATESH, LISA PEÑALOZA, AND A. FUAT FIRAT

INTRODUCTION

Vargo and Lusch (2004a; hereafter V&L) set out on an important course in challenging the traditional view of marketing in their article in the *Journal of Marketing.*[1] The field of marketing, the
authors argue, continues to emphasize the exchange of tangible resources, embedded value, and
transactions, whereas marketing activities increasingly pertain to intangibles, co-creation of value,
and relationships. The appearance of this article in a key journal in marketing should be considered part of a reflective, transformational moment in the discipline. However, though we agree
that challenging the traditional logic of marketing is badly needed for the field to move successfully with currency into the new millennium, we argue for an extension to what V&L have proposed. It is in this spirit that we present our views.

This chapter contributes to the debate regarding a new dominant logic for marketing by
(re)considering the starting point of our disciplinary analysis to be the *market* as a set of culturally
constituted institutional arrangements as opposed to *marketing*, which is a set of activities that
take place within the market, and by advancing a conceptual scheme that views the global economy
as a sign economy. This conceptual scheme is based on a critique that extrapolates from key
historical shifts in the field from a macro-oriented focus on distribution to a micro-oriented focus
on technique; from material, logistical concerns to concepts; and from the exchange of products
and services to the exchange of meanings and symbolic practices. Thus, we title the paper, "The
Market as a Sign System." It must be noted here that in this chapter we do not attempt to deal with
the entire set of issues raised in V&L's article, for that would require a very long critique and
analysis. What we attempt has a twofold purpose: to shift the focus of our disciplinary concerns
from marketing to a more comprehensive and globally inclusive notion of *market*, and to consider the "market as a sign system."

Our approach is quite timely, if not overdue, especially in the context of the shifting cultural
landscape in the United States, as well as global developments that impel us to examine markets
historically and in culturally varied settings. We consciously introduce the global context not
only on account of these contemporary changes, but also because it is pertinent to historical
developments. To this day, one can go to different parts of the world and witness markets that
have existed for centuries (e.g., the Grand Bazaar in Istanbul) and continue to flourish alongside
innovative concept stores such as Niketown and the ESPN Zone. It is in this larger context of the

market as a sociohistorically situated institution that we interject the importance of the sign system in rendering markets intelligible.

To begin, we review key features of V&L's service-dominant (S-D) logic and the logic of modern marketing as points of departure in sketching out our own ideas. We then shift the focal point of study from marketing to markets, elaborating the theory of the market as it has developed at the nexus of some key social transformations. That is, we describe properties of the sign economy, as they are manifested in markets in consumption and marketing practice, and discuss the various domains in which they are played out: ideology, institutionalization, and globalization.

Paradoxically, the term *market* is everywhere and nowhere in our literature. We often write of this or that market, yet have restricted our view of the market to economic exchange when it is only one of several types of sign systems. By fleshing out the unit of analysis of markets and studying them carefully and comparatively, we hope to advance theoretical, methodological, and practical understanding in our field. First, our proposed study offers a more comprehensive, nuanced account of market(ing) discourse and phenomena. Second, our view of the market system is better adapted to global trends of technology and sociopolitical dynamics. Third, the logic of the market is better able to grapple with changes in marketing activity and forms of organization. Finally, this work directs attention to marketing thought and practice in relation to the embodied, sensorial, material world, and in doing so, opens up the field considerably.

THE LOGIC OF VARGO AND LUSCH

V&L recognize that substantive transformations are occurring in cultures and markets that can be ignored only at our own peril. This is clear from the following key points made in various sections of their article:

1. They alert the reader to the economic shift from a product-oriented approach to a service-oriented approach. Thus, "[t]he authors believe that the new perspectives are converging to form a new dominant logic for marketing, one in which service *provision* rather than goods is fundamental to *economic exchange*" (p. 1 abstract, emphases added).

2. They define the term *service* broadly, that is, not in opposition to tangible products but rather inclusive of them: "[T]he service-centered dominant logic represents a reoriented philosophy that is applicable to all marketing offerings, including those that involve tangible output (goods) in the process of service provision" (p. 2).

3. They further elaborate this last point by stating that their aim in the article is to develop marketing thought which "points toward a more comprehensive and inclusive dominant logic, one that integrates goods with services and provides a richer foundation for the development of marketing thought and practice" (p. 2).

4. More concretely, V&L invoke from the previous work of Constantin and Lusch (1994) the distinction between operand resources and operant resources as a basis for their current approach. Thus, operand resources are "resources on which an operation or an act is performed" (the conventional approach), and operant resources are those "which are employed to act on operand resources [in order to] produce effects," (a proposed approach) (p. 2). They later build upon this distinction, positing in the first of their propositions (foundational premise 1, p. 6) that the essence of a service-centered approach to marketing is the application of knowledge and skills as operant resources.

5. Finally, they characterize all economies as services economies, stating, "[s]ervices and the operant resources they represent have always characterized the essence of economic activity" (foundational premise 5, p. 10).

Collectively, these perspectives provide foundational points from which our chapter branches out, with the final statement in the preceding list providing a lead into our main argument. First, V&L use the term *service economy* in moving from an emphasis on products to services in understanding market exchange. In contrast, we put forward the term *market*, in which the sign is key in understanding exchange. Second, for V&L the ingredients of marketing action, as contained in the operant sources, are knowledge and skills, which are the intangible drivers within a market economy. In contrast, our use of the sign system captures this intangibility, but views it slightly differently, as but part of the broader symbolic elements of exchange in a market economy.

Our contribution consists of three main arguments: First, marketing scholars should shift their attention from marketing to markets, with the latter situated within contemporary institutional and sociohistorical contexts. Second, and most important, having set the premises of the context of study, we turn to its central assertion: As markets become more aestheticized, spectacular, embodied, and personalized, it is instructive to view the global market economy as a sign economy. Third, with the development of information and communication technologies, marketing scholars must attend more comprehensively to the informationalization of global markets.

FROM MARKETING TO MARKETS

In one of the stranger omissions of the discipline, the term *market* has not been employed with much seriousness or rigor. The reigning notion of marketing is that it is an activity geared to satisfying the wants/needs of consumers. Although Kohli and Jaworski (1990) use the term *market orientation* in their seminal article, they limit it to marketing research as an aid in developing marketing strategic techniques. The very word *marketing* as the label for our discipline is used to signify the actions people within firms take in implementing their decision strategies about products and services. Thus, marketing is viewed as a set of functions performed by the marketer that cater to customer needs.

We view this approach as overly mechanistic, functional, and reductive. It sacrifices understanding for tactics, and thus has left unspecified perhaps our most fundamental object of study—*markets*. Furthermore, such a view of marketing is limited, because it does not reflect the complex, rapidly changing realities of the marketplace, and these limitations become even more serious in a global environment.

Here are some reasons why we, as marketing scholars, should enlarge our vision of the field from marketing to markets. First, marketing limits our discipline to firm-level activities, whether we are dealing with products or services. In contrast, markets expand our discipline to a larger realm of discourse and practice where the issues are wider and deeper and their potential treatment is much more impactful. As an aside, we must take note that several social science disciplines are actively pursuing the study of markets in their larger context and are gaining greater ground as a result of this enlarged focus. Examples include Marchand (1998) in history, Goldman and Papson (1998) in sociology, and O'Barr (1994) in anthropology.

Second, the study of marketing has been strongly United States–centric, with the issues largely limited to how U.S.-based marketing concepts and techniques can be transported abroad and what modifications are necessary to better suit local needs. In contrast, the study of markets levels the field for scholars, wherever they might be situated, and enables them to discuss issues and phenomena on a more truly global scale. Although the field of international or global marketing was intended to perform this disciplinary function, it has failed to do so, largely because it has become an extension of domestic marketing with an international flavor, and the scholarly contributions have not been foundational, but rather have taken a U.S. firm perspective.

The main concern we have about the discipline of marketing is that our dominant focus has been limited to firm-level decision making.[2] As such, our discipline has become more and more normative, and our primary charge seems to be to make appropriate recommendations to marketing managers as to what the best strategies should be in marketing their products and services. As an implicit extension of this approach, we seem to be obliged to represent U.S.-based firms in their global operations, or larger firms rather than entrepreneurs, within the U.S. context. It is very difficult to comprehend why we should operate from a managerial perspective, or why the entire discipline should do so. A more meaningful intellectual position for us would be to study markets analytically and critically as scholars of the discipline and provide an analysis of market forces and behaviors. This does not mean that we cannot do normative work, or that we cannot work from a managerial perspective. Our call instead is etching out space within the mainstream of the discipline to do research that provides an in-depth analysis of markets and various actors and institutions within market systems.

There is a certain existential tension in what we currently do: We feel morally compelled to generate scholarship that focuses on satisfying consumers' needs, but at the same time are pulled in the direction of assisting marketers in their attempts to get the attention of customers and convert them into buyers of their offerings. In this sense, whether we admit it or not, marketing scholarship has become synonymous with the science of customer persuasion and the logistics of developing marketing strategy and implementing market exchanges. A more meaningful theoretical stance would be to produce scholarship that provides an objective analysis of how markets function and how they contribute to the general economic and social welfare. Perhaps it is time to abandon the so-called marketing concept as it is currently professed, or at least expand the concept to include the interests of all market agents and take into account social welfare.

By focusing on the study of markets, we need not be concerned about taking sides. In fact, this is where we can really learn from the social sciences, and especially the field of economics. Economists study the theory of the firm not with the notion of how to make firms more prosperous, but with the goal of understanding how firms operate under different conditions of supply and demand (whether they work with products or services), and how they maximize their opportunities under certain conditions and assumptions. Similarly, consumer choices are modeled without necessarily trying to suggest how consumers should behave. Economists make a distinction between positive and normative science, and they are none the worse for it. A positive science of marketing (not to be confused with positivism, as in logical positivism) gives us the vantage point of studying markets more, not less, analytically.

By opening our discipline to the study of markets, not only can we contribute to marketing, understood as a set of firm-level practices, but we are also free to engage in a discussion of more fundamental issues concerning the formation of new markets, new institutional structures in retailing and distribution functions, and the nature and effects of global communications and cultural differences on organizational forms. In other words, we can truly develop richer theories of markets and market behaviors.

Finally, as important as distinctions between product marketing and services marketing are, the study of markets allows us to go further conceptually, for both can be addressed equally effectively, as proposed by V&L. What is more important is that we can study marketing techniques as a major component of markets and also study other aspects of markets, such as their institutional structures and the social bases of consumption patterns. In other words, our knowledge base becomes much enlarged.

THE LEGITIMACY OF THE MARKET

The legitimacy of the market lies in the value it creates for the producer, the consumer, and various intermediaries. Historically, we have seen a progression in terms of how value has been defined and conceptualized. In traditional societies, products and services were acted on in terms of their *use value*. With the rise of industrialism and modernity, use value has been eclipsed by *exchange value*. In more recent times, we have begun to realize that both are embedded in *sign value*.

As V&L note, the contemporary marketing paradigm has developed around the creation and management of exchange value. Much of the marketing and economics literature assumes that markets exist because of the exchange value that permeates all transactions. The discipline of economics simplifies this by representing the market equilibrium as the meeting points of supply and demand. Accordingly, the price mechanism is at the heart of economics, and economic theory uses marginal analysis in the determination of prices and equilibrium positions. Marketing academics view their role similarly, in terms of consummating exchanges between the marketer and the customer, where a marketer can be any member of the distribution channel and the customer is at the end of the line. In summary, we see that there has been a historical progression from use value to exchange value. In examining the basis of exchange value, V&L have identified two market forces that enable such a value creation: standardization and customization. These two are opposed, in the sense that the more one attempts to standardize, the less scope there is for customization. In addition, the imperatives of moving into a service-centered economy are such that, as firms move progressively into a service orientation, the burden of commerce shifts rather paradoxically from standardization to greater customization, which results in increasing costs for the provider.

One way to transcend the confines of this dichotomous way of thinking is to reconsider both use value and exchange value as derivations of sign value. A couple of intermediate conceptual moves are required, however. We must take into account processes of commoditization and consumerization. The theoretically meritorious idea of freeing the individual through the market, in which independent exchanges occur and exchange values are realized for all involved, requires both. *Commoditization* refers to the separation of the objects or items of use from their producers and the processes by which they are created. Commoditization is necessary so that those who exchange for them can possess them without any linkages or obligations, thus being "free" agents. The commodities stand on their own and are imbued, in themselves, with the qualities that their possessors seek and develop in them. Thus, possessing and using them is an independent act that involves only the possessor and the commodity and nothing or no one else.

Second, *consumerization* refers to the separation of the individual from the process of production of what is used. Consumerization is another necessity for the existence of modern marketing. Freedom to have and use commodities of all kinds depends upon non-reliance on one's own production and the ability to consume what others produce and are willing to exchange. This separation of commodities consumed from production means that individuals relate to most of the items they consume in modern society solely as consumers. Thus, as people become consumers, acquiring more of what they use and buying more of the means of their existence, the market expands.

The preceding principles illustrate the logic of modern marketing and, derivatively, of modern markets. Clearly, V&L's "new logic" does not violate any of these principles. They are still talking of "customers" and "consumers." Although they indicate that "marketing is a process of doing things in interaction with the customer" and make the consumer a co-producer and more active in this process, the role of marketers in this process is still *provision,* the provision of "specialized knowledge and skills," instead of "goods." Commoditization and consumerization overlap with V&L's notions of standardization and customization, but they are not the same. There is no indication that these specialized knowledge and skills are not commodities, especially because V&L are still talking of wealth accumulation through the exchange of capital for services.

THE LOGIC OF THE MARKET

Markets are foundational economic and social organizations of commerce in many cultures. Whether we refer to capitalist economies, command economies, or traditional economies, markets have come to dominate the socioeconomic order in the modern era. With the rise of globalism, both as an ideology underlying the modern markets and as the structural conditionality of modern commerce, we must take into account the global market system and understand its dynamic properties. Doing so raises many questions: What is the market? What are the contemporary market forces—locally, nationally, and globally? Why are some markets more attractive and/or different than others? What markets do firms invest in and why? How are markets evolving and changing?

In addressing these questions our larger goal is to develop a "theory of the markets" or "theories of markets" that takes into account variations across market structures and dynamics over time. In this chapter, our starting point is the market as an institutional/social arrangement within which marketing activities as currently understood take place. Markets can be product markets, service markets, or a combination thereof. We agree with V&L that contemporary markets are becoming service dominant. But we must ask whether this phenomenon is global or more representative of the so-called developed world.

Various disciplines have approached the notion of the market differently. Economists view the market as a network of exchanges between buyers and sellers, mediated by agreements on price under conditions of scarcity to provide an efficient allocation of resources (Slater and Tonkiss 2001, p. 2). Simply put, the focus of the market is to study supply-and-demand of goods and services under different conditions of competition and related assumptions.

Sociologists view markets differently but not entirely so (Fligstein 2003). They are less concerned with the actual exchange mechanisms governed by supply-and-demand dynamics. Their primary interest is in the social processes and structures that govern, and are affected by, economic output, labor capital relationships, and power hierarchies.

Anthropologists are also concerned with markets—but more specifically market *places,* a distinction crucial to marketers. "Market places are visible public [settings] that happen at a regular time and place" (Slater and Tonkiss 2001, p. 7). Thus, anthropologists are concerned with spatial and temporal locations where products and services are exchanged, bought, and sold. Market places are culturally constituted physical entities with visible social actors. For anthropologists, the materiality of markets as culturally constituted reality and their symbolic properties are very important.

Thus, different disciplines are situated along the line from viewing the market as an abstraction to that of a concrete expression such as the market place. As marketing scholars, we should go beyond the view of marketing as an activity to include this entire range from the market as an idea to market place as a material reality. We will thus be better able to comprehend the market in all its conditionalities and dimensionalities.

In summary, we believe that the essence of marketing is not simply the actions, but the institutionalization of the actions within a cultural and ideological milieu. This is what we mean by the logic of the market. We grant that the economics of the market clearly dictate many marketing actions: selling, buying, advertising, pricing, distributing, and so on. However, in the economic framework, marketing becomes a disembodied set of practices, viewed as if the issue were simply the manipulation of supply and demand. Instead, in studying markets, we argue for the imperative of examining the institutionalization of all economic and marketing discourses and practices, with attention to their historical, ideological, and culturally constituted character. We emphasize the social, symbolic aspects of transactions as well as the rituals associated with these transactions. Finally, an important part of this approach is comparative, as theoretical gains can be made by examining variations across societies and time periods while paying attention to similarities and shared dimensions and principles as a function of emerging global informational and institutional imperatives and constraints.

THE SIGN ECONOMY

In this section, we map out the key features of the sign economy and describe the functioning of markets in relation to marketers and consumers. We view the contemporary system of commerce in terms of the sign economy. We agree with V&L that the dominant logic of marketing should shift away from a product orientation. Moving toward a service orientation as the realm of application of marketing knowledge and skills is one step closer to viewing the economy as a system of signs, in that both depart from a material emphasis for exchange. However, although shifting attention to services enables us to grasp the intangible basis of exchange, this does not go far enough because our focus remains positioned within an economy described in terms of production and distribution. Goods *and now services* remain reduced to standard units of accounting, priced according to prevailing economic principles of supply and demand. Within this framework, marketing is equated with satisfying needs. Yet, as we argue, this view is unable to address who determines these "needs" or the conditions on which things and activities become "needed."

In our reconceptualization, signs are viewed as more fundamental units for the necessities of life, with marketing taking a key role, in conjunction with consumers, in constituting social needs and desires. As such, we are able to look at marketing in new ways, replacing the naïve objectivist view of the commercial world in which marketers "discover" the preexisting needs of consumers who are adeptly capable of articulating them. Indeed, as illustrated with the high percentage of product and service failures, there are many breakdowns for marketers in carrying out this formula, because it limits their activities to the articulation and delivery of "needed" items and does not fully capture their role in *constituting* consumers' needs and desires in the marketplace.

In contrast, our reconceptualization consists of more nuanced, interactive, enacted markets jointly produced by consumers, marketers, and other culturally constituted forces. Consumers and marketers are positioned within the culturally constituted economic systems they produce as they engage in exchanges according to mutually negotiated systems of language and meanings. In this view, firms are no longer identified with the products and services they produce; rather, they operate within significatory systems as interorganizational alliances oriented around various symbolically oriented transactions.

Paradoxically, as marketers continue to compete by adding a plethora of features, which competitors emulate, their products and services become commodified and largely undifferentiated in terms of their functionalities. What then distinguishes one product from another is the image and symbolism built into it. Noting that most market offerings (we include services with products here) become similar to each other, with functionalities virtually indistinguishable at the margin, marketers and consumers distinguish them based on different value elements that, following Baudrillard (1981), we label as *sign* value. The growing importance of sign value is why branding and advertising have become sine qua non in contemporary marketing.

Thus, in the sign economy we put forward, we recognize that signs of all types are conceived and exchanged in markets and each (type of) market is itself a category constructed in the context of a particular sign system. In these particular markets, particular signs manifest particular operationalizations of skills and knowledge in products and services. Yet most important, we direct attention to the meanings and values that give the signs their currency. That is, what is more important than skills and knowledge, or products and services, are the meanings and values underlying these two sets, or levels, of market symbols, which together constitute the micro elements of the life world. Moreover, in our conceptualization of the market as sign economy, the market is the mechanism for the exchange of meanings and values for money. Incorporating Simmel's (1978) exposition of the multiple plays of money, at once abstract and concrete, we direct attention to it as a constitutive factor in the marketplace. Thus, tracking flows of money is critical to appreciate the capital gains accruing to corporations, their transfer from consumers, otherwise masked in V&L's exchange of services for services.

Aestheticization of the Markets

As marketing activities infiltrate more and more into social life in search of meaning complexes, markets assume a cultural character, and the role of marketing becomes one of aestheticization. To meet consumers' needs, the marketing enterprise increasingly provides opportunities for aesthetic consumption through everyday products for use by consumers in assembling their identities and social positions. For consumers this entails a heightened attention to the senses, to meanings, and to experience—somewhat akin to the feeling while being on vacation. Even brands are not merely names attached to products and services but rather market symbols comprising multiple layers of meaning intelligible in terms of social groups and the distinctions between them.

One of the consequences of the market as a sign system is that consumption becomes more visible and spectacular. First, consumption becomes more public, and private consumption assumes a more public character. The *image* becomes a central driver of consumption. Other aspects of consumption are its embodiment and personalization. These qualities have been touched on in the literature on the service economy, but we must go further than to say consumption is increasingly experiential to emphasize agentic qualities of consumer behavior and consumer subjectivity.

Contributing to the decreasingly private character of consumption is the ritualized shopping for goods and the public display of goods. Shopping takes on much more than provisioning or mere entertainment; it involves more expressive qualities. This is further exemplified in the public display of plentiful goods. Expectations for various social positions, roles, and activities are engendered in shop windows, catalogs, and store displays. Normal everyday life pales in comparison to its idealized representations in advertising and market display, and consumption becomes more elaborate, larger, and better than life itself.

Another feature of consumption is that it is celebratory. Consumption of goods and services becomes a matter of celebrating one's life in terms of realizing one's identity and social positioning. This is somewhat related to the leisure economy, but goes further, as it touches on all other aspects of social life. In this day and age when jobs are deskilled and people's lives are saddled with stresses relating to work and economic activities, they are less able to fully produce identity in the workplace. A more satisfactory release from the mundane, sterile, or oppressive nature of work is to celebrate what is left after work hours. The argument here is that life in the modern industrial cultures can become very structured and mechanical, devoid of human content. In such a culture, the rational order is represented by the industrial structure, and nonrational order is oriented toward the private nonwork life (Habermas 1984). As the structures of work environ-ments continue to be stripped of aesthetic appeals, individual workers/consumers find the stimu-lation of marketing signs as some relief from such a structured environment. Furthermore, the consumer not only finds some refuge in the aesthetic aspects of life, either by directly participat-ing in artistic-sounding endeavors or by seeking aesthetic experiences in everyday consumption practices, but comes to thrive there, defining him- or herself and his or her social groups in markets and in terms of consumption.

In summary, as people engage in consumption for certain kinds of fulfillment, consumer be-havior becomes more *aestheticized*. As such, consumers purchase goods and services increas-ingly for their symbolic value, with functional value being designated as just another set of symbols that are important but less distinctive in consumer behavior. In a dialectic fashion, consumers and marketers engage in symbolic posturing, constantly co-producing sign values.

Consumption within the Sign System

We discussed previously that consumption begins to take a privileged position over production and becomes a key driver of the sign economy. Our view of markets interprets transactions between two parties in terms of shared or even contested meanings. This view triangulates with, but departs from, what V&L talk about when they describe relationship marketing. We share attention to intangible elements of exchange, but go further to emphasize the symbolic meaning and value systems underlying the purely monetary gains emphasized by the economic view of market exchange.

Notably, signs are considered essential in making consumption decisions in Levy's (1981) classic article, yet we go much further in asserting that the whole economy is better understood as a sign economy. In this sense, the sign economy moves from a goods-production industry to an "image-production industry." Not coincidentally, images can be produced faster than goods. As Baudrillard (1981) has shown, images can be multiplied, copied, and reproduced with rapid intensity. In this cycle of production and reproduction, what is privileged is not the technical knowledge of producing goods or even services, but rather being adept at negotiating the shift-ing surface of cultural knowledge, whose main ingredients are speed, motion, and instantaneity of change. Contrast this with the Taylorism (Taylor 1911) of an earlier period, in which produc-tion meant decomposing processes into known components and creating an assembly line of processes integrated within a scientific, technical paradigm. Although the scientific production of Taylor ruled the economy for nearly three quarters of a century, as appropriate for linear, integrated production processes, it is simply not as effective in the sign economy in which mod-eling processes that are ephemeral, fluid, and reliant on symbolic systems of thought, expres-sion, and interaction is crucial.

We anticipate much resistance to the notion of the sign economy and the centrality of markets to our field. First, it goes against the grain of modernistic thinking that such ephemeral and tran-sitory objects as signs could determine the nature of the economy. The sign is considered at best an epiphenomenon, subservient to the more important, tangible, and substantive logic of the economic system. Second, there is an inherent discomfort and moral indignation that a sign could be so powerful as to dictate the functioning of an economic system. However, for many market-ing practitioners and academics steeped in such things as language (as opposed to rationalism), signification (as opposed to representation), interpretation (as opposed to analysis), and argu-mentation (as opposed to the iron logic of data), it is compelling that the system of signs provides a better framework for understanding contemporary human affairs.

Does it mean that we are doing away with factories, manufacturing systems, and technical processes such as research? Certainly not. These processes certainly do exist. But they, too, have become subject to the symbolic system. Marketing practices are viewed in dialectic with consumer behavior in constituting markets, in the sense that both are best understood as cultural practices appropriate to their sociohistorical context. Research, far from discovering consumers' characteristics and needs, is better understood as investigating and establishing the conditions from which consumer desires are intelligible. In turn, consumers selectively render marketing practices, as appropriate to their life worlds.

THE IDEOLOGY OF MARKETS

In the framework we present here, we move away from consumption as want satisfaction, the traditional view within the field of marketing, to characterize consumption within the sign system. Although we describe consumption as exhibiting increasingly playful qualities, we do not view it as mere play. Through the range of consumption from the minutiae of daily life to heightened experiences of vacations or extreme consumption, social categories are negotiated and reproduced in and through what we call the ideology of the market.

Historically, Western capitalism has put an emphasis on production as virtuous and consumption as wasteful (Firat and Venkatesh 1995; Weber 1948). The logic here is that one produces value through production and accumulation, and both produce collective economic and social value to society. However, this approach ignores important factors in the economic arrangement —exactly when, where, and how value is created and fulfilled. Whereas the conventional argument takes production as a value-creating activity for granted, we turn this into a series of questions. In answering them, meaning is a vital but neglected element, as production does not create value unless whatever is produced is also consumed. The transfer of value factor from production to consumption has not gone unnoticed by marketing academics and practitioners. Yet, we argue that this is not simply a practical matter of extending the production to one extra step of marketing and distribution by including consumers as participants in the process. We believe that inherent to capitalism is an ideological position in which consumption is central. That is, the value aspect of the economy is no longer limited to productive functions in capitalism; instead, consumption is elevated to the culmination and consummation of economic exchange, which we view as fundamentally composed of signs. The growing tendency among consumer researchers of the world to focus on *brands* as the drivers of consumption activity is yet another indication of the increasing proliferation and hegemony of the sign system. Thus, in displacing key elements of production to signification, we are better able to direct attention to relations between marketers and consumers, particularly the constitution of the life world in consumer/marketer interactions and the ways in which, through their interactions, marketers and consumers constitute each other.

SIGN ECONOMY AND THE INFORMATIONALIZATION OF MARKETS

New technologies of information and communication are transforming global economic and social systems. We highlight three features of these transformations: (1) the emergence of the Internet and the rise of the informational economy, (2) the way the new technologies are reshaping the symbolic order into a global networked society, and (3) the impact on the organization of production termed the weightless economy. Together, these three forces constitute the conceptual groundwork for our paradigm shift to a sign economy. At the end of this section, we trace the cumulative impact of these three forces into an emerging global condition.

Informational Capitalism

The emergence of the Internet illustrates some major developments in the constitution of contemporary markets as signs. In a path-breaking treatise on the global information economy, Castells (1996, p. 13) lays down some important elements of the information economy of interest to marketing scholars. According to him, "The information technology revolution has been instrumental in allowing the implementation of a fundamental process of restructuring of the capitalist system." He makes a key distinction between modes of production (i.e., capitalism) and modes of development (i.e., industrialism, postindustrialism, and informationalism). Thus, one can have industrial capitalism, which will be different from postindustrial capitalism or informational capitalism. Associated with modes of production and modes of development are modes of social formation.

For Castells, the mode of production is related to the mode of consumption and surplus. Thus, by examining the interaction of the social order and the economic order, we are better able to understand how consumption and surplus are managed and negotiated within a given economy. The mode of development is concerned with consumption via the market system and also influences the technological processes that impinge upon both production and consumption. Thus, in his terminology, "industrial" is oriented toward economic growth—that is, maximizing output—and "informationalism" is oriented toward technological development—that is, toward the accumulation of knowledge and toward higher levels of complexity in information processing. For Castells, informationalism is linked to the expansion and rejuvenation of capitalism, just as industrialism was linked to the mode of production.

Castells (p. 66) further demonstrates that the informational economy is truly global because the

> core activities of production, consumption and circulation, as well as their components (capital, labor, raw materials, management, information, technology, markets) are organized on a global scale, through a network of linkages between economic agents. It is informational *and* global because, under the historical conditions, productivity is generated through and competition is played out in a global network of interaction.

The Dawn of the Networked Society

A second feature emerging from the diffusion of global information technology and providing the substantive basis for informational capitalism is knowledge management. Knowledge management is an attempt to intensify information management within a network context.

The basic issues in knowledge management are that as organizations and economies are moving into knowledge-based environments, these environments are not only becoming complex but highly technologically dependent. A very crucial manifestation of a knowledge environment is the networked economy (Castells 1996). The networked economy is not merely a transaction-based economy, but a knowledge-sharing community of alliances and competitors that rely on rapidly developing technological landscapes.

Networked computers link databases, communication systems of production and distribution, and marketing, which together link various fragmented flows of data and information. To keep pace with these technological developments, human beings require superhuman power to manage these developments by themselves. However, by developing appropriate meta-knowledge systems, they manage networked knowledge environments. As the networked environments become more complex, the knowledge systems also become more complex. Much of this complexity arises because the networked environments are not physical environments but virtual environments.

Weightless Industries

The third feature associated with our paradigm shift to the sign economy is the movement to "weightless industries," as proposed by Quah (1999). Quah uses this term in reference to economic activity whose value does not lie in a physical end product. Examples are intellectual property such as ideas and designs, computer software, entertainment products, telecommunications, and better ways to transmit information, all of which he calls *dematerialized* products or, putting it another way, intangibles. Success in such a weightless economy comes from being able to organize and manipulate information in ways that generate extra value and is closely linked to success in applying information technology.

Together, these features of informationalization, network coalescence, and dematerialization are transforming markets toward the sign economy. Although these developments overlap somewhat with the conditions V&L delineated as bringing about the shift toward an S-D logic, we employ them toward different ends. Key concerns here are with the signs that constitute information, their various types, and how they are employed, as not all skills and knowledge have market meaning and value. This is illustrated time and time again in the wide disparities in pay between teachers and professional athletes or other celebrities; in distinctions between products and consumers, for that matter; and even in the successes or failures of various organizations and markets. The research issues stem not from skills and knowledge per se, but rather from their subsets, how they are organized, and how they take on market currency in the interactions of marketers and consumers on a global scale.

Globalization

Globalization is not a new phenomenon and has existed for several centuries through the clash of civilizations. Even so, four recent trends in globalization are noteworthy for our purposes: the information communication revolution, the rise of nonregulated capitalism, the fall of communism, and the freeing of countries in the Southern Hemisphere from colonial rule.

In arguing our case, we have positioned markets as a more appropriate unit of analysis for our field, subsuming the view of marketing as technique, and building from the V&L's emphases on intangible transactions, co-creation of value by consumers and marketers, and relationships. Markets composed of signs are situated within a global context, not as mere epiphenomenon, but rather as a contemporary condition of commerce. Forces contributing to the development of the sign economy, such as informational capitalism, network formation, and the weightless economy, are changing the way we view the world and the place of capitalism within it. As such, the time is right, indeed past, to set aside the dichotomy between products and services that has occupied marketers' attention for more than a quarter century in order to appreciate market transformations within the global economic domain.

First, as discussed previously, the world is changing as a result of the worldwide communications revolution. An important manifestation is the Internet. Its intensification of global communication has had a profound impact on the way marketing is conducted and subsequently on the structure and dynamics of markets.

Yet communications technology is not the only force demanding careful reconsideration of current thinking on global capitalism. In recent decades, the international order has moved away from regulated capitalism toward an idealized version of free-market capitalism. In understanding these global processes, we must distinguish the market economy from the democratic political system in which it is housed. Only then is it possible to appreciate the various ways in which countries in the world are embracing capitalism (e.g., China, United Arab Emirates) while maintaining somewhat altered forms of their political systems. We view these movements toward incorporating capitalist tendencies into various cultural systems as positive outcomes in creating a market economy. However, these developments remain outside the standard definition of capitalism as the three P's: the right to private property, the market as a clearinghouse for prices, and the quest for profits. On the face of it, these are economic factors, yet our more critical view illuminates them as various features of a global sign economy that is coterminous with various political systems.

The fall of communism is another misspecification, because it superimposes a dichotomous, Cold War rhetoric over a much more dynamic, complex reality. The "triumph of capitalism" ignores the many inherent conflicts between democracy and capitalism experienced in many postcolonial nations. Chua (2003) documents in several nations in Africa, Latin America, and Asia how numerical minorities who possess the majority of the assets in their nations clash with the majorities, the latter emboldened by democratic "rights" and "access."

DISCUSSION AND IMPLICATIONS

The first implication of our work stems from its substantive attention to the nexus of meanings and values at the center of market exchanges. More specifically, in directing attention to the working of the sign economy in producing markets via discourses and practices, we add an important dynamic more fundamental than that of the function/activity focus of the field. That is, though useful strategically, the tactical focus of the 4 P's is limited by its attention to products, as V&L note.

The second implication of this work stems from its more comprehensive and nuanced treatment of the market rather than the partial views emphasizing either marketers or consumers characterizing work in the *Journal of Marketing* and the *Journal of Consumer Research,* respectively. In a related point, significant theoretical development is made possible in comparing markets. Recognizing the socially constructed nature of markets draws attention to the importance of examining variations across societies and across time periods, while appreciating shared dimensions and principles as a function of emerging global institutional imperatives and constraints.

Third, in emphasizing the joint roles of market agents in constituting markets, we join forces with V&L and Kotler (1986) in working to replace disciplinary conventions favoring autonomous marketers and consumers with more interactive marketers and consumers co-creating value. Yet we go additional steps, emphasizing the ways in which they co-create meaning as well as value; their interdependence, as co-created subject positions; and the ways in which they jointly produce the marketplace. This reconceptualization provides a better understanding of market agents, their activities, and the impacts of marketing and consuming phenomena on society. For example, regarding the dynamics of power within markets, our work paradoxically better empowers marketers and consumers at the same time it humbles both groups of agents, because by examining markets, we see more clearly the complex ways in which each is beholden to the other, which complements the partial views emphasizing the respective powers and limitations of each.

The final implications of this work lie in its contributions to marketing managers. In line with the discussions regarding meaning and value at the heart of markets, and consumers as co-producers, is the necessary rethinking of the role of marketing as one of designing processes (Firat, Dholakia, and Venkatesh 1995) rather than providing products or services. Expertise in designing processes that allow and facilitate consumer involvement and participation in constructing significations and the resulting services and products is likely to become the key role and social usefulness of marketers.

Appreciating meanings and values of signs as fundamental elements at the heart of market exchanges better informs managers of what it is they are doing. We direct attention to how marketers build markets in their interactions with consumers, and replace the partial views of managing demand, managing the 4 P's, and achieving consumer satisfaction per the market concept. That is, from the perspective of our work, the marketing concept and consumer satisfaction are viewed as two signs with tremendous currency in market discourse. Like all signs, they have multiple referents, and this ambiguity accounts for much of market failures. Specifically, though appearing simple, achieving consumer satisfaction is anything but simple, as a function of the gaps in firms' attempts to operationalize consumer satisfaction as consumer-centered. Instead, consumer satisfaction must be completely overhauled to reflect the joint market enactment by consumers and marketers.

A second major application of interest to marketing managers is branding. We argue that as the sign system becomes intensified globally, research on branding should examine broader issues concerning how systems of signs are developed vis à vis particular social groups, and how they are used by members and nonmembers in negotiating not only identity, but also social relations within and across nations.

FUTURE DIRECTIONS

Future directions from this research stem from the need to completely revamp our understanding of marketers, consumers, and market organizations. So many basic concepts of consumer satisfaction, information processing, decision making, and strategic marketing development are predicated on individual, semiautonomous marketing and consuming agents. These concepts will be radically altered in replacing them with socioculturally constituted marketers and consumers who enact markets interactively, in and through the manipulation of signs. First, our view of marketers situated within the symbolic discourses and practices that they partially create opens up exciting research questions and possibilities of new configurations regarding the nature of their subjectivity and agency within participative markets. Second, our view of consumers challenges the conceptual house of cards built upon the framework of the individual, inviting reconceptualizations that give emphasis to consumers as agents positioned within groups with particular historical and social trajectories. Consumers, too, are situated within the market dynamics of symbolic discourses and practices that they partially create with marketers. Third, global branding represents another important area of study, as the full range of market stimuli must be reconsidered as jointly produced by marketers and consumers via the circle of market research and iterations of enacted symbolic discourses and practices. Fourth, the study of market organizations must be opened considerably to incorporate marketers repositioned within webs of interorganizational alliances, with links traversing nation-states and subcultures, consumers, and other organizations, and consumers positioned not as outside "targeted" subjects, but rather as in-house co-constitutors of market signs. Finally, even the conduct of research begs scrutiny, with calls to better calibrate researchers' cultural positions in relation to those they study.

NOTES

1. Vargo and Lusch (2004b) published another article in the *Journal of Service Research* that clarifies certain issues raised in their *Journal of Marketing* article. Since both articles are closely related and for reasons of space, we limit our attention in this chapter to Vargo and Lusch (2004a).

2. There are journals devoted to broader institutional/societal/cultural issues such as *Journal of Macromarketing, Consumption, Markets and Culture,* and *Journal of Consumer Policy,* but they have not yet become incorporated into mainstream marketing thought.

REFERENCES

Baudrillard, Jean (1981), *For a Critique of the Political Economy of the Sign.* St. Louis, MO: Telos.

Castells, Manuel (1996), "The Rise of the Network Society," *The Information Age, Economy, Society and Culture,*Vol. I. Oxford: Blackwell Publishers.

Chua, Amy (2003), *World on Fire: How Exporting Free Market Democracy Breeds Ethnic Hatred and Global Instability.* New York: Doubleday.

Constantin, James and Robert F. Lusch (1994), *Understanding Resource Management.* Oxford, OH: The Planning Forum.

Firat, A. F. and Alladi Venkatesh (1995), "Liberatory Postmodernism and the Re-enchantment of Consumption," *Journal of Consumer Research,* 22 (December), 239–67.

———, Nikhilesh Dholakia, and Alladi Venkatesh (1995), "Marketing in a Postmodern World," *European Journal of Marketing,* 29 (1), 40–56.

Fligstein, Neil (2003), *The Architecture of Markets: An Economic Sociology of Twenty-First-Century Capitalist Societies.* Princeton, NJ: Princeton University Press.

Goldman, Robert and Stephen Papson (1998), *Nike Culture.* Thousand Oaks, CA: Sage.

Habermas, Jürgen (1984), *The Theory of Communicative Action, (Vol I: Reason and Rationalization of Society.* Boston: Beacon Press.

Kohli, Ajay K. and Bernard J. Jaworski (1990), "Market Orientation: The Construct, Research Propositions, and Managerial Implications," *Journal of Marketing,* 59 (April), 1–18.

Kotler, Philip (1986), "The Emergent Prosumer," *The Futurist* (September/October), 24–28.

Levy, Sidney (1981), "Interpreting Consumer Mythology: A Structural Approach to Consumer Behavior," *Journal of Marketing,* 50 (Summer), 49–61.

Marchand, Roland (1998), *Creating the Corporate Soul: The Rise of Public Relations and Corporate Imagery in American Big Business.* Berkeley, CA: University of California Press.

O'Barr, William (1994), *Culture and the Ad: Exploring Otherness in the World of Advertising.* Boulder, CO: Westview Press.

Quah, Danny T. (1999), "The Weightless Economy in Growth," *The Business Economist,* 30 (1), 40–53.

Simmel, Georg (1978), *The Philospohy of Money,* trans. Tom Bottomore and David Frisby. London: Routledge & Kegan Paul.

Slater, Don and Fran Tonkiss (2001), *Market Society: Markets and Modern Social Theory.* Malden, MA: Blackwell Publishers, Inc.

Taylor, Frederick W. (1911), *The Principles of Scientific Management.* New York: Harper.

Vargo, Stephen L. and Robert F. Lusch (2004a), "Evolving to a New Dominant Logic for Marketing, *Journal of Marketing,* 68 (January), 1–17.

——— and ——— (2004b), "The Four Service Marketing Myths: Remnants of a Goods-Based, Manufacturing Model," *Journal of Service Research,* 6 (May), 324–35.

Weber, Max (1948), *The Protestant Ethic and the Spirit of Capitalism,* trans, Talcott Parsons. London: Routledge.

EXAMINING MARKETING SCHOLARSHIP AND THE SERVICE-DOMINANT LOGIC

WILLIAM L. WILKIE AND ELIZABETH S. MOORE

We are pleased to have the opportunity to offer our thoughts on this very fine initiative by Stephen Vargo and Robert Lusch (2004; hereafter V&L). Beyond its important substantive thesis, we extend our appreciation for several attributes of their article, including its (1) reliance on historical context, (2) careful attention to trends in thought development, and (3) search for both underlying forces and coherence in our field. We found much in the article that educated us, and much with which we concur. In addition—not surprising for any major undertaking so constrained by space limits—we also found several issues that we think merit further discussion.

Before delving into these, however, some brief background will help to explain our basic perspective. The commentary in this essay actually springs from a project that we've been involved in for some years: exploring aspects of the basic question, "What is marketing, anyway?" In our project we have been searching for meaningful ways to comprehend the totality and significance of our chosen field of study. Based on our work to date, we would highlight two particular points whose implications strike us as especially worthy of further examination on the S-D logic proposal. These are:

1. The S-D logic has a strong explicit focus on the firm, but this may lead to difficulties for more aggregate conceptions of the field of marketing.
2. The S-D logic appears to be seeking to offer a central gathering point from which marketing scholarship can proceed.

In this essay we mull over some ramifications of each of these points, not in an effort to debate or diminish the significance of S-D logic, but instead to better consider its promise and potential, as well as any pitfalls that may be lurking out there. In addition, Professor Lusch has recently led an American Marketing Association (AMA) effort to update the official definition for *marketing*. Our S-D logic discussion turns out to provide a natural basis for a brief commentary on the new definition, which we offer in the last section of this essay.

ISSUE 1: S-D LOGIC'S STRONG FOCUS ON THE FIRM IN LIGHT OF THE AGGREGATE MARKETING SYSTEM

The Aggregate Marketing System

The positioning of S-D logic is intended to form a fundamental reconceptualization of marketing. This makes it extremely important for our field and calls for careful consideration of any areas that might not have been sufficiently addressed by S-D logic at its present stage of development. As noted, we've identified aggregated levels of marketing as one such area and discuss our concerns here.

As background, we refer to our project's findings reported in the *Journal of Marketing's Special Millennium Issue*, under the title "Marketing's Contributions to Society" (Wilkie and Moore 1999). To capture the totality of an entire society, we (building on perspectives from an earlier era) proposed and explored the concept of an Aggregate Marketing System (AGMS), a huge, powerful, yet intricate complex operating to serve the needs of its host society. The AGMS is recognized as different in each society, an adaptive human and technological institution reflecting the idiosyncrasies of the people and their culture, geography, economic opportunities and constraints, and sociopolitical decisions. The three primary sets of actors within the system are (1) marketers, (2) consumers, and (3) government entities, whose public policy decisions are meant to facilitate the maximal operations of the AGMS for the benefit of the host society. As pointed out in the classic volume by Vaile, Grether, and Cox many years ago (1952), marketing systems perform two distinct macro tasks for their societies: (1) delivering the standard of living for the citizenry and (2) creating a marketplace dynamism that fosters and supports continual innovation and improvement such that the standard of daily life is enhanced over time.

We recognize that S-D logic is clearly not opposed to these goals and, in fact, is likely supportive of them. However, as a central organizing concept for the marketing field, how well does S-D logic represent more aggregated views of the system of marketing in our society? Does it have answers to the key issues encountered in this sphere? This is not entirely clear at the moment.

The Focus on the Firm as a "Level of Analysis" Decision

One of the fundamental characteristics of the S-D logic approach is that it represents a theoretical shift in marketing's *level of analysis*, here moving from the surface level of goods to the underlying level of service as the root focus for the field. We concur that shifting this level of analysis is feasible and that it does succeed in bringing us to a deeper and more generalized understanding of what is essential to marketing.

However, we want to highlight a different level-of-analysis issue that to our knowledge has not yet been addressed. We believe that this issue is of great importance and must be both recognized and carefully evaluated by marketing thinkers. This level-of-analysis issue reflects the fact that the V&L approach has marketing as fundamentally—and perhaps entirely—conceptualized as a firm-based set of activities or processes. For example, V&L (p. 5) state:

> The focus of marketing on core competences inherently places marketing at the center of the integration of business functions and disciplines.

Here—and in much of the material immediately preceding and following—it is clear that S-D logic is being rooted in organizational theory and that marketing is being conceived of as managerial in nature, grounded inside each organization employing it.

To be clear, it is not our position that this is *wrong*. Given the predominance of the managerial marketing perspective for the past half century, it certainly appears natural enough and might well even be the preference of many marketing scholars today if they were confronted with the need to choose. However, we do see it to be *incomplete*: Some significant questions do arise from this sole focus on the firm. We'll raise them here by asking, "Where does this take us with respect to more aggregated views of marketing?" It is our belief that S-D logic must be capable of dealing with a more aggregated perspective on marketing if it is to be viable and dominant.

For example, public policy is not mentioned at all in the S-D logic discussion. Although this is not a fatal flaw given the goals of the article, it does leave us with some uncertainty as to the capacity of this approach to deal with issues of the broader contexts and performance of marketing. To be clear, we know that V&L are aware of such broader issues, but it does not appear that these issues have been systematically considered in the work presented. We believe that this is precisely because the managerial perspective within a firm does not need to consider these questions in order to act in that firm's interest.

Given its nature, S-D logic is likely to fare well on some aggregate issues, but perhaps not on others. For example, several significant aggregate issues that should be discussed from an S-D logic perspective include the following:

- The *dynamic nature of the system*, bringing innovation, productivity gains, economic growth, and enhanced consumer welfare over time. We suspect that S-D logic will fare well on this dimension.
- The *role of existing characteristics of the AGMS*. Among current characteristics of the AGMS are an extensive and embedded infrastructure, practiced performance (expertise), and strong existing relationships that bring trust, confidence, and allow both risk taking and efficiency. Again, we believe that S-D logic will likely fare well on portions of this, though its treatment of embedded infrastructure is not currently obvious.
- The *competitive nature of the AGMS*. This dimension raises a potential difficulty. For example, when eight or twelve firms compete in a market, how do we assess the "marketing" that is occurring? It would appear inefficiencies would be natural in such settings. It is not clear how S-D logic would approach such a systemic analysis. Extended to public policy, how would antitrust enforcement likely be affected?

In fact, the competitive nature of our AGMS presents some further interesting questions to ponder, in which all three AGMS actors are implicated—marketers, consumers, and governments. We first discuss these in terms of marketers, then in terms of consumers and public policies.

"What Are the Essential Marketing Motivations?" We Wonder . . .

It seems to us that the greatest risk of equating the field of marketing with the managerial decisions being made inside all organizations is that the goals of those organizations are also being adopted by marketing thinkers, but without any external or neutral appraisal. That is, there is a "behind the scenes" accumulation across organizations that is just ignored when we think about our field. This leads to something akin to a lack of direction, or blanket approval, with regard to the reality of what the marketing world in total is undertaking, because we are never actually considering the larger aggregates of marketing activity. Having said this, let us be quick to clarify that we are aware that S-D logic seeks to place laudable service-related goals at the heart of each organization, much to its credit. Is this entirely possible, however? And, if it is only partially realistic, wouldn't it be worthwhile for all marketing scholars to appreciate any ramifications of falling short of this goal? Let us consider some issues that come to mind as we ponder this question:

• *When we adopt the goals of each organization, exactly whose perceived interests are being served, and does this matter to marketing?* A brief consideration of egregious examples found in political campaigning, lobbying, fraudulent schemes, bid rigging, energy gouging, channel stuffing, and so on is sufficient to alert us to the fact that this is not a minor matter and that many organizations are highly imperfect entities with a highly mixed set of motivations. Also, though S-D logic does not recommend this, in most organizations persons other than marketers are setting priorities. (Note: we recognize S-D logic's laudable objectives; however, we are concerned about marketing's fitting itself so neatly within the confines of individual organizations without regard to what else is going on both internally and externally.)

• *What about pricing under S-D logic?* This received little direct attention in V&L, yet it seems to us to be a necessary link to truly appraise the value of marketing programs. For example, we just recently heard of an analysis showing that—across providers—most users of cell phones end the month with a large number of unused calling minutes and that most customers were not enrolled in the plan best for them in terms of their actual phone usage. Would S-D logic propose that firms seek to better align these contracts, even though this might cost them revenue from their present customers? We can see that it might, but given the industry's cost structure and practices, how strongly would this be advocated, and how would it be advocated? More generally, for customers who exhibit unawareness/inertia in existing service relationships, would S-D logic propose that firms revise terms to better serve their partners' interests? If not, is S-D logic actually treating "service" in a complete manner? (Note: again, we realize what the current marketing world is doing with respect to pricing; we are just wondering whether S-D logic would recommend that it be done differently.)

• *We, together with many others in our field, conceive of ourselves as business academics, with interests in the actions, performance, and contributions of private and not-for-profit organizations in general.* This may not apply to S-D logic very directly, but we would ask what this logic might say about issues such as outsourcing, environmental concerns, demarketing, and other issues reflecting dimensions that might not be easily captured within single firm/customer relationships.

• In general, we are trying to raise the issue of what marketing is actually *doing* in our world, and much of this relates to the twin issues of marketplace competition and pressure for profitability and stock market price gains. Note that any such assessments of marketing performance are likely to benefit if taken from more aggregated perspectives, and these have yet to be provided. In the abstract, therefore, we ask, "Might it be possible for a marketer to pursue S-D logic yet simultaneously detract from the overall performance of the aggregate marketing system?" We are afraid the answer is yes.

• Finally, this line of thinking has helped us to realize how very much the managerial thrust of our field has relied on the Marketing Concept over the past half century. Because we have overtly characterized our field's mission as meeting the needs of customers, we have not had to continuously monitor what has actually been undertaken by the huge numbers of marketers who are working in parallel day after day after day. Also, our students over this entire time have been provided with a "comforting cloak of virtue" with which to learn about, and then themselves conduct, this field of endeavor. Again, this is no indictment of the S-D logic concept itself, but it does seem to be quite in keeping with the Marketing Concept, and we would be interested in better understanding their relationship.

How Well Does S-D Logic Comport with Essential Issues in Consumer Behavior?

On balance, we have come away with the thought that S-D logic appears to fit the business-to-business marketing context quite well. At the start, we wish to applaud V&L's intention to better suit offerings to consumers' wants and needs. We do see this characteristic of the marketing system to help create the dynamism that fosters increasing benefits (e.g., innovations, quality enhancements, improved value) that improve daily living in our society (see Wilkie and Moore 1999 for extended discussion). However, because consumer research has been our "home territory" within marketing, we do have several reactions and observations concerning consumer marketing.

Theoretical Bases in Consumer Research

It was interesting for us to find that S-D logic's emphasis on service follows very naturally from the essential thrust of much theory and method exhibited in consumer research since the 1950s and 1960s. For example, the popular area of multi-attribute models (e.g., Wilkie and Pessemier 1973) conceives of an individual's brand attitudes as being composed of weighted beliefs about the object's delivery of valued outcomes for that consumer. This position has also been long maintained in the economist Kelvin Lancaster's (1972) theory of characteristics of goods, in Russell Haley's (1968) proposal for benefit segmentation as a marketing tool, and in the considerable work on decompositional methods in multidimensional scaling, including conjoint benefit bundles (e.g., Green and Wind 1973), as well as in the laddering methodology mentioned in V&L (Reynolds and Gutman 1988). Thus, S-D logic's emphasis on service does clearly comport with much of consumer behavior theory. However, as a dominant logic for marketing itself, the close identification with every organization (firm) raises some other difficult issues that are worth exploring.

Marketing's Inputs into Consumers' Resource Allocation Decisions

One of the major tasks confronting every consumer with a finite budget is to decide on how to allocate his or her purchases, as well as the time and effort to be expended on each. But what if we ask, "How well do marketers help consumers with their budget- and effort-allocation decisions?" Our short answer: "Very poorly." In the aggregate (i.e., all marketers taken together) our marketing system simply proposes far too much consumption for any individual to come close to undertaking. The system acts as if consumer resources and wants are infinite and insatiable: Every product and service category is advocated as worthy of consumption for virtually every consumer. It thus becomes mandatory for every consumer to ignore most marketing programs, resist many others, and respond positively to only a relative few (see Wilkie 1994, chapter 2, for a discussion of this perspective). Our point here is that the extreme heterogeneity of marketing activity cannot possibly serve an individual consumer well in terms of personal allocation choices (excepting in a partially informative sense), and this characteristic surely makes it difficult to equate each marketer's best interest with each consumer's best interest, which is what seems to lie at the heart of the S-D logic thesis.

This same issue arises if we narrow our focus to firms within specific product or service categories. Within each category, marketers as a set are offering each consumer completely conflicting advice as to which sources (both brand and retailer) to select. The system's marketers are also often employing intrusive persuasive attempts, demanding attention and consideration from consumers who would not be best served by the option being advocated. This is not a criticism but a descriptive characteristic of our marketing system. And although S-D logic does advocate improvements, it has yet to grapple with this aggregate difficulty.

"Information Asymmetry" Is a Fundamental Characteristic of the Consumer Environment

The study of consumer behavior—as well as applied work within the public policy sphere of consumer protection—provides overwhelming evidence of a substantial disparity between the resources that marketers and consumers bring to the marketplace. Consider that each marketer specializes in only a few categories, brings financial investment to bear, and possesses considerable expertise and experience with respect to both the entity being sold and the selling processes that will work most effectively. Moreover, marketing managers typically provide only partial information to customers—those inputs that reflect most positively on the offered alternative.

The information asymmetry characteristic then reflects the gap between this expertise and the activity of the marketer relative to the typical prospective buyer (Maynes 1997). On the other side of transactions, we often find a consumer who has had to spread his or her attention across a wide range of categories, is limited in time and financial resources, and probably possesses little expertise or experience with either the entity being sold or the selling processes involved. (Even when consumers are relatively experienced or sophisticated, some gap will still inherently exist.) Beyond this, some consumers will at times be subject to forces of impulsivity, social influence, compulsion, financial straits that demand credit availability, and so forth. These additional forces can exacerbate the base condition of information asymmetry between sellers and the consumer. It is important to recognize that information asymmetry is a natural outgrowth of a specialization-based economic system and not a criticism of marketing or marketers themselves. However, information asymmetry does yield enhanced powers to marketers in influencing and directing transactions toward their benefit. So, although individual marketing managers view consumer success as challenging to achieve, as can be seen clearly in the aggregate, marketers hold great potential power to influence consumers' perceptions, purchase choices, and actual consumption portfolios.

What are the implications for S-D logic, then? Primarily, that marketers will have considerable responsibilities for determining how best to serve consumers' needs. Furthermore, if consumers often are not aware of their own needs and best options for satisfying them, they will be unable to communicate reliable information about them. Thus, it is possible that oftentimes outside observers, including marketers, will not be able to know how best to serve those consumers either. Moreover, because each marketer's self-interests call for affirmative sales efforts and a financial stream back to the firm, and because multiple marketers will be competing for a single choice, it is not at all clear to us that an S-D logic–based marketing system will be able to meet consumers' needs in anything like an optimal fashion. Thus, although S-D logic might well improve performance, we are concerned that the remaining gap is still likely to be large. We would point to this topic as a very significant and complex research question (i.e., What is the upper capacity of S-D logic to truly serve each customer's best interests?).

Internally Inconsistent Consumer Motivations

Consumers' motivations are not always straightforward, which further complicates the challenge for S-D logic to achieve its goals in the consumer marketplace. Consider the extremely large number of products and services that holds potential for social or physical harm (as well as benefits, to be sure). In the food industry, for example, we find that many consumers will at times pursue taste at the expense of health or nutrition, leading to such dangerous long-term effects as obesity, heart attacks, and diabetes. How would an S-D logic marketing approach differ for the firms in this industry? What would McDonald's, for instance, be advised to do to better serve their customers' best interests? Should its menu offerings be sharply altered toward healthy intake only? Should some obese individuals even be refused service? These kinds of issues spiral into further difficulties when we consider product usage issues that might impact on other persons than the purchaser. What about gun manufacturers, or cigarette makers, or alcohol purveyors? How far is it reasonable to ask S-D logic marketers to go in pursuit of truly serving the best interests of their customers, and how different would it be if they did? (Note: these are interesting questions. We don't presume to have answers for them, but they seem fair issues for further consideration in terms of the central tenets for our field.)

Do Consumers Really Want Relationships?

Two of the eight foundational premises (FPs) at the heart of S-D logic involve the customer as co-producer (FP_6) and relationship marketing (FP_8).[1] Each proposes very close, even symbiotic ties between marketer and customer. With respect to co-production, we can appreciate this as a definitional point regarding the process orientation of S-D logic. Also, the concept of co-production does seem to fit many business-to-business marketing situations.

However, we are not sure how frequently this concept of co-producer is descriptively true for the actual motivations and behaviors of consumers themselves. Consider, for example, how many consumers fail to read owner's manuals and never bother to learn how to employ the many options available in modern electronics products. Why do they not? Clearly their perception is that they are completely at liberty to care for and use their purchases in whatever manners they wish. They do not perceive themselves as holding continued responsibility to sellers; we suspect that most consumers would be shocked to be chastised for "falling down on the job" for their new purchases!

With respect to relationship marketing, we have quite parallel reactions. Here it appears that S-D logic must also account for additional motivations and consumption habits of the consumer marketplace. In general, we would recommend a careful consideration of the types of costs or drawbacks that a consumer might associate with stronger and more numerous marketer relationships. Chief among these are issues related to a loss of consumer freedoms. For example, some consumers value privacy highly and could see intimate marketer relationship efforts as unduly intrusive. Many consumers also value the pleasures associated with spending and acquiring and might wish to retain perceived anonymity while doing so. Furthermore, curiosity and variety-seeking are common motivations for consumers, and strong single-source relationships might restrict perceived freedoms in this area. Relatedly, consumers react positively to innovations and might be restricted from pursuing some of these by the bounds of such relationships. If switching costs are higher (as would seem to be desirable from the S-D logic business model), consumers' enjoyment in learning about new offerings through shopping or browsing, Web surfing, discussions with friends, and so forth might likewise be seen to be restricted.

Finally, we again must refer to the fact that there are multiple competing marketers wishing to have relationships with each consumer, and it is not obvious to us that in many categories a typical consumer would want to forgo this appealing facet of the marketplace. Most consumers do switch brands, shop at multiple stores, and have "consideration sets" consisting of more than one alternative during purchase processes for most acquisitions. Does S-D logic seek to change these consumer practices? If so, S-D logic managers might want to consider the possibility that consumers are natural polygamists: They desire to be affectionate but are not pledging to be necessarily faithful to a single marketer relationship. If we consider this issue from an aggregated perspective again—especially considering the twin forces of positive change in offerings as well as direct competition among multiple firms seeking a consumer's patronage—it is more clear why it might be questionable for a consumer to stick to a single-source relationship and refuse to consider what else is out there that is available to them.

ISSUE 2: THE NEW DOMINANT LOGIC AS THE FOCAL POINT FOR MARKETING SCHOLARSHIP

Our second basic issue to consider with regard to S-D logic has to do with today's world of academic marketing scholarship. As background, our basic perspectives are captured in the Fall 2003 *Journal of Public Policy and Marketing* article titled "Scholarly Research in Marketing: Exploring the '4 Eras' of Thought Development" (Wilkie and Moore 2003). In this effort we examined the development and evolution of marketing thought across the past 100 years, including the growth of the knowledge infrastructure (e.g., journals, associations, conferences) and the trends and paradigms characterizing thought progression in the field.

We were pleased to find Vargo and Lusch (2004) to be quite consonant with our own ideas in many respects, including portions of the historical analysis. The dates they cite in their historical portion correspond to important turning points that we characterized as well, with a turn to the marketing management orientation around 1950, and another major set of changes occurring about 1980. Because of a different focus from V&L, we did not assess the substantive domain of managerial thought in recent times and did not cover S-D logic–related issues to any appreciable extent. However, we did identify several other characteristics that pertain to this essay. First, our Era III (1950–1980) was characterized by twin forces that came to dominate marketing thought (and that still do today): (1) the aforementioned marketing-as-management orientation and (2) the scientific approach that came to dominance in marketing about the same time as the managerial focus, with a huge impact on how thought development has been pursued in the field in the years since. Second, our Era IV (1980 to present) has been characterized by several key trends, including the globalization of marketing thought and a fragmentation of the mainstream of marketing thought. Third, over the entire period we observed that the issues and approaches taken up in marketing thought have tended to reflect the larger developments of the society of the time (e.g., world wars, economic depression, baby boom). Fourth, also across the entire period, we noted that marketing thinkers have exhibited highly volitional choices as to which topics and approaches they adopt and study.

Thus, the case mounted by V&L is generally in keeping with two of our observations (adopting the managerial perspective and drawing from real developments in marketing), which augers well for positive recognition among marketing academics. S-D logic's very ambitious goal to represent the central focus for the marketing field, however, also raises our other two observations (involving fragmentation of the mainstream of marketing thought, plus the highly volitional orientation of thought leaders), and on these we are less sanguine.

Modern Scholarship in Marketing: The Fourth Era of Thought Development

Our analysis characterizes the time from 1980 to the present as Era IV (Wilkie and Moore 2003). Evolving out of predecessor Era III (1950–1980), this modern period is characterized by a body of marketing thought that is both focused at micro levels (i.e., individual firms and customers) and driven by scientific premises and methods. In addition, three major developments character-ize this time, each with implications for the impact of S-D logic.

Trend 1: Marketing Education Goes Global

Era IV has seen a dramatic globalization of business concepts, as entire blocs of nations have moved toward market-based systems and away from centralized command and control. The Rus-sian Association of Business Education now numbers more than fifty schools, all formed within the past fifteen years, and the Central and Eastern European Management Association now has more than 100 member schools, up from only thirteen in 1989. In China, more than sixty new master of business administration (MBA) programs have been accredited in only the past ten years, and these MBA programs now receive the largest number of applications of any field of graduate study in China (Wilkie and Moore 2003). Growth is not limited to transitional nations, moreover, with substantial developments also occurring in the European Union as well as else-where around the world.

What does this have to do with S-D logic? This is an interesting question to consider, because it might involve the "context-adaptive" character of our field. Does the concept hold up well for societies that are dramatically different in terms of size, infrastructure presence, monetized mar-kets, growth, and/or sociopolitical policies? How appropriate is it for different stages of eco-nomic growth? Furthermore, must S-D logic be adapted for cultures in which negotiation is the norm? These types of questions are increasingly important as the world continues to globalize in the future.

Trend 2: An Outpouring of New Marketing Journals

Our historical analysis revealed an interesting development at the start of Era IV—in just the five short years from 1980 to 1984, the number of research-based journals in marketing more than doubled, from seven to fifteen (Wilkie and Moore 2003). This burst of activity reflected more than growth in the field: Most of the new entries were specialized outlets aimed at narrower constituencies within the marketing field. For example, *Marketing Science,* the *Journal of Public Policy and Marketing,* and the *Journal of Product Innovation and Management* all began at this point. This growth in journals has continued in the ensuing years: Baumgartner and Pieters (2003) report forty-nine marketing-related journals in their recent analysis of citation patterns in the field. But what does this have to do with S-D logic? We see little direct implication but have significant indirect concerns emanating from this evidence of increased specialization within the academic community of marketing, which has in turn led to a fragmentation of the field of thought.

Trend 3: A Fragmentation of the Mainstream of Marketing Thought

We view S-D logic as an effort to bring a new coherence to marketing thought and accept this to be a worthy goal. At the same time, marketing is an extremely broad field that is presently charac-terized by research specialization and a fragmentation of work and interests. This is a serious issue for scholarship in our field (Wilkie and Moore 2003). It is worth considering what implica-tions this holds for how S-D logic will be received and by whom.

First, we believe that this fragmentation is a by-product of many marketing scholars having cho-sen to pursue science in their work, striving for greater theoretical depth and methodological rigor in extending specific streams of inquiry. In the context of the Brinberg-McGrath framework (1985), we have seen marketing scholarship move increasingly to focus on the theoretical and method-ological domains in its research focus. This movement has been taken at the expense of the substantive domain, into which marketing management most easily falls.

Consider what leading marketing academics are engaged in today and in what they are most intensely interested. The two major research conferences in the field focus on consumer research (the Association for Consumer Research [ACR]) and quantitative methods (Marketing Science). Meanwhile, the major conferences of the American Marketing Association—our field's main-stream marketing organization—have clearly lost their status as leading academic research con-vocations. Notably, it must be recognized that the emphasis at the ACR and Marketing Science conferences is on academic rigor and discovery, not application. And, although some findings presented there do have relevance to marketers, the predominant thrust is not managerial (in the sense that the value of a paper would be judged in terms of its impact on marketing practice).

Turning to the top four academic journals in marketing, we see a very similar situation. Only the *Journal of Marketing (JM)* would be seen as a natural outlet for the S-D logic article, or for almost anything else seeking to speak directly to marketing strategy issues: The *Journal of Mar-keting Research (JMR), Journal of Consumer Research (JCR),* and *Marketing Science (MS)* are clearly positioned more directly within quantitative or behavioral science. (Note: the reality at *JCR* is that marketing's managerial concerns are not at the center of concern: In our historical study we examined the first twenty years of JCR and found only three of nearly 900 articles to have the word *marketing* in the title [Wilkie and Moore 2003].)

Does any of this vitiate the basic S-D logic claims? Not precisely, but it does raise the question of how deeply foundational this perspective will be seen to be by many members of marketing academia, in that it does not capture very well what they are doing. Attention to this issue could thus be worthwhile on the part of S-D logic advocates concerned with reaching out across the marketing academic discipline. To illustrate what we mean here, let us consider an example from Vargo and Lusch (2004, p. 14) that recommends changes for the college curriculum:

> The consumer behavior course might evolve to increased emphasis on relationship phe-nomena such as brand identification, value perception, and the role of social and relational norms in co-production and repeat patronage.

Some faculty members probably do teach consumer behavior with an approach that fits well with this proposed curriculum and might readily adopt it. However, even though the statement is very brief and maybe even mild, other academics will surely object. What is it about this state-ment that might be potentially unattractive for the consumer behavior course?

Several points immediately appear. Some consumer researchers would object that it does not approach consumer behavior as a phenomenon to be studied in its own right, despite the fact that consumer spending accounts for about two-thirds of gross domestic product in the United States. Others would object that it appears not to reflect the theoretical underpinnings of this field—such topics as consumer motivation, perception, learning, search, decision making, and so forth—instead stressing quite derivative issues such as repeat patronage. Still others would point out that it fails to reflect the consumer's perspective on consumer behavior, but instead is "a marketer egocentric view" that simply substitutes issues of importance to a manager.

We should note that one of us is an author of three editions of a consumer behavior textbook (e.g., Wilkie 1994), and that we have given much thought to this issue. Our view is that all of these criticisms are valid. Educators in the marketing field continuously face the issue of just how dominant vocational job training should be within our college curriculum. On the flip side, educators also face a serious question about how deeply our students ought to be educated in the basic disciplines underpinning marketing. Given the large presence of overtly applied managerial courses already in the curriculum, we believe that the consumer behavior class needs to be an academic offering that meets all of the objections just listed. We believe that this is not only the best approach to advance marketing thought, but also that its presence in the curriculum provides a strong background for future managers to draw on in their work. This point is subtle but central to scholars: It would probably be wise for S-D logic proponents to consider it further, as at present this curriculum suggestion seems to be out of step with the academic values that drive the members of both ACR and Institute for Operations Research and Management Sciences (INFORMS).

Note that the root character of S-D logic does fit well with both ACR and INFORMS. Moreover, there is no fundamental problem with the topics being advocated: They could certainly be included in the coverage of a consumer behavior course. Rather, this difficulty relates to the "dominant" label, and the willingness to override the academic priorities of a specialized research area. More specifically, this problem stems—as we indicate throughout this essay—from the implicit assumption that all of marketing thought should revolve around how to make a firm successful, rather than reflect a broader perspective on our field. In this example, as written, S-D logic simply does not advocate enough study of "consumers as consumers."

CLOSING COMMENTARY: ON THE NEW DEFINITION OF MARKETING

Background on the Issue

Just recently the AMA convened a process (under Professor Robert Lusch) to update the definition of *marketing*.[2] The first formal AMA definition had been developed in 1935, was retained for fifty years until being modified in 1985, and has now been modified again in 2004. Here are the three definitions:

> (Marketing is) the performance of business activities that direct the flow of goods and services from producers to consumers (1935).

> (Marketing is) the process of planning and executing the conception, pricing, promotion, and distribution of ideas, goods and services to create exchanges that satisfy individual and organizational objectives (1985).

> Marketing is an organizational function and a set of processes for creating, communicating and delivering value to customers and for managing customer relationships in ways that benefit the organization and its stakeholders (2004).

Examining these definitions in turn reveals a narrowing of focus over time, quite in accord with the historical trends discussed both in Wilkie and Moore (2003) and V&L (2004). Notice that until 1985 the field's definition was pluralistic, thereby easily translatable to more aggregated issues such as competition, system performance, and contributions to consumer welfare. The 1985 change then firmly turned focus toward the manager's tasks as embodied in the 4 P's. (In addition, by focusing on the concept of mutually satisfactory exchanges it implicitly defined marketing to be in the best interests of consumers.) Overall, these changes made it more difficult to adopt more aggregated perspectives on the field.

The new 2004 definition is much in the same spirit, with a singular focus on the individual organization acting alone. This is not simply our reading, but is also clear from the leaders of the initiative. For example, according to Professor Greg Marshall, who headed the AMA's Academic Division: "What we (now) have is more strategic. Now it says marketing is really something that makes the organization run" (in Keefe 2004, p. 17).

Needed: A Definition for Marketing Scholarship?

The conception of marketing as a strategic and tactical activity undertaken within individual organizations is a most reasonable view for marketing managers to take, and the modern S-D logic thrust will move the impacts of this activity into higher and more central positions within organizations. However, what should marketing academics be doing? Is it incumbent to adopt this view of the field of marketing? In our view, this organizational focus for the entire field of marketing does not speak to the concerns of many (even most) scholars who are concerned with the development of knowledge about marketing, including those focusing on consumer behavior, research methods and models, and larger impacts on societies. As we discuss in our "4 Eras" article, we perceive a great need for marketing academia to deal with its own issues of current fragmentation, including special attention to the content and cultivation of doctoral programs (Wilkie and Moore 2003).

When interviewed about the definitional development process, Professor Lusch spoke directly to the societal portion of this issue when reflecting on the diversity of the views offered during the process:

> Some view [marketing] as a managerial activity, but others view it as a broad societal activity . . . Europeans and Australians, for example, were most likely to argue that marketing is a societal process. . . . I don't disagree, but . . . because it's used to introduce students to the discipline, we needed something comprehensible (in Keefe 2004, p. 18).

We have long admired Professor Lusch's views and work and realize that he has had to make conscious choices with this definition. It is telling, however, that the AMA seems to be pointing toward introductory students with the definition. To the extent that this is the case, perhaps it is not intended to be very directive to scholarly pursuits in marketing, and thus our concerns about the definition are actually not very serious. For what it is worth, though, we would like to take this opportunity to weigh in on the side of those who suggested that marketing is best understood as a societal process with great impacts on the day-to-day lives of the people it serves. We further believe that these impacts should clearly be identified and studied as an integral portion of the academic field we call marketing.

In closing, we again congratulate Professors Vargo and Lusch on their fine contribution to marketing thought. We appreciate having had the opportunity to share our thoughts and recommendations in this essay.

NOTES

1. Foundational premise 6 (p. 10) is "The customer is always a co-producer." Foundational premise 8 (p. 11) is "A service-centered view is customer oriented and relational."

2. Readers interested in pursuing this topic should consult a very informative article (Keefe 2004) in *Marketing News*.

REFERENCES

Baumgartner, Hans and Rik Pieters (2003), "The Structural Influence of Marketing Journals: A Citation Analysis of the Discipline and Its Subareas over Time," *Journal of Marketing*, 67 (April), 123–39.

Brinberg, David and Joseph E. McGrath (1985), *Validity and the Research Process*. Beverly Hills, CA: Sage Publications.

Green, Paul E. and Yoram Wind (1973), *Multi-Attribute Decisions in Marketing*. Hinsdale, IL: Dryden.

Haley, Russell I. (1968), "Benefit Segmentation: A Decision-Oriented Research Tool," *Journal of Marketing*, 32 (July), 30–35.

Keefe, Lisa M. (2004), "What Is the Meaning of 'Marketing'?" *Marketing News* (September 15), 17–18.

Lancaster, Kelvin (1972), *Consumer Demand: A New Approach*. New York: Columbia University Press.

Maynes, E. Scott (1997), "Consumer Problems in Market Economies," in *Encyclopedia of the Consumer Movement*, Stephen Brobeck, ed. Santa Barbara, CA: ABC-CLIO, 158–63.

Reynolds, Thomas J. and Jonathan Gutman (1988), "Laddering Theory, Method, Analysis and Interpretation," *Journal of Advertising Research*, 28 (February/March), 11–31.

Vaile, Roland S., E.T. Grether, and Reavis Cox (1952), *Marketing in the American Economy*. New York: Ronald Press Company.

Vargo, Stephen L. and Robert F. Lusch (2004), "Evolving to a New Dominant Logic for Marketing," *Journal of Marketing*, 68 (January), 1–17.

Wilkie, William L. (1994), *Consumer Behavior*, 3rd ed. New York: John Wiley & Sons.

——— and Elizabeth S. Moore (1999), "Marketing's Contributions to Society," *Journal of Marketing*, 63 (Special Millennium Issue), 198–218.

——— and——— (2003), "Scholarly Research in Marketing: Exploring the '4 Eras' of Thought Development," *Journal of Public Policy and Marketing*, 22 (Fall), 116–46.

——— and Edgar A. Pessemier (1973), "Issues in Marketing's Use of Multi-Attribute Models." *Journal of Marketing Research*, 10 (November), 428–41.

21

SOME SOCIETAL AND ETHICAL DIMENSIONS OF THE SERVICE-DOMINANT LOGIC PERSPECTIVE OF MARKETING

GENE R. LACZNIAK

In the January 2004 issue of the *Journal of Marketing,* Vargo and Lusch (2004; hereafter V&L) formally unveiled their service-dominant logic (S-D logic) framework for understanding marketing theory and practice. Their perspective postulates a comprehensive, service-centered conception of marketing that is grounded in eight foundational premises (FPs). The S-D logic exhibits a great flexibility because it can incorporate beneath its umbrella many of the evolving literatures in marketing including customer relationship marketing (CRM), value and supply chain analysis, total quality management, service management models, network analysis, and others. If not revolutionary, the S-D logic approach is importantly evolutionary, as it envisions all economic exchange as consisting of intangible elements (i.e., skills and knowledge) rather than mostly tangible resources. It also interjects the customer as a co-producer rather than mainly a receiver of imbedded value through products purchased, and it takes a relational perspective of consumers and marketers rather than a more static transactional approach. As the full details of the S-D logic approach for marketing are set forth elsewhere in this volume, I truncate my own description of the paradigm itself. However, my overall impression of this framework is captured well by the comments of Hunt (2004, p. 28), who wrote, "As bespeaks an important and potentially seminal article, Vargo and Lusch's argument is historically crafted, properly interdisciplinary and logically sound. Their position deserves a careful read and thoughtful evaluation."

Consistent with this call for further evaluation, I would submit that the S-D logic approach implies certain social and ethical dimensions about the marketing process that need to be specified and discussed as the S-D logic perspective is further refined and extended. Therefore, this essay engages some of the social-ethical issues implied in the S-D logic conception of marketing. It is also intended to begin a sustained dialogue about the macro implications of a service-centered model as the basic analytic framework for marketing activity. The comments offered here should be seen not as a criticism of the S-D logic but as friendly amendments to the thoughtful and pioneering work of V&L.

My reading of the S-D logic finds little to suggest that its views imply stakeholders should be ignored or that its net influence will be antisociety. On the contrary, its conception of the customer (and employees) as operant resources to be partnered with for the long term rather than manipulated (like operand resources) predominantly for short-run value-added, is both insightful and encouraging from a societal standpoint. However, without further articulation, the S-D logic can be interpreted too comfortably as an unqualified endorsement of the "invisible hand" school of thought (Jennings 2003, pp. 53–54), in which society always is best served when shareholder benefits are maximized by exchange. The S-D logic appears to be richer and more flexible than this inherently narrow view. Therefore, this article sets forth to extrapolate some of the social-ethical elements and macro implications of the S-D logic approach and challenges other academics to continue and extend that conversation.

Using especially foundational premises (FPs) 3, 4, 6, and 8 of V&L as the starting points for my commentary, this essay proposes to supplement and amplify portions of the S-D logic approach by specifically developing the following four related points:

1. The "higher order benefits" of service provision referenced in the S-D logic framework must be understood and explored not only for consumers but for society as a whole.
2. The learning (i.e., marketplace) feedback that accrues to organizations from their service provisions should be more broadly conceived than merely financial feedback.
3. Although it is both insightful and useful to envision the customer as a co-producer in the marketing process, stakeholders should also be conceived as co-participants in the consumption, value creation, and delivery process of marketing exchange.
4. For service provision to be truly "customer oriented and relational," it must foster a level of trust that embodies authentic rather than only contractual customer expectations.

Each of these points is illustrated with examples and grounded in [ethical] theory as appropriate.

WHERE DOES SOCIETY FIT INTO THE S-D LOGIC FRAMEWORK?

In FP$_3$ (goods and distribution mechanisms for service provision), tangible goods are relegated to functioning as appliances for service provision. The S-D logic approach creatively conceives of tangible goods predominantly as platforms for the provision of higher-order benefits to consumers (V&L, p. 9). This denotation is necessary to fully develop later points about [intangible] knowledge development and exchange as a foundational dimension of marketing. Presumptive in these observations are an associated evaluation (i.e., marketing research) to be conducted by the firm about the effectiveness of how well desired benefits are being provided to consumers. At several points in their essay, V&L make reference to undertaking such analysis. For example, they write, "The service-centered view of marketing perceives marketing as a continuous learning process (directed at improving operant resources)" (p. 4). However, on an aggregate level, it seems also imperative to further delineate the influence of service provisions not only for the "value proposition" received by consumers but for society as a whole. This is because many services have not only ramifications for the primary parties to the exchange but also secondary and tertiary effects on the larger social system. For example, substantial numbers of consumers are satisfied (more or less) with products they might have ordered as a result of spam advertising conducted over the Internet. Presumably, spam advertising continues to grow because it generates sales. Yet the majority of consumers might wish spam advertising to be severely restricted or eliminated entirely (i.e., a secondary effect) despite the presence of many consumers who are happy (i.e., providing positive marketplace feedback) about the economic exchange. The federal "can spam" legislation as well as a wide variety of state and federal initiatives directed at mitigating Internet advertising via e-mail are testimony to such attitudes. Similarly, large sport utility vehicles (SUVs) apparently generate a notable level of "higher-order benefits" to buyers given their growing sales revenue for dealers and their popularity as a vehicle category. Nevertheless, due to large SUV gasoline consumption rates, their capacity for taking up extra parking space, and the incremental crash danger to others from these suburban trucks, various social critics wonder whether various costs of the vehicle's use by owners, created internal to the service provision, are not being externalized on society.

It seems important to remember from a macro, social standpoint, that although consumers and marketers are "co-creating" the parameters of a service provision—to use the language of the S-D logic model—marketers, due to their familiarity with the category of exchange they participate in, often have greater expertise than the buyer participants in the co-production of the service. The upshot of this situation is that, in some instances, a *higher* social responsibility falls to the (more informed) marketer participant concerning areas of the exchange where they hold greater expertise. For example, with regard to safety issues, service provision appliances such as all-terrain vehicles (ATVs) or personal watercraft (e.g., Jet Skis) have inherent safety/operational issues that require marketer disclosure regardless of how the buyer is trying to refine (i.e., co-produce) the exchange. Similarly, in the financial services sector, because of the complexity of some transactions (e.g., various methods for expanding the magnitude of consumer credit for the marginally creditworthy), marketers have a duty not to deceive or mislead concerning the implications for these consumers of undertaking additional debt. Therefore, marketer-sponsored counseling ought to be conducted to better inform the buyer, no matter how the consumer is trying to shape this exchange. Within the purview of the S-D logic approach, my point is that as consumers show a greater disposition to help customize and define the service exchanges with various marketers, sellers, as responsible co-producers, still have a duty to disclose substantive dimensions of the exchange if they involve relevant consumer rights issues such as safety, informed choice, and the buyers' rights to redress.

Also looming in the background above the fray of the many autonomistic, micro-level exchanges that are occurring, are numerous questions at the macro level about how the higher-order benefits to consumers inherent in the service provision are affecting the society as a whole. In other words, I raise the issue of how the marketing system is helping co-create economic exchange, with an eye to fairness and justice for all. A good example of such a system-outcomes problem is the so-called digital divide. According to many social observers, it appears that a fairly substantial segment of the U.S. general public (mostly low income, probably with lower education, and largely with less financial literacy) has been "virtually" isolated without easy access to broadband networking. Many of the favorable exchange opportunities provided by an increasingly robust and dynamic e-commerce market are closed off to this group. Clearly this outcome is the fault of no one marketer or group of marketers. But it is a reality nonetheless that has resulted from how resources are being employed in the marketing system. Future manifestations of the S-D logic framework should begin to address such questions concerning distributive justice, if it appears that the exchange system is evolving in a manner whereby the opportunity to participate in categories of exchanges that lead to higher-order benefits are somehow systematically restricted for certain segments of buyers (e.g., the elderly, immigrants, the handicapped) thereby disadvantaging them as equal access consumers.

HOW SHOULD SUCCESS BE EVALUATED WITHIN THE S-D LOGIC FRAMEWORK?

In FP_4 (knowledge is the fundamental source of competitive advantage), it is postulated that knowledge is the basic operant resource and represents the basis for compelling value propositions to consumers. This concept is another valuable contribution of the S-D logic framework. V&L observe that the firm's success in the knowledge discovery process is always being gauged against similar information being provided to the competition. Specifically, "The firm primarily knows whether it is making better value propositions from the feedback it receives from the marketplace in terms of firm financial performance" (V&L, p. 5).

This FP is an important part of the S-D logic model because it articulates how individual firms can judge how they are being successful within the parameters of the S-D logic framework. "The process of competition and the information provided by profits result in competition being a knowledge discovery process" (V&L, p. 9). And therefore, as knowledge is leveraged for the purpose of competitive advantage, it becomes a source of power (i.e., a sustainable value proposition) for a given firm. In commenting on this element of the S-D logic, Day (2004, p. 18) insightfully states that the central role of knowledge in this framework "raises the question of who will be advantaged or disadvantaged as the competitive landscape changes."

This last observation raises another significant social-ethical concern about the S-D logic model. Specifically, the learning feedback gleaned from the marketplace about "knowledge discovered" from service provision ought to be evaluated more broadly than only the financial performance records of individual service providers. Inherently, it is important to observe that the S-D logic framework does not endorse profit maximization or the view that the return on investment is the exclusive measure of management success or even that short-run financial measures are of the most critical importance. But one can get that impression based on some of the comments made about evaluation within the S-D logic model. V&L write, "This logic views financial results not as an end result but as a test of a market hypothesis about a value proposition" (p. 3). Similarly, the authors write that one measures "marketplace feedback by analyzing financial performance from exchange to learn how to improve the firm's offering to customers and improve financial performance" (p. 5). In this regard, an important observation about the S-D logic model is that although financial feedback is necessary, as it is both useful and convenient owing to its quantitative nature, true learning about better value propositions in the long run involves a discernment about outcomes that goes beyond financial accounting. The societal concept of marketing, first popularized by Kotler in the 1970s and endorsed in a variety of textbooks since then, conceives of a marketing system in which "organizations determine the needs and wants of target markets and then strive to deliver superior value to customers in a way that maintains or improves the customers *and the society's well being*" (Armstrong and Kotler 2003 [emphasis in the original]). Measures of a firm's success that go beyond financials and incorporate broader constituencies into the evaluation process might include treatment of stakeholders (more about this in the next section), a firm's track record of providing employment, and a company's willingness to undertake responsibilities of corporate citizenship such as volunteerism by executives and employees as well as charitable giving and other community-building activities.

The S-D logic framework is not contrary to a societal orientation, because service provision well delivered generates positive financial feedback as one of its by-products rather than as a philosophy driving the model itself. V&L suggest that the S-D logic approach, with customer responsiveness properly integrated into a firm's marketing philosophy, "positions service, the application competences for the benefit of the consumer, as the core of the firm's mission" (p. 14). In this way, the consumer is well served, and financial success accrues as an outcome of effective resource utilization, allowing the firm to discharge socially beneficial activities as well, if it so chooses. Nevertheless, it is important that future discussions of the S-D logic model do not simply (and falsely) reduce themselves to short-run financials as the primary measure of whether successful "knowledge discovery" is taking place in the firm or whether knowledge is being translated into beneficial service provision. Instead, more thought should be given to other possible feedback measures of wider scope, including emerging approaches such as the balanced scorecard (Kaplan and Norton 1992) and the "triple bottom line"—a system of evaluation that measures not only financial performance but also the firm's social impact and environmental track record as it conducts operations (Rubinstein 2003).

WHAT ROLE DOES A STAKEHOLDER ORIENTATION HAVE IN THE S-D LOGIC MODEL?

One of the most insightful elements of the S-D logic model, captured in FP_6, is the conception that "the customer is always a co-producer." This perspective is a dynamic point because it vests the customer as a full partner in the oversight of marketing exchange. This is a notable insight in the evolution of marketing thought because it is directly contrary to the traditional paradigm of "customer as target"; it is also far more consistent with partnership frameworks of marketing such as relationship marketing, the building of customer equity and various service management approaches to customer satisfaction. Given the consumer's undeniable desire for greater service customization, improved vendor responsiveness, and the better management of after-transaction relationships, the idea of envisioning customers as co-producers is the ultimate in embracing them as fully integrated partners in the marketing process.

Yet, one could contend that, from a macro standpoint, seeing the customer as a co-producer is only the first step of a more cosmopolitan view of marketing. Looking at the business system as a whole, all stakeholders could, and possibly should, be viewed as co-participants in the service provision. The S-D logic model already grants that "all employees are identified as service providers" (V&L, p. 14). Recall that stakeholders are *any* group that has a vested interest in the outcomes influenced by the operations of an organization (Freeman 1984; Laczniak and Murphy 1993). Typical stakeholder groups include primary parties (i.e., those having first claim) such as investors, employees, customers, and sometimes suppliers/distributors, as well as secondary stakeholders such as the host community and the public at large. Using the S-D logic terminology, one might compellingly argue for also viewing employees, customers and suppliers/distributors as co-producers of the service provision and the host community as an operant resource contributing to effective exchange and helping shape value propositions that include society as a co-beneficiary of service interactions. Additional theorizing that links the FPs of this paradigm to stakeholder thinking could prove to be one of the richest conceptual outcomes of S-D logic.

V&L are absolutely correct when they state (p. 11) that "the normative goal of marketing is customer responsiveness." But this raises an implied question of why customer responsiveness is important to begin with. From a macro standpoint, part of the answer to that lies in the consumers' basic right to engage in their pursuit of happiness and acceptance of that right by society as a legitimate activity. (As an aside, it is worth remembering that the "pursuit of happiness" is enshrined as the basic tenet of the U.S. Constitution.) Just as customers have inalienable rights, the society at large also has rights that need to be protected as service provision and knowledge exchange take place within our economic system. Among those rights is the expectation of society not to be disadvantaged by costs of business operations that might be externalized to society as exchange occurs and consumers pursue their happiness. Obvious examples of such externalized costs include the environmental damages from energy production and consumption and the medical costs stemming from the use of tobacco products. One of the basic ways to provide checks and balances on business so as not to shortchange society is by giving voice to parties with legitimate claims in the business decision process via the acceptance of a stakeholder orientation.

From a social-ethical standpoint, the basic payoff of a stakeholder orientation being adopted by business firms is that it keeps the rights and opinions of other parties, affected as co-beneficiaries of the service interaction, represented in the dialogue among sellers and customers as they engage in exchange. In the language of the S-D logic model, this would involve systematically examining how operand resources are used and how operant resources (i.e., people) are treated from an ethical standpoint. My reading of the S-D logic framework finds nothing in the V&L conception that is opposed to the stakeholder orientation. V&L (p. 13) write that "even relatively discrete transactions come with social, if not legal, contracts." But how these "social contracts" would be specifically defined and embodied into the evolving S-D logic deserves further conversation among marketing academics. The stakeholder orientation ought to be a central part of that dialogue.

WHAT IS THE NATURE OF TRUST IN A SERVICE-CENTERED VIEW OF MARKETING THAT IS BOTH CUSTOMER ORIENTED AND RELATIONAL?

In FP_8, V&L postulate a service-centered view of marketing that conceives of all activities of the firm as integrated in their market responsiveness in order to satisfy customers, thereby leading to profits as a result of maximizing consumer involvement. This proposition is unpacked by V&L in order to establish a firm's marketing activities as essential to co-creating the services required to satisfy consumer needs (p. 12). Such a view of marketing is clearly customer oriented and relational, but it also should be accorded an added social dimension. For example, as previously referenced, V&L (p. 12) observe, "even relatively discrete transactions come with social, if not legal contracts (often relatively extended) and often implied, if not expressed warranties." These warrants further suggest that "promises and assurances that the exchange relationship will yield valuable service provision, often for extended periods." The compelling question, of course, has to do with the nature of the social obligations to all potential consumers referenced by V&L or, put another way, what is the essence of genuine customer orientation and relationship marketing? There already exists a considerable marketing literature that addresses some of this question. One prominent example would include the work of Hunt and Morgan (1994), in which the virtue of trust lies at the heart of customer orientation. If a firm is really customer oriented in its service-centered view, it must foster an inherent, genuine trust among consumers that can be relied on regardless of the circumstance. In other words, long-run customer satisfaction that is "relational" depends on a trust that is authentically dependable for the consumer. Brenkert (1997), in an insightful essay, distinguishes between two kinds of trust. The first type of trust is *contractual trust;* it is relatively minimalist. It is contractual in the sense that the seller promises to discharge whatever service responsibilities have been formally negotiated. Furthermore, the consumer can believe that the service provided is "safe" and meets the basic purposes of implied product warranties; that is, the product or service will function in the manner expected by the consumer for a reasonable period of time. This kind of contractual trust can be juxtaposed with *authentic trust,* which is a broader category of trust, linking back to the stakeholder orientation discussed previously. Authentic trust (labeled *attitudinal trust* by Brenkert [1997]) is a superordinate form of trust in which the consumer can rely on the seller to "try to do the right thing" regardless of the circumstances and irrespective of the law. For example, in the case of consumer credit, although it might be profitable for some financial service companies to provide high-interest loans to particular debt-impaired consumers, authentic trust might impel the seller to counsel the consumer not to take on the additional debt. Similarly, in the food products industry, whereas a "low-carb" promotional appeal might be profitable to a particular seller, given the popularity of diets such as the

Atkins, many low-carb appeals make little nutritional sense. For instance, in the case of already low-carb light beer, authentic trust might impel the marketer to forgo this promotional appeal despite its potential profitability. In other words, authentic trust means that consumers have a relationship with a co-producing seller whereby that marketer, given their greater exchange expertise, can be counted on to look out for the best interests of the particular consumer segment (i.e., beer drinkers). As the S-D logic evolves, further discussion about the meaning of an authentically trustful customer orientation in the context of relationship marketing needs to occur.

SUMMARY AND CONCLUSION

In the end, the S-D logic perspective on marketing offers an exciting and evolutionary paradigm with great potential for pulling together various emerging perspectives (e.g., customer relationship marketing, the network approach to business-to-business marketing, customer equity management). Perhaps this is the theoretical calculus binding the various strands of thinking that seek to describe the strategic models that characterize marketing in the emergent new economy of the twenty-first century. The S-D logic framework could be the one paradigm that unites them all. Of their model, V&L (p. 12) write, "What precedes and what follows the transaction if a firm engages in a relationship (short or long term) with customers is more important than the transaction itself." Consistent with looking at the aftereffects of the transaction, the S-D logic paradigm, which already is so participatory and empowering to consumers as to include them as co-producers, should also explicitly look at its impact on society as a whole. As Gummesson (2004, p. 21) observes concerning the S-D logic, "The more marketers dare to recognize the complexity and ambiguity of marketing phenomena in this theory the more useful it will be." We can only hope that the social and ethical elements of marketing's provision of service are an important part of future discussion as marketing academics probe the "complexity and ambiguity" that lies at the depth of the S-D logic framework.

REFERENCES

Armstrong, Gary and Philip Kotler (2003), *Marketing,* 6th ed. Upper Saddle River, NJ: Prentice-Hall.

Brenkert, George G. (1997), "Marketing Trust: Barriers and Bridges," *Business and Professional Ethics Journal,* 16 (1–3): 77–98.

Day, George S. (2004), "Achieving Advantage with a New Dominant Logic," *Journal of Marketing,* 68 (January), 18–19.

Freeman, Edward R. (1984), *Strategic Management.* Marshfield, MA: Pitman Publishing Inc.

Gummesson, Evert (2004), "Service Provision Calls for Partners Instead of Parties," *Journal of Marketing,* 68 (January), 20–21.

Hunt, Shelby (2004), "On the Service-Centered Dominant Logic for Marketing," *Journal of Marketing,* 68 (January), 21–22.

———— and Robert M. Morgan (1994), "The Commitment-Trust Theory of Relationship Marketing," *Journal of Marketing,* 58 (July), 20–38.

Jennings, Marianne M. (2003), *Business Ethics,* 4th ed. Mason, OH: Thompson/Southwestern.

Kaplan, Robert S. and David P. Norton (1992), "The Balanced Scorecard—Measures that Drive Performance," *Harvard Business Review,* 70 (1), 71.

Laczniak, Gene R. and Patrick E. Murphy (1993), *Ethical Marketing Decisions: The Higher Road.* Needham Heights, MA: Allyn & Bacon.

Rubinstein R. (2003), "A Keynote: Triple Bottom Line Investing," *International Journal of Business Performance Management,* 5 (2/3), 109–13.

Vargo, Stephen L. and Robert Lusch (2004), "Evolving to a New Dominant Logic for Marketing," *Journal of Marketing,* 68 (January), 1–17.

22

THE NEW DOMINANT LOGIC OF MARKETING

Views of the Elephant

Tim Ambler

The development of any discipline must be reviewed from time to time, and marketing scholars should be grateful to Vargo and Lusch (2004a; hereafter V&L) for setting an important debate in train. They suggest that marketing is evolving to a new dominant logic in which service provision, as distinct from services, is the basis of economic exchange, namely marketing. They have invited others to contribute their own strategic visions of how marketing is evolving.

V&L open with Kotler's (1972) perspective of marketing—namely, that "marketing management seeks to determine the settings of the company's *marketing decision variables* that will maximize the company's objective(s) in the light of the expected behavior of noncontrollable *demand variables*" (p. 42, emphasis added). Kotler reminds us that "to market" is a transitive verb; it is what companies, or perhaps marketing managers, do. The inference is that it is an activity that is no more than moderated by the objects being marketed. Furthermore, it is much more than *economic exchange*, a term that better describes sales. As the relationship marketing perspective has shown, the exchange itself might be a relatively small part of the marketing continuum.

Bartels (1970, p. 253) attempted "The General Theory of Marketing" and concluded

> (1) that management behavior, incorporating both economics and social technology, is an ultimate focus of marketing theory; (2) that the roots of marketing theory are in the cultural context of society; and (3) that the structure of a theory includes components which reflect, among other things, the viewpoint of the particular theorist.

This chapter adopts the Bartels view and seeks to disentangle marketing (i.e., marketer behavior) from the perspectives of different commentators and from its context. It opens with a brief historical summary. The viewer's spectacles (i.e., the viewer's training and experience) define to some extent what that person sees. For example, the economist will see marketing as an economic activity, whereas the psychologist will analyze what is taking place in the minds of customers and, less commonly, in the minds of the marketers. Next, the chapter discusses whether, and if so how much, the product context changes marketing itself. V&L point to the development of services, as distinct from goods, marketing and then make perhaps too subtle a switch from a "services" to a "service-centered" perspective. The question is whether the "marketing elephant" is changing or whether we are merely seeing the same beast from different points of view.

All human activities evolve, and this must include marketing. Marketing academics provide guidance to practitioners, and that requires them to predict the direction of marketing evolution. In a world with increasing diversity, choice, and complexity, an overarching theory, or dominant logic, of marketing would make sense of the potential confusion and would help teaching and practice.

Alternatively, marketing theories might be no more than a collection of other disciplines applying themselves to the same elephant. In that case, there would be no overarching single marketing "dominant logic," and academics could remain within their own almae maters. To some extent we see this today with behaviorists and economists resolutely pursuing independent approaches. To muddy the water further, this whole debate could be a matter of deconstruction leading to questions rather than fundamental truth. After we have unpeeled the layers of subjectivity and context, nothing might remain. I conclude, however, that marketing theory does have some underlying cohesion, which I attempt to describe.

HISTORICAL SUMMARY

Marketing has existed since the dawn of commerce, even though it was not called as such. Merchants did not simply buy and sell; they developed long-term relationships and what would now be termed brand equity. They might not have been introspective about their business methods, but if they had not known how to satisfy customers while making a profit for themselves, commerce would not have survived. They must always have wanted customers to return and buy again.

Both in China and the West, business historically had negative overtones. Confucius regarded businesspeople as necessary but second rate. The Ming dynasty had no interest in international trade. In the West, the earliest usage of *marketing* in the *Oxford English Dictionary* is "How filthy markettinges they use, how unhonest gaines they make with their massinges" (Norton 1561). According to the *OED*, the first use of *marketing* in the sense of a corporate function was not until 1958.

At the dawn of the Renaissance, St. Thomas Aquinas and his followers, known as the Scholastics, developed what was probably the first formal analysis of buyer motivation. They did not call it "marketing," not least because they were writing, as St. Augustine did a millennium earlier, in Latin. One Scholastic, St Bernardino of Siena (1380–1444), distinguished among *virtuositas* (function), *raritas* (scarcity or market price, i.e., economic benefits), and *complacibilitas* (psychological benefits). Merchants were entitled to take all three into account in determining the *justum pretium* (just price) of goods (Blaug 1991).

These three core components of buyer benefits have been rediscovered by each new generation of marketing scientists: functionality (the problem the product solves), efficiency of spending (value for money), and psychosocial rewards, e.g., social standing. Here, I use "product" to mean the goods and/or services being marketed.

In the eighteenth century, the first early economists, then called "physiocrats," emerged in France. In their perception, as reported by Adam Smith, who developed his thinking while in France, three great inventions principally underlie our societies: writing enabled legislation, money binds relationships, and the "Economical Table" (i.e., the market) completes them both "but of which our posterity will reap the benefit" (Marquis de Mirabeau cited by Adam Smith 1993, p. 390). Although the focus was on goods, and especially the distinction between manufactured and agricultural goods, services were not ignored.

Lovelock and Gummesson (2004) charted a fascinating portrayal of the development of thinking about services marketing from Adam Smith through, thirty years on, Say's use of the term

Table 22.1

Intellectual Foundations per Howard (1983)

Purpose	Descriptive	Prescriptive
Logical Foundation: Empirical	Customer	Functions within the firm (marketing, organization, financial, manufacturing, research, and development)
Logical Foundation: Axiomatic	Competitor	Contribution Present value

immaterial for services and, a further sixty years on, the Marxian perception that services are merely an extension of goods. It is this that V&L are reversing by suggesting that goods are merely part of service. In the Marxian view, transport and repair are not separate services but part of the production of the base goods. Until recently, customers in the People's Republic of China were reluctant to pay for pure services, and consultants, for example, used to cast around for some tangible goods to include in their packages.

The point here is that marketing is as old as commerce, and the intellectual study of marketing is several centuries old, too. The distinctive contribution of the twentieth century was the introduction of the specialist marketer. Whether the earliest was Procter & Gamble's first brand manager for Camay soap in 1926 is an open question; other brands were professionally managed before then. Even so, we can be confident that it was only in the past 100 years that businesses and academics have had to train professional specialist marketers. Accordingly, the trainers needed better to understand the nature and theory of marketing.

Since then confusion has grown as to whether marketing is what the specialist marketers do or what the whole company does to satisfy customers and thereby achieve its own goals (Webster 1992). As Kotler (2003) has pointed out, many specialist marketers only deal with one of the classic 4 P's, namely promotion. Price, product, and place (distribution) are mostly managed by other parts of the organization.

Theories of markets (microeconomics) and buyer behavior (psychology) are generally seen as the progenitors of marketing theory, and these two disciplines still dominate academic departments. Yet they are only indirectly relevant to marketing in the sense that it is what marketers do, or should do. A better understanding of markets and buyer behavior should improve marketing skills, but so should the ability to forecast the weather if you are in the ice cream business. These theories should not be confused with marketing itself.

Nevertheless, the perhaps unlikely bedfellows of economists, or physiocrats, and psychologists duly came together, and the union of these 2 P's produced the 4 P's. Marketers were taught to ensure they sold the right product (and packaging) at the right price, with the right promotion in the right place. Although the 4 P's have been increasingly disparaged over their half-century life to date, they remain a, if not the, dominant ideology among practitioners. They are easy to follow and apply. Marketing plans today are often either in strategy/tactics, 4 P's, or some combined format.

Howard (1983, p. 91) represented the psychological and economic foundation of marketing within a 2×2 model as follows (see Table 22.1). His perspective was based on a psychological approach to the first row, where marketing knowledge owes less to mathematical theory than the application of economics to the last row. The columns distinguished description (e.g., customer behavior) from what marketers should do. He attributed the earliest application of marketing performance being evaluated in financial present value terms, i.e., discounted cash flow, to Howard (1963).

Table 22.2

Marketing Theory Framework per Sheth, Gardner, and Garrett (1988)

Schools of Thought	Noninteractive	Interactive
Economic	Commodity Functional Regional	Institutional Functionalist Managerial
Noneconomic	Buyer Behavior Activist Macromarketing	Organizational Systems Social Exchange

Sheth, Gardner, and Garrett (1988) also structured marketing theory in a 2×2 model (interactive/economic), but each cell, elegantly, contained three "schools of thought" (see Table 22.2). They discuss the distinction between a theory and a school of thought and conclude it is not material. Reviewing each of those twelve schools of thought would occupy too much of this chapter. The first of the two main dimensions contrasts both ends of the exchange (i.e., the dyad) with a one-sided perspective called "noninteractive." Relationship marketing would fall under the former interactive category. The second dimension distinguishes those who see marketing as essentially money making from those who take a wider view.

Although Sheth, Gardner, and Garrett (1988) see the first stage of marketing theory, in the 1960s, say, as concerning consumer behavior, the extent to which managers were really driven by that is arguable. Managers are usually preoccupied by what they themselves have to do, and the early textbooks, in supplying the 4 P's framework, met that need.

They suggest that the first paradigm shift in marketing theory emerged in the 1980s in the form of "strategic marketing." The objective became competitive advantage and the primary performance measure was market share. Practitioners and academics both observed that those brands with the largest market share were also most profitable (e.g., Gale 1994). So marketers were advised to establish "competitive advantage" (Porter 1979, 1985), preferably sustainable. The famous Five Forces analysis of the competitive context was originally six: (1) threat of entry, (2) changing conditions, (3) powerful suppliers and buyers, (4) strategic action, (5) substitute products, and (6) jockeying for position (Porter 1979). The last became "industry competitors" and the second and fourth dropped off. Suppliers and buyers were separated.

The Five Forces model remains perhaps the most popular tool for market analysis, replacing SWOT (strengths, weaknesses, opportunities, and threats), but it is open to question how useful market analysis is for marketers. Analyzing relative strengths and weaknesses does not necessarily determine what action to take and does not provide a clear template for managerial action in the way the 4 P's framework does.

Nevertheless, the idea that market share drives profitability gained considerable credibility when it was promoted by PIMS, a Cambridge-based econometric organization founded by General Electric and Harvard Business School. After much academic controversy, Gale (1994), previously chief executive of PIMS, recanted and admitted that the link between market share and profitability was correlational, not causal. Both, he now claimed, were driven by relative perceived quality, which in turn was driven, with time lags, by actual quality.

At about this point, academics around the world, and especially in Scandinavia, began to realize that marketing, which had begun by taking the customer's point of view, had ironically itself lost that perspective. The 4 P's were a production-line approach to the marketing mix, and strategy was preoccupied with competitors and market share. Furthermore, they showed marketing as short-term transactions when much of marketing only makes sense when it is seen as enduring over time (i.e., marketing beginning rather than ending with the sale). Experiencing the brand takes place after the sale. Marketers seek to maximize the pleasure from the brand experience in order to maximize future sales.

The Fall 1983 edition of the *Journal of Marketing* had provided a boost to theory development with articles by Arndt, Day and Wensley, Deshpandé, Howard and Hunt, many of which suggested that the traditional microeconomic, or neoclassical, view of marketing was inadequate. Alderson's (e.g., 1965) influence was apparent in the focus on social exchange but, as identified by Anderson (1982), emphasis was beginning to shift from transactions to relationships with Arndt's (1983) political economy paradigm, a direct antecedent of the evolving relational, or relationship marketing, paradigm.

The Scandinavian "IMP Group" (i.e., those concerned with International Marketing and Purchasing of industrial goods) provided a further antecedent stimulated by the Hakansson interaction model (1982). Gummesson (1987, 1993) and Grönroos (1990) have linked this development with relationship marketing (Berry 1983).

This rediscovery of the customer perspective and the importance of the continuing relationship paved the way for the increasing emphasis on services. This was reinforced by the shift from manufacturing to services in terms of their relative shares of gross domestic product (GDP). It also paved the way for business becoming more customer-centric, as is evidenced by the huge increase in customer satisfaction research and customer relationship management (Webster, Malter, and Ganesan 2004).

We can welcome the return of the marketing wheel to customers, relationships, and services (according to the Bible, the marketing of services preceded the marketing of goods) but that does not exclude the brand, competitor, transactional, and goods perspectives, as well. Marketing, in short, is becoming more complex as it grows up.

DO THE VIEWER'S OWN SPECTACLES DEFINE WHAT HE OR SHE SEES?

A striking aspect of V&L and the commentaries is the extent to which the authors write from their established points of view. Day (2004), for example, sees "market driven" and Prahalad (2004) sees co-creation of value; references show precisely these concepts in their recent works. That does not make one wrong or another right. It only indicates that academics view the marketing elephant in the way that each has become accustomed, or trained, to do. To comprehend the whole elephant one must include all valid perspectives, and even then some aspects might be missing.

Famous marketing academics are themselves brands- and market-driven. They compete by drawing attention to themselves and away from competitors and strive to improve the experience of those who consume their brands. Those with commitments to brand equity, for example, are unlikely to support the more recent articles suggesting that brand equity is old hat and should be subsumed, or replaced, by customer equity (e.g., Rust, Lemon, and Zeithaml 2004).

This zero-sum (total market share always equals 100 percent) approach to marketing theory is false because each new perspective, so long as it is valid, adds to understanding the elephant; it does not invalidate the preceding ones. Marketing theory, like marketing itself, should add value by incremental accretion and should not necessarily replace alternatives unless those alternatives can be shown to be false.

TO WHAT EXTENT DOES THE PRODUCT CONTEXT CHANGE MARKETING ITSELF?

In making space for services marketing (e.g., Lovelock 1981), theorists sought to differentiate goods from services as not just being different products but requiring alternative marketing theory. More recently, Lovelock and Gummesson (2004) and Vargo and Lusch (2004b) have challenged the traditionally cited distinguishing features of services, namely intangibility, heterogeneity, inseparability, and perishability. Their analysis shows that these four attributes can also belong to goods. Lovelock and Gummesson propose an alternative basic distinction between goods and services in that ownership of the underlying assets changes in the case of goods but not in the case of services. Selling cars, for example, requires the marketing of goods, whereas providing taxis requires the marketing of services.

Neat as that is, it does not deal with the sale of goods and services combined, as is increasingly the case with more sophistication of products. After-sales service, and the lack of need for it, is an integral part of the brand package for a car.

Furthermore, the buy or rent alternative is not fundamentally important for the marketing of goods. In the days when television sets were unreliable, customers were more likely to rent, with backup services from the renter, than buy. In the modern defense industry, armed forces pay for weapons or tanks or planes as they use them. For cash flow, budgetary, and ease of maintenance reasons, it can easier to pay for the weaponry only while it is available for use. Thus the buy or rent decision is an incidental financial or operational matter, subsidiary to the marketing of the product itself and to the relationship between the manufacturer and the customer.

However, marketing power stations is a very different business from selling financial services. The providers of marketing training courses soon discover that they need to specify the product context (e.g., pharmaceutical or business-to-business) if they are to attract customers in this specialist world. Marketers in one specialist field see themselves as requiring very different skills from those in another.

The implication of all this is that marketing is certainly moderated by the type of product being marketed. The balance of GDP in most developed countries is moving from tangibles (goods) to intangibles (services), but that does not mean that marketing itself, or our understanding of it, is changed.

Of course, the V&L approach was not just a services versus goods dialectic. They are suggesting that goods can be seen as service, as distinct from services, provision in much the way Marx represented services in a goods context. Furthermore, V&L attribute the "interactive" (Sheth, Gardner, and Garrett 1988) understanding to the service-centered logic, but a noninteractive, partisan, and production push logic, to goods (Table 2, p. 7). This is unfair: Both sides of the dyad can be used or not used in all perspectives of marketing. It has nothing to do with the nature, or perceived nature, of the product being marketed.

The distinction between *services* and *service* is semantically small and, perhaps, therefore confusing but crucial. Vargo and Lusch are arguing, in effect, that the dominant logic is switching from the product (goods and/or services) to what the product does for the customer, the service, from the customer's point of view. Understanding the transactions and relationships from the customer's side is indeed part of marketing, but it is only part. The marketer has to marry the customer's "service" with the company's goals, costs, and capabilities.

More important, service defined in this way can be deconstructed to functional effectiveness, cost/benefits, and psychological benefits, which is where San Bernardino came in 600 years ago. Returning full cycle does have a certain elegance.

So the question being raised is not whether the service-centered perspective is the dominant logic but whether it is a novel view of the elephant.

THE NEW FINANCIAL ECOLOGY

In reviewing the historical development of marketing thinking, this chapter proposes that new concepts should be tested for validity and whether they add anything new. Those that survive should be added to the basket of theory as distinct from replacing previous theories. Relationships build from the experience of transactions, communications, and interactions; they are not a separate discipline. Similarly, the products, and the extent to which they are goods and/or services, moderate marketing practice.

At the same time, the theory of marketing did change in the twentieth century in the sense that it now needed to guide the actions of professional marketers, a separate group that did not previously exist and is not now limited to for-profit businesses. Charities and political parties have chief marketing officers, and so has the UK Inland Revenue. Taxpayers are now customers of the state as well as being shareholders.

We are therefore left with the question of whether complexity and diversity, together with the continuing importance of context, explain the evolution or whether something else is happening as well. Whether it is just another view of the elephant is explored in the next section, but first we should consider if the growing strength of the financial function might be changing what marketers do (i.e., marketing itself). As Howard (1963) noted, marketing now has to show how it improves the present value of future profits. Marketers see themselves in increasing thrall to the chief financial officer (CFO) and look to marketing academics to help them justify their budgets, and even their existence, in financial terms. They are looking for techniques to show the financial productivity of marketing, and marketers are being pressed for accountability.

Maybe firms should not be blinkered by short-term financial considerations and the wider social, or stakeholder, view of the firm should prevail, but marketing now has to find a better way to exist within the firm's financial ecology. In the Sheth, Gardner, and Garrett (1988) portrayal, the economic-interactive cell is becoming dominant. In the financial ecology, marketing is not seen as fundamental but as a cost that must be justified.

The key to survival in this marketing-hostile ecology is the intangible asset created by good marketing, namely brand equity or reputation. Only transactional marketing, and not all of that, can prove a short-term quarterly, or even annual, payback. The recognition of the long-term nature of marketing, and customer relationships and lifetime value, requires the short-term gains to be seen in the context of any change in the size or value of the marketing asset.

This is key. Each period of marketing activity is marked by the inheritance of the asset from previous periods, the results from the activity during the period, and the handing over of the asset to the next period. Suppose a marketing expenditure of $100,000 resulted in a net contribution (after deducting marketing costs) of $200,000. The typical CFO would be well pleased. Suppose, however, that the marketing was of low quality and brand equity had depreciated during the period by $500,000 in consequence. The now better-educated CFO would take the opposite view. The combination of a marketing-hostile financial ecology and the concept of the marketing asset radically changes what marketers must do to gain acceptance for their work. For the purpose of this arithmetic, it makes little difference if we use the financial value of the brand (brand valuation) or customer equity (Rust, Lemon, and Zeithaml 2004) because they both discount future cash flows.

If cash flow has taken over from the customer, insofar as dominating what marketers actually do, then finance is providing the new dominant logic for marketing. In that case, marketing should be redefined as the sourcing and harvesting of cash flow. In any organization, commercial or charitable, governmental or private, marketing has the role of satisfying customers so that they not only continue but more and more want to hand over their money.

This perspective is consistent with the now widespread view that the prime objective for companies is shareholder value. That value can be best enhanced by first providing value to employees and customers. Some would argue that this financial perspective is too narrow. Companies serve stakeholders, not just shareholders, and companies and marketing have wider responsibilities to the societies in which they operate. We should not have to choose between financial performance and corporate social responsibility, but often we do. One can take a moral stance about the superiority of one or the other, but when it comes to survival, cash flow counts for more than reputation. So an argument exists that corporate social responsibility must be satisficed to the extent that cash flow permits (i.e., cash flow remains dominant).

Furthermore, promoting this understanding of marketing within the financial, top management, analyst, and investor communities reduces the perception that marketing is merely a luxury for the firms that can afford it. If marketing is the sourcing and harvesting of cash flow, there is no organization that can *not* afford it.

A BRIEF DECONSTRUCTION

Assuming the financial perspective is valid, we need to consider whether it is just another point of view or whether it has some dominant characteristics. Perhaps the financial perspective is merely contextual and/or subjective. The death of Jacques Derrida in October 2004 has prompted some reassessment of his ideas of deconstruction (*Dictionary of Social Sciences* 2002).

The responses prompted by V&L, including this one, are exercises in specifying the identity of marketing and the temporal differences as it evolves, if it does, over time. Derrida saw language, in this case the papers, as presenting at best a partial understanding of meaning and to achieve that, the outer wrappings of context and subjectivity, need to be stripped away.

We are in murky territory because the opinion of what is context and what is substance could itself be subjective. Accordingly, Derrida, like Socrates and the Jesuits, preferred to question rather than provide answers. To understand marketing we need to ask *why* marketers do what they do, as distinct from how they do it. Are marketers really driven by customer satisfaction or do they seek customer satisfaction in order to build cash flow?

If we deconstruct V&L, and the ensuing commentaries in that light, we find a valuable aggregation of theories associated with marketing such as economics and relationships. The product does make a difference to the way marketing is conducted (the mix) and products are certainly changing. The idea of service needs to be unpicked from services and value (meaning satisfaction) from value (meaning financial valuation).

Day (2004) explicitly says that dominant logic depends on what we mean by marketing but concludes that, to be successful, marketers have to be customer centered and market driven. Deighton and Narayandas (2004) promote stories as illustrations of theory. One can envisage that the culture within which marketers operate is created by the stories they tell each other. Stories from the marketplace should be informing marketing theory. Stories, as much as or even more than cash flow, might explain not only what marketers do, but also why they do it.

We can test whether a logic is temporal by whether it provides as good an explanation of marketing 200 years ago as it does today. Stories would seem to meet that criterion. Perhaps service does, too.

Gummesson (2004) broadly adopts the same approach as V&L, as might be expected from the preceding discussion, with an emphasis on relationships, specifically partnerships. Hunt (2004) adopts a more competitive, resource-advantage approach, which is important but could be regarded as contextual. Similarly, Prahalad (2004) promotes his and Ramaswamy's perspective of experience-centric co-creation of value. This is a valuable insight for how marketers should proceed rather than why.

Rust (2004) is also supportive of V&L and highlights the contribution that information technology can make to the way marketers conduct their business. Finally, Shugan (2004) takes "a more humble" (p. 26) but pragmatic approach in proposing research into concrete problems, daily challenges, and the impact of marketing on operations. This is another valuable contribution but, in my analysis, more contextual than fundamental.

As noted at the beginning of this chapter, we have an important set of views of the elephant, each adding to the others but based more on the experience of the authors than changing marketing theory. The one exception, which I would add to the cash flow priority, is the Deighton and Narayandas (2004) suggestion of the significance of stories.

CONCLUSIONS

Competitors and especially customers have regained the high ground in marketing thinking, and just as services have increased their share of GDP, so services have rightly achieved a higher profile within the discipline. V&L are right to draw attention to that. This does not mean that marketing is evolving to a service-dominant logic for the discipline as a whole or, at the other extreme, that it is fragmenting. Adding new concepts has made it more complex and diverse.

The new financial ecology adds to, as distinct from replacing, existing theory and provides a framework for evaluating marketing. Marketing performance should not be measured by sales, or even by profits, alone but should consider short-term cash flow alongside changes to the marketing asset. It therefore integrates the longer-term nature of marketing with the short-term need for accountability.

It can be expressed another way—namely that the primary aim of marketing is to build the marketing asset, which in turn will take care of short-term profits. So perhaps building brand equity in order to maximize long-term cash flow is the new dominant logic.

REFERENCES

Alderson, Wroe (1965), *Dynamic Marketing Behavior.* Homewood, IL: Richard D. Irwin, Inc.

Anderson, Paul F. (1982), "Marketing, Strategic Planning and the Theory of the Firm," *Journal of Marketing,* 46 (Spring), 15–26.

Arndt, Johan (1983), "The Political Economy Paradigm: Foundation for Theory Building in Marketing," *Journal of Marketing,* 47 (Fall), 44–54.

Bartels, Robert (1970), *Marketing Theory and Metatheory.* Homewood, IL: Richard D. Irwin.

Berry, Leonard L. (1983), "Relationship Marketing," in *Emerging Perspectives on Services Marketing,* L.L. Berry et al., eds. Chicago: American Marketing Association, 25–28.

Blaug, Mark (1991), *St. Thomas Aquinas (1225–1274).* Aldershot, UK: Edward Elgar.

Day, George S. (2004), "Achieving Advantage with a New Dominant Logic," *Journal of Marketing,* 68 (January), 18–19.

Deighton, John and Das Narayandas (2004), "Stories and Theories," *Journal of Marketing,* 68 (January), 19–20.

Dictionary of the Social Sciences (2002), Craig Calhoun, ed. Oxford University Press. *Oxford Reference Online.* http://www.oxfordreference.com/views/ENTRY.html?subview=Main&entry=t104.e422. Accessed 11 October 2004.

Gale, Bradley T. (1994), *Managing Customer Value: Creating Quality and Service that Customers Can See.* New York: The Free Press

Grönroos, Christian (1990), "Relationship Approach to Marketing in Service Contexts: The Marketing and Organizational Behaviour Interface," *Journal of Business Research* 20, 3–11.

Gummesson, Evert (1987), "The New Marketing: Developing Long-Term Interactive Relationships," *Long Range Planning* 20 (4), 10–20.

——— (1993), "Relationship Marketing: A New Way of Doing Business," *European Business Report* 3Q (Autumn), 52–56.

——— (2004), "Service Provision Calls for Partners Instead of Parties," *Journal of Marketing,* 68 (January), 20–21.

Hakansson, H. (1982), *Interactional Marketing and Purchasing of Industrial Goods: An Interaction Approach.* New York: John Wiley & Sons.

Howard, John A. (1983), "The Marketing Theory of the Firm," *Journal of Marketing,* 47 (Fall), 90–100.

——— (1963), *Marketing: Executive and Buyer Behavior.* New York: Columbia University Press.

Hunt, Shelby (2004), "On the Service-Centered Dominant Logic for Marketing," *Journal of Marketing,* 68 (January), 21–22.

Kotler, Philip (1972), *Marketing Management,* 2nd ed. Englewood Cliffs, NJ: Prentice Hall.

——— (2003), Lecture on board the Marketing Forum, UK, September.

Lovelock, Christopher H. (1981), "Why Marketing Management Needs to Be Different for Services," in *Marketing of Services,* J.H. Donnelly and W. R. George, eds. Chicago: American Marketing Association, 5–9.

——— and Evert Gummesson (2004) "Whither Services Marketing? In Search of a New Paradigm and Fresh Perspectives," *Journal of Service Research,* 7(1), 20-41.

Norton T. (1561), "Marketing," Oxford English Dictionary (online) from tr. J. Calvin *Instit.* IV. xviii. f. 147. http://dictionary.oed.com/cgi/entry/00302203?query_type=word&queryword=Marketing&first=1&max_to_show=10&sort_type=alpha&result_place=1&search_id=IV18-5dtFS7-1049&hilite=00302203. Accessed October 3, 2005.

Porter, Michael E. (1979), "How Competitive Forces Shape Strategy," *Harvard Business Review,* 57 (2, March/April), 137.

——— (1985), *Competitive Advantage.* New York: The Free Press.

Prahalad, C.K. (2004), "The Co-creation of Value," *Journal of Marketing,* 68 (January), 23.

Rust, Roland T. (2004), "If Everything Is Service, Why Is This Happening Now, and What Difference Does It Make?" *Journal of Marketing,* 68 (January), 23–24.

———, Katherine N. Lemon, and Valarie A. Zeithaml (2004), "Return on Marketing: Using Customer Equity to Focus Marketing Strategy," *Journal of Marketing,* 68 (January), 109–27.

Sheth, Jagdish N., David M. Gardner, and Dennis E. Garrett (1988), *Marketing Theory: Evolution and Evaluation.* New York: John Wiley & Sons.

Shugan, Steven M. (2004), "Finance, Operations, and Marketing Conflicts in Service Firms," *Journal of Marketing,* 68 (January), 24–26.

Smith, Adam (1993), *Wealth of Nations.* Oxford: Oxford University Press (originally 1776).

Vargo, Stephen L. and Robert F. Lusch (2004a), "Evolving to a New Dominant Logic for Marketing," *Journal of Marketing,* 68 (January), 1–17.

——— and ——— (2004b), "The Four Service Marketing Myths," *Journal of Service Research,* 6 (4), 324–35.

Webster, Jr., Frederick E. (1992), "The Changing Role of Marketing in the Corporation," *Journal of Marketing,* (October), 1–17.

———, Alan J. Malter, and Shankar Ganesan (2004), "Can Marketing Regain Its Seat at the Table?" Marketing Science Institute working paper 03–113, March.

23

MORE DOMINANT LOGICS FOR MARKETING

Productivity and Growth

Donald R. Lehmann

Considering where marketing is headed is an interesting activity (cf. Lehmann and Jocz 1997). For such a ubiquitous concept as marketing, it is interesting that there is considerable disagreement about what marketing is, or at least should be. Indeed, what marketing means has evolved over time from primarily a transportation activity to one focused on selling (including advertising and promotions) to a strategy of connecting with customers through brands and customer experience.

The issue of what marketing is led the American Marketing Association in 2004 to again revise its definition of the term to the following: "Marketing is an organizational function and a set of processes for creating, communicating, and delivering value to customers and for managing customer relationships in ways that benefit the organization and its stakeholders." This definition nicely encompasses nonprofit as well as for-profit firms. However, it is fairly general (e.g., marketing is seen as both a function and a set of processes) and does not provide a sense of the key essence of the term.

Recently Vargo and Lusch (2004a) proposed service as the central concept in marketing, essentially bridging the often mentioned but artificial distinction between goods and services (Vargo and Lusch 2004b). This view has much to commend it, and they develop eight foundational premises that arise from it. Because any specific view provides both highlights and shadows, however, it is hard to capture everything in a single concept. For that reason this chapter highlights two other key constructs that are critical to marketing: metrics and the productivity of marketing and growth.

SOME CONCERNS WITH THE SERVICE PROVISION PERSPECTIVE

1. Is It about Experience or Services? (What's in the Name?)

The service perspective advocated by Vargo and Lusch (2004a) makes real sense but could suffer from baggage associated with the term *service*, which often is seen as opposite the term *product*. At one level everything is about benefits. This means it is the use one makes of the product, and not the product per se, that matters. In other words, goods provide service (or more generally, experiences; see Schmitt 2003). However, there are important exceptions to this. First, meaningless attributes (i.e., ones with no functional value) can play a role in purchase decisions without providing any useful "service." Moreover, an entire class of possessions, collectibles, is significant in terms of expenditures and yet provides no active service. Of course, mere possession can provide pleasure, but the sense of active benefit conveyed by the term *service* is lacking. Still, to the extent service is defined as customer experience, service is then essentially the value the customer receives from a purchase.

It is also true that even so-called service industries provide products. Airlines have seat sizes and leg rooms as well as meals or the lack thereof (products). H&R Block prepares tax returns (a physical product). Indeed, just as one can interpret products as providing service, services generally provide products. Therefore, it is important not to allow semantic confusion to equate a services perspective with services per se. The efforts to decouple those concepts by Vargo and Lusch (2004a, b) are most welcome.

2. Using the Mix to Make Them Buy It versus Customer as King

It is prudent and desirable to spend effort to determine what customers want and to try and provide it. At some point, however, a firm needs to sell its offering. Tools such as sales forces, promotions, and advertising become primarily one-way communication channels. Service provision and value provision, by contrast, suggest a passive, almost subservient view of the relation between a firm and its customers, in which "pushing" the offering seems unseemly. For for-profit concerns at least (as well as nonprofits with a mission such as health improvement), the task is, more than satisfying current needs, to "create" demand.

3. Customer versus Firm View

Marketing has in the past oscillated between market focused and product focused. The current services and experience orientations represent the result of the pendulum having swung toward the customer (market) focus. As such, the notion of value to the customer is highlighted and the focus on value to the firm somewhat diminished.

At many levels of the organization, this might be appropriate (i.e., for customer-contact personnel to be closely connected to and concerned about customers). At the top level of an organization, however, the firm's welfare is paramount. Note this does not mean other stakeholders, including society and the environment, are not important but rather that these serve more as constraints, or alternatively are weighted somewhat less than firm goals. Put differently, firm performance is not just a reward for connecting with customers; for a publicly held, for-profit firm it is the reason to connect. Satisfying/pleasing/delighting customers then is often a necessary but not sufficient condition.

METRICS AND MARKETING PRODUCTIVITY

Based on Marketing Science Institute's research priorities for the past six years and conversations with chief executive officers (CEOs) and chief marketing officers (CMOs), it is obvious that productive use of marketing spending is a critical issue. Indeed, several authors have suggested that the marketing function has "lost a seat at the table" (i.e., is not involved in key decisions) (Webster 1992). Rather it has been marginalized into a department of cents-off coupons and ad copy design (Lehmann 1997). The impetus for metrics that make marketing matter (Ambler 2003) has only intensified with increased global competition and recessions, not to mention the birth of the Internet. As a result, it seems clear that one key logical response is to demonstrate the produc-

Figure 23.1 **Metrics Value Chain**

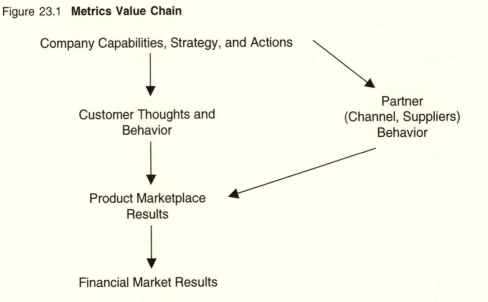

tivity of marketing in ways people outside the marketing department (e.g., chief financial officers [CFOs]) find persuasive.

It is important to emphasize that a focus on metrics and marketing productivity does not imply a short-run orientation. Neither does it preclude the use of measures that have great diagnostic value (e.g., awareness, attitudes) that are not directly relevant to CFOs or CEOs. Rather the focus suggests the development of a system of measures that (1) link together and (2) dominate in measures which matter broadly in the organization.

A useful way to consider metrics is in the form of a value chain (Lehmann 2005b; Srivastava, Shervani, and Fahey 1999). Figure 23.1 presents such a chain, leaving out important aspects such as competition and the general environment, both of which have important impacts throughout the chain. The top level is what the company does in terms of capabilities/processes (e.g., market orientation), strategy (e.g., focus on new product development or umbrella branding), and actions (i.e., the 4 P's). The second level is where the direct effect is felt. Consumer's thoughts (awareness, perceptions, attitudes, intentions, value to the customer, customer-based brand equity, satisfaction) are affected by the company's actions, as is their behavior (purchase incidence and quantity, word of mouth). This link is probably the one that has been most studied. Ironically, it is also the one furthest from the financial market results that drive CEOs and CFOs.

Important, but less formally considered, is the link to partners. There is a large literature on channels and alliances, but much of this focuses on relationship characteristics (trust, satisfaction). These tend to be critical diagnostically but again are not the goal; rather, measurers of channel support (advertising, promotion pass-through, featuring, stocking) are critical for this perspective.

The third level, and the one considered the ultimate by many in marketing, is product-market performance. Key metrics include sales, share (of market, requirements, wallet), and price and price premium– (versus market, generic, private label) as well as revenue premium–based brand equity (Ailawadi, Lehmann, and Neslin 2003). Other measures include growth and the sales from and success rate of new products. When disaggregated to the customer level, net revenue (cash flow) over time, appropriately adjusted for acquisition and retention cost plus retention and expansion, becomes customer lifetime value (CLV) (i.e., the value of the customer to the firm).

Thus, this perspective emphasizes the value of customers and brands to the firm (CLV, firm brand equity) versus value to the customer and customer level (psychological brand equity). Put differently, the emphasis is on current and future "revealed preference" behavior rather than the critical (in a diagnostic and causal sense) but largely "means to an end" measures of attitudes and opinions. Although this makes many researchers (especially those trained in psychology) uncomfortable, this more economic perspective has the potential to resonate with a critical group of stakeholders: CFOs and CEOs.

The final level in the chain is the financial market. This applies primarily to publicly held, for-profit firms. In fact, an operational definition of a nonprofit organization is one for whom the ultimate results are behavioral or attitudinal rather than financial; financial stability and fund raising are means to an end of product-market behavior rather than vice versa. Financial metrics include various return ratios (e.g., return on investment [ROI], return on assets) and Economic Value Added (EVA) as well as stock market–based measures (market capitalization, MVA, Tobin's q).

Taking the chain as given, the logic of marketing is to use resources effectively to create changes that lead to strong financial performance. Although it is perhaps "a bridge too far" to relate the impact of a single promotion to stock price, developing empirical generalizations (e.g., via meta-analyses) of the links is a worthwhile goal. Even in the absence of such calibration, however, keeping the chain in mind will influence thinking and behavior in a generally positive direction.

THE GROWTH IMPERATIVE

Growth (e.g., through new product development) is generally seen as good. Of course, growth can be wasteful and environmentally unfriendly. Indeed, there are trade-offs involved in any action.

Market capitalization depends on the P/E ratio, which in turn depends on discounted cash flow. Constant cash flow leads to a below-market P/E ratio. As a consequence, firms are under pressure to grow.

In the past, much of the growth in firms has been generated by mergers and acquisitions. This is a feasible means to growth for a large, well-resourced firm purchasing small, underfunded firms. Presuming the firm bought was (1) operating reasonably effectively and (2) more aware of its value than the acquiring firm given information asymmetry, however, there is little advantage to the deal. Even when an advantage is realized, the gain is largely one-time. In addition to this, many mergers have already occurred, so the opportunities to grow this way are limited in some areas, in part by antitrust laws. Add to this fallout from corporate scandals at Tyco, Enron, and so on, and a clear limit to growth by merger appears to have been reached.

The other main growth engine has been cost cutting in general. The idea is to increase earnings, which in turn increases stock price. However, cost cutting has largely run its course and backlashes are starting to emerge (e.g., against cramped airline seating and lack of meals; against automated call centers by customers; against off-shoring by society, or at least its politicians).

That leaves one avenue for improved financial performance: growing the revenue from businesses already in operation, often referred to as organic growth. In addition to the proven but risky new-product route, companies are increasingly looking at brands and customers as platforms for growth. Brand extensions (a form of new products) and customer expansion are important growth engines. Put differently, if new customers are not acquired and current ones do not buy more, or at least more profitably, there is no growth. Under this view, brands and customers are key assets for generating revenue growth.

In the extreme, it is growth and not metrics that matter. Given a choice between a good system of metrics, an ROI of 30 percent, and 3 percent growth and a haphazard system, an ROI of 20 percent, and 35 percent growth, which would you take? Put differently, superior growth covers up mediocre spending productivity, but superior productivity can't hide mediocre growth. More to the point, however, growth and productivity are synergistic. Both lead to superior financial performance, and the absence of either retards it.

THE ROLE OF NEW PRODUCTS

A related issue here involves new products and demand creation. In the search for growth, firms often focus on new products. In this context, a question arises concerning whether the new product is market driven (i.e., servicing customers' current needs) or is it market driving (providing offerings that target passive or latent—as opposed to active/current—needs [i.e., creates demand])?

Consider a latent (or nonexisting) need. At one point in time, few had a need for a microwave. (One could put dinner a conventional oven and do something while it cooks or almost immediately cook and eat and then get to do something, meaning in the end there is limited advantage to a microwave.) Was it service to customers to further the move to an eat-and-run society, or was it a service to microwave manufacturers and retailers? Of course, after people become accustomed to new products, they often acculturate and come to consider them indispensable. Hence, service to consumers as they might become is different than service to them as they currently are. Still, it is hard to argue that most new products are introduced because firms know they will serve future customers well after their utility functions have been altered. Rather, it seems firms introduce new products to generate revenue growth in the short run and hopefully in the long run, with customer adoption being a requirement/constraint.

One other aspect of new products worth mentioning is their impact beyond the customers who buy them. New products create sometimes unattainable wants among those who do not have them. They benefit some firms and their employees and hurt others. Their use can also benefit some customers and harm others (e.g., drug side effects). Moreover, products use resources that could be used differently or preserved. Therefore, in the spirit of serving customers, the impact of new products on a variety of stakeholders should be considered (Lehmann 2005a).

WHAT ABOUT NONPROFITS?

One obvious question is, what do the twin perspectives of financial performance and growth mean for nonprofit organizations? First, financial performance becomes a requirement and product-market performance becomes the goal, essentially reversing those stages in the value chain. Put differently, nonprofit firms generate money in order to have a desired impact in the world, not vice versa. That impact can be more people behaving in a certain way (e.g., members or believers, people exposed to the arts or science, people seeking and adhering to treatment for various diseases). It can also be improved services (e.g., more effective cancer treatment, more effective instructional material) or societal impacts (e.g., a cleaner environment, more knowledge, a less divisive society) or electing candidates to office. Organizations with such goals then see finances as a means to an end.

Regarding growth, many have growth goals (e.g., religious). Others, however, might not. Some groups like to stay small and exclusive (e.g., country clubs). In this way, they resemble many privately (and family-) owned businesses. For these, the goal is often (appropriately) stability and survival (i.e., serving current customers).

SUMMARY

In summary, a services- (or experience-) based view of marketing is important and insightful. Indeed, it is the dominant logic for nonprofit firms. Still, for for-profit firms, the logic of marketing must be consistent in goal and measure with firm goals. This means, for better or worse, the dominant logic for a marketing profession that wants to "matter" must be financial result in general and growth in particular oriented.

This logic dictates, among other things, an asset-management orientation. In particular, new product development, brands, and customers stand as the three critical pillars of current revenue and future growth. Furthermore, the need for efficiency suggests that assets must be used in an integrated rather than isolated fashion. Hence, new products must pass screens in terms of impact on the brand (brand equity, cannibalization) and customers (acquisition/trial, repeat/retention, share of wallet). Similarly, brand- or customer-inspired strategies should make sense in terms of each other and new products (in terms of relative advantage, compatibility, and risk).

Hopefully marketing will coalesce around financial performance and growth generation as central tenets. In the past, marketing has had central components migrate to other areas such as new product development (lost to research and development and design), the supply chain (lost to operations), strategy (lost to management), and CRM (lost, at least in significant portion, to information technology, which has largely been unsuccessful in showing positive results despite huge expenditures). If marketing proves irrelevant to finance, fails to develop the intangible assets of customers and brands, and proves unhelpful in generating revenue growth, then there is not much left (back to promotions and ad copy, anyone?). Though a bit overdramatic, it is reasonable to suggest that if we lose this "battle" (i.e., fail to demonstrate economic advantage to marketing activities), marketing will lose the "war" and become increasingly marginalized. Though a focus on the service provided in an exchange is a good way to enable these goals, it is not on its own, quite enough.

REFERENCES

Ailawadi, Kusum, Donald R. Lehmann, and Scott Neslin (2003), "Revenue Premium as a Measure of Brand Equity," *Journal of Marketing,* 67 (October), 1–17.

Ambler, Tim (2003), *Marketing and the Bottom Line,* 2nd ed. London: Financial Times Prentice Hall, Pearson Education.

Lehmann, Donald R. (1997), "Some Thoughts on the Futures of Marketing," in *Reflections on the Futures of Marketing,* Donald R. Lehmann and Katherine E. Jocz, eds. Cambridge, MA: Marketing Science Institute, 121–136.

——— (2005a), "It's New but Is It Good? A Macromarketing Perspective on New Products," *Journal of Macromarketing,* forthcoming.

——— (2005b), "Marketing Metrics," in *Review of Marketing Research,* Naresh Malhotra, ed., forthcoming.

——— and Katherine E. Jocz, eds. (1997), *Reflections on the Futures of Marketing*, Cambridge, MA: Marketing Science Institute.

Schmitt, Bernd H. (2003), *Experiential Marketing: A Revolutionary Approach to Connecting with your Customers.* New York: John Wiley & Sons.

Srivastava, Rajendra K., Tasaddoq A. Shervani, and Liam Fahey (1999), "Marketing, Business Processes, and Shareholder Value: An Organizationally Embedded View of Marketing Activities and the Discipline of Marketing," *Journal of Marketing,* 63 (Special Issue), 168–79.

Vargo, Stephen L. and Robert F. Lusch (2004a), "Evolving to a New Dominant Logic for Marketing," *Journal of Marketing,* 68 (January), 1–17.

——— and ——— (2004b), "The Four Service Marketing Myths," *Journal of Service Research,* 6, May, 324–35.

Webster, Frederick E., Jr., (1992), "The Changing Role of Marketing in the Organization," *Journal of Marketing,* 56 (October), 1–17.

24

AN ECONOMICS-BASED LOGIC
FOR MARKETING

Thorbjørn Knudsen

INTRODUCTION

In the article "Evolving to a New Dominant Logic for Marketing," it is argued that marketing inherited a model of exchange from economics (Vargo and Lusch 2004). The authors find promise in recent emergent perspectives that focus on intangible resources, the co-creation of value, and relationships. These perspectives, it is argued, are converging to a new service-dominant logic, indeed, a fundamental shift in worldview. I argue in this chapter that this new service-dominant paradigm in marketing (Vargo and Lusch 2004) is entirely consistent with a co-evolution taking place in economics, which is a rather confirming event. It is also a basis for exchange of ideas. Marketing has a lot to gain from the extant economics and strategy literatures on issues relating to co-creation of value and resource advantage. Marketing is also uniquely situated to contribute to this research by unraveling how advantages in the factor market translate into advantage in product markets, and vice versa.

POSSIBLE SOURCES OF THE NEW DOMINANT LOGIC
OF MARKETING

Economics Has Provided a Useful Idea of Productive Services

In order to unravel the changing worldview, we must see into, through, and beyond the extant marketing literature (Vargo and Lusch 2004). What is it we see, then? According to the authors, we see that the old dominant worldview was shot through with a goods-centered view drawn on the logic from economics. Early marketing thought apparently grew out of economics and inherited its core assumptions, including its focus on tangible goods (Vargo and Lusch 2004).

Although it is true that early marketing grew out of economics, it was a different kind of economics than the authors consider, mainly influenced by the now-forgotten German Historical School (Hodgson 2001; Jones and Monieson 1990). It was an overly applied field of study whose interest was in the description of changing institutional arrangements. This is not the kind of economics Vargo and Lusch (2004) have in mind. Rather, they consider classical economists. The purpose of considering the works of Malthus, Smith, Mill, and Say is to expose a focus on tangible goods as the dominant logic of economics. Apparently, it is assumed that marketing thought is still constrained by the infusion of classical economics that, along with other approaches, influenced the nascent marketing discipline in the 1880s and 1890s.

The article under consideration, however, downplays the status of intangible services in the writings of the classical economists. Labor, which is a factor of production, was always valued in terms of the intangible services it provided. Indeed, both the classical and the neoclassical economists wrote about goods that could be entirely intangible. The idea of productive services remains a cornerstone of the neoclassical theory of production, and the idea that consumers value the services of goods rather than their tangible attributes has a long pedigree in economics (Tirole 1988; Zeuthen 1955). Even though the general equilibrium approach in neoclassical economics defines production functions and utility functions in terms of quantities of various goods and factors of production, this simplification is introduced for reasons of analytical convenience (Tirole 1988). There is no implication that services are ignored in economics. By contrast, services enter in the kind of neoclassical models that consider the quality of goods and factors of production as choice parameters (Sutton 1991; Tirole 1988).

The idea of services flowing from goods and factors of production grew out of classical economics and became common currency in neoclassical economics (Becker 1996; Debreu 1959; Tirole 1988; Zeuthen 1955). The new service-dominant logic of marketing is therefore consistent with the old dominant logic of neoclassical economics. An upshot of this discussion is that the old commodity-centered logic of marketing does not come from neoclassical economics; it is probably best viewed as an early influence from the overly applied institutional economics of the German Historical School. Apart from setting the historical record straight, this observation has important implications. As marketing adopts the new service-dominant logic, there are possible gains of trade between marketing and economics.

Economics Has Provided a Useful Idea of Co-creation of Value

In consumer theory, economists have provided a clear and useful conception of the co-creation of value. It is here worth quoting Becker (1996, p. 26), a Nobel laureate in economics, on the new theory of consumer choice:

> In the traditional theory, households maximize a utility function of the goods and services bought in the marketplace, whereas in the reformulation they maximize a utility function of objects of choice, called commodities, that they produce with market goods, their own time, their skills, training and other human capital, and other inputs.

From the inception of the discipline, economists have considered both the tangible and the intangible attributes goods. More recently, beginning with Lancaster (1966), they have provided a useful conception of the co-creation of value. Consumers co-create products by adding their own time, skills, and human capital to the goods they acquire in the marketplace. It appears that Vargo and Lusch's (2004) reading of the emergent new paradigm in marketing is entirely consistent with a parallel development taking place in economics.

This parallel development in thought becomes even more transparent if we look into the body of literature on the theory of the firm, including the property rights view and transaction cost economics (Alchian 1977; Coase 1937; Hart 1995; Williamson 1975, 1996). To this literature, the idea of co-creation of value is of fundamental importance. The nature of the argument is well-known in recent contributions to industrial marketing, in particular concerning issues of managing marketing channels. A buyer wants a tailor-made product and chooses to trade with one of many potential sellers. The parties make a contract specifying the terms of trade. The contract is incomplete because it is too costly to specify all possible contingencies. To make the product, the seller makes an investment that is specific to the relation between the buyer and the seller, and the buyer also invests in the relation in several ways. Because of the joint investment in the relationship, value is co-created. But this is not the end of the story. Along the way, either the seller or the buyer might see an advantage in reneging the terms of the contract (a holdup problem). For example, the seller could say that costs unexpectedly increased, or the buyer could claim that demand weakened. Either way, to the extent that the buyer and seller anticipate this risk, the deal might fall through. The threat of holdup might lead to an inefficient outcome. The source of the inefficiency is, in this case, a failure to achieve co-creation of value. Transaction cost economics argues that it might be advantageous to merge the businesses in order to protect the co-created value—that is, the solution will be vertical integration. Thus, an explanation for the existence of firms (vertical integration of independent traders) turns on the idea that transaction costs might prohibit the co-creation of value. From a marketing perspective, it is also worth noting that transaction costs typically relate to marketing activities; they were originally referred to as marketing costs (Coase 1937).

As the examples indicate, economists have provided a clear and useful concept of co-creation of value. Perhaps the most well-known example is the concept of economies of scope. In all of these examples, the underlying principle is that of a significant advantage in combining resources (i.e., complementarities). The new dominant logic of marketing is therefore consistent with the logic of economics also on this score. Vargo and Lusch (2004) rightly highlight the issue of co-creation of value as integral to the new dominant logic in marketing. In advancing this issue, marketing might benefit from the useful ways of modeling complementarities that have been developed in economics. Marketing also has a crucial role to play in elaborating on the ways in which complementarities are an essential aspect of the relation between firms and customers.

Economics Has Provided a Useful Idea of Resource Advantage

Vargo and Lusch (2004) refer to recent works on resource advantage and core competences. These works relate to the influential body of literature on the resource-based view (RBV) of strategy. The idea of resource advantage goes back to the RBV, which in turn goes back to Chicago industrial organization economics and the economist Edith Penrose (1959). Notably, Penrose (1959) focused on the services flowing from resources. Because resources hold unrealized potentials of services, entrepreneurial creativity might lead to discovery of superior resource value, even in a commonly held resource (Penrose 1959).

The RBV asserts that firms attain competitive advantage if they possess valuable resources and sustain this advantage if the resources in question continue to be in limited supply (Barney 1991; Dierickx and Cool 1989; Lippman and Rumelt 1982, 2003a, 2003b; Peteraf 1993). Most previous efforts in this line of research have been directed toward the identification of conditions that secure the value of a bundle of resources (i.e., limits to imitation and substitution) (Barney 1991; Peteraf 1993), and, more recently, co-specialization between those resources that are common and those resources that are in limited supply (Lippman and Rumelt 2003a, 2003b).

Vargo and Lusch (2004) should be recommended for their emphasis on resource advantage as a promising topic for marketing. If this line of inquiry is pursued, marketing has a lot to gain from the extant literature on dynamic capabilities and resource-based theory. Again, marketing is also uniquely situated to contribute to this research. One of the crucial unsolved problems in the RBV is how advantages in the factor market translate into advantage in product markets, and vice versa (Priem and Butler 2001). Recent contributions have begun unraveling this problem (Lippman and Rumelt 2003a, 2003b), but a lot remains before we have a secure theory of competitive advantage, encompassing both demand and supply conditions. One of the important new insights is that complementarities between common resources and valuable resources in limited supply are sources of competitive advantage. This insight could be expanded by identifying the contribution to competitive advantage of complementarities between firms and customers. It is here that marketing is in a unique position to combine an analysis of customers with an analysis of the firm's resource base.

CONCLUSION

Vargo and Lusch (2004) should be praised for their focus on resource advantage and their emphasis on intangible resources, the co-creation of value, and relationships as a possible strong basis for the evolution of marketing thought. A further reason to find promise in this new service-dominant logic, as outlined by Vargo and Lusch (2004), is that it invites development of a shared theoretical basis for the many fragmented areas of marketing study. As briefly outlined here, there is a complementary evolution in economic thought that is consistent with the evolution of service-dominant logic in marketing. This observation invites exploration of possible gains of trade between marketing and economics. A possible starting point for such exploration is the idea of co-creation of value. Here, marketing is uniquely situated to develop insights regarding the ways in which demand- and supply-side linkages influence the creation value.

Vargo and Lusch (2004) in part motivated the shift toward a service-dominant logic in marketing by reference to empirical observation (i.e., an observed shift away from tangibles and toward intangibles) and a shift in orientation, away from producers and toward customers. Even though a recent shift can be observed in the direction of heeding service receivers, there is little theoretical support for the claim that either the provider or the receiver of a service is universally central to realizing the joint value of an exchange relationship. Rather, the relative weight to be placed on each side of the exchange relation appears to depend on specifics relating to the mode of exchange and the form of market within which exchange takes place.

Taking this perspective on co-creation of value between providers and receivers of a service seriously points to a very ambitious research agenda for developing a theory of the market to complement the body of literature on the theory of the firm. A fundamental question for such a theory of the market would be to account for the origins of the observed diversity of market forms and modes of exchange. Economics has a head start in this endeavor (McMillan 2002), but marketing stands to gain enormously from a joint venture.

REFERENCES

Alchian, Armen A. (1977), *Economic Forces at Work*. Indianapolis, IN: Liberty Press.

Barney, Jay B. (1991), "Firm Resources and Sustained Competitive Advantage," *Journal of Management*, 17 (1), 99–120.

Becker, Gary S. (1996), *Accounting for Tastes*. Cambridge, MA: Harvard University Press.

Coase, Ronald H. (1937), "The Nature of the Firm," *Economica*, 4(16), 386–405.

Debreu, Gerard (1959), *Theory of Value: An Axiomatic Analysis of Economic Equilibrium*. New York: John Wiley & Sons.

Dierickx, Ingemar and Karel Cool (1989), "Asset Stock Accumulation and the Sustainability of Competitive Advantage," *Management Science*, 35 (12), 1504–11.

Hart, Oliver (1995), *Firms, Contracts and Financial Structure*. Oxford: Oxford University Press.

Hodgson, Geoffrey M. (2001), *How Economics Forgot History: The Problem of Historical Specificity in Social Science*. London and New York: Routledge.

Jones, D.G. Brian and David D. Monieson (1990), "Early Development of the Philosophy of Marketing Thought," *Journal of Marketing*, 54 (January), 102–13.

Lancaster, Kelvin J. (1966), "A New Approach to Consumer Theory," *The Journal of Political Economy*, 74 (2), 132–57.

Lippman, Steven A. and Richard P. Rumelt (1982), "Uncertain Imitability: An Analysis of Interfirm Differences in Efficiency under Competition," *Bell Journal of Economics,* 13 (2), 418–38.

——— and ——— (2003a), "The Payments Perspective: Micro-Foundations of Resource Analysis," *Strategic Management Journal,* 24 (10), 903–27.

——— and ——— (2003b), "A Bargaining Perspective on Resource Advantage," *Strategic Management Journal,* 24 (11), 1069–86.

McMillan, John (2002), *Reinventing the Bazaar: A Natural History of Markets.* New York & London: W.W. Norton & Company.

Penrose, Edith T. (1959), *The Theory of the Growth of the Firm.* London: Basil Blackwell and Mott.

Peteraf, Margaret A. (1993), "The Cornerstones of Competitive Advantage: A Resource-Based View," *Strategic Management Journal,* 14 (3), 179–91.

Priem, Richard L. and John E. Butler (2001), "Is the Resource-Based 'View' a Useful Perspective for Strategic Management?" *The Academy of Management Review,* 26 (1), 22–40.

Sutton, John (1991), *Sunk Costs and Market Structure. Price Competition, Advertising, and the Evolution of Concentration.* Cambridge, MA: The MIT Press.

Tirole, Jean (1988), *The Theory of Industrial Organization.* Cambridge, MA: The MIT Press.

Vargo, Stephen L. and Robert F. Lusch (2004), "Evolving to a New Dominant Logic for Marketing," *Journal of Marketing,* 68 (1), 1–17.

Williamson, Oliver E. (1975), *Markets and Hierarchies: Analysis and Anti-Trust Implications: A Study in the Economics of Internal Organization.* New York: The Free Press.

——— (1996), *The Mechanisms of Governance.* Oxford: Oxford University Press.

Zeuthen, Frederik (1955), *Economic Theory and Method.* Cambridge, MA: Harvard University Press.

25

FROM GOODS- TOWARD SERVICE-CENTERED MARKETING

Dangerous Dichotomy or an Emerging Dominant Logic?

RODERICK J. BRODIE, JAQUELINE PELS, AND MICHAEL SAREN

INTRODUCTION

In their recent *Journal of Marketing* article, Vargo and Lusch (2004; hereafter V&L) propose that a new dominant logic for marketing is emerging that is based on a service-centered perspective. This involves a shift in emphasis from a goods-centered logic that is based on tangible resources, embedded value, and transactions to one that focuses on intangible resources, the co-creation of value, and relationships.

Although there has been considerable discussion about the increasing importance of the service-centered perspective, including books by Grönroos (2000), Gummesson (2002), and Hunt (2000, 2002), V&L's article makes two important contributions. First, they develop eight foundational premises that underpin the emerging service-centered logic:

1. Skills and knowledge make up the fundamental unit of exchange.
2. Indirect exchange masks the fundamental unit of exchange.
3. Goods are distribution mechanisms for service provision.
4. Knowledge is the fundamental source of competitive advantage.
5. All economies are service economies.
6. The customer is always the co-producer.
7. The enterprise can only make value propositions.
8. A service-centered view is inherently customer oriented and relational.

Second, they make an important distinction between *operand* resources (those on which an operation or act is performed, i.e., physical resources such as machinery, raw materials, and other factors of production) and *operant* resources (those that act on other resources, i.e., human resources involving skill and knowledge). Whereas the goods-centered logic is based on operand resources, the service-centered logic shifts its focus to operant resources. To distinguish between these two types of resources V&L, in Table 2 of their article, use six dimensions: primary unit of exchange, role of goods, role of customer, determination and meaning of value, firm–customer interaction, and source of economic growth. This table provides the basis of taxonomy to classify firms' marketing practices according to the two logics.

Although there has already been extensive discussion about the relevance of the V&L article, this has largely been at a conceptual level. What is now needed is empirical research to investigate the extent that service-centered practice is being adopted and emerging as a dominant practice. It is our view that this empirical investigation should be challenged by competing explanations, and we draw on the experience of the Contemporary Marketing Practice (CMP) research group to provide this. The purpose of the CMP research group's research program has been to profile marketing practice in a contemporary environment, and to examine the relevance of relational marketing in different organizational, economic and cultural contexts. It has undertaken research in more than fifteen countries in North America, South America, Europe, Asia, and Australasia over the past eight years.[1] In doing so, it has investigated the adoption of service-centered marketing and its associated relational marketing practices.

An important characteristic of the CMP research has been that it has avoided taking a particular theoretical perspective and has used a framework that has allowed for multiple perspectives. For example, although the CMP research shows that more than three-quarters of the firms have an emphasis on services, many of these firms have an equally important emphasis on goods. What is more challenging is that firms that emphasize multiple marketing practices have better performance characteristics. Hence, we question whether the focus on the shift of goods toward services is really the key issue, and whether it could create a dangerous dichotomy in which much of what is valuable with a goods-centered view is neglected.

The alternative "goods *and* services" view assumes marketing is characterized by multiple complex processes in which there are a wide range of possible contingencies. The successful firms are those that allow for flexibility and can adapt to different opportunities. For these opportunities, some will have a better fit with a goods-centered logic, some will have a better fit with a service-centered logic, and some have a better fit with both. This type of thinking is referred to by organizational and strategic management researchers as *configuration* or *contingency theory*. Recent empirical research by Vorhies and Morgan (2003) explores the relevance of this perspective to marketing.

However, a competing interpretation could be made from the CMP research that would support V&L's position of the shift of "goods *toward* services." This is that the firms that are currently employing multiple marketing practices are at a stage in an evolutionary process in which the service-centered logic is still emerging. Eventually, there will be a transformation, in which the emerging service-centered logic will dominate, but this has not happened yet. During the transformation period, goods-centered logic will still have an important role, but as the information economy becomes established, the new logic will dominate and V&L's eight fundamental propositions will emerge as the basis for contemporary marketing practice.

In this essay, we develop the ideas around the pluralistic "goods *and* services" view as a competing explanation to V&L's "goods *toward* services" view. We draw on the two aspects of the pluralistic philosophy that have guided the CMP research program. First, we examine the implications of *pluralism from a theoretical perspective*. What is of particular interest is that much of the insight from the CMP research has come from allowing for opposite but not necessarily competing views about the nature of marketing practice (i.e., transaction and relationship marketing). This has meant the CMP studies were able to reveal multiple opposite yet co-existing marketing practices.

Second, we examine the *pluralism of multimethod design*. We have found that by working with a group that is comfortable with both the positivist and the interpretative research paradigms has allowed for greater insight about marketing practice. By taking a pluralistic position we avoid the central methodological problem of getting "boxed" into the explanatory dimensions of the chosen paradigm. We consider that the philosophical problem of paradigmatic incommensurability is overstated. Thus, we challenge Kuhn's (1970, p.103) view of the role of paradigms that "the differences between successive paradigms are both necessary and irreconcilable. . . . The normal-scientific tradition that emerges from a scientific revolution is not only incompatible but often actually incommensurable with that which has gone before."[2] Although there are greater problems in undertaking research guided by this holistic view, the benefit has been a deeper understanding of the current marketing practices.

The essay proceeds as follows. First we examine the origins of the CMP research program and then discuss the development of the classification scheme. We then examine the theoretical and empirical implications for using the classification scheme to investigate the nature of marketing practice and whether a service-dominant logic is emerging.

CREATIVE TENSION BETWEEN PRACTICE AND THEORY

The initial motivation to develop the CMP theoretical framework came from the needs of executive education and our experience with practicing managers. This provided the necessary creative tension to challenge the thinking that characterized the academic literature in the 1990s.

There was considerable debate about what should be included in marketing courses for executive students at the University of Auckland in the 1990s. A large part of the Department of Marketing's teaching was to mid-career managers who were working and taking courses part-time. The students came from a representative cross section of consumer goods, business-to-business goods, consumer service, business-to-business service, and nonprofit organizations. The organizations also varied in ownership, size, age, growth rate, export status, and technology use. The advantage with working with practicing managers was they could immediately compare their classroom experiences with the management practices in their organizations. This meant they were very demanding about the relevance of their education.

During the 1990s considerable change was taking place in the business environments of most organizations. In New Zealand in the late 1980s there had been radical market deregulation. Consequently markets were becoming more global and technologically sophisticated, and consumers were more demanding. Competition was more intense, and as a result the emphasis on the service aspects of products were increasingly becoming the basis for competitive advantage. In this new market environment information and communication were important to all businesses. In addition the traditional boundaries between industries were less relevant and new types of business organizations based on partnerships, alliances, and networks were replacing hierarchical organizational structures. Furthermore businesses were placing an increased emphasis on financial return and understanding how value was being created in these new organizational structures.

With the increasing prevalence of these new organizational structures, there was debate as to whether the traditional marketing management courses based on hierarchical organizational structures were still relevant. The marketing management approach that emerged in the 1950s had become the central theme in marketing education, and was still dominant in the 1990s in New Zealand. This was reflected in the use of North American textbooks and their various Australasian adaptations (e.g., Kotler 1997; McCarthy and Perreault 1997; Stanton 1997), the first editions of which were published in the 1960s. The basic model for these textbooks was a large hierarchical consumer goods organization. Little attention was directed to the marketing of services and industrial products, let alone attention to customers at the individual level. Although the textbooks had been modified to accommodate the service and industrial markets, they still failed to fully embrace the emerging relational marketing practices. The focus was primarily on managing transactions and the associated marketing mix (the 4 P's) rather than on relationships.

V&L describe the managerial approach to marketing (goods-centered logic) as being characterized by a decision-making and problem-solving approach that assumes the need to be customer focused and to let the marketplace determine value (see V&L, Table 1). This is contrasted with the emerging relational view that marketing should focus more on social and economic processes and the development of relationships. These relationships might extend beyond customers to suppliers, channel intermediaries, and other market contacts. In the 1990s, the term *relationship marketing* was used to express this view. The relationship marketing approach started to gain support in the literature, with several special journal issues appearing on the topic and a several useful books becoming available (e.g., Berry 1983; Christopher, Payne, and Ballantyne 1991; Grönroos 1990; Houston, Gassenheimer, and Maskulka 1992; Sheth, Gardner, and Garrett 1988). In addition, new courses in executive education such as services marketing, quality management, supply chain management, customer value management, and so on were being offered. Because of the limited space in the curriculum, these courses were being introduced at the expense of the traditional courses; thus, the issue of what was *most* relevant became paramount. The question arose as to whether a relationship marketing course should be the foundation marketing management course in our executive curriculum rather than the traditional marketing management course.

A second challenge came from research about managerial practice. Nicole Coviello's doctoral research in the early 1990s (supervised by Rod Brodie) used in-depth case studies and survey research to examine the nature of marketing in rapidly internationalizing entrepreneurial technology-based firms. Her findings indicated that the more successful firms facilitated their growth through use of network relationships, whereas less successful firms relied on a more transactional, or 4 P's approach to the market. At the same time, however, it was apparent that all firms employed a pluralistic approach to marketing practice involving a combination of classic transactional practices and a range of different relational practices. Unlike the debate that was being undertaken among academics about which was the correct paradigm (i.e., transaction versus relationship marketing), the managers involved in Coviello's research appeared comfortable with multiple practices. Although some might have emphasized network marketing activities, they also saw a role for 4 P's management. This comfort with multiple perspectives was also confirmed through casual interactions with executive students and through their assignment work examining the marketing practices of their organizations.

What became apparent from the previously mentioned experiences was that the dichotomous view of transaction versus relationship marketing was overly simplistic. Rather, it appeared that there were various aspects of marketing being practiced, aspects that required both theoretical and empirical delineation.

INTEGRATING ALTERNATIVE ACADEMIC VIEWS[3]

In response to this challenge, a University of Auckland group including Rod Brodie and Nicole Coviello, together with their colleagues Richard Brookes and Victoria Little, decided to formalize a research program. The program's objective was to profile marketing practice in a contemporary environment and to examine the relevance of relational marketing in different organizational, economic and cultural contexts. Because of the experience with practicing managers, a guiding principle was to employ multiple perspectives. The first stage of this research program was to develop a classification scheme of marketing practice that allowed for multiple theoretical perspectives, including both the traditional transactional marketing management paradigm and the "newer" relational paradigms.

The traditional marketing management paradigm is summarized in the American Marketing Association's 1985 definition as follows:

> Marketing is the process of planning and executing the conception, pricing, promotion, and distribution of ideas, goods, and services to create and satisfy individual and organizational objectives.

In contrast, the so-called new paradigm referred to as *relationship marketing* had a greater emphasis on marketing as a social and economic process. For example, Grönroos (1994, p. 9) defines the purpose of relationship marketing as follows:

> To identify and establish, maintain, and enhance relationships with customers and other stakeholders, at a profit, so that the objectives of the partners involved are met; and this is achieved by a mutual exchange and fulfillment of promises.

Similar to V&L, who identified seven streams of research (see V&L Table 1), Coviello, Brodie, and Munro (1997) identified six streams of research from which the new relationship marketing paradigm had emerged:

1. Services marketing (e.g., Berry 1983; Grönroos 1990)
2. Interorganizational exchange relationships
   a. Industrial Marketing Purchasing (IMP) (e.g., Ford 1990; Håkansson 1982; Håkansson and Snehota 1995)
   b. Buyer–seller relationships, resource dependency theory, social exchange theory (e.g., Anderson and Narus 1990; Dwyer, Schurr, and Oh 1987; Wilson 1995)
3. Channels
   a. Vertical marketing systems (e.g., Bucklin 1970)
   b. Control mechanisms (e.g., Brown, Johnson, and Koenig 1995)
   c. Channel relationships (e.g., Buzzell and Ortmeyer 1995)
4. Network relationships (e.g., Axelsson and Easton 1992; Johanson and Mattsson 1985, 1988)
5. Strategic management and value chains (e.g., Normann and Ramírez 1993)
6. Information technology and between organizations (e.g., Scott Morton 1991)

Common to each of these six streams of research is the focus on management processes. Together they lead to an alternative view. Within this view, marketing becomes an integrative activity involving personnel from across the organization, with emphasis on facilitating, building, and maintaining relationships over time.

To develop the comprehensive classification scheme, it was necessary to take a pluralistic view about the theoretical contributions of these multiple streams of research. However, rather than taking the view that the different perspectives were competing paradigms that were mutually exclusive (i.e., paradigm incommensurability), a multiparadigm approach was taken. The resultant comprehensive classification scheme involved bringing together literatures from the managerial North American schools of thought, and the process-based European schools of thought. Thus the classification scheme was derived from multiple streams of research in marketing and its related disciplines.

Content analysis of previous researchers' use of the various terms associated with marketing identified two common themes, and nine dimensions were identified of *relational exchange* and *management activities*. Five dimensions had themes associated with relational exchange:

1. Purpose of exchange
2. Nature of communication
3. Type of contact
4. Duration of exchange
5. Formality in exchange

And the remaining four dimensions had themes related to management activities:

1. Managerial intent
2. Managerial focus
3. Managerial investment
4. Managerial level

Following identification of these dimensions, the sources of literature were reanalyzed to more clearly define each dimension in the context of marketing practice. Four rather than two different aspects of marketing practice are used to distinguish between traditional marketing management and relationship marketing. The first relates to the traditional marketing management activities and thus is similar to what V&L have referred to as the goods-centered logic:

- *Transaction marketing:* managing the marketing mix to attract and satisfy customers.

The second three encompass relational marketing activities that are closely aligned to what V&L have referred to as the service-centered logic:

- *Database marketing:* using technology-based tools to target and retain customers;
- *Interaction marketing:* developing interpersonal relationships to create cooperation and interaction between buyers and sellers for mutual benefit; and
- *Network marketing:* developing interfirm relationships to allow for coordination of activities among multiple parties for mutual benefit, resource exchange, and so forth.

With the emergence of informational technology (IT) developments, it became necessary to revise and update the original framework. Therefore Coviello, Milley, and Marcolin (2001) extended the CMP classification to include a fifth aspect of marketing practice associated with IT-enabled interactivity. As a result of a conceptualization process similar to that used to develop the original CMP framework, a further aspect of marketing practice, *e-marketing,* was introduced. This new, IT-enabled marketing practice is defined by Coviello, Milley, and Marcolin (2001, p. 26) as "using the Internet and other interactive technologies to create and mediate dialogue between the firm and identified customers." The final classification scheme, which is included as Appendix 25.1, is made up of nine rows and five columns.

In summary, it was only because the CMP classification scheme embraced the *multitheoretical approach* that a comprehensive taxonomy of marketing practice could be developed. This has been made possible because the authors did not take the view that the alternative types of marketing practices are mutually exclusive, nor did they seek to synthesize the contributions from the different paradigms *(paradigm integration).* Rather, a *multitheory* position was adopted.

The *multitheory* position does not seek to place distinct boundaries between each aspect of marketing, nor does it imply they are independent and mutually exclusive. Rather, it attempts to highlight the similarities and differences between each type of marketing, as determined by the relational exchange and management dimensions derived from the literature. More importantly, emphasis is placed on identifying dimensions relevant to actual marketing practice, rather than replicating all the constructs underlying the nature of relationships per se. In doing so, we also question the clarity of the normative distinction between theory and practice by holding that constructs inherent in any one logic create a "cordon" of knowledge that delineates a particular view or conceptualization not only of theory, but also of practice. We, in the academic community, are not only theoreticians but also practitioners, and are strongly influenced in our worldview by our "community of practice." Thus, the CMP program demonstrates how a pluralistic approach to research is required both to broaden the researchers' view and to identify, recognize, and categorize the fullest possible range of relevant empirical phenomena.

MULTIMETHOD DESIGN

One of the characteristics of the CMP research group is the diversity in methodological experience of the researchers. These range from those with quantitative skills who were more comfortable with a positivist philosophy and those with qualitative skills who were more comfortable with the various interpretative philosophies. Hence, the research can draw on a broad range of experience in using different research methods (i.e., in-depth case studies, standardized questionnaires with large samples). We believe that it is this "team-research pluralism" that allowed us to achieve a more comprehensive understanding of what is occurring in terms of marketing practices around the world. It is only by using a multimethod research approach that the multiplicity of marketing practices can be adequately investigated and traditional views challenged. Thus, a more holistic understanding of the complex phenomenon can be developed.

In applying multimethod research, the CMP group initially used sequential designs with alternative methods being employed in sequence, using results to feed into the next stage in the sequence. For example, the initial interpretive research based on Nicole Coviello's doctoral work was then used to help develop CMP framework and the survey research that followed. However, the preferred CMP approach is to use a parallel design in which methods are carried out in parallel with results feeding into each other. For example, most CMP surveys are undertaken with middle managers who act as participant observers for their organizations. In addition to responding to a structured questionnaire, they are required to reflect on the practices in their organizations and, in so doing, provide qualitative assessments. When analyzing the results, the researcher can move back and forth between the statistical analysis of the quantitative data and the qualitative analysis of individual and groups of cases. When the research is reported, text units and other qualitative summaries of groups of cases can be used to augment the quantitative findings.

In other words, the CMP group adopted a multiparadigm philosophy rejecting both the paradigm incommensurability position (which would have led to choosing one paradigm) and the paradigm integration (which would have led to ignoring the paradigmatic conflict). Instead the CMP team, by embracing a multiparadigm philosophy, seeks to encourage the interplay between applying a positivistic *and* an interpretativist approach. Indeed, this approach is not inconsistent with the "pure" positivist methodology of "conjecture and refutation," or even the Hegelian dialectic of thesis and antithesis.

Successful multimethod design and implementation is challenging because it requires working with a group that is comfortable with both the positivist and the interpretative research para-

Table 25.1

Approach to Marketing by Firm Type

Cluster	Consumer goods (%)	B2B goods (%)	Consumer service (%)	B2B service (%)
Transactional (goods-centered logic), n = 103	38.9	34.9	40.6	26.7
Relational (service-centered logic), n = 98	11.1	30.1	29.0	40.8
Pluralistic (goods- and service-centered logic), n = 107	**50.0**	**34.9**	**30.4**	**32.5**
Total	100.0	100.0	100.0	100.0

Source: Adapted from Coviello et al. (2002).

digms. Because there are few researchers who have a broad enough background to have skills in multiple methods, it means that teams need to be built with individuals with different skills and research experiences. This leads to several team management issues and the need to have processes that facilitate cooperation and overcome conflict.

EMPIRICAL CHALLENGE

As mentioned previously, by using a theoretical framework that has multiple perspectives, the CMP group could examine the relative importance of different marketing practices. The implications of this approach are illustrated in the recent article published in the *Journal of Marketing* (Coviello et al. 2002). The study examined 308 firms in the United States and four other Western countries to understand how different types of firms relate to their markets. The research identified three groups of firms: those that have marketing practices that were predominantly transactional (goods-centered logic), those that have marketing practices that were predominantly relational (service-centered logic), and those that have marketing practices that were pluralistic being both transactional and relational (goods- and service-centered logic).

Each group contained approximately one-third of the sample, and within each group were the four types of firms (consumer goods, consumer services, business-to-business [B2B] goods, and B2B services). The results did not show a dominance of a service-centered logic for any of the four types of firms (see Table 25.1). Rather, large numbers for all the four types of firms were in the Pluralistic Cluster (goods- and service-centered logic). This includes 50 percent of the business-to-consumer (B2C) goods firms, 35 percent of the B2B goods firms, 30 percent of the B2C service firms, and 33 percent of the B2B service firms. What is more challenging is that the firms that reported the pluralistic marketing practices had superior performance characteristics.

CHALLENGING V&L'S THEORETICAL POSITION

The results in Table 25.1 do not contradict the importance of the service-centered logic. However, they do challenge its singularity and whether it will emerge as a dominant logic (i.e., "goods *toward* services"). An alternative explanation can be made in which marketing is based on a pluralism of marketing practices (i.e., "goods *and* services"). As mentioned previously, this logic is more closely aligned to what organizational and strategic management researchers refer to as *configuration* or *contingency theory*. The theory suggests that rather than there being the dominance of one strategy, practice or perspective, a wide range of possibilities can coexist due to the diversity of opportunities. Thus, successful firms are those that allow for flexibility and can adapt to different opportunities. Some of those opportunities will fit best with a goods-centered logic, some will fit best with a service-centered logic, and some will fit best drawing on both goods- *and* service-centered logics.

To resolve the question of whether the "goods *toward* services" logic will supersede the "goods *and* services" logic, empirical research is needed. One starting point would be to undertake research to examine what evidence there is to support V&L's eight fundamental propositions. However, if this investigation is going to be free from bias, it is important that a set of alternative propositions that support the "goods *and* services" logic be investigated as competing explanations. For example, if we take V&L's fundamental premise 3—"Goods are distribution mechanisms for service provision"—alternative propositions could be "services are distribution mechanisms for goods suppliers"; "services have limited or no goods components"; and "goods have limited or no service components." Research might reveal that all four situations apply.

To more thoroughly examine V&L's theoretical position, we suggest that this investigation could build on the CMP research. Keeping with the CMP philosophy, the investigation should be characterized by having strong competing explanations (i.e., "goods *and* services" versus "goods *toward* services"). Table 2 in V&L's article provides a starting position to develop a conceptual framework for the investigation. The table distinguishes the use of *operand* resources (those on which an operation or act is performed), which characterize goods-centered logic, and the use of *operant* resources (those that act on other resources), which characterize service-centered logic. The six dimensions (primary unit of exchange, role of goods, role of customer, determination and meaning of value, firm–customer interaction, and source of economic growth) provide the basis for a classification scheme for marketing practices. It is important to note that the classification scheme does not need to assume that a firm's use of *operand* resources and *operant* resources are mutually exclusive. Thus, as with the CMP research, three groups of firms could be investigated: those that have a predominant use of *operand* resources, those that have a predominant use of *operant* resources, and the pluralistic firms that use both. What would be of particular interest is the proportion of firms within these three groups and the characteristics of the types of firms in the three groups. Also of interest would be the consistency of the CMP groupings of "transactional," "relational," and "pluralistic" firms with the "resource use" grouping.

We suggest the investigation should follow the CMP philosophy of multimethod design (i.e., use of in-depth case studies and other qualitative methods in conjunction with standardized questionnaires with large samples). Whereas the quantitative methods provide a valuable cross-sectional profile of current marketing practices, the qualitative methods provide understanding about how marketing practices are changing and the reason behind the changes. We believe that only by adopting this pluralistic approach can a comprehensive understanding about how marketing practice is changing be developed.

SUMMARY

The purpose of this essay is to challenge V&L's theoretical position by reviewing the research undertaken by the CMP group. We discuss the origins of the CMP research program and the development of the classification scheme that allowed us to gain insight into the multiplicity of marketing practices that are taking place. We then examine some of the CMP findings that suggested an alternative competing logic of "goods *and* services" rather than "goods *toward* services." This is based on the pluralism of marketing practices and aligns more closely to what organizational and strategic management researchers have referred to as *contingency theory*. Rather than any dominance, it suggests that marketing is characterized by multiple complex processes reflecting a wide range of possible contingencies and opportunities. Successful firms are those that allow for flexibility and can adapt to different opportunities, some requiring a goods-centered logic, some requiring a service-centered logic, and some that might require both.

To examine whether there is a shift to "goods *toward* services" that will supersede the "goods *and* services" logic, there is the need for empirical research. We suggest that this investigation could build on the CMP research. Central to this research is the need to examine the relevance of V&L's eight fundamental propositions and to challenge these propositions with alternative propositions. However, at a more fundamental level, research is needed to focus on marketing practice. V&L's distinction between operand and operant resources could be used as the basis for a classification scheme in this investigation. We also suggest that there are considerable advantages from using a multiple-method research design. Although there are greater problems in undertaking research guided by this position, by adopting this holistic view we suggest that a deeper understanding of the current marketing practices can be achieved.

In conclusion, although we have challenged the "goods *toward* services" position that has been advocated by V&L, the "jury is still out" and further investigation into the following questions is needed:

- Are the firms that are currently employing multiple marketing practices at a stage in an evolutionary process that will eventually lead to transformation, where ultimately the service-centered logic will dominate?
- Have V&L created a dangerous dichotomy because the diversity of marketing opportunities mean there will always be the need for "goods *and* service" practices?

NOTES

The authors thank their colleagues Nicole Coviello, Richard Brookes, and Victoria Little at the University of Auckland for their useful suggestions.

1. This research has resulted in a stream of articles (see http://cmp.auckland.ac.nz), including the article published in the *Journal of Marketing* (Coviello et al. 2002).

2. It is beyond the scope of this essay to provide a detailed discussion of the reasons why we consider the issue paradigmatic incommensurability to be overstated. However, there is an emerging literature that is supporting this position (e.g., Burrell and Morgan 1979; Gioia and Pitre 1990; Lewis and Grimes 1999; Schultz and Hatch 1996).

3. This section draws closely on material from Coviello, Brodie, and Monroe (1997) and Brodie and colleagues (1997).

REFERENCES

Anderson, J.C. and J.A. Narus (1990), "A Model of Distributor Firm and Manufacturer Firm Working Partnerships," *Journal of Marketing,* 54 (1), 42–58.

Axelsson, B. and G. Easton (1992), *Industrial Networks: A New View of Reality.* London: Routledge.

Berry, L.L. (1983), "Relationship Marketing," in *Emerging Perspectives of Services Marketing,* L.L Berry, G.L. Shostack, and G.D. Upah, eds. Chicago: American Marketing Association, 25–28.

Brodie, R.J., N.E. Coviello, R.W. Brookes, and V. Little (1997), "Toward a Paradigm Shift in Marketing? An Examination of Current Marketing Practices," *Journal of Marketing Management,* 13 (5), 383–406.

Brown, J.R., J.L. Johnson, and H.F. Koenig (1995), "Measuring the Sources of Marketing Channel Power: A Comparison of Alternative Approaches," *International Journal of Research in Marketing,* 12, 333–54.

Bucklin, L. (1970), *Vertical Marketing Systems.* Glenview, IL: Scott, Foresman.

Burrell, G. and G. Morgan (1979), *Sociological Paradigm and Organizational Analysis.* London: Heinemann.

Buzzell, R.D. and G. Ortmeyer (1995), "Channel Partnerships Streamline Distribution," *Sloan Management Review* (Spring), 85–96.

Christopher, M., A. Payne, and D. Ballantyne (1991), *Relationship Marketing: Bringing Quality, Customer Service, and Marketing Together.* Oxford: Butterworth Heinemann.

Coviello, N.E., R.J. Brodie, P.D. Danaher, and W. Johnston (2002), "How Firms Relate to their Markets: An Empirical Examination of Contemporary Marketing Practices," *Journal of Marketing*, 66 (2), 33–46.

———, ———, and H.J. Munro (1997), "Understanding Contemporary Marketing: Development of a Classification Scheme," *Journal of Marketing Management,* 13 (6), 501–22.

———, R. Milley, and B. Marcolin (2001), "Understanding IT-Enabled Interactivity in Contemporary Marketing," *Journal of Interactive Marketing,* 15 (4), 18–33.

Dwyer, F.R., P.J. Schurr, and S. Oh, (1987), "Developing Buyer–Seller Relationships," *Journal of Marketing,* 51 (2), 11–27.

Ford, D. (1990), *Understanding Business Markets: Interaction, Relationships, and Networks.* London: Academic Press.

Gioia, D.A. and E. Pitre (1990), "Multi-Paradigm Perspectives on Theory Building," *Academy of Management Review,* 15, 584–602.

Grönroos, C. (1990), "The Marketing Strategy Continuum: Toward a Marketing Concept for the 1990s," *Management Decision,* 29 (1), 9.

——— (1994), "From Marketing Mix to Relationship Marketing: Toward a Paradigm Shift in Marketing," *Asia-Australia Marketing Journal,* 2 (1), 9–29.

——— (2000), *Service Marketing and Management: A Customer Relationship Approach,* 2nd ed. Chichester, UK: John Wiley & Sons Ltd.

——— (2002) *Total Relationship Marketing,* 2nd ed. Oxford: Butterworth Heinemann.

Gummesson, Evert (2002b), *Total Relationship Marketing,* 2nd ed. Oxford: Butterworth-Heinemann.

Håkansson, H., ed. (1982), *International Marketing and Purchasing of Industrial Goods: An Interaction Approach.* Chichester, UK: John Wiley & Sons Ltd.

——— and I. Snehota (1995), *Developing Relationships in Business Networks.* London: Routledge.

Houston, F.S., J.B. Gassenheimer, and J.M. Maskulka (1992), *Marketing Exchange, Transactions, and Relationships.* Westport, CT: Quorum Books.

Hunt, S.D. (2000), *Foundations of Marketing Theory: Toward a General Theory of Marketing.* Thousand Oaks, CA: Sage Publications.

——— (2002), *A General Theory of Competition: Resources, Competences, Productivity, Economic Growth.* Thousand Oaks, CA: Sage Publications.

Johanson, J. and L-G. Mattsson (1985), "Marketing Investments and Market Investments in Industrial Networks," *International Journal of Research in Marketing,* 2, 185–95.

Kotler, P. (1997), *Marketing Management: Analysis, Planning, Implementation, and Control.* Englewood Cliffs, NJ: Prentice Hall.

Kuhn, T.S. (1970), *The Structure of Scientific Revolutions.* Chicago: University of Chicago Press.

Lewis, M.W. and Grimes, A.J. (1999), "Metatriangulation: Building Theory from Multiple Paradigms," *The Academy of Management Review,* 24 (4), 672–90.

McCarthy, E.J. and W.D. Perreault (1997), *Basic Marketing: A Managerial Approach.* Homewood, IL: Richard D. Irwin.

Normann, R. and R. Ramírez (1993), "From Value Chain to Value Constellation: Designing Interactive Strategy," *Harvard Business Review* (July/August), 65–77.

Scott Morton, M.S. (1991), *The Corporation of the 1990s, Information Technology and Organisational Transformation.* Oxford: Oxford University Press.

Schultz, M. and M.J. Hatch (1996), "Living with Multiple Paradigms: The Case of Paradigm Interplay in Organizational Culture Studies," *Academy of Management Review,* 21, 529–57.

Sheth, J.M., D.M. Gardner, and D.E. Garrett (1988), *Marketing Theory: Evolution and Evaluation.* New York: John Wiley & Sons.

Stanton, W.J. (1997), *Fundamentals of Marketing.* New York: McGraw Hill.

Wilson, D.T. (1995), "An Integrated Model of Buyer–Seller Relationships." *Journal of the Academy of Marketing Science,* 23 (4), 335–45.

Vargo, S.L. and R.F. Lusch (2004), "Evolving to a New Dominant Logic for Marketing," *Journal of Marketing,* 68 (January), 1–17.

Vorhies, D.W. and N.A. Morgan (2003), "A Configuration Theory Assessment of Marketing Organization Fit with Business Strategy and Its Relationship with Marketing Performance." *Journal of Marketing,* 67 (January), 100–115.

Appendix

Five Aspects of Marketing Practice Classified by Exchange and Managerial Dimensions

	Transaction Marketing	Database Marketing	e-Marketing	Interaction Marketing	Network Marketing
Purpose of Exchange	Economic transaction	Information and economic transaction	Information-generating dialogue between a seller and many identified buyers	Interpersonal relationships between a buyer and seller	Connected relationships among firms
Nature of Communication	Firm "to" mass market	Firm "to" targeted segment or individuals	Firm using technology to communicate "with" and "among" many individuals (who might form groups)	Individuals "with" individuals (across organizations)	Firms "with" firms (involving individuals)
Type of Contact	Arms-length, impersonal	Personalized (yet distant)	Interactive (via technology)	Face-to-face, interpersonal (close, based on commitment, trust, and cooperation)	Impersonal-interpersonal (ranging from distant to close)
Duration of Exchange	Discrete (yet perhaps over time)	Discrete and over time (occasional yet personalized)	Continuous (but interactivity occurs in real time)	Continuous (ongoing and mutually adaptive, short or long term)	Continuous (stable yet dynamic, could be short or long term)
Formality in Exchange	Formal	Formal (yet personalized via technology)	Formal (yet customized and/or personalized via interactive technology)	Formal and informal (i.e., at both a business and social level)	Formal and informal (i.e., at both a business and social level)

319

Managerial Intent	Customer attraction (to satisfy the customer at a profit)	Customer retention (to satisfy the customer, increase profit, and attain other objectives, e.g., increased loyalty, decreased customer risk)	Creation of information technology–enabled dialogue	Interaction (to establish, develop, and facilitate a cooperative relationship for mutual benefit)	Coordination (e.g., interaction among sellers, buyers, and other parties across multiple firms for mutual benefit, resource exchange, market access)
Managerial Focus	Product or brand	Product/brand and customers (in a targeted market)	Managing information technology–enabled relationships between the firm and many individuals	Relationships between individuals	Connected relationships among firms (in a network)
Managerial Investment	Internal marketing assets (focusing on product/service, price, distribution, promotion capabilities)	Internal marketing assets (emphasizing information and database technology capabilities)	Internal operational assets (information technology, Web site, logistics); functional systems integration	External market assets (focusing on establishing and developing a relationship with another individual)	External market assets (focusing on developing the firm's position in a network of firms)
Managerial Level	Functional marketers (e.g., sales manager, product manager)	Specialist marketers (e.g., customer service manager, loyalty manager)	Marketing specialists (with) technology specialists and senior managers	Employees and managers (from across functions and levels in the firm)	Senior managers

Source: Contemporary Marketing Practice, http://cmp.auckland.ac.nz.

26

THE SERVICE-DOMINANT LOGIC FOR MARKETING

A Critique

RAVI S. ACHROL AND PHILIP KOTLER

INTRODUCTION

Consumers do not buy soap because of the carbolic fatty acids from which it is made, nor is it the aloe vera or perfume that they need. Consumers buy soap because soap provides cleanliness, skin conditioning, and a fresh feeling, and sometimes because the bottle looks so pretty in the powder room! In other words, consumers do not buy products for their intrinsic physical properties but for the *services* they provide.

From that simple truth Vargo and Lusch (2004; hereafter V&L) articulate a scientific logic, which has its roots in the origins of marketing thought, and propose to chart its direction into the future. V&L argue that marketing has evolved over its 100 years from a goods-dominant, discreet-transaction logic (inherited baggage from its economic origins) to a service-dominant view that emphasizes intangibility, exchange processes, and relationships.

Few would disagree with that nutshell view of marketing progress. It is a view that is ingrained in much of conventional marketing theory. It is a view endorsed in varying degree by the eight marketing scholars who wrote commentaries to go along with the V&L article featured in the *Journal of Marketing.*

There are several reasons why the V&L thesis can be positioned as timely, visionary, and paradigmatic. Rust (2004) notes in his commentary that the output of the world's leading economies has changed from 30 percent service to approximately 70 percent service. Venerable goods manufacturers are turning into *young* service companies. General Motors makes more profit form its auto-loan services division than from its core auto-sales business. IBM has transformed itself from computer manufacturing to marketing of computing services. Shugan's (2004) commentary echoes such evidence. In today's service-dominated economies, most transactions involve high-end services such as health care, legal, financial, entertainment, information, transport, and communications. The service components of products add more customer value than the manufactured components. The service sector employs nearly all marketing students (albeit, Shugan qualifies, the best marketing students are still employed by the stagnant consumer-packaged goods manufacturing sector).

V&L's service-centered view of marketing is relevant for all these reasons, but they are in fact all the wrong reasons. At the outset V&L resolutely state that the service-centered logic is *not* about marketing in service industries or about the value added to products by services or about services as distinct from goods. They criticize services marketing theory as burdened with a need to *distinguish* how services differ from products as marketable commodities, and demonstrate what is unique about the consumer behavior and the marketing management of services.

The service-centered argument is that there is only one unit of exchange in marketing and that is a service—whether a human provides it or it is provided by a product, it is a service nevertheless. V&L cite several authors before them who have argued the case that consumers do not buy products for their physical properties but for the services that the products render (notably Gummesson 1995; Rust 1998). V&L claim that the service-centered view is not about two parallel streams of knowledge but about a unifying dominant logic driven by the service side.

The V&L thesis is a bold interpretation of what a service-centered view of marketing encompasses. It casts a spotlight on several concepts that are important to the fabric of current marketing theory and that can benefit from frequent restatement. What is bold, provocative, and potentially controversial is its claim that the service-centered view provides a synthesizing foundation to these recent developments in marketing theory, a synthesis that amounts to a "fundamental worldview" and "dominant logic" for the discipline—a tall claim that inspires tall expectations and invites tall scrutiny.

New theories, criticism, and controversy are the lifeblood of science. Most great advances in theory emerged from controversial positions, including such "heretical" notions that the earth is round, not flat! But radical new strides for a discipline rarely come as airtight, full-blown arguments (Einsteins of the world excepted), and can be prematurely rejected or politely ignored because of too many ambiguities and vague areas, loose ends, or exaggerated claims. Critical scrutiny is essential to the rigorous development and broad acceptance of new scientific paradigms. And even if eventually the consequences of the service-centered view are short of paradigmatic, critical debate is sure to spin off important advances and modifications in the normal science of marketing as we know it today. It is in this spirit that we offer this critical analysis of the V&L thesis.

Before we turn to a critical analysis of the elements of the service-centered view, we first need to get a sense of what V&L imply is the domain and defining character of the service-centered view.

WHAT IS THE SERVICE-CENTERED LOGIC, REALLY?

We begin this chapter by observing that consumers do not buy soap because they have a craving for soap, but because it provides assorted sensory satisfactions such as cleanliness, skin conditioning, a fresh feeling, and possible symbolic and aesthetic satisfactions associated with brand, advertising, and packaging. That is, we buy products for the services they provide, not for their tangible or compositional properties per se.

The problem with this logic is that having been said, it becomes obvious, a simple truth. V&L cite Bastiat (1860; cited in V&L, pp. 6–7), an early critic of the goods-centered logic of economics, and it is noteworthy that the quote laments its triviality even as it heralds its omniscience: "The great economic law is this: Services are exchanged for services. . . . It is trivial, very commonplace; it is, nonetheless, the beginning, the middle, and the end of economic science."

Unfortunately the important questions of science are rarely about the obvious—that is, that which needs no explanation. Science *is* explanation. Where every thing is the same, or can be reduced to a common denominator, there is little to explain. We hasten to acknowledge that the term *goods* is no less trivial or commonplace. But then, is there profound conceptual meaning hidden in the differences between two pieces of trivia? Despite the claim to the contrary, practically every rationale that V&L put forward is grounded in the goods versus services distinction. So the challenge remains: Can the service-centered view be articulated in ways that are nontrivial statements?

As the article articulates its logic, it leans heavily on goods versus service distinctions (e.g., p. 5, fundamental premises 3 and 5) in ways that can be criticized as creating two currencies from the two faces of a coin. V&L set the stage to their eight "fundamental propositions" by distinguishing the goods-versus-service orientations (p. 5). The goods orientation is summarized in five points and the service-centered view in four. These statements are reproduced in the following numbered lists. To drive home our criticism about whether the goods-service debate is one of substance or merely stylistic and rhetorical, we substitute the term *services* for *goods* and vice versa to see if there is any loss of meaning.

The goods orientation looks like this (substitutions in italics, original in square brackets):

1. The purpose of economic activity is to *offer* [make] and distribute *services* [things] that can be sold.
2. To be sold, these *services* [things] must be embedded with utility and value during the production and distribution processes and must offer to the consumer superior value in relation to competitors' offerings.
3. The firm should set all decision variables at a level that enables it to maximize the profit from the sale of *service* output.
4. For both maximum production control and efficiency, the *services* should be standardized and *offered at a centralized location* [produced away from the market].
5. The *service* [good] can then be inventoried until it is demanded and then delivered to the consumer at a profit.

Except for point 5, substituting the term *services* for *goods* does not cause any logical or practical inconsistencies or problems of meaning. Even point 5 has a logical interpretation—we oftentimes argue that because service cannot be inventoried, the customer or demand is inventoried (held in queue). For example, for efficiency in delivering high-value services, customers and demand are inventoried via appointment systems and waiting and preparation rooms in hospitals, surgical centers, and doctor offices. Likewise, demand is inventoried by off-peak pricing. Thus the logic of point 5 can be paraphrased in services terminology as follows: The customer and demand for services can then be organized like sequential inventories until the service can be delivered economically to the customer at a profit.

Next consider what happens if we substitute *product* for *service* in V&L's statement of the service-centered orientation (as before, substitutions are in italics and original in square brackets):

1. Identify or develop core competences *in manufacturing and product technologies*, the fundamental knowledge and skills of an economic entity that represent potential competitive advantage.
2. Identify other entities (potential customers) that could benefit from these *manufacturing and product* competences.

3. Cultivate relationships that involve the customers in developing customized *products that offer* competitively compelling value propositions *and* [to] meet specific needs.
4. Gauge marketplace feedback by analyzing financial performance from exchange to learn how to improve the firm's *product* offering to customers and improve firm performance.

The point is simple: The professed distinction between the service-centered and product-centered views is not based on a fundamental logic system. Neither, we submit, is a distinctive logic to be found in the eight fundamental propositions that V&L derive. There might be some value in seeing the service-centered view as offering a more relevant and metaphorically correct language system for marketing, but that is a long way from a dominant logic system. Even as a language system it starts with a rather shaky definition.

V&L define *services* as the "application of specialized competencies (knowledge and skills) through deeds, processes, and performances for the benefit of another entity or the entity itself" (p. 2).

The definition can be criticized from several angles, but two are especially pertinent to its position in a logic for all of marketing. First, it is not written in a way that readily recognizes pure services *as well as* services provided via goods. (To make it fit both involves a torturously expansive interpretation of the term *application*.) Second, it is more provider oriented than consumer oriented: As a foundational concept for marketing, it is a backward step from the current *exchange* paradigm. The exchange paradigm distances itself from the marketing management paradigm in that it highlights a mutually beneficial process between two parties. V&L's definition, in contrast, highlights that which one entity does for the benefit of another. The application of specialized competencies and knowledge for one's own benefit (presumably meaning the act of consumption) still does not encompass a mutuality of interest among parties in an end-to-end exchange-consumption relationship.

However, debating the issues in an unstructured, open-ended discussion is likely to have us talking past one another and arguing in circles. The discussion needs to be grounded in an appropriate analytical structure. It is one thing to evaluate the differences in a service-versus-goods orientation, or the nature of operant versus operand resources in marketing decision making, or a relational-versus-transactional view of customers and consumption as theoretical arguments. It is quite another to claim that they add up to a dominant logic for all of marketing. To evaluate that, we submit the relevant analytical framework should be a philosophy of science. One must analyze what the various concepts and distinctions have to say about the service-centered view's ontological, epistemological, and pragmatic meaning (Hunt 2003).

Ontology asks the question "What is the fundamental nature of the service-centered logic?" Is it the claim that the service-centered world is the "real world" of marketing, that it is the way "reality" is experienced by consumers? What does it say about the elemental units of analysis in marketing—the product, the consumer, the firm?

Epistemology wants to know "How do we come to know a service-centered truth?" Is it a formal logic that we can use to test and verify derivative propositions by their internal consistency with the rules by which the logic is constructed? Or is it an empirical science whose truth or falsity can be tested via conventional methods of science?

Pragmatics ask, "How is the service-centered view useful to marketing as an empirical science?" This is the question related to the service-centered view as an applied science. In short, how does it contribute to improving the practice of marketing?

It is presumptuous to imagine that these weighty questions can be answered in an essay-length critique. Our purpose here is the easy one: to frame and give substance to some key questions. We focus primarily on the ontological questions, but this discussion inevitably covers issues in epistemology. This chapter will not evaluate pragmatic issues.

THE ONTOLOGY OF SERVICE-CENTERED MARKETING

What can we deduce from V&L about the ontology of a service-centered view of marketing? This is not an easy task, as the authors tread much ground in their article without explicitly painting a reality picture. On the one hand, they state that a "dominant logic or worldview is never clearly stated but more or less seeps into the individual and collective mind-set of scientists in a discipline" (p. 2). It suggests that a dominant logic is an ideational process of becoming aware of and perceiving the world in a certain way. Nevertheless, V&L must be analyzed for its implicit if not explicit ontological structure and assumptions. We believe a would-be dominant logic in marketing must make meaningful statements about its concept of the fundamental units of analysis— product or service, the consumer and consumption, and the firm.

The Product/Service

V&L's ontology of the product can be deduced from foundational premises 3, 5, and 7. Like most of their arguments, this ontology is also grounded in the limitations of classical economic theory concepts.

V&L argue that from the days of Adam Smith and Alfred Marshall, economics has been tied to tangible goods as the unit of production, value, exchange, and wealth. Needless to say this is an exaggeration. The *language* of economics might be about *goods,* but economic theories define concepts in such abstract terms that they are little bound to the tangible objects we call goods or consumers or firms or technology. The economic good is a "price" and a "quantity." Certain assumptions about standardization and differentiation determine the "demand function," but these are abstract properties that apply equally to goods and services.

V&L's core conceptualization is that a product is *matter embodied with knowledge* and a *distribution mechanism for providing a service.* The wheel and pulley reduce the need for physical strength, the safety razor replaces barber services, washing machines replace laundry services, the computer substitutes for the direct services of accountants, attorneys, physicians, and teachers.

The examples are evocative. But there is some irony in that every illustration is about *products substituting for a direct service.* It needs little telling that the efficiencies driving the economic engine of industrialized society have been the progressive shifting of direct services to services provided by goods. True that postindustrial society has a new and higher-value range of direct services that are driving the economy, but already in sectors of the service-heavy economy (e.g., health care), the scramble is on to find cost-effective goods-mediated alternatives (chemical, mechanical, and electronic devices).

The kinds of theoretical and pragmatic issues that underlie the economic opportunities of, as well as the frictions between, goods and direct services cannot be easily explained away by saying that in the end everything is a service. This type of analysis that x is a more basic form than y is not an end in itself, because, as we have learned about the atom, there is always a more basic x. Theoretically, *basic* is only as basic as the level of the phenomena or level of explanation.

The more basic the elemental relationships, the greater the generality of their explanations. That is the great hope and appeal of "general theory." But it is often the case in the social sciences that the more general the theory, the weaker its pragmatic power to explain. For example, one advantage that comes from the service view of the product is that it says quite loudly that if a better soap-like or not-soap provider-of-cleanliness-and-associated-sensations is discovered, soap might become obsolete. It does not tell us where or how to discover such an alternative, but it serves as a useful caution and competitive refrain. Most will recognize this as the old generic need view of the product, well narrated in the classic buggy whip versus automobile story. V&L acknowledge Shostack (1977, p. 74) in this connection. But Shostack also concluded that if either *product* or *service* does "not adequately describe the true nature of marketing entities, it makes sense to explore the usefulness of a new structural definition."

Whether we speak *good* or *service*, the most widely accepted *basic x* in marketing is surely *satisfaction.* Consumers do not purchase goods *or* services because they need either, but because they provide satisfactions. And if we dig deeper into what constitute the sources of satisfaction, we come full-circle to concepts like *utilities* or *value.* V&L critically examine both these concepts (p. 5 and FP$_7$). They reject the concepts of utility and value-added as tied to the goods orientation. They propose a model based on *value propositions* and *co-production.*

V&L's treatment of value hinges on a distinction between value-added (value-in-exchange, embedded value) and value-in-use. They associate value-added with economic concepts dating back to Adam Smith and early marketing thought based on the creation of form, place, time, and possession utilities (Weld 1916). They associate value-in-use with consumption itself and argue that the consumer alone determines value and participates "in creating it through the process of co-production" (p. 11).

It is one thing to emphasize that until it is converted into a sale, what a firm has to offer, whether tangible or intangible, is no more than a value proposition. And it bears emphasizing that the consumer is a co-producer, that production does not end with the sale but begins with the consumer and extends through the consumption process. But it is quite another thing to argue that value proposition and co-production are more elementary conceptual alternatives to consumer utility and value. Can customization and co-production in an ideal exchange change the basic utilities that need to be delivered to create value for the customer and the firm?

In our opinion, form, time, place, and possession utility remain fundamental to the value-creation and value-consumption process in the conventional as well as in a service-centered logic. What is changing is the relative importance of time, place, and possession utility versus form utility, in the analysis of value to the consumer. Thanks to the enormous efficiencies of the modern economic engine the cost of "form" has become a smaller and smaller component of most consumer products. What the V&L thesis should point to is not the need to discard concepts of utility, but how we can refine our focus on the relative importance and our depth of understanding of the critical utilities in today's marketplace.

For example, for a while it has been apparent that time is an increasingly important element in the bundle of benefits that consumers purchase. But do we know much about what time-value is to a consumer? How do consumers trade off and what price-points can we attach to off-the-shelf delivery, delayed delivery (e.g., Internet purchases), or produce-to-order delivery (e.g., furniture)? What about the time-value of customer co-production—whether it is by way of product co-design, product setup, ease of use and maintenance, ease of service appointments, or waiting for service, and so on?

It seems to us that the service-centered view should naturally highlight the nature and scope of possession utilities today. The traditional view of possession utility as transfer of ownership is limiting. There are many dynamic components of value (and dissatisfiers) to product or service "possession" that we have studied in a disjointed fashion. The role of convenience in use, information value, prestige and symbolic value, post-purchase dissonance, after-sale service, recyclabiltiy, and residual or resale value are a few. Product leasing introduces a new and alternate concept of possession value. What is the real information value of products? Why do so few people care to read product manuals? How much information value do we consume from the powerful computers we buy when many do little more than word processing and surfing the Internet?

In summary, as far as the ontology of the product in modern marketing thought is concerned, we submit that there is not much leverage to be had in hammering the distinction between goods versus services (FP_1, FP_3, and FP_5). A fundamental assumption of the exchange paradigm is that marketing is about the marketing of anything of value between two or more persons or parties. When we say "products" in marketing, it is well understood we mean goods, services, organizations, places, people, ideas, and symbols. Anything of value to the parties involved is a valuable product, including a meaningless ownership share in the Green Bay Packers, a book of blank pages, a pet rock, or psychic services over the phone.

The Consumer and Consumption

V&L's ontology of the consumer can be cobbled together from fundamental propositions 2, 3, 6, and 8. FP_2 argues that preindustrial exchange was direct, one-to-one, skill-for-skill, services-for-services exchange. Industrialization and moneterization removed the consumer from the direct exchange equation and "masked the fundamental unit of exchange."

The service-for-service economy is a romantic fiction we often indulge in about preindustrial society. Strictly speaking it applies only to premoney or barter economies. Today knowledge and information are key sources of service creation, delivery, and wealth. In contrast, barter economies were dominated by power and physical assets as the sources of wealth and the basis of exchange. Skill sets were rudimentary, and ownership of land, animals, plants, and so on were the keys to exchange. Service providers and traders in agrarian economies fawn over the powerful and the elite (owners of material wealth) but pay rudimentary attention to the service needs of the less fortunate. Those who exchanged their services (labor or skill) directly for services-embedded-in-goods did so typically because they had little else to exchange for. To this day in the less-developed economies of the world, the services and products sold to the masses are frequently substandard, adulterated, and shorted.

Absent market discipline, the service-for-service model of exchange is inefficient and inequitable. We argue that industrialization was a boon to the average consumer. FP_2 as an indictment of the bureaucracy of large organization is fine, but to say that industrialization and the moneterization have *masked the true nature of exchange* is not a useful interpretation. Modern economies have complex multilayered systems of exchange. The systems have their shortcomings but have created enormous value and improved standards of living. The marketing task is to explain the nature of modern institutions and the market processes in which they are imbedded, so their limitations can be managed. In this regard V&L make us reexamine our assumptions regarding the consumer as the (1) ultimate source or "creator" of value and (2) co-producer.

The consumer creates value by consumption. Only consumption can create value. "Value creation is only possible when a good or service is consumed. An unsold good has no value" (Gummesson 1998, p. 247).

That is true. But it is worth a word of caution here. Modern exchange is a complex hierarchy of value creation—a complex hierarchy of consumption, if you will. Around the consumption of automobiles and mineral water by the ultimate consumer is a vast network of consumption by business customers and government agencies. Much value is also created during and after consumption in the form of maintenance services, resale and recycling services, and so on. Indeed, consumption creates consumption.

We believe the V&L argument is a great impetus to look more closely at how and how much value creation is done by the consumer in the consumption process, and how this is shifting among service deliverers, support services, and postconsumption services. Much has been written about outsourcing business services. Do we have a theory of outsourcing consumption by ultimate consumers? What happens when we outsource lawn mowing (i.e., replace the service-vehicle lawn mower with the service lawn-service)? Is this a pure income effect? How far is this income effect likely to reach? What is the theory of the leisure society, the theory of the convenience shopper? Is this theory unique? Or is it the same price, quality, differentiation, distribution, communication, and so on theory of pizza consumption? Or is this theory similar to the theories about efficiency, innovation, uncertainty-flexibility, and so on underlying the outsourcing of business functions? Is the consumer a microfirm?

Consider next the central role of consumer as co-producer in the V&L thesis. We note here that consumption by the ultimate consumer is surrounded by a network of consuming business and governments. It follows that the consumer as co-producer is also projected into a network phenomenon. In modern markets, co-production is a delegated function. V&L seem to speak disapprovingly of the "microspecialized" world of today, but the fact remains that few have the knowledge, time, or energy to be enjoined to, or engaged with, their lives as consumers to any extant beyond the perfunctory.

No doubt there are consumers who live to consume, but the majority, we suspect, consume to live. The number of consumers who say they hate shopping continues its secular increase. Consumer participation rate in market research studies continues its secular decline. Except for cult brands like Harley-Davidson and Apple, the majority of consumers participating in relationship marketing programs do so because of financial benefits they receive.

To conclude, the fact remains that the foundation of efficiency in exchange in modern economies is based on mass production of standardized goods in anticipation of demand. The demand itself is whetted and massaged into consumer choices available to the ultimate consumer by numerous actors and regulators in the value chain. This might mask the fundamental nature of service-for-service exchange, but there is little reason to lament that in itself. Likewise, co-production by the consumer is a delegated function. The majority of firms must rely on marketing research as the "co-production" mechanism and on the "feedback it receives from the marketplace in terms of financial performance" (p. 5) to know how good its value propositions are.

If the analyses emerging from the service-centered view are pointing us in a particular direction, it is toward understanding of the consumer and consumption as a network phenomenon. The consumer chooses to participate in various consumption networks. The degree of embeddedness varies greatly. The consumer delegates various levels of the consumption decision making and the consumption process itself, and his or her role as co-producer, to members of the network. A great opportunity before marketing seems to be to adapt consumer behavior theory to understanding how and why consumers make their network choices, change them, and decide how much time, energy, and involvement they are willing to devote to their memberships.

To the end of FP$_3$, V&L touch on concepts commonly used to describe the consumption process, concepts like satisfaction, self-fulfillment, esteem, and experiences. But the authors classify these as higher-order needs and thus seem to say that the service aspect of consumption is associated with the basic functions of the product (e.g., transportation-automobiles). As we point out here, the generic need definition of products or services in terms of generic needs is a useful perspective but not very rich in explanatory content. In contrast, one would think that the service-centered view would uncover much more fertile ground by focusing on consumption experiences as its ontology of consumption.

Indeed, do we know much about how consumers *experience* product performance and use? The service-centered view, which sees a product as a vehicle for service delivery, should be especially sensitive to the *sensations* that mediate the product experience (service delivery). Our research is full of social, psychological, and environmental influences on consumer decision making, and our textbooks continue to recycle the wisdom of Maslow and Freud, but there is practically nothing on how our senses of sight, sound, touch, smell, and taste mediate the product or service experience.

As the marketing literature toys with higher-order forms of satisfaction, such as delight and experiential and virtual consumption, it seems a whole new area for theory and research lies ahead of us that would explicitly incorporate the physiological and cognitive role of our five senses in mediating consumption.

The Firm

V&L's view of the firm can be deduced from foundational premises 1 and 4. Typically, the premises seek to distance themselves from the so-called goods orientation of classical economics to suggest that the "new view" is a significant evolution.

In economics, the firm itself is a "production function," what we fondly call the black box. Ronald Coase and Oliver Williamson sought to define its boundary conditions, and agency and contract theory have added the ghost of a managerial dimension. But the firm in economics remains largely an ontological mystery. It is in the disciplines of organization behavior and strategic management that a managerial theory of the firm and competition are most developed, and not surprisingly, these are the sources from which marketing has drawn the most (especially its literature in the tradition of the marketing management paradigm). Thus, more valid points of departure would be the marketing management and competitive strategy views of the firm.

In articulating its viewpoint the service-centered view draws on strategic management theory, aligning itself with the resource-based (RB) theory of competition. The resources it emphasizes are knowledge and information. Furthermore, V&L suggest the distinction between operand versus operant resources is important to understanding the nature of the service-centered logic.

The alignment with RB theory provides an interesting positioning. V&L make much of the fact that value is created *only* by the consumer. Firms only make value propositions. As it turns out there is a spirited debate in the RB literature along similar lines, phrased in terms of "value capture" (commonly known as "value-added" in manufacturing) versus "value creation" (customer use value or utility). Critics charge that RB theory is flawed because it does not contain an explanation of value creation (Priem and Butler 2001). Supporters respond that RB theory is about the value of resources in the firm and how they are deployed to capture profit (Makadok 2002). Value creation is neither a necessary nor sufficient condition for value capture. (Interestingly, the illustrations Makadok employs to make this point smack of the old preoccupation with *efficiency* at the peril of ignoring *effectiveness*.)

RB proponents seem to ignore the fact that the concept of value capture (the difference between revenues earned and the cost of goods sold) cannot be sheared off from value creation. Half the equation for value capture (i.e., revenues) is nothing other than customers exercising their assessment of value in use. Makadok (2002) is content with the position that the explanation of customer use value is exogenous to RB theory and the discipline of strategic management, something that he assigns to the realm of marketing, psychology, sociology, and such.

Thus, the point V&L make about the critical role of consumers and consumption in validating (putting a monetary stamp of approval on) the value created via product innovation and manufacturing cannot be overemphasized. It is a point that seems to go a-begging no matter in how many ways and how often it has been made. But V&L go to the other extreme and imply that consumption is the only source of value. It is true that an unsold good, especially an unsold service, has no value. But sold goods and services that do not generate an economic surplus for the firm (an efficient and sustainable difference between revenues and cost of goods sold) will sooner or later exit the market.

Thus, there is a ready-made complementarity gap to plug marketing and strategic management together as far as RB theory is concerned. V&L propose to do this by two mechanisms: the distinction between operand and operant resources, and the proposition that knowledge and information are the key strategic resources of today.

V&L observe that the past fifty years have shown that resources are dynamic functions of human ingenuity and not static or fixed in nature. They go on to argue that the classical preoccupation with tangible resources (land, minerals, animals, and plants) as the source of value and wealth is misplaced. These are but operand resources to which operant resources (human ingenuity) are applied to make them valuable.

No doubt distinctions of the kind that "resources *are* not; they *become*" (Zimmermann 1951) offer rare food for the intellect. Penrose (1959, pp. 24–25) made a point when she noted that "it is never *resources* themselves that are the 'inputs' to the production process, but only the *services* that the resources can render," and might very well, if you will pardon the levity, have persuaded some manufacturer barons from feeding labor into blast furnaces during times of fuel shortages! But we argue that the distinction between operand and operant resources is not important ontologically. In theory no resource is inherently operand or operant; it is only a function of the level of explanation and the role (*explananda* or *explanandum*) that the variable (resource) plays in the theoretical scheme. Labor and capital are both operand *and* operant resources. So are knowledge and information. When resources are created or acquired, they are operands. When they are applied to a problem, they are operants. Resources have tangible and intangible dimensions, and their productivity in use is a function of training, organization, management, and human ingenuity.

V&L rightfully point out that a large part of classical economics is based on the assumption that resources have value because they are scarce (i.e., limited in supply). To wit, the air has no value on the surface of the earth, but great value in space or deep under the ocean. But what was especially true for land for Malthus and Riccardo is no less true today by virtue of the realization that intangibles assets—such as knowledge, information, human capital, core competency, management and organization—are far more valuable than coal or grain (but not petroleum or platinum). They *are* and they have *become* far more valuable because they are scarce relative to their uses, not because they are operand or operant. Real estate in Manhattan still costs a lot more than the services of the vast majority of the working/operant class, the Bill Gateses excluded.

In any event, differences with language terms, economic or otherwise, is a weak argument. It is not irrelevant, but neither is it substantive or compelling. A substantive argument would be that a service-centered view changes the nature of the production function, the demand function, equilibria, or such, in some specified way. In this regard, there is more substance in V&L's fundamental proposition 4, in which the case is made that operant resources are primarily knowledge and information.

The emerging literature in information economics is driven by differences in the development and production costs and revenue functions of today's information products. It highlights such unique market phenomena as network effects or externalities, customer lock-in and the life term value of customers (e.g., Shapiro and Varian 1998).

Likewise, the concept of the firm as information processor and knowledge creator is also a new and exciting area of inquiry. It is of much less significance to know that knowledge is an operant resource than to know how firms can nurture knowledge in productive ways. Knowledge as individual human talent does not necessarily add up to organizational knowledge, capabilities, and performance; witness the periodic collapse of the great giants of industry staffed and managed by the best and the brightest.

In both of these areas, the focus of theoretical frameworks has been on how network structures and linkages nurture or impede the flow and utilization of relevant information, and the creation and application of new knowledge (e.g., the work of Burt 1980 and Granovetter 1973 in information networks, and Achrol and Kotler 1999 in organizational networks). We argue that rather than get sidetracked with labeling conventions of what is operant and what is operand, the logic of the new marketing paradigm should focus more intently on networks and information flows of all kinds. This would represent a real evolution from the current exchange paradigm in marketing and not just an abstract improvement over the largely ceremonial theory of the firm in classical economics.

The focus on the network as the fundamental unit of analysis is a significant ontological step from the theory of the firm as well as dyadic exchange theory. It is especially important today because marketing as well as firm environments are being pervaded by network phenomena. Firms have been downsizing and outsourcing large chunks of their resource and functional domains. Vertical marketing systems are evolving sophisticated cooperative and relational managerial systems in contrast to the old manufacturing-firm-dominated hierarchies. The networks seek to include and involve consumers as integral elements of the relational system. Consumers find their consumption environment is increasingly complex, interlinked, and networked. They are outsourcing consumption services and delegating decision making. They are operating as microfirms in a larger network of business firms.

These exciting and far-reaching changes are causing major shifts in the allocation of functions, including innovation, manufacturing, marketing, and value added/created in the network. Unfortunately, subsuming all of this under the "service" label does not add anything to the explication of the network or the theories that might be useful in explaining network phenomena.

Then how useful is the service-centered RB theory of the firm for marketing? We believe it is important from a language-of-science point of view. We believe the language of science has important epistemological and pragmatic consequences, though they are not fundamental to explanation itself. The language of science serves to highlight and bring into relief certain features of the subject phenomena, thus inviting theoretical explanation and incorporation in empirical sets and operationalizations. However, analyzing the implications of the service-centered view as a language system for marketing is beyond the scope of this article.

CONCLUSION

There is little doubt that marketing theory and concepts have made remarkable strides over their history. Yet we are far from a mature science with a unified body of knowledge and methodologies. Can the varied and patchy body of marketing knowledge be reduced and codified into a contemporary logic? The critical analysis in this chapter would lead us to believe that for direction we need to look beyond the *service* word and visualize the key elements of the conceptual system in which the service-centered logic claims to be embedded—elements such as knowledge resources, relationships, and networks. The discussion section of V&L's article provides an excellent overview of these leading-edge theories in marketing, but it is far from clear that the service-centered logic is an important driver of these theories or an overarching framework that ties them together in a way that makes the whole greater than its parts. A semantic reorganization of concepts that does not advance our understanding of theoretical mechanisms and interconnections underlying marketing phenomena is a superfluous distraction. In other words, in trying to understand what *is* the service-centered logic implied by V&L, we found the *service* word to be a distraction.

Nevertheless, one cannot deny V&L's argument that at the root of every consumption experience is indeed a delivered service. One cannot deny the large shift in the relative component of service compared with product in modern economies and delivered value. One cannot deny that marketing theory and practice can benefit by according a higher profile and theoretical cognizance for service in its phenomenology and epistemology.

Even if there are insufficient grounds to elevate service to occupy a role as a dominant or instrumental logic in marketing epistemology, there is an important semantic role in modifying the language of marketing to more closely reflect the phenomenon underlying consumption. Language plays a powerful, oftentimes subconscious, role in the way we view the world. The use of what is sometimes pejoratively called "politically correct" terms has had a great impact in eliminating subtle ethnic-, gender-, and age-related biases in society that are often perpetuated by language queues. Likewise, language can have a purposive influence in expanding and adding dimension to the ways in which we view and behave toward phenomena in the world around us.

We argue that explicating and expanding the service-centered logic so that the ideational and behavioral meanings of service (the service-centered gestalt) are enhanced holds much more promise than seeking to subsume emergent ideas and theory in marketing. The former can be achieved by developing theory and research about the service dimensions in each area of marketing. For example, if consumers consume only the service provided by services and products alike, then what are the sensory mechanisms that mediate the service experience?

The other advantage of language in a science like marketing stems from its formative role. Marketing might be called a "living science," because we often face the curious situation of studying phenomena that we sometimes create. Marketing is a phenomenon that is enacted. It is not an objective reality that exists independent of the people or organisms that inhabit it, but is fashioned and enlightened by these people. For example, there was no relationship marketing before it was "discovered" and given life and shape by marketing academics, consultants, and managers.

But there are disadvantages in adopting a service-oriented language for marketing. First, even if we conceptualize products as delivered service, we must not forget that the *service* choice is constrained by design, features, storage space, operability, discardability/recyclability, price, and a host of other factors that follow directly from the tangible nature of the service-product. Failing to keep the tangible dimensions of the service-product in clear perspective risks building more and better service for the sake of service, a service orientation similar to the product orientation as in the parable of building a better mousetrap. In a way, that is the story of the American Express card versus Visa.

Second, the language of science might be easier to change than language itself. It might be relatively easy to acculturate marketing scientists to see a food processor or chef as a "service appliance" that consumers use to process food. Or to see food as a "service vehicle" that delivers taste sensations, energy, and nutrition, and see candlelight, music, tablecloth, and so on as the "service platform." But can one reasonably expect practicing managers to think of a six-pack of beer in terms of a six-server: a six-service vehicle of thirst-quenching, bitter-flavorful, pleasure-inducing, social-intoxicant? Can one reasonably expect the dictionaries of tomorrow to define a good as matter embedded with knowledge?

Saying that every product is a service in material disguise ignores the enormous creative energy and technological progress represented by the tangible means of delivering services invented by the industrial revolution. To suggest that only "services are exchanged for services" and that that is the core logic of marketing science is as true of the barter economy as of the information economy, but it also trivializes everything that has happened in between.

Pushing to label the emerging marketing paradigm a service-centered (or knowledge-centered, relationship-centered, or network-centered) dominant logic will probably do more harm than good to its evolution by imposing restrictions on peripheral vision of the kind that this-is-not-service-centered, really.

Theoretical diversity rather than uniformity is a positive sign of the health of a relatively new science like marketing. Theoretical diversity might also be the only way for a science that not only encompasses a vast phenomenology but also is constantly changing and evolving in interaction with the "science" itself. Thus marketing might need many worldviews: the view of firms, exchanging dyads, networks and consumers; the view of products, technologies, and the services they and humans provide; managerial views, personal consumer views, and social and public policy views.

Some philosophers like Popper, Feyerabend, and Lakatos forcefully argue for theoretical diversity and against dominant paradigms such as the *Einheitswessen* (unified science) of the logical positivists, or Kuhn's weltanschauung (worldview). Popper (1959) points out that because we never know for certain that our theories are correct, we should proliferate our theories as much as possible to encourage the growth of scientific knowledge.

In the remarkable words of the remarkable Wroe Alderson, the entire marketing process can be described as a series of transformations of the meaningless heterogeneity of the materials found in nature (agglomerations) into the meaningful heterogeneity of goods (assortments) found in consumer households. It is unlikely any dominant logic will *serve* to explain a heterogeneity processing system well!

REFERENCES

Achrol, Ravi S. and Philip Kotler (1999), "Marketing in the Network Economy," *Journal of Marketing,* 63 (Special Issue), 146–63.

Bastiat, Fredric (1860), *Harmonies of Political Economy,* Patrick S. Sterling, trans. London: J. Murray.

Burt, Ronald S. (1980), "Models of Network Structure," *Annual Review of Sociology,* 6, 79–141.

Granovetter, Mark (1973), "The Strength of Weak Ties," *American Journal of Sociology,* 78 (May), 1360–80.

Gummesson, Evert (1995), "Relationship Marketing: Its Role in the Service Economy," in *Understanding Services Management,* William J. Glynn and James G. Barnes, eds. New York: John Wiley & Sons, 244–68.

——— (1998), "Implementation Requires a Relationship Marketing Paradigm," *Journal of the Academy of Marketing Science,* 26 (Summer), 242–49.

Hunt, Shelby D. (2003), *Controversy in Marketing Theory.* Armonk, NY: M.E. Sharpe.

Makadok, Richard (2002), "The Theory of Value and the Value of Theory: Breaking New Ground versus Reinventing the Wheel," *Academy of Management Review,* 27 (1), 10–13.

Penrose, Edith T. (1959), *The Theory of the Growth of the Firm.* London: Basil Blackwell and Mott.

Priem, R.L., and J. E. Butler (2001), "Is the Resource-Based View a Useful Perspective for Strategic Management Research?" *Academy of Management Review,* 26, 22–40.

Popper, Karl R. (1959), *The Logic of Scientific Discovery.* New York: Harper and Row.

Rust, Roland (1998), "What Is the Domain of Service Research?" *Journal of Service Research,* 1 (November), 107.

——— (2004), "If Everything Is Service, Why Is this Happening Now, and What Difference Does It Make?" Invited Commentaries, *Journal of Marketing,* 68 (January), 23–24.

Shapiro, Carl and Hal R. Varian (1998), *Information Rules: A Strategic Guide to the Network Economy.* Boston: Harvard Business School Press.

Shostack, G. Lynn (1977), "Breaking Free from Product Marketing," *Journal of Marketing,* 41 (April), 73–80.

Shugan, Steven M. (2004), "Finance, Operations, and Marketing Conflicts in Service Firms," Invited Commentaries, *Journal of Marketing,* 68 (January), 24–26.

Vargo, Stephen L. and Robert F. Lusch (2004), "Evolving to a New Dominant Logic for Marketing," *Journal of Marketing,* 68 (January), 1–17.

Weld, Louis D. H. (1916), *The Marketing of Farm Products.* New York: Macmillan.

Zimmermann, Erich W. (1951), *World Resources and Industries.* New York: Harper and Row.

PART VI

MOVING FORWARD WITH A SERVICE-DOMINANT LOGIC OF MARKETING

The book closes with chapters that direct the marketing discipline toward service-dominant (S-D) logic (what some have referred to as the "new dominant logic" of marketing). Not all will agree with the specific direction in which these authors point, but virtually all will probably agree that they suggest that marketing will unfold into a much richer discipline, both from a theoretical and a practical perspective.

"Many-to-Many Marketing as Grand Theory: A Nordic School Contribution" (chapter 27) by Gummesson emphasizes the unifying role of networks in the development of general or grand theory in marketing. Because of their capacity to allow for complexity, context, and dynamism, Gummesson believes networks have a universal capacity to explain. Gummesson argues for what happens between parties in relationships is interaction and that it become a central construct in marketing theory. It is then the relationships and interactions embedded in them that result in networks that he views as the core construct in marketing. Developing a very holistic and systems view, he suggests that marketing is a subset of organizations, which are a subset of society, which is consequently a subset of life. In concluding the chapter, Gummesson develops a tentative grand theory of marketing that he refers to as "many-to-many marketing." This theory describes, analyzes, and utilizes the network properties of marketing. Generally, we find Gummesson's position very consistent with S-D logic. We believe that S-D logic provides the justification for network formation: mutual service exchange. Network theory, in turn, provides the foundation for understanding the process of interactivity and emergent structure.

Grönroos, in chapter 28, "What Can a Service Logic Offer Marketing Theory?" suggests that, rather than exchange as the core concept of marketing, the core become the tripartite concepts of services, interactions, and relationships with customers. Thus, his ideas have much in common with Gummesson's. He suggests two basic rules of marketing: (1) Marketing activities must take place where the customers are and where the customers are influenced by them; and (2) the customers of a firm, not its marketing department, decide which of the firm's resources and activities are marketing resources and activities. Not surprisingly, then, Grönroos's position argues the "logic of service is to support the customers' value-generating processes." Marketing must do more than communicate value propositions; it must "make sure that value indeed is created in the customers' processes." Grönroos is of course correct; value creation, through service exchange, is the purpose beyond the proposition.

An integrative chapter, by Sawhney, with many examples grounded in industry and firm practice, is presented in chapter 29, "Going beyond the Product: Defining, Designing, and Delivering Customer Solutions." The crux of Sawhney's thinking is that customers have no interest in offer-

335

ings per se but really want solutions to problems. As simple as this sounds, it is very enlightening, as well as confirming of S-D logic. From this perspective, the firm must start with customer outcomes and work backward to solve them. Sawhney encourages firms to develop a "solutions mind-set." Vivid examples are given of a solutions-centric mind-set, the nature of solutions, defining customer outcomes, and mapping customer activity cycles. Especially instructive is his description of activity blueprinting, which is a form of qualitative research that develops descriptions of how real customers buy, use, and consume products. Importantly, he does not ignore firm performance and offers guidelines for designing repeatable solutions for profit. Further, in one of the more difficult tasks for which there is little innovative thinking, Sawhney shares his insights into how to price solutions based on customer value. Not to ignore the significant research opportunities coming out of solutions marketing, he suggests an innovative research program that not only advances theory but also the practice of marketing.

Immediately after the publication of the original S-D logic article (reprinted as chapter 1), we began to receive inquiries about how acceptance of it would change the practice of marketing or marketing strategy. Rust and Thompson, in chapter 30, "How Does Marketing Strategy Change in a Service-Based World? Implications and Directions for Research," argue that the driving force behind S-D logic is information technology. They believe that the service and information revolutions are two sides of the same coin. "It is the ability to generate, transform and distribute information that ultimately enables firms to provide services to customers." This results in a move from a product-centered mind-set to a customer-centric mind-set.

A natural movement, then, is to focus on customer equity or the long-term value of a customer. The authors show how this influences strategic efforts, competitive advantage, the measurement of the financial impact of marketing, the nature of product utility, and marketing planning. They further suggest three key avenues for future research focusing on firm behavior: (1) the impact of information technology on business performance, (2) transforming information technology resources into superior customer equity and management skills, and (3) the impact of customer equity on the value of the firm. Coupled with this, they suggest needed consumer behavior research: (1) the impact of offering more flexibility, more choices, and transferring more power to customers; (2) the psychological effects of product customization; and (3) when and how to offer customization as a mechanism to co-production.

Reflecting on decades of experience in service marketing and as leaders of perhaps the most prestigious and high-impact university-based research center in North America focused on service, Brown and Bitner share their thoughts on furthering a services revolution in marketing. Chapter 31, "Mandating a Services Revolution for Marketing," stands out due to its detailed focus on actual industry illustrations. Throughout the chapter they argue that a corporate strategy of getting closer to customers requires a service-centered view cutting across and involving all functions of the firm. Clearly, this is entirely consistent with S-D logic. The authors show how a framework developed at the ASU Center for Services Leadership, the "services marketing triangle," can be used to provide strategic guidance to firms. Three points of the triangle include customers, providers (employees, agents or subcontractors), and the company. They use the linkages among these groups to discuss the role of external marketing, which results in "making promises"; internal marketing, which "enables promises"; and interactive marketing, which helps in "keeping promises."

Concluding the book is a chapter in which we begin to more systematically lay the foundation for the development of a general theory grounded in S-D logic. We argue that (1) the fundamental subject matter is exchange, but each time a seller or buyer exchanges they change and they learn via this process; thus, exchange is pro-knowledge discovery; (2) organizational and consumer goals cannot be optimized or maximized but only can be improved upon one step at a time; (3) the external environments are not uncontrollable as suggested by the dominant paradigm but rather are resources that can be drawn on for support (after resistances are overcome); (4) consumers are not operand resources to market to and target but are operant resources to market with and co-produce with; and (5) value-in-exchange exists but value-in-use is more customer-centric.

The inverted paradigm replaces the highly tactical marketing mix with a more strategic orientation. Rather than (1) price making the firm develop value propositions (ideally co-created with the customer), (2) products are not offered but service(s) and appliances are used to co-produce with the customer, (3) promotion that focuses on persuasion and propaganda is largely replaced with conversation and dialogue that is truly open, two-way, and co-productive, and (4) place is not composed of distribution to but the development of supply and value networks to collaborate and co-produce with partners and customers. In brief, just like those that began to view earth as round and not flat, our proposed framework for the formation of a general theory of marketing is radically different from the dominant paradigm.

27

MANY-TO-MANY MARKETING AS GRAND THEORY

A Nordic School Contribution

Evert Gummesson

INTRODUCTION: RESEARCHSCAPES IN MARKETINGLAND

Vargo and Lusch (2004a, p. 15) state that "the academic focus is shifting from the thing being exchanged to one on the process of exchange. Science has moved from a focus on mechanics to one on dynamics, evolutionary development, and the emergence of complex adaptive systems." Services marketing, relationship marketing, customer relationship management (CRM), and one-to-one marketing, and in addition to those quality management and the balanced scorecard, have all contributed in this direction. But their potential has not been properly tapped; they have neither become as comprehensive nor been as successfully implemented as I had hoped. My conclusion is that a major hurdle is lack of grand theory, in which the parts, links, and changes of marketing can be addressed and be given meaning.

Being critical to the current state of marketing theory, the chapter advocates that three variables —relationships, networks, and interaction—should form the basis for future marketing theory. It shows how this conclusion came about through an inductive and interactive approach, including both practical experience and research of observed gaps between real-life marketing and marketing theory, textbooks, and education. In this chapter the center of attention is networks.

Many-Faceted Researchscapes

The landscapes in which researchers work—their *researchscapes*—have many properties. Officially, we focus on the intellectual, rational, and methodological issues, although we experience other angles in the practice of research. There are institutional conditions, and there are the psychology and sociology of science. Researchscapes include individual researchers and teams as well as individual and collective perceptions of what is good and bad science; career paths, budgets, university bureaucracies and political regulations; and evaluations by journal reviewers and grants, awards, promotion, ranking and certification bodies. The life in researchscapes is shaped by not only a drive to add to scientific knowledge, but also a desire for recognition, position, power, and wealth—sometimes even crossing the line of scholarly decency. These human features contribute to explain how concepts and theories are developed and disseminated, and even systematically marketed through both unobtrusive modesty and hard-pressure sales techniques. Furthermore, past and present accounts of a discipline might be written to boost the reputation of an elite of those who have acquired the power and privilege to define priorities and set academic agendas.

It is common to ignore that any scientific paradigm is founded on a mix of objective, subjective, intersubjective, and qualitative assumptions. Mainstream research adheres to an approved foundation and treats it as rock-solid scientific truth. On its axioms, academic researchers perform elaborate dances of factor analysis, conjoint analysis, and Lisrel, often in the innocent belief that they are doing "rigorous, objective research." Although these performances per se might be of high professional standard, they remain applications of techniques, all with their strengths and weaknesses.

Doubtful Axioms

Among the axiomatic pillars in marketing are exaggerated and simplistic reliance on a "free" market economy; the marketing concept of customer needs and satisfaction as the highway to profits; maximization of short-term profit (shareholder value) as the purpose of business; unlimited growth as beneficial; corporate citizenship diluted to charity; and blindness to the effects of unethical and criminal action and black economies. Furthermore, accounts of the past and present of marketing often suffer from unwarranted claims of generalization. It is commonly assumed that the U.S. history of marketing is the world history, and sweeping characterizations and categories of doubtful content are offered. For example, the industrial era succeeded the agricultural era (we never consumed as much of agricultural products as we do today); we now have a service economy (we have never had so many manufactured products as we have today, and the industrialization of services has only just begun); the scarcity is not goods and services but customers (pure water, pure air, and natural foods are scarce even to the rich; medical services, legal services, and education are scarce to the majority of the world population); services are intangible and therefore service quality is difficult to manage and measure, whereas goods quality is a piece of cake (rooted in stone mythology of services marketing); and previously everything pretty much sold itself but today we have entered fierce global competition; and so on.

Although these doctrines have been the object of debate and dialog, they explicitly or implicitly underpin the accessible and palatable species of theory, *textbook theory,* which constitutes the gist of the education of new generations of marketers.

Theory Generation with an Open Source Code

This chapter offers my ongoing and tentative contribution to a grand theory. It is my very personal travel report from a lifelong journey in Marketingland. I would like you—to be frank, demand of you—to consider it with an open mind. I hope you will get inspired by it, even buy it—but I am not trying to sell it to you. To use Internet lingo, it is like the Linux operating system: It has an open source code. Anybody is welcome to contribute with constructive improvements or alternatives, but destructive criticism is not encouraged.

My interests could also be expressed as theory generation with a desire to understand more and to contribute to better marketing theory. There is a commonly upheld distinction of discovery and theory generation versus theory testing. Seen as a never-ending process, theory generation and theory testing merge. Translated into a leading strategy from total quality management it is "continuous improvement."

A Journey through a Rough Countryside

Marketingland is intersected with mountains and canyons. There are gorges between scholarly theory, textbook theory, and practice. What I found early as a marketing practitioner forever made me doubt the credibility of academic research in marketing, marketing textbooks, and the wisdom of professors. Several key issues that I encountered in business practice and as a private consumer were absent in the literature. Prompted by my job, I first looked for services and business-to-business (B2B) topics. In the 1970s, services marketing and management started to gain a critical mass of researchers, and service research skyrocketed in 1980s. Contributions came from the UK, the United States, France, and my own corner of the world, what later became known as the Nordic School (Grönroos 2000a, 2000b). Service research particularly added to marketing theory by stressing interaction and the relationship with the customer in the service encounter. It was also the beginning of a divisive categorization between goods and services, even if many claimed that goods and services always appear in tandem, and what should be marketed is the services or value rendered by a supplier, whether they consist of activities (services) or things (goods). A certain service mythology started to establish itself and has not as yet been laid bare, even if voices have been raised in recent articles (Lovelock and Gummesson 2004; Vargo and Lusch 2004b). My own initial research concerned professional services, where services and another less-studied area, B2B, joined forces.

Relationships have always been important in business practice and have gradually stepped forward in the new theoretical developments of marketing of services and B2B since the 1970s. It was not until the 1990s, however, that relationships really came into focus under the label of "relationship marketing," later also to be named "one-to-one marketing" and "customer relationship management" (CRM). It became obvious that relationships were also significant in consumer goods marketing. In combining relationship marketing with information technology (IT) into CRM, providers found the right set of circumstances to sell huge software packages in which to store, integrate, and process information about customers with the purpose of targeting markets more efficiently. However, the 1960s marketing management "theory" lingered as the guiding framework, and frequently CRM seems to have become a novel way of molding and managing captive customers rather than cooperating with customers.

Although the role of the customer had started to be redefined, especially the customer being an active party in marketing and not just a pawn managed by suppliers, and customer-to-customer interaction (C2C) had appeared in service models, it has had no particular impact on general marketing management theory.

Contributions to grand theory also go beyond marketing and ally with other management disciplines. Quality management moved its focus from the technical aspects of engineering and manufacturing to customer-perceived quality. In practice, customer satisfaction and quality became synonymous. At long last models of service quality emerged, supplementing the then sixty-year-old tradition of product-oriented quality management. The balanced scorecard offered a framework for thinking beyond the short-term financial considerations. Other factors, notably customers, employees, and development were added to the balance sheet as antecedents to future profit.

VANTAGE POINTS FOR GRAND MARKETING THEORY

In a synthesis of my journey, three aspects of marketing theory have attracted my attention in particular. First, among all the phenomena and concepts *relationships, networks,* and *interaction* stand out as more generic than others. Second, through my experience of the difficulties to integrate new discoveries such as services marketing, B2B, the changing role of the customer, and the new IT with extant marketing theory, the need for a fundamentally new theory of marketing on a higher level of abstraction, a *grand theory,* is urgently felt. Third, and primarily inspired by new developments in the natural sciences and their validity for social sciences, I conclude that marketing needs to be put into a *wider context;* its myopic and insular state is long outdated. These three vantage points—networks, grand theory, wider context—are further reviewed in the next sections.

The Core Variables of Marketing

Relationships are important to everybody and ubiquitous in private, professional, and commercial life. From our own experience we have an intuitive perception of what relationships are and the many shapes they can assume. There is an affluence of synonyms—*contacts, ties, links, bonds, friends, acquaintances,* and others—that are part of everyday language. They link people or organizations; they might be temporary or sustaining. Although it might feel comforting to have clear definitions of the words we use, it is part of my scientific credo that essential phenomena of life—such as relationships—are fuzzy and overlapping by nature and therefore cannot be given simple, clear-cut definitions. When relationships embrace more than two people or organizations, complex patterns and contextual dimensions will emerge—*networks.* We therefore also talk about networks of relationships. What happens between the parties in the relationships is called *interaction.*

A common research strategy is to reduce the abundance of data into something simple and manageable. But we certainly do not need reduction of complexity and context, discarding disturbing data—anomalies—that refuse to get into neat, preconceived boxes. Within the strategies for grounded theory (Glaser 2001, 2003), it means that we search for variables that absorb the essence of a phenomenon—without disfiguring its nature. Generation of grounded theory starts with inductive, empirical emergence of data and patterns that can form a hierarchy of core and subcore variables. Examples of such condensed expressions in natural sciences are atoms, electrons, quarks, molecules, protons, neutrons, and Einstein's famous formula $E = mc^2$ (energy equals mass times the squared speed of light).

Without going further into the search and analysis process, I settled for relationships, networks, and interaction as potential core variables. My conclusion became that in a future grand theory of marketing, networks should be tentatively appointed the core variable, with relationships and interaction as the two subcore variables on the next tier of a hierarchy of variables (Figure 27.1). I found that networks could harbor the other two, whereas neither relationships nor interaction could. I found support for this in natural sciences; networks might be the best available way of describing and analyzing life in a generic sense.

An alarming observation is that none of these three variables are part and parcel of traditional marketing management and its marketing mix theory, although they have entered everyday language in marketing. The dramatic impact these should have on marketing theory has failed to appear in the core of general scholarly marketing theory and textbook theory.

Grand Theory—or Being Stuck in the Middle

Another aspect emphasized in grounded theory is shown in Figure 27.2. The major contribution from scholarly research is its ability to condense data; define variables, categories, and concepts

Figure 27.1 **The Core and Subcore Variables of a Future Grand Marketing Theory**

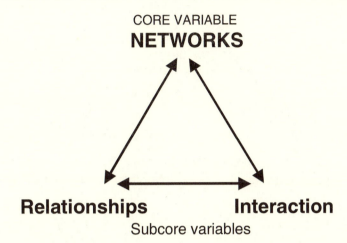

CORE VARIABLE
NETWORKS

Relationships   Interaction
Subcore variables

on a progressively higher level of abstraction; and configure them into theories that provide guide-lines for the understanding of marketing reality. It is a value-adding process, taking raw data from description to conceptualization and generalization.

Few marketing academics seem to devote themselves to making syntheses of the knowledge that is produced. We are part of a systemic whole, but yet business systems are fragmented and are better characterized by *holes* than by *wholes*. New findings are not integrated with extant knowledge. The big marketing textbooks offer their textbook theory as a compilation of frag-mented aspects, like services marketing, B2B marketing, and relationship marketing/CRM being added and presented as special applications on an allegedly general theory.

When this chapter focuses on grand theory in marketing, the underlying assumption is that theory on a higher level of abstraction is helpful in research, education, and practice (Gummesson 2002a). However, grand theory can only be relevant and helpful if it emerges out of substantive detail. Therefore, ongoing iterations between grounded data and abstract thinking are a symbiotic process. The whole is not the sum of more and more details; it is synergetic integration. Genuine grand theory can be compared to a world map where we can see the continents and the seas and how they relate to each other. Before this grand map can be drawn, the detailed shapes of the seas and continents must be correctly identified. The map can be hierarchically presented on the level of the landscape that is suited for a specific use.

The multiple arrows in Figure 27.2 symbolize the emergence of theory in iterative, nonlinear, and dynamic processes. We have to take data all the way up to an abstract level at which we might be able to offer grand theory. Natural scientists seem to be more inclined to develop grand theory than marketers. Despite seminal achievements during the past hundred years, natural scientists continue their search for more inclusive, integrative, and unifying theories. The latest is superstring theory, which integrates the theory of relativity and quantum mechanics on a yet higher level of abstraction. They even go as far as to talk about the "theory of everything," although, not surpris-ingly, the rationale of such a claim is disputed (Barrow 1992). The goal is to find an all-embrac-ing theory, even if that might be a direction more than an attainable goal. According to physics and mathematics professor Brian Greene (2004, p. 328), "We envision each new theory taking us closer to the elusive goal of truth, but whether there is an ultimate theory—a theory that cannot be refined further, because it has finally revealed the workings of the universe at the deepest possible

Figure 27.2 **Iterative Climbing of the Theory Ladder**

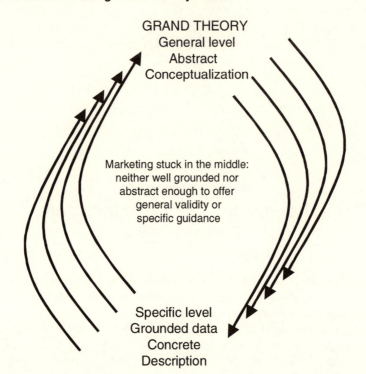

GRAND THEORY
General level
Abstract
Conceptualization

Marketing stuck in the middle:
neither well grounded nor
abstract enough to offer
general validity or
specific guidance

Specific level
Grounded data
Concrete
Description

level—is a question no one can answer." In a similar vein, I consider it high time to work more with syntheses of the material that comes out of research in marketing and marketing practice.

My unsettling conclusion is that *marketing is stuck in the middle.* It is neither well grounded in data nor abstract enough to have general validity. It offers neither a general overview nor specific guidance. It is not sufficiently linked to data on a concrete level of description because research techniques deployed to access the real world are imperfect, and some are routinely promoted by tradition and an exaggerated belief in numbers. We need better access through presence and involvement; we need more deep-going observation and action research. My personal package of research approaches, which I label *interactive research* because the approaches each require various types of interaction, consists of case study research, grounded theory, action research, ethnography, and narrative research (see further Gummesson 2001).

In my view, research in marketing performed both by academia and commercial research institutes has become techniques oriented in a wild goose chase for simplistic cause-and-effect proof. Real-world complexity and context is lost on the way. This is especially so when the research rests on approximate, probabilistic, truncated, and operationalized data, generalized inside the black box of subjective respondent perceptions, as is the input from questionnaire-based statistical surveys. Natural sciences dissolve the artificial demarcation line between qualitative and quantitative; in fact, the new mathematics can be characterized as more qualitative than quantitative. According to Fritjof Capra (1997, p. 134), one of the physicists who endeavors to find bridges between natural sciences and social life, modern natural science is more concerned with "the qualitative features . . . rather than the precise values of its variables at a particular time. . . . The new mathematics . . . represents a shift from quantity to quality."

Natural sciences work with systems theory, chaos theory, dissipative structures, fractal geometry, autopoiesis with self-healing and self-organizing systems, and others. These theories are geared to accepting and addressing complexity, context, dynamics, indeterminism, and ambiguity. They are looking not for simplistic and partial cause-and-effect links but for patterns and wholes. Anomalies—data that refuse to fit into existing equations, models and theories—are not discarded for the sake of researcher convenience. In line with chaos theory, even a miniscule anomaly can disrupt a seemingly robust system.

There is little grand theory of marketing today that develops continuously and is solidly grounded and conceptually advanced. Microeconomics is a grand theory that has lost its credibility through "forcing" (in conflict with the grounded theory requisite of "emergence") and its surreal assumptions. Although some assumptions have gradually been relaxed it is still pursuing the strategy of mathematical rigor—paradoxically primarily using poor quality data that are appointed facts—over relevance and validity. Alderson's (1957) efforts to reconceptualize marketing and offer a coherent and valid theory is quoted with reverence but is not used anywhere. Hunt's (2002) current efforts to design a resource-advantage theory of marketing are commendable, but still too little known and tried. Most efforts to integrate new elements of marketing theory—relationships, services, quality, IT—seem to degenerate into piecemeal efforts to prove unidirectional and static causality.

A Broadened Context for Marketing Theory

Zohar (1997, p. 46) views management in the light of quantum theory and puts emphasis on context:

> The ambiguous and heavily relational boundaries of quantum entities are known as "contextualism." To be known, to be measured, to be used, a quantum entity must always be seen within the larger context of its defining relationships. Change the context, and the entity itself is different. It realises another of its infinite potentialities. It *becomes* something different. Something more. [emphasis in original]

Within this spirit and from having studied relationships and networks on the marketing level, I gradually realized that they are part of a broader context. As marketing is part of life, it should be natural to position it in a life context. In not doing so, the risk is that we will continue to treat marketing from a myopic, piecemeal outlook. Figure 27.3 defines marketing as a subset of the management of organizations, and organizations as a subset of society, which is in turn a subset of life.

In mainstream relationship marketing/CRM, I found both lack of context and the dodging of complexity. With few exceptions (e.g., Christopher, Payne, and Ballantyne 2002; Morgan and Hunt 1994; Reichheld 1996), developments have focused on a simple customer–supplier dyad. In an effort to develop a more complete concept, I defined thirty relationships, the 30Rs (Gummesson 2002b). I gradually came to define relationship marketing as "interaction in networks of relationships" (Gummesson 2004, p.16). I have subsequently ventured to go further and deduce that this was not just a definition limited to relationship marketing; it could be the beginnings of a general definition of marketing on a higher level of abstraction.

NETWORKS

Based on the claims codified in Figures 27.1–27.3, the second half of the chapter starts with the universal role of networks in life and society; narrows it down to organizations, management, and

Figure 27.3 **Marketing Positioned in a Broader Context**

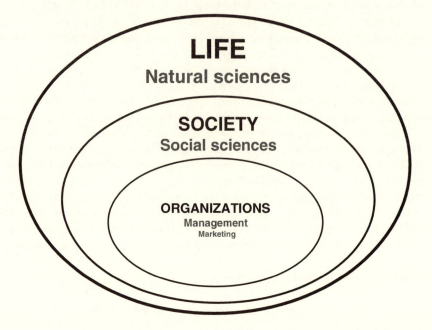

marketing; and proceeds with a tentative account of a new theory: many-to-many marketing.

I sometimes hear or even read that networks are trendy and hyped. I disagree completely. Perhaps they can be considered trendy if by that you mean that they are more in focus these days than before. But the question is: Why are they more talked about?

My explanation is that networks are the basis of life, society, and organizations, and consequently also of management and marketing. We are now discovering this; it is a belated discovery but one of great consequence. In my view it will help us accept marketing complexity and see the larger context, and thus networks can form the foundation of a comprehensive marketing theory, a grand theory. I reached the conclusion by coalescing practical job experience, research experience, and experience as a consumer with network theory from several disciplines.

Networks in Life and Society

The word *system* is derived from the Greek *systema*, meaning "a whole composed of many parts." A way of capturing systemic complexity and context is offered by *network theory*. Network theory is "democratic" as it can be applied by anybody with varying degrees of sophistication. Networks consist of nodes and links between them in which interaction takes place. Networks can be used in a verbal discourse, in graphic representation, or together with matrix algebra and newer forms of mathematics. Network theory is also intuitive as it often reflects how we think and act in practice. For example, driving a car demands instantaneous and constant interaction with other vehicles and people, road conditions, traffic lights, the weather, and so on. It requires immediate observation of detail in a dynamic and nonlinear process, and immediate positioning of the data into the larger context of the whole driving situation. It is interaction in a pulsating and ever-changing network of relationships.

By reviewing individual links and nodes, we aim for the complexity and context of the whole network, recognizing that a network, although structurally consisting of its parts, is something other than the linear sum of its parts. Network theory offers a universal description of life itself: Life consists of networks of relationships within which we interact (Capra 1997; Gummesson 2004).

Network theory has a long history in both social and natural sciences. On social network analysis, see for example overviews by Scott (1991), Degenne and Forsé (1999), and Kilduff and Tsai (2003). Currently natural scientists take a particularly keen interest in generating general network theory. Several scientists transcend boundaries and integrate natural and social sciences (Barabási 2002; Buchanan 2003; Capra 1997, 2002; and Zohar 1997). The Internet, which is a social and technical network infrastructure with a potential to embrace all human beings, contributes through its complex and still little understood properties and fickle dynamics, and it also offers a new tool to survey and analyze networks.

Within network theory a series of concepts, strategies, and conclusions have been developed, such as scale-free networks; the power of preferred hubs; tipping points; epidemic dissemination of information and behavior; Granovetter's (1973) seemingly paradoxical "the strength of weak ties" (weak relationships between people are sometimes more important than strong links); and "six degrees of separation" (we are closer to each other than we intuitively realize).

Network theory has traditionally been concerned with structures, such as those depicted in network graphs. In alignment with the quotation from Vargo and Lusch in the introduction to this chapter—with the key words *process, dynamics, evolution,* and *complex adaptive systems*—network theory is increasingly addressing the complexity of dynamic transformational aspects. In today's natural sciences "complexity theory"—a collective name for a series of developments—is part of the mainstream. Capra (2002, p. 236) notes the affinity between complexity and networks: " 'Complexity' is derived etymologically from the Latin verb *complecti* ('to twine together') and the noun *complexus* ('network'). Thus the idea of nonlinearity—a network of intertwined strands—lies in the very root of the meaning of 'complexity.'"

Complexity is not limited to natural sciences, and the methods and techniques are largely universal. However, it is sparsely treated in management literature; notable exceptions are Stacey (1996), Lissack (1997), and Morgan (1998). Complexity theory is codified in new mathematics, a general vocabulary and grammar that is sympathetic to all types of phenomena. This mathematics is hardly even noted in the quantitative studies favored by mainstream social researchers, who primarily represent old mathematics albeit in an upgraded and digitalized format.

The assumption that the world can be understood through an increasingly more complete series of fragmented "A causes B" studies, in which an independent variable and a dependent variable are unambiguously defined, is mechanistic and not realistic; it is in conflict with life and nature. A more "realistic reality" is that sometimes A causes B, in the next moment B might cause A, or they might interact and cause each other, only to stay away from each other totally in the next moment. Furthermore, A and B live a dynamic flux of and endless number of nodes and links, which directly or indirectly could affect our object of study.

Figure 27.3 claimed that the study of organizations should be considered a part of social sciences, and so it is already to a certain extent. Most would stop there. The reason for bringing in natural sciences is the support I have found in its methodology and scientific approach. Natural sciences—which seem to be much more daring and adaptable than the economic sciences—can teach management researchers useful lessons, and its scientists do not seem bashful of transforming their findings to social and business areas.

In my previous studies of relationships, I came to the conclusion that "society is a network of relationships in which we interact." There is also an overlap between the role of private life as a citizen and commercial life as a consumer. Fukuyama (1995) has stressed the importance of trust and cooperation beyond the family as prerequisites for the wealth of a nation and the efficiency of business. This has recently been echoed by Seabright (2004) in his treatise of the complexity of cooperative networks and the importance of the reciprocity between strangers, making them—if not our friends—so at least our "honorary friends." It is a reaction against the tradition of hierarchical, rule-ridden, and anonymous institutions, where red tape, bureaucratic/legal values, and technicalities govern society for lack of empathy and human values. Schluter and Lee (1993, 2003) propose the transfer from a market economy built on formal institutions and hierarchy to a relational market economy, relational democracy, and relational justice. They argue that "relationism is a conceptual framework as complete and as a robust in policy terms as capitalism and socialism" (1993, p. 193). A relational market economy can accommodate competition, growth, and private ownership. However, it is not anonymous and depersonalized, as is the case in economics, in today's ownership of companies and the operation of government bureaucracies. A crucial concept is "relational proximity," referring to an economy that promotes local activities and resources and demotes the giantism and anonymous power that is characterized by today's global expansion of corporations.

Castells (1996) describes society as networked through the Internet, e-mail, and mobile telecom. However, in line with Naisbitt (1982), we should also consider the *high-tech/high-touch* trade-off, based on the notion of balancing "the material wonders of technology with the spiritual demands of our human nature" (p. 42). Naisbitt's conclusion was as follows: "The more high technology around us, the more the need for human touch" (p. 52). Today, more than twenty years later, his claim rings truer than ever, primarily through the impact that IT now has on social life.

Capra (2002) concludes that "one of the key insights in the systems approach has been the realization that the network is a pattern that is common to all life. Wherever we see life, we see networks" (p. 8), and "Living social systems . . . are self-generating networks of communications. This means that a human organization will be a living system only if organized as a network or contains smaller networks within its boundaries" (p. 93).

What unites natural sciences, social sciences, and marketing is that networks of relationships within which interaction takes place has the potential to describe and explain life more fully than any other approach.

Networks on the Marketing and Management Levels

Networks is a neutral, generic concept and can be applied in numerous ways, broader or narrower, to signify a specific phenomenon. Here is a selection of its usage in marketing literature.

According to Iacobucci (1996, xiii), "a network describes a collection of actors (persons, departments, firms, countries, and so on) and their structural connections (familial, social, communicative, financial, strategic, business alliances, and so on)." Thorelli (1986, p. 37), who analyzed B2B hierarchies and networks, defines network as "two or more organizations involved in long-term relationships." Achrol and Kotler (1999) identify four levels of networks in marketing: internal, vertical, intermarket, and opportunity networks. Möller and Svahn (2003, p. 213) emphasize the difference between macro networks that have emerged spontaneously or are orchestrated by powerful corporations, and strategic nets that are "intentional structures that firms try to design deliberately for specific purposes." Alm (1996, p. 164) talks about organized networks as being more formal than private networks, some type of association: "A set of relationships between people through a common interest." In this spirit we can perceive a nation as a mega network of people with something in common and a company as an organized commercial network with a common business mission. In between the two exist both formally organized networks and spontaneous, free-wheeling networks of consumers and citizens. Zetterberg (2003) sees networks as informal, filling the gap between formal organizations. He points out that a network has no boss who determines what the customer should buy, but customers form networks around their current interests and purchases.

There are also more specific applications. Coyne and Dye (1998, p. 101) define network-based companies and industries as "those that deliver a significant portion of their value to their customers by transporting people, goods, or information from any entry point on a network to any exit point." Examples are airlines (move people and goods between a large number of airports), banks (move money in a network of accounts), and telecom operators (link people for information exchange). When media industry members talk about networks, they usually mean radio and television stations. "Network marketing" and "multilevel marketing (MLM)" signify companies building their operations on private contacts, such as Avon and Tupperware ("home party selling").

MANY-TO-MANY MARKETING

The final part of this chapter presents a tentative grand theory of marketing based on networks and their universal capacity to mirror reality by allowing for complexity, context, and dynamism. Although the principle of establishing long-term relationships with customers as is proposed in relationship marketing, CRM, and one-to-one seems reasonable, companies have had great difficulty in its implementation. From a many-to-many perspective the major reason for the failures is that the customer-and-supplier relationship is looked on as isolated from the rest of the world.

The expression "many-to-many marketing" is used to epitomize the contrast to one-to-one marketing. It is defined as follows (Gummesson 2004, p. 17): "Many-to-many marketing describes, analyzes and utilizes the network properties of marketing." For the sake of comparison, the properties of one-to-one marketing, largely also representing mainstream relationship marketing and CRM, are used (Figure 27.4). The target for one-to-one is a single supplier and single customer relationship, but for many-to-many it is supplier networks interacting with customer networks. The contribution from one-to-one is to put the light on individual interaction in marketing as opposed to unidirectional mass marketing. Many-to-many goes a step further, addressing the whole context of a complex world.

As shown in Figures 27.1–27.3, many-to-many marketing recognizes (1) networks as its core variable and relationships and interaction as subcore variables; (2) the need for grand, unifying theory to which the parts, links, and changes of marketing can be related and given meaning, based on both substantive detail and abstract generalization; and (3) marketing as part of the broader context of life itself.

Here follow seven areas for consideration in a future grand theory of many-to-many marketing:

1. Networks can be used for both structural description and analysis and the understanding of process and dynamics; interaction and its consequences are expressions for the latter aspects.

2. Although networks have been primarily treated in B2B, not only organizations live in networks but also consumers, citizens, and employees. B2B is based on a derived demand from consumers and is therefore an antecedent to B2C marketing. Orthodox B2C marketing treats consumers as anonymous masses or segments who essentially buy products/services as stand-alones, one-by-one. Many-to-many consumer purchasing is part of a context of products/services and membership in networks of friends, family, suppliers, customer clubs, and others. In a

Figure 27.4 **One-to-one and Many-to-many Compared**

One-to-one marketing
According to Peppers and Rogers

Many-to-many marketing
According to Gummesson

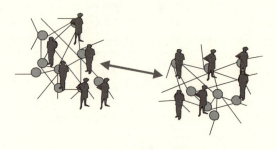

* identify your customers	* identify your networks of relationships
* differentiate your customers	* differentiate your relationships
* interact with your customers	* interact with the network members
* customize	* customize
* form learning relationships	* form learning networks

Source: Gummesson 2004, p. 17; reproduced with permission.
Note: The characteristics of one-to-one are taken from Peppers and Rogers (1999).

consumer-centric and interactive mode, we might equally well say C2B; the initiative is just as much that of the consumer. When the complexity and context of marketing is addressed it is obvious that the roles of producer and consumer are ambiguous, not clear-cut. This has been put forward in services marketing but is also true for other marketing situations in which the networks of contacts and interactions are laid bare and the interdependence between goods and services is recognized. There is also growing understanding of C2C, which has long been addressed in services marketing but has been turbocharged by the Internet. Eventually all this is interrelated—B2B2C2C2B2B . . . —in complex, scale-free networks (Figure 27.5).

3. To establish the broadened context of marketing to the management of a company and to society, networks are classified in market, mega, and nano networks. *Market networks* primarily include customers, suppliers, competitors, and intermediaries. In turn, they are a subset of *mega networks,* the realm of society, governments, media, and strategic corporate issues such as alliances operating beyond the control of marketing and sales. Infrastructural networks belong here, such as road networks, postal service, electricity grids, broadband, and networks for mobile telecommunication, all necessary to provide a supportive environment for marketing. Finally, *nano networks* refer to internal networks, those embracing people who work in an organization.

4. The need for balance between the roles of technology and human beings has perhaps never been more acute than today. The Internet, e-mail, and mobile communication are increasingly directing the lives of society in our roles as citizens, consumers, and employees. Echoing Naisbitt's (1982) demand for high-tech/high-touch balance, we can raise a pressing question: Are people

Figure 27.5 **B and C Linked in a Unified Context**

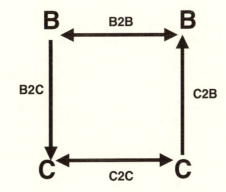

using technology for conceiving a better society, or are people becoming enslaved by technology? I find the issue increasingly relevant to networks; it also aligns social sciences and natural sciences.

5. Businesses are dependent on alliances, outsourcing, knowledge-sharing, and so on to be competitive. This requires a network approach to organization. New businesses are often built on personal networks, at least to some degree. To make many-to-many marketing work, it is necessary to rethink a company's leadership, organization, and systems. Wilkinson and Young (2003, p. 180) compare the network to an orchestra: "Instead of examining ways to command and control a relationship or network of relations, managers are more participants that learn to adapt and respond to what others are doing, similar to how the members of a jazz ensemble interact to coproduce good improvisational music." In a yin and yang mode they discuss *followship* (the female role in dancing) versus *leadership* (the male role); it's "business dancing" (Young and Wilkinson 1994). Good jazz and dancing as well as good marketing require both followship and leadership.

6. Several positions and titles, some long established, indicate the importance of handling relationships and networks: account managers with advertising agencies and financial brokers, key account managers coordinating the contacts with major B2B customers, relationship managers, CRM managers, and network captains. Perhaps the next and more radical step is to exchange the CEO for an NEO, a network executive officer. Networks do not have a chief in the same sense as a traditional hierarchical company. The network requires an NEO with ability to exert both leadership and followship. In fact, my contention is that every successful business leader is already working as a NEO, otherwise he or she would not last long.

7. Marketers must always consider cost, revenue, and bottom line (Ambler 2000). Currently research in marketing metrics and marketing accountability suggests a new wave of interest in marketing's financial role. As an umbrella concept I use *return on networks (RON),* defined as follows (Gummesson 2004, p. 23): "RON (Return on Networks) is the long-term effect on profitability caused by the establishment and maintenance of an organization's networks of relationships." In a similar vein, *intellectual capital* and the *balanced scorecard* offer a measurement format beyond mere short-term finance. Other approaches are *ROM (return on management)* (Simons and Dávila 1998); *customer equity* (Rust, Zeithaml, and Lemon 2000); and *access capital.* From a many-to-many perspective, it might be possible to develop *network equity.* Open questions are as follows: How can we measure RON and network equity? What should be quan-

titative measurements and what should be qualitative assessments? What should be left to experience and intuition?

In the process of designing many-to-many marketing, it gradually dawned on me that this was just the prelude to a much more comprehensive field of study than I had visualized. So far, many-to-many is the closest I have come to a DNA or string theory of marketing. Just as theories of relativity, quantum theory, and string theory form vantage points for scientific inquiry, marketing defined as networks of relationships within which we interact, must ask itself: Where will it take us? Will it, as I believe, give us a more inclusive and condensed platform for marketing?

To find out, we have to take many-to-many seriously, understand its fundamentals, and experiment with its application. For its further evolution I would like to recall the spirit of the open source code of Linux. Its originator, Linus Torvalds, had conceived the beginnings of a new operative system and, rather than protect it, asked others to help develop it. It elicited the brainpower of committed hackers and rapidly grew into the most advanced operating system. Anyone can use it for free and suggest changes—but its originator has remained the network captain.

EPILOGUE

I was once told by Vedic sages that university means *uni*-fication of di-*versity*. In today's practice, *university* means diversification and fragmentation of knowledge, reminding me of George Orwell's prophecy that words by manipulation can come to mean their opposites. New disciplines keep spawning and linking them through interdisciplinary research has proven difficult. I am getting increasingly impatient with those who advocate more rigorous testing of fragmented detail—pretending complexity and context can largely be disregarded—and only marginally sensitive to the systemic whole, the network structures and processes of life, the dynamics and the phenomenon of emergence, and not least individual and collective dimensions of researcher persona and its researchscape. In contrast to the bulk of research in marketing currently being reductionistic and based on fragmentation, many-to-many requires defragmentation where systemic complexity, context, and dynamic processes are addressed.

REFERENCES

Ambler, Tim (2000), *Marketing and the Bottom Line*. London: Financial Times/Prentice Hall.
Achrol, Ravi S. and Philip Kotler (1999), "Marketing in the Network Economy," *Journal of Marketing, 63* (Special Issue), 146–63.
Alderson, Wroe (1957), *Marketing Behavior and Executive Action*. Homewood, IL: Richard D. Irwin.
Alm, Johny (1996), *Nätverksguiden*. Malmö, Sweden: Liber.
Barabási, Albert-László (2002), *Linked: The New Science of Networks*. Cambridge, MA: Perseus.
Barrow, John D. (1992), *Theories of Everything*. London: Vintage.
Buchanan, Mark (2003), *Small World*. London: Phoenix.
Capra, Fritjof (1997), *The Web of Life*. London: Flamingo.
——— (2002), *The Hidden Connections*. London: HarperCollins.
Castells, Manuel (1996), *The Rise of the Network Society*. Oxford: Blackwell.
Christopher, Martin, Adrian Payne, and David Ballantyne (2002), *Relationship Marketing*. Oxford: Butterworth-Heinemann.
Coyne, Kevin P. and Renée Dye (1998), "The Competitive Dynamics of Network-Based Businesses," *Harvard Business Review,* (January/February), 99–109.
Degenne, Alain and Michel Forsé (1999), *Introducing Social Networks*. London: Sage.
Fukuyama, Francis (1995), *Trust*. New York: The Free Press.
Glaser, Barney G. (2001), *The Grounded Theory Perspective I: Conceptualization Contrasted with Description*. Mill Valley, CA: Sociology Press.

———— (2003), *The Grounded Theory Perspective II: Description's Remodeling of Grounded Theory Methodology*. Mill Valley, CA: Sociology Press.

Granovetter, Mark S. (1973), "The Strength of Weak Ties," *American Journal of Sociology*, 78, 3–30.

Greene, B. (2004), *The Fabric of the Cosmos*. New York: Alfred A. Knopf.

Grönroos, Christian (2000a), "Relationship Marketing: A Nordic School Perspective," in *Handbook of Relationship Marketing*, Jagdish N. Sheth and Atul Parvatuyar, eds. Thousand Oaks, CA: Sage, 95–117.

———— (2000b), *Service Management and Marketing*. Chichester, UK: John Wiley & Sons.

Gummesson, Evert (2001), "Are Current Research Approaches in Marketing Leading Us Astray?" *Marketing Theory*, 1 (1), 27–48.

———— (2002a), "Practical Value of Adequate Marketing Management Theory," *European Journal of Marketing*, 36 (3), 325–29.

———— (2002b), *Total Relationship Marketing*, 2nd ed. Oxford: Butterworth-Heinemann.

———— (2004), "From One-to-One to Many-to-Many Marketing," in *Service Excellence in Management: Interdisciplinary Contributions*, Proceedings from the QUIS 9 Symposium, Bo Edvardsson et al., eds. Karlstad, Sweden: Karlstad University, 16–25.

Hunt, Shelby D. (2002), *Foundations of Marketing Theory: Toward a General Theory of Marketing*. Armonk, NY: M.E. Sharpe.

Iacobucci, Dawn, ed. (1996), *Networks in Marketing*. Thousand Oaks, CA: Sage Publications.

Kilduff, Martin and Wenpin Tsai (2003), *Social Networks and Organizations*. London: Sage Publications.

Lissack, Michael R. (1997), "Of Chaos and Complexity: Managerial Insights from New Science," *Management Decision*, 35 (3), 205–18.

Lovelock, Christopher H. and Evert Gummesson (2004), "Whither Services Marketing? In Search of a New Paradigm and Fresh Perspectives," *Journal of Service Research*, 6 (5), 20–41.

Möller, Kristian and S. Svahn (2003), "Managing Strategic Nets," *Marketing Theory*, 3 (2), 209–34.

Morgan, Gareth (1998), *Images of Organization: The Executive Edition*. Thousand Oaks, CA: Sage Publications.

Morgan, Robert M. and Shelby D. Hunt (1994), "The Commitment-Trust Theory of Relationship Marketing," *Journal of Marketing*, 58 (July), 20–38.

Naisbitt, John (1982), *Megatrends*. New York: Warner Books.

Peppers, Don and Martha Rogers (1999), *The One to One Manager*. New York: Currency-Doubleday.

Reichheld, Frederick F. (1996), *The Loyalty Effect*. Boston: Harvard Business School Press.

Rust, Roland T., Valerie A. Zeithaml, and Katrine N. Lemon (2000), *Driving Customer Equity*. New York: The Free Press.

Scott, John (1991), *Social Network Analysis*. London: Sage.

Schluter, Michael and David Lee (1993), *The R Factor*. London: Hodder & Stoughton.

———— and ———— (2003), *The R Option*. Cambridge, UK: The Relationship Foundation.

Seabright, Paul (2004), *The Company of Strangers*. Princeton, NJ: Princeton University Press.

Simons, Robert and Antonio Dávila (1998), "How High Is Your Return on Management?" *Harvard Business Review*, (January–February), 71–80.

Stacey, Ralph D. (1996), *Strategic Management & Organizational Dynamics*. London: Pitman.

Thorelli, Hans B. (1986), "Networks: Between Markets and Hierarchies," *Strategic Management Journal*, 7, 37–51.

Vargo, Stephen L. and Robert F. Lusch (2004a), "Evolving to a New Dominant Logic for Marketing," *Journal of Marketing*, 68 (1) (January), 1–21.

———— (2004b), "The Four Service Marketing Myths," *Journal of Service Research*, 6 (4), 324–35.

Wilkinson, Ian and Louise Young (2003), "A View from the Edge," *Marketing Theory*, 3 (1), 179–81.

Young, Louise and Ian Wilkinson (1994), "Business Dancing—An Alternative Paradigm," *Asia-Australia Marketing Journal*, 2 (1), 67–80.

Zetterberg, Hans L. (2003), "Social Science Theories and the Study of Public Opinion." Paper presented at the annual meeting of World Association for Public Opinion Research (WAPOR), Prague (September 17–19).

Zohar, Danah (1997), *Rewiring the Corporate Brain*. San Francisco: Berrett-Koehler.

28

WHAT CAN A SERVICE LOGIC OFFER MARKETING THEORY?

CHRISTIAN GRÖNROOS

INTRODUCTION

The purpose of this chapter is to discuss what a service logic can offer marketing theory. In services, interactions and relationships with customers are central phenomena, whereas traditionally exchange has been considered the core concept of marketing. According to this view value for customers is embedded in the exchange. The product that is exchanged includes value, and this value is delivered to customers for their use. As Vargo and Lusch (2004) have revealed this view of value seems to be based on a misunderstanding when macroeconomic analysis of value was transferred to microeconomics and from there further adopted by business economics. Value proposition is mixed up with value for customers. In reality, there is no value for customers until they can make use of a product. Value is not what goes into goods and services, it is what customers get out of them; that is, value emerges in the customers' space rather than in the producer's space (Vandermerwe 1996). The notion that only customers can assess value to goods and services was expressed by Levitt (1983) already in the early 1980s. However, this thought was largely ignored by the academic and business communities alike. From the beginning of the 1990s onward, this *value-in-use* notion (see Woodruff and Gardial 1996), as opposed to a value-in-exchange view, has been put forward in the marketing and management literature (see, e.g., Grönroos 2000; Gummesson 2002; Jüttner and Wehrli 1994; Normann 2001; Normann and Ramírez 1993; Ravald and Grönroos 1996; Storbacka and Lehtinen 2001; Vandermerwe 1996; Wikström 1996; Woodruff and Gardial 1996).

This value-in-use notion has been an implicitly, if not explicitly, expressed foundation of service marketing and relationship marketing. In service marketing the concept of interaction between the consumer and various resources and systems of the service firm was introduced as a core phenomenon. In relationship marketing this was extended to relationships over time, where a set of interactions take place. These may include product transfer, repair and maintenance activities, information, personal contacts, customer training, product upgrading, problem solving and service recovery and a number of other activities and processes. The relationship becomes the core of marketing. The firm should attempt to create relationships with its customers, because if that is not the case managing interactions successfully will be less easy and in the worst case no business takes place. In addition, a relationship approach to marketing makes it important for a supplier or service provider to manage a flow of processes aiming at making it possible for customers to perceive value in their consumption or usage processes; that is, to perform as service firms. What service firms do is to manage processes where interactions take place in order to make it possible for their customers to manage their own processes in a value-creating manner (value-in-use). It is no new observation that, especially when taking a relationship approach, all businesses are service businesses (see, e.g., Grönroos 2000; Webster 1994).

To understand the new role of marketing in a service business and relationship context it is important to start with an understanding of what should be achieved by marketing. In short the goals of marketing can be formulated in three steps (compare Grönroos 2000):

1. To get customers to buy a firm's goods or services a first time ("to get customers");
2. To provide these customers with such interactions with goods, services and other touch points with the firm so that they get satisfied enough with the value they get from using the goods or services to consider buying the same goods or services again from the same supplier or service provider ("to keep customers"); and
3. To further cultivate the interactions with these customers so that they give the supplier or service provider a larger share of not only their wallet but also their heart and mind,[1] so that an emotional or attitudinal connection is established ("to grow customers").

Latent relationships between suppliers and customers always exist, but only when achieving the third goal have relationships been perceived and appreciated by customers; they have become manifested. And ultimately it is the customers who determine whether a relationship exists with a supplier or not. Relationship marketing requires that the firm aims at achieving the third goal, but in many cases the firm might not get further than Goal 2. However, in principle for a manifested relationship to exist it is not enough with repeat buying behavior. An emotional or attitudinal component is also required. A firm can practice relationship marketing even though none of its customers, or only part of them, are at the third stage (Goal 3 reached), but relationship marketing as a strategy means that the firm *attempts* to reach the third goal.

Repeat buying might be due to many reasons other than the existence of a relationship. Various bonds, such as geographical closeness, technological superiority or affordable price level may make a customer buy the same goods or services over again from the same supplier or service provider, but as soon as an option with a more convenient location, better technology or more affordable price appears, the customer might be gone (Arantola 2002; Liljander and Strandvik 1995). Inertia, without an emotional connection, may also make customers behave in a relationship-like way. Bonded behavior of the above mentioned types and inertia must not be mixed up with relationships. However, repeat buying behavior does not have to be caused by negative bonds or inertia. If it is not, we have an at least partly manifested relationship. If, in addition to repeat purchasing behavior, there is an attitudinal or emotional connection between the customer and the firm, a well-manifested relationship probably exists and the likelihood that the customer will stay grows (Lindberg-Repo and Grönroos 2004). It goes without saying that a relationship should be mutual. The supplier and service provider must also be committed to its customers. Relationship marketing is not a manipulative approach to marketing. Hence, a relationship in a commercial context can be defined as "mutual understanding and commitment between two parties in the marketplace for the sake of supporting the customer's value processes and creating value for the supplier or service provider."[2]

Figure 28.1 **Customer–Firm Touchpoints**

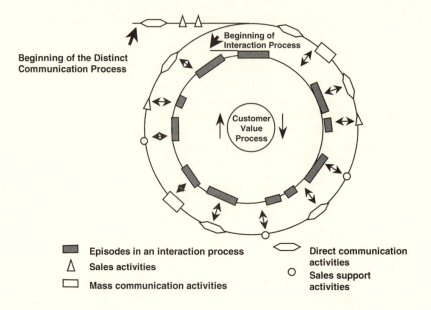

Source: Adapted from Grönroos (2004).

A relationship is developed over time as a result of interaction and communication processes. In Figure 28.1 the content of these processes as well as their value-generating effects for the customer and the supplier or service provider, respectively, are illustrated (see Grönroos 2004).

Customers are exposed to a firm's activities in two separate yet related processes. In the figure these processes are illustrated by the two outer circles: the *distinct communication process* and the *interaction process*. The distinct communication process includes firm-customer touch points that are purely communicational, including sales. Advertising, direct response communication, sales support activities and sales are examples of such activities. The interaction process represents the real world. Episodes in the interaction process are, for example, interactions with goods, service processes, Web sites, call centers, service recovery procedures, payment and invoicing systems, documentation about how to use goods, and so on. Activities in the distinct communication process are aimed at giving promises about the firm's value proposition, whereas the episodes in the interaction process should fulfill promises that have been given. The reality is, of course, more complicated than this. For example, competitor's actions and promises as well as how a customer interprets a communication message and his or her mood and emotions at any point in time will influence promises given by a firm and the fulfillment of them.

Of course, interactions between the customer and the firm in various episodes also communicate something and give promises, and they might even include sales activities. However, the main objective of the episodes of the interaction process is to provide customers with value-supporting solutions (e.g., goods, services, information, and, when needed, service recovery, call center advice, etc.)—that is, solutions that support the customers' processes in a value-supporting way. The arrows between these two circles point out the need to integrate the communication activities in the distinct communication process with episodes in the interaction process. When this integration has been achieved and both the firm and the customer have learned to listen to each other and respond to what they hear, communication in the marketplace may have developed into a *relationship dialogue* (Grönroos 2000).

The innermost circle illustrates the value-generating processes of customers as well as of the supplier or service provider. If the activities on the two outer circles develop favorably, value is generated in the customers' processes as well as created for the supplier or service provider. Hence, if performed well, activities and interactions in both the distinct communication and the interaction process contribute to customers' value creation and this, in turn, should pay back as more value for the firm and its shareholders.

BASIC "RULES" OF MARKETING

Keeping in mind that marketing relates a firm to its customers, whatever is planned and implemented as part of marketing should have an impact on customers. This leads to a first basic "rule" of marketing:

> Marketing activities must take place where the customers are and where the customers are influenced by them.

This should be self-evident, but still this guideline is often violated. All variables of the marketing mix are geared toward achieving sales, whereas only one, Product, can be considered to be partly related to the consumption of goods as well. It is mainly left to the customers themselves to decide whether consumption, which is treated as a black box, influences their willingness to do repeat purchases. In spite of this, it is during consumption that customers assess the value-supporting capacity of goods and services for them. To a decisive degree the foundation for future buying behavior is laid here. However, instead of making the consumption process a marketing arena, it is treated as a black box. The goods as such including add-ons such as warranties and documentation (the Product variable) may not provide enough incentive for a customer to buy again. Customer satisfaction is a key concept in marketing, but what really takes place in the customers' processes when using goods remains unknown and outside the scope of marketing. Branding, to a large degree based on marketing communication, the Promotion variable, is offered as a way of increasing the attractiveness of products. However, branding goods that do not support customers' consumption processes in a value-generating way is an uphill battle, where the marketing budget is under constant upward pressure and the productivity of marketing decreases.

In service firms that are influenced by consumer goods-dominated marketing models, marketing in practice is often dominated by marketing communication. These communication activities may, of course, influence the customers, but in addition the customers are engaged in a number of service processes (service production and delivery processes), which are not managed with a customer focus (i.e., with a marketing concern). The customers are in the service production and delivery processes, but most often marketing is not there.

Hence, goods-dominated marketing models make firms put their marketing efforts only partly in places where their customers are. Consequently, marketing effectiveness can be expected to be lower than it could be. It should be noted that what here is called "marketing activities" refers to not only what is included in the marketing mix or to activities that are planned and managed by the marketing department. In principle, anything could be marketing activities as long as these activities take place in contexts where they are observed and perceived by customers and influence them.

According to the marketing concept, the customers are at the center of marketing. This leads to a second basic "rule" of marketing:

> The customers of a firm, not its marketing department, decide which of the firm's resources and activities are marketing resources and activities.

If marketing should take the customers and their needs and wants and processes as the starting point for developing marketing activities, it is only these customers who can decide what marketing of a given firm consists of. This guideline is also often violated. To take a service example, the customers would probably like the service processes to be smoother, including for example better interactions with service contact employees, whereas the firm's marketing activities are elsewhere, mainly in the form of advertising campaigns and price offers.

SHORTCOMINGS OF THE CONSUMER GOODS-DOMINATED MARKETING LOGIC

Based on the value-in-use assumption, the consumption or usage behavior of customers and their internal value-generating processes become an area of interest for marketers and marketing. If they are not integrated into marketing, only getting customers (Goal 1) can be successfully achieved, whereas keeping and growing customers (Goals 2 and 3) will be given less organized attention or more or less totally forgotten. As relationship marketing demonstrates, keeping and growing customers are at least as vital to success as getting customers. In addition, it is important to keep in mind that while a manipulative marketing approach can make some customers buy a first time, in other cases customers might not even make a trial purchase before the firm has won their minds and perhaps even their hearts.

The goods-dominated marketing logic has drawn buying and consuming apart. Marketing models and the consumer goods-inspired marketing mix revolves around getting customers to buy. Only the Product variable is somehow related to consuming or using goods, but in marketing models even this variable is almost totally geared toward making customers buy. Clearly this is a serious shortcoming in marketing today, in which long-term relationships become more and more important for firms to develop. And even if such relationships are not considered imperative to a firm's success in the marketplace, no firm can survive in the long run without repeat purchases by a considerable number of its customers. Today marketers are persuading customers to buy again mainly by marketing communication and price offers. The goods-dominated logic of marketing does not seem to offer other opportunities. The main reason for this is that this logic does not properly include consuming and the customers' processes as an integral part of its models. Explicitly it deals only with buying.

It seems quite obvious that keeping buying and consuming apart has had negative effects on marketing. Because the consumption process goes unsupported by the firm, this separation of buying from consuming easily has a negative impact on customers' internal value-generating processes and on customer satisfaction. Moreover, it has led to unnecessarily high marketing costs and revenue losses caused by too much money spent on marketing communications and by unnecessarily huge price offers.

Keeping buying and consuming apart does not mean that consuming would not have been an area of interest for marketing research. On the contrary, there is a considerable literature on consumer behavior, but the problem seems to be that this literature is not clearly related to the consumer goods-based theory of marketing with its marketing mix and 4 P's model. One could say that marketing is marketing and consumer behavior is consumer behavior, and the two do not meet.

A SERVICE-BASED LOGIC: THE NORDIC SCHOOL APPROACH

Service marketing research has addressed the importance of customers' consumption processes in a different way. This is, for example, demonstrated by the interest in studying the service encounter and perceived service quality. There is a considerable amount of research that ties together the buying and consuming processes and hence gears marketing to the value-generating processes of customers. In North America, for example, the 7 P's of the marketing mix is an attempt to include company resources such as people, processes, and physical resources (physical evidence) in a marketing model (Booms and Bitner 1982). These variables clearly relate to the service production/consumption interface. In France, a service marketing model, the *Servuction* model (Langeard and Eiglier 1987), also recognized the importance of integrating marketing with the consumers' processes.

Another approach to service marketing which explicitly and extensively integrates buying, consuming and marketing is the *Nordic School* of service marketing thought emanating out of the Nordic countries of Europe (see Berry and Parasuraman 1993; Edvardsson and Gustafsson 1999; Grönroos 1978; Grönroos and Gummesson 1985; Gummesson, 1977). One of the central arguments of the Nordic School, which was developed in the mid-1970s, is that the interactions between the service provider (an organization with people, physical resources, and systems) and the consumer of its services during the simultaneous service production and consumption processes are at the heart of successful marketing. Marketing was found to consist of an *external marketing* part, including some traditional elements of the marketing mix such as marketing communication and pricing, and an *interactive marketing* part, which was geared to the interactions that take place when customers and various resources of the firm, such as people, systems, and physical resources and goods, meet during the consumption of services. (Thus, the interactive marketing term, which now has become popular in the context of interactive media, was originally introduced in service marketing research.) Also, an interest in understanding how customers perceive the service process and its outcome grew, resulting in the *perceived service quality* model introduced by Grönroos (1982 and 1984) in the early 1980s (see also Gummesson 1991). In North America this model was later extended to the *gap model* (Parasuraman, Zeithaml, and Berry 1985; see also a comparison between the Nordic School and American approaches to service quality and an extension of such models in Brady and Cronin 1992) and, for example, the *Servqual* (Parasuraman, Zeithaml, and Berry 1988) and *Servperf* (Cronin and Taylor 1992; see also Liljander 1995) measurement instruments, and subsequently extended to include the *tolerance zone* notion (Berry and Parasuraman 1991; see also Strandvik 1994).

Although value was not explicitly discussed in the 1970s, implicit in the Nordic School of service marketing thought was a value-in-use concept, where the interactions between service providers and customers, not exchange of preproduced service products, were considered the core of marketing. Value is created by the customer in interactions with the service provider and supported by the service provider. In addition to this the outcome of the service production process when used by the customer also contributes to customer value.[3]

Making the management of the interactions between the service firm and its customers (the service encounter) a field of interest for marketing made consumption of a service an equally important marketing issue as buying services. Thus, the black box of consumption was opened up and explored. From a marketing point of view, consuming services was seamlessly integrated with buying services. Interactive marketing is the part of total marketing that is geared toward managing the consumption process in a value-supporting way, in order to increase the likelihood that the customers decide to stay with the firm.

In Figure 28.1 the beginning of the distinct communication and interaction processes were indicated in an arbitrary way. In reality it is difficult to determine when consumption and customers' value creation starts and ends. For example, depending on how broadly consumption is defined, the consumption of an inclusive tour to a tourist destination may begin already when the customer starts thinking about taking the trip or when the first ad by the tour operator is seen. By the same token, the customer's value creation may start from the very beginning of this extended consumption process or at least at the point in time when he or she starts thinking about and reviewing the tour operator's options. There is, so to speak, a mental pre-consumption even before interactions with the tour operator's processes commence. Also, it may be difficult to determine when consumption ends. A similar mental post-consumption may take place. Using the inclusive tour example, one could say that consumption ends not when the customer returns home but when memories of the trip are not brought up in discussions or entering the person's mind anymore.

When both buying and consuming are managed as marketing issues, it is easier to reach all three goals of marketing, i.e., getting customers, keeping customers, and growing customers, and in the best case ultimately create manifested relationships with customers. In addition, when marketing is explicitly extended to the consumption process (interactive marketing), the two basic "rules" of marketing are better appreciated. All resources needed in the interactions with customers during the integrated buying and consumption processes, irrespective of which department they belong to, can be developed and managed with a customer focus ("Rule 1"). Otherwise they easily are thought of and managed as operational sources only (which they of course also are). A customer focus in the service encounters also forces the service firm to get and use customer input for how the service encounters should function from a marketing perspective in order to make customers interested in repeat purchasing ("Rule 2").

In conclusion, according to this logic the service provider should develop such a set of resources and create such interactions with its customers that these interactions between the firm and its customers, together with the outcome of the service process, have a positive impact on the customers' value creation. This increases the likelihood of repeat purchasing and perhaps contributes to the development of relationships between the service provider and its customers. The role of external marketing activities is to get customers, whereas the role of interactive marketing is to keep and grow customers and, in the best case, to lay the foundation for enduring customer relationships.

The logic of service as a perspective is to support the customers' value-generating processes. And due to the importance of the interactions between the service provider and its customers, marketing's role is not only to communicate value propositions but to make sure that value indeed is created in the customers' processes.

WHAT CAN A SERVICE LOGIC OFFER GOODS?

The service logic discussed in the previous section can be summarized in the following way:

1. Because value for customers is created when they consume a service, i.e., in the customers' value-generating processes (value-in-use), the role of the service provider is to support the customers' processes with a set of resources—service employees, systems, physical resources, and the customers themselves and the time they spend in interactions—as well as with service processes and interactions that contribute to value creation in those processes. The *logic of service* is to support customers' processes so that

value for the customers is created in those processes. Consequently, services can be defined as processes in which a bundle of resources are integrated to support customers' processes in order to enable value creation in those processes.

2. Although some of the consumption of a service takes place in isolation from the production and delivery of that service, the consumption process is an integrated part of service production and delivery (the service process).

3. Because the simultaneously occurring part of consumption and production of a service has a decisive impact on the customers' perception of the quality of the service (especially on the functional or process quality dimension) and therefore also on the attitudes of customers toward the service provider and on their future purchasing behavior, reaching all three goals of marketing, managing, and handling activities in the consumption process must be an integral part of the total marketing process of the service provider (interactive marketing as part of total marketing).

Let us examine the case of physical goods in the light of the previously summarized service logic. As a means of illustration, I use cellular phones. The same arguments can easily be made for any type of goods.

1. The reasons for using cellular phones are several: communicating with other people, entertaining oneself in isolation or even together with someone else, taking photographs and perhaps sending them to someone else; making financial transactions; paying for bus tickets, car wash, and car parking; sending and receiving text messages (sms) and e-mails; and so on. According to the value-in-use notion customers consider that they get value in their processes of communicating, playing games, making payments, reading and sending e-mails, and operating on the Internet when the cellular phone indeed facilitates doing so in a secure, uncomplicated, and swift manner. If all these functions do not work properly, a cellular phone with all the technical capabilities for performing these functions is not enough. No support to customers' value creation exists. What is required is call center and customer service activities, access to entertainment content, and an infrastructure with connections to telecommunication operators, financial institutions, and other organizations that enables the performance of the functions technically made possible by the cellular phone itself. Some of these activities (e.g., call center and customer service and entertainment content) can be provided by the manufacturer of the cellular phone, whereas some must be offered by others in a network context.

2. Making it possible for customers to use/consume a cellular phone for some or all of the above-mentioned activities is clearly in the best interest of the producer of the phone. Otherwise the phone is less useful than it could be. Making sure that, for example, customer service is prepared to give proper advice about how to use the phone, that games and other forms of entertainment are easily accessible, and that the Internet connections work so that customers continuously can use the phone are critical to customers' value creation. Some of these resources and interactions are provided by the manufacturer of the cellular phone, whereas others are the responsibility of other organizations. All are required so that customers can use the phone in ways they want, and they have to be available at the very moment the customers need them and try to make use of them.

3. If a cellular phone does not have the technical capability and is not backed up by necessary customer service support or if telecommunication operators and other organizations do not support the use of the existing technical capabilities of the phone in a proper way, customers will shift to other manufacturers which offer more appropriate technical capabilities and support from its own organization and other organizations needed to make value creation possible in the cus-

tomers' processes. Repurchasing will not take place, and bad word-of-mouth will probably occur. In other words, marketing has failed to keep and grow the customers of the firm (reaching Goals 2 and 3 of marketing). And if that is the case, marketing as such has failed.

Even in the case of goods, customers are looking for service. They are spending money *and* time to make it possible to make use of goods for the service they get from a bundle of goods *and* necessary supporting resources required to use these products. The support to their value-generating process that they get from the physical product combined with other required resources *is the service.* In the case of cellular phones these "other required resources" were, for example, call center customer service support, access to entertainment content, and support from telecommunication operators and other organizations needed to use technical capabilities offered by a cellular phone.

CONCLUSIONS

Three conclusions can be drawn from the discussion of what a service logic can offer the marketing of goods.

First, concentrating on the product draws the marketer's attention away from what ultimately is important for the customers: their value-creating processes. The goods are considered *the value,* when in reality they are only value support. It also makes the marketer believe that the goods are the key and often the only source of value for customers, when in fact they perhaps are not even the most important one. As the case of cellular phones demonstrates, the phone is only a starting point for customers' value creation, but the rest of the resources are the ones which make it possible for the customers to create value in their processes.

Second, goods can be seen as a "platform for services" (Edvardsson, Gustafsson, and Roos 2005, p. 118). In the consumer's mind goods render services in the same way as services do (compare also Lovelock and Gummesson 2004). Goods form one type of resources among others in a bundle of resources, consisting of goods and other tangible items, service employees, systems, processes, and the customers themselves and interactions between these resources that are needed to make it possible for customers to create value for themselves. In other words, this bundle of resources, in which the goods are nothing but one resource among others, is required to support the customers' processes so that value is created in those processes. The observant reader realizes that this is a description of a service and of the logic of service. In this respect the cellular phone is equivalent to the beef in a hamburger restaurant. The beef has to be there, and it has to fulfill given requirements, but without the other resources of the restaurant, no restaurant service will exist. The beef will not be bought and consumed. Hence, goods are resources, goods businesses are service businesses, and the marketing of a physical good should be viewed as the marketing of a service.

Third, although I use cellular phones as an illustration here, the same analysis can be made for any type of goods. For the customer to use goods, other resources must accompany them, and the goods are only one resource among others in the process of supporting customers' value-generating processes. However, there are of course situations where a good is of such a nature that, based on a customer's level of competence, it is so simple to use that no support in terms of customer service, customer education or support from other organizations is required. The only resources that are needed are the goods and the customer, although another customer with a lower level of competence might need such support. Buying candy could be an example of a situation in which few customers would need additional support. The only resource customers interact with and is required so that they can create value in their processes is the good. In this case, focusing on the physical product only, in addition to the customer, as the means of customers' value creation can work well, and a marketing approach in which the physical product is the only variable related to the customers' consumption processes can be successful.

However, in a situation as the one just described, the physical product is still a resource required to support the customers' processes. The only thing that differentiates this situation from the case of cellular phones is that no other resources are required. It is still a matter of spending customers' money and time for the support of their processes that this good as a resource can offer. Hence, it is still a matter of spending money and time for a service. In conclusion, goods marketing is a special case of service marketing, a case in which the interactions with customers is solely related to the goods. In this case, in terms of marketing, focusing predominantly or only on the product variable as a means of supporting customers' processes can lead to positive results. But this is only a special case. And even in this case customers are looking for support for some processes of theirs; that is, they are looking for the service the product as a resource can produce.

NOTES

The author thanks his colleague Tore Strandvik at Hanken Swedish School of Economics, Finland, for his useful comments and suggestions.

1. The need for not only a share of customers' wallet (repeat purchasing) but also of their hearts and minds (emotional connection) for a firm to develop a relationship with its customers was put forward in Storbacka and Lehtinen (2001).

2. This definition of a relationship is based on a discussion of what constitutes relationships in a business-to-business context. See Håkansson and Snehota (1995).

3. Similar thoughts can be found in the so-called IMP interaction and network approach to industrial marketing (see, e.g., Håkansson and Snehota 1995), also originally emanating out of the Nordic countries.

REFERENCES

Arantola, Heli (2002), *Relationship Drivers in Provider-Consumer Relationships. Empirical Studies of Customer Loyalty Programs.* Helsinki, Finland: Hanken Swedish School of Economics.

Berry, Leonard L. and A. Parasuraman (1991), *Marketing Services: Competing through Quality.* New York: The Free Press.

———— and ———— (1993), "Building a New Academic Field: The Case of Services Marketing," *Journal of Retailing,* 69 (1), 13–60.

Booms, Bernard H. and Mary Jo Bitner (1982), "Marketing Structures and Organization Structures for Service Firms," in *Marketing of Services,* John H. Donnelly and William R. George, eds. Chicago: American Marketing Association, 47–51.

Brady, Michael K. and J. Joseph Cronin, Jr. (2001), "Some Thoughts on Conceptualizing Perceived Service Quality: A Hierarchical Approach," *Journal of Marketing,* 65 (July), 34–49.

Cronin, Jr., J. Joseph and Stephen A. Taylor (1992), "Measuring Service Quality: A Reexamination and Extension," *Journal of Marketing,* 56 (July), 55–68.

Edvardsson, Bo and Anders Gustafsson (1999), *The Nordic School of Quality Management.* Lund, Sweden: Studentlitteratur.

————, ————, and Inger Roos (2005), "Service Portraits in Service Research: A Critical Review," *International Journal of Service Industry Management,* 16 (1), 107–21.

Grönroos, Christian (1978), "A Service-Oriented Approach to the Marketing of Services," *European Journal of Marketing.* 12 (8), 588–601.

———— (1982), *Strategic Management and Marketing in the Service Sector.* Report 8. Helsinki: Hanken Swedish School of Economics Finland (also published as Report 83–104. Cambridge, MA: Marketing Science Institute, 1983).

———— (1984), "A Service Quality Model and Its Marketing Implications," *European Journal of Marketing,* 18 (4), 36–44.

———— (2000), *Service Management and Marketing: A Customer Relationship Management Approach.* Chichester, UK: John Wiley & Sons.

—— (2004), "The Relationship Marketing Process: Communication, Interaction, Dialogue, Value," *Journal of Business and Industrial Marketing,* 19 (2), 99–113.

—— and Evert Gummesson (1985), "The Nordic School of Services—An Introduction," in *Service Marketing—Nordic School Perspectives.* Series R:2, Christian Grönroos and Evert Gummesson, eds. Stockholm, Sweden: Stockholm University.

Gummesson, Evert (1977), *Marknadsföring och försläljning av professionella tjänster (Marketing and sales of professional services).* In Swedish. Stockholm: Akademiförlaget.

—— (1991), *Kvalitetsstyrning i tjänste- och serviceverksamheter (Quality management in services).* In Swedish. Report 91:4, Service Research Centre, Karlstad University.

—— (2002), "Relationship Marketing and a New Economy: It's Time for Deprogramming," *Journal of Services Marketing.* 16 (7), 585–89.

Håkansson, Håkan and Ivan Snehota (1995), *Developing Relationships in Business Networks.* Routledge: London.

Jüttner, Uta and H.P. Wehrli (1994), "Relationship Marketing from a Value Perspective," *International Journal of Service Industry Management,* 5 (5), 54–73.

Langeard, Eric and Pierre Eiglier (1987), *Servuction. Le marketing des services.* Paris: John Wiley & Sons.

Levitt, Theodore (1983), *The Marketing Imagination.* New York: The Free Press.

Liljander, Veronica (1995), *Comparison Standards in Perceived Service Quality.* Helsinki: Hanken Swedish School of Economics Finland.

—— and Tore Strandvik (1995), "The Nature of Customer Relationships in Services," in *Advances in Services Marketing and Management,* 4, Theresa A, Swartz, David E. Bowen, and Stephen W. Brown, eds. Greenwich, CT: JAI Press, 141–67.

Lindberg-Repo, Kirsti and Christian Grönroos (2004), "Conceptualising Communication Strategy from a Relationship Perspective," *Industrial Marketing Management,* 33, 229–39.

Lovelock, Christopher and Evert Gummesson (2004), "Whither Services Marketing? In Search of a New Paradigm and Fresh Perspectives," *Journal of Service Research,* 7 (1), 20–41.

Normann, Richard (2001), *Reframing Business. When the Map Changes the Landscape.* Chichester, UK: John Wiley & Sons.

—— and Rafael Ramírez (1993), "From Value Chain to Value Constellation: Designing Interactive Strategy," *Harvard Business Review* (July/August), 65–77.

Parasuraman, A., Valerie A. Zeithaml, and Leonard L. Berry (1985), "A Conceptual Model of Service Quality and Its Implications for Future Research," *Journal of Marketing,* 49 (Fall), 41–50.

——, ——, and —— (1988), "SERVQUAL: A Multi-Item Scale for Measuring Consumer Perceptions of Service Quality," *Journal of Retailing,* 64 (1), 12–40.

Ravald, A. and C. Grönroos (1996), "The Value Concept and Relationship Marketing," *European Journal of Marketing,* 30 (2), 19–30.

Storbacka, Kaj and Jarmo R. Lehtinen (2001), *Customer Relationship Management.* Singapore: McGraw-Hill.

Strandvik, Tore (1994), *Tolerance Zones and Perceived Service Quality.* Helsinki: Hanken Swedish School of Economics, Finland.

Vandermerwe, Sandra (1996), "Becoming a Customer 'Owning' Company," *Long Range Planning,* 29 (6), 770–82.

Vargo, Stephen L. and Robert F. Lusch (2004), "Evolving to a New Dominant Logic for Marketing," *Journal of Marketing,* 68 (January), 1–17.

Webster, Jr., Frederick E. (1994), "Executing the New Marketing Concept," *Marketing Management,* 3 (1), 9–18.

Wikström, Solveig (1996), "Value Creation by Company-Consumer Interaction," *Journal of Marketing Management,* 12, 359–74.

Woodruff, Robert B. and Sarah Gardial (1996), *Know Your Customers: New Approaches to Understanding Customer Value and Satisfaction.* Oxford: Blackwell Publishers.

29

GOING BEYOND THE PRODUCT

Defining, Designing, and Delivering Customer Solutions

Mohanbir Sawhney

INTRODUCTION

In recent years, many leading firms have moved away from marketing individual products and services to providing complete customer solutions (Bennett and Tipping 2001; Foote et al. 2001; Slywotsky and Morrison 1998; Wise and Baumgartner 1999). The move toward solutions is particularly noticeable in industries characterized by complex and high-value products and services, such as telecommunications systems, computer systems, aerospace and weapons systems, transportation networks and medical devices (Hobday 1998; Davies and Brady 2000; Gann and Salter 2000). Firms like IBM, UPS, Ericsson, and GE have successfully transformed themselves into providers of end-to-end customer solutions, and have achieved significant growth and financial success from service-intensive solutions (Sawhney, Balasubramanian, and Krishnan 2004).

The move toward solutions is grounded in the insight that customers have no interest in products and services per se—what they really want are solutions to problems they face in their lives and businesses. As Peter Drucker (1974, p. 61) famously reminded us three decades ago, "What the customer buys and considers value is never a product; it is always utility—that is—what a product does for him." True customer focus requires marketers to begin with a customer problem and work toward creating solutions that address these problems. Although the "problem-solution" approach seems logical, few firms follow this logic in practice. Most organizations remain centered around developing and marketing products. The traditional goods-dominant view of marketing still prevails in most firms, where the product is the primary unit of value exchange (Vargo and Lusch 2004).

The purpose of this chapter is to help marketers to think beyond the product by embracing the solutions mind-set. Consistent with the emerging service-dominant logic of marketing, I propose that marketers need to focus on design and marketing of *customer solutions*—offerings that integrate goods and services to provide customized outcomes for specific customers. I present a comprehensive roadmap for defining, designing, and delivering solutions. I begin by contrasting the traditional product-centric mind-set with the solutions-centric mind-set, and highlight the benefits and challenges marketers face in solutions marketing. Next, I propose a definition of solutions and a set of dimensions for classifying solutions. I show how solution providers can develop a deep understanding of customer problems by focusing on customer outcomes and mapping customer activity cycles. I then turn to the challenge of creating profitable solutions and how solution providers can develop a "solutions factory" that develops repeatable solutions. I also outline the capabilities that firms need to develop in moving toward solutions and how they can restructure their organizations to develop and deliver solutions. Next, I discuss how firms can capture value from solutions by employing value-based pricing mechanisms for solutions. I conclude by offering suggestions for a research agenda on solutions marketing.

THE PRODUCT-CENTRIC MIND-SET AND ITS LIMITATIONS

The product-centric mind-set rests on the belief that firms win by creating superior products and by enhancing the features of existing products. Marketing strategies focus on product innovation, product line extensions and new product features. In the product-centric mind-set, services are an afterthought—loss leaders thrown in to enhance the appeal of products. The organization is structured around products, including product development, product marketing and product sales. And success is measured in terms of product revenues and product profitability.

This product-centric mind-set no longer guarantees business success. Product demand is volatile, particularly for high-value capital goods. Product differentiation based on features is difficult to sustain in the face of intense global competition. In many markets like automobiles and computers, existing products are good enough for most customers, offering little incentive for customers to upgrade to newer versions of products. But perhaps most importantly, products are merely means to an end. To help customers achieve their ultimate goals and outcomes, products and services need to be integrated into customer solutions that solve the complete customer problem. This move toward solutions demands a different mind-set.

TOWARD A SOLUTIONS-CENTRIC MINDSET

The product-centric mind-set is being challenged by the emerging service-dominant logic of marketing (Vargo and Lusch 2004). The service-dominant logic turns product-centric thinking on its head. Services are no longer considered separate from products. Instead of services being a loss leader for products, product become platforms for delivering services. Services become a source of profit and the basis for competitive advantage. The focus of marketing evolves from product designs and marketing to the design and marketing of end-to-end customer solutions.

The solutions-centric mind-set is diametrically opposed to the product-centric mind-set on many dimensions. Instead of starting with the product, solutions design begins with an analysis of a *customer problem* and ends with the identification of products and services that will be needed to solve the entire problem. In the solutions mind-set, customer offerings are integrated combinations of products and services designed to provide customized experiences for specific customer segments. Customers segments or vertical markets become the dominant axes for organization and process design. And the firm defines success in terms of customer profitability and share of customer spending. Figure 29.1 contrasts the solutions mind-set with the product mind-set.

A number of leading firms are embracing the solutions-centric mind-set to transform their value propositions from marketing products to providing customer solutions. For instance, Alstom

Figure 29.1 **Contrasting the Product Mind-Set with the Solutions Mind-Set**

Dimension	Product Mind-Set	Solutions Mind-Set
Mental Model	Product leadership—winning by creating innovative products and enhancing features of existing products.	Value leadership—winning by working with partners to create and deliver superior customers solutions
Offerings and Targeting	Standardized "horizontal" offerings targeted at a broad range of customer segments	Customized "vertical" offerings targeted at a precisely defined set of customers and industries
Offering Design	Start with the product or service, and then find customers for the product or service.	Start with the customer problem, and then assemble a set of products and services to solve the customer problem
Organization Structure	Product as primary organizational pivot for sales and marketing. Profit and loss organized around products	Customer accounts and customer segments as primary pivot for sales and marketing. Profit and loss organized around segments and industry verticals
Marketing Operations	• Emphasis on product launches and broad reach advertising campaigns • Marketing function separated from sales, and partners separated from the firm	• Emphasis on deep and ongoing customer engagement • Marketing, sales, and partner functions integrated into customer account teams
Key Performance Indices	• Product revenues • Market share • Product profitability	• Segment/account revenues • Share of customer spending • Segment/account profitability

Transport has shifted its focus from selling passenger trains to offering turnkey "Total Train-Life Management" solutions that includes project management, financing, maintenance, renovations, parts replacement and servicing of train systems (Brady, Davies, and Gann 2004). Similarly, the chemicals and life sciences giant DuPont has embraced the mantra to "go beyond the molecule." DuPont's Safety and Protection business is going beyond providing basic materials for roofing and insulation by thinking in terms of foundation systems, roofing systems, window and door systems, structural integrity systems and building science services. Similarly, UPS has created a multibillion-dollar business called UPS Logistics Services, which creates solutions for supply chain management, reverse logistics, transportation network management and customer relationship management (Sawhney, Balasubramanian, and Krishnan 2004). GE and IBM have also grown profitably by creating solutions for financing and business process outsourcing for their customers. Figure 29.2 provides examples of how companies in a wide range of industries are embracing the shift toward integrated solutions.

BENEFITS AND CHALLENGES IN SOLUTIONS MARKETING

The shift from products to solutions offers several important payoffs for firms. Solutions allow firms to do more business with their existing customers by offering them an expanded portfolio of service-intensive solution offerings. These solution offerings inevitably involve taking on some of the work that customers would have done by themselves, and therefore often represent a far bigger market opportunity than the core product market. John Deere, the agricultural equipment manufacturer, found that the percentage of every dollar spent by farmers on equipment has been declining steadily over the years, and stands at less than 10 percent today. The bulk of the spending is migrating downstream to services. By tapping into this services profit pool, John Deere can potentially increase the size of its market opportunity tenfold. Along the same lines, Wise and Baumgartner (1999) estimate that railway companies buy $1.4 billion of new locomotives annually, but they spend $28 billion a year to maintain and operate their locomotives and infrastructure. By augmenting their core products with complementary services, firms can greatly increase the size of their addressable markets.

Solutions also allow firms to become more embedded in their customers' operations, which

Figure 29.2 **Examples of the Shift to Integrated Solutions**

Company	Traditional Product or Service Focus (1995)	Integrated Solutions (2000)
Alstom Transport— Railways	Products: • Subsystems (e.g., propulsion, traction, drive, electronic information systems) • Rolling stock • Signaling and train control systems	Transport solutions (e.g., train availability): • Systems integrator—turnkey solutions for project management, fixed infrastructure, and finance • Services for maintenance, renovation, parts replacement, and service products—"Total Train-Life Management"
Ericsson—Mobile Communications Systems	Products: • mobile handsets • mobile system • subsystem products: radio base stations, base station controllers, mobile switches, operating systems, and customer databases	Turnkey solutions to design, build, and operate mobile phone networks: • Mobile systems—complete supplier, systems integrator, and partner • Global services—services and business consulting to support a customer's network operations
Thales Training & Simulation—Flight Simulation	Products—stand-alone flight simulators for commercial and military aircraft	Training solutions (e.g., "pay as you train"): • Systems integration • Training services: networked training, independent training centers for training services, and synthetic training environments
WS Atkins— Infrastructure and the Built Environment	Engineering consultancy, project management, and technical services for infrastructure projects	Integrated solutions for the built environment: • The design, building, financing, and operation of infrastructure across industrial sectors • Total Solutions for Industry (TS4i) provides one-stop-shop for design, construction, maintenance, and finance
Cable & Wireless Global Markets— Corporate Networks	Provides "managed network services" for multinational corporations • Network design • Supply telecom infrastructure and applications • Network management	Global outsourcing solutions for a multinational corporation's entire telecom and information technology needs on a global basis: • Network design • Telecom infrastructure and applications • Network management • Ownership of the network • Network operation • Business-process applications • Service-level agreements

Source: Brady, Davies, and Gann (2004).

increases customer loyalty and decreases the probability that customers can replace the firm with a competing supplier. By moving to solutions, firms can overcome the commoditization challenge that plagues products and sustain differentiation more effectively than in their core product markets. The reason—solutions offer many more avenues for differentiation than products because they include a variety of services that can be customized in many unique ways for individual customers (MacMillan and McGrath 1997). In addition, solutions design requires very intimate knowledge of customers and industries. This domain expertise can become a source of competitive differentiation.

However, moving to solutions also presents a number of challenges. A solutions mind-set is difficult for a product-centric company to embrace, because it involves reversing several deeply held assumptions about developing, marketing, selling and supporting the firm's offerings. Consider the sales process for solutions. Solutions are more complex and more customized than products, so selling solutions requires more effort and takes more time than selling products. The sales cycle for solutions is longer because the firm first needs to understand customer problems through intense interaction and dialogue. Then, it needs to design and develop a customized solution for each customer, which is far more time-consuming than selling an off-the-shelf product. In addition to the time and effort, selling solutions requires that salespeople take a consultative approach to selling as opposed to the transactional approach that product salespeople are comfortable with. Transitioning a product-based sales force to a solutions-based sales force requires significant retraining of the sales personnel, and may involve substantial turnover because some salespeople may not be willing or able to change their approach.

In moving from products to solutions, firms also need to manage a number of risks (Sawhney, Balasubramanian, and Krishnan 2004). Perhaps the most important is the competence risk that the firm incurs in entering into a services-intensive business. Firms that excel at products may not do well at services because they lack the appropriate skills. Product firms also potentially face a risk of lower margins, because solutions need to be customized for each customer at an additional cost, unlike products that can be created once and sold to millions of customers without modification. If solution providers do too much one-off customization for each customer, profit margins can suffer. To mitigate the competence risk, solution providers need to progressively enhance their project and program-management capabilities. To overcome the margin risk, solution providers need to proactively pursue the creation of repeatable solutions. These strategies are discussed in more detail when I consider the capabilities and the process for designing and delivering solutions.

THE NATURE OF SOLUTIONS

While many firms talk about "solutions selling" or "solutions marketing," there is little agreement about what constitutes a solution. Solutions are loosely defined as products and services that solve customer problems. I define a solution as "an integrated combination of products and services customized for a set of customers that allows customers to achieve better outcomes than the sum of the individual components of the solution." This definition highlights two key dimensions on which solutions can be categorized—the degree of integration and the degree of customization (Krishnamurthy, Johansson, and Schlissberg 2003).

Degree of Integration

Solutions are more than a simple bundle of products and services. The products and services need to be *integrated* in ways that add value to customers. In fact, the degree of integration across products and services is a key determinant of the incremental value offered by the solution over the sum of the individual parts.

The incremental value customers derive from integration of a solution arises from two sources—*marketing integration* and *operational integration*. Marketing integration refers to integration across the entire customer decision-making and buying cycle, from the pre-sales search to post-sales service and support. Marketing integration is *temporal* in nature, because it spans the sequence of steps that customers go through in searching, evaluating, buying, installing, using, servicing and maintaining a system of products. Customers may benefit from being able to search a single location for all elements of the solution, to buy all the products and services they need from a "one-stop-shop" provider, pay a single bundled price for the solution, have a single provider install and deploy the solution, call a single number for customer support and service, and maintain a single vendor relationship.

In addition to being marketed, sold and supported in an integrated manner, the products and services that constitute the solution also need to work "better together" in technical and operational terms. Without operational integration, integration may just be a marketing slogan, and the solution may amount to little more than "putting lipstick on a pig." In fact, operational integration is the difference between bundling and true integration. Operational integration may mean that individual products are engineered to work better together, or that individual services are delivered using an integrated services platform. The value of operational integration depends on two factors—the effort that customers would need to expend in order to integrate the products and solutions themselves and the value that they place on their time. If the individual products are standardized (e.g., the components of a personal computer), integration is not difficult and customers would place less value on the integration. And the reason that a segment of customers prefers to buy unassembled furniture from companies like IKEA and assemble it themselves is related to the fact that the opportunity cost of their time is low enough to justify the time spent by them in self-assembly.

Degree of Customization

The problem contexts for any two customers are rarely completely identical. Therefore, it is difficult to create a "one size fits all" solution that works for all customers equally well (Sawhney 2003). In fact, the value of a solution derives from the fact that it is customized to the contexts of specific customer segments, and sometimes even for individual customers. Solutions are far more amenable to customization than products, because they are enhanced with services that can be customized in many ways. The degree of customization may range from segment-specific customization to customer-specific customization (Krishnamurthy, Johansson, and Schlissberg 2003). For instance, 3M, a diversified industrial company, offers solutions for eleven specific industries, ranging from architecture and construction to telecommunications and utilities. Financial services firms like Goldman Sachs and Merrill Lynch go even further in their wealth-management services for high net-worth customers, by offering individual-level customized investment solutions and advice. The degree of customization required is a function of the degree of variation in end-user needs and end-use contexts, and the value that customers place on customization.

In summary, the value of a solution can be conceptualized as the sum of:

- The value of individual products and services that make up the solution, *plus*
- The value of marketing and operational integration provided by the solutions vendor, *plus*
- The value of customization for the customer's specific needs and context.

The value of integration and the value of customization represent the difference between the "whole" (the value of the solution) and the "sum of the parts" (the value of component products and services). Figure 29.3 illustrates the classification of solutions on the two key dimensions of integration and customization.

DEVELOPING CUSTOMER UNDERSTANDING
FOR SOLUTIONS DESIGN

Solutions design begins with a deep understanding of the customer *problem* that the solution is designed to solve. To understand customer problems, it is useful to begin at the end—with the *outcomes* that customers seek in solving their problem, and the *activities* that they perform in order to achieve their outcomes. By focusing on customer outcomes and activities, marketers can gain powerful insights for creating compelling solutions.

Figure 29.3 **Dimensions of Solutions Design**

Degree of Customization	Individual Customer	• Bentley • Dell	• Accenture • Siemens One	• BASF OEM solutions • IBM Outsourcing
	Vertical/Segment	• Procter & Gamble • Coca-Cola	• Telecom services • NCR Teradata	• Trilogy Software • Dow Automotive
	None/Limited	• Commodities • Ingredients	• McDonald's Value Meals • Mutual Funds	• Microsoft Office • Sony Home Theater
		No Integration, Single Products	**Marketing Integration**	**Marketing and Technical Integration**

Degree of Integration

Source: Adapted from Krishnamurthy, Johansson, and Schlissberg (2003).
Note: Names are all registered trademarks of respective companies.

Defining Customer Outcomes

The head of Black & Decker once noted, "What do we sell—Drills? No we don't. We sell holes." This quote reminds us of the importance of anchoring the development of solutions on a clear understanding of the outcomes that customers seek as they look for solutions to their problems. By focusing on outcomes, marketers can shift their focus away from individual products or services and think instead of what it would take to solve a complete customer problem. An outcomes focus often points the way to services that can complement the core product or, in some cases, even replace the product with a service-dominant solution.

Focusing on customer outcomes helps marketers to see their business from the customer point of view, which is often very different from the marketer's point of view. As Lorenzo Gambrano, the CEO of the Mexican cement company CEMEX, notes, "We understand that our real business is helping our customers complete their construction projects. At the end of the day, no one wants to buy cement; they want to build a house or a bridge or a road." This outcomes-focused thinking has led CEMEX to think very differently about its business and has enabled CEMEX to create innovative solutions to customer problems (Prahalad 2004, pp. 147–68).

In its search for opportunities to increase its revenues from low-income Mexican customers, CEMEX sent a team of researchers to Guadalajara to uncover problems that low-income customers face in building houses. They discovered that financing was the most important problem for low-income customers. They also found that families employed local unskilled or semiskilled masons who built houses with poor planning and with a lot of wastage. Finally, they discovered that a large proportion of the low-income houses built in Mexico are financed by immigrants repatriating small sums of money from the United States. These remittances are made using money transfer firms who charged high transaction fees and offered poor currency-exchange rates. In addition, there was a risk of theft when relatives collected money from the money transfer agencies in Mexico, and a significant portion of the remittances meant for constructing houses ended up being used for other purposes.

CEMEX has created an innovative solution called Construmex USA to solve these problems. Construmex is a service that allows Mexicans living in the United States to send their money directly to cement distributors in Mexico. Distributors receive the money and deliver cement and other building materials directly to the site. Construmex also offers advice to relatives in Mexico on finding the best distributors, planning a house, and estimating material requirements for the house. Construmex has allowed CEMEX to position itself as a solutions provider and not simply as a seller of cement.

A useful way to shift focus from products to customer outcomes is to think in terms of verbs—what objects *do*—rather than nouns—what they *are* (Vandermerwe 1993). Descriptions framed in terms of what objects do tend to be more expressive and more associative than descriptions framed in terms of their tangible features. This forces marketers to think more deeply about what their products are ultimately designed to accomplish for customers. For instance, when a customer opens an individual retirement account with a brokerage firm, she may really be looking forward to a "comfortable retirement." And when a customer buys a ball bearing in an industrial plant, what they really care about is "trouble-free operations." This is not merely a shift in vocabulary. It is a shift in point of view that requires marketers to see the world of products from the customer's point of view and work backward from there to discover the products and services that might help customers accomplish the outcomes they seek.

Mapping the Customer Activity Cycle

The outcomes that customers seek require them to perform a sequence of activities that are logically connected. This temporally linked sequence of activities that customers engage in to solve a problem is called a *customer activity cycle* (Sawhney 1999; Sawhney, Subramanian, and Krishnan 2004; Vandermerwe 1993, 2000). The customer activity cycle consists of three phases:

1. *Pre or before:* when customers are deciding what to do to get the desired result—searching, evaluating, deciding, acquiring.
2. *During:* when customers are doing what they decided on—installing, using, operating.
3. *Post or after:* when customers are keeping things going—reviewing, renewing, extending, upgrading and updating.

The customer activity can be mapped in detail at each of these stages through an activity-mapping process called activity blueprinting, or customer experience mapping process (Seybold 2001; Shaw 2004; Shaw and Ivens 2002). Activity blueprinting is a form of exploratory research that uses interviews and observation to trace the full stories of how real customers buy, use, and consume products.

To illustrate how customer activity mapping can lead to the identification of new opportunities, consider how Kodak reconceptualized its digital imaging business in terms of the customer activities involved in managing memories (see Figure 29.4). The customer activity cycle begins with "capturing memories" through a camera, a camcorder or a camera phone. These memories are then modified and edited, an activity that has been enabled through digital software for manipulating images. Images can then be instantiated, stored, transmitted, shared, archived, and repurposed. An analysis of these activities pointed Kodak to a number of new value-creation opportunities, such as online photo printing services, home photo printing paper and printers, and services for printing cards and flyers using photos. By seeing itself as being in the business of helping customers manage their memories instead of producing cameras and film, Kodak has been able to create compelling solutions like the EasyShare system of cameras, the Ofoto printing services, and PictureMaker kiosks in pharmacies for self-printing of digital pictures.

DESIGNING REPEATABLE SOLUTIONS FOR PROFIT

A key driver of the value of solutions is the fact that they are deeply customized to the needs and context of specific customers. This means that solutions often require one-off customization work

Figure 29.4 **The Customer Activity Cycle for Managing Memories**

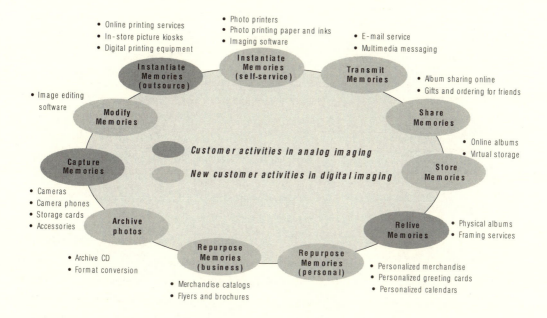

- Online printing services
- In-store picture kiosks
- Digital printing equipment

- Photo printers
- Photo printing paper and inks
- Imaging software

- E-mail service
- Multimedia messaging

Instantiate Memories (outsource)

Instantiate Memories (self-service)

Transmit Memories

- Album sharing online
- Gifts and ordering for friends

- Image editing software

Modify Memories

Share Memories

- Online albums
- Virtual storage

Capture Memories

Customer activities in analog imaging

New customer activities in digital imaging

Store Memories

- Cameras
- Camera phones
- Storage cards
- Accessories

Archive photos

Relive Memories

- Physical albums
- Framing services

- Archive CD
- Format conversion

Repurpose Memories (business)

Repurpose Memories (personal)

- Personalized merchandise
- Personalized greeting cards
- Personalized calendars

- Merchandise catalogs
- Flyers and brochures

for each customer, making it is difficult to create economies of scale in developing solutions. Therefore, a key consideration in the design of solutions is to provide the level of customization valued by customers without significantly compromising operating margins.

The key to overcoming the margin challenge in solutions is to embrace *repeatability* by creating a "solutions factory" for productizing solutions (Brady, Davies, and Gann 2004; Davies and Brady 2000). Instead of economies of scale, solutions firms need to embrace "economies of repetition" by reusing elements of previously designed solutions or by creating solutions platforms that can be used to create flexible offerings from common baseline solutions and a set of flexibly configurable options (Anderson and Narus 1995).

To embrace repeatability, solution providers need to complement their strategic and functional capabilities with *project capabilities*—capabilities that are central to the project-based one-off work that is central to the design and delivery of customized solutions (Davies and Brady 2000). Project capabilities include skills related to customer requirements gathering, conceptual design, cost estimation, bid preparation, project and program management, and organizational learning processes that allow firms to benefit from "economies of repetition" (Hobday 1998).

The development of project-based capabilities requires a fundamental change in the design of the organization. The need to develop specialized project-based and customer-facing capabilities has led firms like IBM, Nokia, and ABB to adopt a "front-back" hybrid organization to develop and deploy solutions (Brady, Davies, and Gann 2004; Foote et al. 2001; Galbraith 2002; Gerstner 2002). This front-back design consists of "front-end" *solutions units* responsible for developing and delivering integrated solutions, "back-end" *product units* that support the front-end units by developing products that go into the solutions and a "strong center" to mediate between the front-end and the back-end units (see Figure 29.5).

The front-end units specialize in project-management capabilities and customer knowledge. They take responsibility for revenue and profit growth for specific customer accounts or specific

Figure 29.5 **Organizing for Solutions: The Front-Back Design**

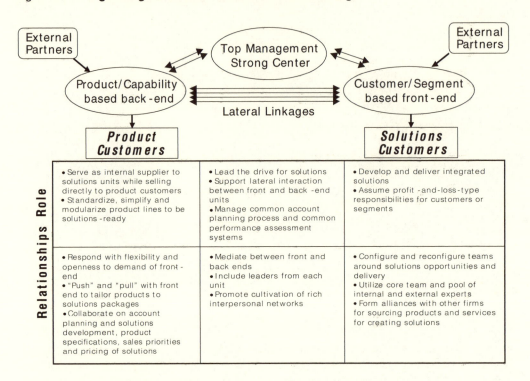

Adapted from: "Making Solutions the Answer." *McKinsey Quarterly*, 2001, 3.

customer segments. They provide a "single face" to the customers, bringing together products and services from the entire firm as well as from third-party partners for customers. Customers are typically served through relationship managers, account managers, or segment managers who have a deep understanding of the customer segment and even individual customer accounts within a specific segment. IBM went through a reorganization of this type under Lou Gerstner from 1993 to 1998, which involved creating a front-end called IBM Global Industries, which was organized around the key industries that IBM serves. These units were given profit-and-loss responsibility for their industries, a significant departure from the past where the geographical units had P&L responsibility (Gerstner 2002).

In the front-back design, the product units become back ends that support the customer-facing front-end units. This often requires a significant change-management challenge, because product units traditionally are the power centers for the organization in many product-centric firms (Foote et al. 2001). Product units are responsible for designing and developing products and for working closely with the front-end solutions units to ensure demand for their products within the solutions. Product units are also responsible for creating platforms that can become the basis for repeatable solutions.

The front-back organization design cannot function well without a clear strategic direction and effective coordination between the front end and the back end. This is the responsibility of the corporate center. This "strong center" is responsible for mediating between the front end and the back end, to ensure that they collaborate closely together. The corporate center should include leaders from the front end as well as the back end of the organization who are tasked with coming up with coordination mechanisms like shared performance scorecards, cross-linked teams, and rotation of personnel between the front end and the back end.

A front-back organization design allows firms to create repeatable solutions by progressively productizing one-off solutions developed by the front end. This allows the firm to create a "solutions factory" that is constantly being provided with one-off solutions as "raw material" that the back-end units can convert into repeatable solutions—the "finished goods" for the solutions factory. This is how IBM creates repeatable solutions (Foote et al. 2001). IBM's Global Industries Units create one-off solutions by working with cutting-edge customers. An integrative leadership team with members drawn from the front end as well as the back end evaluates each one-off solution as a candidate for a productized solution, based on how many other customers, geographies, and industries the one-off solution can be leveraged into. The back-end Global Services unit then develops a codified, standardized, and generalized version of the chosen solutions as a solutions platform. These solutions platforms are then sent off to the front end, which markets the solutions to all of IBM's customers.

The solutions capabilities in the front end and the back end are developed in a phased manner, with initial moves focusing on developing the front end, and later moves focusing on strengthening the back end and refocusing the firm around solutions (Brady, Davies, and Gann 2004). These four stages are as follows:

1. *Initial front-end moves:* At this stage, the firm establishes a pilot project based to move into and learn about new solutions opportunities. The capabilities in the front end are developed by carrying out "one-off" solutions projects for a few vanguard customers.

2. *Expand the front end:* At this stage, the learning from initial projects is captured and transferred to all existing projects as well as to all subsequent projects. The scope and size of the customer-facing front end is increased, and customer segment–based or market-based organizations are formalized. Program-management skills are also enhanced in the front end.

3. *Build the back end:* The focus at this stage is to reorganize internal product units to better support the solutions front-end units, to enter into strategic partnerships that are needed to fill out the solutions offering, and to build capabilities for developing product platforms and service portfolios in the back-end units.

4. *Refocus the entire organization:* Finally, at this stage, the entire firm's activities are oriented around the delivery of integrated solutions. Profit-and-loss responsibilities are shifted from the product units to the front-end customer-facing units. The focus of capability development at this stage is to improve coordination between the front end and back end and to promote strategic learning.

PRICING SOLUTIONS BASED ON CUSTOMER VALUE

Pricing of solutions is a difficult task, for at least four reasons. First, integrated solutions provide value-added services like integration, customization, deployment, maintenance, servicing, and financing. Setting a price on these services is more difficult than pricing tangible products. Second, these value-added services are customized for each customer, so it is difficult to establish a standardized price for solutions. Third, solutions providers take over the responsibility for activities previously performed by customers and ownership of assets previously owned by customers. This transfer of responsibility also involves a transfer of risk from the customer to the supplier,

Figure 29.6 **Value-Based Pricing Mechanisms for Solutions**

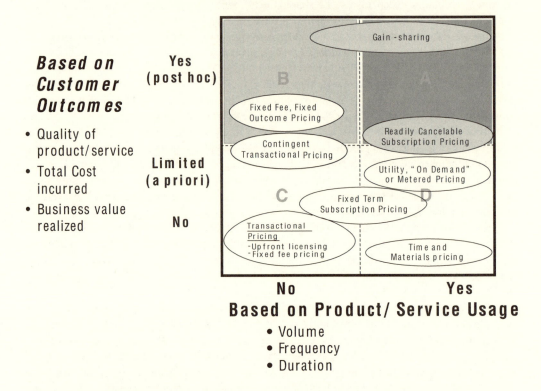

which needs to be incorporated into the price for solutions. Finally, solutions often involve an ongoing relationship between the solutions provider and their customers, as opposed to a one-time transaction involved in selling a product. Pricing mechanisms need to allow for pricing over the entire duration of the relationship.

To overcome these challenges, the price of a solution should be based on the value created by the solution for customers. The logic behind value-based pricing is simple—the value captured by the solutions provider should be indexed to the value created by the solution for the customers (Roegener, Seifert, and Swinford 2001). Value-based pricing begins with a value assessment study to estimate the monetary value of the benefits received by the customer from the solution. These techniques include field value-in-use assessment, indirect survey questions, benchmarks and conjoint analysis (Anderson, Jain, and Chintagunta 1993). Next, the solution provider needs to link the amount and timing of customer payments for the solution to the timing and amount of actual value realized by customers (Sawhney 2002).

Value-based pricing approaches can include pricing approaches based on the *quantity of usage* of a product or service, or on the *quality of customer outcomes* (see Figure 29.6 for a classification of value-based pricing mechanisms for solutions). Quantity-based pricing approaches for solutions include subscription pricing (based on the duration of the solution), utility pricing (based on quantity of usage of a product or service), and time-and-materials pricing (based on quantity of usage of human resources). Quantity-based approaches typically involve payments for solutions on a periodic basis instead of a large up-front payment for a capital good. This mechanism is often called subscription pricing, or "utility pricing," because of its similarity to pricing in utility industries. Subscription pricing can also include a no-fee termination option that allows customers to terminate the subscription payments at any time if they are not satisfied with the service, to mitigate the customer's risk.

Outcome-based approaches go one step further in linking value captured by solution providers with the extent to which value is created for customers. These approaches can include fixed-fee, fixed-time pricing or gain-sharing pricing. Fixed-fee and fixed-time pricing involves mitigating the risk of cost and time overruns in the project, because the vendor provides the guarantee that the cost or the duration of a project will not exceed an agreed-upon amount. For instance, IT and business-process outsourcing contracts often guarantee a fixed price or a fixed amount of cost savings to customers.

The most extreme version of customer value-based pricing is gain-sharing (also called risk and reward sharing). Gain-sharing is a pricing approach where the payments to the solution provider are based entirely on the level of business value realized by the client. In a gain-sharing arrangement, the solution provider and the customer agree to track a predefined set of value metrics, and the payment to the vendor is fully contingent upon the extent to which the customer actually realizes value, as measured on these metrics. Gain-sharing offers several important benefits to customers as well as to solution providers. For customers, gain-sharing provides an assurance that the interests of solution providers are closely aligned with their interests, because the solution provider's financial success depends upon customer success. Therefore, the providers have strong incentives to only undertake work that truly creates value for customer. Further, they have an incentive to find creative ways to collaborate with customers in the joint pursuit of greater value. A second major benefit of gain-sharing arises from the fact that this arrangement shifts financial risk from the customer to the solutions provider. This is particularly important for risky and costly projects, where the financial risk is considerable. And gain-sharing lessens the upfront capital required by cash-strapped customers because it is a "pay as you go" mechanism that could potentially make projects self-funding, because realized savings can be used to pay for future investments in the project (Sawhney 2004).

Gain-sharing also has several potential benefits for solution providers. It provides a basis for competitive differentiation by signaling the confidence that the solution provider has in its ability to successfully deliver value. By putting their own "skin in the game," solution providers can convince customers that they truly believe in their ability to deliver on their promises and on their confidence in their own financial position based on their ability to take on risk on behalf of customers.

Despite these benefits, gain-sharing arrangements are still relatively rare, with only a few examples in advertising, legal services, revenue collection agencies, and IT outsourcing contracts. The barriers to adopting gain-sharing arrangements include the difficulty in objectively measuring the value created by solutions, resistance from purchasing organizations to using unfamiliar pricing approaches, fears of owing the solution provider a lot of money if the projects are *too* successful, and the lack of trust between solution providers and customers. To overcome these barriers, solution providers need to define a clear set of business success metrics for measuring value. They also need to educate the customer's organization about the benefits of gain sharing. And they need to offer to put caps that limit the maximum payout to the solution provider in the event of a runaway success.

Ultimately, gain-sharing arrangements only make sense when the gains from the projects are not a zero-sum game that involve a pure transfer of risk from the customer to the solution provider, because this would create an adverse selection problem for the solution provider if only customers who have no confidence in the solution outcomes opt for gain-sharing arrangements. Gain-sharing is most useful when there are significant *gains to collaboration*—when the solution outcomes derived from close collaboration between solution providers and customers are truly superior to the outcomes that would be achieved if the two parties acted independently. Gains from collaboration can accrue from joint forecasting, joint planning, and joint optimization of operations.

TOWARD A RESEARCH AGENDA IN SOLUTIONS MARKETING

Despite the importance of solutions in the world of practice, academic research on solutions marketing is woefully lacking. This is a domain where practice is well ahead of academic research. This is partly attributable to the fact that academic research in marketing has traditionally focused on high-volume, low-value, frequently purchased consumer packaged goods, while solutions marketing is most relevant in industry settings characterized by low-volume, high-value, technology-intensive capital goods (Davies and Brady 2000). Academic research in marketing has generally paid less attention to business marketing than to consumer marketing, and it seems to have paid even less attention to complex project-based solutions marketing in business-to-business settings.

This paucity of academic research suggests that solutions marketing is an extremely fertile area for academic researchers. Here is a partial list of interesting directions for research in solutions marketing:

• *Financial attractiveness of solutions marketing:* I note here that a move toward solutions has some important benefits (e.g., revenue growth, differentiation, customer retention), but such a move also presents difficult challenges and risks (e.g., competence risk, margin risk). It would be interesting to conduct an empirical investigation to see if the financial benefits of moving toward solutions outweigh the risks and to define the contextual factors that separate winners from losers in migration to a solutions approach. A related research direction would be to identify approaches to mitigating risks in moving toward a solutions-centric approach and the conditions that determine the success of various risk-mitigation approaches (see Sawhney, Balasubramanian, and Krishan 2004 for preliminary thinking on this). Also of interest is the scope decision—how far should the firm go in expanding the scope of the solutions that it provides to customers, and when does the competence stretch required to expand the scope become too much for the firm to handle?

• *Market opportunity analysis for solutions:* Although a move to solutions greatly expands the market opportunity for firms, it also makes the market opportunity analysis process more difficult. It can even be difficult to define the boundaries of the market space for solutions, because there are so many directions along which solutions opportunities can be explored. For instance, firms can move downstream in the customer activity cycle to provide after-sales services to customers. Or they can move upstream to provide pre-sales services and assistance. Or they can take over some of the customers' activities and business processes. Each of these directions is a possible "growth vector" that the firm could explore. Further research is needed to understand how firms can structure their solutions market opportunity portfolios, and how they can prioritize the vectors along which they should explore opportunities for service-intensive growth (Sawhney, Balasubramanian, and Krishnan 2004).

• *Value stream for solutions development:* The flow of value-added activities in product-centric industries has traditionally been conceptualized in terms of Porter's value chain, a representation of the sequence of value-adding activities performed by firms from sourcing of inputs all the way to outbound logistics, distribution and sales of finished products (Porter 1985). However, the value chain for products is quite different than that for products, because the sequence of activities performed in producing one-off, highly complex capital goods-based solutions is often the reverse of that required for mass-produced products (Brady, Davies, and Gann 2004). In mass production, product development comes first, followed by marketing and distribution to customers. In solutions development, by contrast, the sequence begins with understanding the customer's problem and designing a customized solution. This is followed by manufacturing or sourcing components and products that will constitute the solution, integrating the components into a whole system, installing and deploying the solution, operating and maintaining the solution over an extended duration, and providing end-of-life cycle services for the solution. In solutions design, the products that will be needed for the solution are not known a priori, in contrast with product marketing, where the product comes first. Further research is needed to conceptualize the value stream for solutions development along the lines suggested by Brady, Davies, and Gann (2004) by modifying and adapting the value chain framework to the solutions design and development context.

• *Organizing to deliver solutions:* The front-back organization design is an example of the structural changes that are required for firms to organize around solutions design and delivery. The front-back design allows firms to create solutions and customer expertise in the front end while concentrating product and service capabilities in the back-end units (Sawhney 2001). However, managing the linkages between the front end and the back end presents a difficult challenge. Further research is needed to identify the various linking and coordination mechanisms that firms can use to improve the effectiveness of the front-back organization and the conditions under which different mechanisms should be used.

• *Design of optimal value-based pricing mechanisms:* Value-based pricing, particularly gain-sharing mechanisms, represent an important advance in thinking about how value gets created and shared between solution providers and customers. But gain-sharing mechanisms need to be more than a simple transfer of financial and operational risk from the customer to the solution provider—they need to facilitate the creation of superior outcomes through collaboration. Gains from collaboration can come from better allocation of activities between customers and providers, better collaboration in executing the activities, and improved incentives for both parties to create more value from the partnership. We need to learn more designing gain-sharing mechanisms to maximize the potential benefits of collaboration and to learn how to overcome barriers to adopting gain-sharing mechanisms.

These are only a few of the many directions along which academic researchers can enhance our understanding of how to define, design, develop, and deliver solutions more effectively. As we evolve to a new service-dominant logic for marketing, I believe that we also need to evolve to a solution-centric mind-set that encourages marketers to think beyond their products and to explore the vast frontiers of solutions opportunities that surround their products. Hopefully, this chapter will serve as a roadmap for practitioners as well as academics to embark on this exciting journey.

REFERENCES

Anderson, James C. and James A. Narus (1995), "Capturing the Value of Supplementary Services," *Harvard Business Review* (January/February), 75–83.

———, Dipak C. Jain, and Pradeep K. Chintagunta (1993), "Customer Value Assessment in Business Markets: A State-of-Practice Study," *Journal of Business-to-Business Marketing,* 1 (1), 3–29.

Bennett, J.D. Sharma and A. Tipping (2001), "Customer Solutions: Building a Strategically Aligned Business Model," in *Insights: Organization and Strategic Leadership Practice.* McLean, VA: Booz Allen & Hamilton, 1–5.

Brady, Tim, Andrew Davies, and David Gann (2004), "Creating Value by Delivering Integrated Solutions," paper presented at IRNOP VI Project Research Conference, August 25–27, Turku, Finland.

Davies, Andrew and Tim Brady (2000), "Organisational Capabilities and Learning in Complex Product Systems: Toward Repeatable Solutions," *Research Policy,* 29, 931–53.

Drucker, Peter F. (1974), *Management: Tasks, Responsibilities, Practices.* New York: Harper & Row, Publishers, Inc.

Foote, Nathaniel, Jay Galbraith, Quentin Hope, and Danny Miller (2001), "Making Solutions the Answer," *McKinsey Quarterly,* 3, 84–93.

Galbraith, J.R. (2002), "Organising to Deliver Solutions," *Organisational Dynamics,* 31/2: 194–207.

Gann, D.M. and A.J. Salter (2000), "Innovation in Project-Based, Service-Enhanced Firms: The Construction of Complex Products and Systems," *Research Policy,* 29, 955–72.

Gerstner, L.V. (2002), *Who Said Elephants Can't Dance? Inside IBM's Historic Turnaround.* London: Harper Collins Publishers.

Hobday, M. (1998), "Product Complexity, Innovation and Industrial Organization," *Research Policy,* 26, 689–710.

Krishnamurthy, Chandru, Juliet Johansson, and Hank Schlissberg (2003), "Solutions Selling: Is the Pain Worth the Gain?" *McKinsey Marketing Solutions.*

MacMillan, Ian C., and Rita Gunther McGrath (1997), "Discovering New Points of Differentiation," *Harvard Business Review* (July), 3–11.

Porter, Michael (1985), *Competitive Advantage: Creating and Sustaining Superior Performance.* New York: The Free Press.

Prahalad. C.K. (2004), *The Fortune at the Bottom of the Pyramid: Eradicating Poverty through Profits.* Philadelphia: Wharton School Publishing.

Roegener, Eric V., Torsten Seifert, and Dennis D. Swinford (2001), "Setting a Price on Solutions," *McKinsey Quarterly,* 3, 94–97.

Sawhney, Mohanbir (1999), "Making New Markets: Sellers Need to Better Understand Buyers to Achieve the Promise of the Net Economy," *Business 2.0* (May), 10–22.

——— (2001), "Don't Homogenize, Synchronize," *Harvard Business Review* (July/August), 100–108.

——— (2002), "Getting Real about Getting Paid," *CIO Magazine,* September 15.

——— (2003), "The Problem with Solutions," *CIO Magazine,* February 15.

——— (2004), *Trilogy: Customer Value-Based Pricing,* Kellogg School of Management case study, Northwestern University.

———, Sridhar Balasubramanian, and Vish Krishnan (2004), "Creating Growth with Services," *MIT Sloan Management Review,* 45 (Winter), 34–43.

Seybold, Patricia B. (2001), "Get Inside the Lives of your Customers," *Harvard Business Review* (May), 80–89.

Shaw, Colin (2004), *Revolutionize your Customer Experience.* Basingstoke, UK: Palgrave Macmillan.

——— and John Ivens (2002), *Building Great Customer Experiences.* Basingstoke, UK: Palgrave Macmillan.

Slywotsky, A. and D.J. Morrison (1998), *The Profit Zone: How Strategic Business Design Will Lead You to Tomorrow's Profits.* Chichester, UK: John Wiley & Sons.

Vandermerwe, Sandra (1993), "Jumping into the Customer's Activity Cycle: A New Role for Customer Services in the 1990s," *The Columbia Journal of World Business* (Summer), 46–65.

——— (2000), "How Increasing Value to Customers Improves Business Results," *MIT Sloan Management Review* (Fall), 27–37.

Vargo, Stephen L. and Robert F. Lusch (2004), "Evolving to a New Dominant Logic for Marketing," *Journal of Marketing,* 68, January, 1–17.

Wise, R. and P. Baumgartner (1999). "Go Downstream: The New Profit Imperative in Manufacturing." *Harvard Business Review* (September/October), 133–41.

30

HOW DOES MARKETING STRATEGY CHANGE IN A SERVICE-BASED WORLD?

Implications and Directions for Research

ROLAND T. RUST AND DEBORA VIANA THOMPSON

INTRODUCTION

Scholars have recently discussed a paradigm shift in the marketing discipline. For example, Vargo and Lusch's (2004a) recent article, published in the *Journal of Marketing*, argues in favor of an emerging new dominant logic for marketing. This paradigm shift or new logic, sometimes referred to as the "service revolution," relies on the notion that the core element in the exchange between firms and customers is service provision. The boundaries between goods and services are increasingly becoming blurred, and the conventional characteristics that differentiate goods and services have been shown to be artificial and ineffective (Lovelock and Gummeson 2004; Vargo and Lusch 2004b). Thus, a broader perspective of marketing considers physical products as distribution mechanisms for service provision (Vargo and Lusch 2004b). Consumers acquire products to obtain the services that they provide.

The shift toward service can be seen worldwide in several industries. For instance, software companies and personal computers and electronics manufacturers are experiencing a massive change in their business mission, from manufacturing goods to providing services to customers. Companies such as IBM, Dell, Oracle and HP are relying on services as their most importance source of profits. This trend from tangible to intangible products does not seem restricted to high-technology industries, and includes conventional channels such as grocery store chains and car manufacturers. Along with this process, it becomes imperative to review the firm's internal structure, strategic goals and, most importantly, the relationships with customers.

The service revolution affects both macro- and microeconomic levels of our society. At the macro level, for example, the growing service-based economy is changing the requirements for the workforce. The U.S Federal Reserve chairman recently stated that Americans face a never-ending necessity to learn new skills because of the ever-growing *conceptualization* of economic output (*The Washington Post*, 02/21/04). At the micro level, managers from a wide array of industries are being urged to move away from marketing strategies and tactics based on brands and product lines to strategies based on developing relationships with individual customers.

The expression "paradigm shift" implies the notion of change from one philosophical and theoretical framework to another. We believe that several of our theories will need to be revised to incorporate (and explain) all the impacts of a service-based view of the firm. This does not mean, however, that everything we know so far is invalid or outdated; rather, it suggests that we need to rethink some of our key marketing concepts and reevaluate the way marketing strategy is formulated and implemented.

In this chapter, our goal is threefold. First, we address the driving force of this new service logic—information technology (IT). We believe that the service revolution and the information revolution are two sides of the same coin. Second, we describe why the customer equity framework fits a service-based view of the firm and summarize its advantages as the central element of marketing strategy. Lastly, we comment on the impact of this service perspective on firm and consumer behavior and suggest important new areas for investigation.

INFORMATION TECHNOLOGY AND THE SERVICE REVOLUTION

We believe that information technology drives services. It is the ability to generate, transform and distribute information that ultimately enables firms to provide services to customers. Developments in digitization of information and advances in computing and telecommunications have created higher levels of mobilization and unbundling of intelligence, which in turn have altered how value is created in the economy (Sawhney and Parikh 2001). As Sawhney and Parikh (2001, p. 80) summarized, economic value is now linked to improving the utility of information: "where intelligence resides, so too does value." Overall, information technology allows firms to have more complex transactions with customers (transactions that involve a larger volume of information) and complete these transactions at a greater distance from the firm's site (Xie and Shugan 2001). Taken together, these structural changes in the economic system (i.e., developments in information technology in the last 100 years) have promoted new capabilities to leverage knowledge into service and have expanded the intangible aspect of all economic exchanges. In summary, the shift toward services is the result of continuous progress on how information can be manipulated.

We will focus on four main outcomes from information technology that shape firms' capability to offer services: (1) e-service opportunities, (2) demand-driven production systems, (3) personalization of communication, and (4) organizational agility.

The accelerated progress in information technology during the twentieth century developed a wide array of technologies to generate, transport and transform information, such as the Internet, wireless networks, smart cards, agent technologies, customer relationship management programs, supply chain management networks and data mining tools, just to cite a few. These technologies substantially increase firms' capacity to decompose and reassemble information in different ways; they allow the firm to learn and store more information about the market and its customers, which in turn leads to an enhanced understanding of customers' needs and greater ability to offer services and develop relationships with customers.

In our opinion, one of the most important business impacts of such IT developments is the ability to provide service over electronic networks (including Internet, wireless networks, ATMs, smart card networks, etc.), or *e-service*. Today, several industries are transforming their physical products into e-services. As the transport of voice and data become a commodity, telecommunication businesses face the need to provide other services like hosting, maintenance, portals with content for end users, and so on. The same trend appears in personal computer and information products. "The functionality that was once built into computers or sold as software packages can now be delivered over the Internet, much as utility companies deliver electricity through power lines. Just as corporations and consumers no longer need to own their own generators, they'll soon be freed from having to own their own computing hardware and applications" (Sawhney and Parikh 2001, pp. 82–83). For instance, Microsoft is viewing software as a service to which customers can subscribe; Yahoo! offers the ability to store e-mail messages, digital photographs and other files; and Dell Computers recently launched "Dell E Works," which consists of e-services such as e-consulting and Web hosting (Sawhney and Parikh 2001).

Moreover, the development of smart card networks (including electronic tickets, smart cards and online prepayments) has facilitated advance-selling services, where sellers allow buyers to purchase (online or offline) at a time preceding consumption (Xie and Shugan 2001). Advance-selling strategies increase firms' profits by increasing the number of buyers or by allowing a premium advance price (Xie and Shugan 2001), and risk of arbitrage is controlled due to the encryption of personalized information in the card or ticket.

A very important aspect of the nature of e-service resides on its revenue-expansion effect. In contrast with the early e-service applications (traditional e-commerce perspective), which were primarily developed to decrease operational costs and increase efficiency through automation, an emerging view of e-service focuses on its ability to improve the level of customer service (enhance the service experience), increase customer satisfaction and lead to higher profits (Rust and Kannan 2003). Based on this perspective, e-service should be used to foster relationships with customers and increase customer equity, i.e., their lifetime value to the firm. In a recent research project funded by IBM and the Center for Excellence in Service at the University of Maryland, we studied the impact of governmental e-service (e-government) on small businesses in three states of the United States. We found that governmental e-service was significantly improving the performance of small companies through revenue expansion, rather than through cost reduction. Small firms that used governmental online services more frequently generated greater amounts of market intelligence and showed superior financial performance, relative to firms that had a lower usage rate (Thompson, Rust, and Rhoda 2004).

Advances in information technology have also allowed companies to migrate from supply-driven production (build-to-forecast) to complex and flexible demand-driven production systems (build-to-order) (Dedrick and Kraemer 2002). Sophisticated internal information systems can now integrate all the fulfillment processes, from order entry, manufacturing, and billing to delivery. Information technology allows the three main stages of customization to be integrated in a seamless network: elicitation, the mechanism to interact with the customer and obtain specific information; process flexibility to fabricate the product according to the information; and logistics to deliver the right product to the right consumer (Zipkin 2001). Thus, it is the information system connecting the different players in the supply chain that made possible what researchers are calling co-creation of value.

The impact of such flexible production systems that allow consumers to configure their own products is tremendous. Firms are substantially reducing inventory, offering higher levels of customization and giving more power to consumers. Consumers can choose from larger assortments and can match product configurations to their exact preferences, possibly increasing the value of the products they buy. For instance, Levi Strauss sells custom-fitted jeans, Andersen Windows can produce windows to fit any house, and Nike allows you to personalize your own tennis shoes.

A third important outcome of information technology that enhances the quality of firms' services is the opportunity to design communications or marketing programs at the individual level (one-to-one marketing). In this case, the personalization of information is initiated by the firm itself, which can filter information about individual customers. The Internet allows a high level of targetability—the possibility of reaching individual customers at low cost. Furthermore, the interactivity of the Internet allows firms to collect and update information about customers' preferences obtained from on-site surveys and from click-stream data. This intelligence can be later integrated with algorithms in an optimization approach to provide unique content to each customer (Ansari and Mela 2003).

The integration of knowledge about customers' preferences and optimization algorithms has also led to collaborative and content filtering systems, which use data on users' preferences to recommend products or content (Ansari and Mela 2003), such as the ones used by Amazon.com, Yahoo!, Macys, Blockbuster, among others. Firms use these systems to offer recommendation services and other decision aid services (e.g., product comparison services, search engines, matchmaking services, etc.) to help consumers to search for information and make purchase decisions. Research in marketing has shown that the usage of such services significantly reduces consumers' search effort and improves the quality of their purchase decisions (Haubl and Trifts 2000).

The fourth outcome of information technology that directly impacts firms' capability to offer services is corporate agility—the ability to quickly detect and seize market opportunities (Sambamurthy, Bharadwaj, and Grover 2003). Previous research shows that firms with wide-ranging information networks were more responsive in turbulent business environments due to the possibility of quickly leveraging assets and knowledge of suppliers, manufacturers and other partners (Zaheer and Zaheer 1997). Technologies that facilitate interorganizational collaboration such as portals and supply-chain systems are primarily responsible for a higher level of agility in service innovation. Yahoo!, for example, has migrated from a search engine to a portal by developing alliances to provide content and several other services in the Web site. AOL has followed a similar trend and offers a myriad of services from weather information to financial and real estate resources.

Further advances in information technology will happen in the years to come; thus we expect that the service orientation in business will only intensify. All industries, including packaged goods, which historically have focused on short-term transactions, will be able to use information technology tools: (1) to understand customers' needs better and offer customized products or personalized content, (2) to unbundle or bundle different useful pieces of information and deliver them to customers, and finally, (3) to strengthen the customer relationships and increase customer equity.

CUSTOMER EQUITY FRAMEWORK

The essence of the business movement toward service is the shift from product-centered thinking to customer-centric thinking. Service provision aims at developing relationships with customers, increasing their satisfaction, inducing switching costs over time, building customer loyalty, and, ultimately, improving performance by expanding revenues. According to the service logic (enabled by information technology), the key unit of analysis is the value of the relationship between the firm and each individual customer. The lifetime value of the customer base is firms' most important asset. Therefore, as companies become increasingly service-oriented, marketing strategy will need to accompany this shift and become less product-centered and increasingly customer-centered. We propose that the customer equity framework is a flexible, customer-based approach that should be the central element in marketing strategy. By using this approach, firms can focus on marketing actions that lead to the greatest payoff.

In the rest of this section, we will discuss the rationale behind one specific model of customer equity: the framework proposed by Rust, Zeithaml, and Lemon (2000). Our goal is to discuss advantages of this model over other models that measure financial impact of marketing expenditures and point out how it reflects some of the foundational premises of the service-dominant logic presented by Vargo and Lusch (2004a). For those interested in how to implement the customer equity framework, we suggest two sets of readings: Rust, Zeithaml, and Lemon (2000) and Rust, Zeithaml, and Lemon (2004) for broader managerial implementation issues, and Rust, Lemon, and Zeithaml (2004) for statistical and computational details.

Customer equity is the total of the discounted customer lifetime values summed over all the firm's current and potential customers (Rust, Lemon, and Zeithaml 2004). The ultimate goal of the customer equity model is to link marketing actions to the firm's financial return, making marketing a financially accountable investment. Customers' lifetime values to the firm mediate the relationship between strategic actions and return on investments. The chain of effects behind this approach is the following: (1) marketing investments produce improvements in drivers of customer equity (i.e., improvements in dimensions that affect customer satisfaction and retention, such as brand associations, product improvements, etc.), (2) improvements in these drivers lead to improvements in customers' perceptions and enhance customer attraction and retention, (3) attraction of new customers and retention of current customers increase customer equity, and (4) increased customer equity, relative to the cost of marketing actions, results in favorable returns on investment.

The estimation of customer equity is based on data about individual customers' frequency of category purchases, average quantity purchased, brand-switching patterns, and the firm's contribution margin. Model inputs such as drivers of customer equity, estimated shift in customer ratings, size of the total market, competitors and discount rate are obtained through exploratory research. A key piece of information is the estimate of the shift in customers' perceptions induced by a specific marketing action. A shift in a driver of customer equity produces an estimated shift in customer's utility, which in turn produces an estimated shift in the conditional probabilities of choice. The revised choice probabilities are used to compute the customer's lifetime value.

The customer equity framework presents several important advantages over previous models of customer lifetime value and models of financial impact of marketing actions. First, the customer equity framework allows managers to project the comparative impact of alternative marketing expenditures, providing a data-driven basis for trading off marketing actions and making marketing financially accountable. Second, the customer equity framework incorporates customers' switching behavior. To capture the flow of customers from one competitor to another, the model uses a Markov switching matrix, where each customer has a probability of being retained by each brand in the subsequent purchase occasion. This feature of the model allows managers to consider the impact of competitors' actions on a firm's customer equity. Third, the customer equity framework considers the impact of both current customers and prospective, future customers. Thus, it is a forward-looking model that considers customer acquisition and retention. Fourth, to implement the customer equity framework, firms do not need to have longitudinal data on customers' purchases. The model can be implemented with cross-sectional data, using purchase intentions. Fifth, firms can use the customer equity framework to segment their customers in terms of the distribution of customer lifetime value. Finally, the mathematical models behind this approach are easily implemented using standard, commercially available software.

What main changes does the customer equity approach bring to marketing strategy? We believe that the customer equity view changes five important components of marketing strategy, which we briefly describe in the following section.

Focus of Strategic Efforts

In the customer equity perspective, firms use increasingly personalized expenditures to increase the value of an individual customer relationship. So, the focus is on the value of individual customers, rather than on aggregate sales responses, and marketing efforts are closer to one-to-one interactions, rather than to mass-marketing actions.

Competitive Advantage

Previous theories on marketing strategy such as Porter's product differentiation are based on product characteristics. In contrast, customer equity shifts the firm's focus from its products to knowledge of its customers' needs and to drivers of equity. Customer lifetime value, a strategic asset *outside* the firm, becomes the main strategic resource.

Measuring the Financial Impact of Marketing

The customer equity approach shifts the firm's attention from market share and other aggregate measures to measures of current and future individual customer profitability. This shift to measures that capture revenues and costs of serving individual customers allows managers to segment the market based on individual current and/or future profitability to the firm.

Product Utility

Product utility has been traditionally a function of its attributes (attribute-based models have been extensively used in economics and consumer behavior). Market research models, such as conjoint analysis, estimate consumers' choice based on how they trade off different levels of product attributes. This view of product utility assumes a transactional choice and does not take into consideration the context of the customer relationship with the firm. In the customer equity framework, product utility is a function of product value, brand, *and* relationship history, such as switching costs and emotional ties to the company. Product attributes (physical, tangible aspect) are reframed as benefits to the customer (intangible aspect).

Marketing Planning

Historically, firms have organized their marketing departments and marketing planning around products and brands. For instance, advertising campaigns, product differentiation strategies, product line and brand extension efforts are all centered on product and brand managers. Resource allocation is also based on product lines. Conversely, the customer equity framework is centered on customers, so logically, marketing planning activities revolve around customers and drivers of customers' lifetime value. The customer relationship focus on marketing planning relies on the fact that brand equity is not equal across customers and products will inevitably change as technology develops.

　　To conclude our reasoning of why customer equity fits a customer-centric, service-oriented view of marketing strategy, we would like to highlight the links between this approach and three specific foundational premises of the service-dominant logic presented by Vargo and Lusch (2004a). First, according to Vargo and Lusch (2004a), in a service-based world, *knowledge* is the fundamental source of competitive advantage. Consistent with an information-driven approach to strategy, the customer equity approach relies on knowledge about customers' needs to maximize their lifetime value and their contribution to a firm's profits. It is the intelligence about customers that drives a firm's efforts to improve customer equity drivers, which in turn improve acquisition and retention. Second, service-oriented enterprises can only make value propositions, rather than value distribution (Vargo and Lusch 2004a). This proposition directly addresses the notion that products and brands have no intrinsic value by themselves, but only in the context of developing relationships with customers. The customer equity framework is consistent with this proposition. It argues for a replacement of the main marketing asset: from brand equity to the discounted lifetime value of the firm's relationships with all its current and future customers. Finally, a service-centered view is customer oriented and relational (Vargo and Lusch 2004a). The customer equity approach is a relational model to measure (and maximize) firm's financial return from individual relationships with customers.

RESEARCH IMPLICATIONS OF THE SERVICE-DOMINANT LOGIC

Research about Firm Behavior

The cornerstone of the service-dominant logic and the customer equity framework is a customer-centered firm. Therefore, the key resource to competition is knowledge about customers' needs. Hogan, Lemon, and Rust (2002) proposed that the ability to acquire, manage, and model customer information to initiate and maintain profitable customer relationships is the key source of competitive advantage for customer-centered firms. The role of marketing is, then, to maximize the profitability of such relationships.

We believe that three bodies of literature provide useful and insightful conceptual frameworks for research on the strategic behavior of service-oriented firms: the resource-based view of the firm (RBV) (e.g., Peteraf 1993), core competency theory and organizational learning (e.g., Day 1994a, 1994b), and market orientation studies (e.g., Jaworski and Kohli 1990). Taken together, the ideas and empirical results of these research streams are consistent with the simple notion that those who know their customers better profit the most.

RBV and core competency theories assume the firm as a bundle of resources. Resources that are valuable, distinctive, relative to those of competitors, and hard to imitate become the source of competitive advantage. Some of these resources are internal and tangible such as machine capacity, others are internal and intangible, such as bundles of skills and technologies called competencies (e.g., production experience and IT capability), and others are external to the firm's boundaries, such as customer loyalty, mergers and acquisitions (Wernerfelt 1984). The shift from product to service orientation emphasizes one internal core competency as the key to competitive advantage: the firm's capability to acquire and process information about customers and to apply this information to increase customer equity. Using Vargo and Lusch's (2004a) terminology, knowledge about customers is the firm's *operant* resource. Moreover, the organizational learning literature focuses on how firms actually learn information about the market (and customers) and on the strategic benefits of learning. Learning implies more than "simply taking in information" and includes the ability of managers to ask the right questions, absorb the answers into their mental models, share the information and make decisions (Day 1994a, 1994b). Finally, the concept of market orientation (as a corporate culture) remains current and appropriate to understand the behavior of a service-oriented firm. Jaworski and Kohli (1990) defined market orientation as the organization-wide generation of market intelligence pertaining to current and future customer needs, dissemination of the intelligence across departments, and organizationwide responsiveness to it (Jaworski and Kohli 1990, p. 54). We believe that market orientation is the most important source of competitive advantage of service-oriented firms.

Even though these previous literatures seem appropriate to guide our understanding of the service-dominant logic, they cannot fully answer several new important questions. We present below three broad areas that we consider particularly relevant for future research about firm behavior.

What Is the Impact of Information Technology on Business Performance?

The information system literature has long debated this topic, but there is no consensus about how exactly information technology leads to superior performance. Recent managerial literature has challenged the positive effect of information technology on performance. Carr (2003) argues that companies overspend in information technology. For instance, from the 7,500 largest U.S companies, the twenty-five companies that presented the highest economic returns spent, on average, just 0.8% of their revenues on IT. The relationship between information technology and superior performance is a complex one. Future research should investigate the *indirect* effects of IT on economic returns. The strategic value of IT is, probably, linked to how firms use their IT capabilities to generate knowledge, develop relationships with customers and expand revenues, rather than just increase efficiency and cut costs.

How Can Information Technology Resources Be Transformed to Superior Customer Equity Management Skills?

This is a crucial question for the effective implementation of the customer equity model. How can firms make use of available technologies to generate knowledge about their customer base and enhance their level of services? Ansari and Mela's (2003) study on e-customization is a good example. They propose an optimization approach for customization of the design and content of e-mails with customers. Rust and Verhoef (2004) present a hierarchical model to personalize a mix of CRM interventions at the individual level, which led to higher profitability than other common segmentation approaches. Much more work should be done on how managers can use current technologies to foster relationships with customers.

What Is the Impact of Customer Equity on the Value of the Firm?

The ultimate role (and credibility) of marketing in the service-oriented firm will depend on how a superior customer base can potentially affect shareholder value. How does customer lifetime value impact cash flow measures? Does it impact the stock market? Existing theory (e.g., Rust et al. 2004; Rust, Lemon, and Zeithaml 2004; Srivastava, Shervani, and Fahey 1998, 1999) provides conceptual frameworks that integrate marketing and finance and discuss the links between market-based assets, such as customer relationships, market performance (e.g., market penetration, price premium loyalty), and shareholder value. More empirical work documenting this chain of effects is needed.

Research about Consumer Behavior

The service-dominant logic carries important implications for consumer behavior. We will focus here on the proposition that *the customer is always a co-producer* (Vargo and Lusch 2004a). We believe that the assumption that consumers will (and should) have a proactive involvement in their exchanges with service firms is more complex than it seems and actually may have negative consequences to consumer welfare. So, our goal is to incite interest and encourage research on how and to what extent consumers will be co-producers.

First, we think that exchange relationships must be truly considered *from the consumers' point of view*. Fournier, Dobscha, and Mick (1998), in an insightful article titled "Preventing the Premature Death of Relationship Marketing," argue that consumers feel trapped in a confusing, stressful and insensitive marketplace. They say (Fournier, Dobscha, and Mick 1998, p. 42):

> Companies may delight in learning more about their customers than even before and in providing features and services to please every possible palate. But customers delight in neither. Customers cope. They tolerate sales clerks who hound them with questions every time they buy a battery. They muddle through a plethora of products that line grocery store shelves. They deal with the glut of new features in their computers and cameras. They juggle the flood of invitations to participate in frequent-buyer reward programs.

Consumers cannot keep close, one-to-one relationships with all the firms they interact with. Furthermore, many times they do not want to. This is also the case for customization, which is a frequently used strategy in the marketplace that allows consumers' co-production. Consumers do not have the cognitive resources to customize all the products they buy. And several times, they may not want to customize products or to have a personalized connection with the firm. This is a challenge for firms whose primary goal is to maximize customer lifetime value. How to exactly calibrate the optimal amount of customization and personalization? Next, we discuss some potential problems linked to the use of customization as a mechanism of co-production.

Gateway, a direct computer seller, used to offer twenty-three million combinations of computers. The company recently reduced this number (due to costs) to hundreds of possible configurations. Starbucks can currently prepare a cup of coffee in nineteen thousand different ways. The service revolution brings more power and control to consumers, but this empowerment also implies higher levels of purchase involvement, that is, consumers tend to spend a greater amount of cognitive resources configuring products, choosing and trading off alternatives, etc. However, after decades of research in decision making, we know that consumers frequently cannot accurately predict what they want. Thus, the possibility to customize and configure their own products does not lead, necessarily, to better decisions. A recent book by Barry Schwartz (2004) expands on what he calls the paradox of choice: that fact that today's world offers more choices but less satisfaction. Consistent with Fournier, Dobscha, and Mick (1998), Schwartz argues that, under the customer's point of view, opportunities can become so numerous that individuals feel overwhelmed, and the supposedly increased control is experienced as a loss of control.

From the customer's point of view, when companies attempt to give them more flexibility, more options and more power over the exchange process, companies may end up creating more problems. We are currently investigating some of these issues. One of our projects (Thompson, Rust, and Hamilton 2004) examines the effects of increasing the number of features offered by e-services, such as online media players (music and video players), on consumers' evaluations. We tested only those features that are considered important individually. Preliminary results suggest that before usage, consumers prefer media players that offer a high number of features, relative to players that offer a low number of features. Consumers tend to focus on desirability issues, such as "what can this player do for me?" However, after using the service, users of more complex media players (high number of features) indicated lower levels of satisfaction and behavioral intentions (e.g., likelihood to recommend), compared to those obtained from users of simpler players (lower number of features). After using the service, consumers seem to focus more on the usability dimension. Thus, what a priori seems to be a strategy to increase the value of the e-service (adding more features) could actually decrease its value to customers.

Another interesting area of investigation is the psychological effect of customization. We are currently testing the possibility that interfaces where consumers specify at least some of the attributes of the product create an affective cost due to an increased attachment to the forgone options. This option attachment effect has been recently described in the consumer behavior literature (Carmon, Wertenbroch, and Zeelenberg 2003) but has not yet been linked to product customization. According to Carmon, Wertenbroch, and Zeelenberg (2003), as individuals consider or deliberate about options more closely, they become more attached to the options and experience more discomfort (consumers feel bad after considering their options more closely). When customizing the products they buy, consumers are forced to make higher number of choices, increasing the amount of deliberation on the forgone attribute options. The increased deliberation may lead to an enhanced attachment to the options and could cause postchoice discomfort ("choosing feels like losing"). We predict that consumers will not anticipate this option attachment effect. As a result, there may be a gap between consumers' beliefs about the value of product customization and their actual responses to product customization. More specifically, consumers may overestimate the value of customizing their own products. From the consumer's viewpoint, if our predictions are empirically supported, our results may suggest that the best customization strategies are the ones that allow for a closer match with consumers' preferences but *do not* increase consumers' amount of deliberation on the diverse set of options.

To summarize, we think future research should address the following interrelated areas of consumer behavior:

Impact of Offering More Flexibility and More Choices and Transferring More Power to Consumers

How does this empowerment influence satisfaction, quality of life, levels of stress and happiness? Schwartz (2004) presents robust evidence that this empowerment may hurt well-being. We believe these are important aspects of our work as marketers, important issues for public policy and, therefore, topics that marketing researchers should be concerned with.

Psychological Effects of Product Customization

While from the economics point of view, customization has a value-enhancing effect, offering unique value and a closer match to consumers' preferences, customization may increase the complexity of the shopping experience and also induce more attachment to the existent options. Future studies should explore the cognitive and affective costs of customization.

When and How to Offer Customization as a Mechanism to Co-production

For instance, customization probably adds more value for consumers who have the expertise to configure a product, relative to novices. Moreover, consumers may be more willing to configure certain categories of products, where they extract utility from the act of configuring the product itself (e.g., customizing a cruise vacation). Future research should explore these moderator variables on the value of customization. Finally, firms can use different elicitation strategies to link consumers to their production systems. What types of interfaces do work better from the customer's viewpoint? How can firms concurrently increase the match between the product and customer's preferences and decrease cognitive and affective costs to consumers?

SUMMARY

We are witnessing a transition from an economy based on tangible goods to an economy driven by information and service. This movement, enabled by developments in information technology, permeates all sectors, from labor intensive, goods-based industries to information products. Because progress in information technology is not likely to cease, we believe that firms' service orientation will only increase.

The service-dominant logic is customer-centric. Customers are the key assets that lead to superior profitability. We think that the role of marketing in service-oriented firms is to maximize customer equity, that is, to maximize the discounted lifetime value summed across current and future customers. The customer equity framework is an information-based, customer-driven, competitor-cognizant and financially accountable approach to marketing strategy; therefore, it is fully consistent with the foundational premises of the service-dominant logic.

This paradigm shift in marketing, where all products are merely distribution mechanisms of services and consumers are co-producers of value, brings several new challenges for scholars and practitioners. Our goal here was to identify a few of these challenges. We hope that future research will improve marketers' ability to maximize the welfare of both the consumer and the firm.

REFERENCES

Ansari, Asim and Carl F. Mela (2003), "E-Customization," *Journal of Marketing Research*, 40 (May), 131–45.

Carmon, Ziv, Klaus Wertenbroch, and Marcel Zeelenberg (2003), "Option Attachment: When Deliberating Makes Choosing Feel Like Losing," *Journal of Consumer Research*, 30 (June), 15–29.

Carr, Nicholas G. (2003), "IT Doesn't Matter," *Harvard Business Review*, 81 (5), 41–49.

Day, George (1994a), "Continuous Learning about Markets," *California Management Review*, 36 (Summer), 9–31.

——— (1994b), "The Capabilities of Market-Driven Organization," *Journal of Marketing*, 58 (October), 37–52.

Dedrick, Jason and Kenneth L. Kraemer (2002), *The Impacts of Information Technology, the Internet, and Electronic Commerce on Firm and Industry Structure: The Personal Computer Industry*. Irvine, CA: CRITO: Center for Research on Information Technology and Organizations, University of California, Irvine, 1–24.

Fournier, Susan, Susan Dobscha, and David Glen Mick (1998), "Preventing the Premature Death of Relationship Marketing," *Harvard Business Review*, 76 (1), 42–51.

Haubl, Gerald, and Valerie Trifts (2000), "Consumer Decision Making in Online Shopping Environments: The Effects of Interactive Decision Aids," *Marketing Science*, 19 (1), 4–21.

Hogan, John E., Katherine N. Lemon, and Roland T. Rust (2002), "Customer Equity Management: Charting New Directions for the Future of Marketing," *Journal of Service Research*, Special Issue on Managing Customer Equity, John E. Hogan and Katherine N. Lemon, Eds., 5 (1), 4–12.

Jaworski, B. and A. Kohli (1990), "Market Orientation: Antecedents and Consequences," *Journal of Marketing*, 57 (July), 53–70.

Lovelock, Christopher and Evert Gummeson (2004), "Whither Services Marketing? In Search of a New Paradigm and Fresh Perspectives," *Journal of Service Research*, 7 (1), 20–41.

Peteraf, Margeret A. (1993), "The Cornerstones of Competitive Advantage: A Resource-Based View," *Strategic Management Journal*, 14 (3), 179–91.

Rust, Roland T., Tim Ambler, Gregory S. Carpenter, V. Kumar, and Rajendra K. Srivastava (2004), "Measuring Marketing Productivity: Current Knowledge and Future Directions," *Journal of Marketing,* 68 (4), 76–89.

——— and P.K. Kannan (2003), " E-Service: A New Paradigm for Business in the Electronic Environment," *Communications of the ACM,* 46 (6), 37–42.

———, Katherine N. Lemon, and Valarie A. Zeithaml (2004), "Return on Marketing: Using Customer Equity to Focus Marketing Strategy," *Journal of Marketing,* 68 (January), 109–27.

——— and Peter C. Verhoef (2004), "Optimizing the Marketing Interventions Mix in CRM," working paper, University of Maryland.

———, Valarie A. Zeithaml, and Katherine N. Lemon (2000), *Driving Customer Equity.* New York: The Free Press.

———, ———, and ——— (2004), "Customer-Centered Brand Management," *Harvard Business Review,* 82 (9), 110–18.

Sambamurthy, V., Anandhi Bharadwaj, and Varun Grover (2003), "Shaping Agility through Digital Options: Reconceptualizing the Role of Information Technology in Contemporary Firms," *MIS Quarterly,* 27 (2), 237–63.

Sawhney, Mohanbir and Deval Parikh (2001), " Where Value Lives in a Networked World," *Harvard Business Review,* 79 (1), 79–86.

Schwartz, Barry (2004), *The Paradox of Choice: Why More is Less.* New York: Ecco/HarperCollins.

Srivastava, Rajendra K., Tasadduq A. Shervani, and Liam Fahey (1998), "Market-Based Assets and Shareholder Value: A Framework for Analysis," *Journal of Marketing,* 62 (January), 2–18.

———, ———, and ——— (1999), "Marketing, Business Processes, and Shareholder Value: An Organizationally Embedded View of Marketing Activities and the Discipline of Marketing," *Journal of Marketing,* 63 (Special Issue), 168–79.

Thompson, Debora Viana, Roland T. Rust, and Rebecca Hamilton (2004), "Feature Fatigue: When Product Capability is Too Much of a Good Thing," working paper, Department of Marketing, University of Maryland.

———, ———, and Jeffrey Rhoda (2004), "The Business Value of e-Government to Small for Small Firms," working paper, Department of Marketing, University of Maryland.

Vargo, Stephen L. and Robert F. Lusch (2004a), "Evolving to a New Dominant Logic for Marketing," *Journal of Marketing,* 68 (January), 1–17.

——— and ——— (2004b), "The Four Service Marketing Myths: Remnants of a Goods-based, Manufacturing Model." *Journal of Service Research,* 6 (4), 324–35.

Wernerfelt, Birger (1984), "A Resource-Based View of the Firm," *Strategic Management Journal,* 5 (2), 171–80.

Xie, Jinhong and Steven M. Shugan (2001), "Electronic Tickets, Smart Cards, and Online Prepayments: When and How to Advance Sell," *Marketing Science,* 20 (3), 219–43.

Zaheer, A. and Zaheer, S. (1997), "Catching the Wave: Alertness, Responsiveness and Market Influence in Global Electronic Networks," *Management Science,* 43 (11), 1493–509.

Zipkin, Paul (2001), "The Limits of Mass Customization," *Sloan Management Review,* 42 (3), 81–87.

==========

31

MANDATING A SERVICES REVOLUTION FOR MARKETING

STEPHEN W. BROWN AND MARY JO BITNER

We have been intimately involved in founding and contributing to the field of services marketing. Our embracing of the field grew out of a frustration with traditional marketing and its dominant goods focus. We see marketing as a corporatewide strategic discipline requiring a long-term, service-centered view of customers that cuts across and involves all areas and employees of the firm around an integrated vision of success.

In this chapter we make the case that enlightened firms and services-marketing researchers have been working with and studying customers for years in ways quite different than the perspective of traditional marketing. We begin by examining themes that underlie our reasoning for mandating a revolutionary change in marketing, including our own personal experiences. We then share six service-dominant best practices we have observed and contributed to through our work with member companies of the Center for Services Leadership (CSL) at Arizona State University. We believe these best practices can serve as an important foundation for a service-dominant, contemporary marketing.

DATED GOODS-CENTERED PARADIGM

One foundational observation for needed change in marketing stems from our conviction that the traditional goods-centered paradigm of marketing is hopelessly dated and has been so for over twenty-five years. Frustration with this preoccupation led a bold group of young marketing scholars and practitioners to "found" a new field of services marketing in the late 1970s/early 1980s.[1] A key catalyst for the new field was a provocative 1977 *Journal of Marketing* article, "Breaking Free from Product Marketing" by Lynn Shostack, then a vice president at Citibank. This period was characterized by massive deregulation of the U.S. service sector, including banking, health care, telecommunications and transportation. The role of marketing among firms in these industries soared and competitive rivalry, price competition and rising customer expectations assumed great interest. Yet, the early services practitioners and their interested academic colleagues quickly

393

realized that the dominant paradigm of marketing was lacking. In constructing a new services-marketing paradigm, the scholars of this period were often rebuffed by their tradition-bound academic peers. And to this day, among some marketing academics the services researchers are not considered "mainstream."

Today, all developed economies of the world are overwhelmingly services economies. Trade in services has become a global phenomenon and the United States enjoys a huge trade surplus in services. In fact, in some ways we can consider all businesses to be service businesses (Vargo and Lusch 2004). Over the past several decades, services marketing has become the study and practice of building relationships with customers over time through valued deeds, processes and performances. It is time for these ideas and practices—that still seem revolutionary to many—to be more fully integrated within marketing as foundations of the field.

CUSTOMERS ARE A CORPORATE PRIORITY

A second foundational observation is that customers are a C-suite priority. Chief executive officers (CEOs) of many highly successful, growth-oriented companies are preoccupied with customer satisfaction, loyalty and service. They see these corporate objectives as critical challenges but also as keys to their companies' continued profitable growth. In fact a survey of CEOs by The Conference Board in 2002 identified "customer loyalty and retention" as the leading management issue ahead of many other critical issues including reducing costs, developing leaders, increasing innovation and others (Dell 2002). These executives also recognize that strategies for achieving critical customer goals cut across all functions in the organization. A corporate strategy of getting close to customers is beyond the marketing department's traditional, micro and tactical focus. And, it is beyond the traditional short-term focus of most corporate finance departments, the typical inward focus of most operations and supply chain groups, and the narrow, legalistic focus of most human resource departments.

A corporate strategy of getting close to customers requires a long-term, service-centered view that cuts across and involves all functions in new ways of thinking. For example, at Harrah's Entertainment their very successful customer-focused strategy driven by CEO Gary Loveman (a former services management scholar at the Harvard Business School) draws on a highly sophisticated customer database, technology investments to use the data effectively for marketing programs, an unwavering focus on customer loyalty and profitability segmentation, and a deep focus around customer service to grow customer relationships. In Harrah's case, the focus on customer service translates into tying employee rewards directly to customer satisfaction. Each and every employee from slot attendants to valets, from receptionists to chefs, was told: "If your service can persuade one customer to make one more visit a year with us, you've had a good shift. If you can persuade three, you've had a great shift"(Loveman 2003). Clearly the implementation of such a strategy must be cross-functional, involving all employees, around an integrated vision of success.

Academic and practice leaders in the services marketing and management field have recognized this need for cross-functional integration around the customer for several decades. In fact, as early as 1979 Evert Gummesson, one of the pioneers in the field, stressed that the work of the marketing department includes only a small portion of the overall marketing in a service business. Complementing Gummesson's view, Christian Grönroos has articulated that every function in the firm should be customer focused and "doing marketing." Gummesson's and Grönroos's prescription fits well with Peter Drucker's 1954 definition of marketing: "There is only one valid definition of business purpose: to create a satisfied customer . . . Marketing is not only much broader than selling, it is not a specialized activity at all. It is the whole business seen from the point of view of its final result, that is from the customer's point of view." Consistent with this broad view of marketing, the services marketing discipline has evolved quickly over the last twenty-five years, strengthened by its cross-functional, cross-disciplinary, cross-industry and global roots (Berry and Parasuraman 1993; Fisk, Brown, and Bitner 1993; Fisk, Grove, and John 2000). Subtitles of leading services-marketing textbooks illustrate this cross-disciplinary view through taglines such as: "Integrating Customer Focus across the Firm" (Zeithaml and Bitner 2003) and "People, Technology, Strategy" (Lovelock and Wirtz 2004). A perusal of the tables of contents of these books confirms a cross-disciplinary, integrated focus around the customer.

Although the service-centered dominant logic proposed by Vargo and Lusch might seem quite provocative to many marketing thought leaders, it is the way great companies, and enterprises aspiring to be great, have been thinking, planning, and executing for years. From our experiences, the service-dominant logic mirrors corporate strategy in progressive firms. Unfortunately, most of marketing scholarship and practice is far narrower in scope than either the service-dominant logic or corporate strategy. Thus, if marketing is to transform itself to reflect the service-centered dominant logic and corporate strategy, it must broaden its scope and reorient its emphasis to such topics as relationship value, customer equity and lifetime customer value. Further, the recruitment, training and motivating of employees, beyond the sales force, must become a priority because these associates are often the service providers delivering the value and building the relationships with customers.

ASU'S CENTER FOR SERVICES LEADERSHIP

As mentioned in the introduction, much of this chapter is derived from our personal experiences as leaders of ASU's Center for Services Leadership. The CSL was founded in 1985 by the W. P. Carey School's Marketing Department as the world's first university-based Center for research and education in services marketing. As directors of the Center for many years, we have been both active participants and observers of the evolution of services marketing scholarship and practice. The mission of the center is "to be the global thought leader and source for research and education on the topic of competing through service(s)." The thought leadership comes from Center faculty and staff and a global network of scholars, member companies, and alliance relationships. With its funding coming primarily from its member companies (see Table 31.1), most of the CSL's research and executive- and graduate-level teaching has a bias for action and implementation.

Interestingly, the Center of today is quite different than it was in its early years of existence. Originally endowed by a leading Western bank, its name was once the First Interstate Center for Services Marketing. When Wells Fargo Bank merged with First Interstate Bank, the leadership of the Center decided to go forward without a corporate identifier. The dropping of the corporate name also stimulated discussion about a new name among key faculty and business stakeholders. The primary business input came from the center's board of advisors composed of executives from marketing, operations, and finance and CEOs of member companies. Reflecting a more holistic view of customers and services, these business people were cool to having "marketing" stay in the center's name and instead enthusiastically embraced the option of the "Center for Services Leadership." Although our ASU marketing faculty colleagues were not initially as enthusiastic, they did not oppose the name option favored by the board. Over time, all stakeholders have seen the wisdom in the name change.

We share this particular name change example because it represents a microcosm of what has happened to the field of marketing. As currently studied and practiced by many, marketing is far too narrow and not integral to C-suite matters. Yet, the services economy mandates that market-

Table 31.1

Center for Services Leadership: Member Companies

American Automobile Association	J.P. Morgan Chase & Co.
American Express Corporate Services	LensCrafters, Inc.
Andersen Corporation	Marriott International, Inc.
Annenberg Center for Health Sciences	Marsh
AT&T	Mayo Clinic
Avaya, Inc.	McKesson Corporation
Avnet, Inc.	McKinsey & Company, Inc.
Blue Cross and Blue Shield	Neoforma, Inc.
Cardinal Health	neoIT
Caremark	PETsMART
Charles Schwab & Co.	RR Donnelley
The Co-operators	SAP
Evanston Northwestern Healthcare	Siemens
Exult, Inc.	Southwest Airlines Co.
Ford Motor Company	State Farm Insurance Companies
Harley-Davidson Motor Company	Synovate Symmetrics
Harrah's Entertainment	TriWest Healthcare Alliance
Hewlett-Packard Company	United Stationers
Hill-Rom Company, Inc.	Valley Crest Landscape Maintenance
IBM Global Services	Yellow Roadway Corporation
The INSIGHT Group	Zane's Cycles
Intermec	

ing transform its scholarship and practice to embrace what really matters—value co-creation and delivery, customer relationships and customer equity—often provided by employees not generally thought of as marketing or salespeople.

BEST PRACTICES OF REVOLUTIONARY MARKETERS

To catalyze the revolution in marketing thought and practice that Vargo and Lusch suggest in their article, we offer several best practices that already exist and can be adopted by leading organizations and academics to speed our progress. We have observed and studied these best practices working in companies, and they directly support many of the fundamental premises in the Vargo and Lusch article. In addition, these best practices are cross-functional, centered on customers and relationships, and based in sound academic research. Applying services marketing knowledge, skills and best practices in corporate strategy and business education are ways to "lead through the services-dominant logic."

There is no reason these practices should be limited to traditional services businesses only. In fact a quick look at our CSL members listed in Table 31.1 reveals that all types of businesses and industries are focused on competing through services leadership today. One of our strongest, longest and deepest partnerships has been with IBM, traditionally a manufacturer who clearly sees itself today as a services business.

Keeping Promises to Customers

Promises are at the heart of the first best practice. When the layperson or practitioner thinks of marketing, they often think of marketing promotions or "making promises" to customers. Adver-

Figure 31.1 **The Services Marketing Triangle**

Company

Internal Marketing
"Enabling Promises"

External Marketing
"Making Promises"

Providers   Customers
Interactive Marketing
"Keeping Promises"

Source: Adapted from Bitner (1995), Kotler (1994), Grönroos (1990).

tising, personal selling and various sales promotions all make promises to customers about the attributes of an organization's goods or services. Yet, our experiences with companies clearly indicate that making promises is only the first step to successful marketing. In this era of building valued relationships with customers that extend over time, premier marketers are particularly focused on the best practice of "keeping promises."

Through our own research and work with CSL member companies, we have learned that services marketing, and increasingly marketing per se, is all about promises—promises made and promises kept. This important idea is illustrated in Figure 31.1 and represents the strategic framework referred to as the "services triangle." We use the services triangle very effectively in our executive teaching, and it clearly resonates with business executives across industries and across functions.

The three end points of the triangle—the company (or business unit), customers, and providers —represent the parties that work together to develop, promote and deliver services. The providers can be the company's employees, agents or subcontractors who deliver the firm's services. Between the end points of the triangle, the figure shows that three forms of marketing take place— external marketing, interactive marketing and internal marketing. External marketing could be thought of as traditional marketing. It involves all forms of communications to customers in the form of making promises, but it represents only the first step of marketing because the promises made must be kept. The base of the triangle represents interactive marketing, or where the promises are kept or broken by providers, employees, or other parties representing the company. The left side of the triangle illustrates internal marketing. Here, management supplies the training, incentives, technology and other resources to enable the providers to successfully deliver the service. A key to the effectiveness of the triangle is keeping it aligned around the customer.

FedEx is an excellent example of a company that illustrates the best practice of keeping promises to customers through aligning all sides of the triangle. For many years FedEx has promised customers that it will deliver a package by 10:00 A.M. the next business day. Though relatively few associates are involved in the external marketing of making this promise, many participate in some way in keeping the promise, or interactive marketing. From the package pickup to the many activities in the middle of the night at the Memphis airport to the delivery the following morning, thousands of service providers are committed to honoring the promise. FedEx's ability to fulfill the promise by 10:00 A.M., however, is dependent upon management's effectiveness in recruiting, training and motivating associates and providing them with the appropriate technology and equipment to do their job. There are, of course, other living examples of this best practice, including Harrah's Entertainment discussed earlier.

We like the services triangle because it unmasks what goes on in a marketing exchange. It depicts the important roles of the company, customer and service provider in keeping promises. The triangle also relates to one of Vargo and Lusch's fundamental premises in that valued information flows between the interrelated parties of company, customer and service provider to consummate a successful exchange and help build a relationship. The foundation for many of the other best practices discussed in this chapter can be referenced back to the triangle and keeping promises to customers.

Understanding Service from the Customer's Point of View

At the core of keeping promises and aligning the services triangle is an unwavering focus on the customer. Taking the customer's point of view, our second best practice, is critical to strategies on all sides of the triangle.

Much of the research in services marketing centers on understanding services and service quality from the customer's point of view. Similarly, our observation of leading companies that adopt a service-dominant logic is that they quickly embrace the best practice of becoming focused on their customers and customer relationships. These firms learn that providing sustained quality service requires a focus on customers' perceptions—not an internal fixation with standards or costs. They do not just give lip service to the importance of their customers, but they actually listen to them and take action based on what they hear. Acting on what they hear can involve adapting, changing or improving their services, or it might mean managing customer expectations to be more in line with what is possible. Harrah's Entertainment, mentioned previously, has taken the focus on customers further than almost any company we know. They religiously listen to them and collect masses of customer data; they also reward their frontline employees and managers for being responsive to customers. A compulsive drive to serve customers and build relationships is at the foundation of the company's successful strategy. And, fanatical focus on execution makes the strategy a reality.

Taking a customer focus from the beginning, researchers in services marketing have developed many useful tools, theories and frameworks that are commonly taught and used in services marketing and management in both executive and student education. Early work by Len Berry, Valarie Zeithaml, and Parsu Parasuraman in the area of service quality provided a key foundation (Parasuraman, Zeithaml, and Berry 1988). The development of SERVQUAL as a generalizable measure of service quality was a seminal contribution that has been adapted and widely used across industries and around the world. Through this measurement tool, organizations first began to think about and measure service as perceived and experienced by their customers. Later research on critical service encounters confirmed the importance of the "moment of truth" in shaping customer perceptions (e.g., Bitner, Booms, and Tetreault 1990). This research emphasized the role of interpersonal interactions between customers and employees and how, independent of the specific features of the service, the service encounter could build or destroy customer relationships. Today, measuring the quality of service encounters is fundamental for excellent firms that are driven by a services logic.

Services blueprinting is another valuable tool that has evolved over time to help organizations create services that meet their customer's expectations (Shostack 1984, 1987; Zeithaml and Bitner 2003, chapter 8). This tool maps the chronological flow of activities, interactions, and support processes of a service, all in a logical visual picture that starts with the customer's experience. A blueprint visually depicts the service process, points of customer contact, and physical evidence of the service. In our work with companies we have found that this tool, more than any other, provides the greatest revelations for firms seeking to become customer focused. It forces them to take the customer's view; it forces them to see the moments of truth; and it forces acknowledgment of the inevitable cross-functionality of service. Operant resources are clearly evident in a service blueprint, and their connection to the delivered service is also apparent.

Working with CSL member companies we have observed firsthand the tremendous value a firm can achieve through shifting its focus to the customer. We have worked for the past seven years with Yellow Transportation—a long-haul trucking company with a 100-plus-year history. In 1997 the company was viewed as "worst in its industry" by *Fortune* magazine. Through the vision of its leadership team, the company saw the potential to turn the company around by moving from a traditional operations focus of filling trucks and moving "stuff" to a customer-focus where service and information flows were their competitive advantage. Using the tools outlined above as well as others discussed in this chapter, the management team at Yellow Transportation began to: innovate new services in response to its customers' needs; develop training and incentive programs to improve the service of its nearly 20,000 teamsters who are its face to the external world; and measure and track service quality relentlessly. While being customer focused is a "journey, not a destination," Yellow Transportation has come a very long way in a relatively short time. They are now rated "most admired" in their industry class by *Fortune* magazine and have won awards for their technology, innovation, and service. The payback for firms that adopt a service-dominant logic can be tremendous, but management commitment and attention to the details of execution are equally critical. Adopting a customer focus and services logic cannot be the "program of the month."

Recognizing That Employees Are the Product

Interestingly, when firms begin to take service quality, customers and service encounters seriously, they quickly find they have moved beyond the scope of traditional marketing and its preoccupation with brands and product features. It turns out that customer benefits and value creation are often in the hands of their frontline employees, not the marketing department. Firms that lead with service-centered dominant logic understand that "employees are the product" and that "employees are the brand." Internal marketing and cross-functional cooperation between operations, marketing and human resources become essential.

Marriott International is a prime example of a company that has historically acknowledged the important role of its associates. Marriott clearly operates with an underlying service logic. Currently 128,000 employees strong and operating in seventy countries and territories, Marriott International aims to be the "preferred provider" of lodging services worldwide and also the "preferred employer" for hospitality workers. They understand the value of attracting the best workers in their industry in order to provide the best services for customers. In 2004 Bill Marriott was the inaugural recipient of the Global Service Leader Award given by the Center for Services Leadership and the W. P. Carey School of Business at ASU. In his speech accepting the award, Mr. Marriott spoke almost exclusively about employees and their role in making the company successful. Marriott clearly recognizes that their frontline employees make or break the company every day through their attitudes and actions and that their people are the human embodiment of their brand.

The recognition of the pivotal role of employees in creating value and delivering customer satisfaction has led to streams of research in both services marketing and services management. Early on, well-known names in the management and operations fields such as David Bowen, Benjamin Schneider, and Richard Chase led the way. Marketing scholars such as Christian Grönroos and Leonard Berry echoed their views, and the research on the pivotal role of employees has flourished. By chiding us to treat "employees as customers" and "customers as employees" these and other researchers foreshadowed several of Vargo and Lusch's fundamental premises. Current work in employee empowerment, internal branding, and creating a service culture are all outgrowths of this basic recognition that employees are vital to service success. While cross-functional in nature, much of the research on these topics is published in *marketing* journals in the United States and Europe.

Another research contribution, the service-profit chain, evolved from work at the Harvard Business School and also puts the role of the employee front and center for services marketers (Heskett et al. 1994). The service-profit chain connects the dots between internal service quality, employee satisfaction and productivity, customer value, loyalty and profitability. Every executive we know who embraces a service-dominant logic uses a version of the service-profit chain to explain or support his or her strategy. For example, Tony Rucci, Executive Vice President and Chief Administrative Officer of Cardinal Health, a Fortune 25 company, espouses the service-profit chain as an underlying framework for driving his company's success. They have found clear, quantifiable links between employee attitudes and profits. By quantifying the outcomes related to employee initiatives, executives are able to link internal strategies to important customer and profit goals.

In work we have done with AT&T, IBM, Ford Motor Company, and two financial services firms, we have focused on the roles of employees in enhancing service quality. (This work supported doctoral dissertations as well as academic publications.) At AT&T we studied the role of employee adaptability on the front lines and helped the company to identify recruiting and training strategies to foster adaptability and service customization (Gwinner et al. 2005). With IBM, we explored how the use of a flexible frontline work force (e.g., part-time, contingent workers) would affect employees' identification with IBM and the delivery of service to customers. For Ford we examined the role of frontline dealership employees in enhancing or detracting from the company's ability to introduce a new self-service technology that would benefit customers. With the two financial services firms, we investigated how employees' customer service–oriented behaviors are influenced by role conflict and role ambiguity and their perception of how fairly they are treated by their employer (Bettencourt and Brown 2003; Bettencourt, Brown, and MacKenzie 2005). In each of these cases, the companies clearly recognized the critical role their employees played in the success of marketing initiatives. In all four cases, success required cross-functional efforts, a process orientation, and an appreciation for the pivotal value of employees—not a narrow focus around traditional marketing activities.

The critical role of employees, as well as contractors and other partners, is apparent in the services triangle. They occupy one of the three critical points on the triangle and are in many cases responsible for keeping the promises to customers on a daily basis. In addition, they are the target of the firm's enabling activities that are essential to ensuring they can honor the firm's promises.

Involving Customers in Co-producing Services

Increasingly we are witnessing firm's performance being closely tied to the best practice of engaging its customers in co-producing its services or solutions. Elements of co-production exist in most service exchanges, and shifting certain activities from employees to customers often provides substantial benefits to both customers and the firm. The existence of automatic teller machines, for example, reduces employee costs for firms and provides twenty-four hour access to core banking services for customers. As goods-dominant firms begin to reorient their thinking to offering services, one of their biggest challenges becomes how to engage the customer in unique ways represented by this best practice. Vargo and Lusch feature "the customer is always a co-producer" as one of their fundamental premises. This perspective of the customer is markedly different from the traditional marketing view of the customer as a target.

The idea of co-producing is especially relevant to successful business marketers. Center-sponsored research includes a major project with a provider of IT professional services (Bettencourt et al. 2002). Though co-production was extensive in this professional B2B context, the research findings have implications for other settings as well. A basic premise for successful co-production is for the firm to have a deep understanding of its customers, their processes, and their procedures as well as an understanding of the relevant competitive and environmental factors. In our research we found that once one recognizes the importance of customers in creating services outcomes, the steps to proactively manage customer co-production behaviors become readily clear. Having effective or "high-performing" customers can also enhance the providing firm's operational efficiency. When both the firm and customer excel at performing their respective roles, it brings about efficiencies (e.g., cost and time savings) for both parties and can give the provider firm a competitive advantage.

The CSL research and the work of others have indicated that defining the customers' roles requires a "job analysis" of customer responsibilities as is traditionally done for firm employees (Schneider and Bowen 1995). This can be accomplished by addressing questions such as the following: What constitutes the "job" of our customers? What specific tasks and behaviors should our customers be doing during each phase of service delivery that would contribute to the quality of the solution delivered and the bottom line? And then, how do we get customers to actually perform their role responsibilities effectively? Research suggests that the same factors discussed as being important to enhancing employee job performance—specifically, role clarity, motivation and ability—must all be present for customers to perform their co-production role successfully (Bowen 1986).

Firms effectively engaging customers in co-production are typically more effective in keeping their promises. This is depicted in the services triangle in the interaction between customers and providers at the base of Figure 31.1.

Enabling Customers to Serve Themselves

The influx of technology has influenced how customers interact with firms and how goods and services are delivered. In fact, the ultimate form of customer co-production is customer self-service (primarily through technology) and we see it as a best practice. Firms that lead through a services logic realize that technology can enable both their employees and their customers in the delivery of quality service (Bitner, Brown, and Meuter 2000). These companies know that technology cannot be introduced simply as a cost-saving strategy for the firm. Unless cost-savings or other benefits are passed along to customers, they will quickly see through this type of self-centered strategy and take their business elsewhere.

Research that links customer focus with technology-delivered service is prevalent and growing in the services marketing field. It was a logical next step for researchers interested in customer-employee interactions to delve into customer-technology interactions (Meuter et al. 2000).

And, service quality researchers logically wanted to know whether what we had learned about quality in a personal service context would translate into technology-delivered service (Zeithaml, Parasuraman, and Malhotra 2002).

Working with Center member Caremark (formerly AdvancePCS), the nation's largest pharmacy-benefit management company, we developed a model of customer adoption for self-service technologies (Meuter et al. 2005). This model helped the company to implement strategies to engage more customers in their online mail-order pharmacy by recognizing the basic marketing and customer education challenges that needed to be overcome. It was not simply a matter of introducing an efficient and effective technology and then expecting customers to actively self-serve. Once again, the cross-functional integration of marketing, service operations, and technology came together in this project. As services marketers we had to look outside our own discipline for a cross-functional theory and solution. Interestingly, when we presented the results of the research to the company, the audience was composed of senior executives and directors of operations, technology, and marketing.

With CSL member Ford Motor Company, we looked at the issue of self-service from a very different angle. We examined Ford's pilot test of a new virtual service advisor that allows customers to schedule their own appointments and track the status of their vehicles while they are being repaired—all online, through a dealership Web site. In that case we concluded that just as there is a need for a customer rollout plan for a new technology-based service, it is just as important to engage frontline employees through an "employee rollout" plan. Again, the research and the solution suggested to the company were cross-functional in nature.

In our work with member companies over the years and benchmarking others, we have observed a number of best practices that lead to successful implementation of self-service technologies and that support a customer and services lead strategy logic. These lessons include such things as "maintain a customer focus in SST design," "prevent and manage failures," and "provide quality service via the SST" (Bitner, Ostrom, and Meuter 2002). Clearly these lessons go beyond traditional marketing tactics. They are deeply embedded in a service-dominant logic.

Recovering When Failures Occur

The previously discussed best practices are all directed at building positive, long-lasting relationships with customers. Yet, in service interactions, we have found that problems and complaints are bound to occur. The best practice of effectively handling these failures is vital to maintaining and even enhancing customer satisfaction and loyalty. In services, this ability is also closely related to the satisfaction and loyalty of employees interacting with customers. American Express, for example, estimates that more than 30 percent of its investment advisors' clients would defect if the advisor left the company.

Despite the benefits offered by effective service-recovery strategies, research sponsored by the CSL shows that a majority of customers are dissatisfied with the way companies resolve their complaints (Tax and Brown 1998; Tax, Brown, and Chandrashekaren 1998). These results are consistent with other findings indicating most customers have more negative feelings about an organization after they go through the service-recovery process. These revelations have led us to work with firms to help understand service failures from the customers' perspective and develop appropriate strategies to recover and retain the relationship.

Various respected scholars and organizations such as the Marketing Science Institute have called recently for more research attention to the financial consequences of marketing strategies and actions. This "call" is very appropriate for the area of service recovery because some firms and scholars blindly follow the mantra of "make it right for the customer" regardless of the cost. Recognizing the need for research, we are currently working with LensCrafters on a major study examining the financial consequences of service failure and recovery using a massive twelve-year customer database supplemented with store observations, qualitative interviews and survey research.

The best practices of recovering from services failures further illustrate the services triangle in action (see Figure 31.1). In the customer's mind, a failure represents a promise broken, and it is the responsibility of the firm and its service providers to recover.

CONCLUSION

Assuming a marketing professor, practitioner or student has been swayed by this chapter, what can one do to help revolutionize the marketing discipline to adopt the service-dominant logic? We offer four recommendations that we have both experienced and feel have made us better marketing scholars.

1. Get far closer to our laboratory. The laboratory for marketing scholarship is the business world. However, we continue to see too few bridges built between the academic and practitioner worlds. Yet, we have found, and documented in this chapter, that firms are receptive to cooperating with faculty on research projects under the right conditions. In approaching companies, academics must be client-centric, working with firms to determine how the proposed project can be a win-win for both parties.

2. Accept that customers are not the sole province of marketers. When marketing scholars gain entry to a firm for a potential project, it might often be advisable to be identified as a business, rather than marketing, professor. Marketing in many top firms is primarily associated with getting new customers. The retention and development of valued customers is seen as a corporatewide priority, engaging all functional areas. In our own experience, several of the research studies we have conducted with firms have had client leads from areas other than marketing.

3. Become knowledgeable of other business disciplines. Marketing scholars have actively and appropriately pursued their interests in the behavioral and quantitative disciplines, but we often overlook relevant work in management areas such as strategy, operations, human resources and supply chain. With customers and service increasingly being a corporatewide priority in excellent companies, much of our research needs to embrace other disciplines and functional areas of the firm (Brown 2005).

4. Work aggressively to reorient marketing curriculum. If we were to arrange the features of this chapter and the service-dominant logic in one column next to the features of the typical marketing curriculum in another column, the differences would be striking. As marketing scholars, we feel our marketing curricula, as well as our approach to research, needs to be revolutionized. With a more corporatewide and services-logic approach, we envision a wider spread movement to change curricula, moving toward a service-centered dominant approach. We envision schools featuring courses in service-dominant logic; managing cross-functional processes on behalf of customers; service design and delivery; and customer satisfaction, loyalty and advocacy.

We hope that this chapter provokes further thought, discussion and research on the services revolution in marketing. Our experiences as researchers and educators indicates such a revolution is overdue.

NOTE

1. Very early research on services marketing actually began in the 1950s and 1960s, often in the form of doctoral dissertation research.

REFERENCES

Berry, Leonard and A. Parasuraman (1993), "Building a New Academic Field—The Case of Services Marketing," *Journal of Retailing,* 69 (Spring), 13–60.

Bettencourt, Lance A., Amy L. Ostrom, Stephen W. Brown, and Robert I. Roundtree (2002), "Client Co-Production in Knowledge-Intensive Services," *California Management Review,* 44 (Summer), 100–128.

——— and Stephen W. Brown (2003), "Role Stressors and Customer-Oriented Boundary-Spanning Behaviors in Service Organizations," *Journal of the Academy of Marketing Science,* 31 (4), 394–408.

———, ———, and Scott B. MacKenzie (2005), "Customer-Oriented Boundary-Spanning Behaviors: Test of a Social Exchange Model of Antecedents," *Journal of Retailing,* 81(2), 141–158.

Bitner, Mary Jo, Bernard H. Booms, and Mary S. Tetreault (1990), "The Service Encounter: Diagnosing Favorable and Unfavorable Incidents," *Journal of Marketing,* 54 (January), 71–84.

———, Stephen W. Brown, and Matthew L. Meuter (2000), "Technology Infusion in Service Encounters," *Journal of the Academy of Marketing Science,* 28 (1), 138–49.

———, Amy L. Ostrom, and Matthew L. Meuter (2002), "Implementing Successful Self-Service Technologies," *Academy of Management Executive,* 26 (4), 96–109.

Brown, Stephen W. (2005), "When Executives Speak, We Should Listen and Act Differently," *Journal of Marketing,* 69 (October), 1–4.

Bowen, David (1986), "Managing Customers as Human Resources in Service Organizations," *Human Resource Management,* 25 (3), 371–83.

Dell, David (2002), "The CEO Challenge: Top Marketplace and Management Issues—2002," in *The Conference Board Research Report.* New York: The Conference Board.

Fisk, Raymond P., Stephen W. Brown, and Mary Jo Bitner (1993), "Tracking the Evolution of the Services Marketing Literature," *Journal of Retailing,* 69 (Spring), 61–103.

———, Stephen J. Grove, and Joby John, eds. (2000), *Services Marketing Self-Portraits: Introspections, Reflections, and Glimpses from the Experts.* Chicago: American Marketing Association.

Grönroos, Christian (1990), *Service Management and Marketing.* Lexington, MA: Lexington Books.

Gummesson, Evert (1979), "The Marketing of Professional Services: An Organizational Dilemma," *European Journal of Marketing,* 13 (5), 308–18.

Gwinner, Kevin P., Mary Jo Bitner, Stephen W. Brown, and Ajith Kumar (2005), "Service Customization Through Employee Adaptiveness," *Journal of Service Research,* 8 (November), 131–148.

Heskett, James L., Thomas O. Jones, Gary W. Loveman, W. Earl Sasser, Jr., and Leonard A. Schlesinger (1994), "Putting the Service-Profit Chain to Work," *Harvard Business Review,* March–April, 164–74.

Kotler, Philip (1994), *Marketing Management: Analysis, Planning, Implementation, and Control,* 8th ed. Englewood Cliffs, NJ: Prentice Hall.

Lovelock, Christopher and Jochen Wirtz (2004), *Services Marketing: People, Technology, Strategy.* Upper Saddle River, NJ: Prentice Hall.

Loveman, Gary (2003), "Diamonds in the Data Mine," *Harvard Business Review* (May), 109–13.

Meuter, Matthew L., Amy L. Ostrom, Robert I. Roundtree, and Mary Jo Bitner (2000), "Self-Service Technologies: Understanding Customer Satisfaction with Technology-Based Service Encounters," *Journal of Marketing,* 64 (July), 50–64.

———, Mary Jo Bitner, Amy L. Ostrom, and Stephen W. Brown (2005), "Choosing among Alternative Service Delivery Modes: An Investigation of Customer Trial of Self-Service Technologies," *Journal of Marketing,* 69 (April), 61–83.

Parasuraman, A., Valarie Zeithaml, and Leonard L. Berry (1988), "SERVQUAL: A Multiple-Item Scale for Measuring Consumer Perceptions of Service Quality," *Journal of Retailing,* 64 (Spring), 12–40.

Schneider, Benjamin and David Bowen (1995), *Winning the Service Game,* Boston, MA: Harvard Business School Press.

Shostack, G. Lynn (1977), "Breaking Free from Product Marketing," *Journal of Marketing,* 41 (April), 73–80.

——— (1984), "Designing Services That Deliver," *Harvard Business Review,* January–February, 133–39.

——— (1987), "Service Positioning through Structural Change," *Journal of Marketing,* 51 (January), 34–43.

Tax, Stephen S. and Stephen W. Brown (1998), "Recovering and Learning from Service Failure," *Sloan Management Review,* 40 (Fall), 75–88.

————, ————, and Murali Chandrashekaren (1998), "Customer Evaluations of Service Complaint Experiences," *Journal of Marketing,* 66 (April), 60–76.

Vargo, Stephen L. and Robert F. Lusch (2004), "Evolving to a New Dominant Logic for Marketing, *Journal of Marketing,* 68 (January), 1–17.

Zeithaml, Valarie and Mary Jo Bitner (2003), *Services Marketing: Integrating Customer Focus across the Firm,* 3rd ed. New York: McGraw-Hill.

————, A. Parasuraman, and A. Malhotra (2002), "Service Quality Delivery through Web Sites: A Critical Review of Extant Knowledge," *Journal of the Academy of Marketing Science,* 30 (4), 362–75.

32

SERVICE-DOMINANT LOGIC AS A FOUNDATION FOR A GENERAL THEORY

ROBERT F. LUSCH AND STEPHEN L. VARGO

INTRODUCTION

The quest for a general theory of marketing has been elusive. At least in part, this is because marketing is built on economic science, which has its own general theory. But, as discussed in chapter 2, though dealing with related subject matter, this general theory was built for a different purpose and within a different social and academic context than are characteristic of marketing, at least in the past fifty years. The focus of economics was "productive" services, defined in terms of units of tangible output that could be exported and exchanged. This focus and its related theoretical framework served applied marketing reasonably well in its initial concern with the distribution of these tangible goods.

In line with this concern for tangibility and application, marketing thought developed and evolved based on what was tangible, or at least observable, and capable of being acted upon. Goods were tangible and visible. Advertising also was visible, as was price and distribution channels.

However, what was less readily perceptible was that much of what was exchanged was intangible—the direct application of knowledge and skills (i.e., service)—and even when goods were exchanged, their value was partially derived from their being embodied with knowledge and thus had service potential; price (an expression of value-in-exchange) was a quantitative estimate of how valued a party's specialized-resource-based service potential was in a market-based economy; advertising was part of a process of symbolic communication of a party's service potential in the context of a broader, societal-based "sign" system; and distribution channels were mechanisms for the division and exchange of specialized marketing functions. In short, the common denominator of marketing was the intangibles—knowledge and skills, and social and economic processes.

Our concluding point of view in this volume of original essays is that service-dominant logic may be able to serve as a foundation for the development of a general theory of marketing. We base this view on the fact that S-D logic is grounded in the micro-activities of humans—specialization through the development of competences and the subsequent exchange of these competences for competences the individual does not have. However, it also offers justification for the formation of macro institutions and structures—for example, goods, money, organizations, intermediaries, and markets–as natural consequences of this process of specialization and exchange. Stated alternatively, S-D logic demonstrates how micro actions result in macro structures. Consequently, as we will see, S-D logic has the breadth and abstract properties to operate at both the micro and macro level. Additionally, we argue that it has characteristics of generalizability and integration sufficient to be inclusive of competing and sometimes apparently contrary frameworks, some of which are offered by the authors of chapters in this book. Finally, we argue that it is implicitly normative and thus can point managers toward practical actions and organizations to standards for ethical interaction and social well-being.

CHALLENGING THE DOMINANT LOGIC

S-D logic, by viewing service(s) as dominant and goods, organizations, networks, and money as only intermediaries, results in a fundamental inversion of the dominant logic in marketing. As such, it is similar to the reversal in thinking when the dominant logic about planet earth was that it was flat. Over the course of human history and experience, dominant thinking was repeatedly replaced by beliefs that were virtually opposite. Similarly, with the existing dominant paradigm in marketing, the following beliefs are strongly held: (1) entity performance is to be optimized or maximized, (2) the external environments are uncontrollable forces to be reckoned with, (3) consumers are operand resources or objects to be marketed to, and (4) value is embedded in products and then exchanged. Surprisingly, S-D logic takes an opposite perspective: (1) entity performance cannot be optimized but can be improved upon, (2) the external environments are not uncontrollable but are resources that can be drawn upon for support once resistances are overcome, (3) consumers are operant resources and to be marketed and collaborated with (i.e., co-producers or co-creators) as opposed to operand resources that are targeted and marketed to, and (4) value-in-use is superordinate to value-in-exchange.

Though disquieting to some (as illustrated in some of the chapters in this collection) S-D logic goes a step further and challenges the fundamental method for the practice of marketing. This dominant practice has become synonymous with the Four P's, or the marketing mix—product, price, promotion, and place—which are managed to enable the firm to target and capture the customer. However, S-D logic does not abandon the Four P's, just as it does not abandon the role of tangible goods, but rather places them in a more strategic role. This is quite different from current normative marketing practice in which the marketing mix is largely tactical. S-D logic recognizes the Four P's as part of a continuing flow of service(s) embedded in a dynamic marketing system comprising social and economic dynamic "flows" and "processes" in which value is collaboratively co-created with customers and partners. Strategic marketing becomes largely focused on the collaborative co-creation of value with customers and partners.

As shown in Figure 32.1, replacing a tactical product focus, service-dominant logic views the offering as service, which in some circumstances can be transmitted in the form of an appliance that the customer uses to provide self-service; in other circumstance, this service is provided directly (without a tangible transmission mechanism). Replacing price, arguably the most often-employed marketing tactic, is a strategic orientation on a firm's value proposition. S-D logic recognizes that firms can only make a value proposition and that value itself is a continuous process that unfolds over time as consumers participate in the value-creation process. Promotion, also heavily tactical, is replaced by conversation and dialogue (also a continuous flow) as a strategic pathway for improved integrated marketing communication. Channels of distribution (place)

Figure 32.1 **Traditional Marketing Mix versus Service-Dominant Logic**

Traditional Marketing Mix (largely tactical)	Service-Dominant Logic (largely strategic)
Product	Co-creating service(s)
Price	Co-creating value proposition
Promotion	Co-creating conversation and dialogue
Channel of distribution (place)	Co-creating value processes and networks

rather than being a fixed mechanism for distributing product is replaced with a strategic focus on value-creation processes and networks that are constantly developing and evolving. Rather than trying to capture the customer via target marketing, the firm shifts its focus to co-producing or co-creating value with the customer. In fact, Jaworski and Kohli (chapter 8) argue that co-production begins with the front-end process of identifying customer needs/wants with a dialog-based process for co-creating the voice of the customer.

However, S-D logic brings not only the customer to the process of co-creation of value, but also the organization's partners throughout the value creation network. This is primarily because S-D logic views knowledge as the fundamental source of competitive advantage and recognizes that knowledge is not centralized but dispersed throughout the marketing system and society. Consequently, S-D logic recognizes all entities must collaborate with other entities and integrate resources with them.

Collectively S-D logic moves the totality of marketing from a product-centric focus to a customer- and knowledge-centric focus. In fact, S-D logic suggests that marketing be defined as the process in society and organizations that facilitates voluntary exchange through collaborative relationships that create reciprocal value through the application of complementary resources. Marketing is thus seen as the means by which organizations and societies are able to create value by the voluntary exchange of knowledge and skills. Sawhney (chapter 29) coins the concept of a "solutions-centric mind-set" which focuses on the "design and marketing of end-to-end customer solutions." S-D logic explicitly recognizes that solutions require the application of operant resources (knowledge and skills) and the active involvement of customers (and partners). Whether we use the term *customer* or *solutions-centric mind-set*, the goods-dominant (G-D) paradigm is viewed as seriously flawed and inadequate as a marketing framework. In what follows, we try to uncompact the fundamental shift in worldview of marketing and markets[1] to service-dominant. In so doing we hope to show that S-D logic is sufficiently broad and abstract to serve as the foundational basis of a general theory of markets and/or marketing.

THE MARKET(PLACE) AND S-D LOGIC

S-D logic suggests that markets and marketing are primary drivers or creators of society. Individuals without the exchange of service for service are anti-society. With exchange of service comes society and society does not exist without the exchange of the most fundamental resources for human existence (mental and physical competences). Sometimes social and sometimes economic, but most often intertwined, a society involves a complex web of social and economic exchanges of service(s). In modern society this complex is heavily centered on the market as the central forum for exchange.

Consequently, S-D logic is supportive of a starting point of analysis being the market, which Venkatesh, Peñaloza, and Firat (chapter 19) view as a set of institutional arrangements. However, institutions themselves are co-produced and co-production is a central concept in S-D logic. Furthermore, language, knowledge, norms, culture, and scientific paradigms are all part of a network of co-creation activities by individuals and organizations that create society. In a real sense, society can be viewed as a macro-service provision institution. Through the invisible hand of the exchange of service for service, a market-driven society emerges that serves humankind.

As the division of labor develops in the family or household unit, we see the roots of service being exchanged for service. To facilitate this exchange of service(s), humans develop three primary mechanisms: (1) tangible, primarily operand resources that are embedded with knowledge, (2) organizations and networks, which become the integrative mechanisms through which micro-specialists exchange their competences (service), and (3) money, which people exchange for the service(s) they need and want.

Although we recognize that tyrants often controlled early civilizations and open and free one-to-one exchange of services was not the norm (Achrol and Kotler, chapter 26) it is still useful to conceptualize the basic process of service being exchanged for service as suggested by Bastiat (1860/1964)—one party hunting and gathering and another tending to cooking, fabricating clothing, tending the young ones. At some point this household unit begins to exchange with other units. Direct barter might apparently involve trading animal hides for feedstock—tangible good for tangible good. However, what is the tangible good and how did it come about? The tangible good came about because one party applied their specialized knowledge and skills to hunt the animal and skin the hide (i.e., they provided service). Another party applied its specialized knowledge and skills and tended crops or gathered crops (i.e., provided services). But more importantly the tangible goods (animal hide and feedstock) are only of value because of the value that can be extracted or received from them in use. The animal hide provides protection from the cold weather and thus the equivalent to heating services. The feedstock provides nourishment, and thus energy, for the body to function. However, there is one other function the tangible good may provide. It may be a storehouse of value or medium of exchange. First as a storehouse of value it can be inventoried and can be used at another time to trade for other things. Second, as a medium of exchange, it may be used to trade for other things indirectly (i.e., it can be used as money). Cattle or livestock were often used for this function. In fact with loans one would often give a pregnant cow as collateral where the creditor would receive the offspring as interest and then return the cow when the loan was paid. Thus we see even interest or financial services being embedded in tangible matter.

It is because of gain from trade that a medium of exchange is developed. Money emerges initially as tangible and then evolves to being purely abstract. Initially most monetary systems involve some type of scarce metal minted into different sizes. These tangible coins become the medium of exchange. Latter they are represented by paper or notes that are backed by metallic currency. Today they are largely represented by paper or notes not backed by metallic currency and increasingly are digital signals (or purely abstract). Behind these currencies are the character and trustworthiness and integrity of the backer. Essentially what we see in contemporary money is both economic and social exchange (the social exchange being the exchange of trust). Money as a medium of exchange facilitates exchange and trade and goods become convenient and effective marketing channels for services.

Entities learned that there are gains to be made by organization. Coase (1937) developed a theory of organization, which was further developed by Williamson (1975). Firms or organizations develop to lower transaction costs. But because individuals who work in the organization

Figure 32.2 **Service(s) Exchanged for Service(s)**

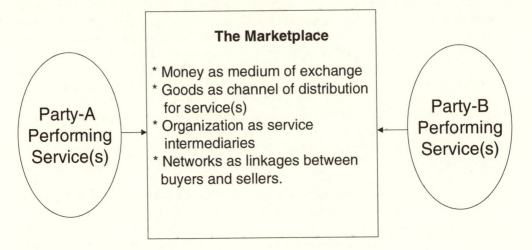

(i.e., sell their services to the organization) can avoid the discipline of the marketplace, they can often be individually nonresponsive to the customer. In short, they are not directly exchanging service for service. As such, they can often shirk responsibility and are not responsive to customer demands. This partially explains the paradox of why many service organizations (government agencies, airlines, phone services, etc.) have a reputation of *not* being service oriented and have low-quality service.

In Figure 32.2 we graphically portray the fundamental notion that service(s) are exchanged for service(s). It is important to note that it is only because of the marketplace and the development of: (1) money as a medium of exchange, (2) goods as channels of distribution for services, (3) organizations as service intermediaries, and (4) networks that link together buyers and sellers, that we have lost sight of the fundamental economic principle of Bastiat (that services are exchanged for services). The world we live in is not about money, goods, and organization; it is about service to each other and humankind (society). Money, goods, organization, and the network are only the exchange vehicles.

SERVICE(S) EXCHANGED FOR SERVICES

A service-centered model of exchange motivates the study of marketing at the most micro level, which is entities exchanging competences or service(s) (refer to Figure 32.2). We suggest this micro-level analysis allows for a more complete understanding of marketing from a holistic, systems, or macro perspective. Consequently, a service-centered model is not anti-macromarketing as some believe.

Macro systems, which undoubtedly should be studied in their own right, come about or emerge from micro phenomena. Systems at higher and higher levels of aggregation constitute a hierarchy of nested levels (Capra 1996; Holbrook 2003; Kiel, Lusch, and Schumacher 1992), for instance, atom, molecule, cell, organism, species, community, ecosystem, biosphere, cosmos (Holbrook 2003). Since marketing deals with human exchange, it is useful to begin the study of marketing with individual human organisms, although these entities themselves consist of particles inside of nuclei of atoms, inside of atoms, inside of molecules, inside of nuclei of cells, inside of cells, inside of tissue, inside of organs, inside of the human organism (Kiel, Lusch, and Schumacher 1992).

Most of marketing from a managerial perspective has begun with the organization as the unit of analysis. However, organizations are a community of human organisms. By investigating the more fundamental unit of individuals and their exchanging of services for services we can inform ourselves on how macro structures such as organizations and societies emerge. There is a temptation to view these macro structures as entities in and of themselves without recognizing that they emerge from the actions of more fundamental actors exchanging their services or competences. The macro structures emerge from co-productive activities of micro-entities.

Division of Labor

The microscopic actions begin with the division of labor. Physical and mental skills are the two basic operant resources that all individuals possess (Vargo and Lusch 2004). As long as all individuals used these resources for self-service and did this independent of other individuals, the world was simple. Isolated man interacting only with nature keeps the world rather static except for naturally occurring physical phenomena. An individual human can at best survive but without others cannot change the world. However, when individuals begin to interact with others and exchange the platform for changing the world is set.

Humans learned that the skills they possess are not equally distributed and thus they began to specialize. This specialization led to a division of labor where entities became more dependent upon each other. Smith (1776/1904) recognized that the extent of the market was a function of the division of labor in society. However, as the division of labor increased, another important development occurred—the connectedness of individuals. As each person specializes we become more dependent and connected to others. Thus both the extent of the market and the density of the network of interconnections is a function of the division of labor in society.

This begins to form the basis of a complex system. And since each entity in this interconnected system is always attempting to do better or to improve its condition the system becomes adaptive. Thus what emerges rather quickly as a result of a division of labor is a complex adaptive system. Soon the environment humans face is not only the natural environment but also the social environment that is made up of the actions of all other entities that are part of this web of interconnectedness.

Learning Through Change

Exchange is pro knowledge discovery because entities enter into exchange to improve their condition. They have very simple hypotheses or expectations that if one takes a certain action (and changes) then he or she will be better off. However, these hypotheses are tested in the crucible of reality. They take actions to enter into exchange and are able to experience the consequences firsthand. These hypotheses can be falsified. Exchange is not only pro knowledge discovery for firms but also for consumers. Firms seeking competitive advantage are constantly seeking ways to lower costs or improve value provided to buyers (Hunt 2000). Seldom mentioned is the fact that buyers also learn in this process. A buyer has the desire to improve its condition and thus via exchange learns what works and doesn't work. This can also stimulate the buyer to use or develop its competences to either be able to acquire more in the marketplace or to better utilize goods acquired in the marketplace to obtain value.

In the exchange process, one of the most important things learned is the relative value of things. Without exchange one has no or little information on value. In a simple bartering economy one is able to learn about how many of A units can be exchanged for B units. Let us say one is not pleased that it has to give up three units of A for one unit of B. What can this entity do to alter this situation? There are several options. It could attempt to develop a production technique that allows one to produce more units of A with the same effort (production innovation); it could do some innovation with A to make it more desirable (product innovation); it could decide it needs to learn to make B for itself; it could decide to search for and hopefully discover C which until now had not been produced or exchanged between entities. In short, by learning the relative value of things exchanged each entity is provided feedback and a signal on how to redirect its efforts (either for internal or external production).

In the preceding highly simple example we should note three things: (1) when each entity exchanges it itself changes or is altered, (2) before each entity could exchange it had to expend mental and/or physical effort which almost always changed other entities and itself, (3) as each entity received feedback from the exchange process it was stimulated or motivated to do things differently and thus to be more creative and generate more knowledge. Contrast this with an entity continuing to be isolated and engaging in self-production. In this situation it would be foolish to suggest that entities would not change or not learn; however, the extent and speed of change of learning would be slower because by not specializing there would be less variety and thus less learning contrasted to when people exchange in a market-based society. In brief, variety is stimulated and fostered when two parties specialize and learn from each other from marketplace exchange.

We live in an out-of-change world. We live in a world where micro entities each seek to be better off by specializing and exchanging their services for the services of others. From these individual actions emerge macro structures such as market segments, lifestyle groupings, fashion movements, and legal and government regulations that become more visible. However, behind all of these macro and visible trends are individuals seeking to improve their stake in life and engaging in exchanges to accomplish this but by so doing stimulating additional change that ripples throughout society. And as this ripple occurs we see more and more creative effort because more and more signals are transmitted about what works and does not work; what creates satisfaction and what creates dissatisfaction; and what produces gain over loss. The system is not perfect but once the power of individuals exchanging based upon their micro specializations starts to roll out throughout the local, regional, national and world economy and society, more and more change occurs and more and more variety manifests itself via the creative learning processes of exchange.

INVERTING THE DOMINANT PARADIGM

Perhaps one of the more pervasive models in marketing is the three circles model that was first developed by McCarthy (1960). In this model, the inner circle is the customer, the middle circle is the firm's marketing decision variables (the Four P's), and the outermost circle is the uncontrollable external environments that generally comprise the competitive, legal, social, technological, and ecological environments. Essentially, this paradigm suggests that the firm set its marketing decision variables in order to market to the customer to maximize profit within the constraints of the external environment. The S-D model of marketing inverts this perspective as outlined below (see Figure 32.3).

Co-Creation

The dominant paradigm in marketing separates the producer from the customer in order to maximize production efficiency, but this production efficiency comes at the expense of marketing

Figure 32.3 **S-D Marketing**

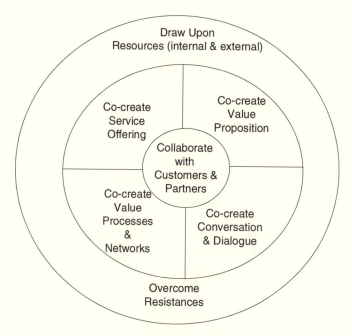

effectiveness. By pursuing a division of labor that led to the separation of parties, including the producer from the customer, a dramatic increase in efficiency resulted. This reinforced an attitude and view that the customer was someone to target and *market to* versus an entity to *market with.* The result was poorer and poorer marketing effectiveness but high cost efficiency for producers. The preceding behavior and attitude has also prevailed in the distribution channels literature, where channel intermediaries were seen as entities that distributed to customers, rather than marketing with them (Constantin and Lusch 1994).

Contrast the preceding with S-D logic, which recognizes customers are operant resources and that knowledge is dispersed throughout the system. Therefore, its focus is one of *marketing with*—collaborating and co-creating value with both customers and supply and value network partners —rather than *marketing to* and delivering value.

Strategic Marketing

The firm's marketing activities, rather then reflecting the dominant and historically prevalent tactical Four P's, should focus on continuous processes that are reflected in four fundamental building blocks of a firm's strategic marketing direction: (1) service offerings, (2) value propositions, (3) conversation and dialogue, and (4) value processes and networks. And all of these should be co-created with customers and partners.

Importantly, they are not intended to replace the Four P's but to provide them strategic direction. Product decisions will be better informed with a service strategy direction; price decisions will be more effective long term when guided by the firm's strategic oriented value proposition; promotion will continue, however, be more effective when conversation and dialogue provide an informed background and perspective on how to promote; and channel decisions will be more effective when they are considered within the context of the entire value network.

These four fundamental strategic building blocks were discussed and elaborated on in this volume by various thought leaders in marketing. We especially recommend studying Rust and Thompson (chapter 30) and Sawhney (chapter 29) for insights on the role of appliances and service(s); Woodruff and Flint (chapter 14), Holbrook (chapter 16), and Berthon and John (chapter 15) for perspectives and frameworks for thinking about value and value propositions; Ballantyne and Varey (chapter 17) and Duncan and Moriarty (chapter 18) for a discussion of concepts related to conversation and dialogue; and Flint and Mentzer (chapter 11) and Lambert and García-Dastugue (chapter 12) for conceptual models that help one to understand the complexity of value processes and networks.

Endogenous Environments

Viewing resources as anything one can draw on for support provides a different perspective for the outer, external environment circle in the three circles model. It essentially suggests that the external environments have the potential to be resources if certain resistances can be overcome. For instance, under a traditional perspective, a firm would not normally consider competition as a resource. However, competition can be a valuable resource in its role of constantly challenging a firm to do a better job for the customer. Also, in some situations, it is possible to collaborate with a competitor such as in joint research and development efforts.

Certainly the legal environment should be viewed as more than an uncontrollable environmental variable. A strong legal system can be a resource a firm can use to protect its rights. Similarly, new legislation can either be viewed negatively or as a resource that provides an opportunity to develop new or improved services. Witness the growth in auto safety that grew out of federal legislation.

The social environment is also often considered an uncontrollable externality. While we cannot control all aspects of the social environment, this does not mean it cannot be a resource to the organization. The growth of social movements, alternative lifestyles, changing attitudes and opinions about work, and so on are all potentially resources that the firm can draw upon for support if certain resistances can be overcome.

Few firms can claim that they control the technology and science of an industry. But, viewing the technological environment as completely uncontrollable and other than a potential source of support is myopic. Technology, even what may appear as unrelated technology, can be a major resource. Consider the influence of the integrated circuit and silicon chip on improvements in everyday products ranging from automobiles to televisions to refrigerators.

Finally, the ecological or physical environment is normally considered to be uncontrollable but can also serve as a potential source of support. Because of the cost of waste disposal and its ecological impact the firm may be forced to redesign production processes and products to eliminate waste or what the Japanese call *muda*. However, in so doing firms have found that they become more efficient and can actually lower, rather than increase, production costs. Consequently, because firms have been forced to consider the externalities and the impact on the physical environment, the physical environment has actually become a major source of support for eliminating waste in the organization. Coincidentally many of these firms are able to promote to customers the good things they are doing for the ecological environment. Perhaps as important, their workers (a primary firm resource) are exposed to fewer harmful chemicals and pollutants, which improves their quality of life and potentially their contribution.

Under the G-D model, the Four P's are set (within the constraints of the external environment) in order to make an offer to the customer and optimize profit. With the S-D model, the customer is a collaborator and co-producer and the external environments are resources. Rather than trying to maximize profit, the firm using the S-D logic lens views financial performance as feedback to gauge (along with other measures) the extent that it is serving the customer and/or market.

THE PURPOSE OF THE FIRM, ETHICS, AND PUBLIC POLICY

In *Evolving to a New Dominant Logic for Marketing* (Vargo and Lusch 2004), we draw upon the historical writings of Fredric Bastiat (1860/1964) to anchor the logic that the essence of economic activity is the exchange of service(s) for service(s). In two fundamental propositions we show how indirect exchange, via organizations, mask the fundamental nature of economic activity and in another we discuss how goods are mechanisms for the delivery of services. Delving deeper into these two fundamental propositions we show how the purpose of the corporation is not to create wealth as many students of business believe. The purpose of the corporation, we argue, is to provide a mechanism for man to exchange service(s) for service(s) in order to improve his standard of living, or stated alternatively, to exchange one's skills in the form of a job for a medium of exchange (money) that in turn the entity uses to enter into exchanges with the corporation to obtain the services needed to be better off. Organizations exist to integrate and transform micro specialized competences into services that are demanded in the marketplace.

The modern corporation is given license or legitimacy to operate in society as long as it provides a fair venue for the exchange of service(s) for service(s). For this to be accomplished individuals and collectivities must generally be satisfied with both work and consumption. If corporations create wealth but fail to provide a fair venue for the exchange of services for services (both via jobs and consumption), then the corporation will lose its legitimacy. Since all institutions are co-produced this would be inevitable. Although it is difficult to predict the form of action society would take—orderly or revolt and chaos—the change to a different form of economic organization would ultimately occur. Similarly, the modern democratic government is given license or legitimacy to operate in society as long as it provides a fair mechanism for the collection of tax revenues in return for the provision of public services.

As a potential theory of the firm, S-D logic is highly prescriptive regarding ethical issues. The goods-dominant logic on the contrary offers little ethical guidance. We believe this is important because markets operating without normative ethical guidelines will have imperfections and externalities that can at least in part be avoided by embracing S-D logic.

Normative Guidelines

As opposed to the relatively weak normative guidance of G-D logic, S-D logic offers the following guidance:

1. The firm should be transparent and make all information symmetric in the exchange process. Since the customer is someone to collaborate with, anything other than complete truthfulness will not work.
2. The firm should strive to develop relationships with customers and should take a long-term perspective. Firms should thus always look out for the best interest of the customer and protect the customer's long-term well-being.
3. The firm should view goods as transmitters of operant resources (embedded knowledge); they are intermediate "products" that are used by other operant resources (customers) as appliances in value-creation process. The firm should focus on selling service flows.
4. The firm should support and make investments in the development of specialized skills and knowledge that is the fountainhead of economic growth.

Not surprisingly, some may argue that we can hardly expect the firm in a free enterprise system to be so righteous. However, we argue that behaving in this manner provides the firm with a source of competitive advantage. At the same time a focus on these principles provides a marketer a moral compass to gauge his or her actions by. Finally, we suspect that a marketing curriculum designed along S-D logic and its normative principles will make marketing more appealing as a life pursuit and allow marketers to make even stronger contributions to society. In brief, S-D logic is pro-society.

If all or most firms were to: (1) be transparent and truthful to the customer, (2) be the guardian and do what is best for long-term customer welfare, (3) focus on selling service flows and not tangible stuff, and (4) continually invest in the development of human skills, then we would argue we would have less societal ills or things that government may be prompted to address. In fact a brief journey over the last 100 years will show that the major legislation directed at marketing was largely because firms did not follow the preceding norms.

Public Policy

Much of macro marketing is focused on public policy and legislation directed at controlling marketing. There has been legislation on price fixing, price discrimination, deceptive pricing, deceptive advertising, product liability, product safety, credit disclosure and fair credit policies, bait-and-switch promotional tactics and a host of other legislative actions. However, we would suggest that virtually all of these were directed at controlling and reprimanding firms for not telling the truth and not thinking of long-term customer welfare. In fact, as we have mentioned (Vargo and Lusch 2004) even if firms want to be only transaction focused, we have evolved into a society where more is expected. Firms cannot disclaim warranty and cannot choose to not take a long-term view at how a product may be misused. Exchange is relational, even if the firm prefers otherwise. We are not saying that all firms will eventually adopt S-D logic. However, even if they don't, S-D logic can provide public policy makers and federal court judges with normative guidelines on how firms should behave.

Societal implications of S-D logic, however, go beyond marketing per se. There is considerable concern about global pollution and other environmental waste issues that are caused or related to tangible products. If a firm focuses on selling the tangible product and not the service flow it forgets about the system within which the tangible good is used as an appliance for service delivery or production. For instance, if an auto manufacturer sold service flows, then it would necessarily have to think about total ownership costs to include fuel, repair costs, and other factors that can be ignored if you are just selling "stuff." Thus S-D logic is pro-environment.

Furthermore, S-D logic, with its focus on the improvement of human mental and physical skills, is pro-education. S-D logic recognizes human and mental skills as the fountainhead of economic growth and human progress. Thus it encourages firms to invest in these resources, support schools and colleges, and generally be pro-education.

In summary, S-D logic is intentionally managerial in focus; however, it provides normative guidelines or rules of action that, if followed by firms, will create more consumer welfare and satisfaction, a cleaner environment, and a pro-education society. Isn't this better than a goods-dominant logic with band-aid legislation directed at mandating firms to do what they would do if they followed the S-D logic normative guidelines? Although not all firms will abide by these norms, who can deny them as worthy goals and a useful framework by which to organize our actions?

CAN S-D LOGIC BE INTEGRATIVE?

Is S-D logic sufficiently broad to provide a foundation for a general theory of marketing? It is probably too early in its development to be sure. However, we do believe Hunt's view of the fundamental *explananda* of marketing (Hunt 1983) that S-D logic goes further than the current goods-dominant logic. We also believe the increased focus on the network as perhaps a unifying unit of analysis for marketing thought (Gummesson, chapter 27; Achrol and Kotler (1999) and chapter 26 this volume) can be embraced by S-D logic.

Hunt's Fundamental Explananda

Hunt (1983) suggests that a general theory of marketing should be capable of explaining four fundamental *explananda* of marketing. S-D logic is able to address each of these fundamental *explananda* as follows:

FE1. The behaviors of buyers directed at consummating exchange.
- S-D logic argues that entities buy service(s) in exchange for providing service(s), most often using organizations, networks, money and goods as intermediaries, in order to (improve) their standard of living.

FE2. The behaviors of sellers directed at consummating exchanges.
- S-D logic argues that entities organize service providers (employees and partners) that do not have a ready one-to-one trading outlet for their competences and transform these competences into services (either embedded in tangible goods or unembedded) that customers want or need. Firms seek competitive advantage using their competences to obtain relative lower resource cost and/or higher relative value for customers.

FE3. The institutional framework directed at consummating and/or facilitating exchanges.
- S-D logic embraces co-production as universal. It would argue that the institutional framework is always co-produced. In the case of the traditional marketing institutions (such as primary and facilitating channel intermediaries) there is always a sharing and co-producing of marketing functions. In the case of social institutions (such as norms, language, sign systems, etc.) co-production is essential for the institutions to be accepted and diffused through society.

FE4. The consequences on society of the behaviors of buyers, the behaviors of sellers, and the institutional framework directed at consummating and/or facilitating exchanges.
- S-D logic argues that buyers and sellers as they exchange create change at the micro level that creates emergent macro structures to include society. Furthermore, human interaction and networks largely through private market and public market exchange lead to co-creating institutions in society. As such, markets and marketing are the primal force in creating society and institutions.

Networks

Gummesson (chapter 27) suggests that networks provide a unifying role in the development of general or grand theory in marketing. Because of their capacity to allow for complexity, context, and dynamism, he suggests that networks have a universal capacity to explain. Achrol and Kotler (chapter 26) suggest that "the focus on the network as the fundamental unit of analysis is a significant ontological step from the theory of the firm, as well as dyadic exchange theory." These same authors (Achrol and Kotler 1999, p. 161) have suggested:

> As the twenty-first century dawns, the Industrial Revolution is fast giving way to the Information Revolution. Many giant, vertically integrated manufacturing firms, which were the product of the Industrial Revolution, are morphing into internal and external networks. These managed networks promise superior information processing, knowledge creation, and adaptive properties to conventional firms.

Achrol and Kotler (1999), citing Drucker (1993) observe "the twenty-first century is shaping up to be a knowledge-driven society in which the basic economic resource is not materials, labor, or capital, but knowledge" (p.146).

S-D logic embraces these views. We agree that the network is rising in importance in many economies throughout the world. However, the network, just as the organization, goods, and money, is merely the transmission mechanisms for the exchange of service(s) for service(s). As S-D logic argues in foundational premise #1 (Vargo and Lusch 2004; and chapter 1), "the application of specialized skills and knowledge is the fundamental unit of exchange." It is the network that is increasingly being used to exchange these specialized skills and knowledge (services). Nonetheless, most often, just like with the industrial organization the network organization will mask the fundamental unit of exchange and where value is created or resides. As S-D logic argues in foundational premise #2 (Vargo and Lusch 2004; and chapter 1), "indirect exchange masks the fundamental unit of exchange." Networks assist in the work of service delivery, just as do goods, money and organizations. However, the value is not in the network per se. In fact, Hakansson (2004, pp. 91–92), an early pioneer in network theory, recognizes resources are valued for the services they make possible.

> Irrespective of whether physical objects or services are exchanged, Penrose (1959) concluded that physical resources, such as products, are not valued for anything more than the services they create. Thus, all exchange activities are conducted in order to realize services. Business exchange activity is characterized in that it is through exchange that the potential services of resources are released and value arises. In other words, the outcome of the business exchange activity is the services rendered and the goal of business activity is to actualize the potential services buried in the innermost recesses of the included resources. . . . The objective is to create value through the release of the services habituated within resources.

Finally, S-D logic agrees with the observation that the twenty-first century is shaping up to be a knowledge-driven society. S-D logic places a primary focus on operant resources, and knowledge is an operant resource. S-D logic in foundational premise #4, "knowledge is the fundamental source of competitive advantage," recognizes that the foundation of competitive advantage and economic growth and the key source of wealth is knowledge. Central to S-D logic is the embracing of the view of services "as the application of specialized competences (knowledge and skills) through deeds, processes, and performances for the benefit of another entity or the entity itself" (Vargo and Lusch 2004, p. 2). Because of this embracing view of services S-D logic argues in foundational premise #5 that "all economies are service economies." Thus not only is the twenty-first century primarily about knowledge as a source of wealth but the history of the division of labor, the growth of society, and market-centered exchange is primarily about knowledge and learning. As Vargo and Lusch (2004, p. 10) observe:

> The hunter-gather macrospecialization was characterized by the refinement and application of foraging and hunting knowledge and skills; the agricultural macrospecialization by the cultivation of knowledge and skills; the industrial economy by the refinement of knowledge and skills for large-scale mass production and organizational management; and the services and information economies by the refinement and use of knowledge and skills about information and the exchange of pure, unembedded knowledge.

Achrol and Kotler (1999) believe that "the very nature of network organization, the kinds of theories useful to its understanding, and the potential impact on the organization of consumption all suggest that a paradigm shift for marketing may not be far over the horizon" (p. 162). S-D logic would position supply and value networks as replacing the traditional focus on organization and channels of distribution (place). However, S-D logic goes further since it views the customer and partners as entities to *market with versus market and/or distribute to.* Hence S-D logic places a strong focus on collaboration that is consistent with Achrol and Kotler's (1999) perspective that networks are embedded with "dense lateral connections, mutuality, and reciprocity, in a shared value system that defines 'membership' roles and responsibilities" (p. 148). Consequently, network organizations and S-D logic are synergistic.

In the development of a paradigm shift that many are expecting, S-D logic provides more of a foundation than network theory. S-D logic in addition to its focus on value-creation processes and networks puts a strategic focus on the marketing mix by emphasizing service(s) offerings and flows, value propositions, and communication and dialog (see Figure 32.2). However, S-D logic also reverses the logic of viewing external environments as uncontrollable and views them as resources to draw upon for support (see Figure 32.3). Importantly, network organizations can help to establish connections to these external environments and transform them into a resource, again emphasizing that network theory and S-D logic are synergistic.

CONCLUDING COMMENT

General theories are long in coming to an academic discipline. When developed they come under extreme scrutiny. Although we do not purport that S-D logic at its current stage of development is a general theory. However, for the reasons elaborated upon in this chapter we believe that it provides the foundational basis for the development of a general theory. S-D logic is open source code and we hope others will add to this effort in the hope that what evolves and develops is a fully integrative and complete general theory of marketing.

NOTE

1. Gummesson (chapter 27) similarly urges a focus on flows, processes, and dynamics by suggesting the core concepts of a future grand theory of marketing are networks, relationships and interaction. In contrast, Grönroos (chapter 28) places a heavy emphasis on interaction and relationship as central phenomena.

REFERENCES

Achrol, Ravi S. and Philip Kotler (1999), "Marketing in the Network Economy," *Journal of Marketing*, 63 (special issue), 146–63.

Bastiat, Frederic (1860), *Harmonies of Political Economy*, trans. Patrick S. Sterling. London: J. Murray.

———— (1964), *Selected Essays on Political Economy*, (1848), trans. Seymour Cain. George B. de Huszar, ed. Reprint, Princeton, NJ: D. Van Nordstrand.

Capra, Fritjof (1996), *The Web of Life: A New Scientific Understanding of Living Systems*. New York: Anchor Books.

Coase, Ronald H. (1937), "The Nature of the Firm," *Economica*, 4, 386–405.

Constantin, James A. and Robert F. Lusch (1994), *Understanding Resource Management*. Oxford, OH: The Planning Forum.

Drucker, Peter F. (1993), *Post Capitalist Society*. Oxford: Butterworth Heinemann.

Hakansson, Haken and Frans Prenkert (2004), "Exploring the Exchange Concept in Marketing" in *Rethinking Marketing*, H. Hakansson, D. Harrison, and A. Waluszewski, eds. West Sussex, New York: John Wiley & Sons, 75–98.

Holbrook, Morris (2003), "Adventures in Complexity: An Essay in Dynamic Open Complex Adaptive Systems, Butterfly Effects, Self-Organizing Order, Coevolution, the Ecological Perspective, Fitness Landscapes, Market Spaces, Emergent Beauty at the Edge of Chaos, and All That Jazz," *Academy of Marketing Science Review*, 2003 (6), http:www.amsreview.org/articles/holbrook06–2003.pdf. Accessed April 3, 2005.

Hunt, Shelby D. (1983), "General Theories and the Fundamental Explananda of Marketing," *Journal of Marketing*, 47 (Fall), 9–17.

———— (2000), *A General Theory of Competition: Resources, Competences, Productivity, Economic Growth*. Thousand Oaks, CA: Sage Publications.

Kiel, Douglas L., Robert F. Lusch, and B. G. Schumacher (1992), "Toward a New Paradigm for Marketing: The Evolutionary Exchange Paradigm," *Behavioral Science*, 37, 59–78.

McCarthy, Jerome E. (1960), *Basic Marketing: A Managerial Approach*. Homewood, IL: Richard D. Irwin.

Penrose, Edith T. (1959), *The Theory of the Growth of the Firm*, London: Basil Blackwell and Mott.

Smith, Adam (1904), *An Inquiry into the Nature and Causes of the Wealth of Nations* (1776). Reprint. London: Printed for W. Strahan and T. Cadell.

Vargo, Stephen L. and Robert F. Lusch (2004), "Evolving to a New Dominant Logic for Marketing," *Journal of Marketing*, 68 (January), 1–17.

Williamson, Oliver E. (1975), *Markets and Hierarchies: Analysis and Anti-trust Implications*. New York: The Free Press.

ABOUT THE EDITORS AND CONTRIBUTORS

Ravi S. Achrol (PhD, Kellogg Graduate School of Management, Northwestern University) has been Professor of Marketing in the School of Business at George Washington University since 1991. From 1981 to 1991 he served on the faculty of the University of Notre Dame. During 2001–02 and 2002–03 he held the Kmart Endowed Chair in Marketing at West Virginia University. His areas of research interest include distribution channels, marketing strategy, interorganizational relations, and network organization. His research articles have been published in the *Journal of the Academy of Marketing Science*, *Journal of Marketing*, *Journal of Marketing Research*, *Journal of Public Policy & Marketing*, *Journal of Retailing*, *Social Science Research*, *Journal of Business Strategy*, and various other publications.

Tim Ambler is Senior Fellow at London Business School. His research covers international marketing and the measurement of brand equity, marketing, and advertising performance. His books include *Marketing and the Bottom Line* (2000, 2nd edition 2003), *Doing Business in China* (2000, 2003), *The SILK Road to International Marketing* (2000) and *Marketing from Advertising to Zen* (1996). He has published in the *Journal of Marketing*, *Journal of Marketing Research*, *International Journal of Research in Marketing*, *Journal of Advertising Research*, and *International Journal of Advertising*. A member of the *Journal of Marketing* Editorial Review Board and Economics Committee of the Advertising Association, he is a Chartered Accountant and previously Joint Managing Director of International Distillers and Vintners (IDV), now part of Diageo plc. During his various marketing roles in IDV, in the United Kingdom and internationally, he was involved in the launch of Baileys, Malibu, and Archers and the development of Smirnoff vodka worldwide.

Eric Arnould is on the faculty of the Norton School of Family and Retailing Sciences, University of Arizona, where he holds the PETsMART Chair of Retailing. Dr. Arnould obtained his doctorate from the University of Arizona in 1982. He has taught at Odense University in Denmark; University of South Florida at Tampa; University of Nebraska-Lincoln; EAP-ESCP, Paris; University of Ljubljana, Slovenia; and others. Also, he has consulted on agriculture and natural resources management issues in many African countries. His work is published in journals including the *Journal of Consumer Research*, *Journal of Marketing Research*, *Journal of Marketing*, *Journal of the Academy of Marketing Science*, *Journal of Retailing*, and *Psychology and Marketing*. Dr. Arnould has served as Associate Editor of *Journal of Consumer Research*, and has served on the editorial boards of journals such as the *Journal of Macromarketing*, *Journal of Marketing*, and the *Journal of Retailing*. His most recent research interests are in the areas of relational aspects of services, consumer resources and the co-production of marketing outcomes, consumer culture theory, applications of multimethod consumer research, and channels structure and marketing organization.

David Ballantyne is an associate professor of marketing at the University of Otago, School of Business, in New Zealand, and an International Fellow at the Centre for Relationship Marketing and Service Management, Hanken Swedish School of Economics in Helsinki. He is a coauthor with Martin Christopher and Adrian Payne of *Relationship Marketing: Bringing Quality, Customer Service and Marketing Together* (1991), the first text published internationally in this rapidly expanding field of inquiry. A second edition was published in 2002 as *Relationship Marketing: Creating Stakeholder Value.* Dr. Ballantyne is a past director of the Total Quality Management Institute of Australia, and has held senior executive positions in marketing research, public relations, strategic marketing, and service management. He is a member of the British Academy of Management and a member of the editorial review boards of the *Journal of Business-to-Business Marketing, Management Decision,* and the *International Marketing Review.* His research interests are internal marketing, knowledge management, and dialogue as a co-creative learning mode in marketing.

Pierre Berthon is Professor of Marketing at Bentley College. He has held academic positions at Columbia University in the United States; Henley Management College, Cardiff University; and University of Bath in the United Kingdom. Dr. Berthon's research focuses on electronic commerce and marketing strategy in information-intensive contexts. His work has appeared in journals such as *Sloan Management Review, California Management Review, Information Systems Research, Journal of the Academy of Marketing Science, Journal of Business Research, Journal of International Marketing, Technological Forecasting and Social Change, Journal of Interactive Marketing, Business Horizons, Marketing Theory, Journal of Advertising Research, Journal of Business Ethics,* and others. A number of his papers have won awards in the United States and the United Kingdom.

Mary Jo Bitner is Professor of Marketing and PETsMART Chair in Services Leadership in the W.P. Carey School of Business at Arizona State University (ASU). At ASU, she also serves as Academic Director for the Center for Services Leadership (CSL), where she was one of its founding faculty members and a leader in its emergence as a university-based center for the study of services. Her research is published in leading marketing and business management journals, including *Journal of Marketing, Journal of the Academy of Marketing Science, Journal of Retailing, Academy of Management Executive,* and others. Her research focuses on managing customer experiences, service encounters, and customer adoption and usage of self-service technologies. Dr. Bitner is coauthor of *Services Marketing: Integrating Customer Focus across the Firm*, 4th edition (2006), a leading text in services marketing used worldwide. In 2003 she received the American Marketing Association's Career Contributions to the Service Discipline Award.

Ruth N. Bolton is Professor of Marketing, W.P. Carey Chair in Marketing, at the W.P. Carey School of Business, Arizona State University. Dr. Bolton currently studies how organizations can grow the value of their customer base over time, focusing on high-technology services sold to business-to-business customers. She previously held academic positions at Vanderbilt University, the University of Oklahoma, Harvard University, University of Maryland, and the University of Alberta. She also spent eight years with Verizon, working on projects in its telecommunications and information services strategic business units. Dr. Bolton's earlier published articles investigate how organizations' service and pricing strategies influence customer satisfaction, loyalty, and revenues. She received her BComm, with honors, from Queen's University (Canada), and her MSc and PhD from Carnegie-Mellon University. She currently serves on the editorial boards of *Marketing Science* and *Journal of Marketing,* and also as a Trustee for the Marketing Science Institute.

Stephen W. Brown holds the Edward M. Carson Chair in Services Marketing and is Professor of Marketing and Executive Director of the Center for Services Leadership at the W. P. Carey School of Business at Arizona State University. He is also a Winspear Visiting Scholar at the University of Victoria and holds an honorary doctorate degree from Hanken Swedish School of Economics. He is a past recipient of the American Marketing Association's annual Career Contribution to Services Marketing award. His research interests focus on services marketing, strategic marketing, and building services revenues in goods-dominant companies. He has published in the *Journal of Marketing, Journal of Marketing Research, Journal of Applied Psychology, Journal of the Academy of Marketing Sciences, Journal of Service Research,* and *Sloan Management Review.* He is a past chair of the Board of the American Marketing Association and currently serves on the boards of directors of several companies.

Roderick Brodie is a Professor in the Department of Marketing at the University of Auckland, New Zealand. His research experience is in the areas of marketing strategy, branding, marketing research, services, marketing science, and forecasting. His publications have appeared in leading international journals including *Journal of Marketing, Journal of Marketing Research, International Journal of Research in Marketing, Management Science, Journal of Service Research,* and other international journals. He is an editor of *Marketing Theory* and is currently on the Editorial Boards of the *International Journal of Research in Marketing*, the *Journal of Service Research*, and the *Australasian Journal of Marketing*.

George S. Day is the Geoffrey T. Boisi Professor, Professor of Marketing, and Codirector of the Mack Center for Technological Innovation at the Wharton School of the University of Pennsylvania. Prior to joining the Wharton School he was Executive Director of the Marketing Science Institute. He is also a Director of the American Marketing Association Foundation and the Sheth Foundation. He has received various awards including two Alpha Kappa Psi Foundation awards and two Harold H. Maynard awards for best papers in the *Journal of Marketing*, as well as the Charles Coolidge Parlin Award, the Paul D. Converse Award, and the Mahajan Award, and was selected as the outstanding marketing educator for 1999 by the Academy of Marketing Science. In 2003 he received the American Marketing Association/Irwin/McGraw-Hill Distinguished Marketing Educator award.

Tom Duncan founded the Integrated Marketing Communication (IMC) graduate program at the University of Colorado in 1993. He now teaches at the Daniels College of Business (University of Denver) where he is Director of the first master of business administration program in IMC in the United States. Before becoming a college professor, Duncan spent fifteen years in industry, working on both the agency and client sides of marketing communication. He began at Leo Burnett worldwide headquarters in account management, where he worked for clients such as Procter & Gamble, KFC, and Union Carbide. On the client side he was Manager of Marketing Services for Peter Eckrich & Sons (a manufacturer of processed meats) and was Vice President of Marketing for Jeno's, Inc. (frozen Italian foods). He is the coauthor of several books including *Driving Brand Value.* The second edition of his newest book, *Principles of Advertising and IMC,* was published in 2004. His writings and research have been appeared in *Direct Marketing, Advertising Age*, *Journal of Advertising Research*, *Journal of Marketing*, and *Journal of Advertising*. His bachelor's and master's degrees in advertising are from Northwestern University, and he earned a doctorate at the University of Iowa.

Michael Etgar is a professor of Marketing at the Graduate School of Business Administration, the College of Management, Rishon LeZion in Israel. He serves as director of research in the school. He holds a doctorate in Marketing from University of California at Berkeley and has served as a faculty member at UC Berkeley, New York University, and at State University of New York, Buffalo. Recently he was a visiting scholar at the Graduate School of Business at University of Northern Florida. He has published more than 100 articles in leading journals such as the *Journal of Marketing Research, Journal of Marketing, Management Science, Journal of Retailing,* and the *Journal of Risk and Insurance*. His main research interests lie in the areas of channel management, retail management marketing strategy, and international marketing.

Daniel J. Flint is Associate Professor of Marketing in The Department of Marketing and Logistics at The University of Tennessee, Knoxville. He has a doctorate from the University of Tennessee, an MSA from Central Michigan University, and a BS in Engineering from Annapolis. His research has appeared in top journals covering both marketing and logistics such the *Journal of Marketing, Journal of Business Logistics, Industrial Marketing Management, International Journal of Physical Distribution and Logistics Management,* and others, and has coauthored book chapters and numerous conference papers. He has industry experience as an industrial sales engineer for Alcoa and is a former naval flight officer and aircraft maintenance division officer. He primarily teaches executives, PhDs, and MBAs, and frequently works with marketing and sales managers on issues related to customer value management in industrial and logistics settings. His general research interests include customer value prediction, customer value management, and marketing/logistics innovation.

Christian Grönroos is Professor of Service and Relationship Marketing at Hanken Swedish School of Economics, Finland, part-time Professor of Service Management at Lund University, Sweden, and a previous visiting professor at Arizona State University and The University of Auckland. He has published numerous articles on service marketing and management, relationship marketing, service quality, internal marketing, service productivity, and other areas related to the broad field of service research. His book *Service Management and Marketing: A Customer Relationship Approach* (2000) has been translated into several languages. He has also taught service marketing in executive programs on four continents. In 1999 he was the first scholar outside North America to receive the American Marketing Association SERVSIG Career Contribution to the Services Field Award.

Evert Gummesson is Professor of Marketing at the Stockholm University School of Business, Sweden. He is a fellow of the University of Tampere, Finland, and a fellow and honorary doctor of the Swedish School of Economics and Business Administration, Helsinki, Finland. He has twenty-five years of experience as marketing manager and management consultant. His research is directed to services, quality, relationship marketing, and CRM. In 1977 he published the first book on services marketing in Scandinavia; in 2000 he received the American Marketing Association's Award for Leadership in Services Marketing; and in 2003, the Chartered Institute of Marketing, UK, included him in its list of the fifty most important contributors to the development of marketing. His book *Total Relationship Marketing* has won two prizes, and his new book *Many-to-Many Marketing* was published in 2004. He has authored more than twenty books and over 100 articles.

A. Fuat Firat is Visiting Professor of Marketing at the University of Southern Denmark-Odense. His research interests cover areas such as macro consumer behavior and macro marketing, postmodern culture, transmodern marketing strategies, gender and consumption, marketing and development, and interorganizational relations. He has won the *Journal of Macromarketing* Charles Slater Award for best article with coauthor N. Dholakia, and the *Journal of Consumer Research* best article award with coauthor A. Venkatesh. He has several books including *Consuming People: From Political Economy to Theaters of Consumption*, coauthored by N. Dholakia, and is Co-Editor-in-Chief of *Consumption, Markets & Culture*.

Sebastián J. García-Dastugue is Assistant Professor at Universidad de San Andrés, in Buenos Aires, Argentina. His research interests are in supply chain management, logistics, and the use of information systems for decision making. His research has been published in *Journal of Business Logistics, The International Journal of Logistics Management* and *Industrial Marketing Management*. He has more than ten years of experience in industry. He worked for Ryder Argentina, Cementos Avellaneda, Solutions Informatiques Francaises, and Sud America Seguros. Dr. García-Dastugue holds a BA in MIS from Universidad CAECE, an MBA from IAE Universidad Austral, and a PhD from The Ohio State University.

Morris B. Holbrook is the W. T. Dillard Professor of Marketing in the Graduate School of Business at Columbia University. Since 1975, he has taught courses at the Columbia Business School in such areas as marketing strategy, consumer behavior, and commercial communication in the culture of consumption. His research has covered a wide variety of topics in marketing and consumer behavior with a special focus on issues related to communication in general and to aesthetics, semiotics, hermeneutics, art, entertainment, music, motion pictures, nostalgia, and stereography in particular. Recent books include *The Semiotics of Consumption* (with Elizabeth C. Hirschman, 1993), *Consumer Research* (1995), and *Consumer Value* (edited, 1999).

Shelby D. Hunt is the Jerry S. Rawls and P. W. Horn Professor of Marketing at Texas Tech University. A past editor of the *Journal of Marketing* (1985–87), he is the author of numerous books, including *Foundations of Marketing Theory: Toward a General Theory of Marketing* (2002) and is one of the 250 most frequently cited researchers in economics and business (Thompson-ISI). Three of his *Journal of Marketing* articles won the Harold H. Maynard Award for the best article on marketing theory. He has also won the 2004 Sheth Foundation/*Journal of Marketing* award for an article that made "long-term contributions to the field of marketing." His 1994 "Commitment and Trust" *Journal of Marketing* article, with Robert M. Morgan, was the most highly cited article in economics and business in the 1993–2003 decade (Thomson-ISI). For his contributions to theory and science in marketing, he received the 1986 Paul D. Converse Award from the American Marketing Association, the 1987 Outstanding Marketing Educator Award from the Academy of Marketing Science, the 1992 American Marketing Association/Richard D. Irwin Distinguished Marketing Educator Award, and the 2002 Society for Marketing Advances/Elsevier Science Distinguished Scholar Award.

Bernard J. Jaworski is a Cofounder and Senior Leader of Marketspace™ and is President of Monitor Executive Development. He previously was the Jeanne and David Tappan Marketing

Fellow and a tenured, Full Professor of Marketing at the University of Southern California. He has also served on the faculty at the University of Arizona and was a Visiting Professor at Harvard Business School. His most recent book is *Best Face Forward* (2005).

Joby John is Professor and Chair of the Marketing Department at Bentley College. He has a B.S. (Pharmacy), an MBA, and a PhD (Marketing). He is a former marketing officer at Pfizer and BAT, India. John has lectured in a dozen countries on topics such as services marketing, customer-focused management and cross-cultural issues. He has published more than fifty journal and conference papers and most recently three books: *Services Marketing Self-Portraits: Introspections, Reflections and Glimpses from the Experts; Interactive Services Marketing;* and *Fundamentals of Customer-Focused Management: Competing through Service.* Joby is a past President of the American Marketing Association's Boston Chapter and a past chair of the Services Marketing Special Interest Group of the American Marketing Association.

Kartik Kalaignanam is a doctoral student in Marketing in the Mays Business School at Texas A&M University. His research interests are in marketing strategy, strategic alliances, outsourcing, and e-commerce. His professional experience spans sales and marketing management in the home appliances, sportswear, and Internet industry.

Ajay K. Kohli is the Isaac Stiles Hopkins Professor of Marketing at Emory University's Goizueta Business School. Dr. Kohli's research on market orientation, sales management, and industrial marketing appears in leading academic journals. He has received several research awards including the Alpha Kappa Psi award (with Dr. Jaworski), the Sheth Foundation/*Journal of Marketing* award (with Dr. Jaworski), and the Jagdish N. Sheth Award (with Dr. Jaworski and Dr. Menon). Thompson-ISI lists him among the 100 most cited scientists in Economics and Business during1993–2003. Dr. Kohli has also taught at the Harvard Business School and The University of Texas at Austin. He has served as the founding Dean and Director of Emory University's doctoral program in business. He has worked full-time in industry for six years, and consulted with or led executive education programs for a number of companies in the United States, Europe, Asia, and Latin America.

Philip Kotler (MA, University of Chicago, PhD, MIT) is the S. C. Johnson Distinguished Professor of International Marketing at the Kellogg School of Management, Northwestern University, Evanston, Illinois. He published his twelfth edition of *Marketing Management*, the world's leading textbook in teaching marketing to MBA students. He has also published *Principles of Marketing, Strategic Marketing for Nonprofit Organizations, Marketing Places, Kotler on Marketing, Marketing Insights A to Z, Lateral Marketing, Social Marketing, Museum Strategies and Marketing, Standing Room Only, Corporate Social Responsibility,* and several other books. His research covers strategic marketing, innovation, consumer marketing, business marketing, services marketing, distribution, e-marketing, and social marketing. He has been a consultant to IBM, Bank of America, Merck, General Electric, Honeywell, and many other companies. He has received honorary doctorate degrees from ten major universities here and abroad.

Thorbjørn Knudsen is a Professor at the Department of Marketing, University of Southern Denmark. He has specialized in dynamic change in business organizations. Dr. Knudsen has published widely on topics relating to evolutionary and institutional theory as well as formal models of economic architecture and adaptive search.

Gene R. Laczniak is the Wayne and Kathleen Sanders Professor of Business at the Straz College of Business Administration at Marquette University. He is a former chair of the Marketing Department and former Associate Vice President/Provost for Academic Affairs. He has been a Visiting Professor or Visiting Fellow at the University of Western Australia (Perth). Dr. Laczniak's research focuses on the influence of competitive strategy upon society and especially the question of ethics. He has published more than 100 articles and papers, including placements in the *Journal of Marketing, Journal of Marketing & Public Policy, Long Range Planning, Journal of Business Ethics,* and the *Journal of the Academy of Marketing Science.* Dr. Laczniak has coauthored six books. He served on the editorial review board of the *Journal of Marketing* for fifteen years and currently serves on four other editorial review boards, including the *Journal of Business Ethics, Journal of Macromarketing,* and the *Journal of World Business.* He has served as a member of the Board of Directors of several local, not-for-profit organizations. His bachelor's degree is from Marquette University, and he holds an MBA and PhD from the University of Wisconsin-Madison.

Douglas M. Lambert is the Raymond E. Mason Chair in Transportation and Logistics and Director of The Global Supply Chain Forum at The Ohio State University. Dr. Lambert has served as a faculty member for more than 500 executive development programs in North and South America, Europe, Asia and Australia. He is the author or coauthor of seven books and more than 100 articles, the most recent of which appeared in the December 2004 *Harvard Business Review.* In 1986, Dr. Lambert received the CLM Distinguished Service Award for his contributions to logistics management. He holds an honors BA and MBA from the University of Western Ontario and a PhD from The Ohio State University. Dr. Lambert is coeditor of *The International Journal of Logistics Management.*

Donald R. Lehmann is George E. Warren Professor of Business at the Columbia University Graduate School of Business. He has a BS degree in mathematics from Union College, Schenectady, New York, and an MSIA and PhD from the Krannert School of Purdue University. His research interests include individual and group choice and decision making, empirical generalizations and meta-analysis, the introduction and adoption of new products and innovations, and measuring the value of marketing assets such as brands and customers. He has published in and served on the editorial boards of *Journal of Consumer Research, Journal of Marketing, Journal of Marketing Research, Management Science,* and *Marketing Science,* and was founding editor of *Marketing Letters.* He has published numerous journal articles and six books: *Market Research and Analysis, Analysis for Marketing Planning, Product Management, Meta-Analysis in Marketing, The Futures of Marketing,* and *Managing Customers as Investments.* Dr. Lehmann has served as Executive Director of the Marketing Science Institute and as President of the Association for Consumer Research.

Sidney Levy is Coca-Cola Distinguished Professor of Marketing and Special Assistant to the marketing department head, Eller College of Management, University of Arizona. His PhD is from the University of Chicago. He was licensed as a psychologist in Illinois. He joined the Northwestern University faculty in 1961 and taught for 36 years, chairing the Kellogg School marketing department from 1980 to 1992. He is the Charles H. Kellstadt Emeritus Professor of Marketing. In 1988, he was named American Marketing Association/Irwin Distinguished Marketing Educator. In 1982 he became a Fellow and Life Member of the Association for Consumer Research. He was elected president of the Association for 1991. In 1997, HEC-University of

Montreal named him a Living Legend of Marketing. In 2000, he received the Converse Award for contributions to Marketing, noting the enduring influence of his 1959 *Harvard Business Review* article "Symbols for Sale."

Robert F. Lusch is professor of marketing and marketing department head in the Eller College of Management at the University of Arizona. He holds a PhD from the University of Wisconsin-Madison and served on the faculty at the University of Oklahoma for twenty-five years and Texas Christian University for four years. A past editor of the *Journal of Marketing*, past chairperson of the American Marketing Association, and dean of two major business schools, he is a prolific author in the areas of marketing channels, retailing and marketing strategy. In 1997 and 2005 he was the recipient of the Harold H. Maynard Award for the "best article on marketing theory" appearing in the *Journal of Marketing* and was selected as the Academy of Marketing Science Distinguished Educator in 1997. In 2001 he won the Louis W. Stern award for outstanding contributions to the marketing channels literature. His research has appeared in many journals such as the *Journal of Marketing Research, Journal of Marketing, Journal of Consumer Research, Journal of Retailing* and the *Journal of Macromarketing*. In addition he has authored twenty books and research monographs.

Sreedhar Madhavaram is a doctoral candidate and Instructor of Marketing at Rawls College of Business, Texas Tech University, Lubbock, Texas. His research interests include marketing strategy, organizational knowledge, and marketing education. His work has been published in the *Journal of Business and Industrial Marketing* and in the proceedings of the American Marketing Association and the Association of Consumer Research.

Avinash Malshe is Assistant Professor of Marketing at the University of St. Thomas, Minneapolis. His research focuses on marketing strategy, strategy implementation and the interface of firm strategy and customers. Dr. Malshe's current research investigates the paradox of "marketplace paranoia" and its impact on firm-level outcomes. Other research investigates customer loyalty and service relationships. He has presented his research at several major conferences including Association for Consumer Research and American Marketing Association. Avinash has industry experience in brand management and sales management and currently teaches courses in the areas of marketing strategy and consumer behavior.

John T. (Tom) Mentzer is the Harry J. and Vivienne R. Bruce Chair of Excellence in Business in the Department of Marketing and Logistics at the University of Tennessee. He has written more than 180 papers and articles and seven books. He was recognized in 1996 as one of the five most prolific authors in the *Journal of the Academy of Marketing Science*, and in 1999 as the most prolific author in the *Journal of Business Logistics*. He is on the editorial review boards of numerous journals. He is a past President of the Council of Logistics Management. He was formerly President, and is presently Chair of the Board of Governors, of the Academy of Marketing Science, and is a Distinguished Fellow of the Academy of Marketing Science. Dr. Mentzer was the 2004 recipient of the Council of Logistics Management Distinguished Service Award.

Elizabeth S. Moore (PhD, University of Florida) is Associate Professor of Marketing at the University of Notre Dame. Her research interests are in marketing and society, consumer behavior of households, and marketing to children. Her research has appeared in the *Journal of Marketing, Journal of Consumer Research, Journal of Public Policy & Marketing, Journal of the Academy of Marketing Science, Journal of Business Ethics* and *Journal of Macromarketing*. She currently serves on the editorial board of the *Journal of Public Policy & Marketing*. She has received awards for her research, including the "Best Article" Award (2002) and the "Ferber" Award (Honorable Mention), both from the *Journal of Consumer Research*, and the "Kinnear" award from the *Journal of Public Policy & Marketing*. Prior to joining Notre Dame, she served on the faculty at Illinois where she received the Outstanding Undergraduate Teacher Award in the College of Commerce, and at Notre Dame was recently presented with the BP Amoco Outstanding Teacher Award.

Fred Morgan (PhD, Michigan State University) is the Ashland Professor of Marketing at the University of Kentucky. He has also served on the marketing faculties of the University of Oklahoma, Wayne State University, and the University of Missouri-Columbia and has been a visiting faculty member at the University of California-Berkeley, the University of Michigan, and the University of San Francisco. His research interests center on the impact of the legal environment on marketing and business strategy and the effect of distribution practices on product liability exposure. His research appears in several academic journals, including the *Journal of Marketing*, the *Journal of Consumer Research*, the *Journal of Public Policy & Marketing*, the *Journal of the Academy of Marketing Science*, and the *Journal of Retailing*.

Sandra Moriarty was a Cofounder of the Integrated Marketing Communication master's program at the University of Colorado. She has also taught at Michigan State University, the University of Kansas, and Kansas State University and has worked in government public relations, owned an advertising and public relations agency, directed a university publications program, and edited a university alumni magazine. She was a Fellow at the Freedom Forum Media Studies Center at Columbia University in 1993. Professor Moriarty has published widely in scholarly journals on marketing communication and visual communication topics and has authored nine books on advertising, graphics, and integrated marketing communication including *Driving Brand Value: Using Integrated Marketing to Manage Profitable Stakeholder Relationships,* with coauthor Tom Duncan. International translations include Chinese, Korean, Japanese, and Russian. She has spoken to groups and presented seminars in most European countries, as well as Mexico, Japan, Korea, New Zealand, and Turkey.

Richard L. Oliver (PhD, Wisconsin-Madison, 1973) is a Professor of Management (Marketing) at the Owen Graduate School of Management, Vanderbilt University. His research interests include consumer psychology with a special focus on customer satisfaction, customer loyalty, and postpurchase processes. He holds the position of Fellow of the American Psychological Association for his extensive writings on the psychology of the satisfaction response and is the author of *Satisfaction: A Behavioral Perspective on the Consumer* (Irwin/McGraw-Hill) and coeditor of *Service Quality: New Directions in Theory and Practice* (Sage). He has published numerous articles in the major marketing journals as well as in selected psychological outlets. He previously taught at the Wharton School, University of Pennsylvania, and Washington University in St. Louis.

Jaqueline Pels is a Professor in the Department of Marketing at the University Torcuato Di Tella, Buenos Aires, Argentina. Her research experience is in the areas of business-to-business marketing, relationship marketing, professional services, and marketing theory. Her publications have appeared in leading international journals including *European Journal of Marketing, Journal of Business in Industrial Markets, Journal of Relationship Marketing, Journal of Marketing Theory and Practice,* and *Journal of Global Marketing,* among others. She is Latin America editor for *Marketing Theory* and for the *Academy of Marketing Science Review* and currently on the Editorial Boards of the *Journal of Marketing, Journal of International Marketing, Journal of Relationship Marketing,* and *Journal of Business in Developing Nations,* among others.

Lisa Peñaloza is Associate Professor of Marketing at the University of Colorado, Boulder. Her research is concerned with how consumers express culture in their consumer behavior and, in turn, how marketers negotiate various cultures of consumers. Market subcultures examined in her work relate to ethnicity/race, nationality, gender/sexuality, and industry. Her most recent work is a documentary film exploring the role of the market in the development of the Mexican American community in San Antonio, Texas. Her work has been published in the *Journal of Consumer Research, Journal of Marketing, Public Policy & Marketing, International Journal of Research in Marketing,* and *Consumption, Markets and Culture.*

Linda L. Price is Professor of Marketing at the University of Arizona and holds a PhD from the University of Texas-Austin. Dr. Price's research is published in *Journal of Consumer Research, Journal of Marketing, Organization Science,* and other leading journals. Her research combines qualitative and quantitative methodologies to examine the active, emotional, imaginative aspects of consumers' decisions and activities, and the social and cultural context of marketplace behaviors. Dr. Price is coauthor of *Consumers*, a textbook on global consumer behavior, now in a second edition. She has been an invited plenary speaker at numerous national and international forums. Dr. Price regularly serves on the editorial boards of several leading journals, and her research has been funded by a variety of agencies including the U.S. Department of Agriculture, and the Marketing Science Institute. She has also worked as a consultant with a variety of firms varying from small non-profit organizations to Fortune 500 businesses.

Roland T. Rust holds the David Bruce Smith Chair at the University of Maryland's Robert H. Smith School of Business, where he heads the Marketing Department and directs the Center for Excellence in Service. His lifetime achievement honors include the American Marketing Association's Churchill Award for Lifetime Achievement in Marketing Research, the American Advertising Association's Outstanding Contributions to Research in Advertising award, the American Marketing Association's Career Contributions to the Services Discipline Award, Fellow of the American Statistical Association, and the Southern Marketing Association Distinguished Marketing Scholar Award. He has won best article awards for articles in *Marketing Science, Journal of Marketing Research, Journal of Marketing* (three times), *Journal of Advertising,* and *Journal of Retailing,* as well as Marketing Science Institute's Robert D. Buzzell Best Paper Award (twice) and the Berry-American Marketing Association Book Prize. He is founder and Chair of the American Marketing Association's Frontiers in Services Conference, founding Editor of the *Journal of Service Research*, and editor of the *Journal of Marketing.*

Michael Saren is a Professor of Marketing at the Leicester University Management Centre. Prior to this he was Professor of Marketing at the University of Strathclyde. He is currently working on several research projects including an investigation into subcultural consumption, branding and identity and is UK Area editor of the journal *Marketing Theory.* His work has been published in many academic management journals in the United Kingdom, Europe, and the United States, including the *International Journal of Research in Marketing, Omega,* and *British Journal of Management.*

Mohanbir Sawhney is a globally recognized scholar, author, and speaker in technology marketing, innovation, and e-business strategy. He has pioneered the development of concepts like business-to-business hubs, metamarkets, collaborative marketing, communities of creation and business synchronization. Crain's Chicago Business named him a member of 40 under 40. A Fellow of the World Economic Forum, he has coauthored three books and many influential articles in leading academic as well as managerial journals. He has received several awards for his research and teaching, including the 2001 Accenture Award for the best paper published in the *California Management Review* and the 1998 Outstanding Professor of the Year Award at Kellogg. His consulting and speaking clients include dozens of Fortune 500 companies as well as governments. He also serves on the advisory boards of several startup companies.

Debora Viana Thompson is a PhD Candidate at the Robert H. Smith School of Business, University of Maryland. Her research interests are consumers' information processing, the impact of technology on choice and consumption, and e-services. Her dissertation proposal investigates how consumers trade off product capability and usability in their product evaluations and was a winner in the 2005 Marketing Science Institute's Alden G. Clayton Doctoral Dissertation Proposal Competition. She has presented at conferences such as the Association for Consumer Research Conference and the American Marketing Association Frontiers in Services Conference. Before starting the doctoral program at the University of Maryland, Ms. Thompson worked as a market research analyst (1997–2000) at the Center for Research in Management in the Federal University of Rio Grande do Sul-Brazil, conducting customer satisfaction surveys and segmentation studies for large companies in southern Brazil.

Rajan Varadarajan is Distinguished Professor of Marketing and holder of the Ford Chair in Marketing and E-Commerce in the Mays Business School at Texas A&M University. His primary teaching and research interest is in the areas of strategy. His research on strategy has been published in the *Journal of Marketing, Journal of the Academy of Marketing Science, Academy of Management Journal, Strategic Management Journal,* and other journals. Dr. Varadarajan served as editor of the *Journal of Marketing* from 1993 to 1996 and the *Journal of the Academy of Marketing Science* from 2000 to 2003. He currently serves on the Editorial Review Boards of the *Journal of Marketing, Journal of the Academy of Marketing Science, Journal of International Marketing,* and other journals. He is a recipient of several honors and awards, including the Academy of Marketing Science Distinguished Marketing Educator Award (2003), American Marketing Association Mahajan Award for Career Contributions to Marketing Strategy (2003), and Texas A&M University Distinguished Achievement Award in Research (1994).

Richard Varey is Professor of Marketing and Chairperson of the Department of Marketing at the Waikato Management School, Hamilton, New Zealand. He is a member of the Editorial Boards of several journals, including the *Journal of Communication Management, Journal of Marketing Communications, Corporate Reputation Review, Journal of Management Development, PRism,* and *International Journal of Applied Marketing.* He is a guest reviewer for a wide range of management journals, conferences, and publishers, and a member of the Advisory Committee and Visiting Professor of the Corporate Communication Institute at Fairleigh Dickinson University, Madison, New Jersey. Dr. Varey's research interests are marketing as a social interaction system, the political economy of market systems, participatory and ethical communication and information systems management, and management studies methodology. He applies critical social theory, critical social psychology, and communication theory in his work. Dr. Varey teaches relationship marketing and marketing communications.

Stephen L. Vargo is Associate Professor of Marketing at the University of Hawaii at Manoa. He has an MS degree in social psychology and a PhD in marketing. His primary areas of research are consumers' evaluative reference scales and marketing theory and thought. He is published in the *Journal of Marketing, Journal of Service Research, Journal of Macromarketing*, the *Marketing Management Journal,* and other major marketing journals and books. He has been awarded the Harold H. Maynard Award by the American Marketing Association for "significant contribution to marketing theory and thought." Dr. Vargo currently serves on the Editorial Review Boards of the *Journal of Marketing, Journal of Service Research,* and the *International Journal of Service Industry Management.* He has previously taught at the University of Maryland; the University of California, Riverside; and California Polytechnic State University, San Luis Obispo. Prior to entering academics, he had an extended career in entrepreneurial business and consulted for a variety of major national, regional, and local corporations and governmental agencies.

Alladi Venkatesh is a Professor of Management and Associate Director of the Center for Research on Information Technology and Organizations (CRITO) at the University of California, Irvine. His current research interests are Marketing and Aesthetics, Technology and Culture, Social Informatics, and the Sign Economy. His postmodern work has appeared in the *Journal of Consumer Research* (received the best article award in 1998), *International Journal of Research in Marketing, Journal of Macromarketing,* and the *European Journal of Marketing.* His technology-related publications have appeared in the *Journal of Marketing, Management Science,* and the *Communications of the ACM.* His chapters have also appeared in the book series edited by Stephen Brown. He is currently Co-Editor-in-Chief of an interdisciplinary journal, *Consumption, Markets and Culture.*

Frederick E. Webster, Jr. (PhD, Stanford) is the Charles Henry Jones Third Century Professor of Management, Emeritus, Tuck School of Business at Dartmouth College and Jon Underwood Distinguished Research Fellow in Marketing, Eller College of Management, University of Arizona. He has also served as Executive Director of the Marketing Science Institute, as a Director of the American Marketing Association, and on the editorial boards of several marketing journals such as *Journal of Marketing, Marketing Letters,* and *Marketing Management.* His research in buyer behavior, marketing strategy and organization, business-to-business marketing, and sales force management has resulted in more than seventy-five articles and book chapters and a dozen books. Most recently, his primary research focus has been on the changing role of marketing in the firm. He has had lecturing and consulting assignments with leading companies and universities in more than twenty-five countries and he currently serves on several corporate and not-for-profit boards.

William L. Wilkie is the Aloysius and Eleanor Nathe Professor of Marketing at the University of Notre Dame. His research centers on marketing and society, consumer behavior, and advertising. Dr. Wilkie has received several honors, including the American Marketing Association's highest recognition, the Distinguished Marketing Educator Award. At Notre Dame, he has received the special President's Award and the BP/Amoco Outstanding Professor Award, as voted by the graduating seniors of the College. Dr. Wilkie has served as President of the Association for Consumer Research, and on the editorial boards of the *Journal of Marketing, Journal of Marketing Research, Journal of Consumer Research,* and *Journal of Public Policy & Marketing.* One of his articles has been named a Citation Classic in the Social Sciences by the Institute for Scientific Information. Prior to Notre Dame, he served on the faculties at Purdue, Harvard, and Florida, as an in-house consultant at the Federal Trade Commission's Bureau of Consumer Protection, and as

Research Professor at the Marketing Science Institute. Dr. Wilkie's undergraduate degree is from Notre Dame. At Stanford, where he was a Fellow in the Stanford-Sloan Executive Program, he earned MBA and PhD degrees.

Robert B. Woodruff is the Proffitt's, Inc. Professor of Marketing and Head of the Department of Marketing and Logistics at The University of Tennessee. His research spans interests in customer value and satisfaction theories, market opportunity analyses, and customer-value-based marketing strategies. Dr. Woodruff has published more than sixty books, book chapters, and essays, and refereed journal articles and conference papers on these topics. He currently serves on the Editorial Review Boards of the *Journal of Marketing, Journal of the Academy of Marketing Science, Journal of Consumer Satisfaction, Dissatisfaction and Complaining Behavior,* and the *Journal of Strategic Marketing.* Through consulting, teaching/learning, and research partnerships, Dr. Woodruff has worked with managers in more than two dozen companies in consumer, industrial, product, and service industries. This work focuses on market opportunity analyses, customer value and satisfaction information processes, and marketing strategy planning.

INDEX